liz
suburbia

SACRED
HEART

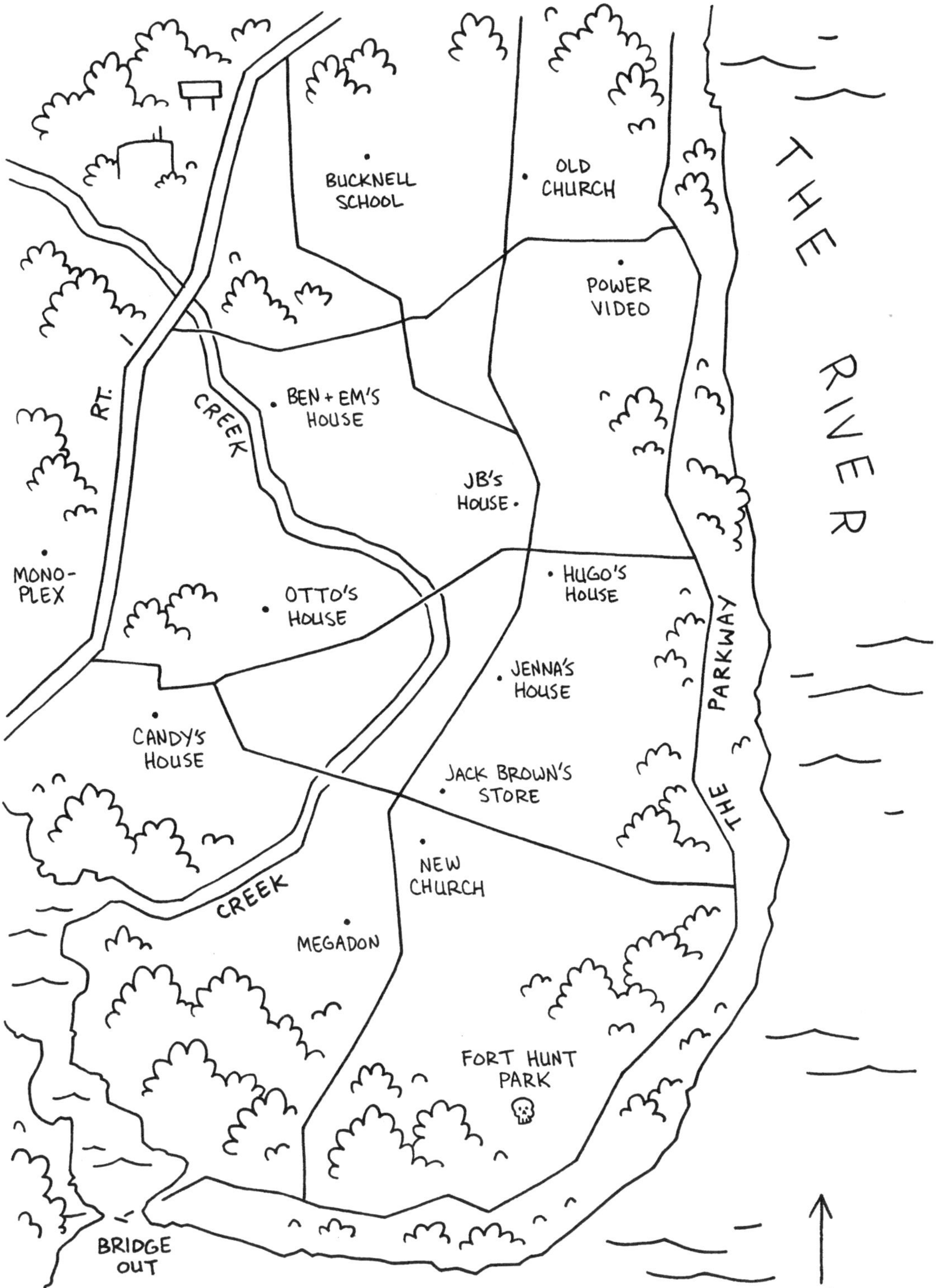
BUCKNELL SCHOOL
OLD CHURCH
POWER VIDEO
THE RIVER
RT. 1
CREEK
BEN + EM'S HOUSE
JB's HOUSE
MONO-PLEX
OTTO'S HOUSE
HUGO'S HOUSE
JENNA'S HOUSE
THE PARKWAY
CANDY'S HOUSE
JACK BROWN'S STORE
NEW CHURCH
CREEK
MEGADON
FORT HUNT PARK
BRIDGE OUT
N

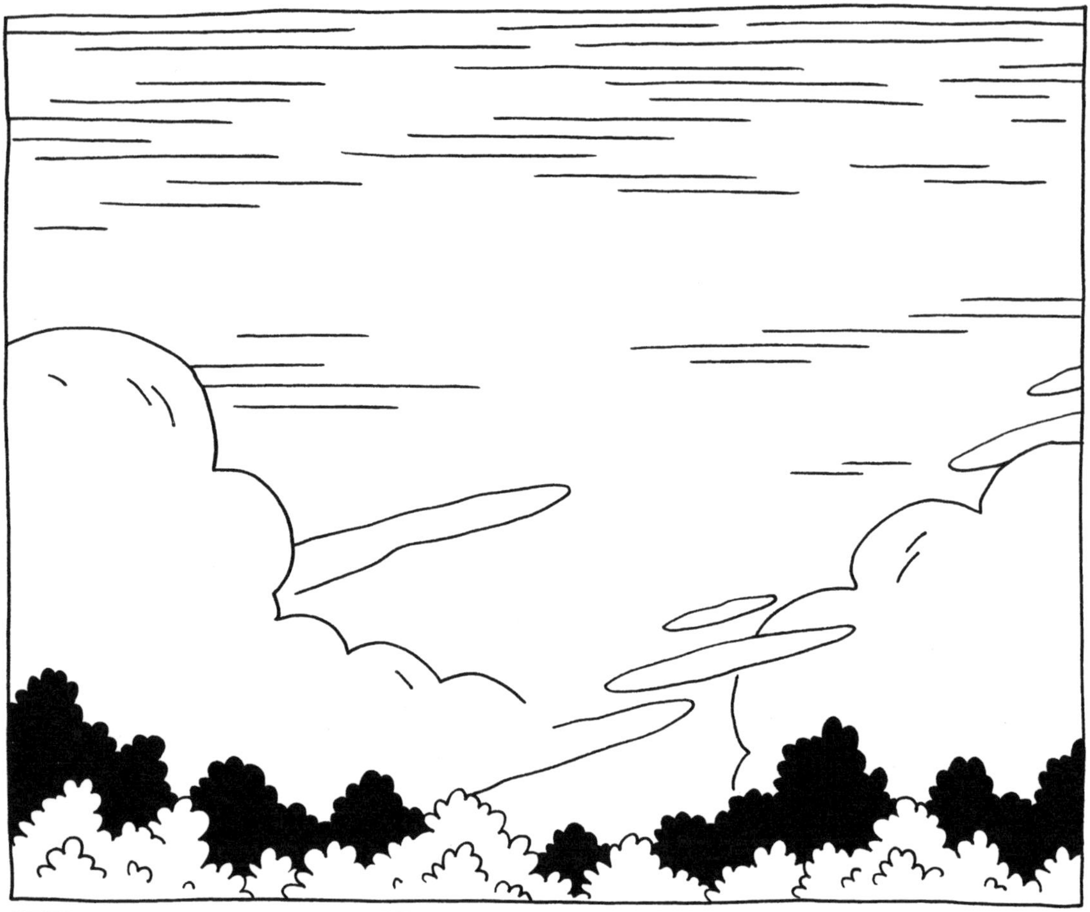

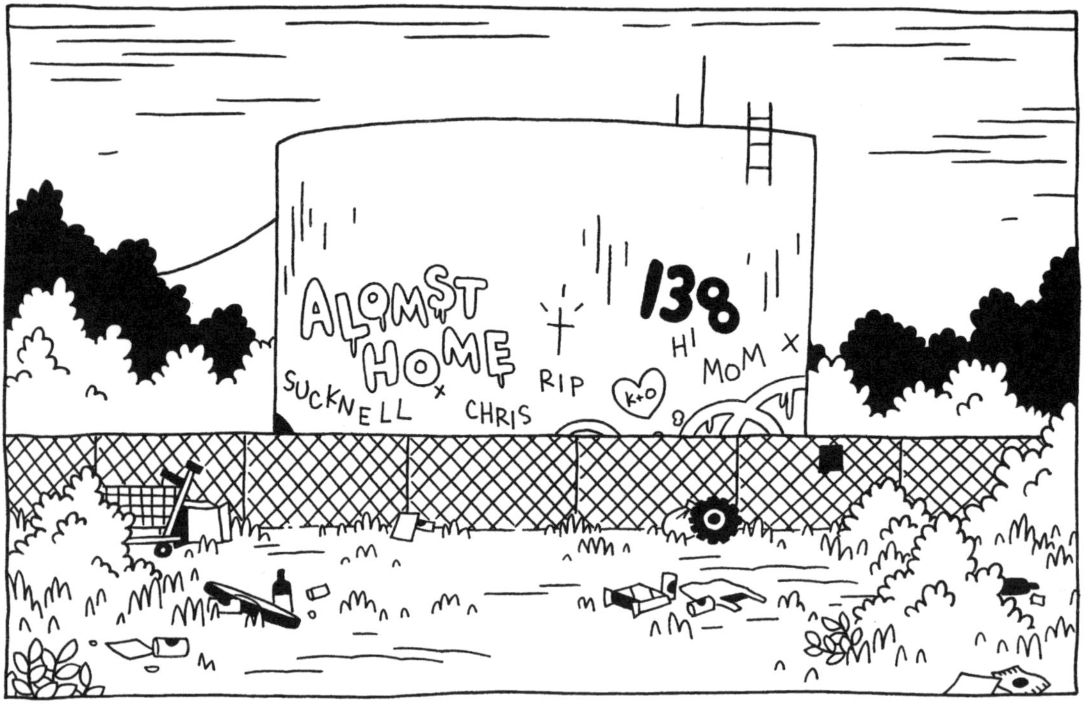
ALOMST HOME
138
RIP
HI MOM
SUCKNELL
CHRIS
K+O

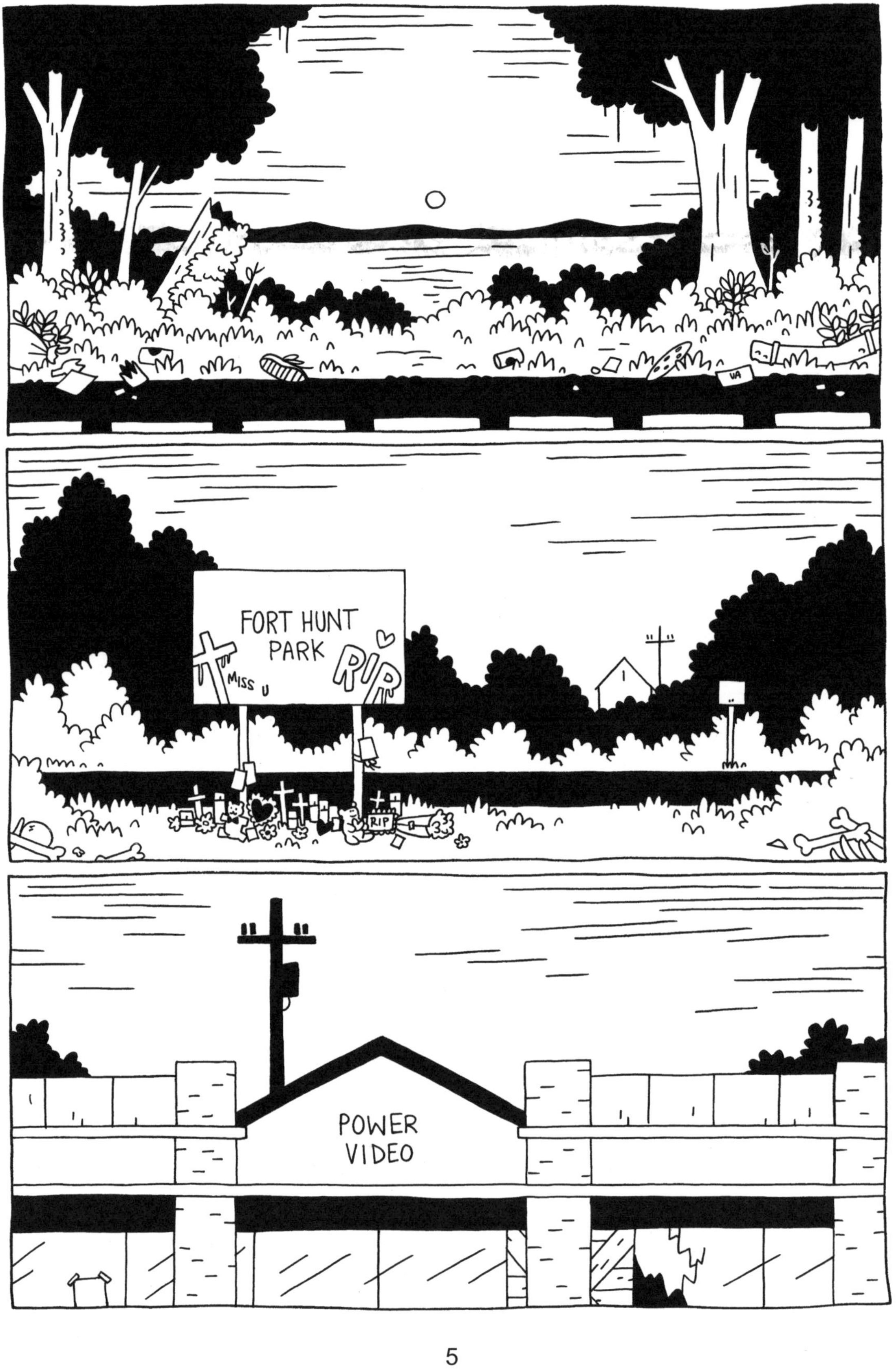
UA
FORT HUNT PARK
MISS U
RIP
RIP
POWER VIDEO

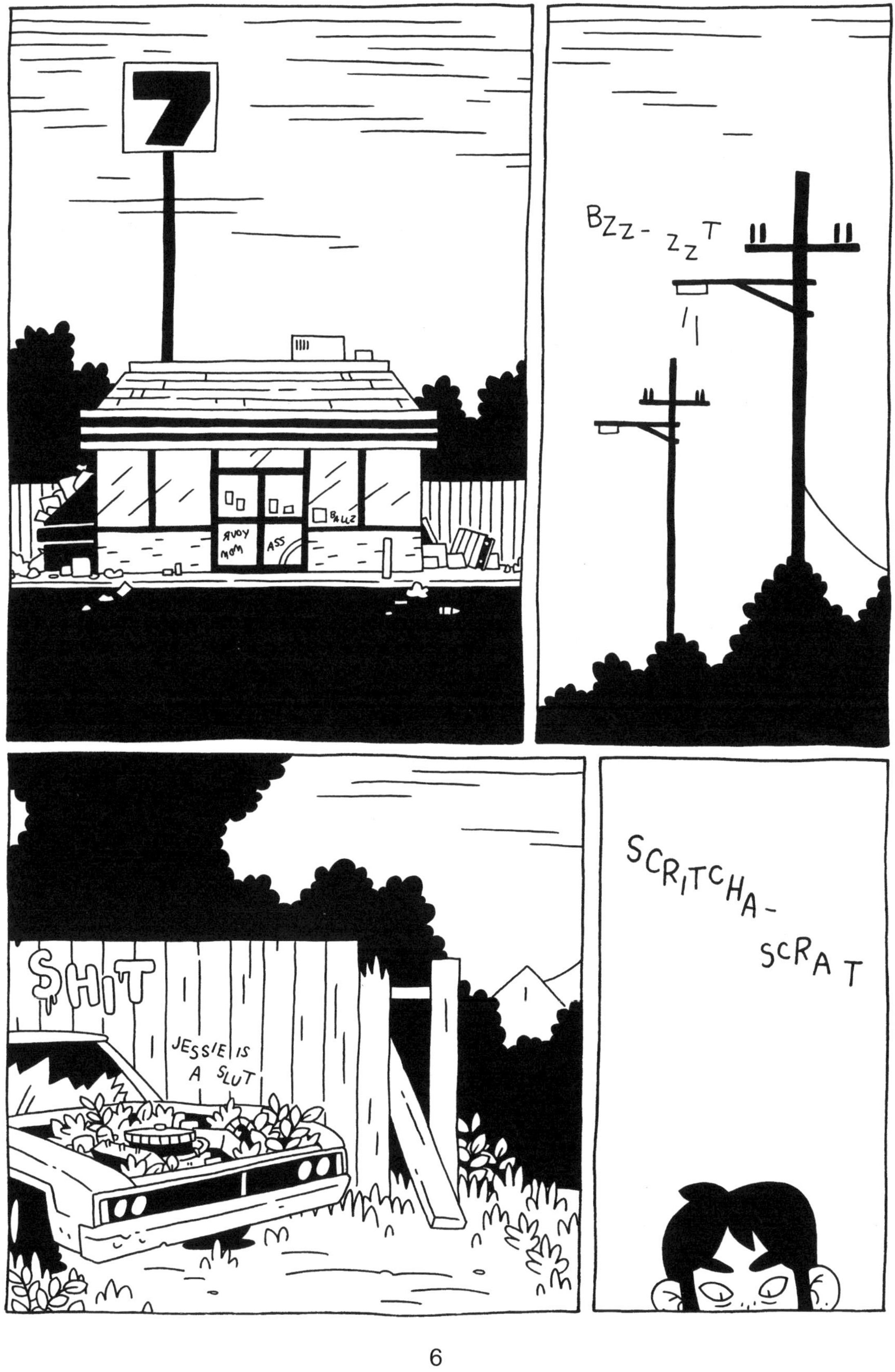

7
MOM
ASS
BALLZ
BZZ- ZZT
SHIT
JESSIE IS A SLUT
SCRITCHA-SCRAT

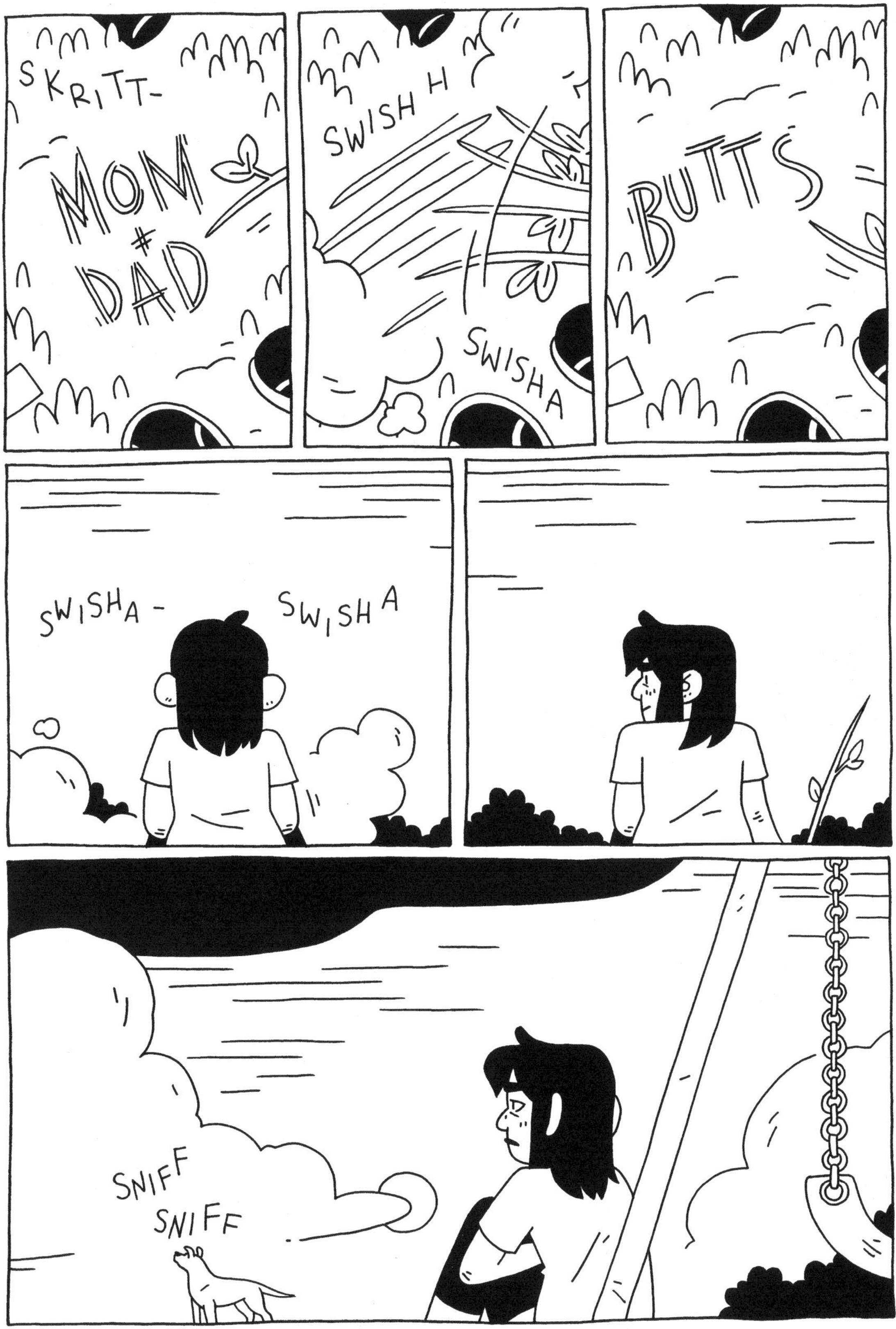
SKRITT-
MOM + DAD
SWISHH
SWISHA
BUTTS
SWISHA-
SWISHA
SNIFF
SNIFF

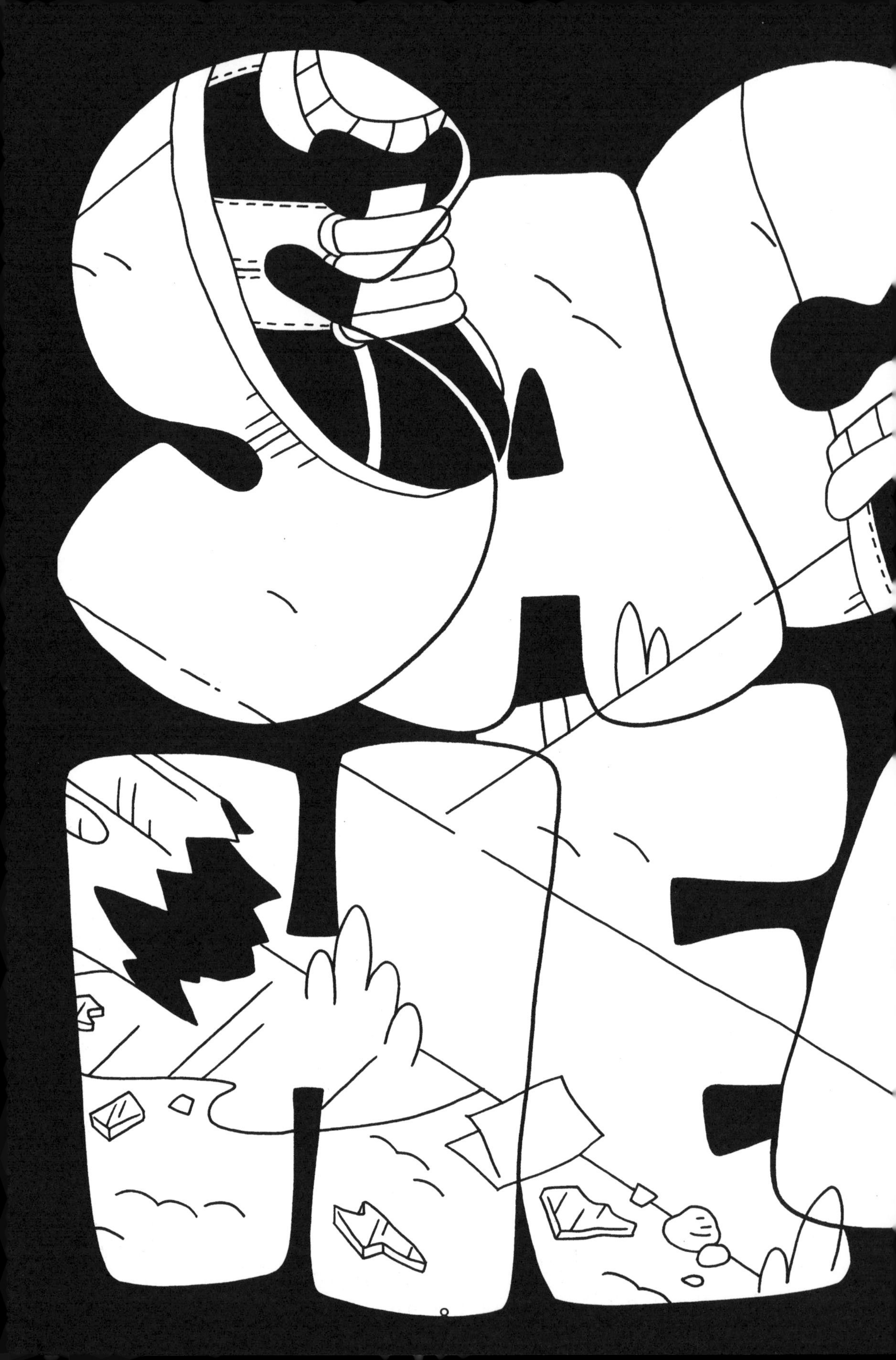

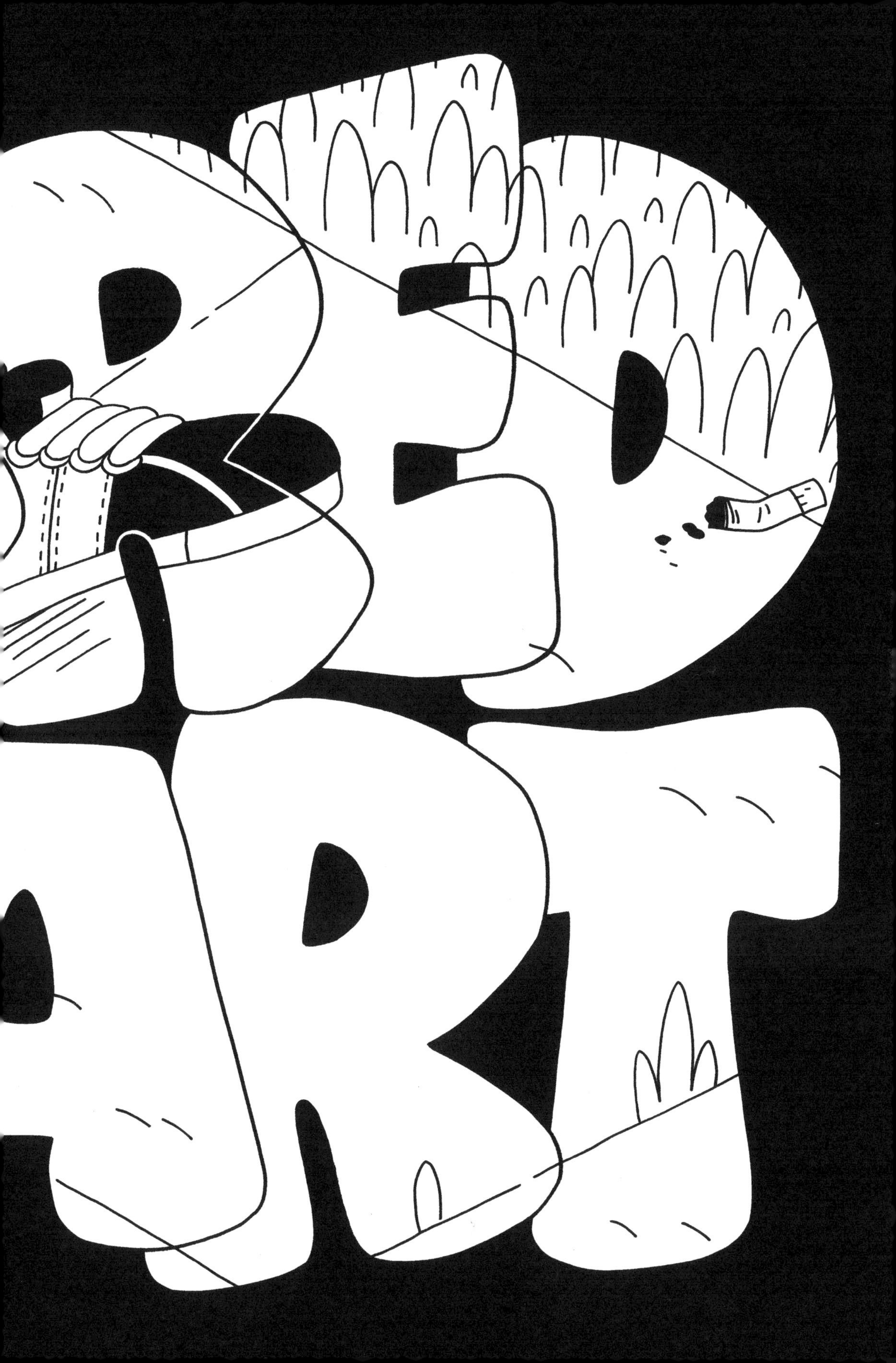

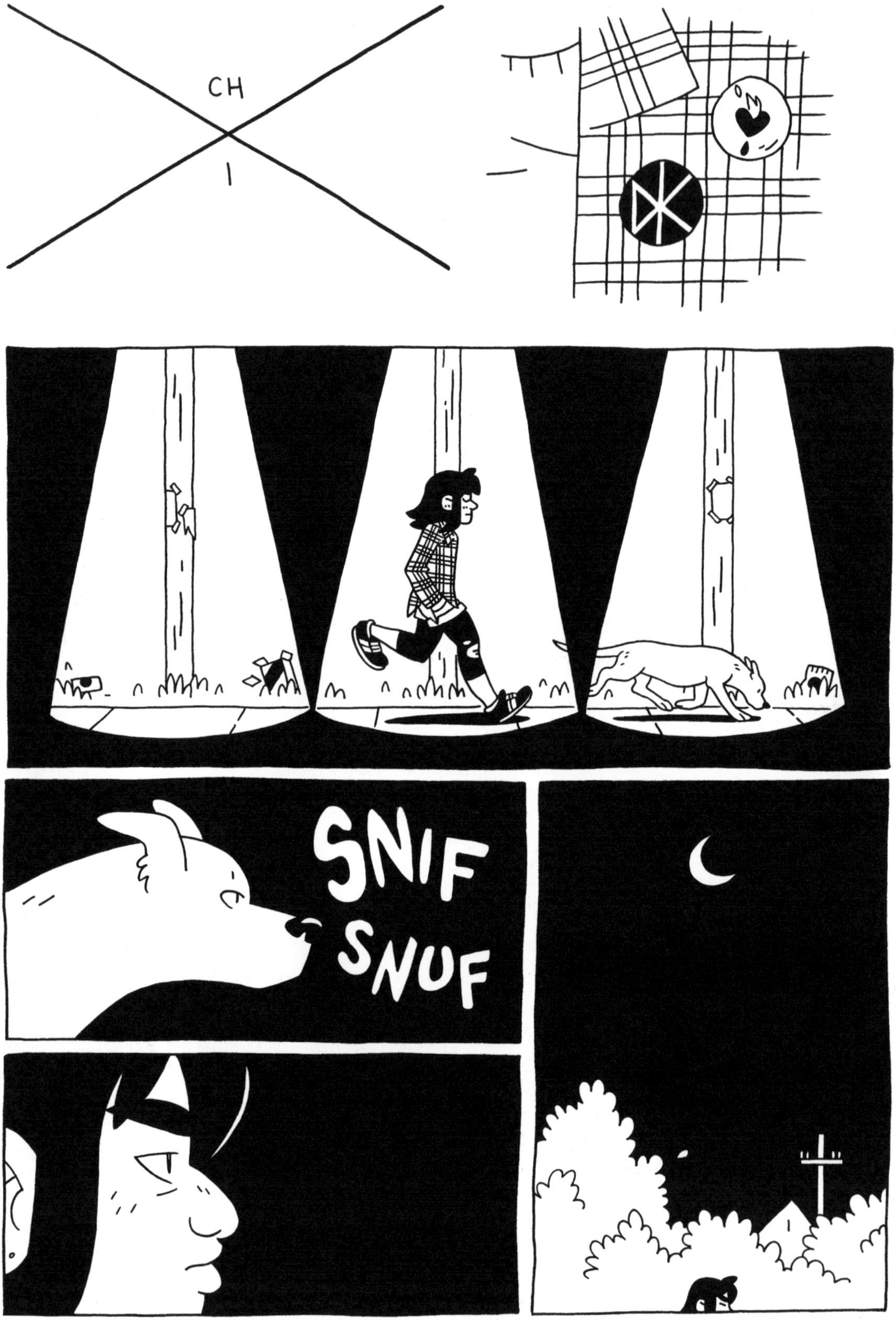
CH
I
SNIF
SNUF

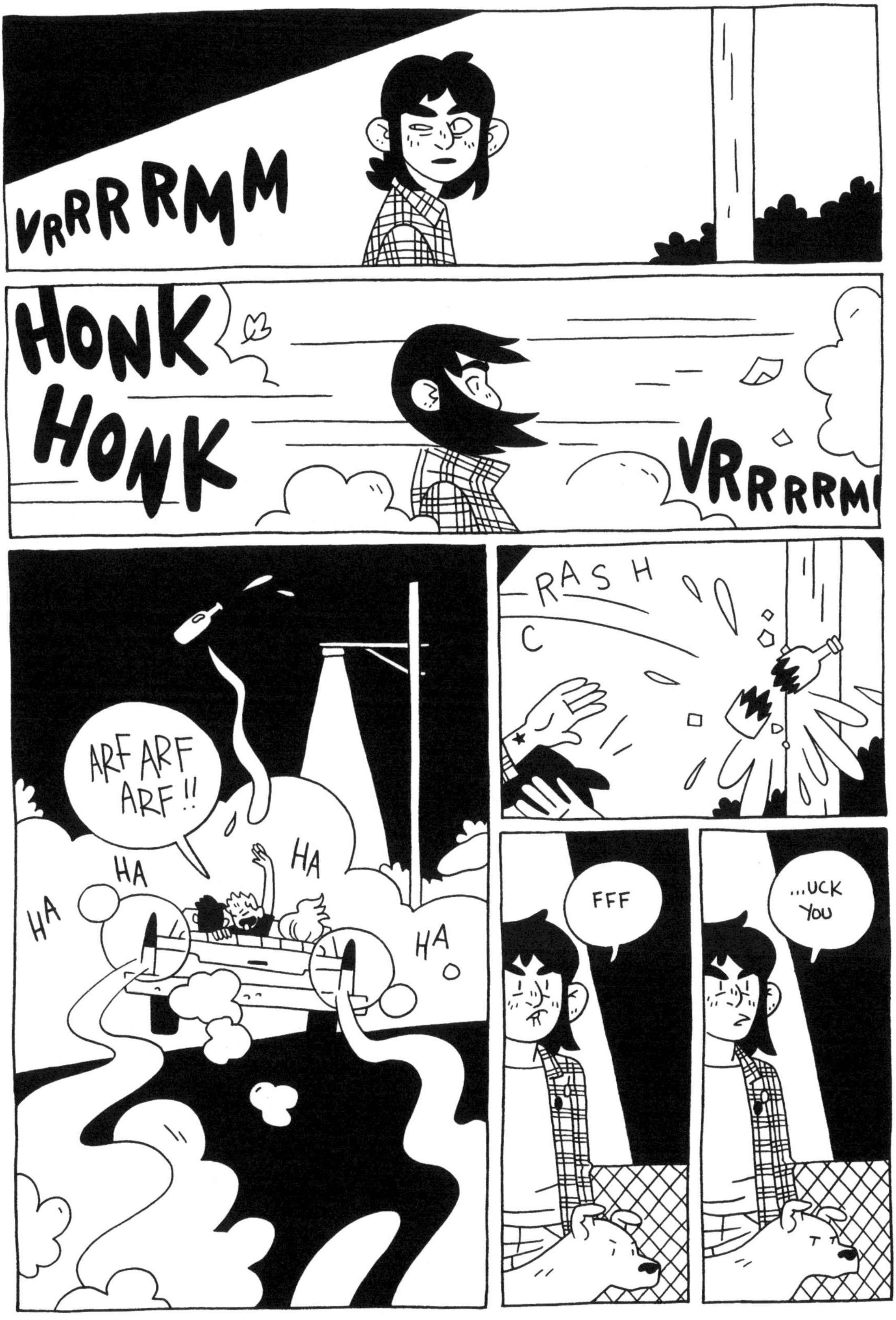
VRRRRMM
HONK
HONK
VRRRRM
ARF ARF ARF!!
HA
HA
HA
HA
C
RASH
FFF
...UCK YOU

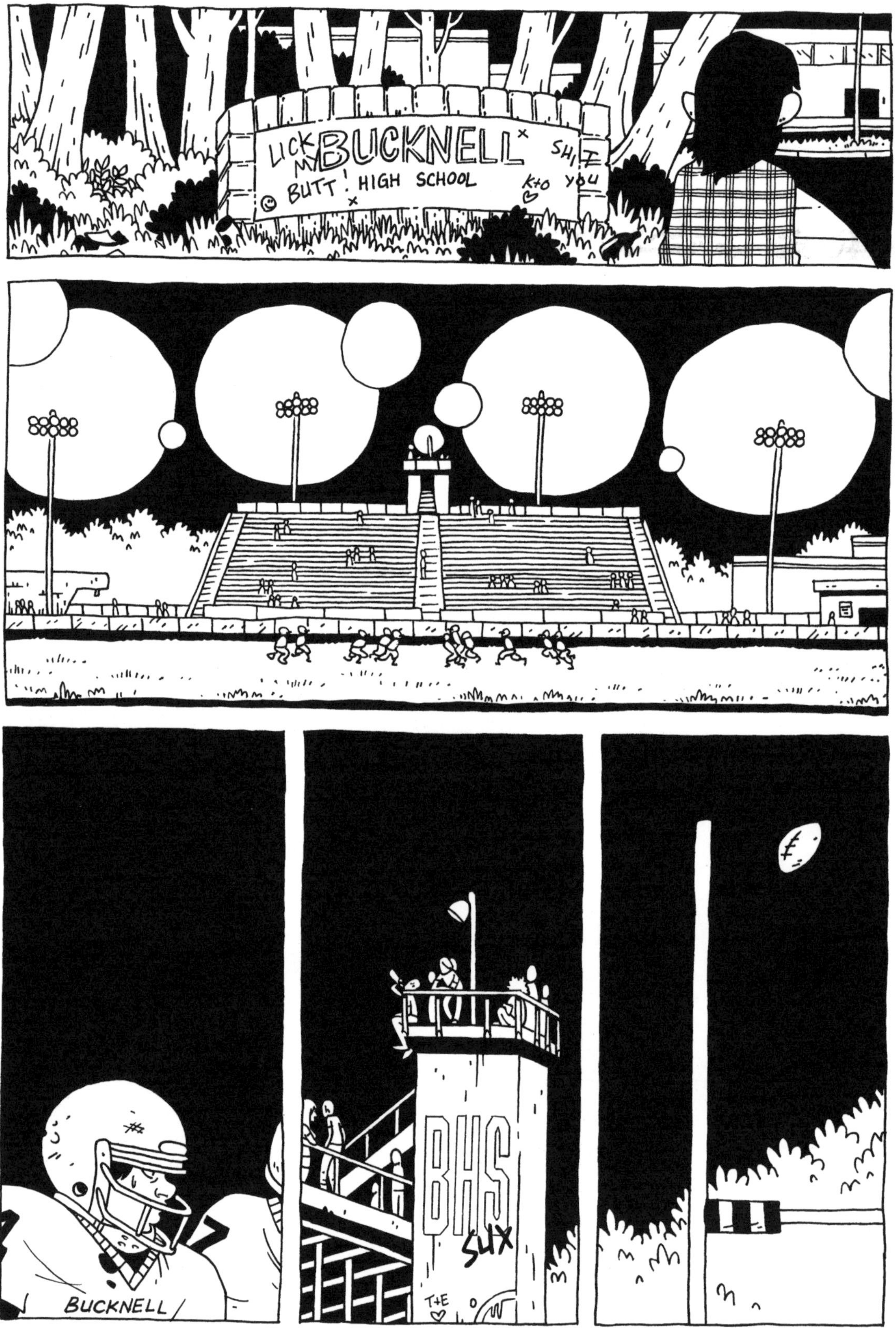
LICK MY
BUCKNELL
SHIT
BUTT!
HIGH SCHOOL
K+O
YOU
BUCKNELL
BHS
SUX
T+E

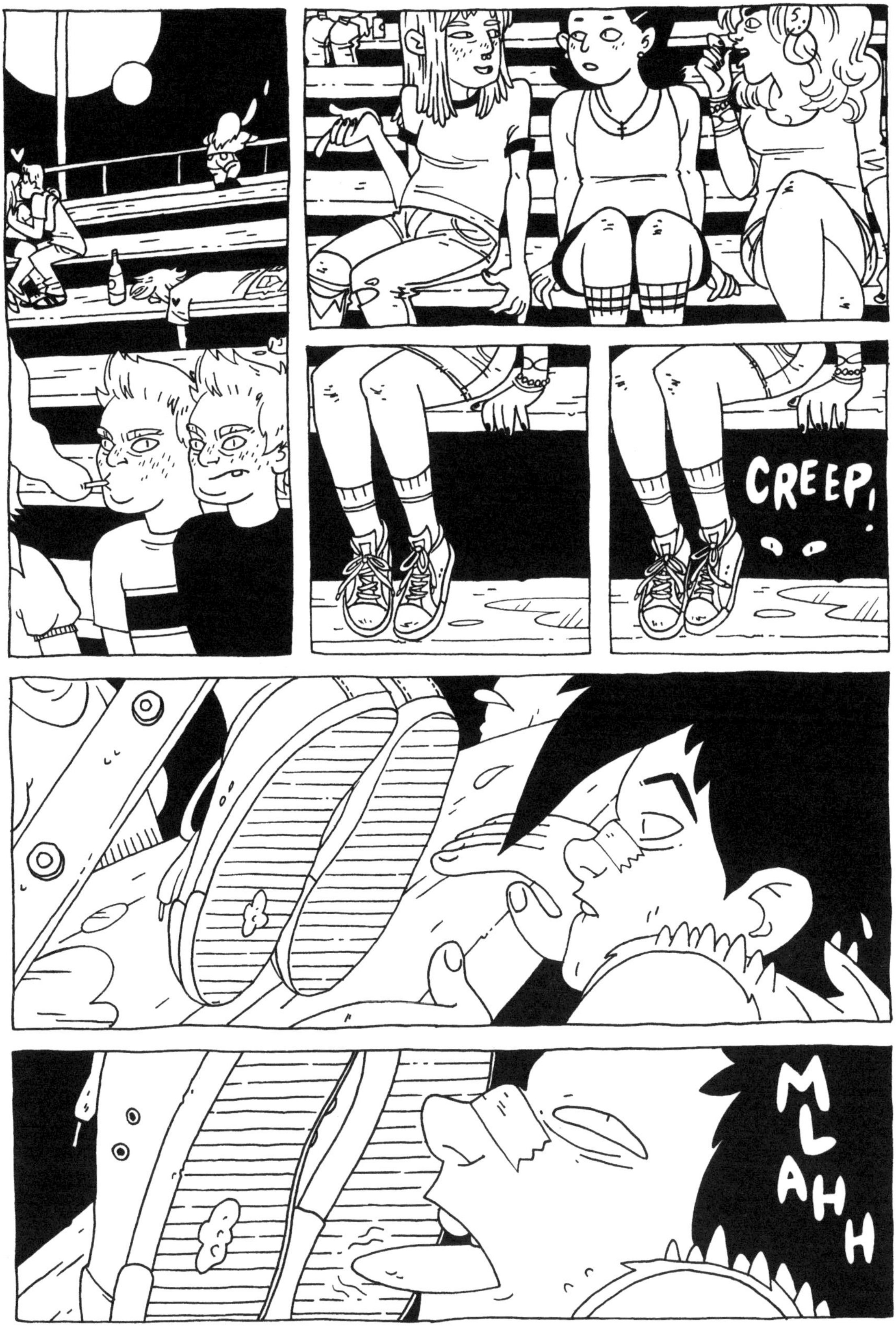
CREEP!
MLAHH

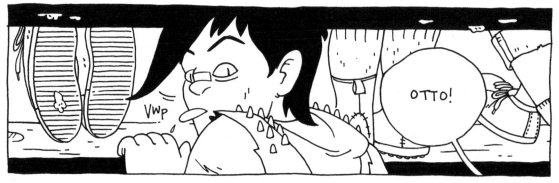

VWP

OTTO!

OH! HI BEN.

DIDN'T THINK I'D SEE YOU HERE...

I'M LOOKING FOR EMPATHY, HAVE YOU SEEN HER AROUND?

†VOID†

NOPE

JOHN McCLANE! KISSES!

GREAT.

WHAT HAPPENED TO YOUR NOSE?

14

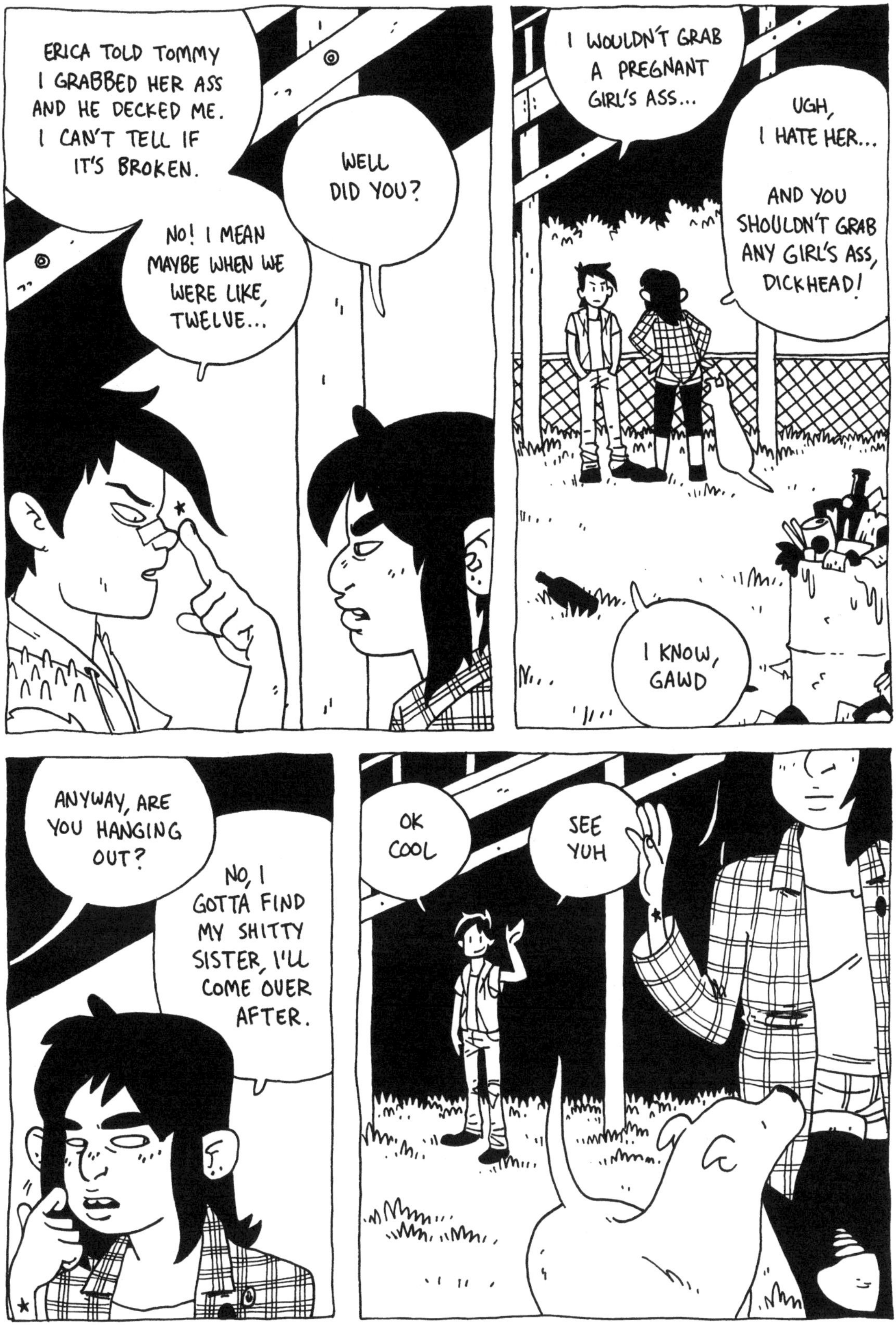
ERICA TOLD TOMMY I GRABBED HER ASS AND HE DECKED ME. I CAN'T TELL IF IT'S BROKEN.
WELL DID YOU?
NO! I MEAN MAYBE WHEN WE WERE LIKE, TWELVE...
I WOULDN'T GRAB A PREGNANT GIRL'S ASS...
UGH, I HATE HER...
AND YOU SHOULDN'T GRAB ANY GIRL'S ASS, DICKHEAD!
I KNOW, GAWD
ANYWAY, ARE YOU HANGING OUT?
NO, I GOTTA FIND MY SHITTY SISTER, I'LL COME OVER AFTER.
OK COOL
SEE YUH

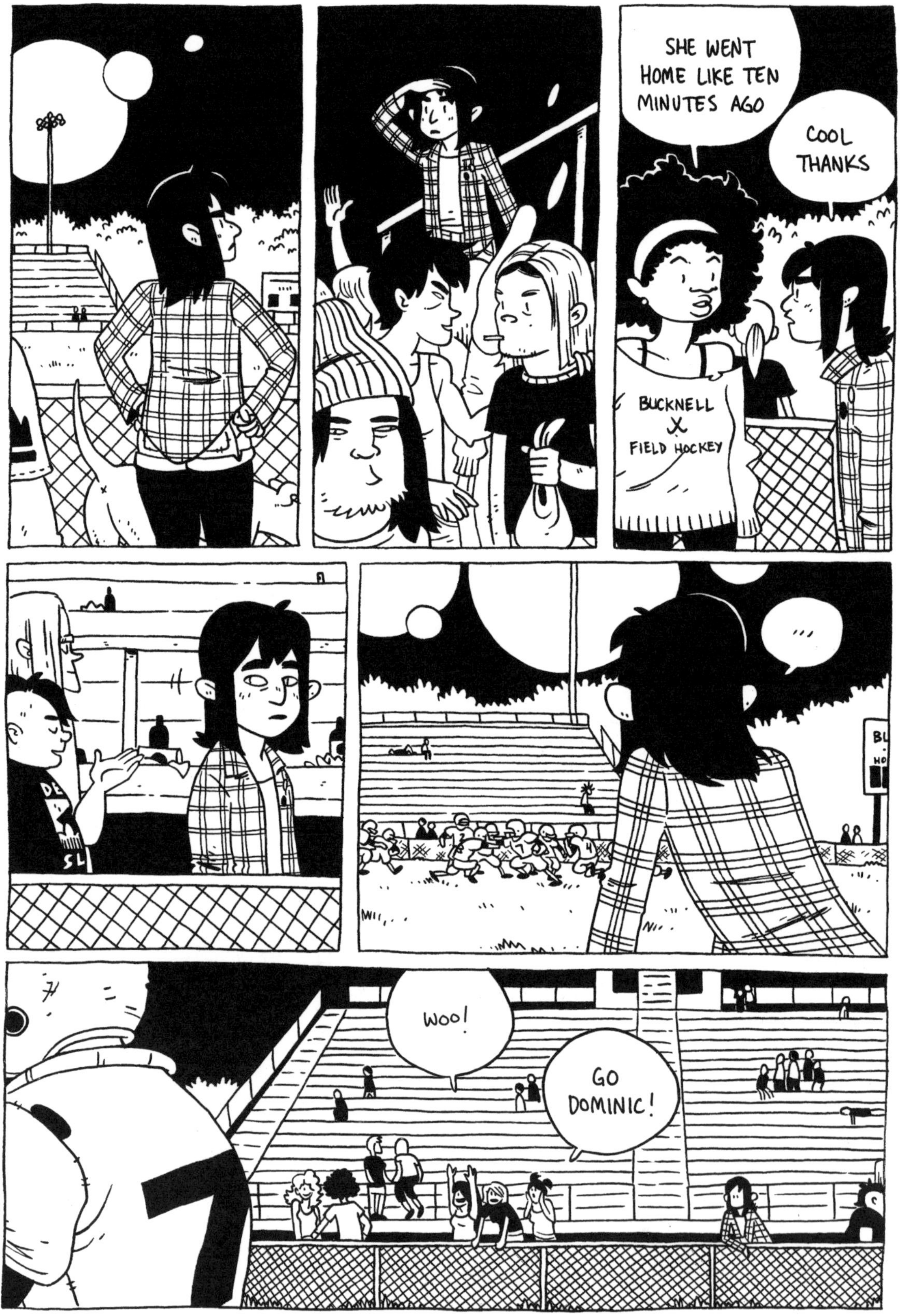
SHE WENT HOME LIKE TEN MINUTES AGO
COOL THANKS
BUCKNELL FIELD HOCKEY
...
WOO!
GO DOMINIC!

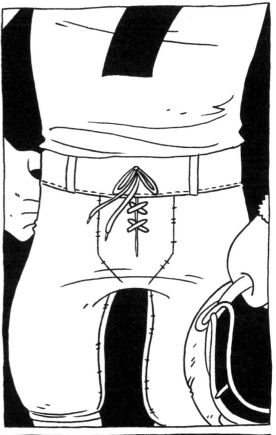

AHEM

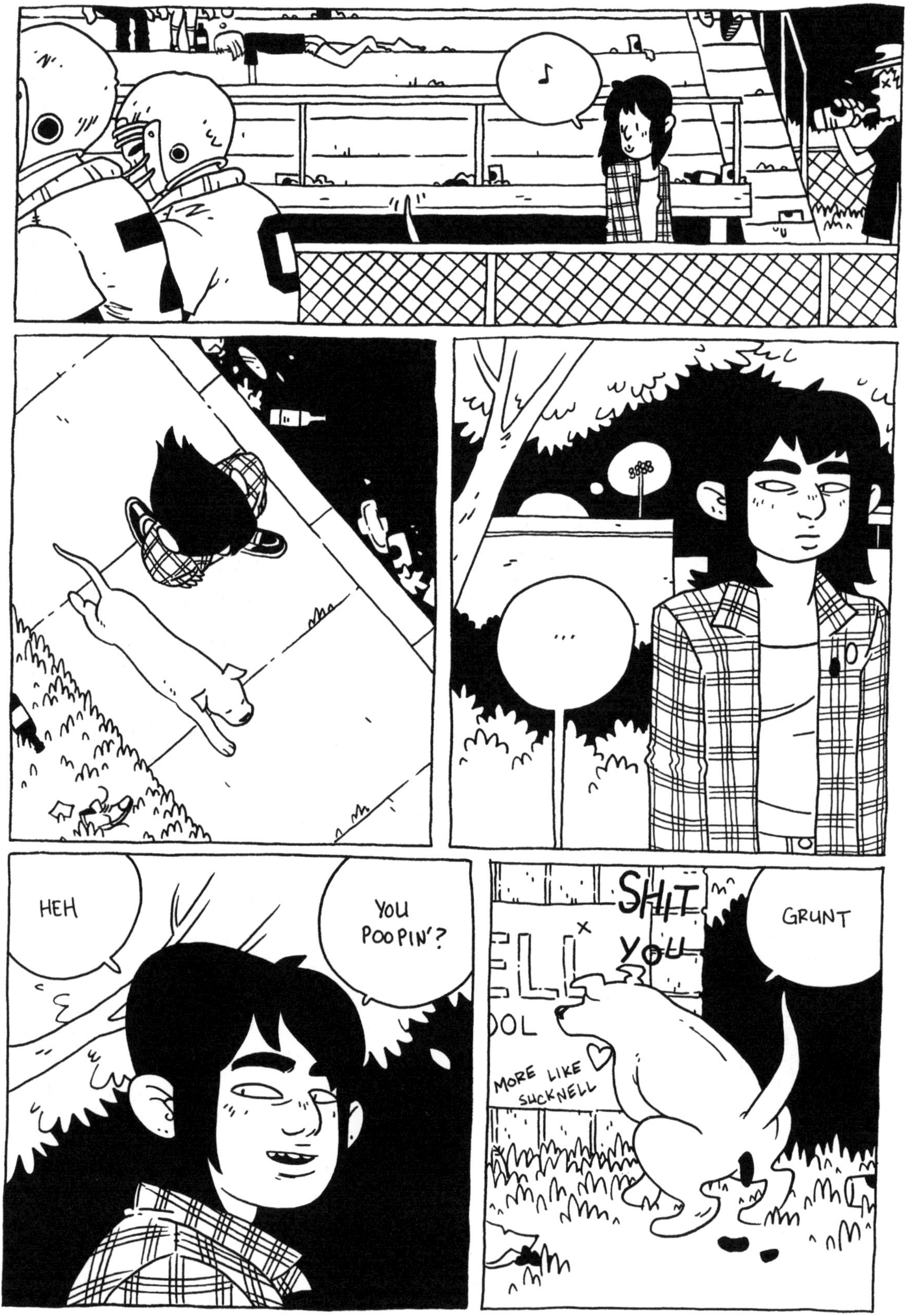
♪
...
HEH
YOU POOPIN'?
SHIT YOU
ELL
OOL
MORE LIKE SUCKNELL
GRUNT

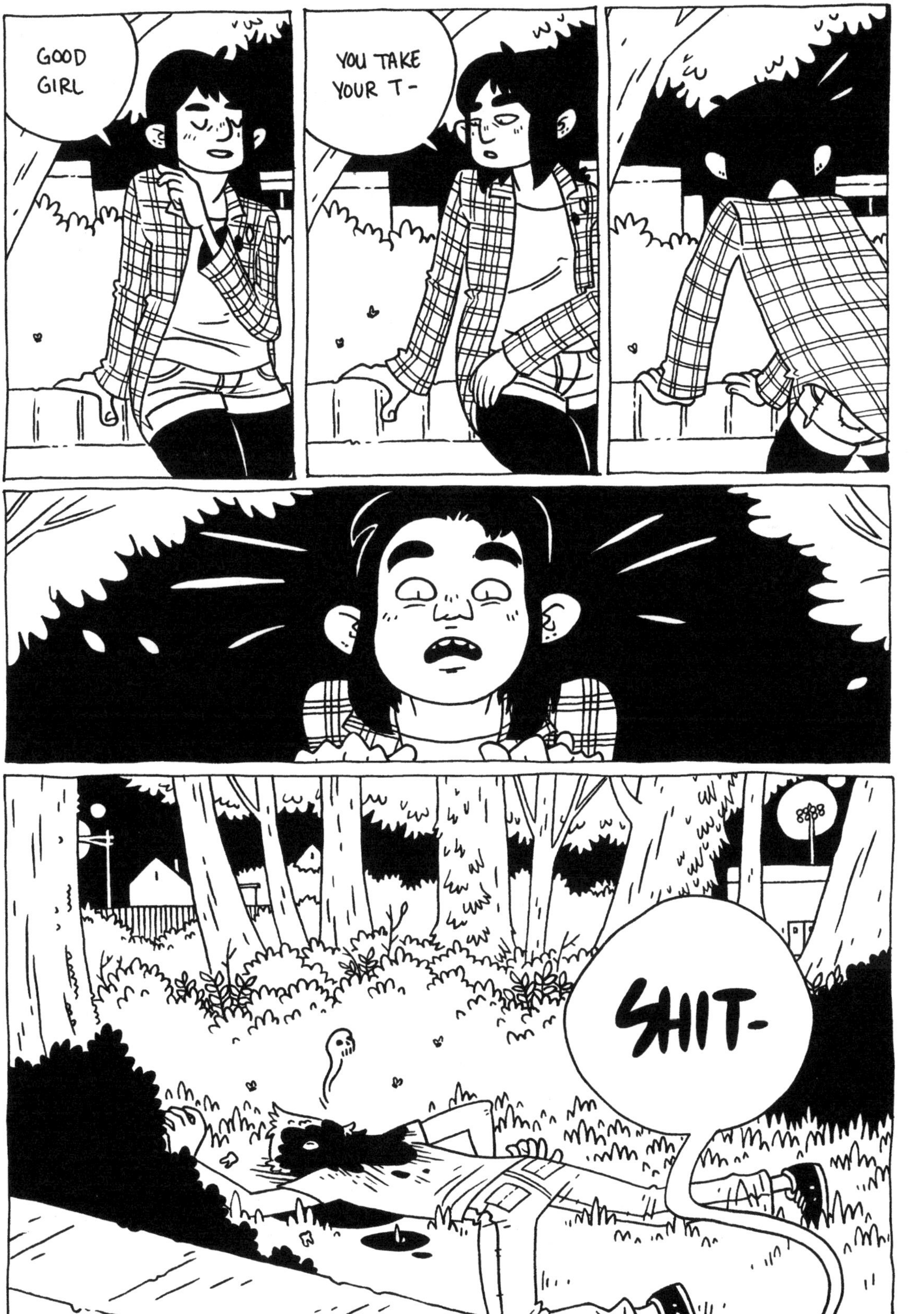
GOOD GIRL
YOU TAKE YOUR T-
SHIT-

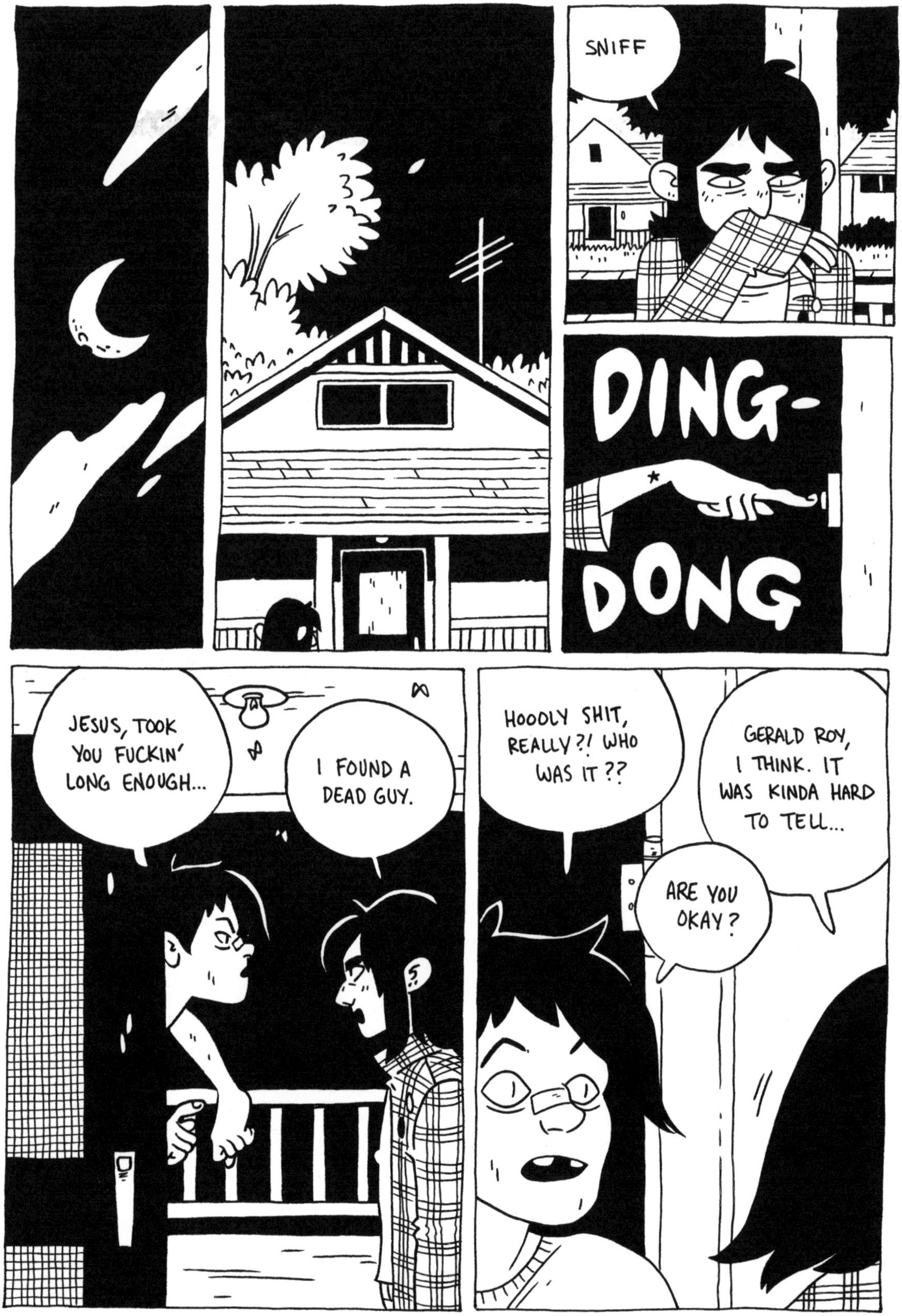
SNIFF
DING-DONG
JESUS, TOOK YOU FUCKIN' LONG ENOUGH...
I FOUND A DEAD GUY.
HOOOLY SHIT, REALLY?! WHO WAS IT??
GERALD ROY, I THINK. IT WAS KINDA HARD TO TELL...
ARE YOU OKAY?

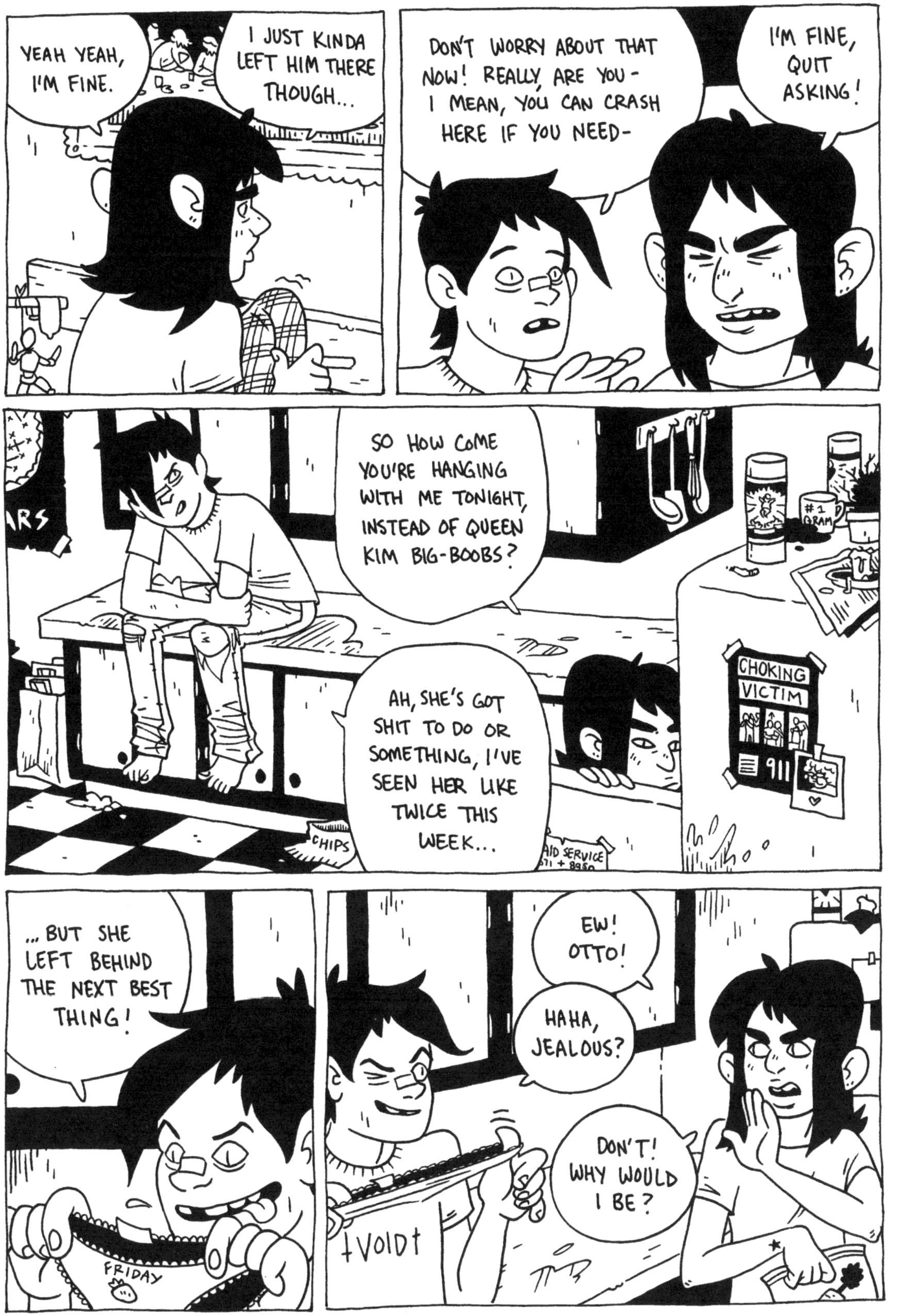
YEAH YEAH, I'M FINE.
I JUST KINDA LEFT HIM THERE THOUGH...
DON'T WORRY ABOUT THAT NOW! REALLY, ARE YOU- I MEAN, YOU CAN CRASH HERE IF YOU NEED-
I'M FINE, QUIT ASKING!
SO HOW COME YOU'RE HANGING WITH ME TONIGHT, INSTEAD OF QUEEN KIM BIG-BOOBS?
AH, SHE'S GOT SHIT TO DO OR SOMETHING, I'VE SEEN HER LIKE TWICE THIS WEEK...
CHOKING VICTIM
911
#1 GRAM
CHIPS
...BUT SHE LEFT BEHIND THE NEXT BEST THING!
FRIDAY
EW! OTTO!
HAHA, JEALOUS?
DON'T! WHY WOULD I BE?
VOID

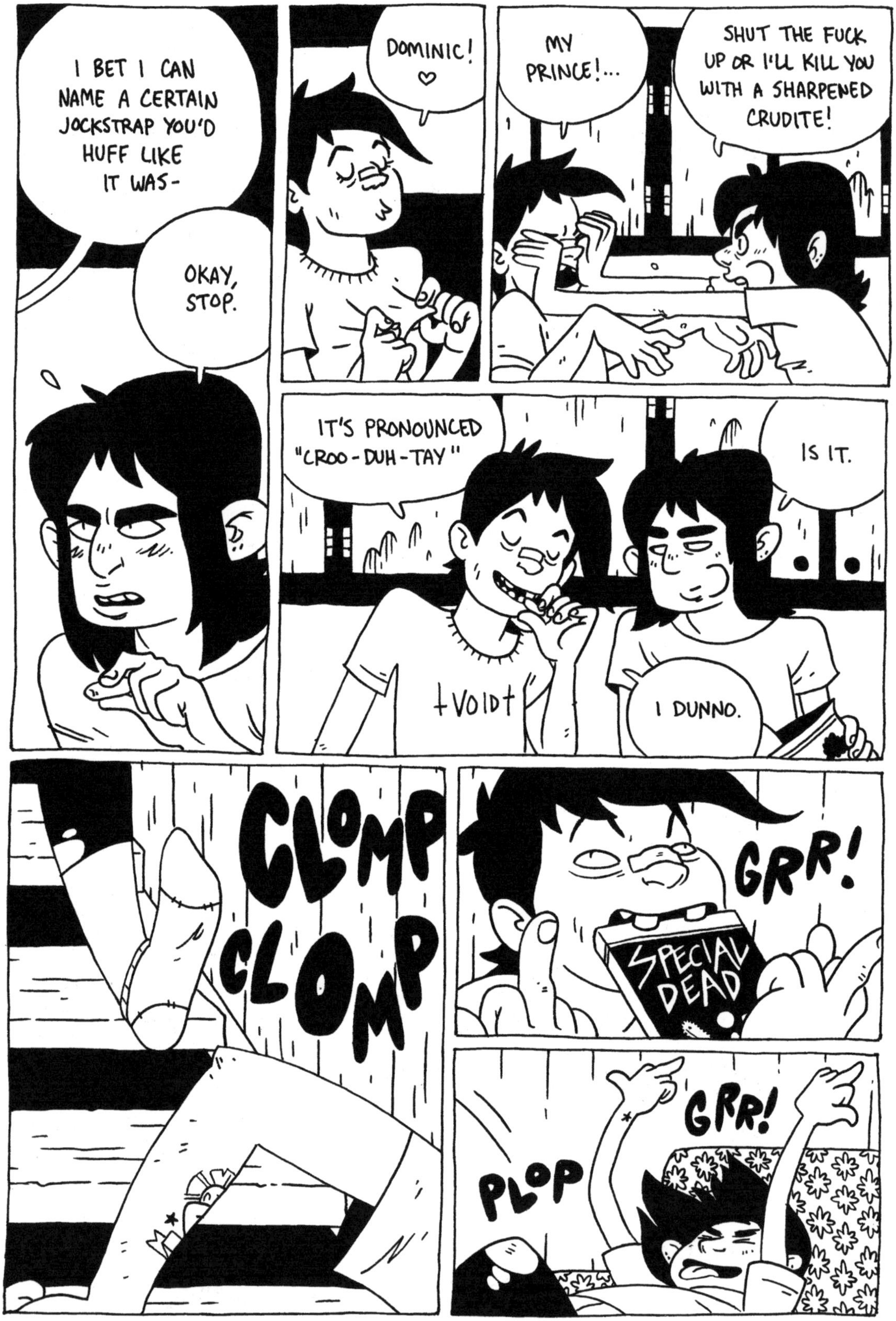
I BET I CAN NAME A CERTAIN JOCKSTRAP YOU'D HUFF LIKE IT WAS-
OKAY, STOP.
DOMINIC! ♡
MY PRINCE!...
SHUT THE FUCK UP OR I'LL KILL YOU WITH A SHARPENED CRUDITE!
IT'S PRONOUNCED "CROO-DUH-TAY"
IS IT.
+VOID+
I DUNNO.
CLOMP CLOMP
GRR!
SPECIAL DEAD
PLOP
GRR!

YOU EVER RIDE A ZOMBIE HORSE, BOY?

I HAVE

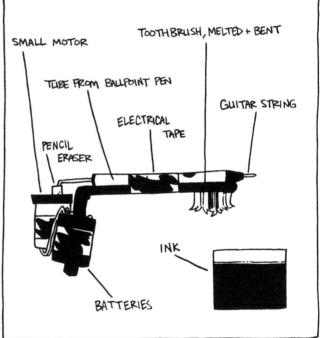

SMALL MOTOR

TOOTHBRUSH, MELTED + BENT

TUBE FROM BALLPOINT PEN

GUITAR STRING

ELECTRICAL TAPE

PENCIL ERASER

INK

BATTERIES

AIN'T NO FUN

THIS ISN'T VERY GOOD...

ARE YOU KIDDING? THIS IS GREAT!

HOW ABOUT WE WORK ON LOLA SOME?

OH! HEY NOW!

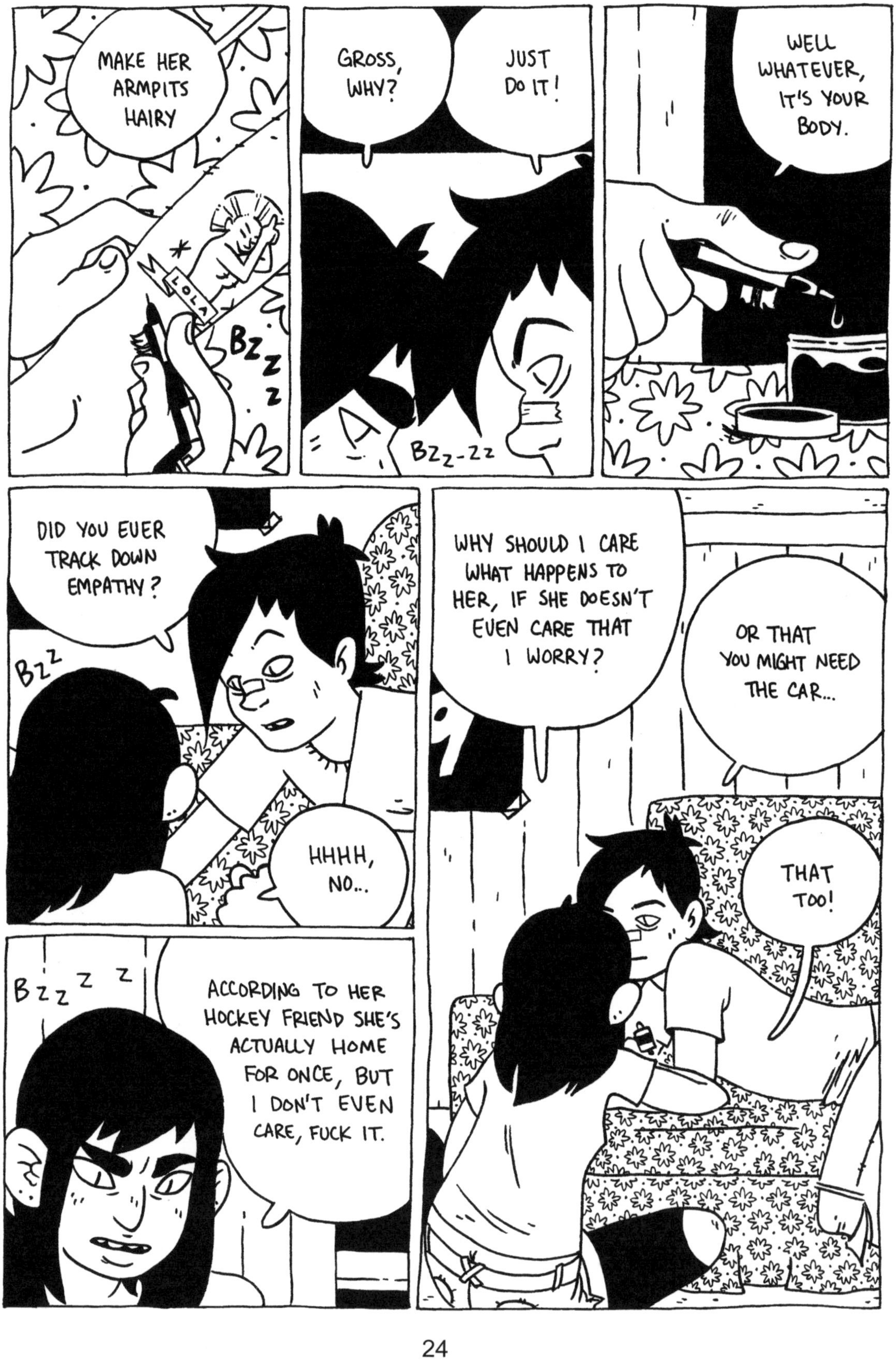
MAKE HER ARMPITS HAIRY
LOLA
BZZZ
GROSS, WHY?
JUST DO IT!
BZZ-ZZ
WELL WHATEVER, IT'S YOUR BODY.
DID YOU EVER TRACK DOWN EMPATHY?
BZZ
HHHH, NO...
WHY SHOULD I CARE WHAT HAPPENS TO HER, IF SHE DOESN'T EVEN CARE THAT I WORRY?
OR THAT YOU MIGHT NEED THE CAR...
THAT TOO!
BZZZ Z
ACCORDING TO HER HOCKEY FRIEND SHE'S ACTUALLY HOME FOR ONCE, BUT I DON'T EVEN CARE, FUCK IT.

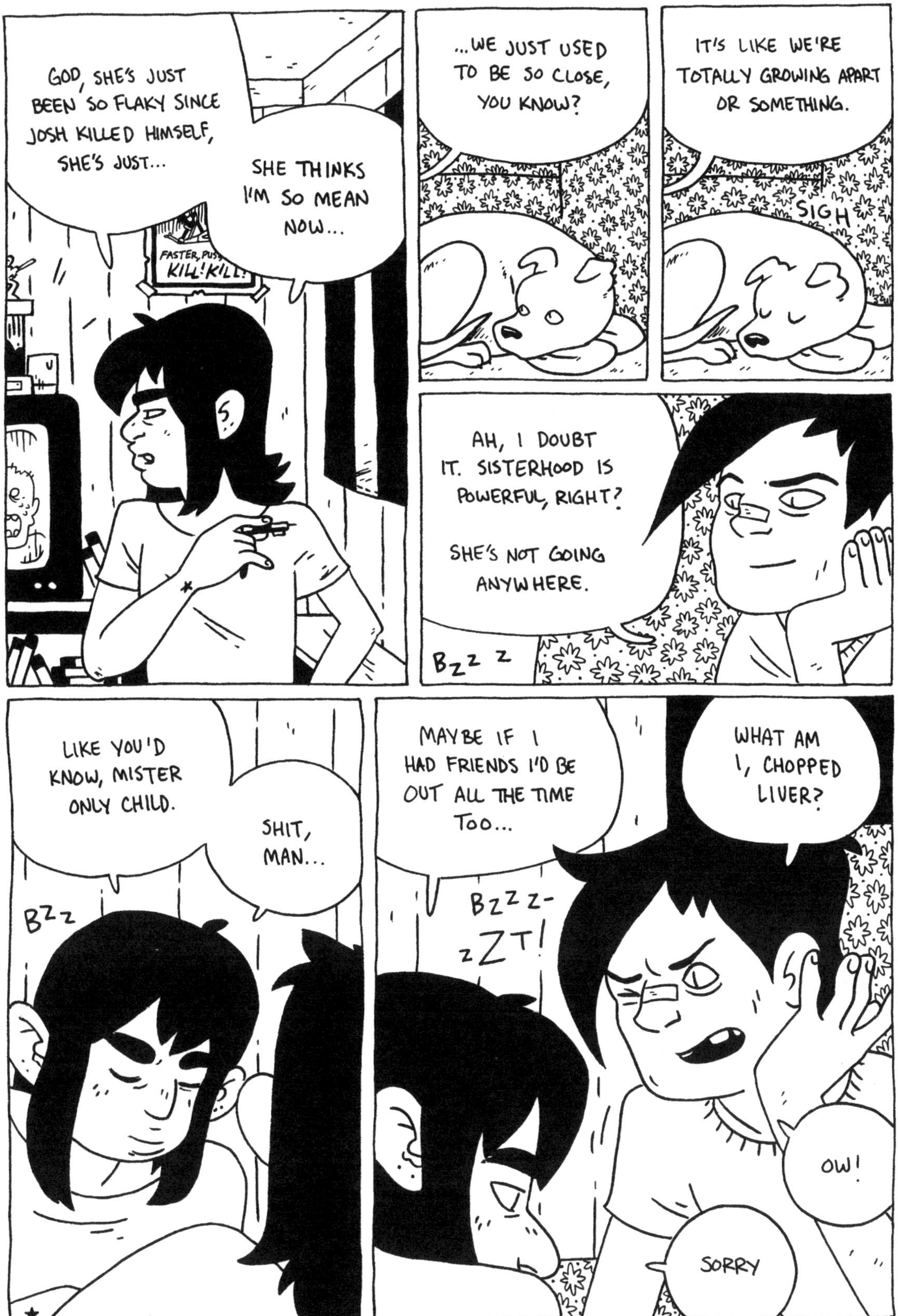
GOD, SHE'S JUST BEEN SO FLAKY SINCE JOSH KILLED HIMSELF, SHE'S JUST...
SHE THINKS I'M SO MEAN NOW...
...WE JUST USED TO BE SO CLOSE, YOU KNOW?
IT'S LIKE WE'RE TOTALLY GROWING APART OR SOMETHING.
SIGH
AH, I DOUBT IT. SISTERHOOD IS POWERFUL, RIGHT?
SHE'S NOT GOING ANYWHERE.
BZZ Z
LIKE YOU'D KNOW, MISTER ONLY CHILD.
SHIT, MAN...
BZZ
MAYBE IF I HAD FRIENDS I'D BE OUT ALL THE TIME TOO...
WHAT AM I, CHOPPED LIVER?
BZZZ-
zZT!
OW!
SORRY

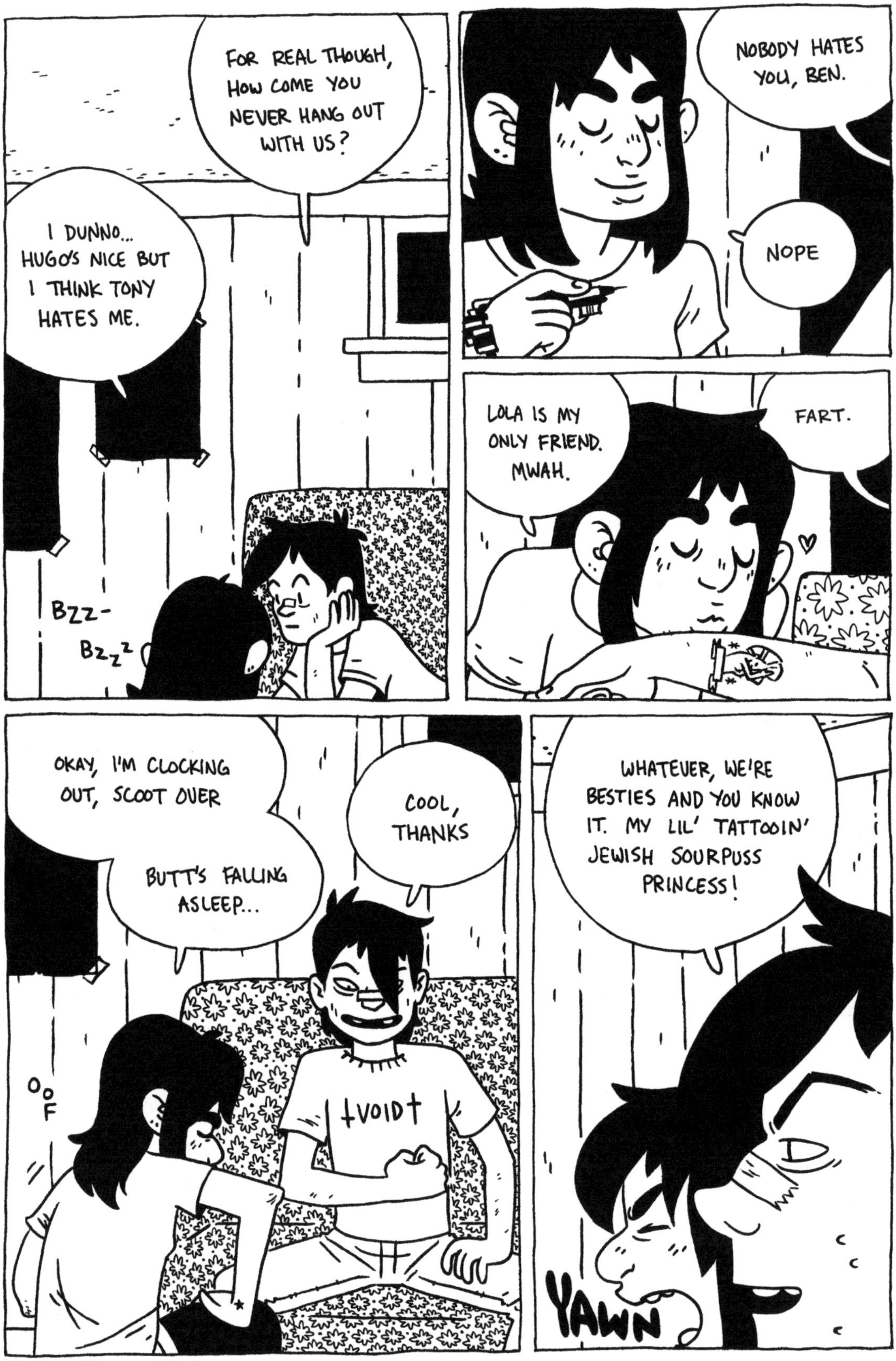
FOR REAL THOUGH, HOW COME YOU NEVER HANG OUT WITH US?
I DUNNO... HUGO'S NICE BUT I THINK TONY HATES ME.
BZZ-
BZZZ
NOBODY HATES YOU, BEN.
NOPE
LOLA IS MY ONLY FRIEND. MWAH.
FART.
OKAY, I'M CLOCKING OUT, SCOOT OVER
BUTT'S FALLING ASLEEP...
COOL, THANKS
OOF
VOID
WHATEVER, WE'RE BESTIES AND YOU KNOW IT. MY LIL' TATTOOIN' JEWISH SOURPUSS PRINCESS!
YAWN

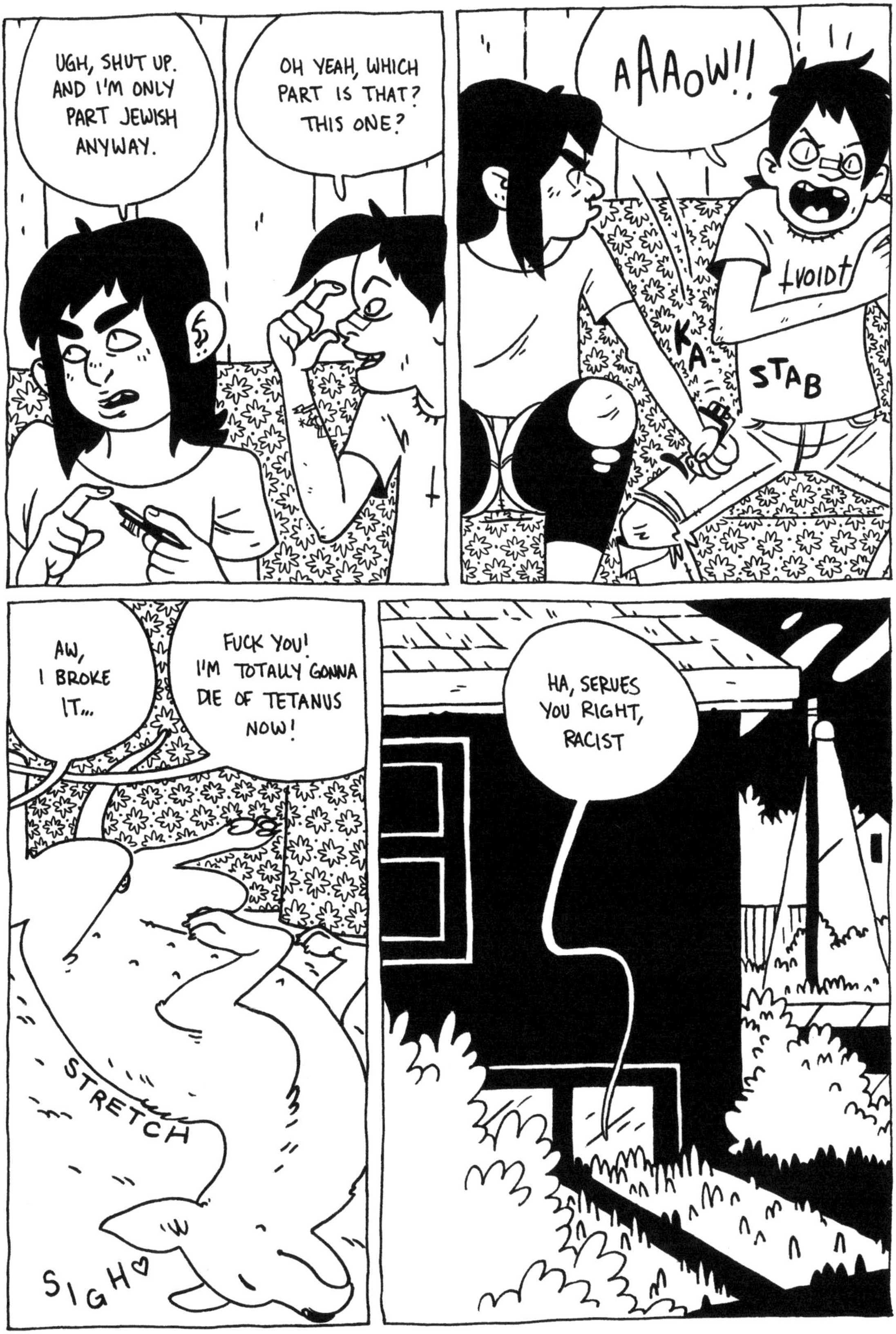
UGH, SHUT UP. AND I'M ONLY PART JEWISH ANYWAY.
OH YEAH, WHICH PART IS THAT? THIS ONE?
AAAOW!!
+VOID+
KA-
STAB
AW, I BROKE IT...
FUCK YOU! I'M TOTALLY GONNA DIE OF TETANUS NOW!
STRETCH
SIGH♡
HA, SERVES YOU RIGHT, RACIST

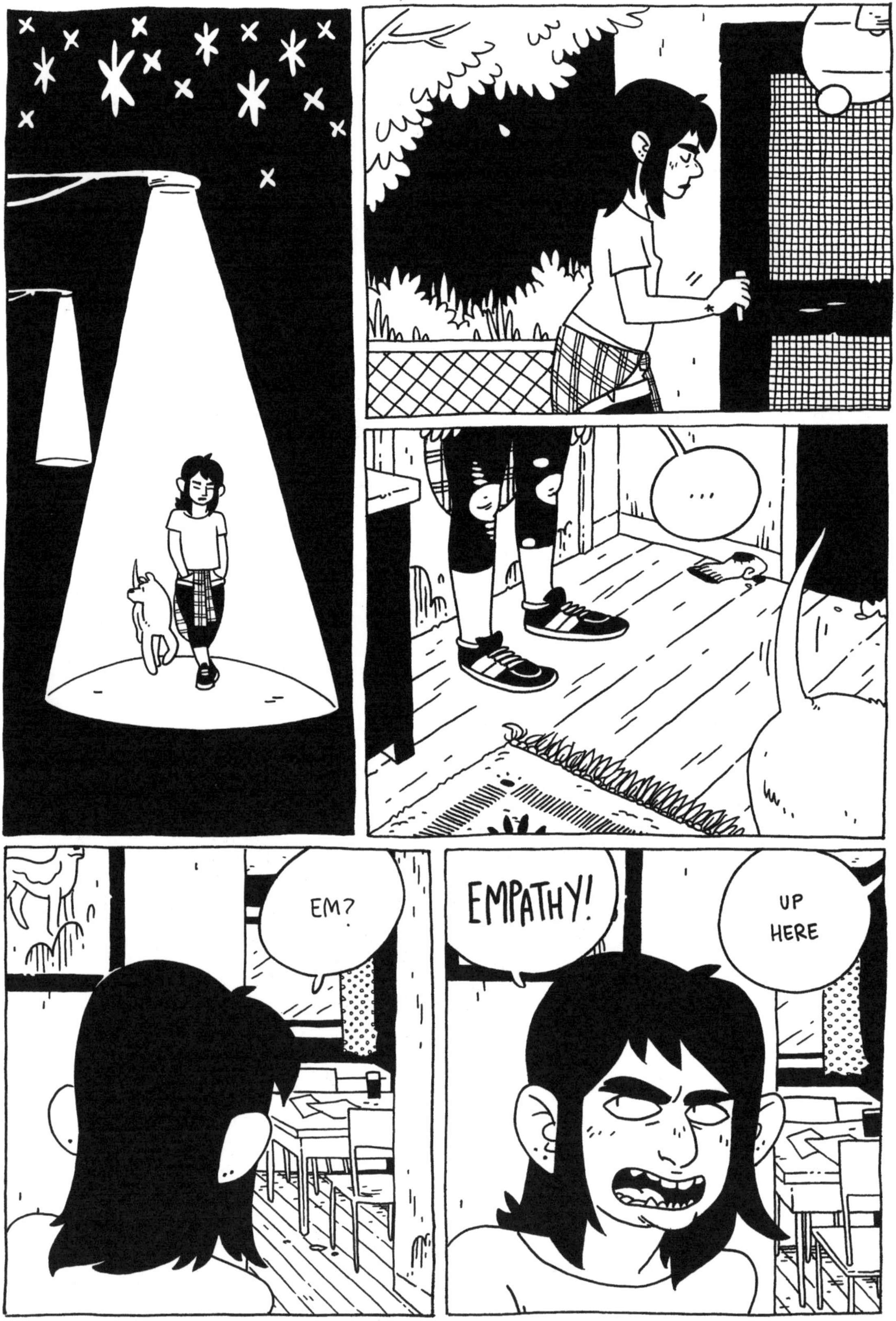
...
EM?
EMPATHY!
UP HERE

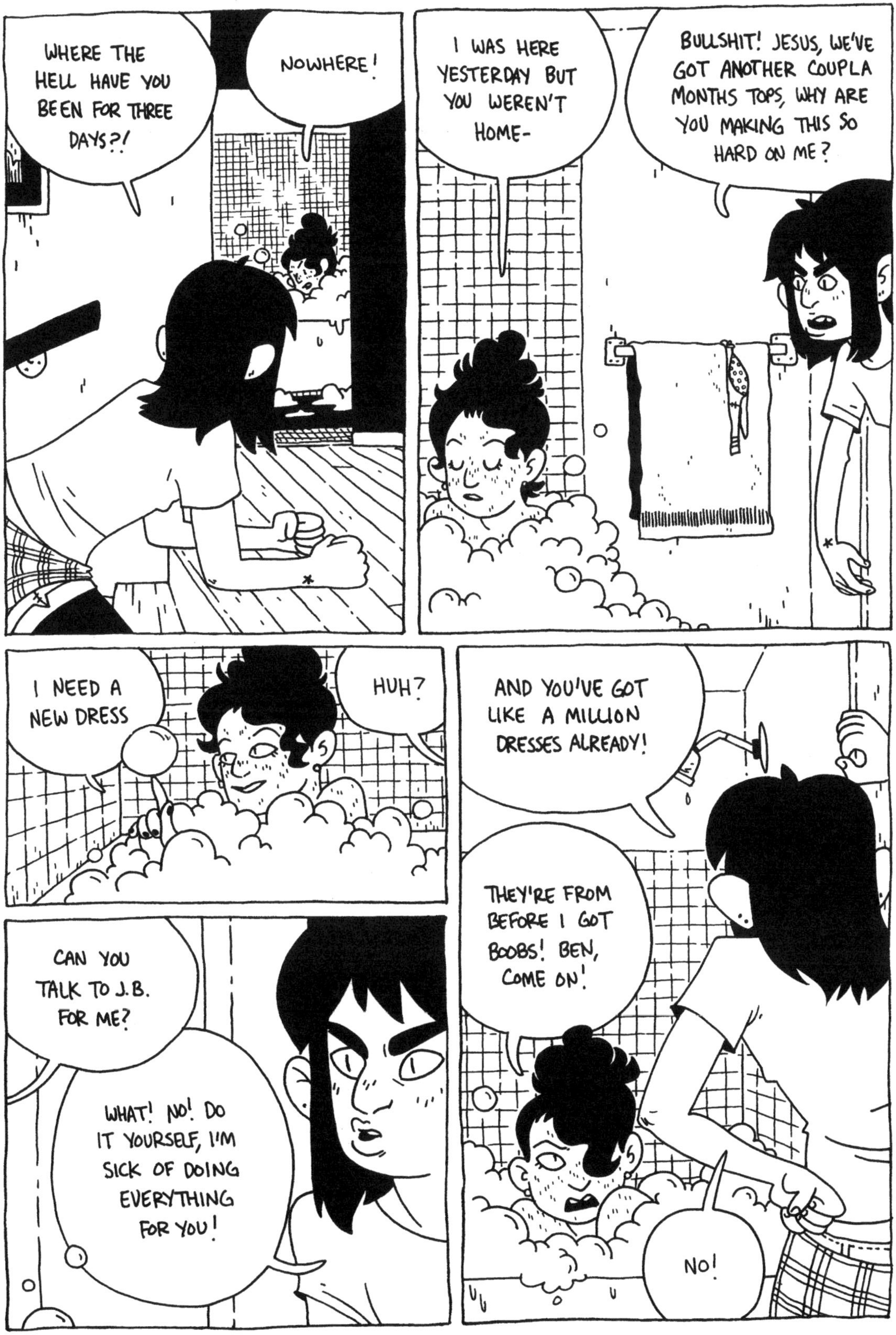
WHERE THE HELL HAVE YOU BEEN FOR THREE DAYS?!
NOWHERE!
I WAS HERE YESTERDAY BUT YOU WEREN'T HOME-
BULLSHIT! JESUS, WE'VE GOT ANOTHER COUPLA MONTHS TOPS, WHY ARE YOU MAKING THIS SO HARD ON ME?
I NEED A NEW DRESS
HUH?
AND YOU'VE GOT LIKE A MILLION DRESSES ALREADY!
THEY'RE FROM BEFORE I GOT BOOBS! BEN, COME ON!
CAN YOU TALK TO J.B. FOR ME?
WHAT! NO! DO IT YOURSELF, I'M SICK OF DOING EVERYTHING FOR YOU!
NO!

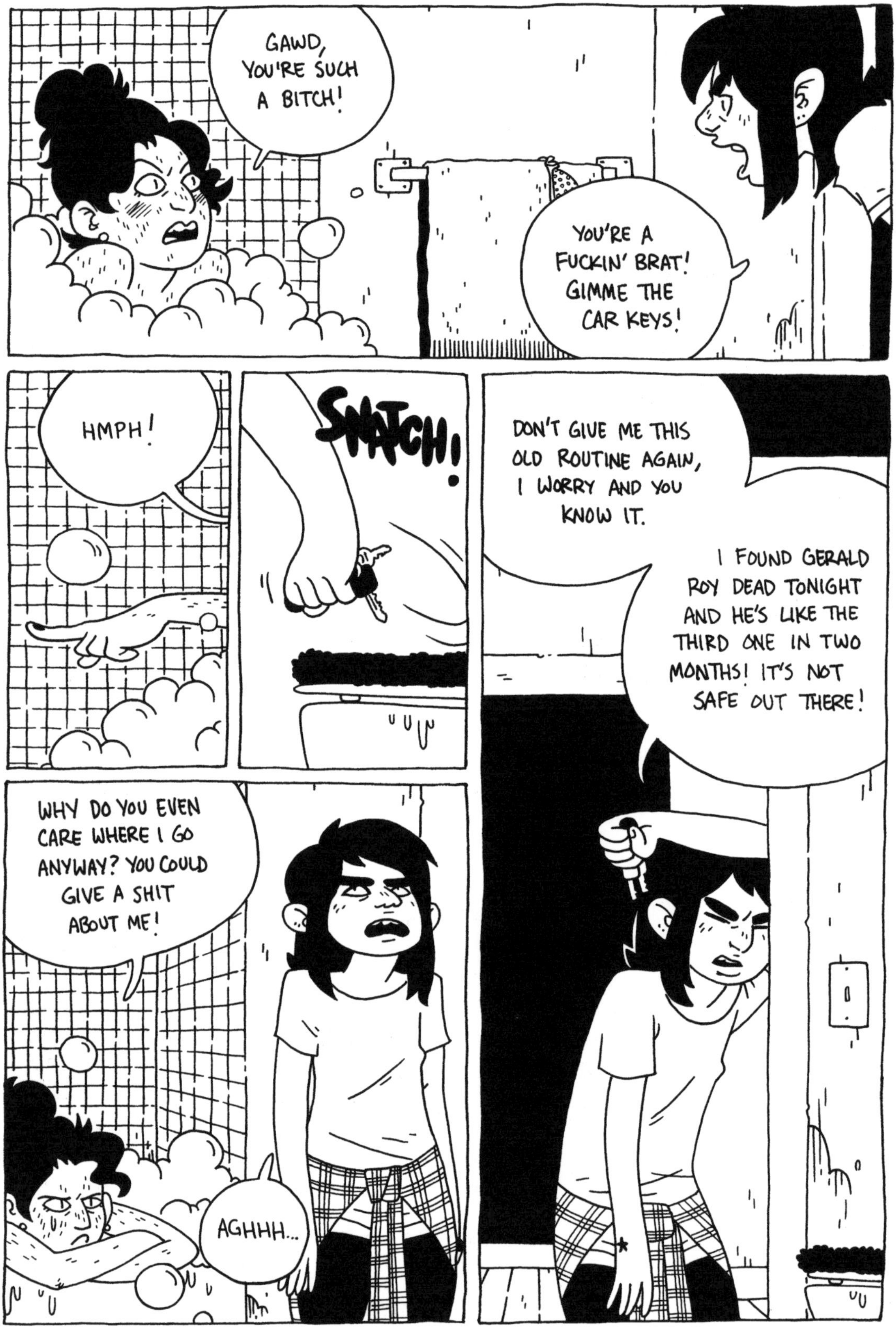
GAWD, YOU'RE SUCH A BITCH!
YOU'RE A FUCKIN' BRAT! GIMME THE CAR KEYS!
HMPH!
SNATCH!
DON'T GIVE ME THIS OLD ROUTINE AGAIN, I WORRY AND YOU KNOW IT.
I FOUND GERALD ROY DEAD TONIGHT AND HE'S LIKE THE THIRD ONE IN TWO MONTHS! IT'S NOT SAFE OUT THERE!
WHY DO YOU EVEN CARE WHERE I GO ANYWAY? YOU COULD GIVE A SHIT ABOUT ME!
AGHHH...

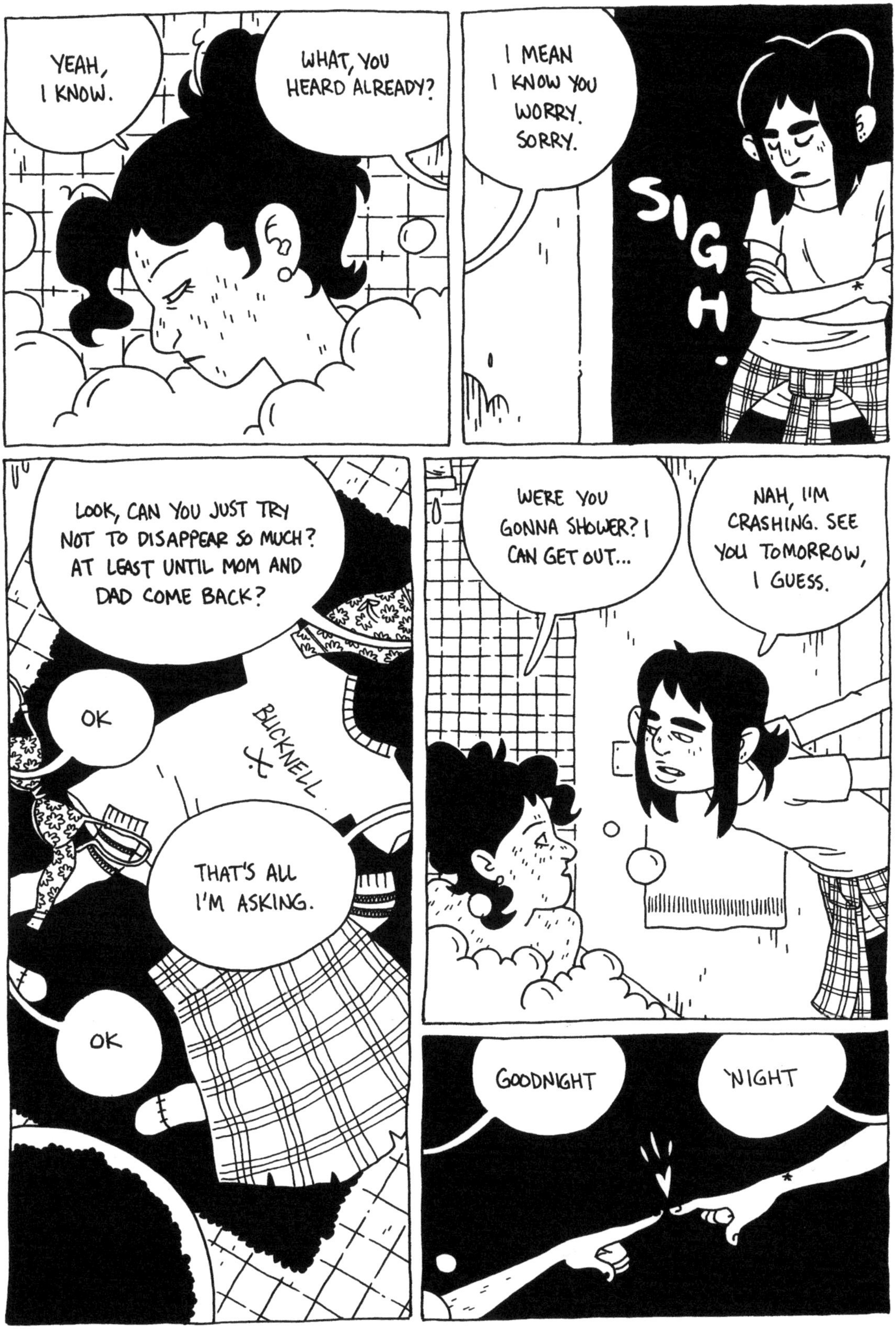
YEAH, I KNOW.
WHAT, YOU HEARD ALREADY?
I MEAN I KNOW YOU WORRY. SORRY.
SIGH.
LOOK, CAN YOU JUST TRY NOT TO DISAPPEAR SO MUCH? AT LEAST UNTIL MOM AND DAD COME BACK?
OK
BUCKNELL
THAT'S ALL I'M ASKING.
OK
WERE YOU GONNA SHOWER? I CAN GET OUT...
NAH, I'M CRASHING. SEE YOU TOMORROW, I GUESS.
GOODNIGHT
'NIGHT

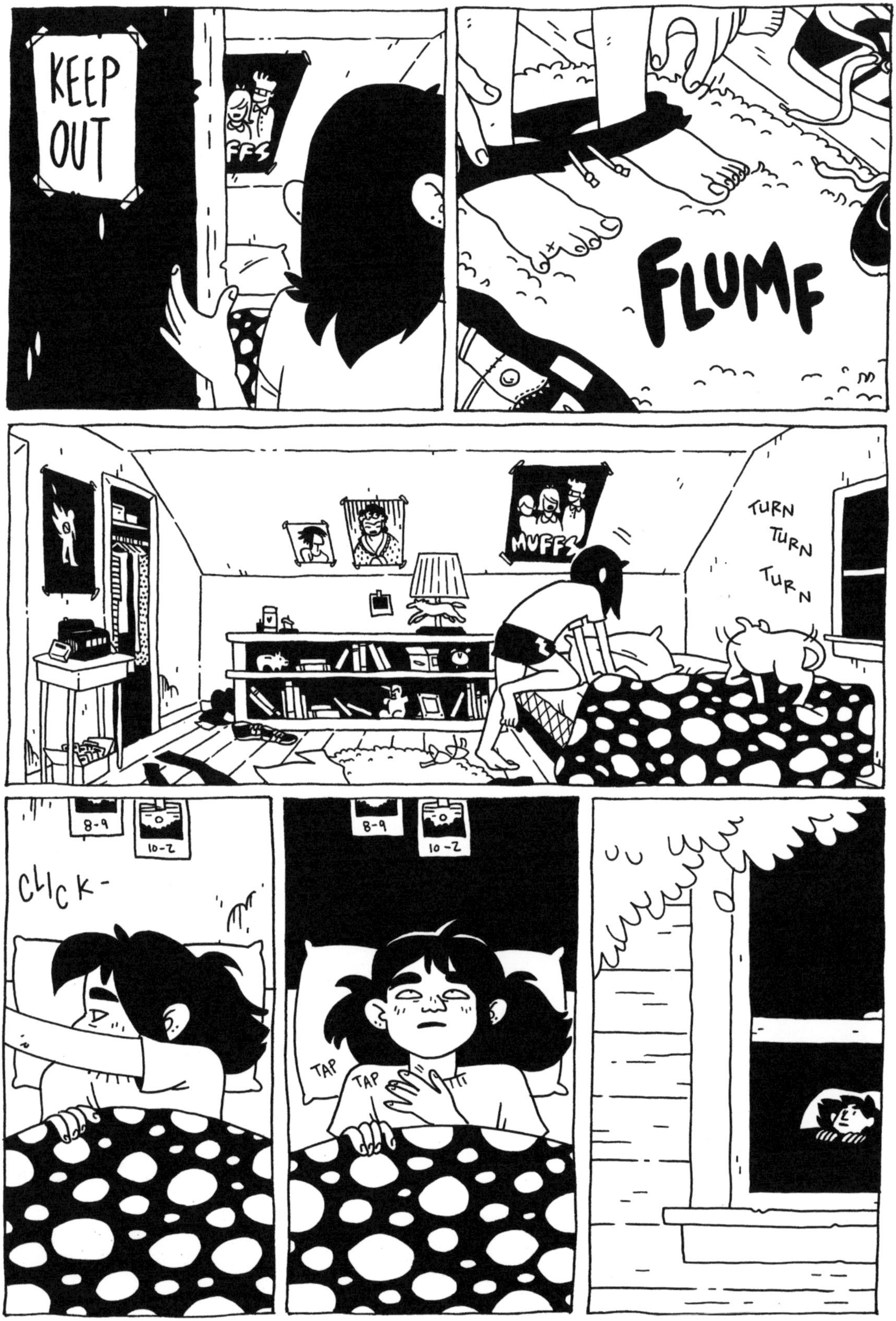
KEEP OUT
FFS
FLUMF
MUFFS
TURN
TURN
TURN
8-9
10-2
CLICK-
8-9
10-2
TAP
TAP

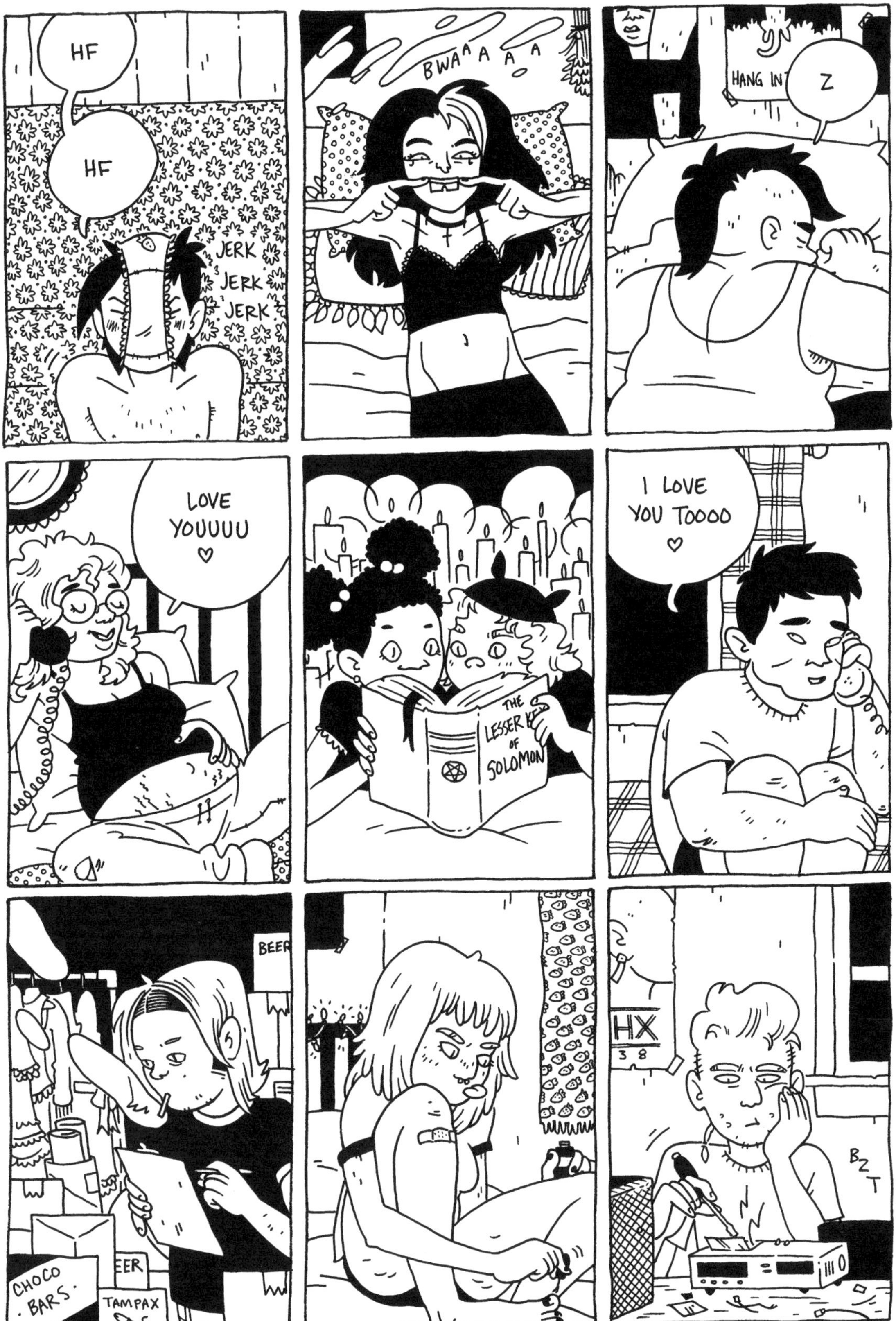
HF
HF
JERK
JERK
JERK
BWAAAAA
HANG IN
Z
LOVE YOUUUU ♡
THE LESSER KEY OF SOLOMON
I LOVE YOU TOOOO ♡
BEER
CHOCO BARS
EER
TAMPAX
HX
3 8
BZT

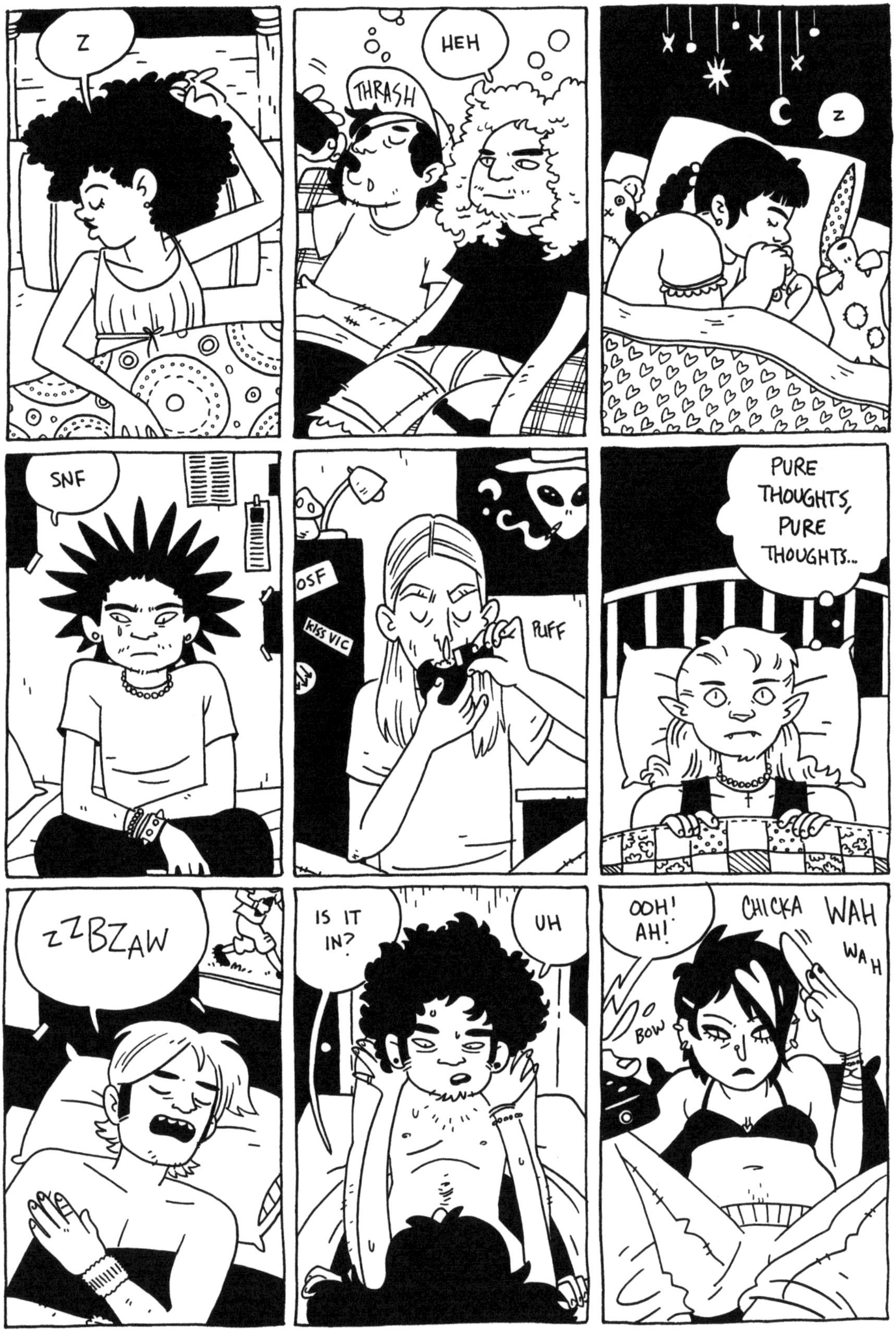
Z
THRASH
HEH
Z
SNF
OSF
KISS VIC
PUFF
PURE THOUGHTS, PURE THOUGHTS...
ZZBZAW
IS IT IN?
UH
OOH! AH!
BOW
CHICKA
WAH
WAH

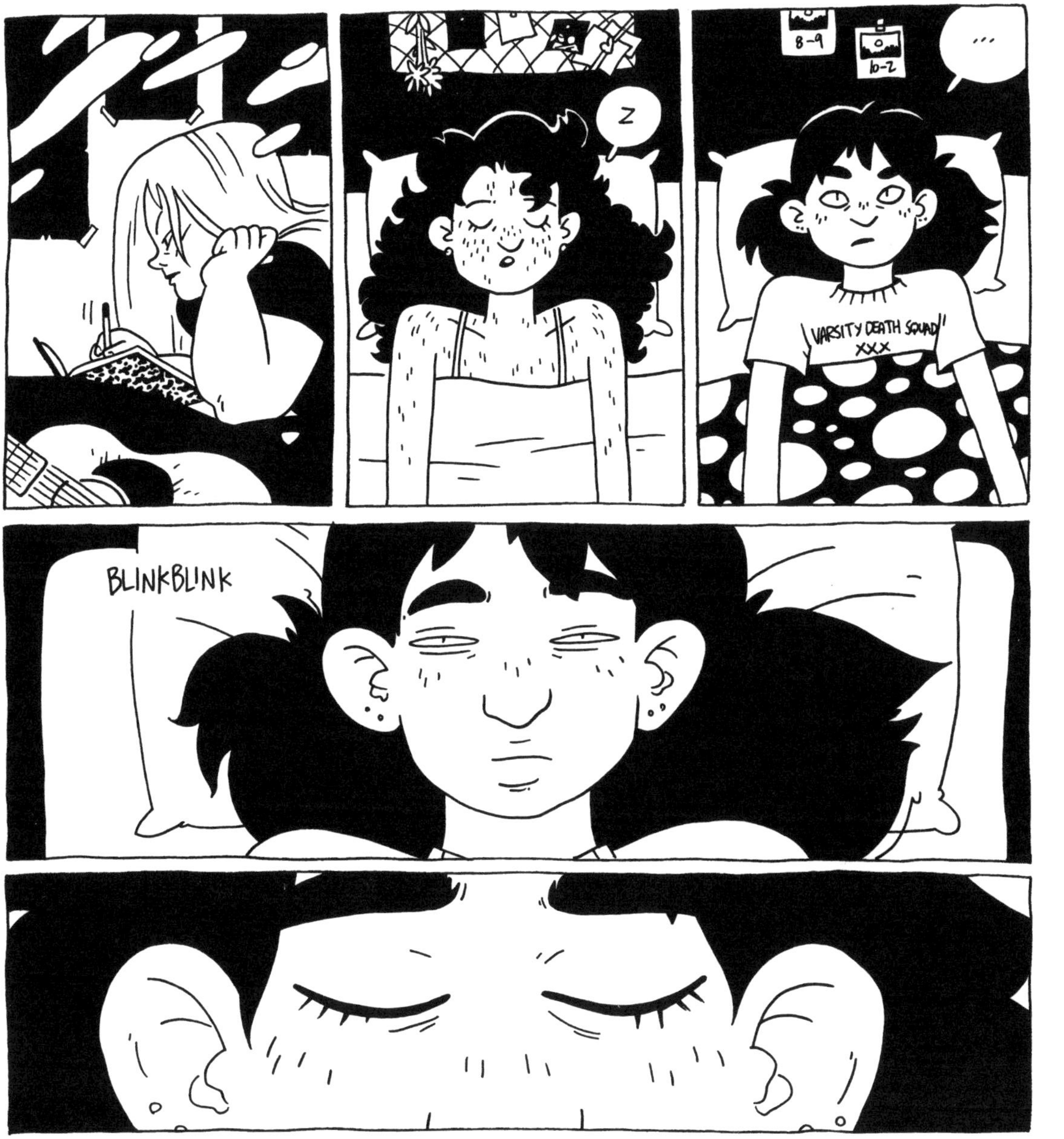
Z
8-9
10-2
...
VARSITY DEATH SQUAD
XXX
BLINKBLINK

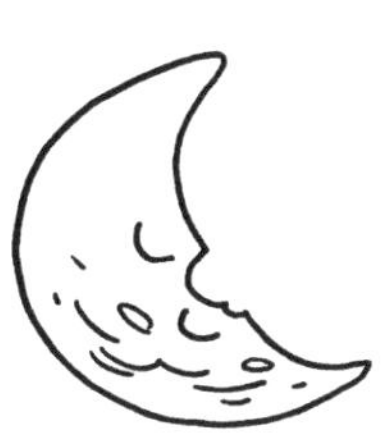

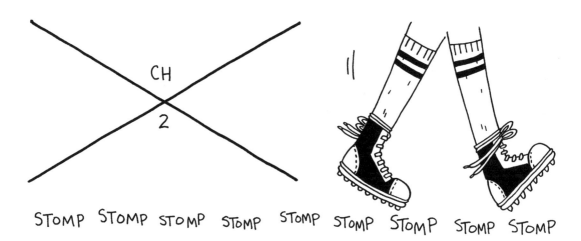

CH

2

STOMP STOMP STOMP STOMP STOMP STOMP STOMP STOMP STOMP

STOMP
STOMP
STOMP
STOMP

BEN! HEY!

WHERE'S OTTO?

UH, INSIDE I THINK...

STOMP

STOMP

I MEAN I HAVEN'T GONE IN YET—

OKAY THANKS BYE

STOMP STOMP

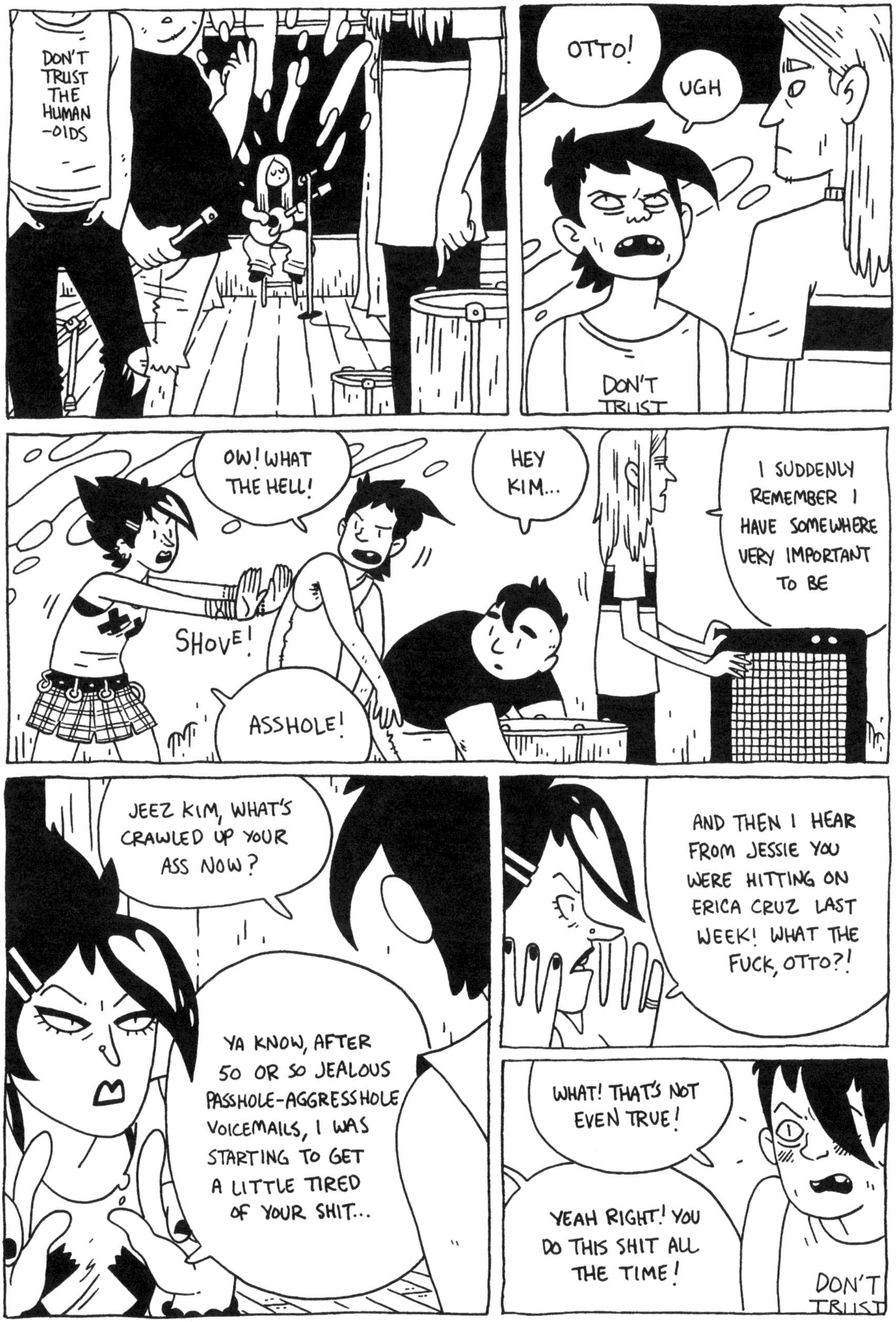
DON'T TRUST THE HUMAN-OIDS
OTTO!
UGH
DON'T TRUST
OW! WHAT THE HELL!
HEY KIM...
I SUDDENLY REMEMBER I HAVE SOMEWHERE VERY IMPORTANT TO BE
SHOVE!
ASSHOLE!
JEEZ KIM, WHAT'S CRAWLED UP YOUR ASS NOW?
YA KNOW, AFTER 50 OR SO JEALOUS PASSHOLE-AGGRESSHOLE VOICEMAILS, I WAS STARTING TO GET A LITTLE TIRED OF YOUR SHIT...
AND THEN I HEAR FROM JESSIE YOU WERE HITTING ON ERICA CRUZ LAST WEEK! WHAT THE FUCK, OTTO?!
WHAT! THAT'S NOT EVEN TRUE!
YEAH RIGHT! YOU DO THIS SHIT ALL THE TIME!
DON'T TRUST

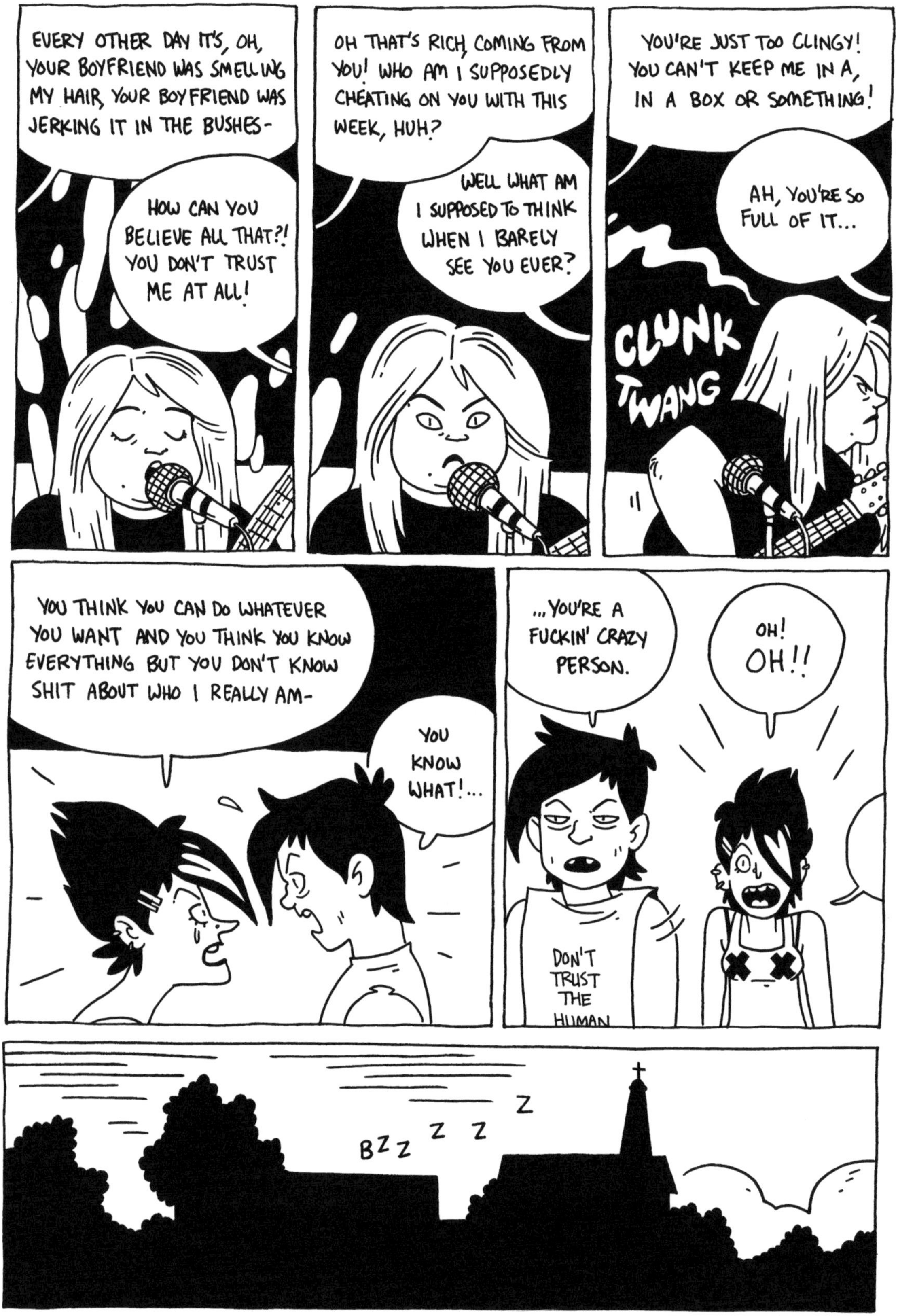
EVERY OTHER DAY IT'S, OH, YOUR BOYFRIEND WAS SMELLING MY HAIR, YOUR BOYFRIEND WAS JERKING IT IN THE BUSHES-
HOW CAN YOU BELIEVE ALL THAT?! YOU DON'T TRUST ME AT ALL!
OH THAT'S RICH, COMING FROM YOU! WHO AM I SUPPOSEDLY CHEATING ON YOU WITH THIS WEEK, HUH?
WELL WHAT AM I SUPPOSED TO THINK WHEN I BARELY SEE YOU EVER?
YOU'RE JUST TOO CLINGY! YOU CAN'T KEEP ME IN A, IN A BOX OR SOMETHING!
AH, YOU'RE SO FULL OF IT...
CLUNK
TWANG
YOU THINK YOU CAN DO WHATEVER YOU WANT AND YOU THINK YOU KNOW EVERYTHING BUT YOU DON'T KNOW SHIT ABOUT WHO I REALLY AM-
YOU KNOW WHAT!...
...YOU'RE A FUCKIN' CRAZY PERSON.
OH! OH!!
DON'T TRUST THE HUMAN
BZZZ Z Z Z

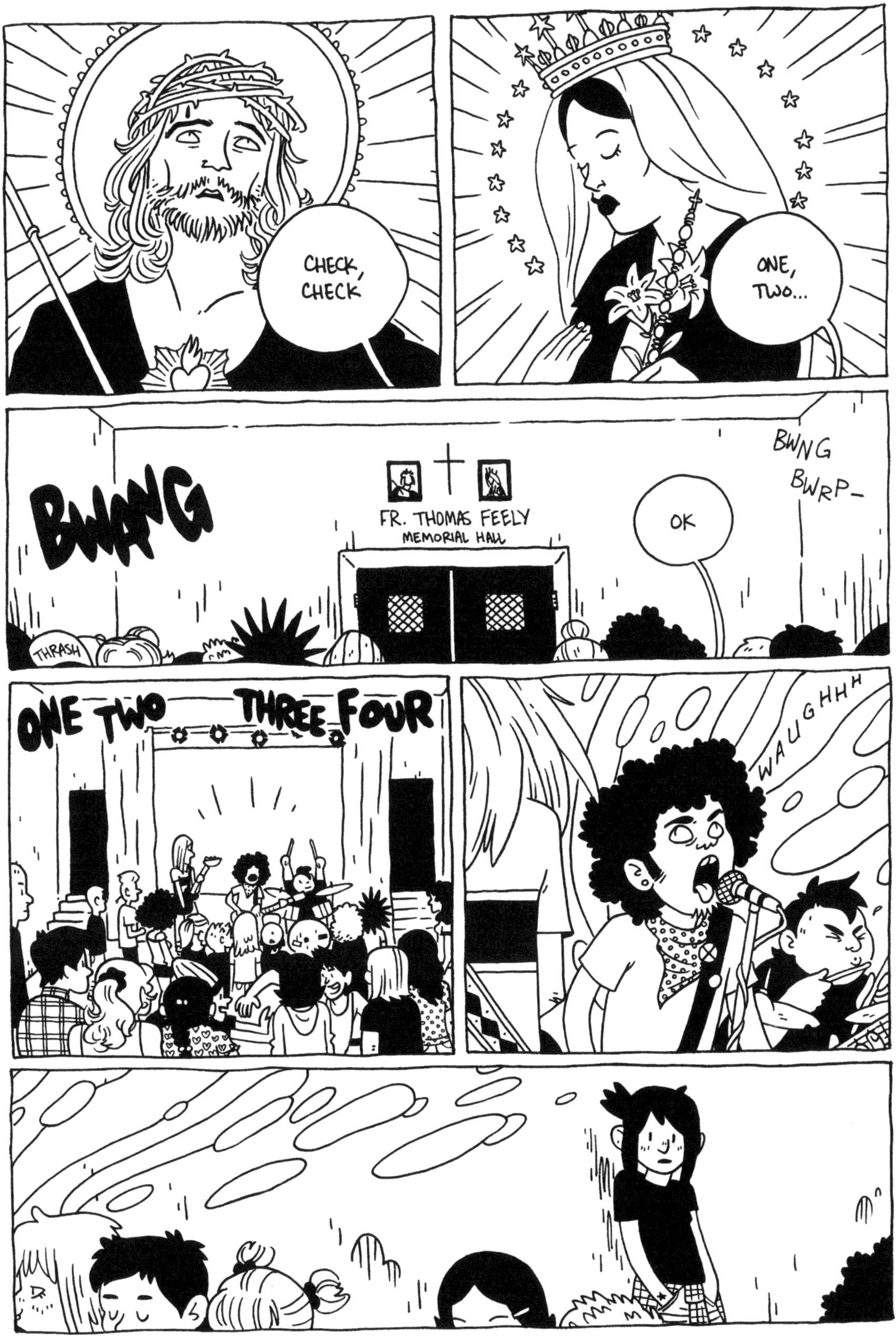

CHECK, CHECK
ONE, TWO...
BWANG
FR. THOMAS FEELY
MEMORIAL HALL
OK
BWNG
BWRP-
THRASH
ONE TWO THREE FOUR
WAUGHHH

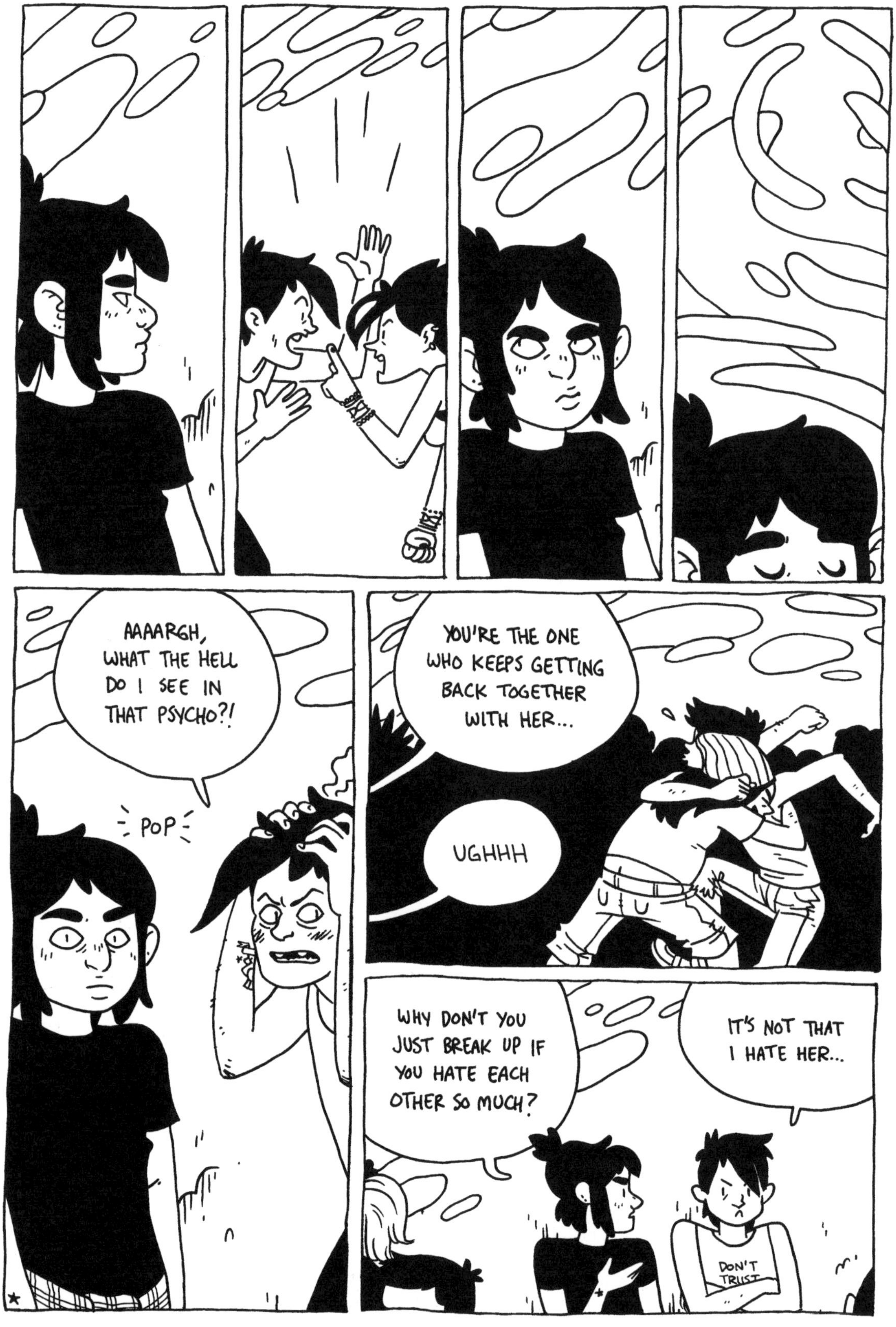
AAAARGH, WHAT THE HELL DO I SEE IN THAT PSYCHO?!
POP
YOU'RE THE ONE WHO KEEPS GETTING BACK TOGETHER WITH HER...
UGHHH
WHY DON'T YOU JUST BREAK UP IF YOU HATE EACH OTHER SO MUCH?
IT'S NOT THAT I HATE HER...
DON'T TRUST

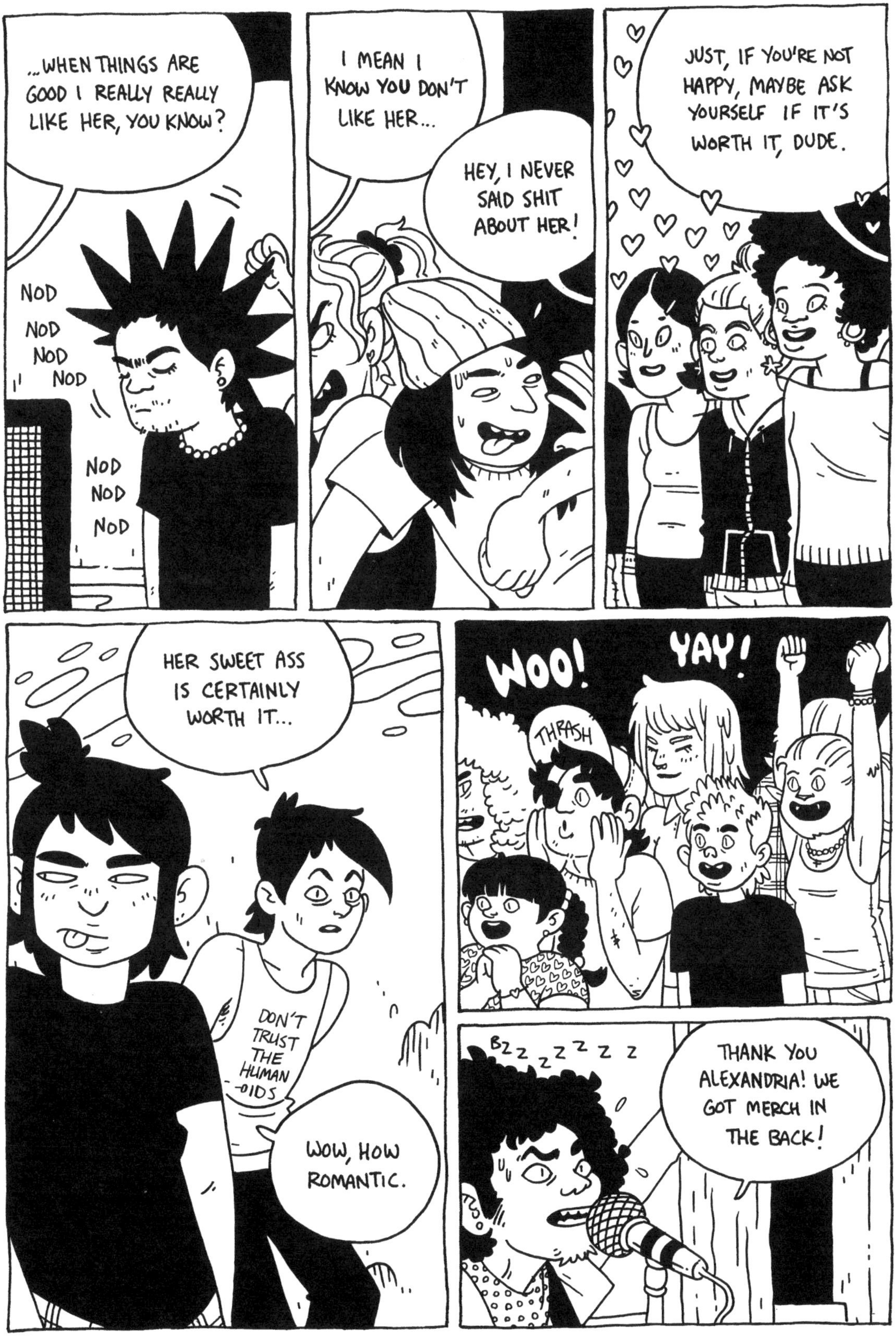
...WHEN THINGS ARE GOOD I REALLY REALLY LIKE HER, YOU KNOW?
NOD
NOD
NOD
NOD
NOD
NOD
NOD
I MEAN I KNOW YOU DON'T LIKE HER...
HEY, I NEVER SAID SHIT ABOUT HER!
JUST, IF YOU'RE NOT HAPPY, MAYBE ASK YOURSELF IF IT'S WORTH IT, DUDE.
HER SWEET ASS IS CERTAINLY WORTH IT...
DON'T TRUST THE HUMAN -OIDS
WOW, HOW ROMANTIC.
WOO!
YAY!
THRASH
BZZ Z Z Z Z Z
THANK YOU ALEXANDRIA! WE GOT MERCH IN THE BACK!

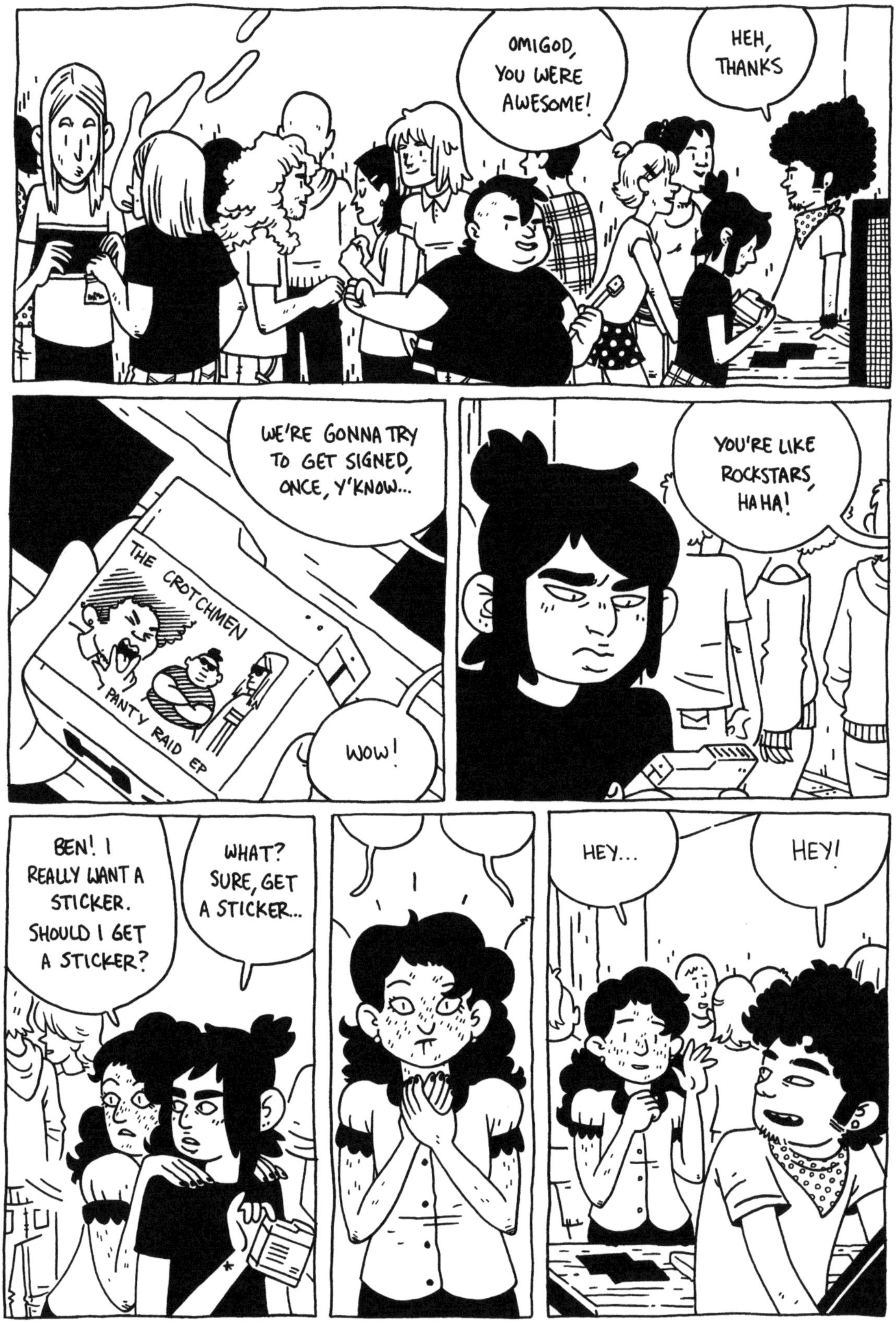
OMIGOD, YOU WERE AWESOME!
HEH, THANKS
WE'RE GONNA TRY TO GET SIGNED, ONCE, Y'KNOW...
THE CROTCHMEN
PANTY RAID EP
WOW!
YOU'RE LIKE ROCKSTARS, HAHA!
BEN! I REALLY WANT A STICKER. SHOULD I GET A STICKER?
WHAT? SURE, GET A STICKER...
HEY...
HEY!

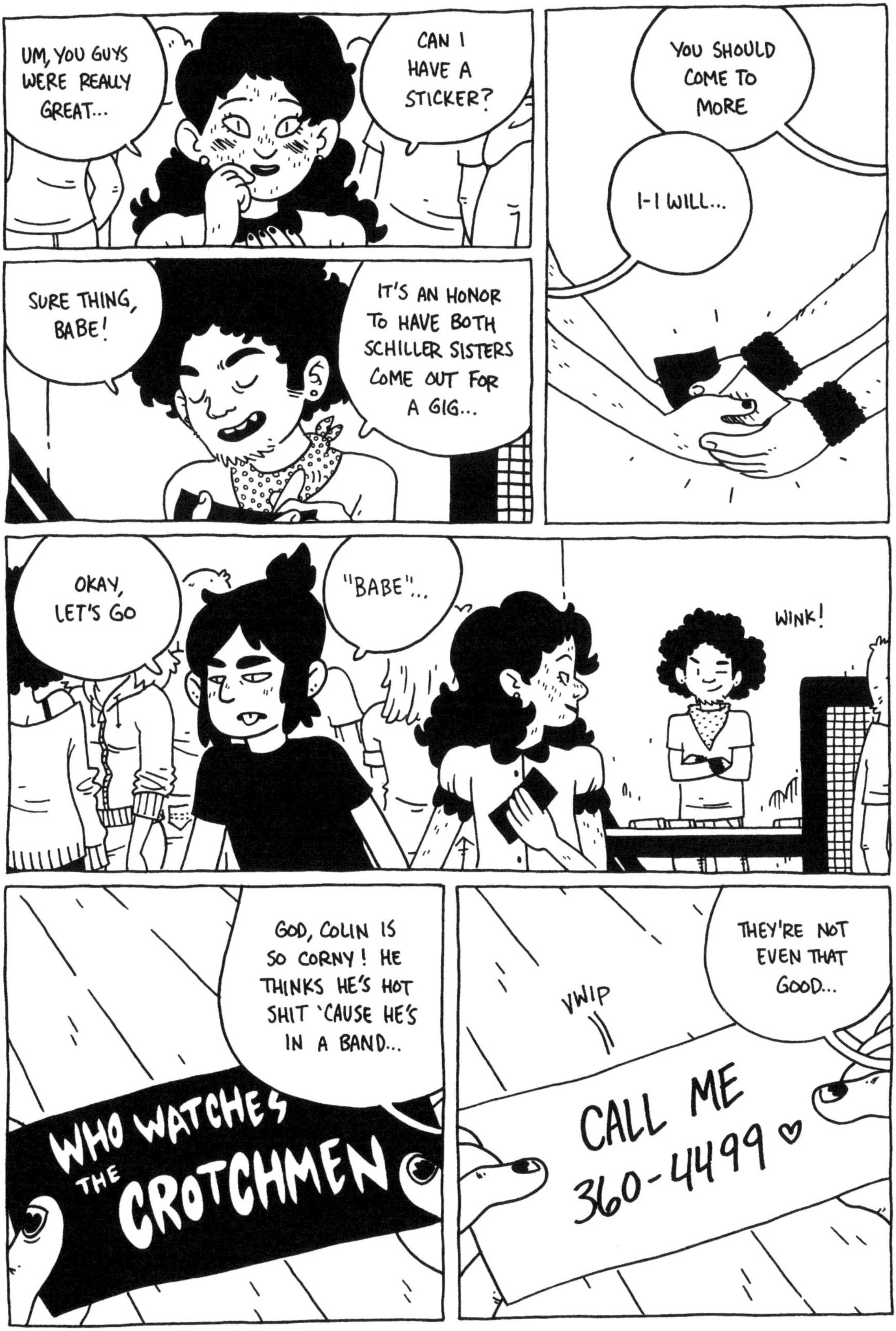
UM, YOU GUYS WERE REALLY GREAT...
CAN I HAVE A STICKER?
SURE THING, BABE!
IT'S AN HONOR TO HAVE BOTH SCHILLER SISTERS COME OUT FOR A GIG...
YOU SHOULD COME TO MORE
I-I WILL...
OKAY, LET'S GO
"BABE"...
WINK!
GOD, COLIN IS SO CORNY! HE THINKS HE'S HOT SHIT 'CAUSE HE'S IN A BAND...
WHO WATCHES THE CROTCHMEN
THEY'RE NOT EVEN THAT GOOD...
VWIP
CALL ME 360-4499

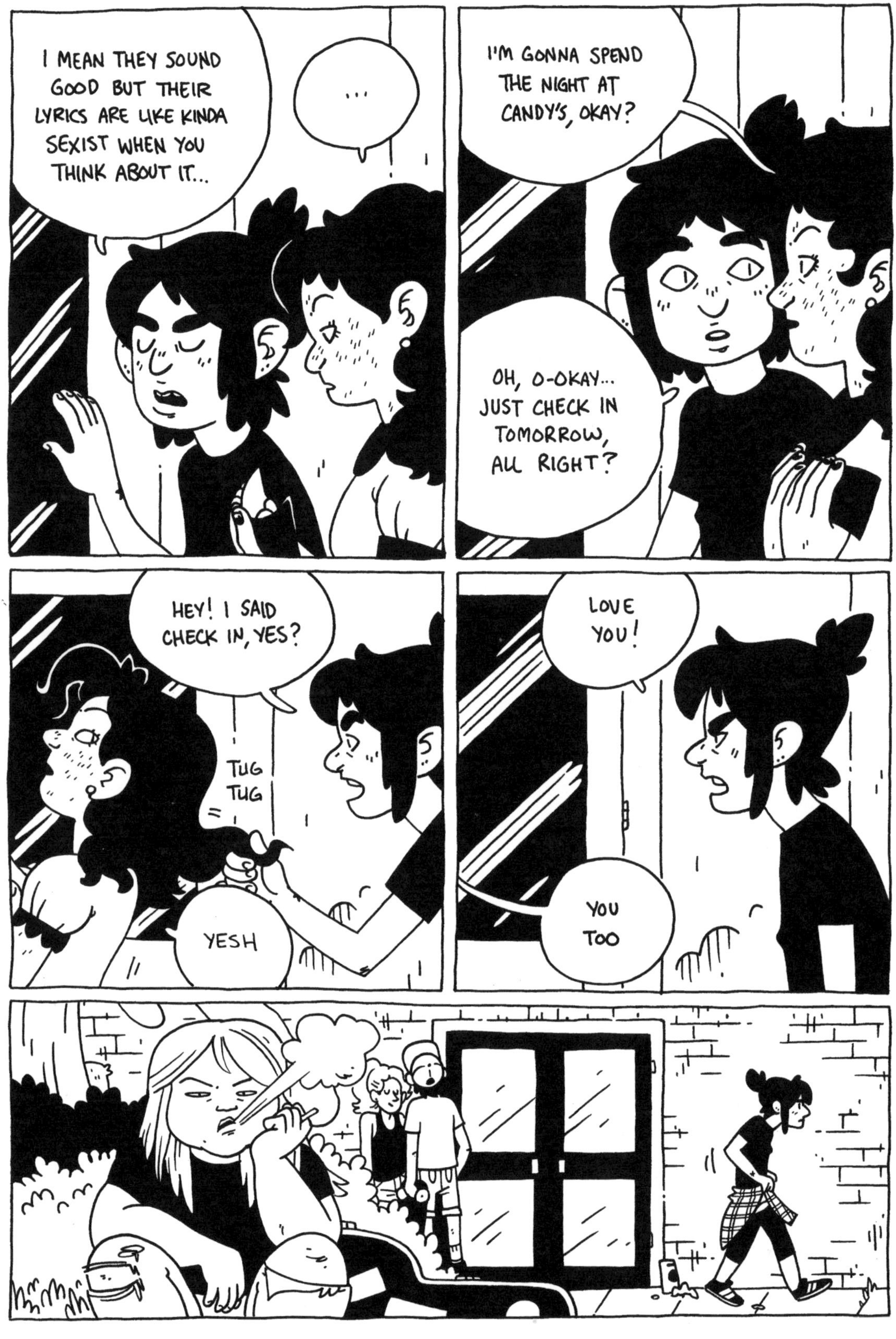
I MEAN THEY SOUND GOOD BUT THEIR LYRICS ARE LIKE KINDA SEXIST WHEN YOU THINK ABOUT IT...
...
I'M GONNA SPEND THE NIGHT AT CANDY'S, OKAY?
OH, O-OKAY... JUST CHECK IN TOMORROW, ALL RIGHT?
HEY! I SAID CHECK IN, YES?
TUG TUG
YESH
LOVE YOU!
YOU TOO

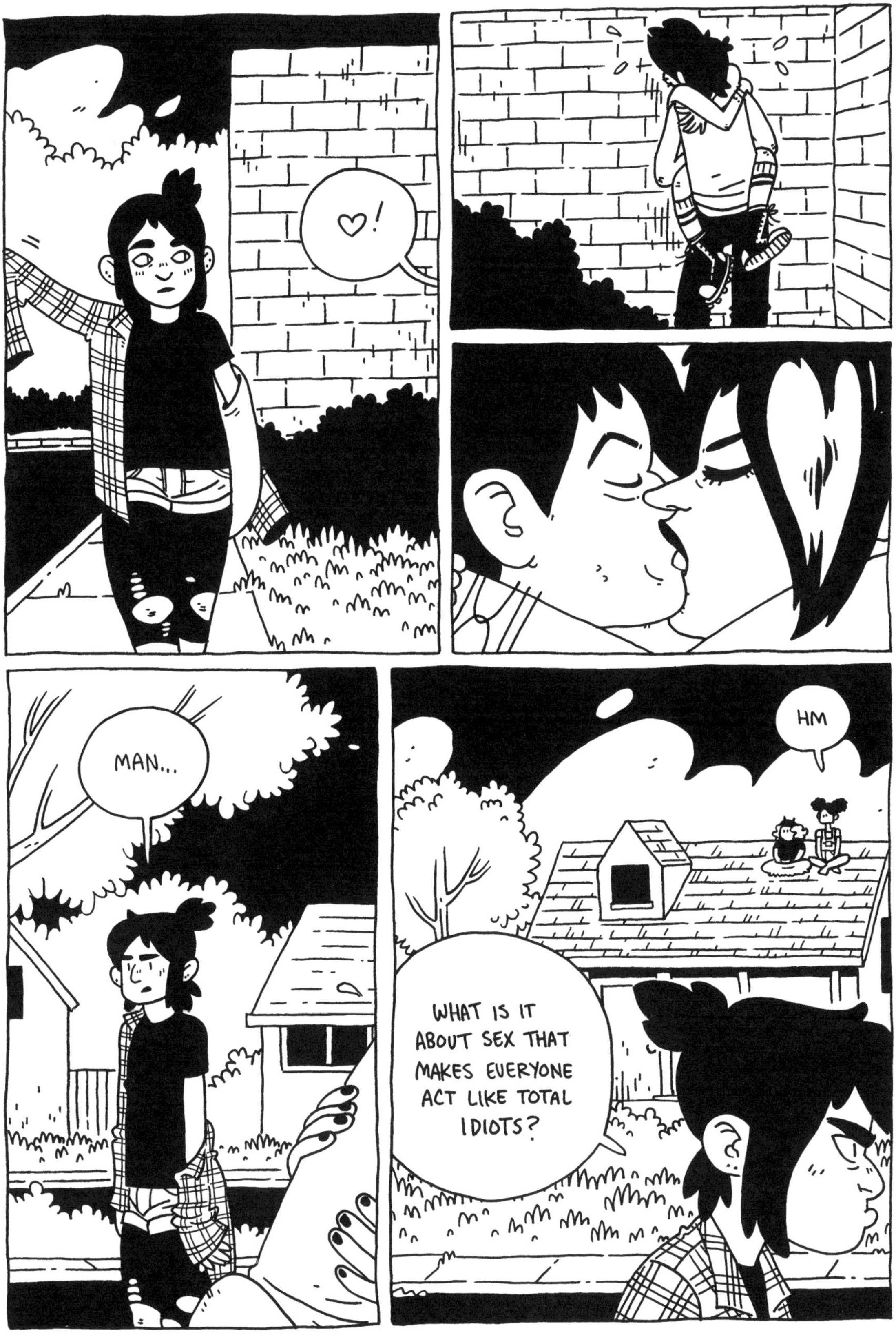
♡!
MAN...
HM
WHAT IS IT ABOUT SEX THAT MAKES EVERYONE ACT LIKE TOTAL IDIOTS?

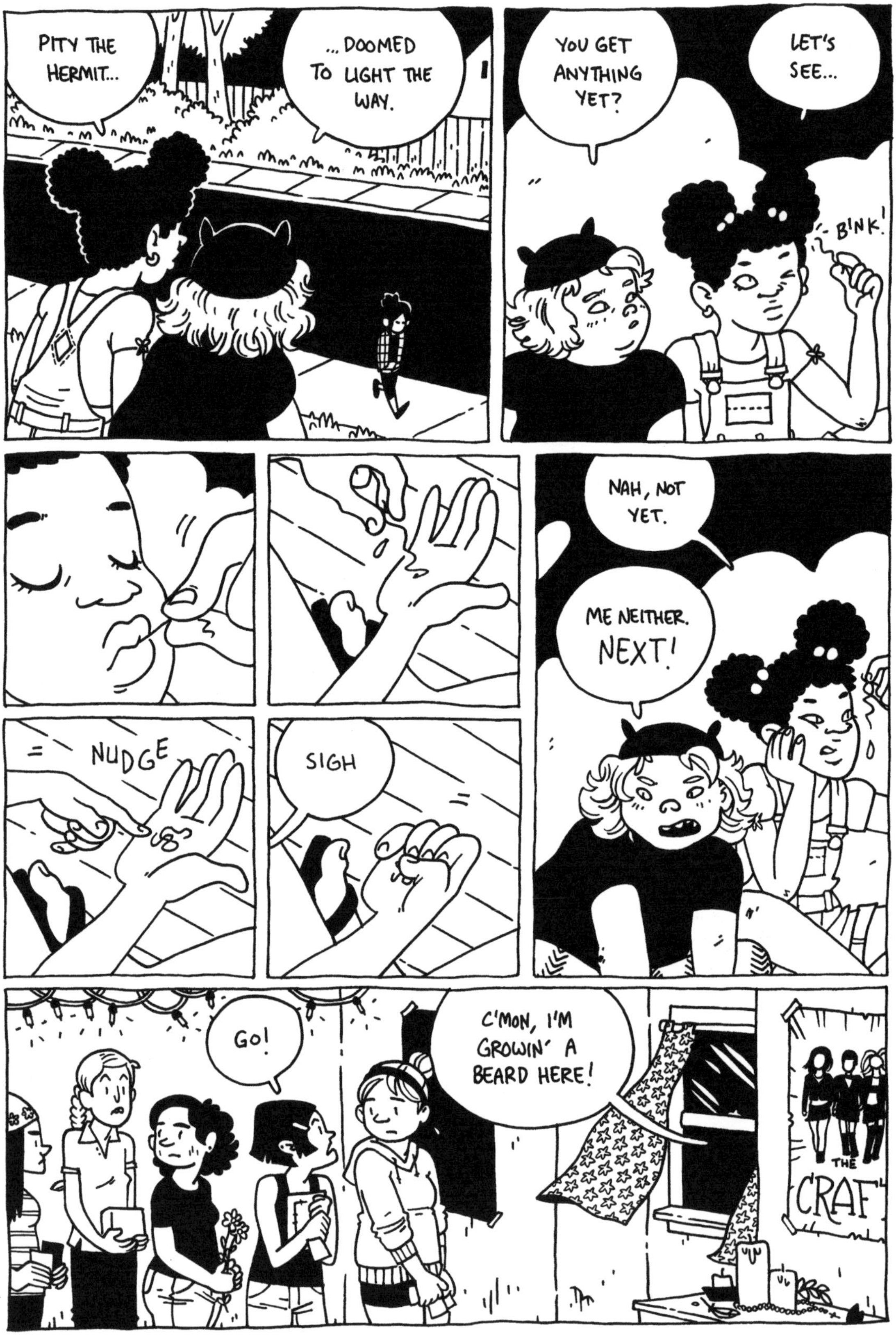
PITY THE HERMIT...
...DOOMED TO LIGHT THE WAY.
YOU GET ANYTHING YET?
LET'S SEE...
BINK!
NAH, NOT YET.
ME NEITHER. NEXT!
NUDGE
SIGH
GO!
C'MON, I'M GROWIN' A BEARD HERE!
THE CRAF

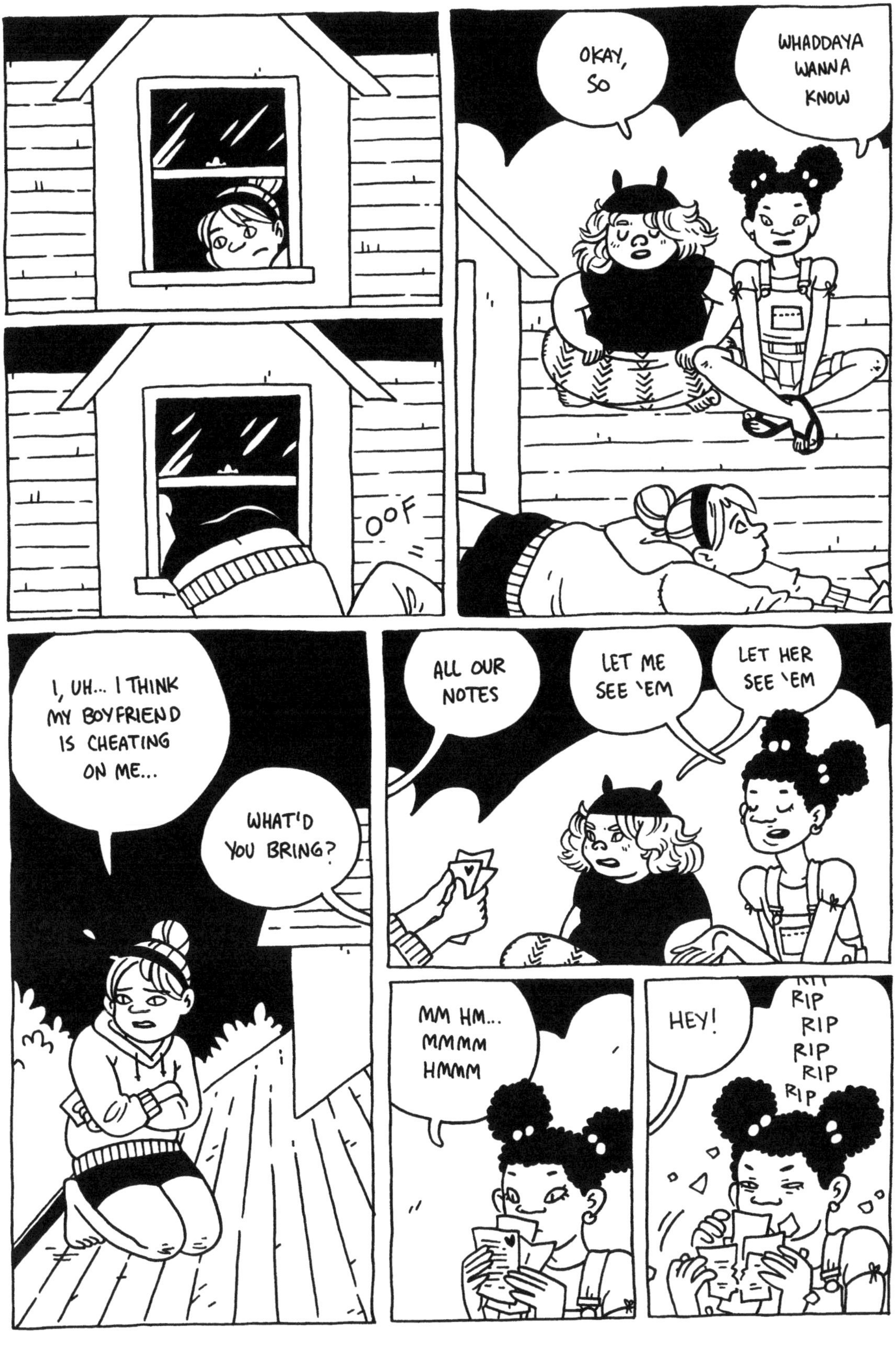
OOF
OKAY, SO
WHADDAYA WANNA KNOW
I, UH... I THINK MY BOYFRIEND IS CHEATING ON ME...
WHAT'D YOU BRING?
ALL OUR NOTES
LET ME SEE 'EM
LET HER SEE 'EM
MM HM... MMMM HMMM
HEY!
RIP
RIP
RIP
RIP
RIP
RIP

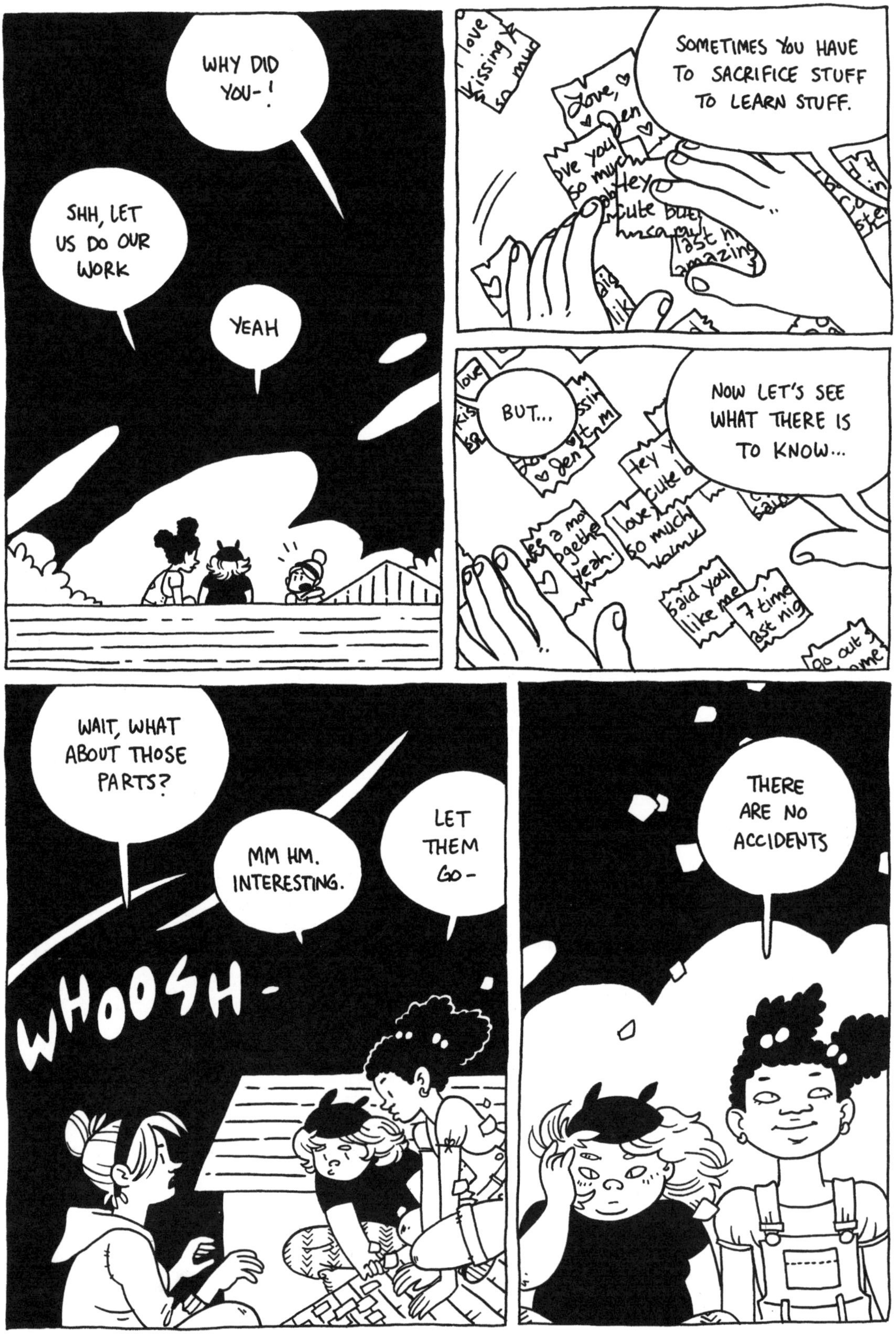

WHY DID YOU-!
SHH, LET US DO OUR WORK
YEAH
SOMETIMES YOU HAVE TO SACRIFICE STUFF TO LEARN STUFF.
BUT...
NOW LET'S SEE WHAT THERE IS TO KNOW...
WAIT, WHAT ABOUT THOSE PARTS?
MM HM. INTERESTING.
LET THEM GO-
WHOOSH-
THERE ARE NO ACCIDENTS

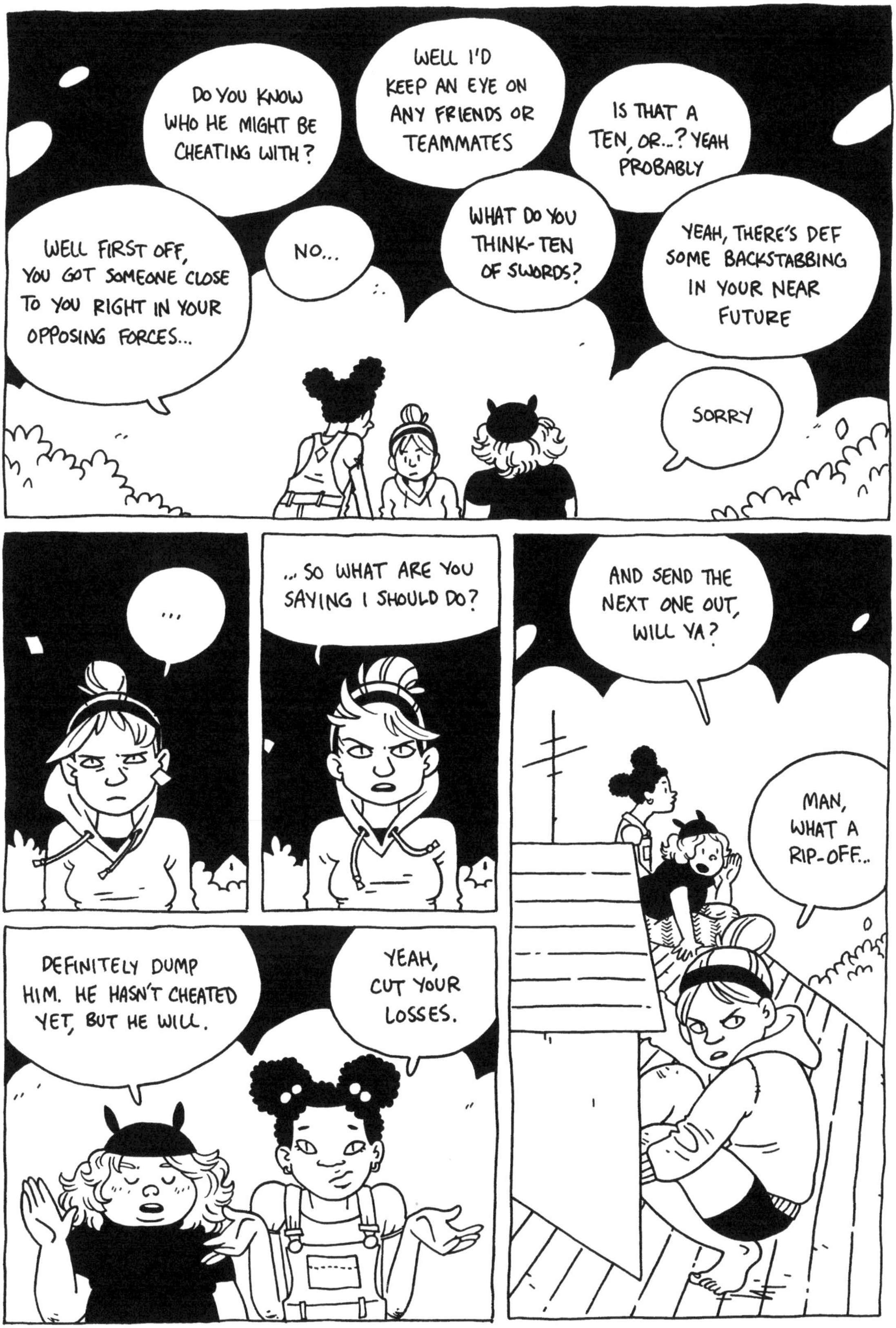
DO YOU KNOW WHO HE MIGHT BE CHEATING WITH?
WELL I'D KEEP AN EYE ON ANY FRIENDS OR TEAMMATES
IS THAT A TEN, OR...? YEAH PROBABLY
WELL FIRST OFF, YOU GOT SOMEONE CLOSE TO YOU RIGHT IN YOUR OPPOSING FORCES...
NO...
WHAT DO YOU THINK- TEN OF SWORDS?
YEAH, THERE'S DEF SOME BACKSTABBING IN YOUR NEAR FUTURE
SORRY
...
... SO WHAT ARE YOU SAYING I SHOULD DO?
DEFINITELY DUMP HIM. HE HASN'T CHEATED YET, BUT HE WILL.
YEAH, CUT YOUR LOSSES.
AND SEND THE NEXT ONE OUT, WILL YA?
MAN, WHAT A RIP-OFF...

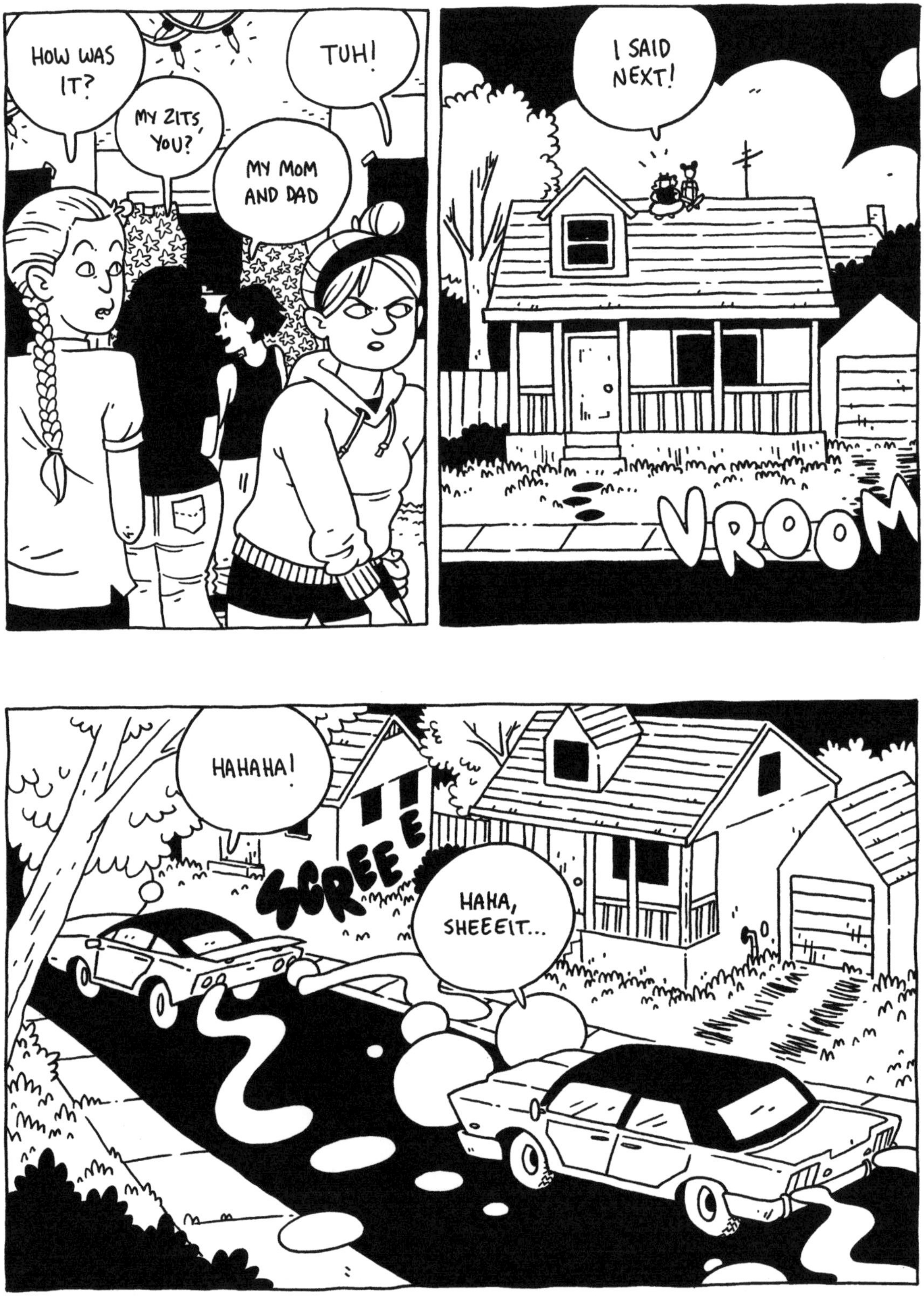
HOW WAS IT?
MY ZITS, YOU?
MY MOM AND DAD
TUH!
I SAID NEXT!
VROOM
HAHAHA!
SCREEE
HAHA, SHEEEIT...

CH
3
BRNNNG
SHIT!
BRNNNG...
OKAY, OKAY...
BRNNNG!!
DUDE, IT'S WADE
OH HEY MAN, WHAT'S UP?
HORROR FLICK AT THE MONOPLEX, TONIGHT, WANNA GO?
SURE. CALL A CHAPERONE THOUGH, I DON'T WANT YOU TO DATE-RAPE ME
FUCK YOU! OKAY, HANG ON-

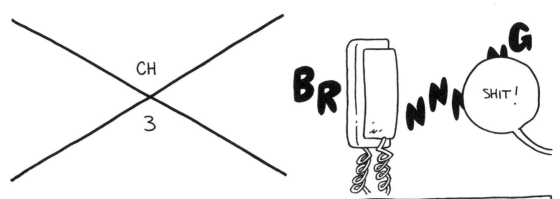

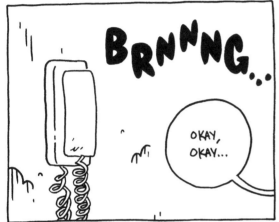

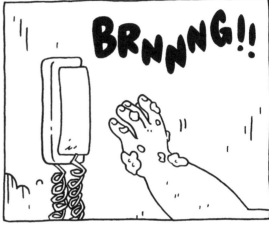

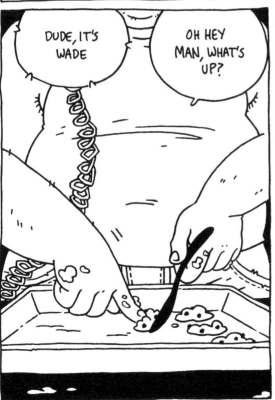

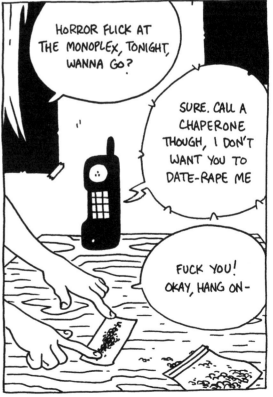

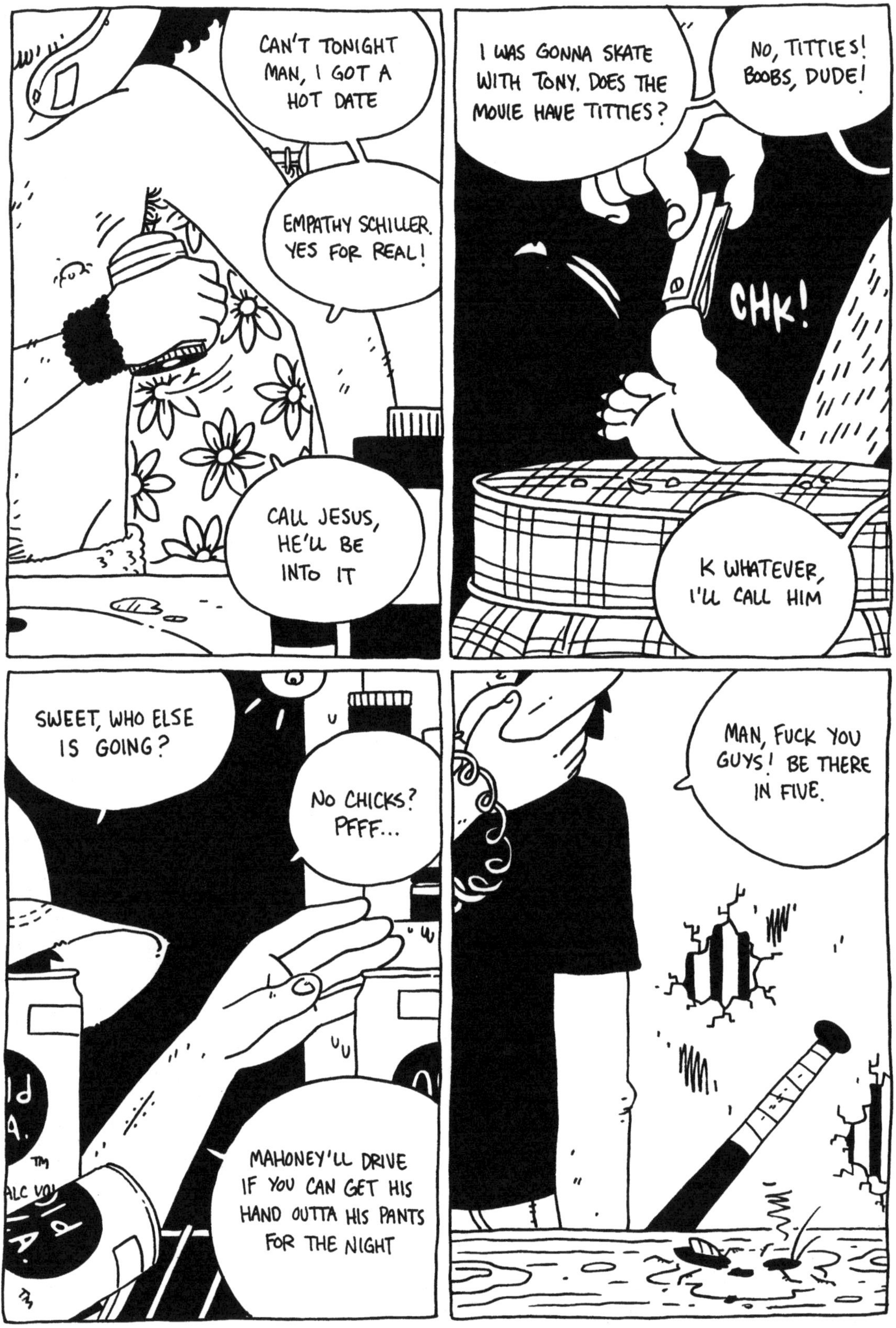
CAN'T TONIGHT MAN, I GOT A HOT DATE
EMPATHY SCHILLER. YES FOR REAL!
CALL JESUS, HE'LL BE INTO IT
I WAS GONNA SKATE WITH TONY. DOES THE MOVIE HAVE TITTIES?
NO, TITTIES! BOOBS, DUDE!
CHK!
K WHATEVER, I'LL CALL HIM
SWEET, WHO ELSE IS GOING?
NO CHICKS? PFFF...
MAHONEY'LL DRIVE IF YOU CAN GET HIS HAND OUTTA HIS PANTS FOR THE NIGHT
MAN, FUCK YOU GUYS! BE THERE IN FIVE.

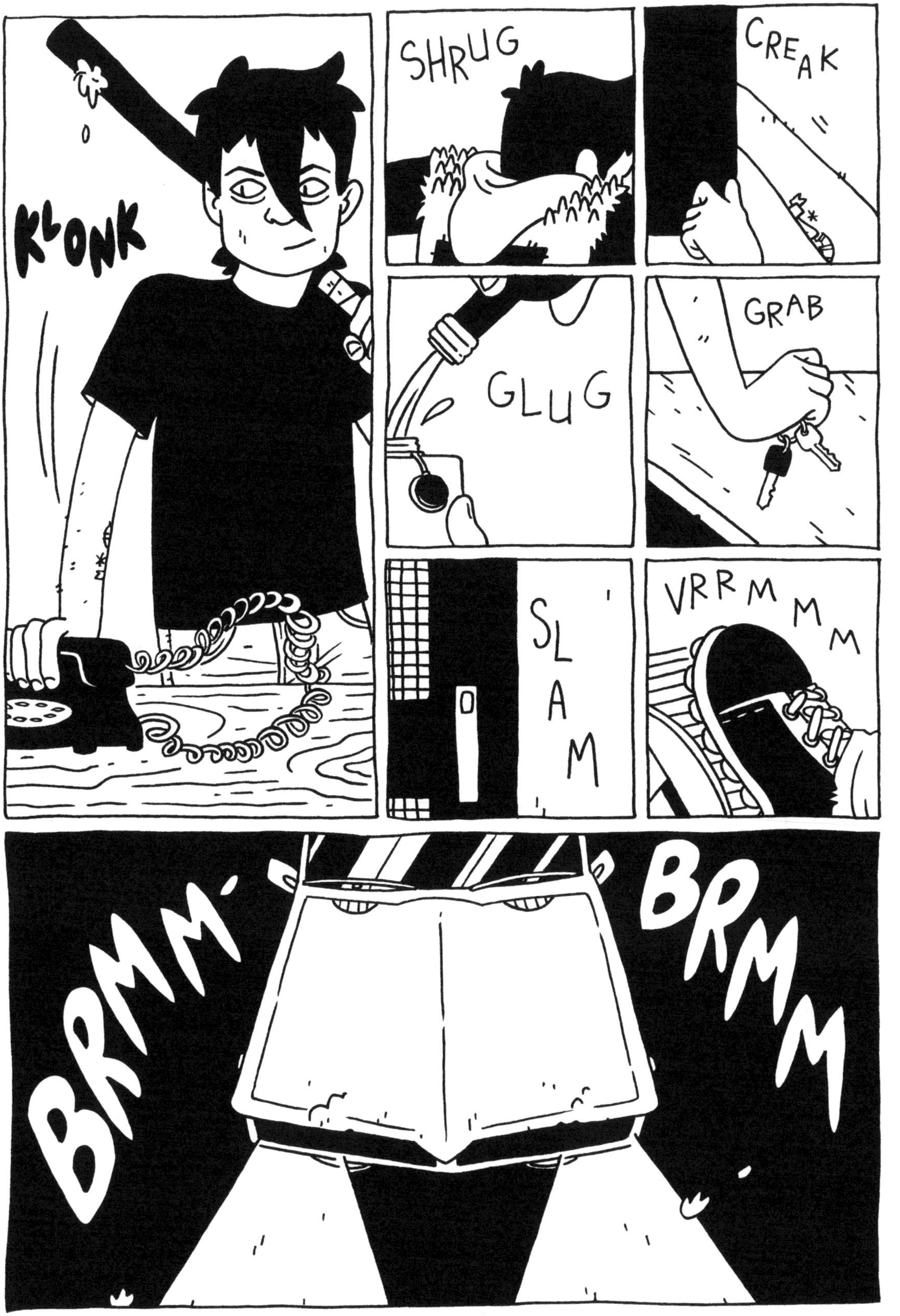
KLONK
SHRUG
CREAK
GLUG
GRAB
SLAM
VRRMMMM
BRMM
BRMM

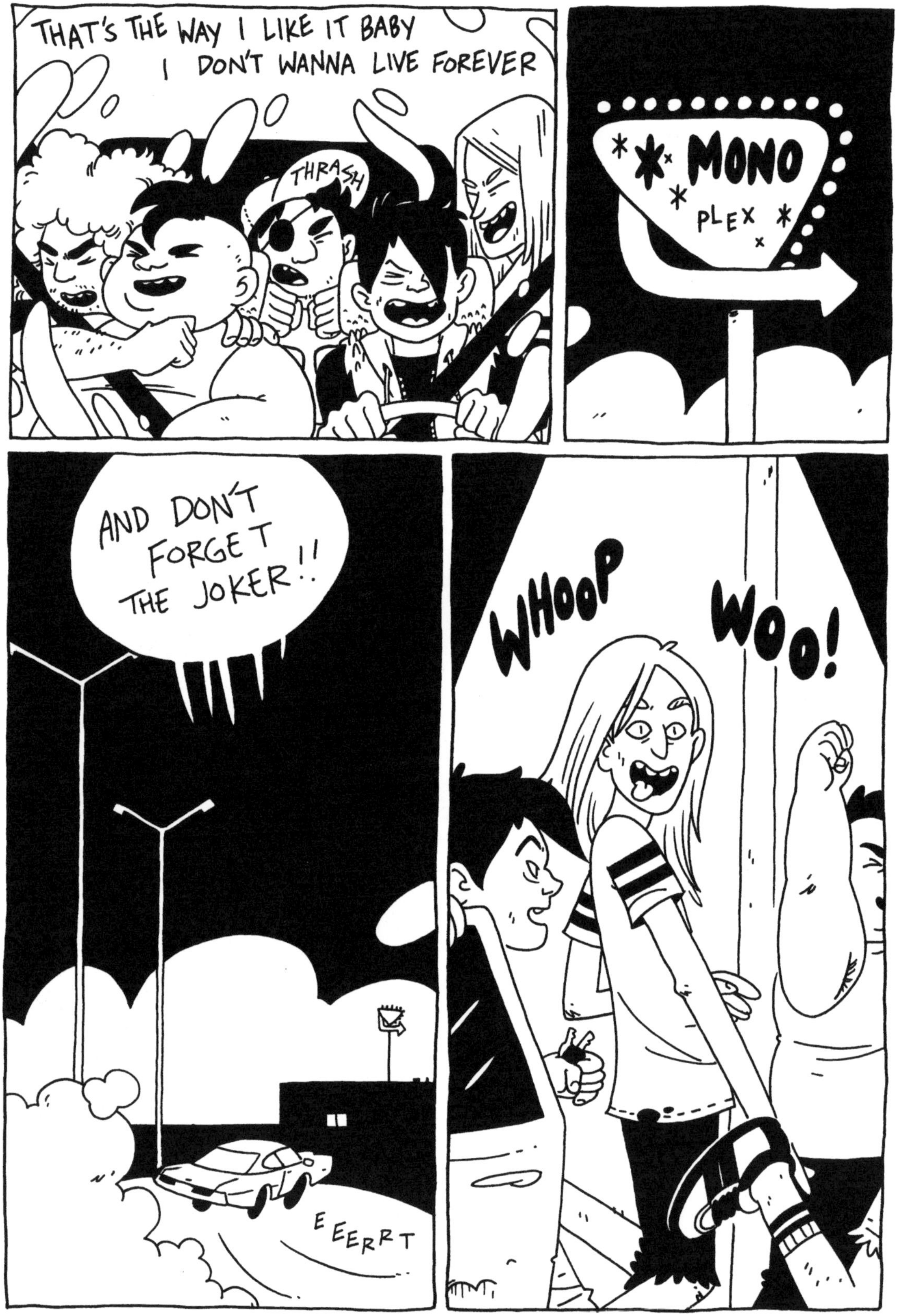
THAT'S THE WAY I LIKE IT BABY
I DON'T WANNA LIVE FOREVER
THRASH
MONO
PLEX
AND DON'T FORGET THE JOKER!!
EEERRT
WHOOP
WOO!

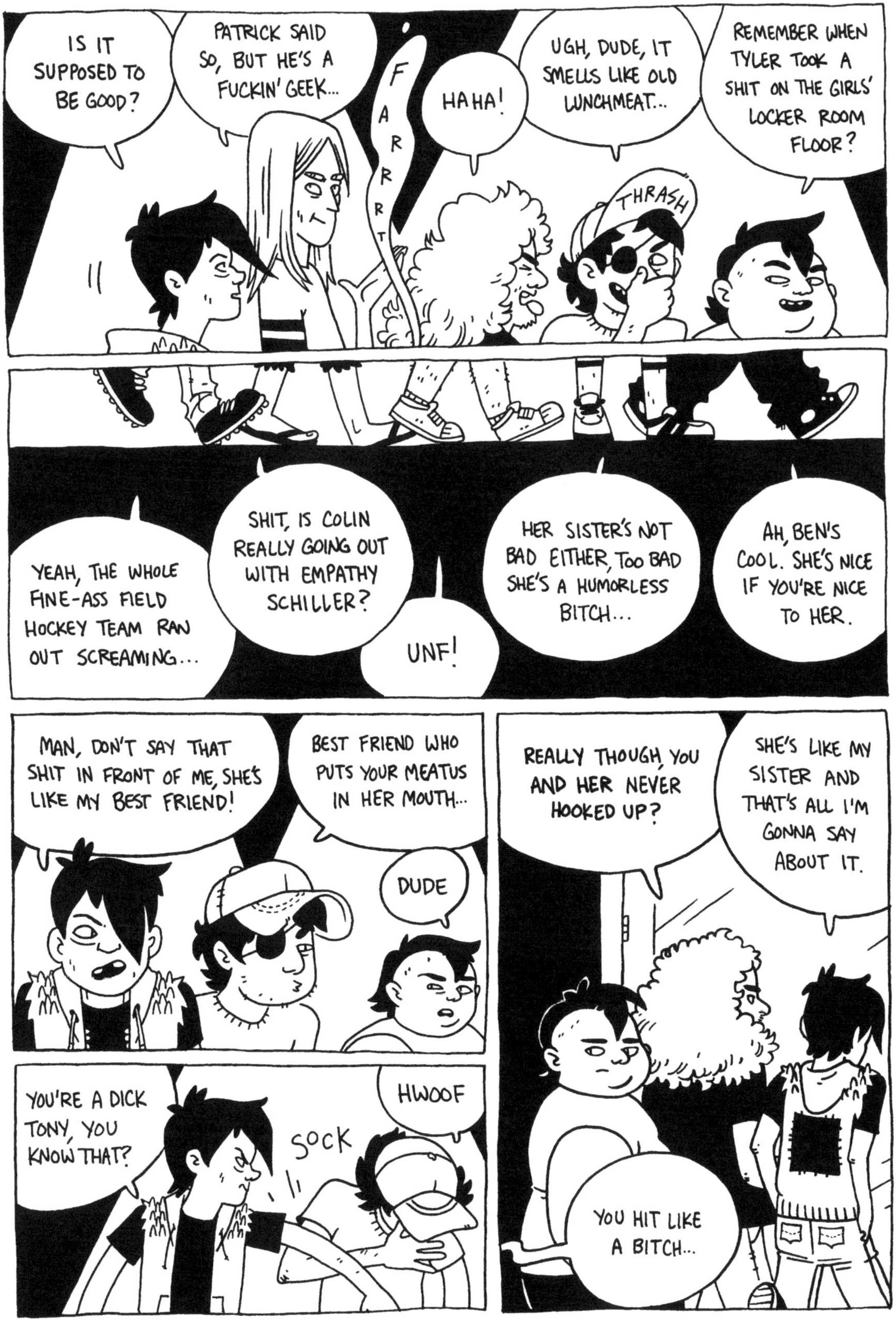
IS IT SUPPOSED TO BE GOOD?
PATRICK SAID SO, BUT HE'S A FUCKIN' GEEK...
FARRRT
HAHA!
UGH, DUDE, IT SMELLS LIKE OLD LUNCHMEAT...
THRASH
REMEMBER WHEN TYLER TOOK A SHIT ON THE GIRLS' LOCKER ROOM FLOOR?
YEAH, THE WHOLE FINE-ASS FIELD HOCKEY TEAM RAN OUT SCREAMING...
SHIT, IS COLIN REALLY GOING OUT WITH EMPATHY SCHILLER?
UNF!
HER SISTER'S NOT BAD EITHER, TOO BAD SHE'S A HUMORLESS BITCH...
AH, BEN'S COOL. SHE'S NICE IF YOU'RE NICE TO HER.
MAN, DON'T SAY THAT SHIT IN FRONT OF ME, SHE'S LIKE MY BEST FRIEND!
BEST FRIEND WHO PUTS YOUR MEATUS IN HER MOUTH...
DUDE
YOU'RE A DICK TONY, YOU KNOW THAT?
HWOOF
SOCK
REALLY THOUGH, YOU AND HER NEVER HOOKED UP?
SHE'S LIKE MY SISTER AND THAT'S ALL I'M GONNA SAY ABOUT IT.
YOU HIT LIKE A BITCH...

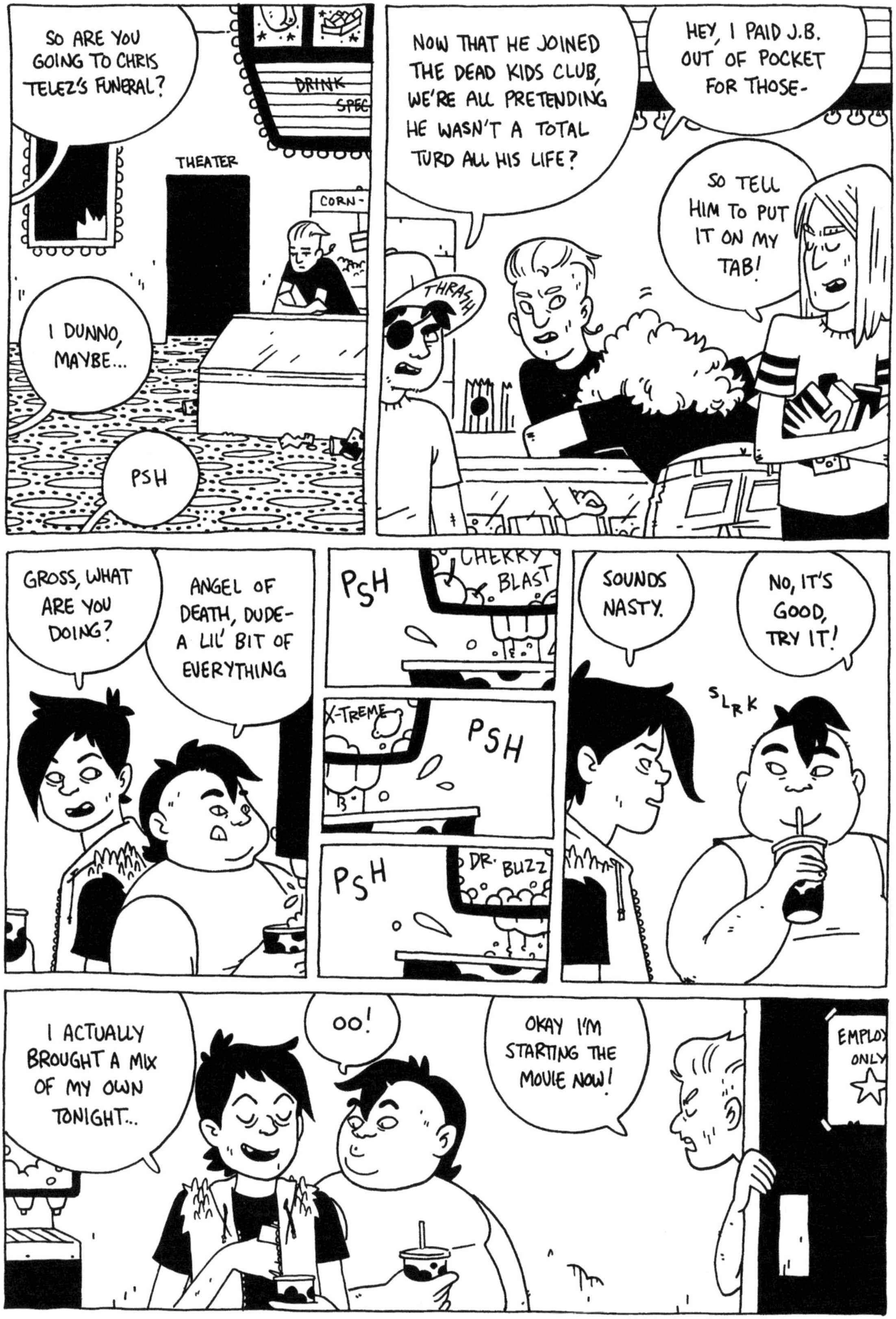
SO ARE YOU GOING TO CHRIS TELEZ'S FUNERAL?
DRINK SPEC
THEATER
CORN-
I DUNNO, MAYBE...
PSH
NOW THAT HE JOINED THE DEAD KIDS CLUB, WE'RE ALL PRETENDING HE WASN'T A TOTAL TURD ALL HIS LIFE?
HEY, I PAID J.B. OUT OF POCKET FOR THOSE-
SO TELL HIM TO PUT IT ON MY TAB!
THRASH
GROSS, WHAT ARE YOU DOING?
ANGEL OF DEATH, DUDE- A LIL' BIT OF EVERYTHING
PSH
CHERRY BLAST
X-TREME
PSH
PSH
DR. BUZZ
SOUNDS NASTY.
NO, IT'S GOOD, TRY IT!
SLRK
I ACTUALLY BROUGHT A MIX OF MY OWN TONIGHT...
OO!
OKAY I'M STARTING THE MOVIE NOW!
EMPLOY ONLY

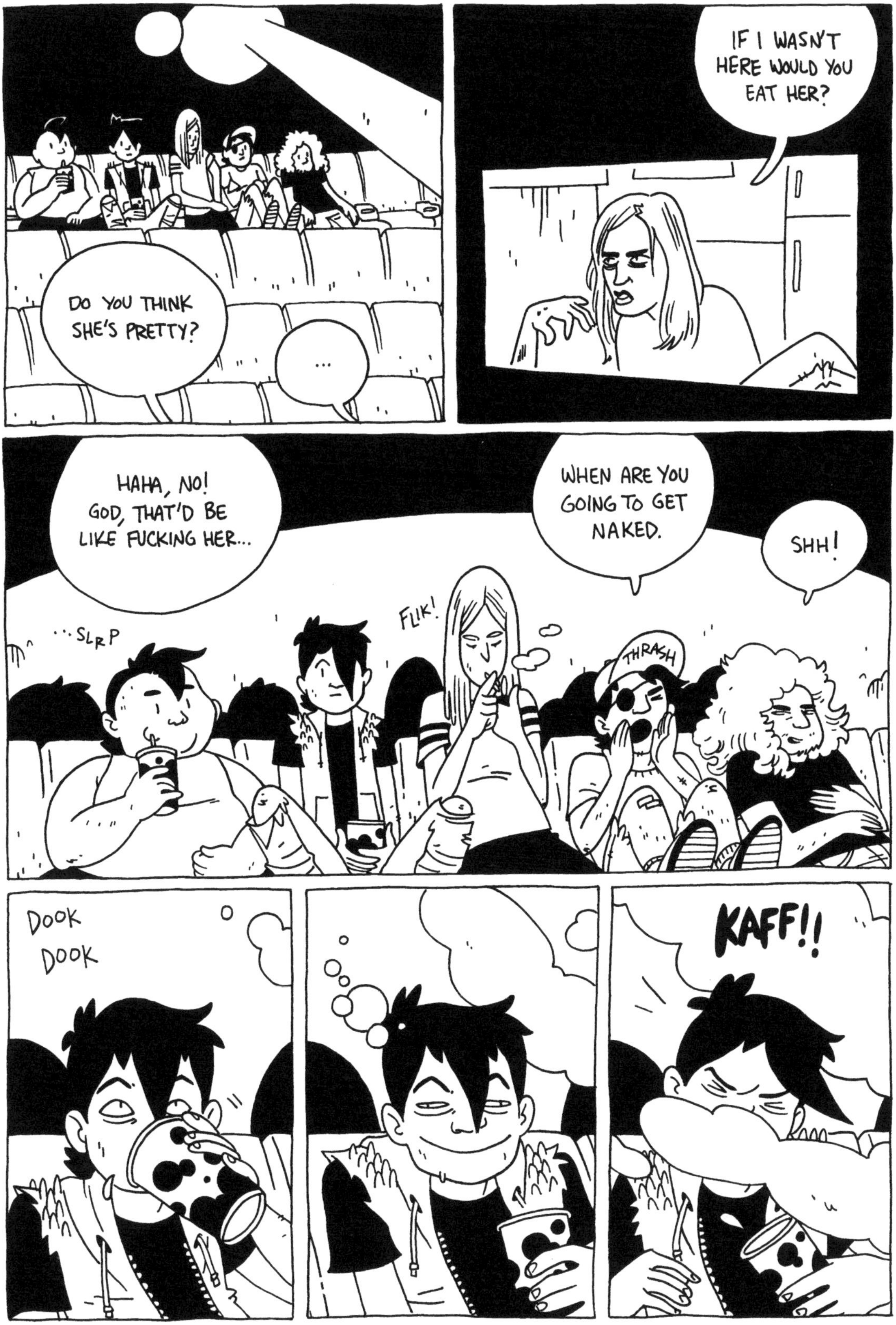

DO YOU THINK SHE'S PRETTY?
...
IF I WASN'T HERE WOULD YOU EAT HER?
HAHA, NO! GOD, THAT'D BE LIKE FUCKING HER...
...SLRP
FLIK!
WHEN ARE YOU GOING TO GET NAKED.
SHH!
THRASH
DOOK DOOK
KAFF!!

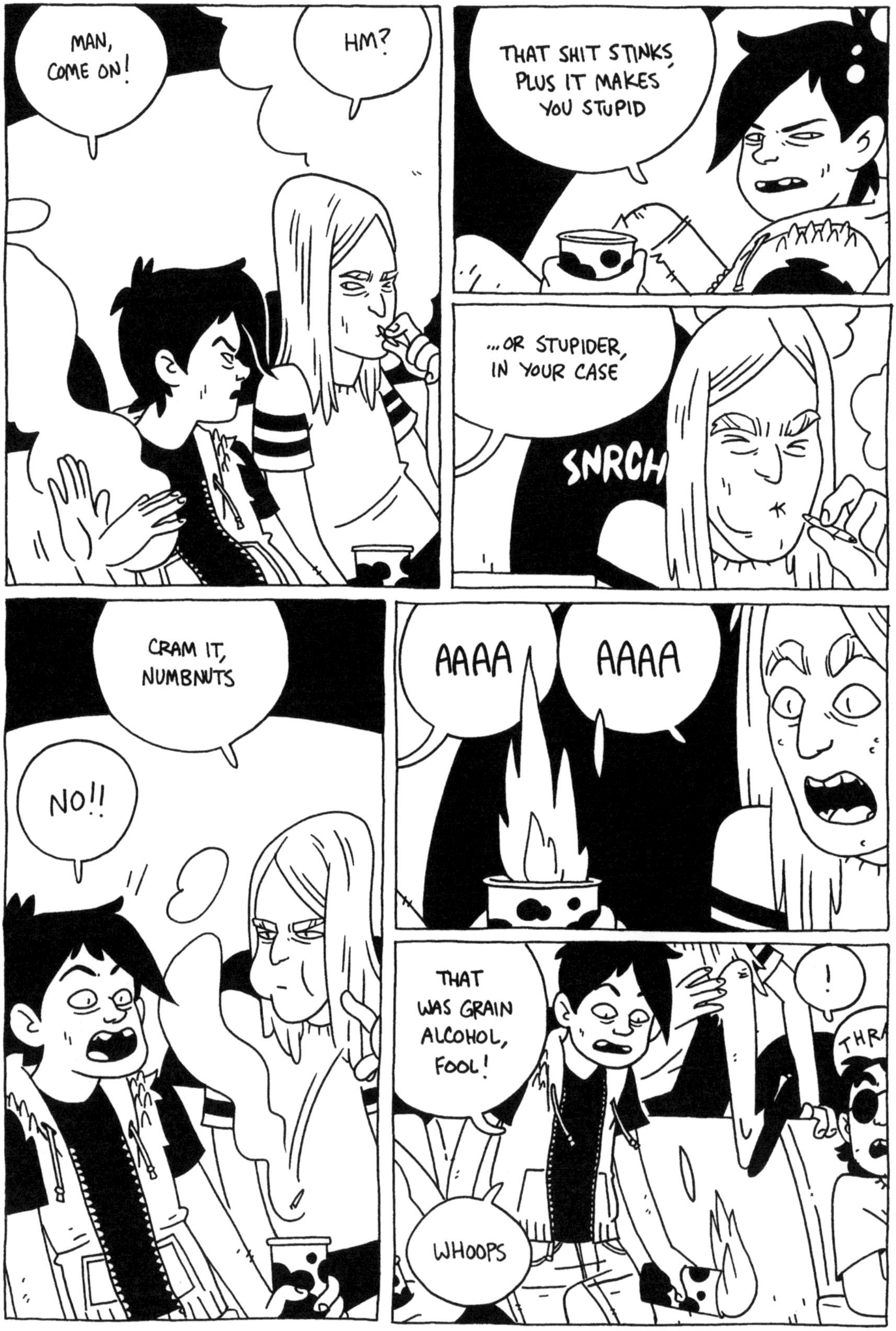
MAN, COME ON!
HM?
THAT SHIT STINKS, PLUS IT MAKES YOU STUPID
...OR STUPIDER, IN YOUR CASE
SNRCH
CRAM IT, NUMBNUTS
NO!!
AAAA
AAAA
THAT WAS GRAIN ALCOHOL, FOOL!
!
WHOOPS

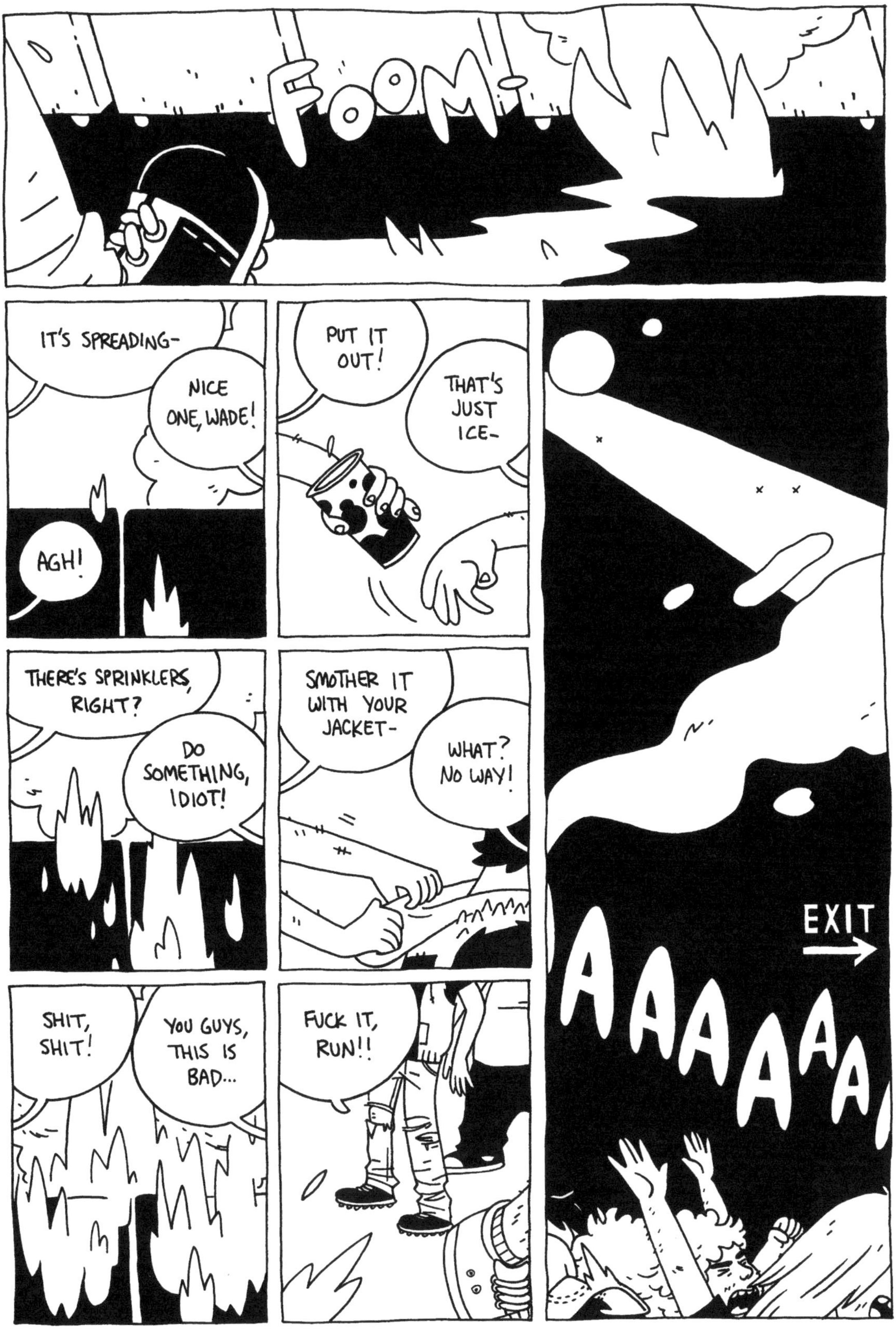
FOOM!
IT'S SPREADING-
NICE ONE, WADE!
AGH!
PUT IT OUT!
THAT'S JUST ICE-
THERE'S SPRINKLERS, RIGHT?
DO SOMETHING, IDIOT!
SMOTHER IT WITH YOUR JACKET-
WHAT? NO WAY!
SHIT, SHIT!
YOU GUYS, THIS IS BAD...
FUCK IT, RUN!!
EXIT
AAAAAA

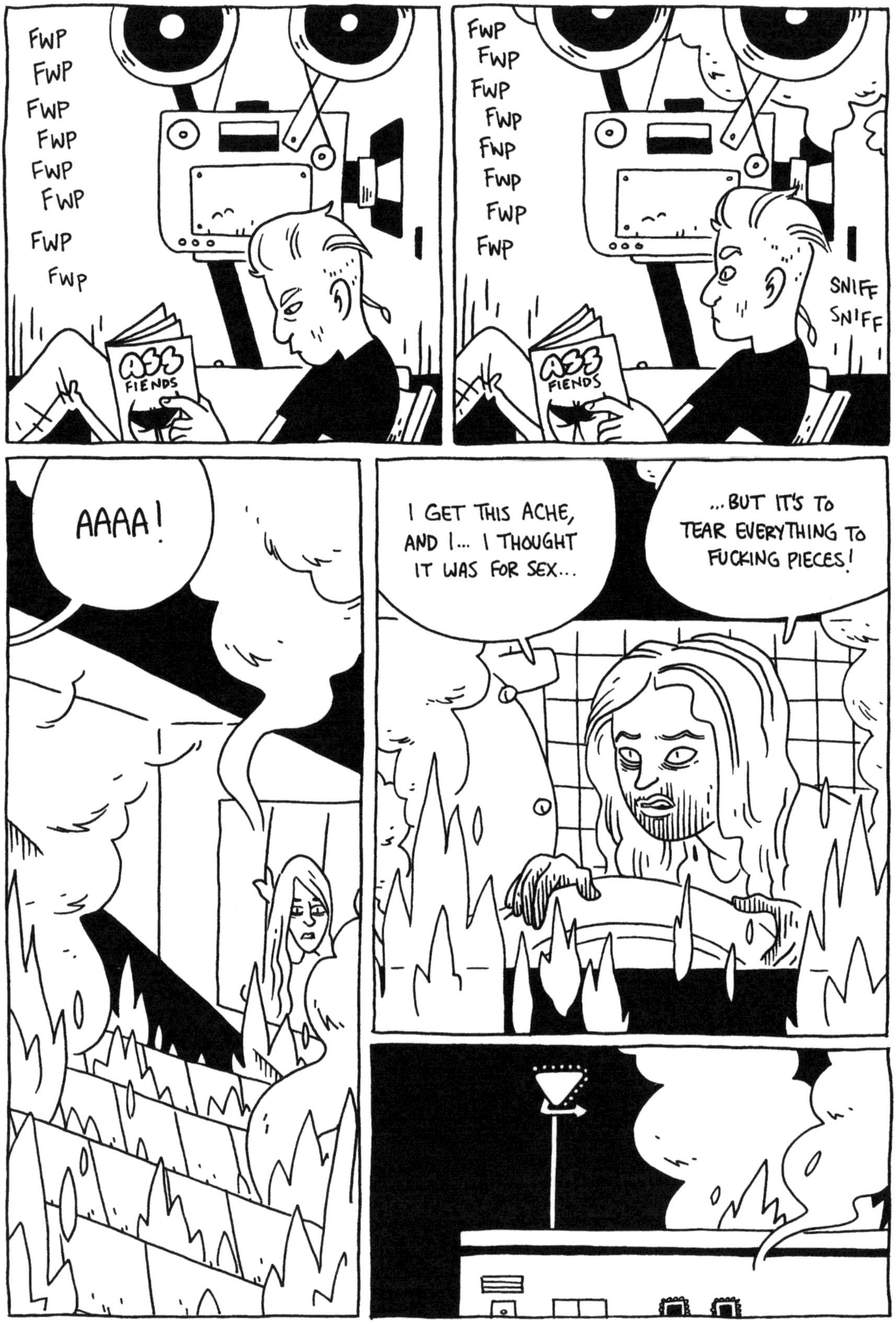
FWP
FWP
FWP
FWP
FWP
FWP
FWP
FWP
ASS FIENDS
FWP
FWP
FWP
FWP
FWP
FWP
FWP
FWP
SNIFF
SNIFF
ASS FIENDS
AAAA!
I GET THIS ACHE, AND I... I THOUGHT IT WAS FOR SEX...
...BUT IT'S TO TEAR EVERYTHING TO FUCKING PIECES!

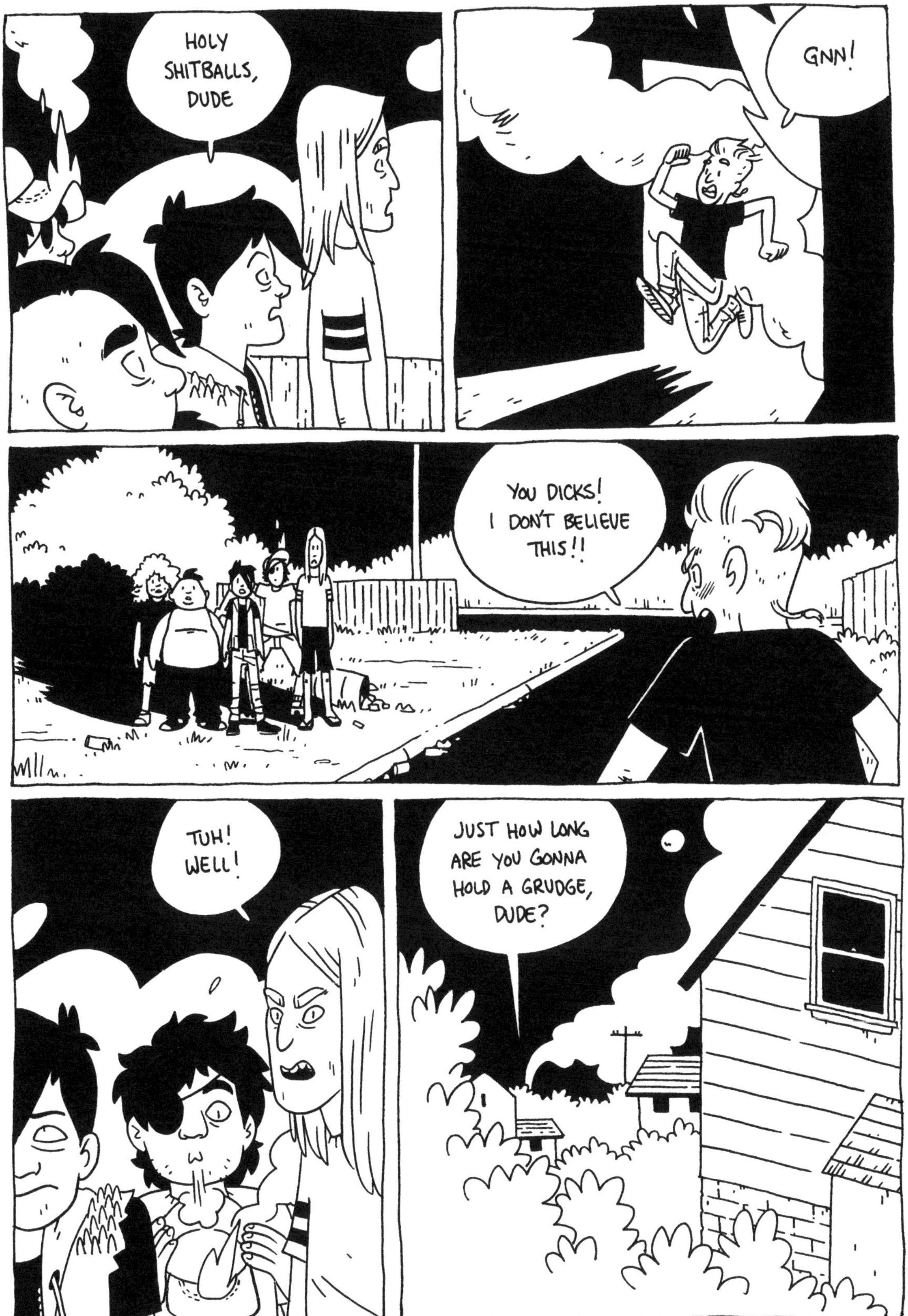
HOLY SHITBALLS, DUDE
GNN!
YOU DICKS! I DON'T BELIEVE THIS!!
TUH! WELL!
JUST HOW LONG ARE YOU GONNA HOLD A GRUDGE, DUDE?

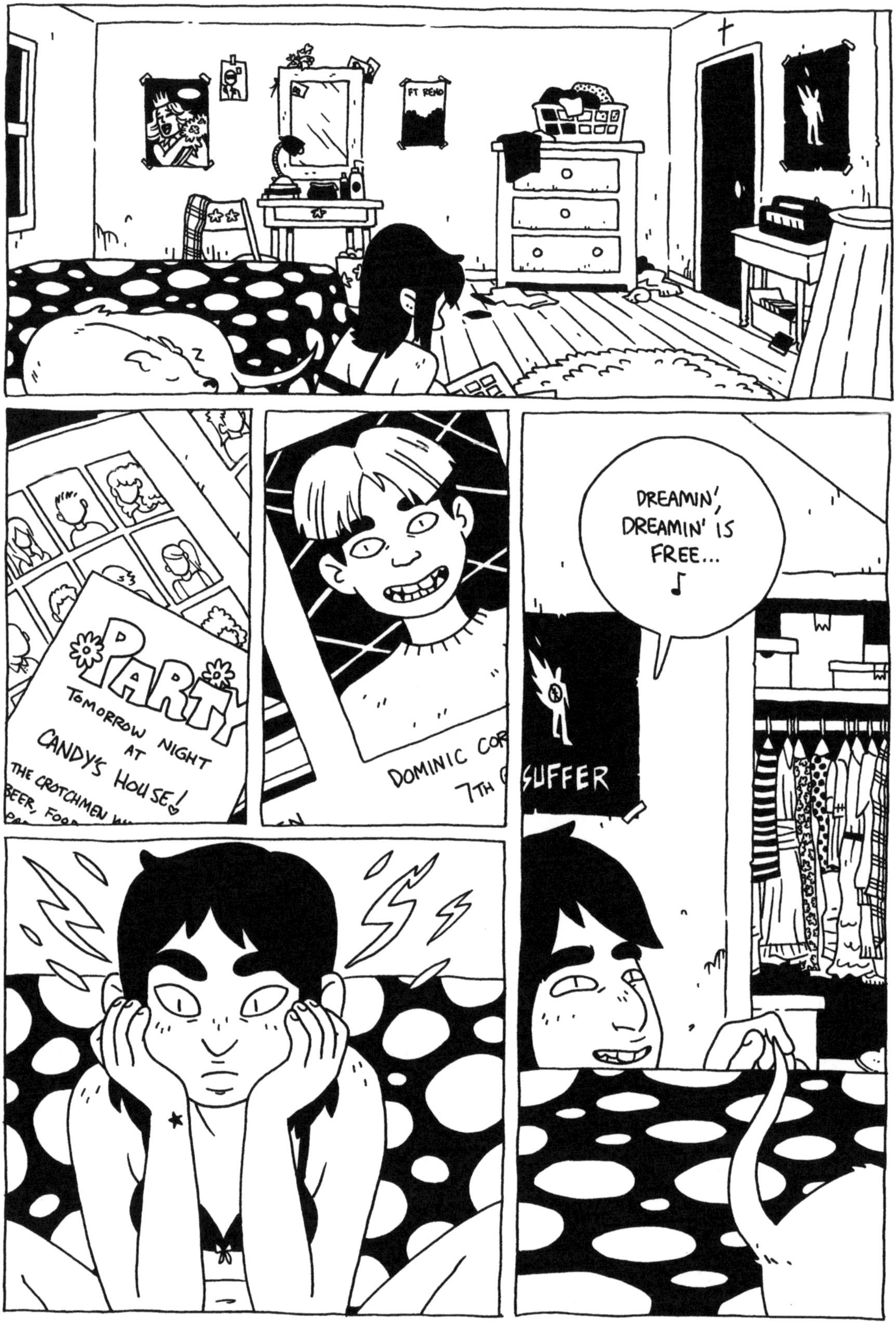
FT RENO
PARTY
TOMORROW NIGHT
AT
CANDY'S HOUSE!
DREAMIN', DREAMIN' IS FREE...

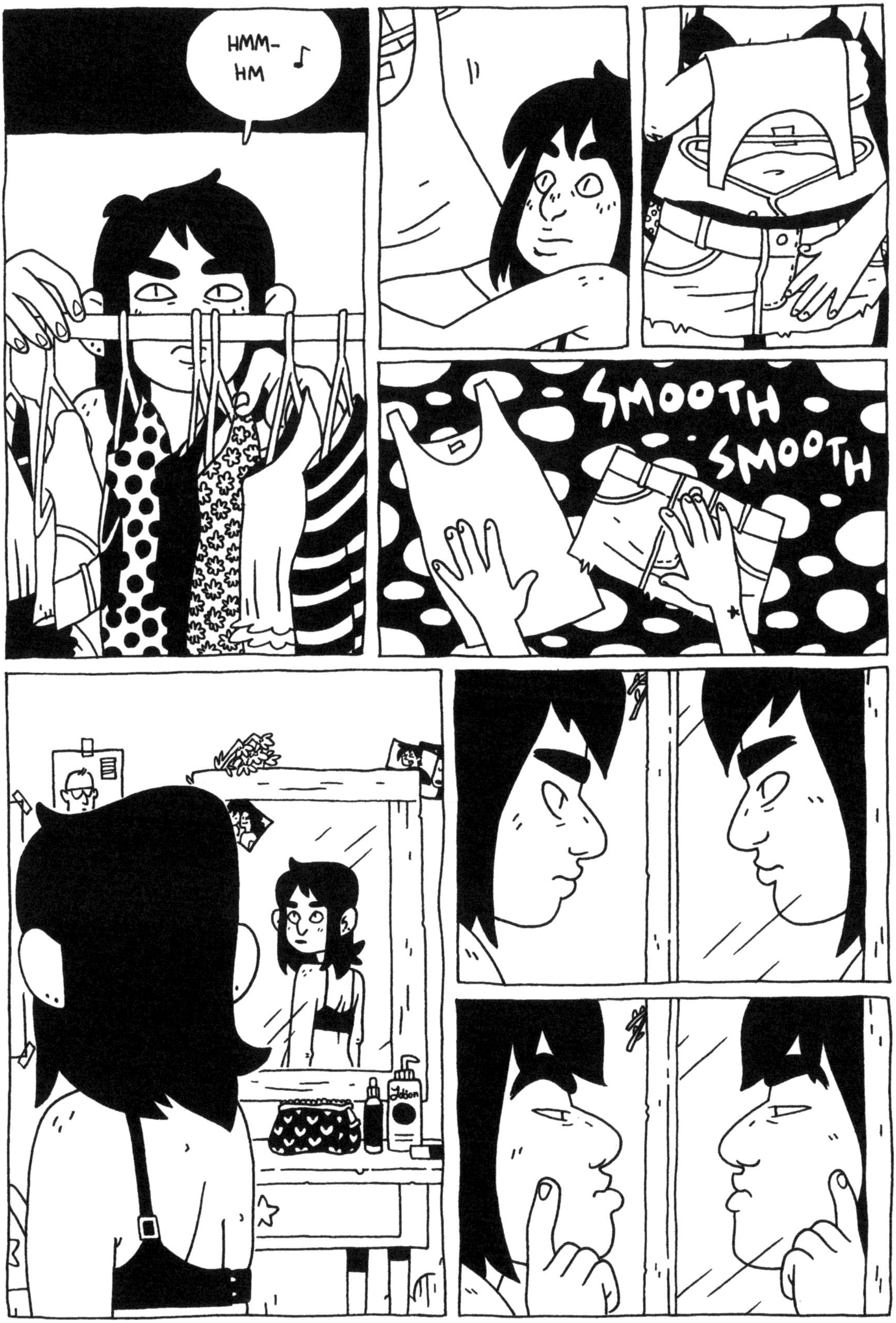
HMM-HM ♪
SMOOTH SMOOTH
Lotion

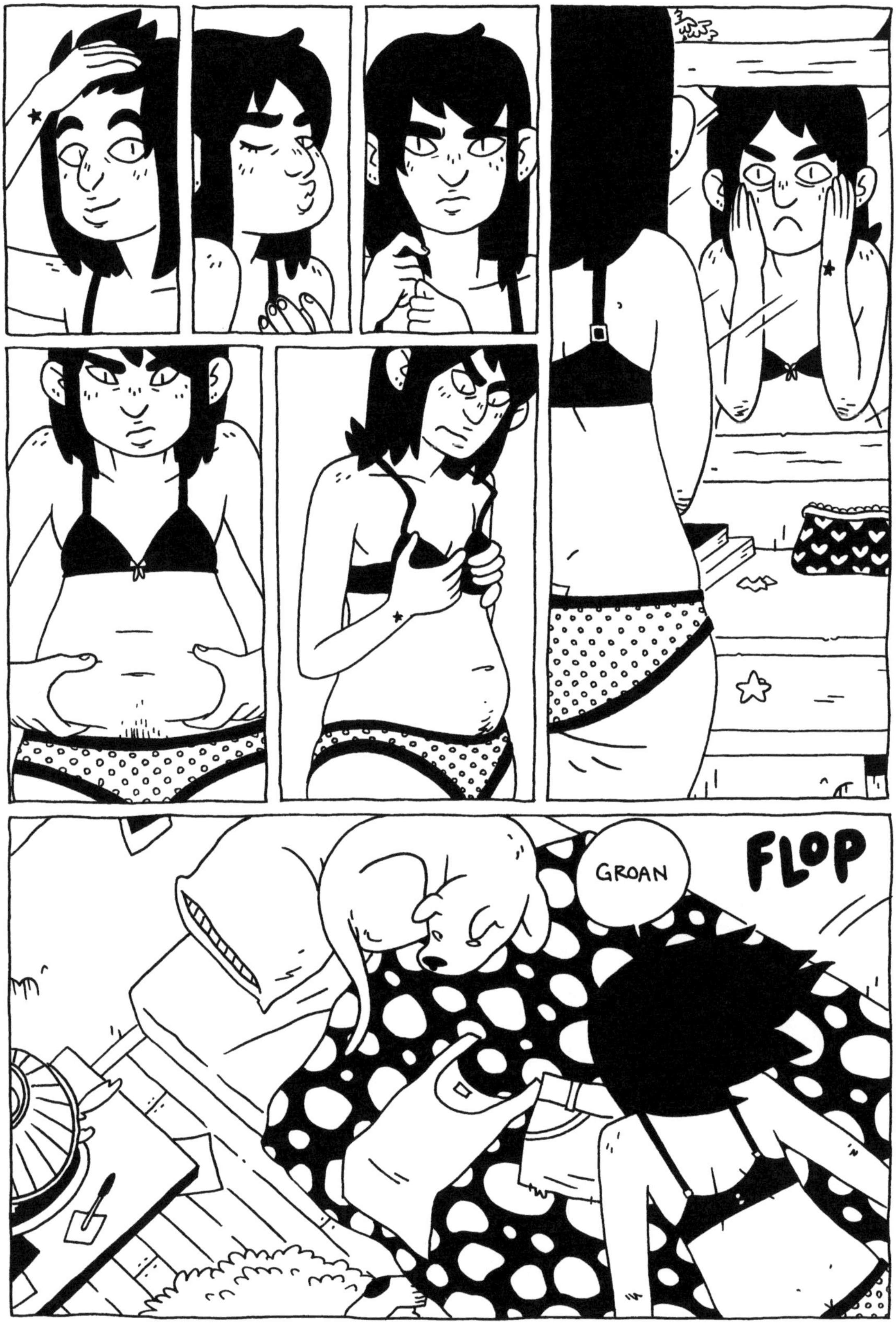
GROAN
FLOP

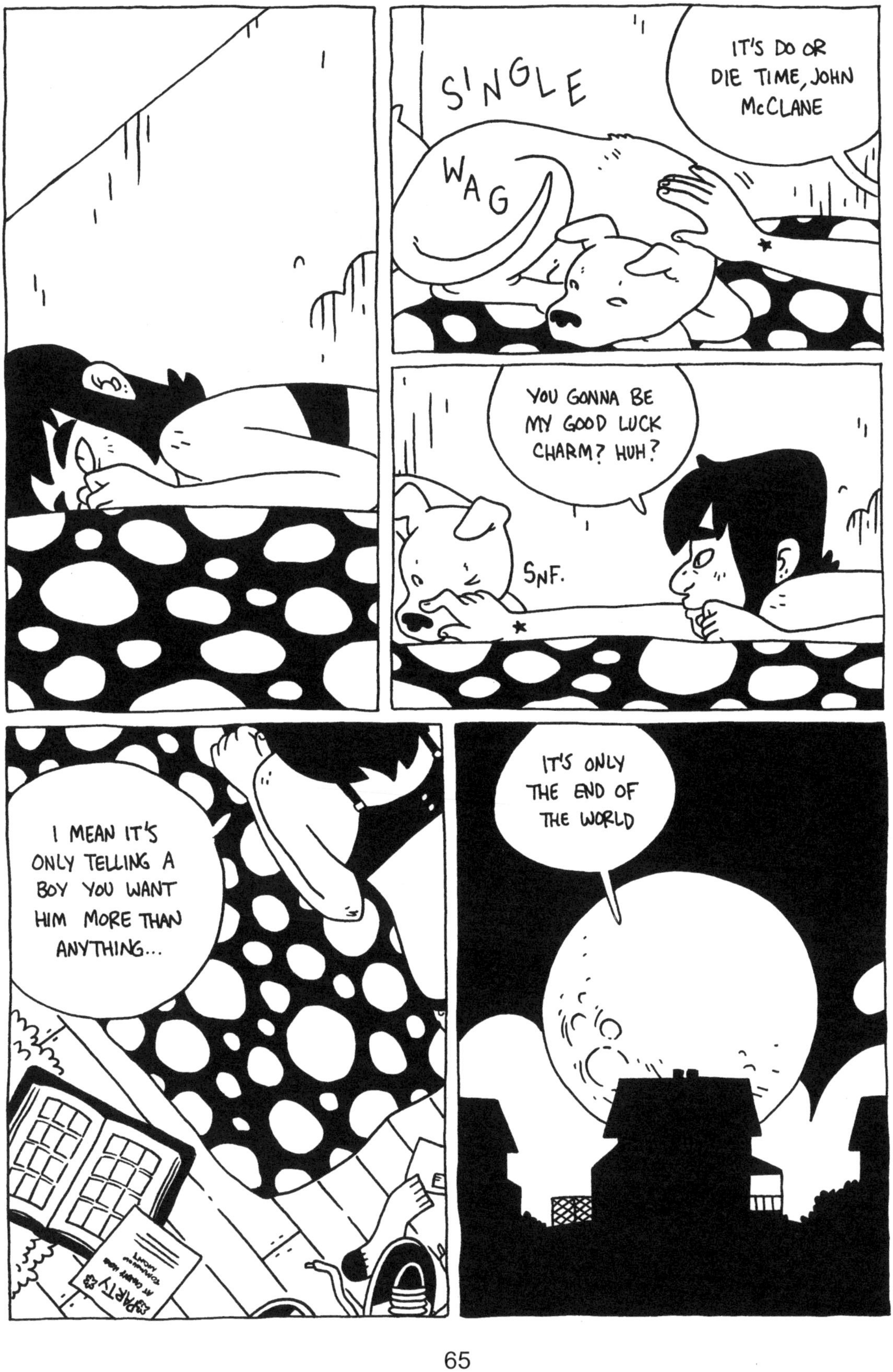
SINGLE
WAG
IT'S DO OR DIE TIME, JOHN McCLANE
YOU GONNA BE MY GOOD LUCK CHARM? HUH?
SNF.
I MEAN IT'S ONLY TELLING A BOY YOU WANT HIM MORE THAN ANYTHING...
IT'S ONLY THE END OF THE WORLD

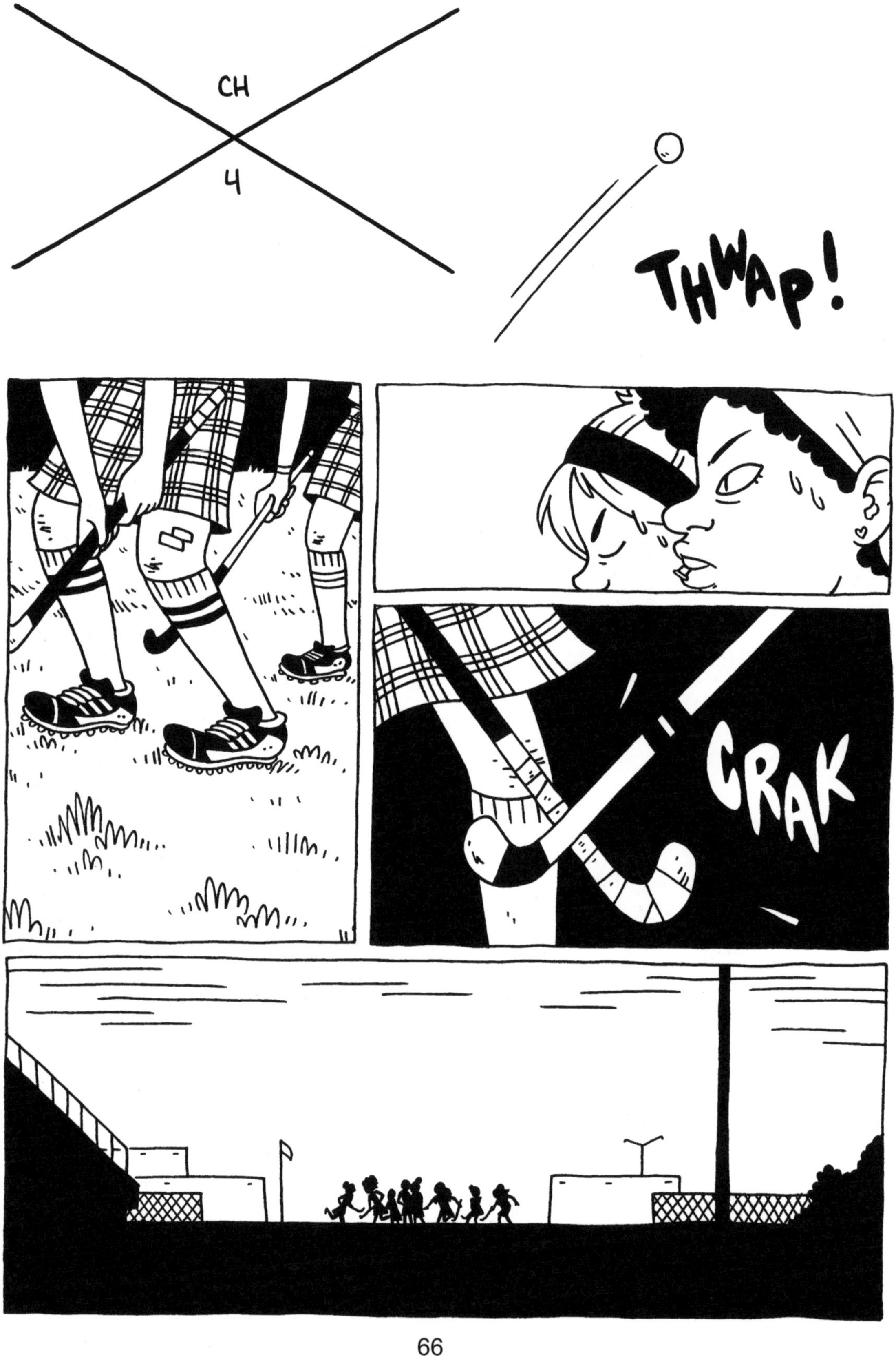
CH
4
THWAP!
CRAK

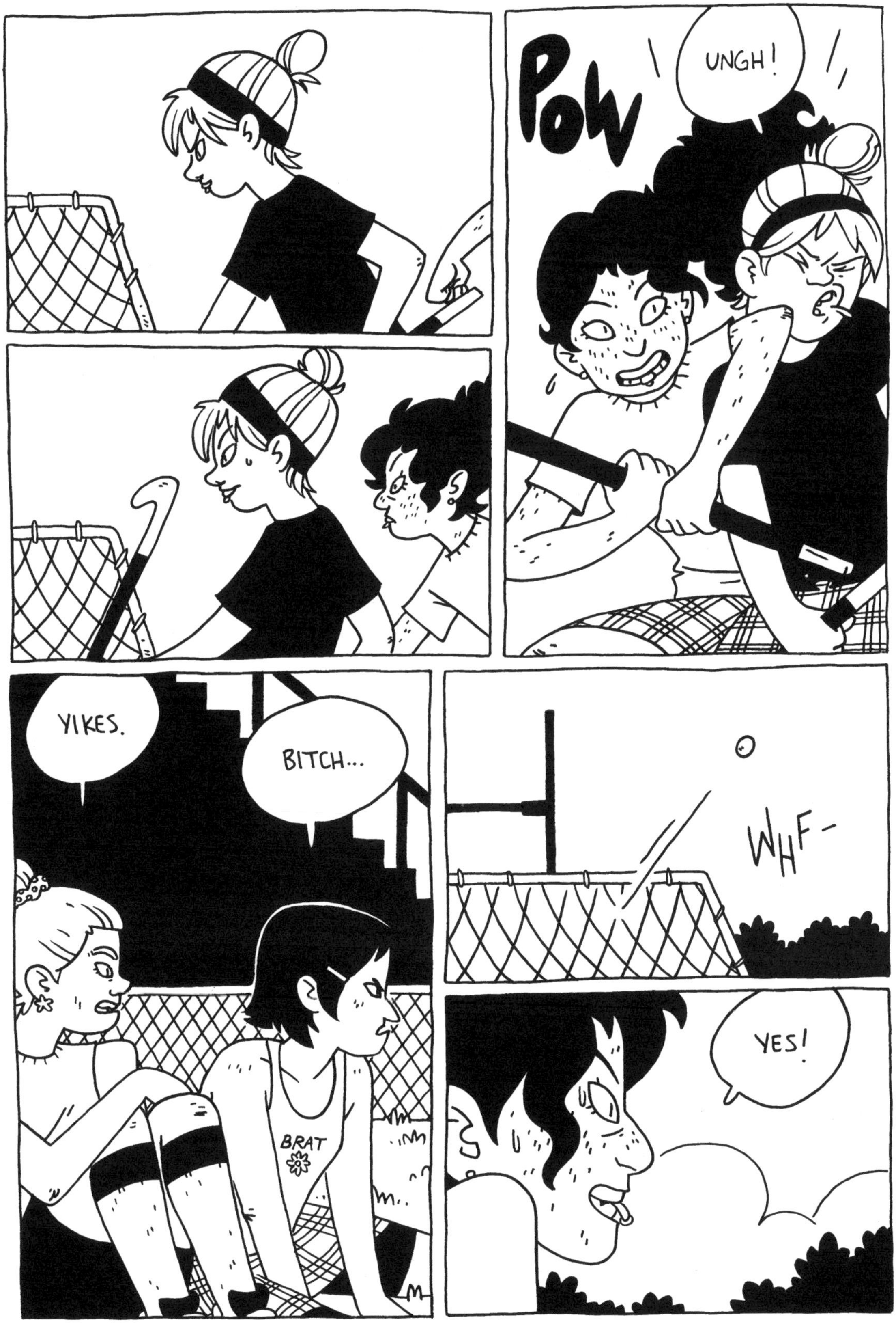
POW
UNGH!
YIKES.
BITCH...
WHF-
YES!
BRAT

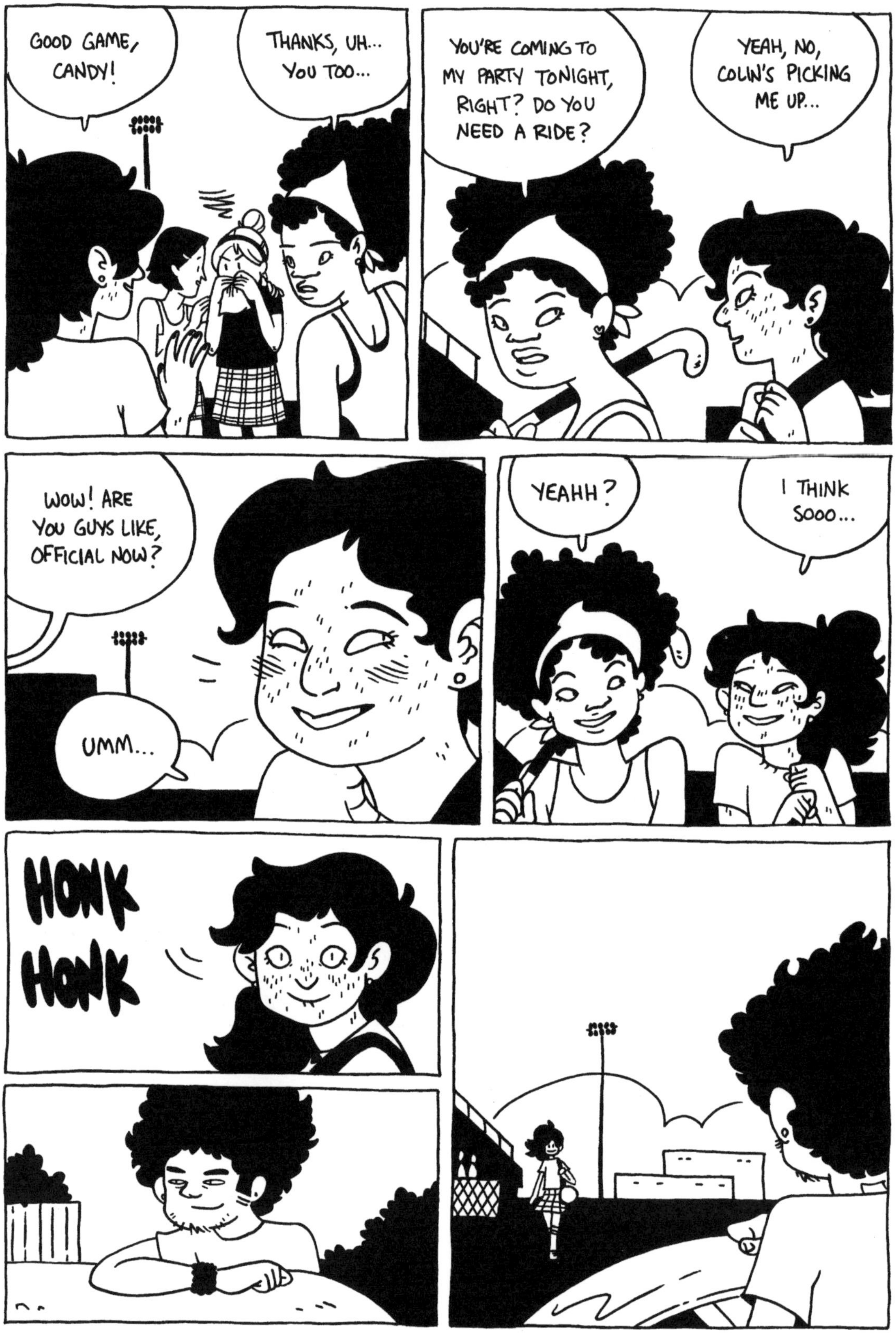
GOOD GAME, CANDY!
THANKS, UH... YOU TOO...
YOU'RE COMING TO MY PARTY TONIGHT, RIGHT? DO YOU NEED A RIDE?
YEAH, NO, COLIN'S PICKING ME UP...
WOW! ARE YOU GUYS LIKE, OFFICIAL NOW?
UMM...
YEAHH?
I THINK SOOO...
HONK HONK

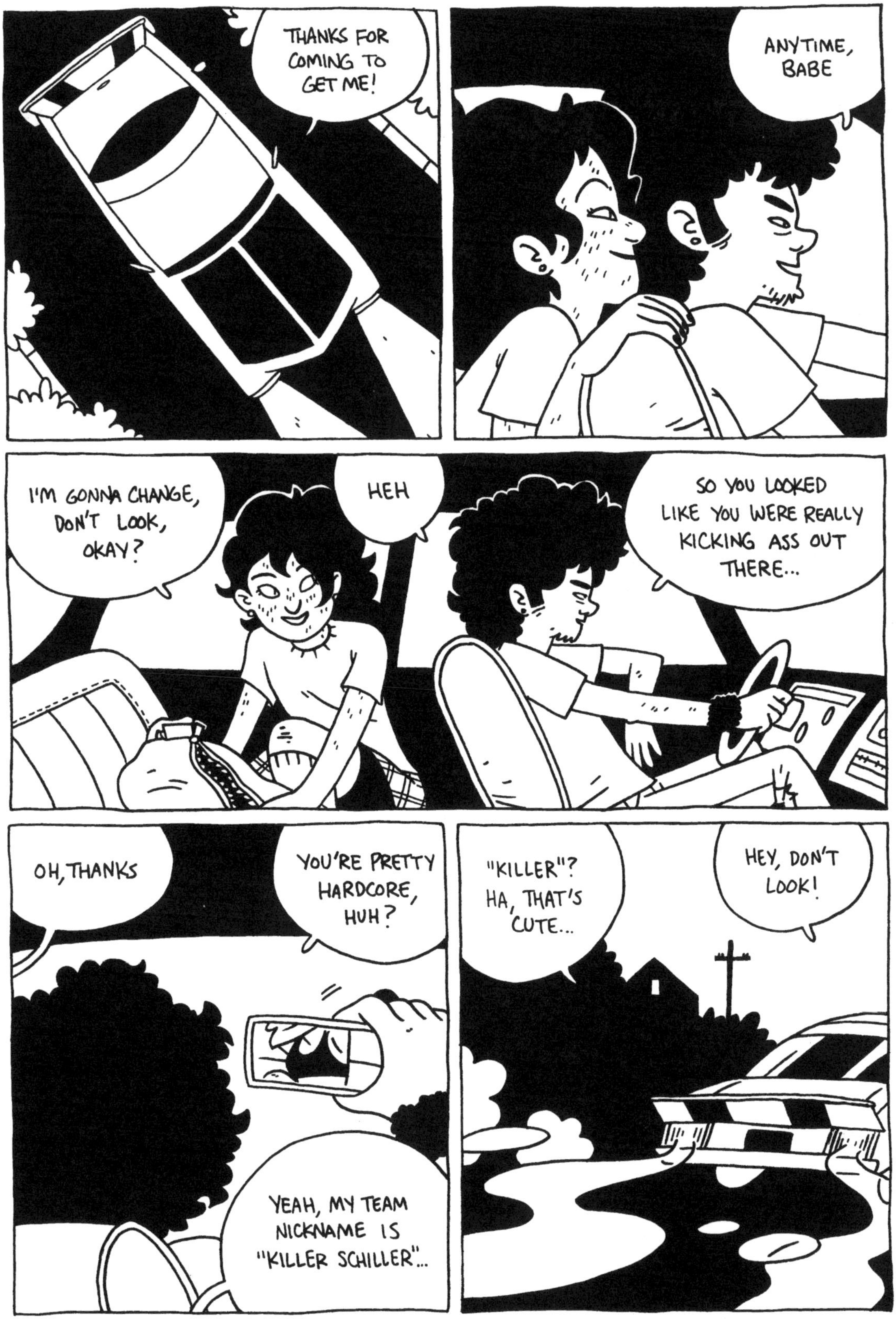
THANKS FOR COMING TO GET ME!
ANYTIME, BABE
I'M GONNA CHANGE, DON'T LOOK, OKAY?
HEH
SO YOU LOOKED LIKE YOU WERE REALLY KICKING ASS OUT THERE...
OH, THANKS
YOU'RE PRETTY HARDCORE, HUH?
YEAH, MY TEAM NICKNAME IS "KILLER SCHILLER"...
"KILLER"? HA, THAT'S CUTE...
HEY, DON'T LOOK!

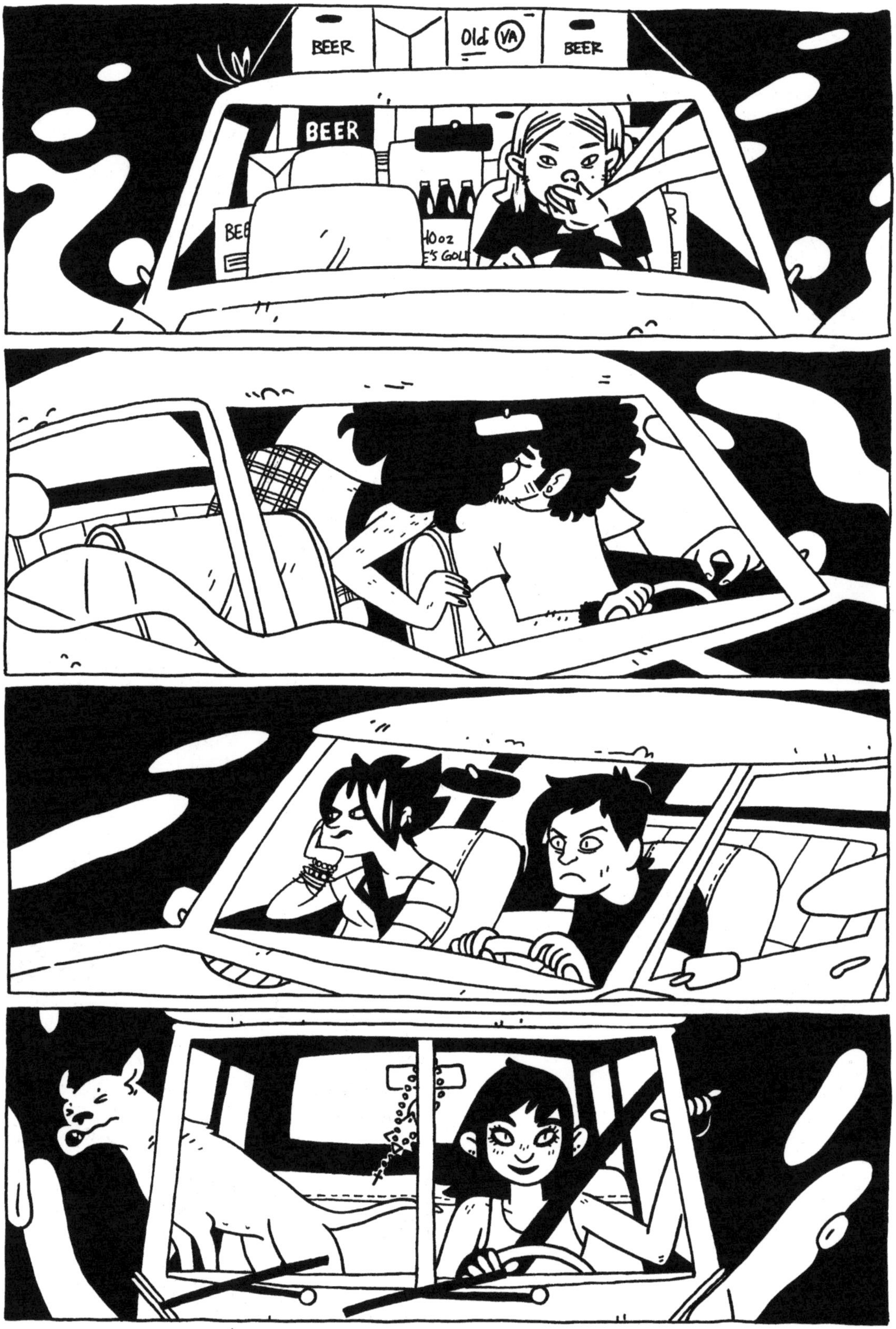
BEER
Old VA
BEER
BEER
40 oz

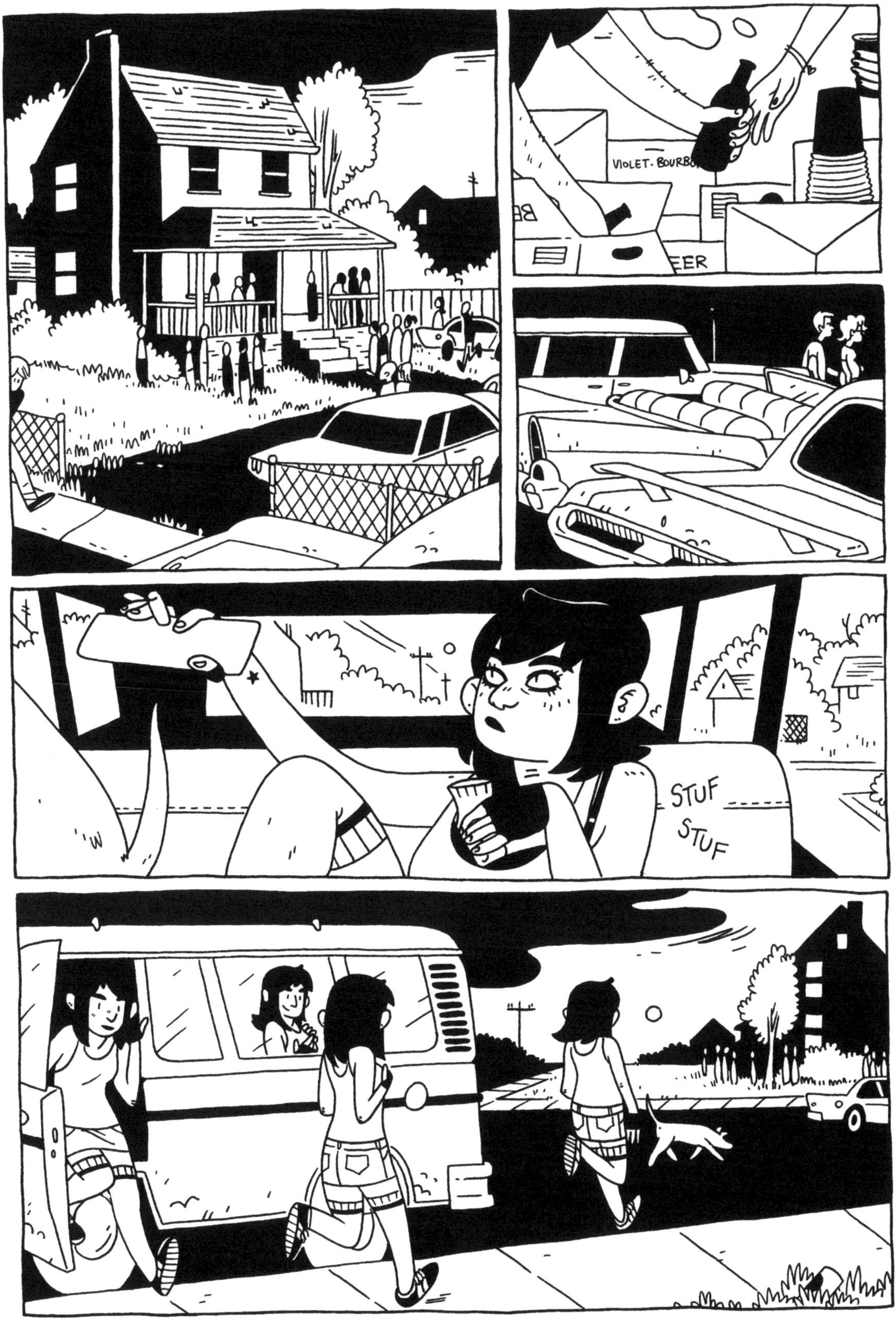
VIOLET. BOURBO
EER
STUF
STUF

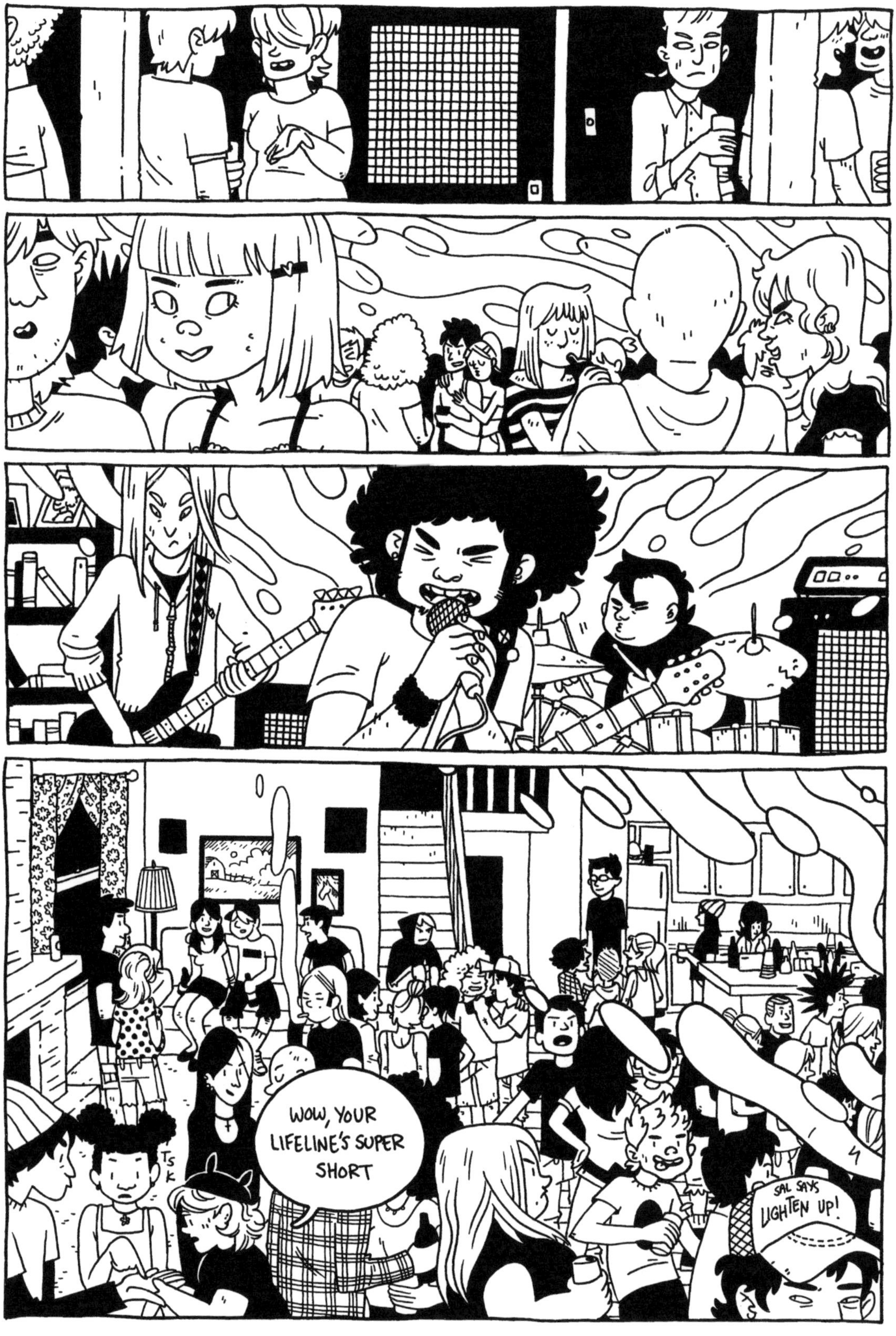
TSK
WOW, YOUR LIFELINE'S SUPER SHORT
SAL SAYS LIGHTEN UP!

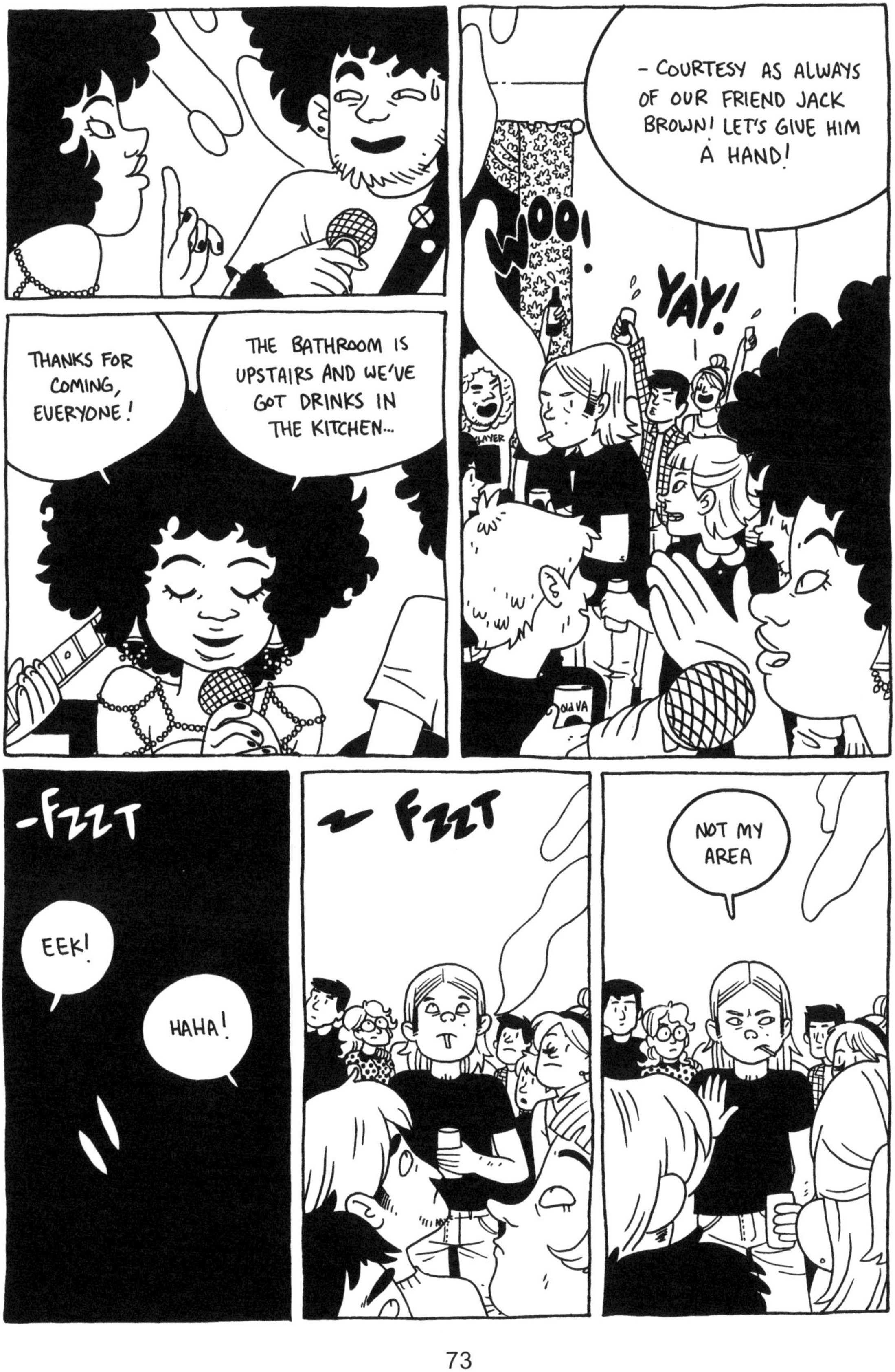
- COURTESY AS ALWAYS OF OUR FRIEND JACK BROWN! LET'S GIVE HIM A HAND!
WOO!
YAY!
THANKS FOR COMING, EVERYONE!
THE BATHROOM IS UPSTAIRS AND WE'VE GOT DRINKS IN THE KITCHEN...
SLAYER
OLD VA
-FZZT
EEK!
HAHA!
FZZT
NOT MY AREA

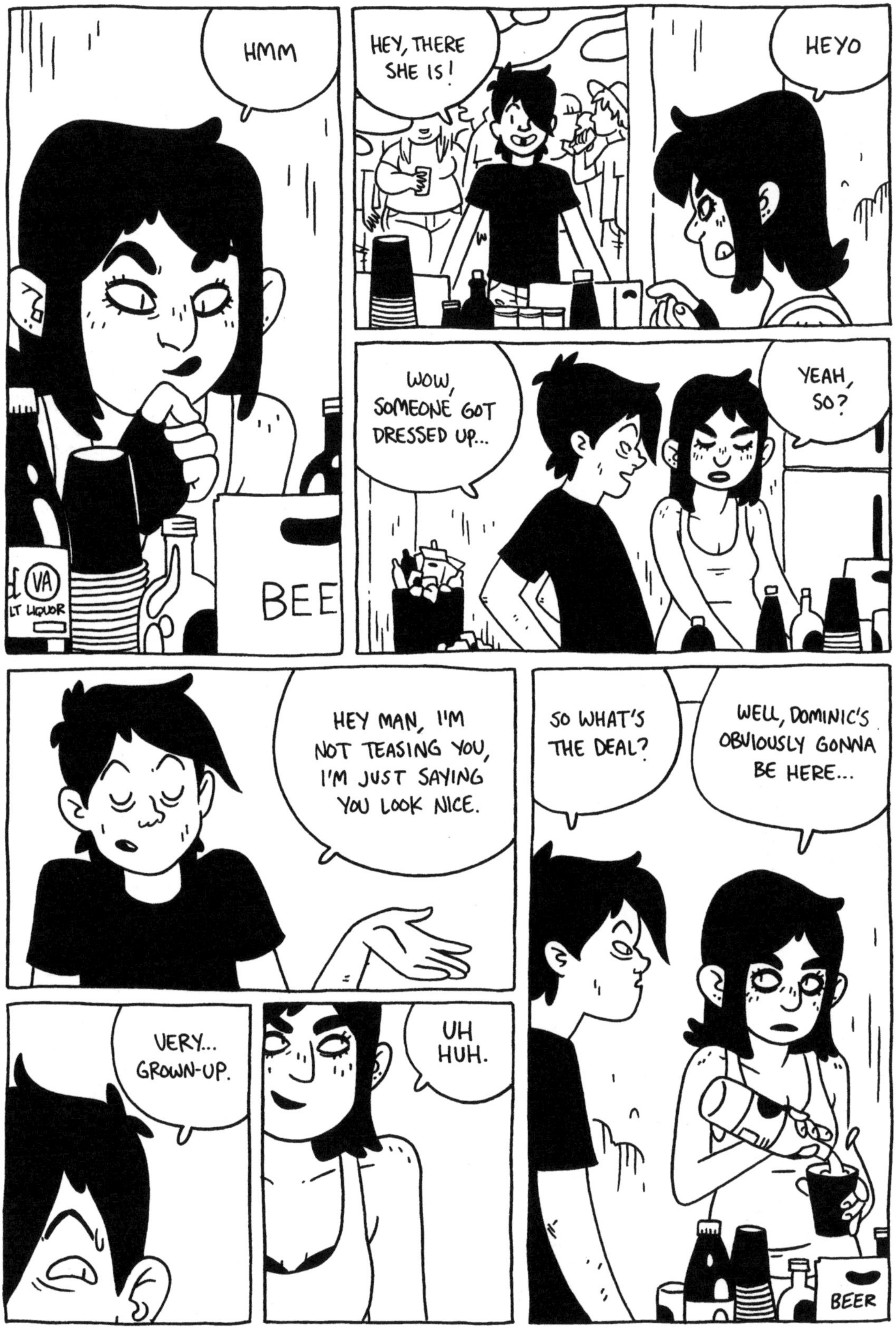
HMM
VA
LT LIQUOR
BEE
HEY, THERE SHE IS!
HEYO
WOW, SOMEONE GOT DRESSED UP...
YEAH, SO?
HEY MAN, I'M NOT TEASING YOU, I'M JUST SAYING YOU LOOK NICE.
VERY... GROWN-UP.
UH HUH.
SO WHAT'S THE DEAL?
WELL, DOMINIC'S OBVIOUSLY GONNA BE HERE...
BEER

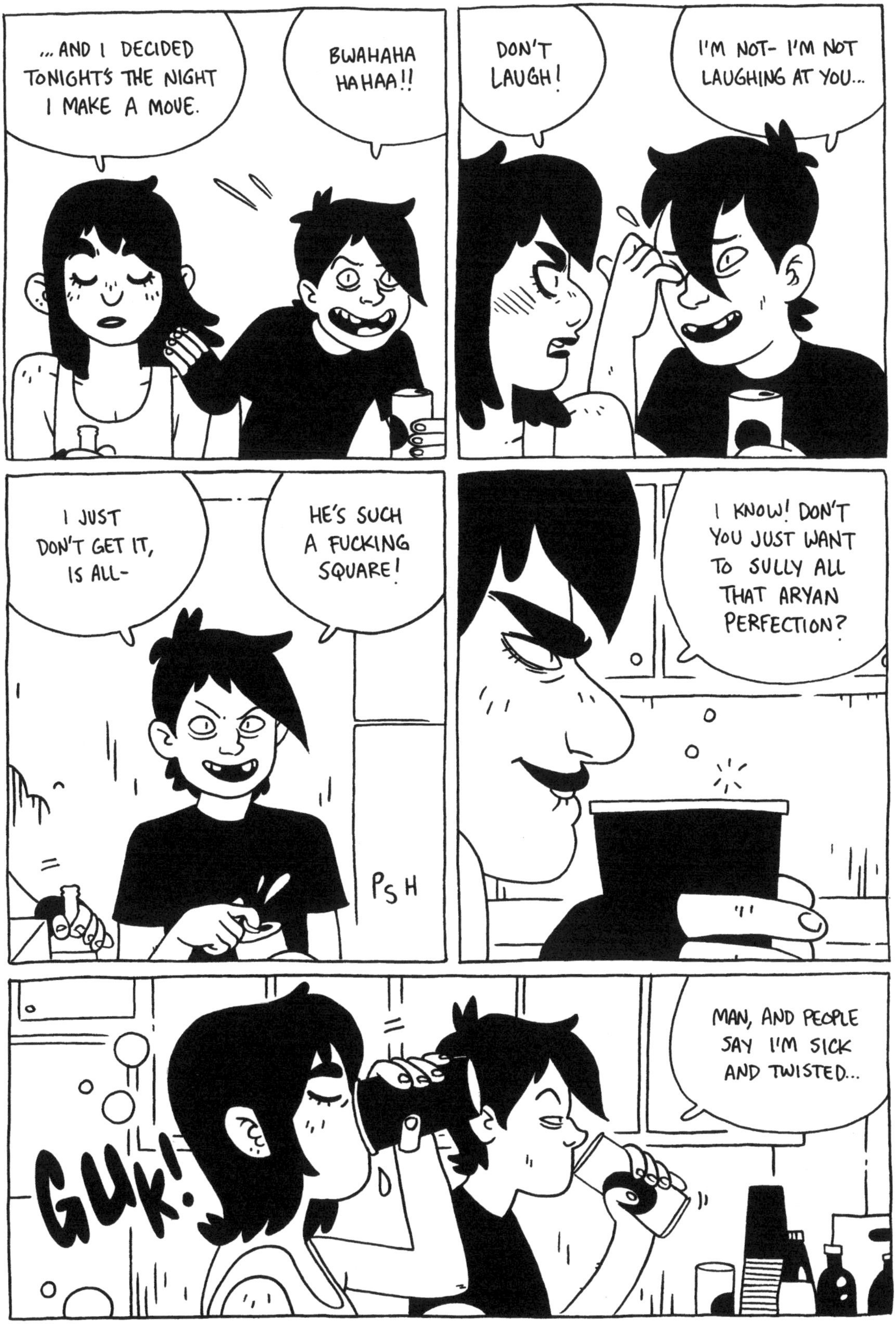
...AND I DECIDED TONIGHT'S THE NIGHT I MAKE A MOVE.
BWAHAHA HAHAA!!
DON'T LAUGH!
I'M NOT- I'M NOT LAUGHING AT YOU...
I JUST DON'T GET IT, IS ALL-
HE'S SUCH A FUCKING SQUARE!
PSH
I KNOW! DON'T YOU JUST WANT TO SULLY ALL THAT ARYAN PERFECTION?
GUK!
MAN, AND PEOPLE SAY I'M SICK AND TWISTED...

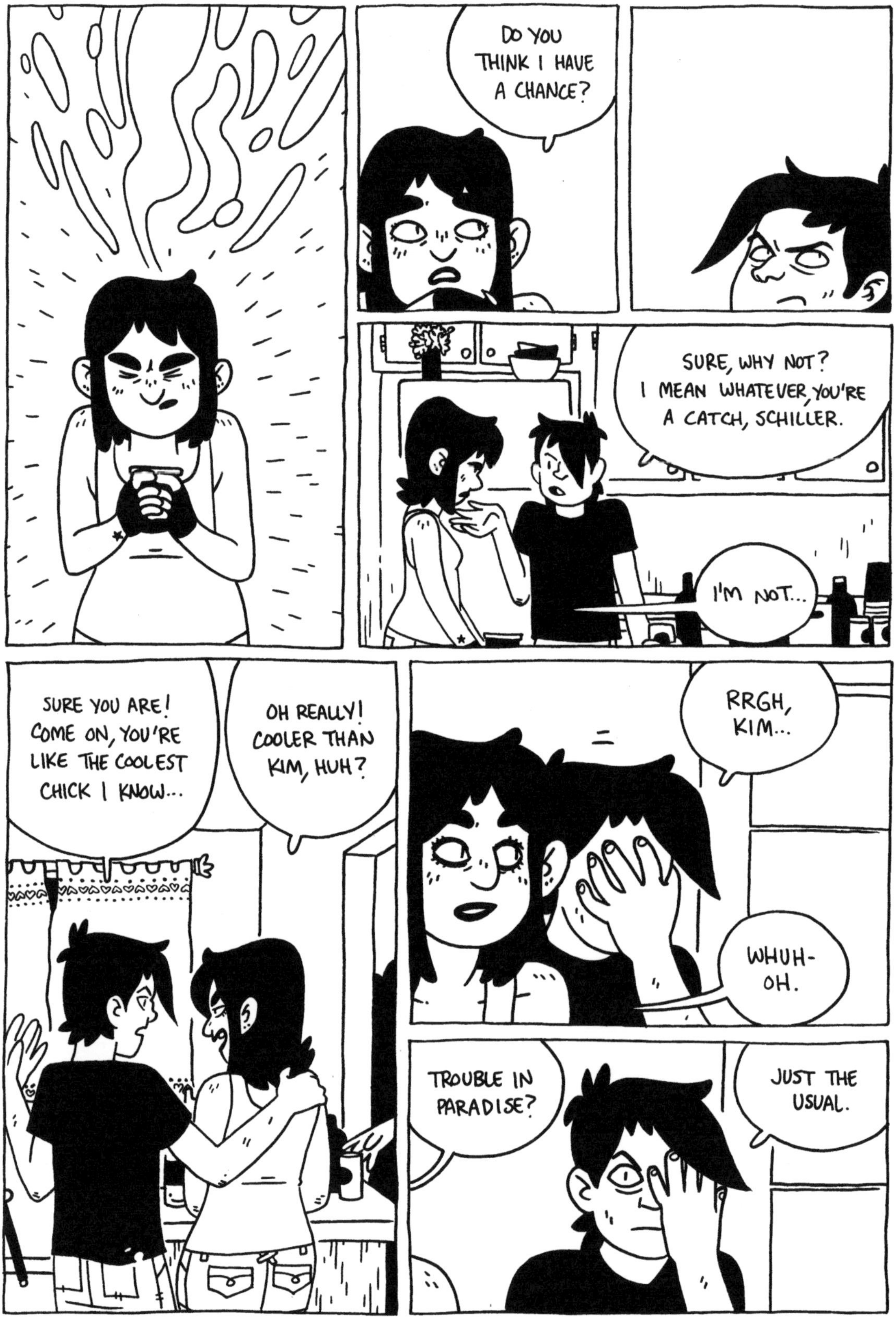
DO YOU THINK I HAVE A CHANCE?
SURE, WHY NOT? I MEAN WHATEVER, YOU'RE A CATCH, SCHILLER.
I'M NOT...
SURE YOU ARE! COME ON, YOU'RE LIKE THE COOLEST CHICK I KNOW...
OH REALLY! COOLER THAN KIM, HUH?
RRGH, KIM...
WHUH-OH.
TROUBLE IN PARADISE?
JUST THE USUAL.

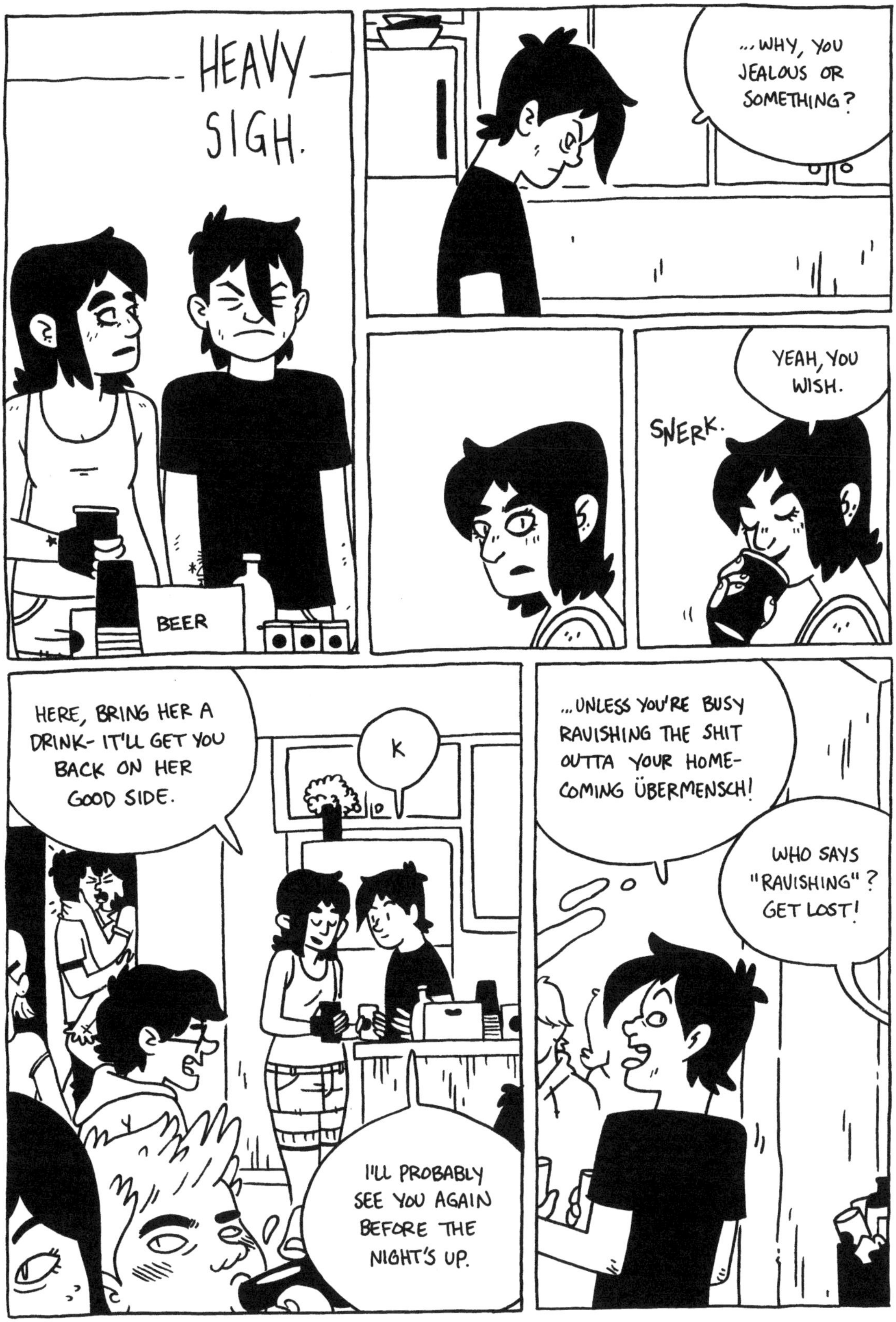
HEAVY SIGH.
BEER
...WHY, YOU JEALOUS OR SOMETHING?
SNERK.
YEAH, YOU WISH.
HERE, BRING HER A DRINK- IT'LL GET YOU BACK ON HER GOOD SIDE.
K
I'LL PROBABLY SEE YOU AGAIN BEFORE THE NIGHT'S UP.
...UNLESS YOU'RE BUSY RAVISHING THE SHIT OUTTA YOUR HOME-COMING ÜBERMENSCH!
WHO SAYS "RAVISHING"? GET LOST!

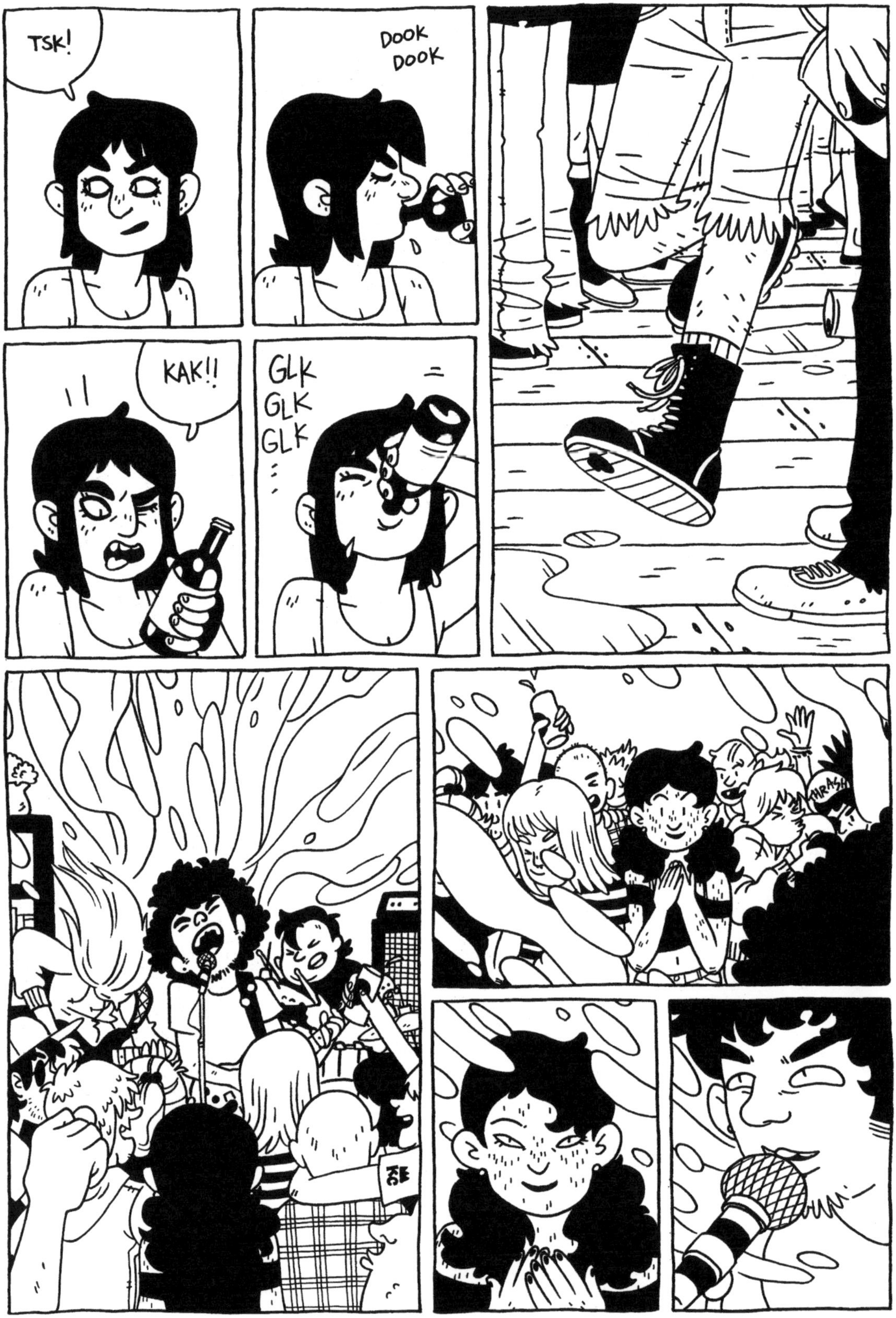
TSK!
DOOK DOOK
KAK!!
GLK GLK GLK

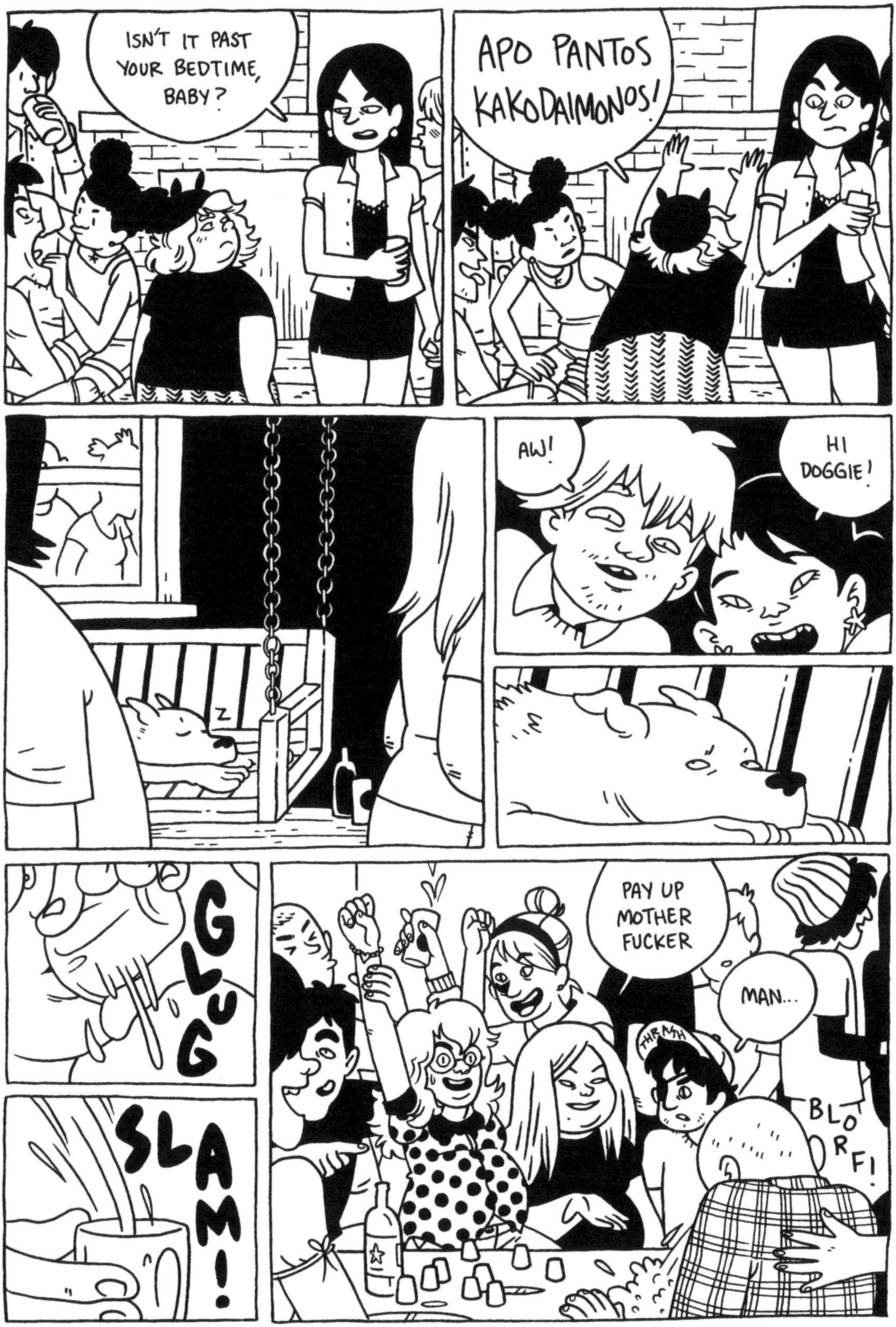
ISN'T IT PAST YOUR BEDTIME, BABY?
APO PANTOS KAKODAIMONOS!
AW!
HI DOGGIE!
Z
G L U G
SLAM!
PAY UP MOTHER FUCKER
MAN...
THRASH
BLORF!

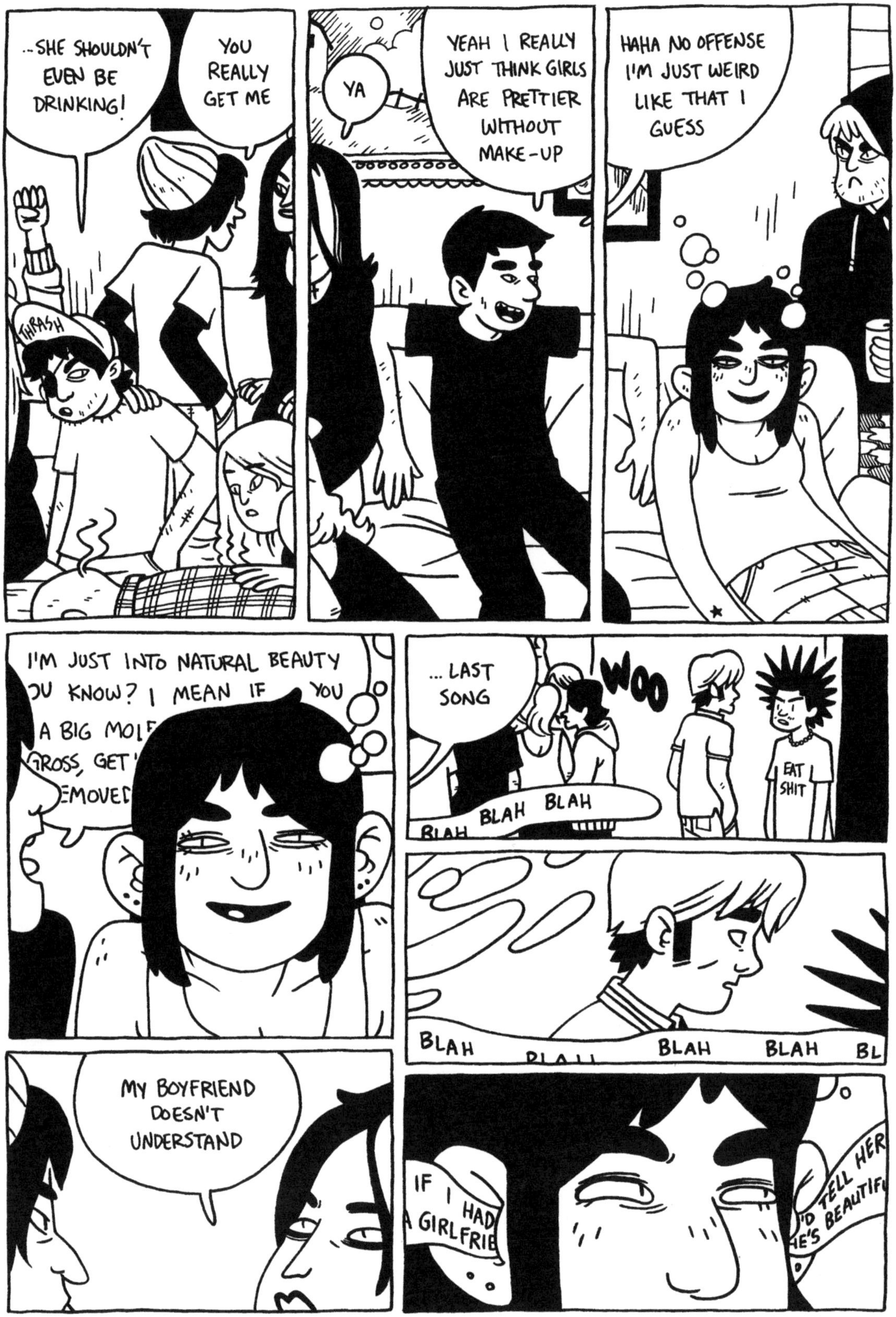
...SHE SHOULDN'T EVEN BE DRINKING!
YOU REALLY GET ME
THRASH
YA
YEAH I REALLY JUST THINK GIRLS ARE PRETTIER WITHOUT MAKE-UP
HAHA NO OFFENSE I'M JUST WEIRD LIKE THAT I GUESS
I'M JUST INTO NATURAL BEAUTY
...LAST SONG
WOO
EAT SHIT
BLAH BLAH
BLAH BLAH BLAH BL
MY BOYFRIEND DOESN'T UNDERSTAND
IF I HAD A GIRLFRIE
TELL HER HE'S BEAUTIF

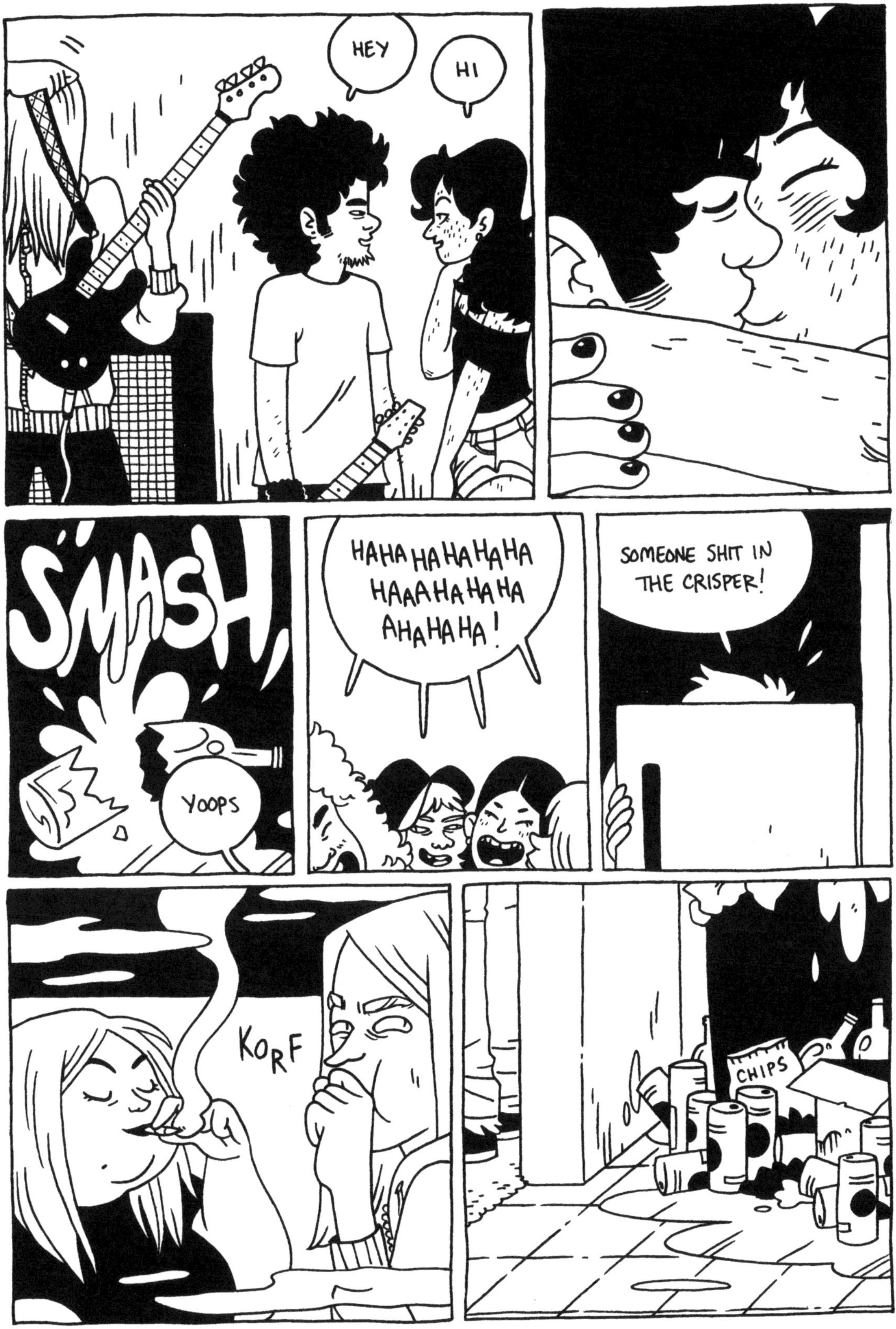
HEY
HI
SMASH
YOOPS
HAHA HAHAHAHA HAAAHAHAHAHA AHAHAHA!
SOMEONE SHIT IN THE CRISPER!
KORF
CHIPS

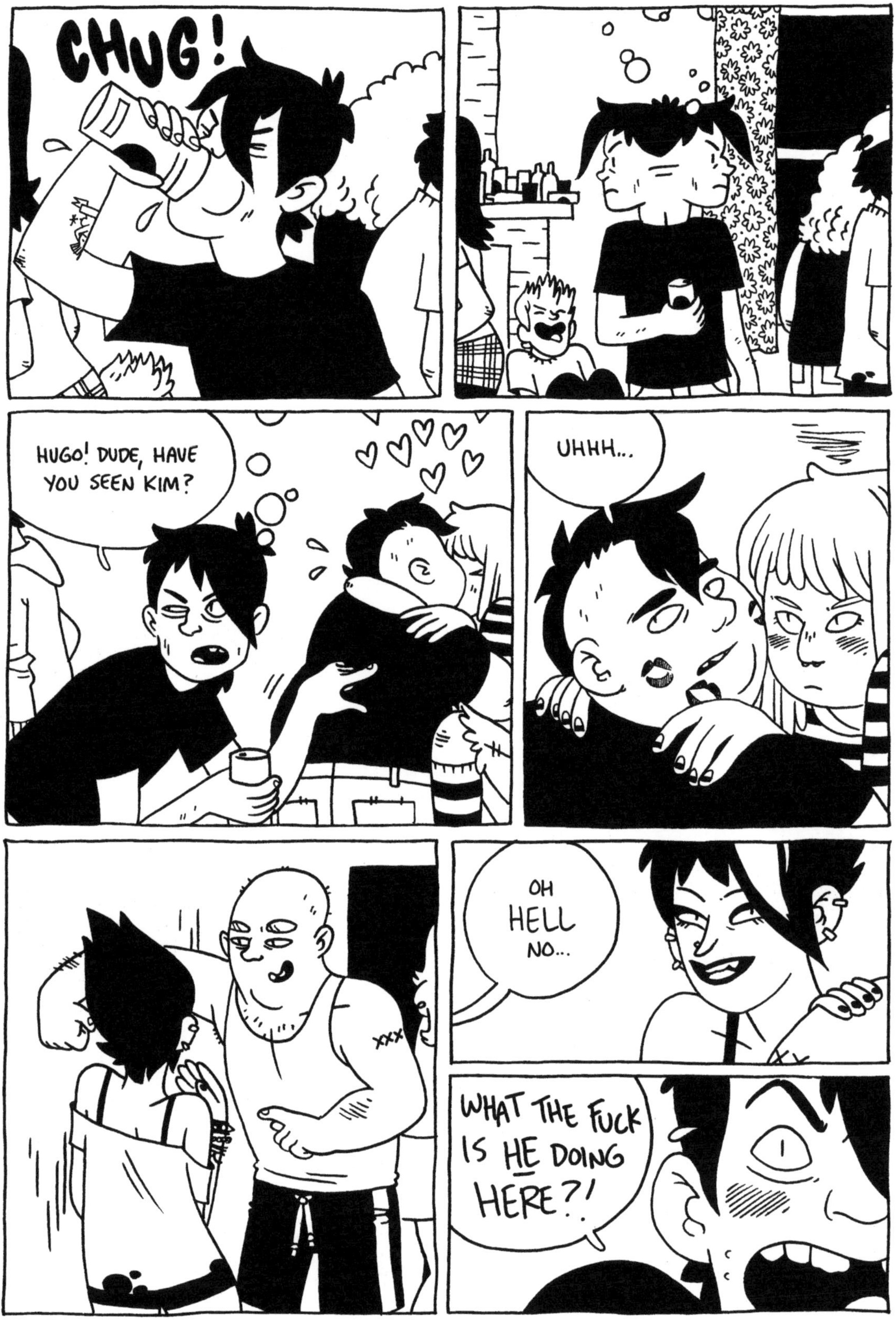
CHUG!
HUGO! DUDE, HAVE YOU SEEN KIM?
UHHH...
OH HELL NO...
WHAT THE FUCK IS HE DOING HERE?!

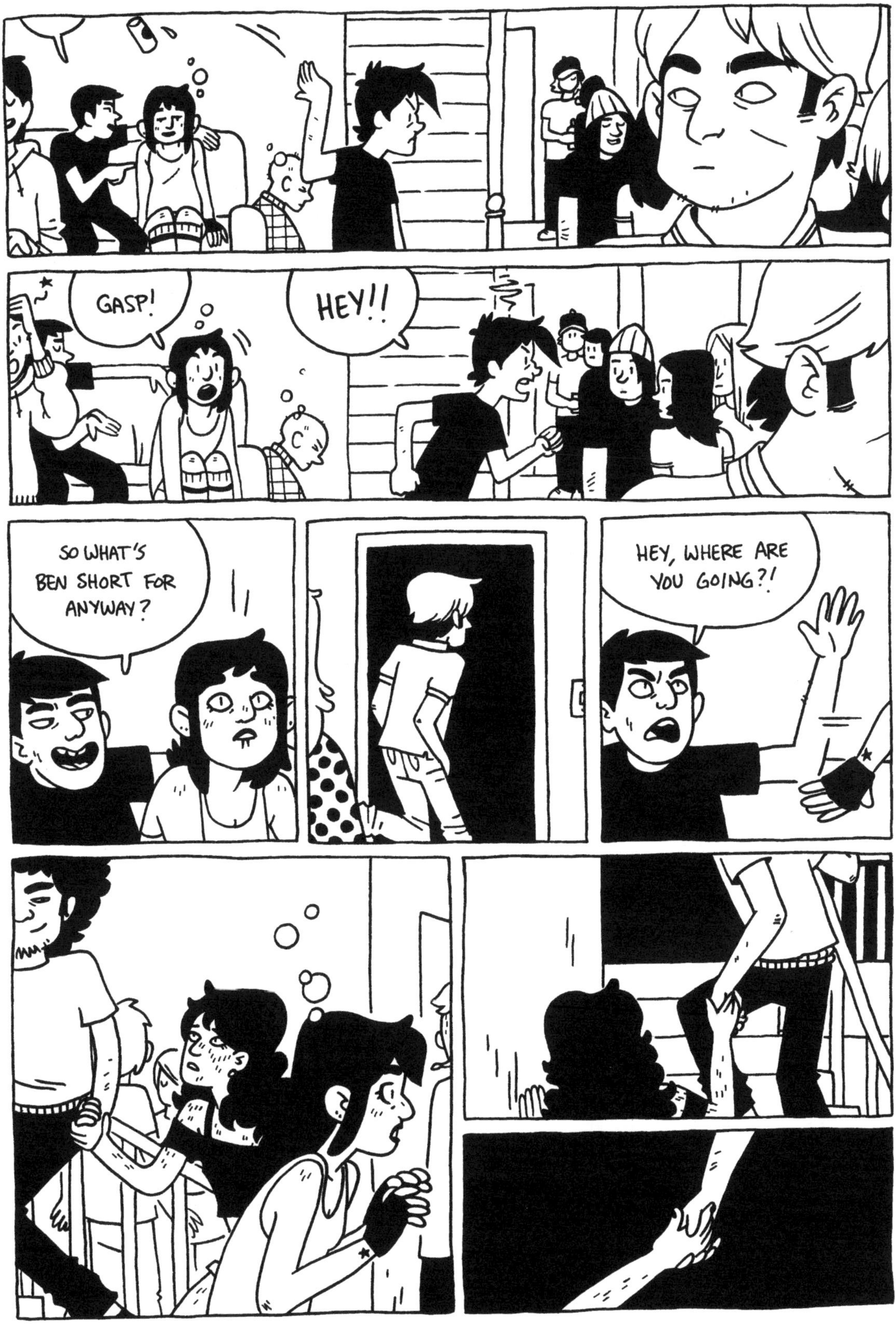
GASP!
HEY!!
SO WHAT'S BEN SHORT FOR ANYWAY?
HEY, WHERE ARE YOU GOING?!

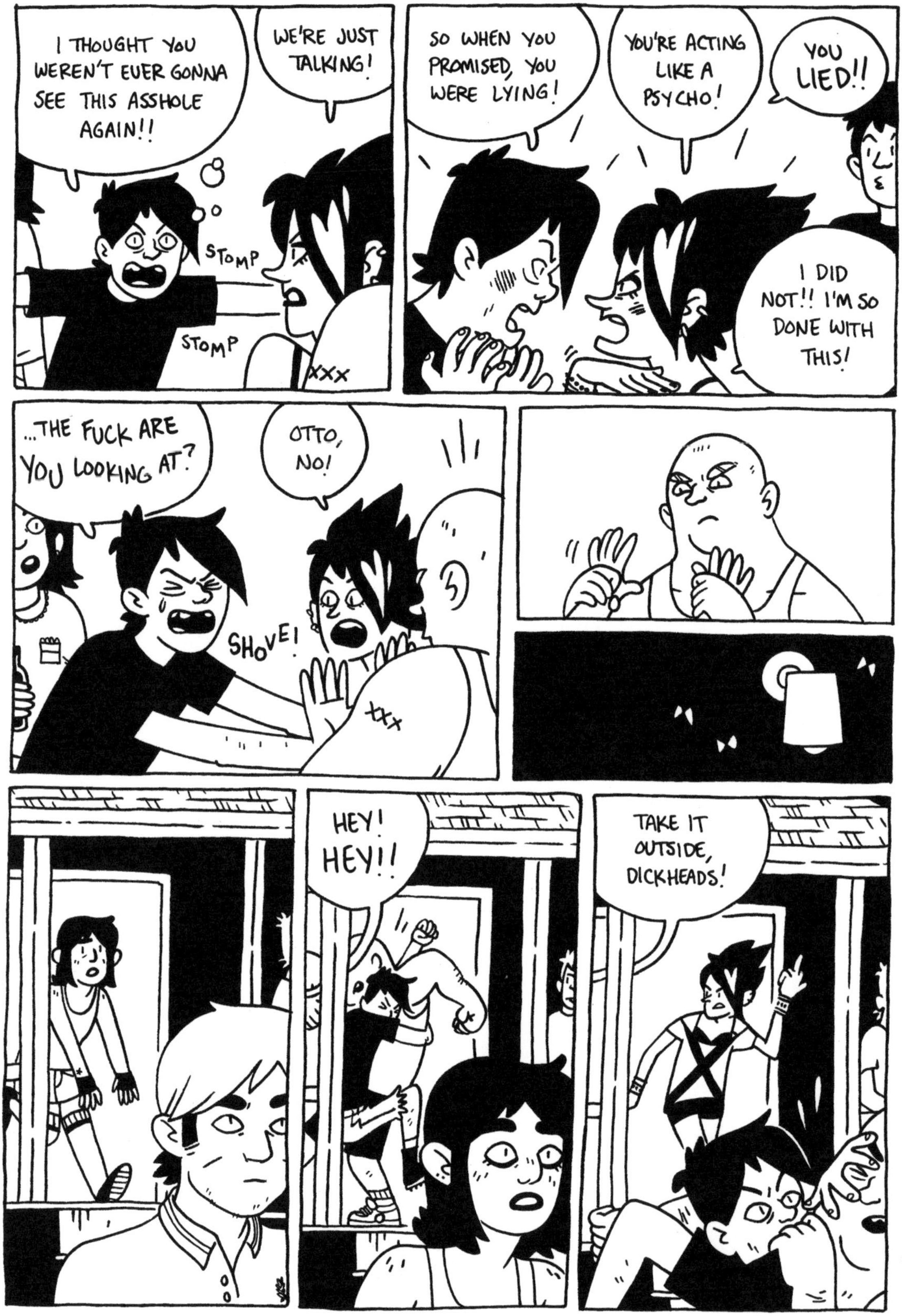

I THOUGHT YOU WEREN'T EVER GONNA SEE THIS ASSHOLE AGAIN!!
WE'RE JUST TALKING!
STOMP
STOMP
XXX
SO WHEN YOU PROMISED, YOU WERE LYING!
YOU'RE ACTING LIKE A PSYCHO!
YOU LIED!!
I DID NOT!! I'M SO DONE WITH THIS!
...THE FUCK ARE YOU LOOKING AT?
OTTO, NO!
SHOVE!
XXX
HEY! HEY!!
TAKE IT OUTSIDE, DICKHEADS!

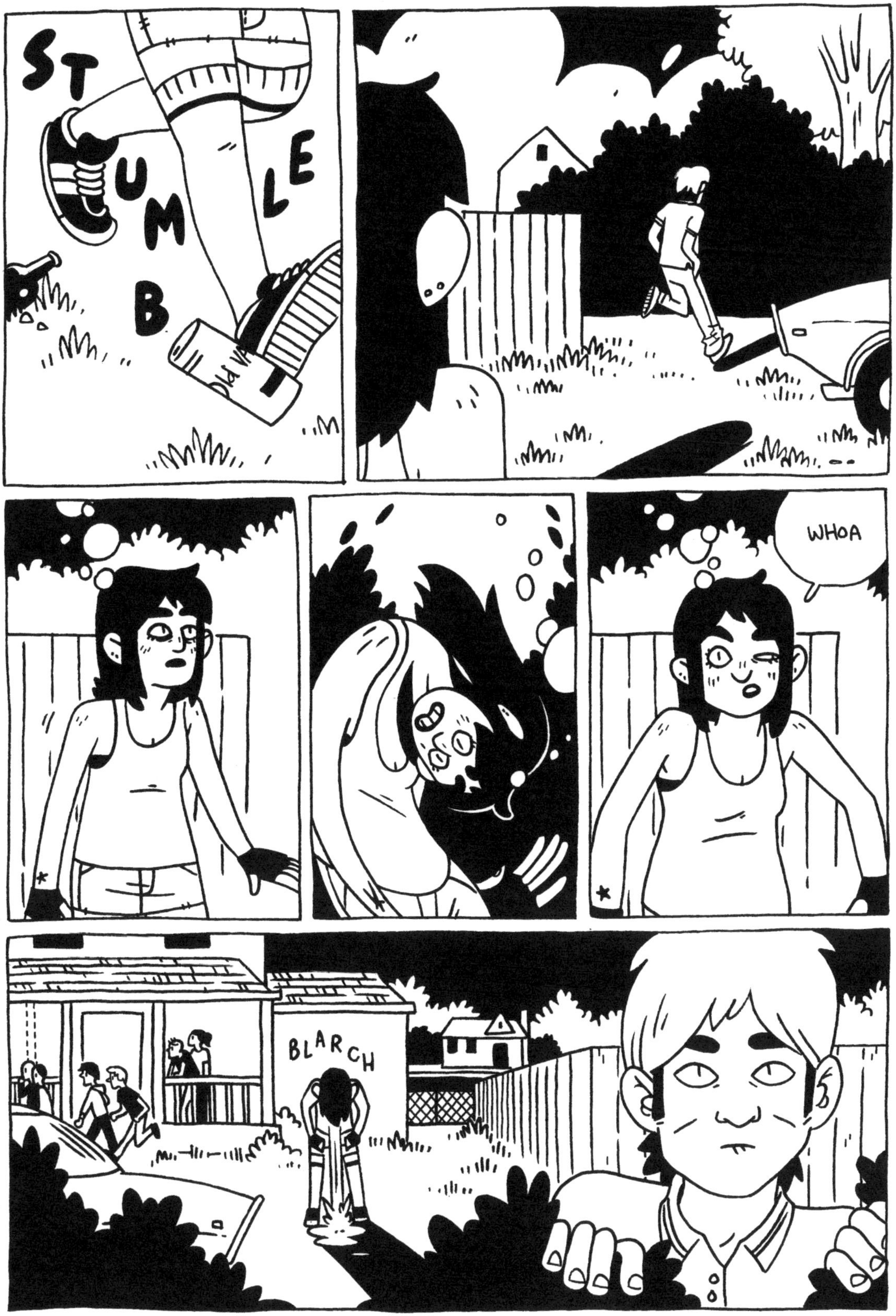
STUMBLE
WHOA
BLARCH

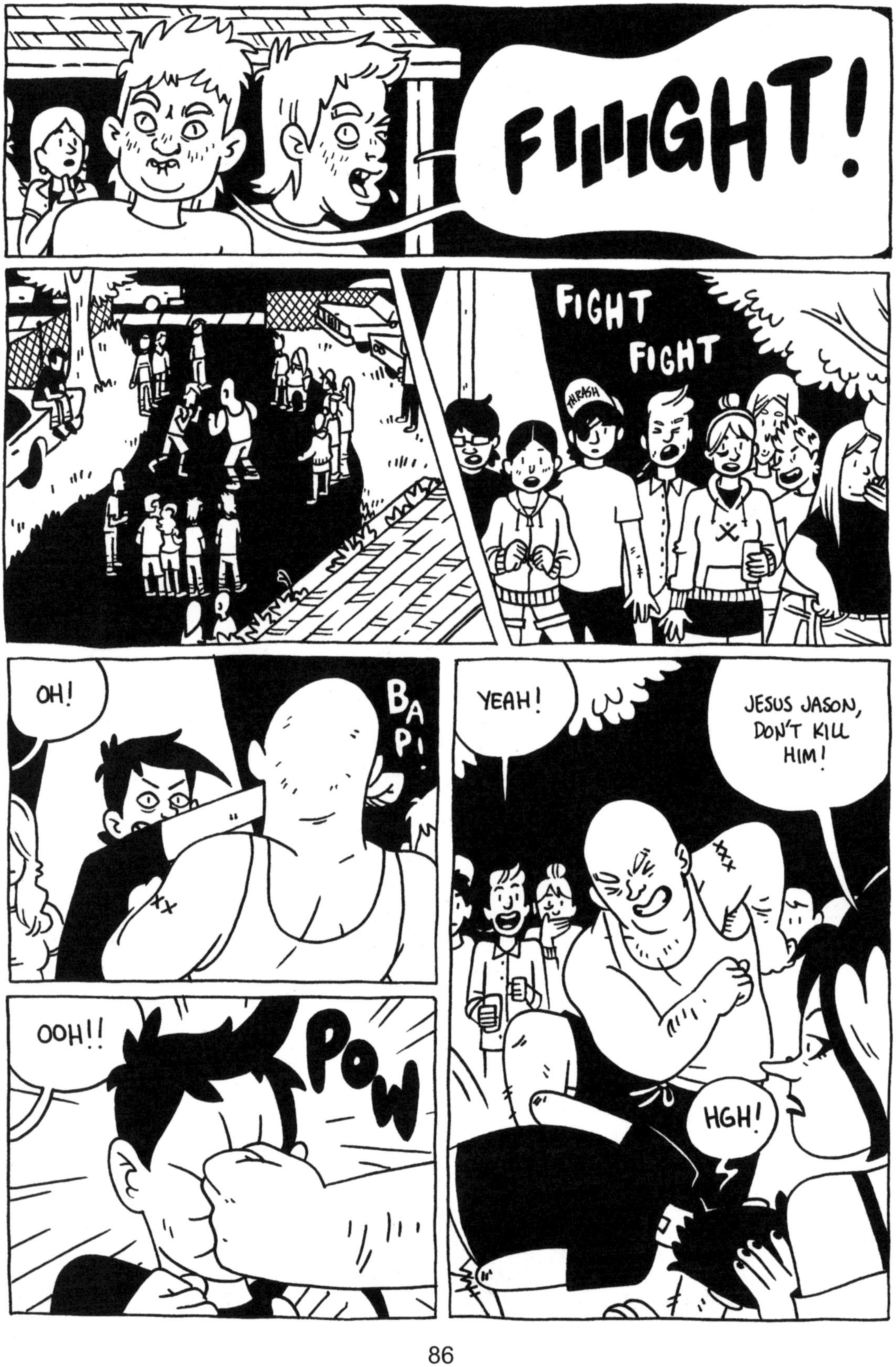
FIIIIGHT!
FIGHT
FIGHT
THRASH
OH!
BAP!
YEAH!
JESUS JASON, DON'T KILL HIM!
OOH!!
POW
HGH!

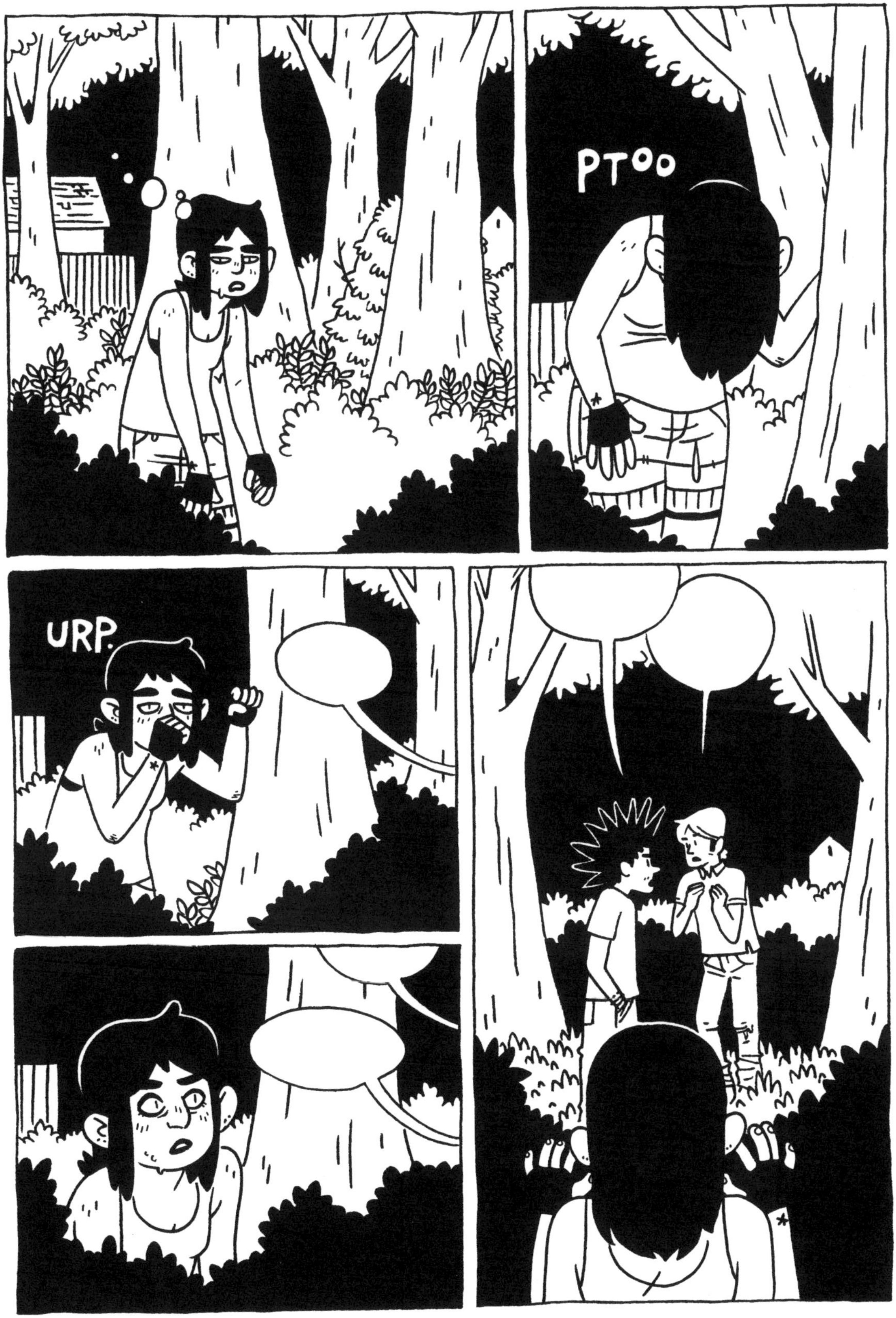
PTOO
URP.

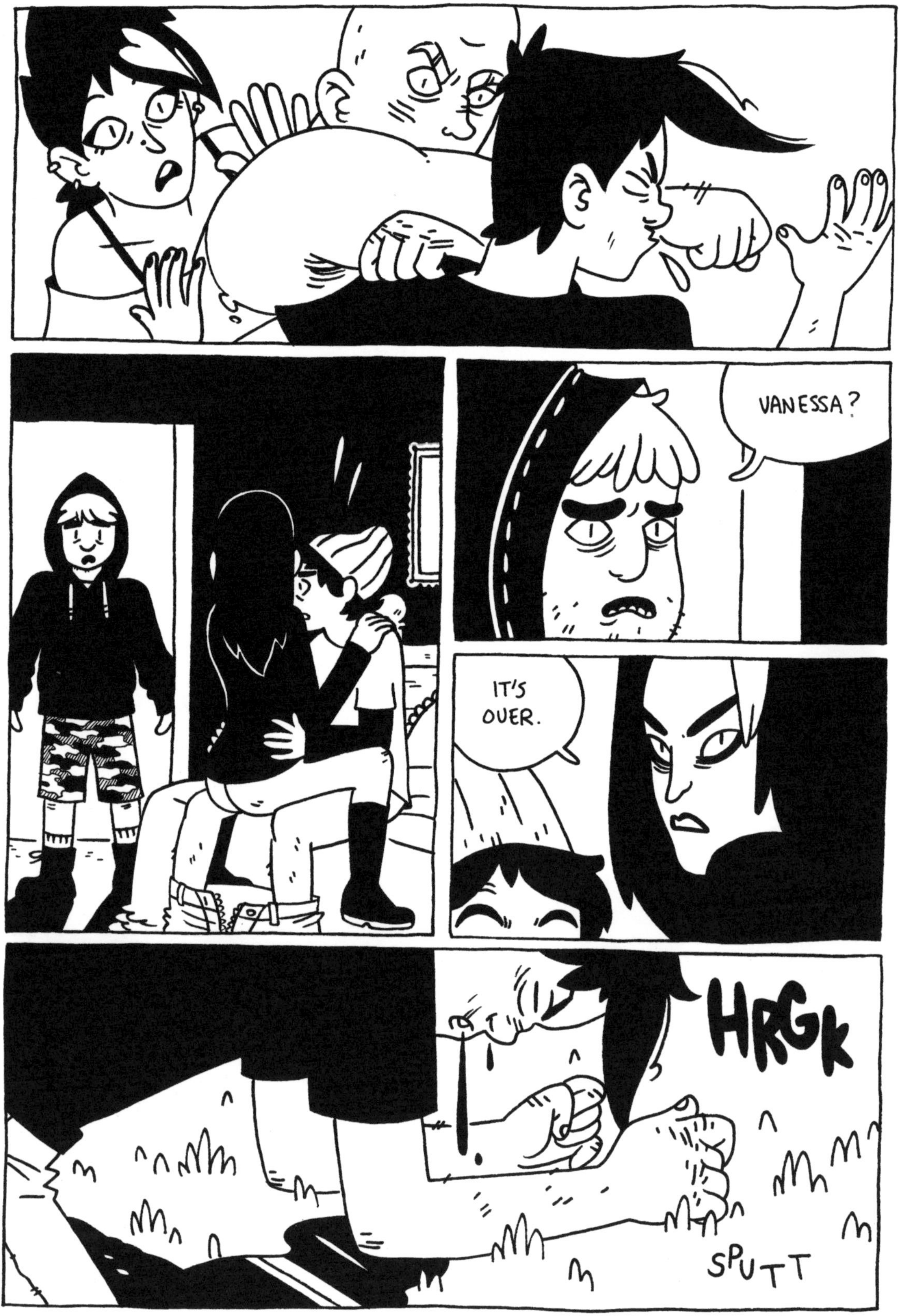
VANESSA?
IT'S OVER.
HRGK
SPUTT

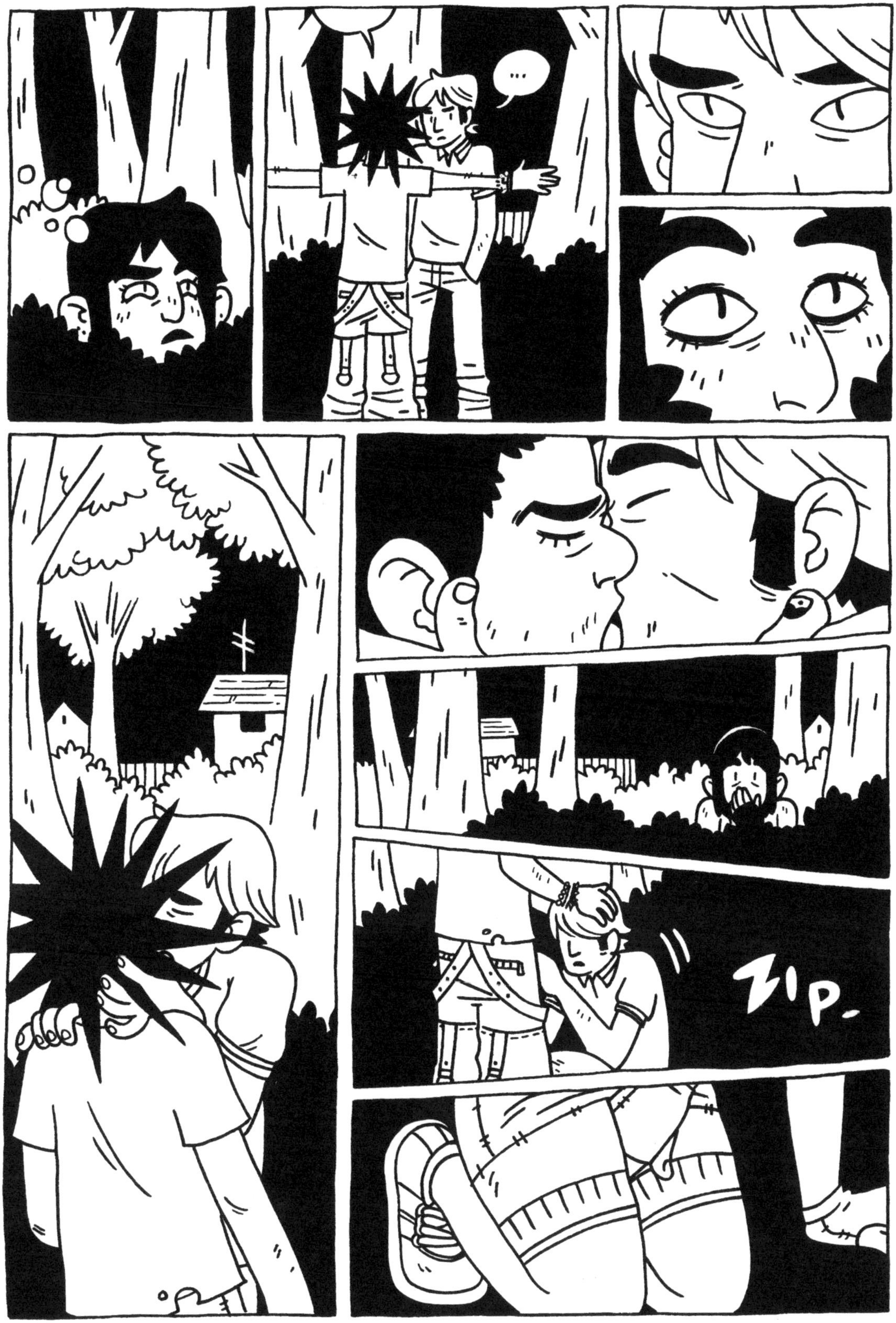
...
ZIP.

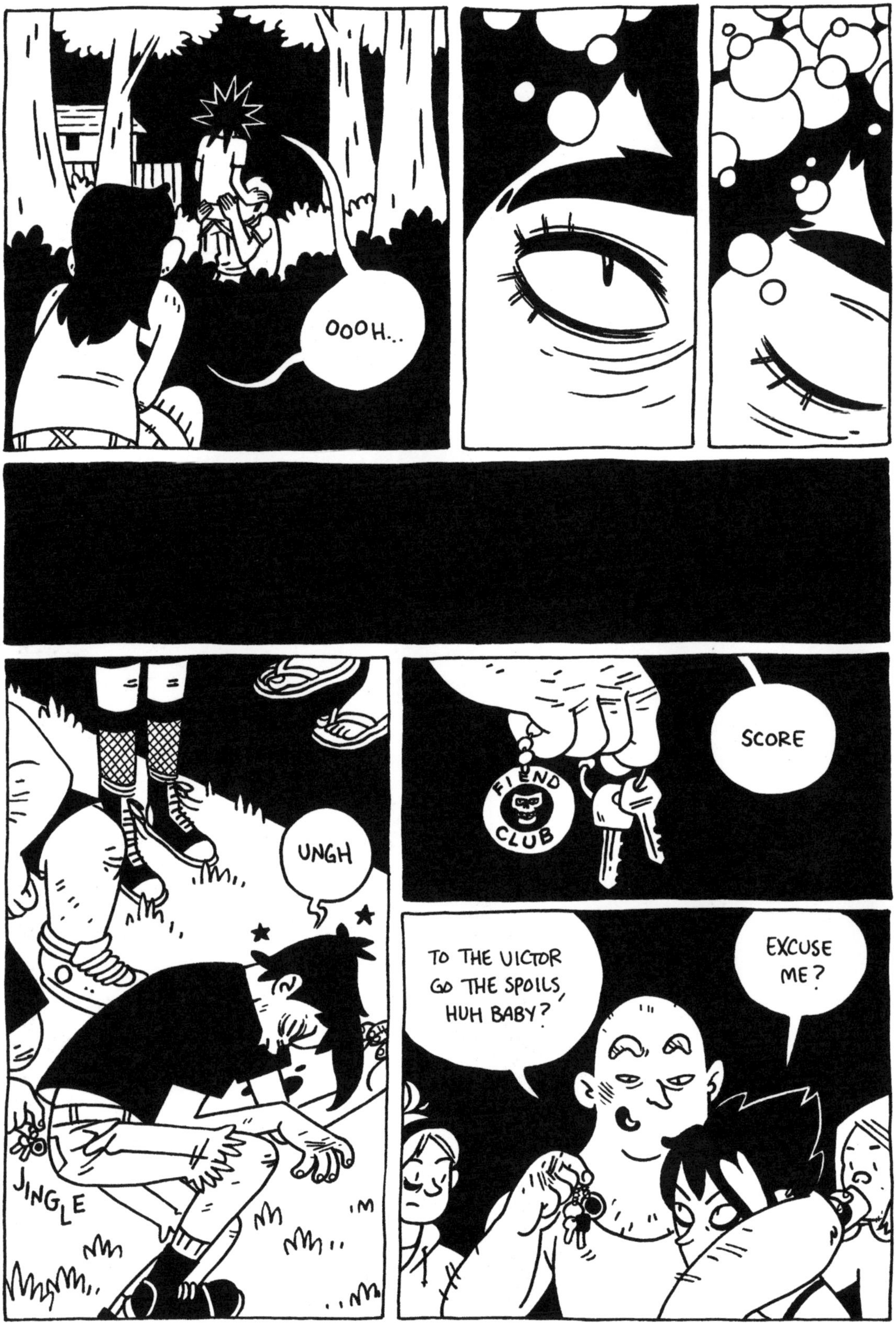
OOOH...
UNGH
JINGLE
SCORE
FIEND CLUB
TO THE VICTOR GO THE SPOILS, HUH BABY?
EXCUSE ME?

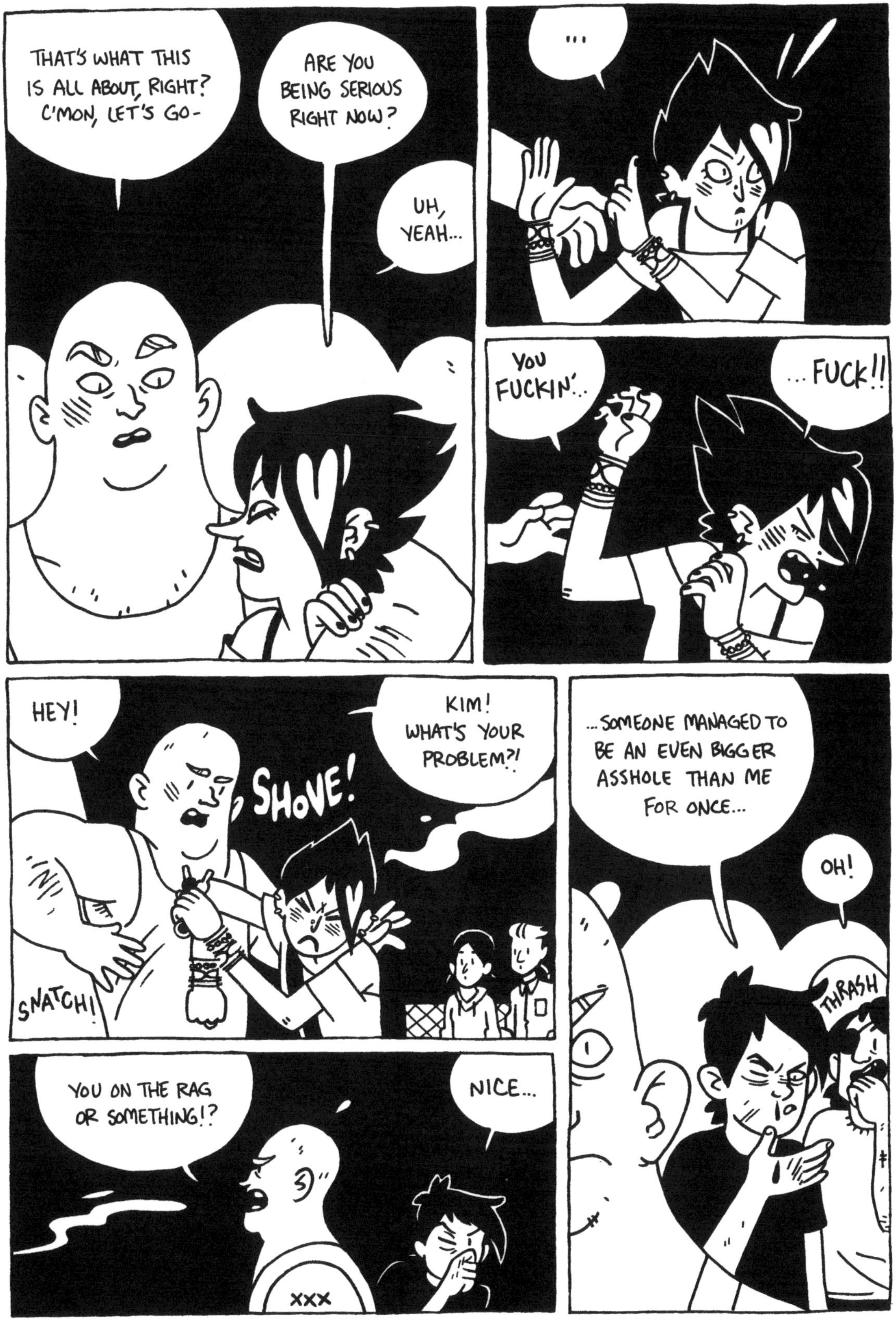
THAT'S WHAT THIS IS ALL ABOUT, RIGHT? C'MON, LET'S GO-
ARE YOU BEING SERIOUS RIGHT NOW?
UH, YEAH...
...
YOU FUCKIN'...
...FUCK!!
HEY!
SHOVE!
KIM! WHAT'S YOUR PROBLEM?!
SNATCH!
...SOMEONE MANAGED TO BE AN EVEN BIGGER ASSHOLE THAN ME FOR ONCE...
OH!
THRASH
YOU ON THE RAG OR SOMETHING!?
NICE...
XXX

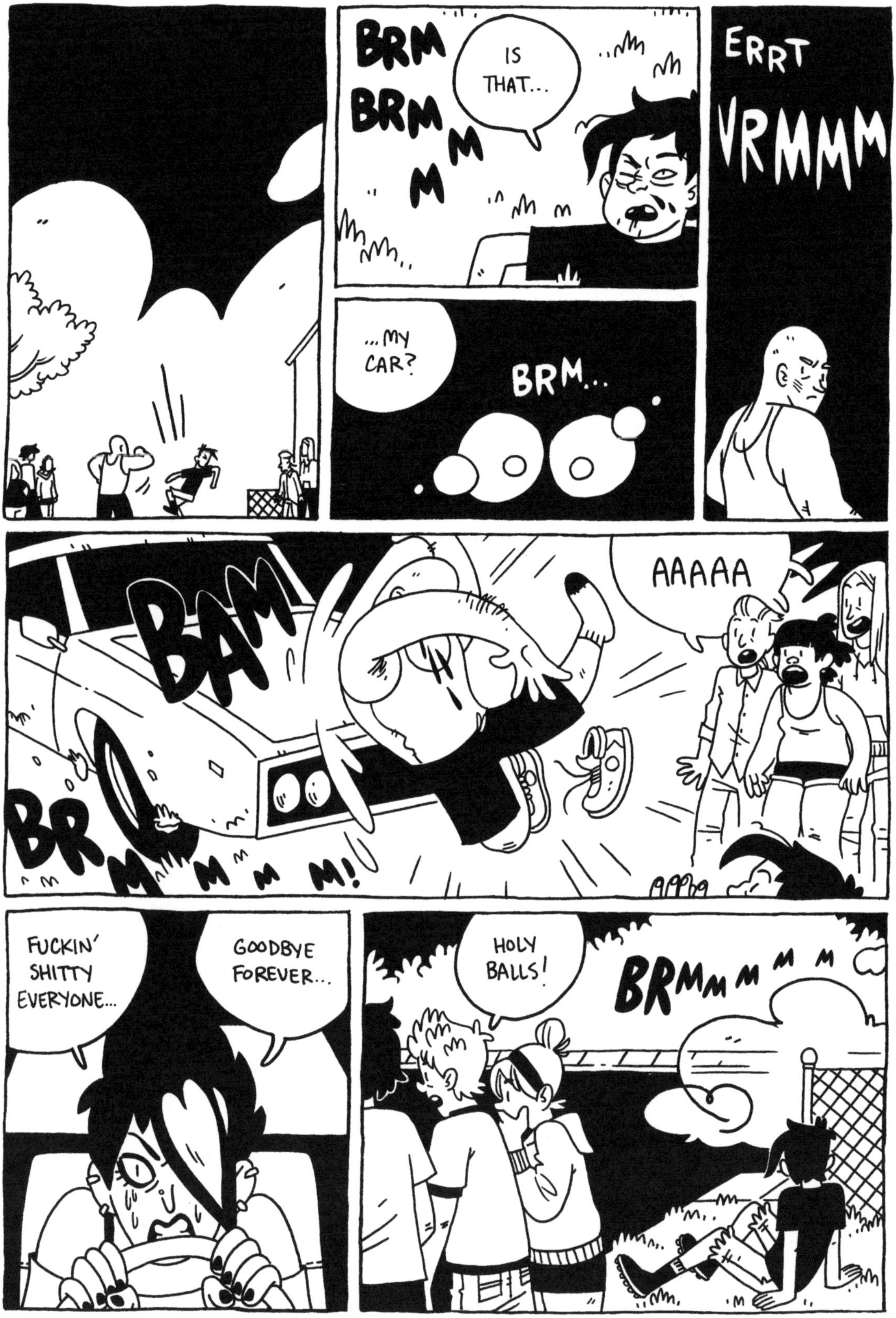
BRM
BRM
M
M
IS THAT...
ERRT
VRMMM
...MY CAR?
BRM...
BAM
AAAAA
BRMMMM!
FUCKIN' SHITTY EVERYONE...
GOODBYE FOREVER...
HOLY BALLS!
BRMMMMM

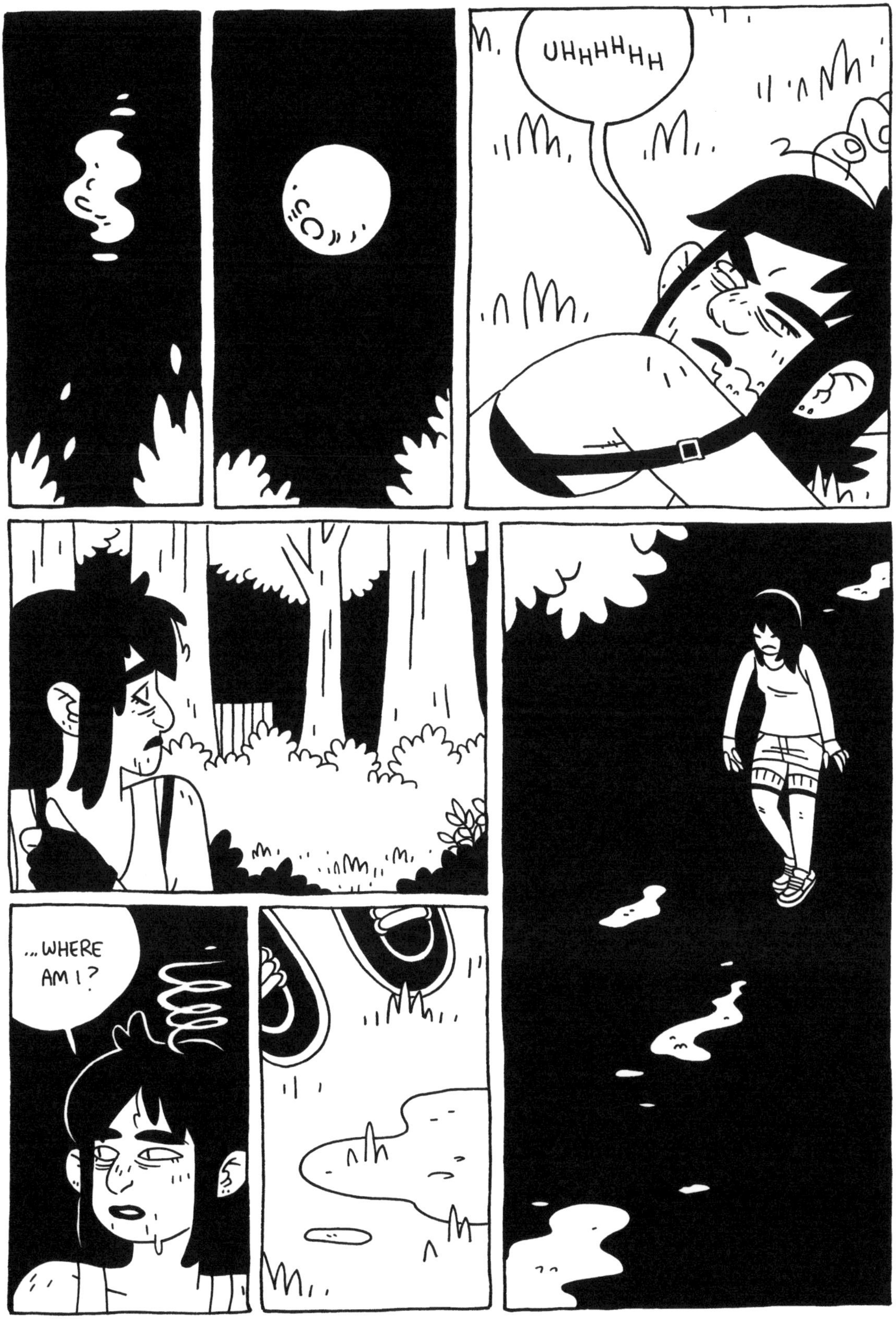
UHHHHHH
...WHERE AM I?

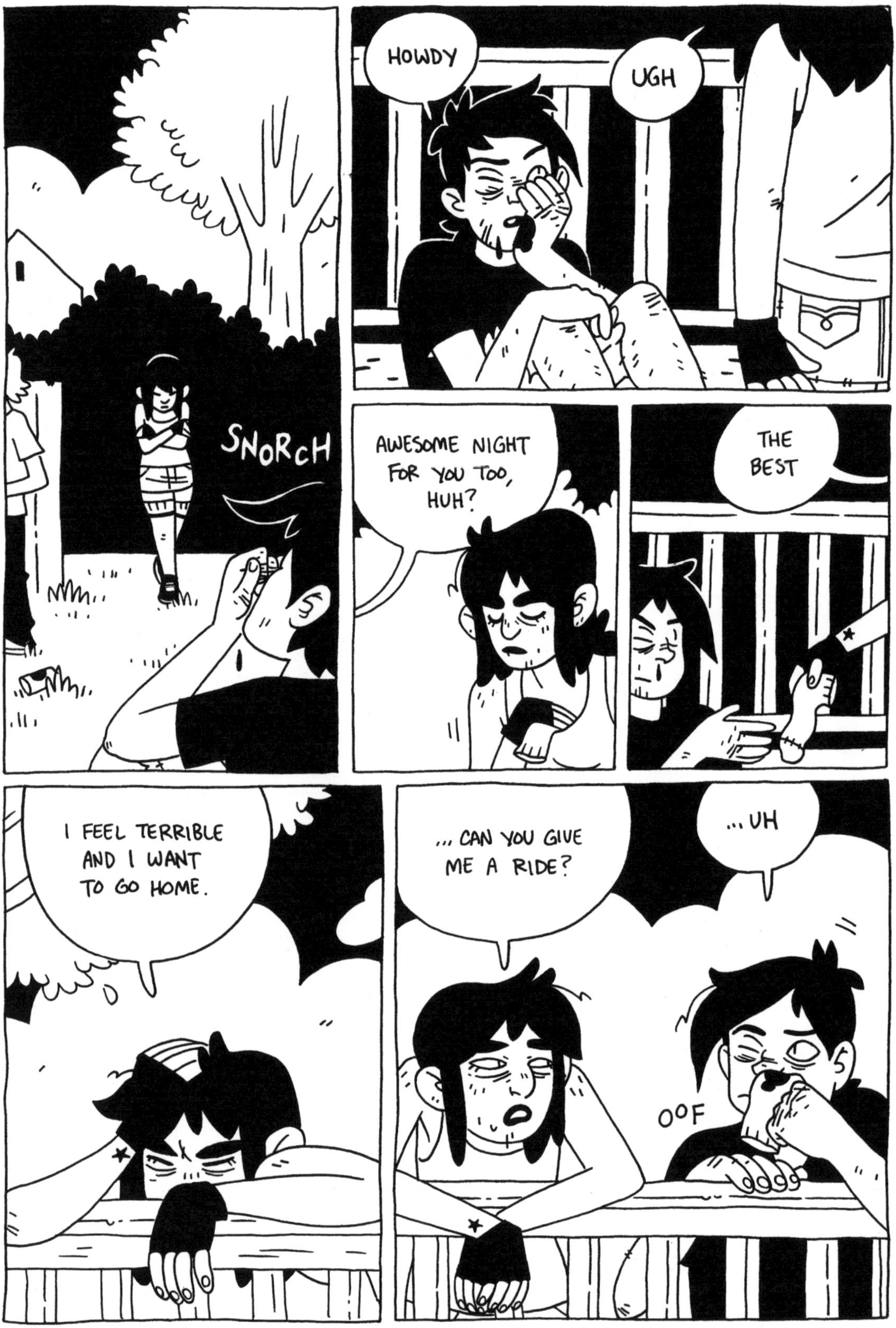
SNORCH
HOWDY
UGH
AWESOME NIGHT FOR YOU TOO, HUH?
THE BEST
I FEEL TERRIBLE AND I WANT TO GO HOME.
... CAN YOU GIVE ME A RIDE?
... UH
OOF

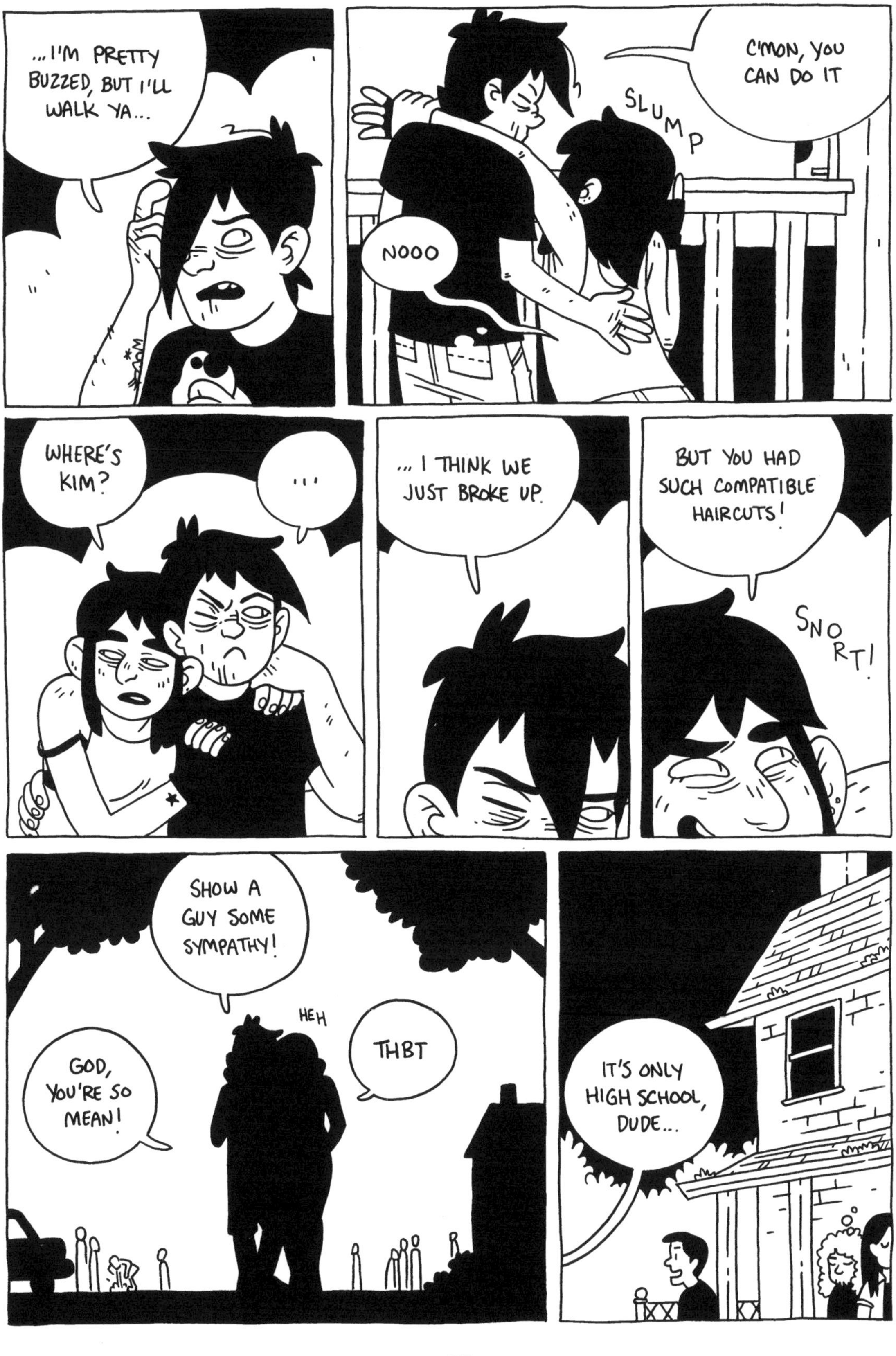
...I'M PRETTY BUZZED, BUT I'LL WALK YA...
C'MON, YOU CAN DO IT
SLUMP
NOOO
WHERE'S KIM?
...
...I THINK WE JUST BROKE UP.
BUT YOU HAD SUCH COMPATIBLE HAIRCUTS!
SNORT!
SHOW A GUY SOME SYMPATHY!
HEH
THBT
GOD, YOU'RE SO MEAN!
IT'S ONLY HIGH SCHOOL, DUDE...

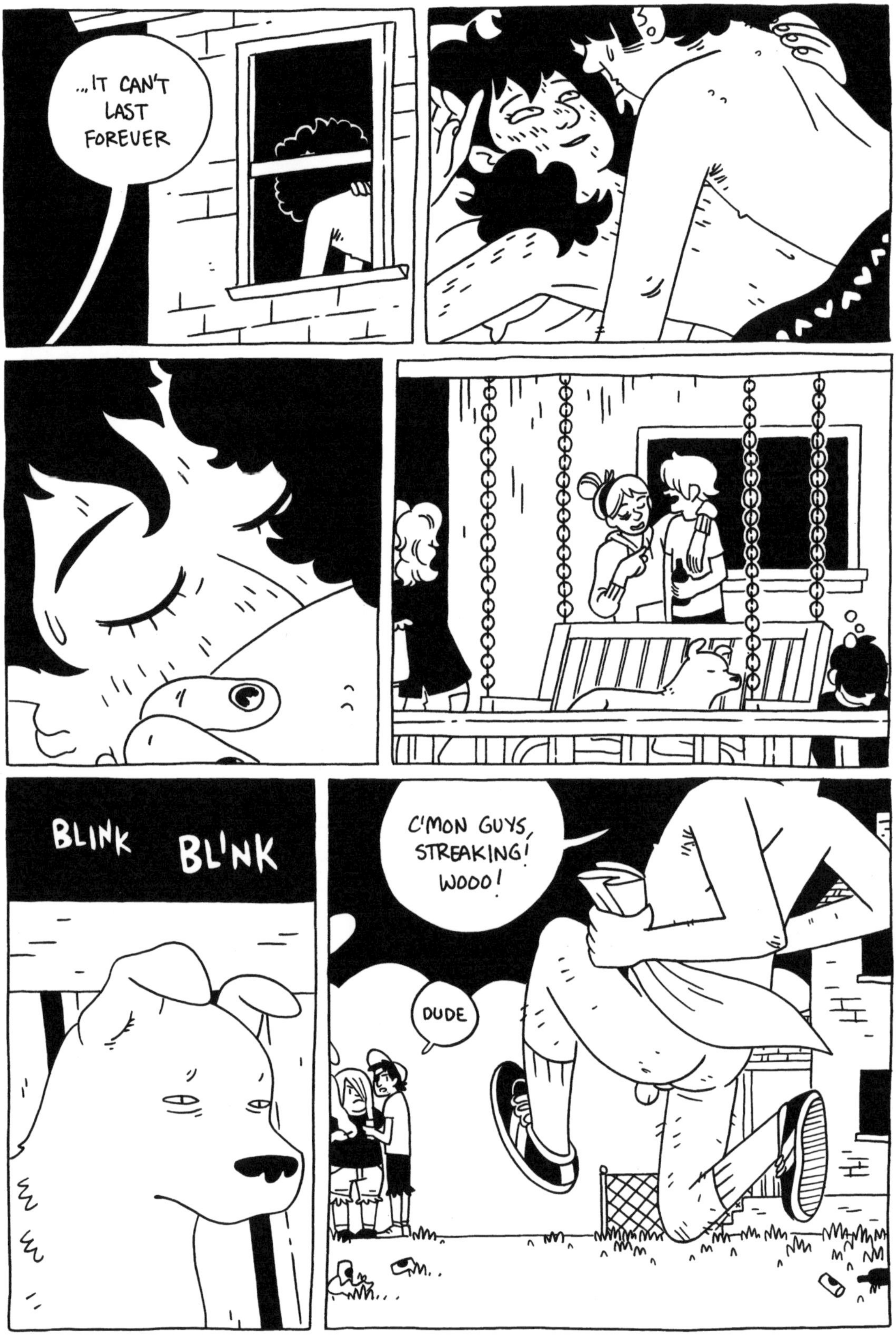
...IT CAN'T LAST FOREVER
BLINK
BLINK
C'MON GUYS, STREAKING! WOOO!
DUDE

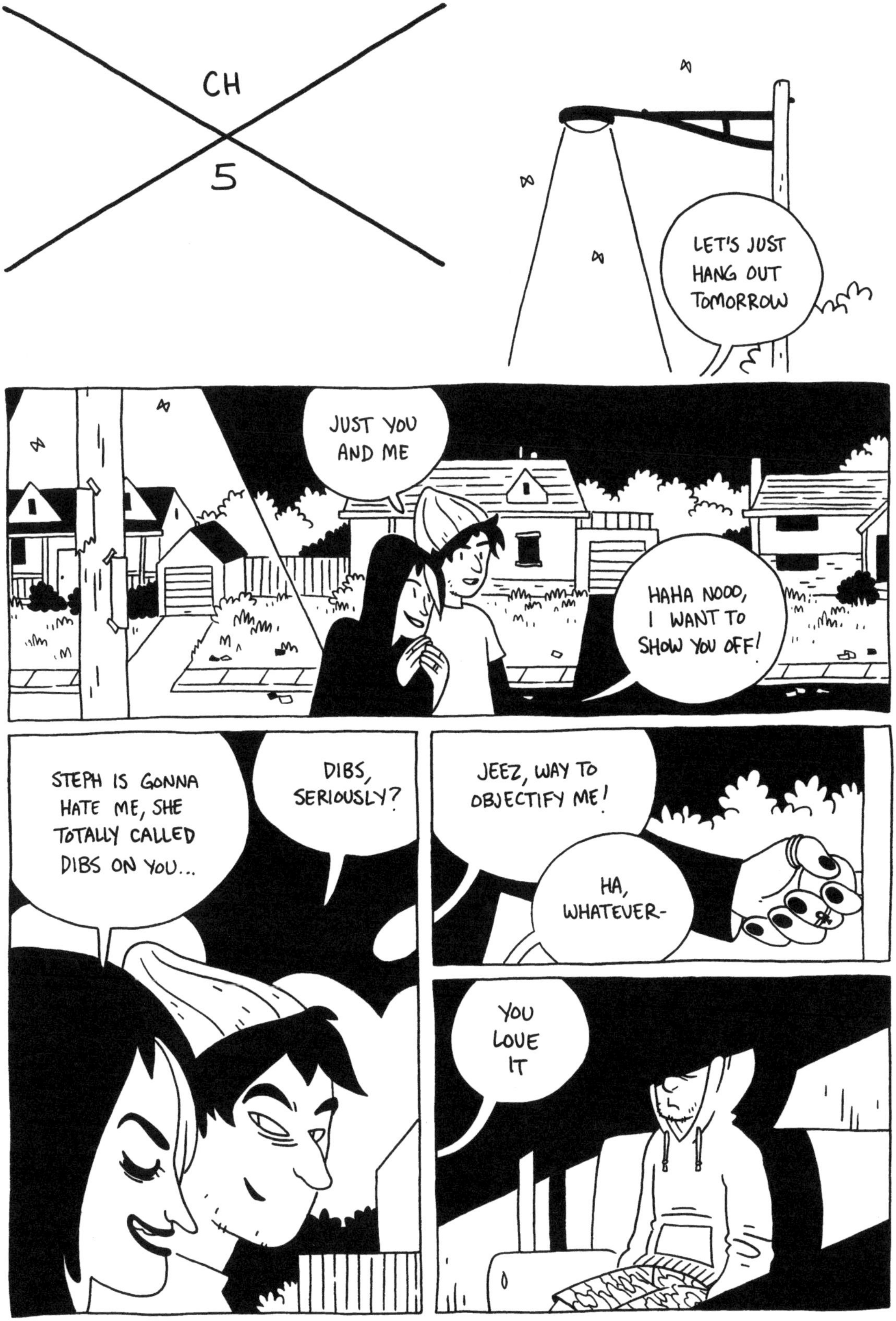
CH 5
LET'S JUST HANG OUT TOMORROW
JUST YOU AND ME
HAHA NOOO, I WANT TO SHOW YOU OFF!
STEPH IS GONNA HATE ME, SHE TOTALLY CALLED DIBS ON YOU...
DIBS, SERIOUSLY?
JEEZ, WAY TO OBJECTIFY ME!
HA, WHATEVER-
YOU LOVE IT

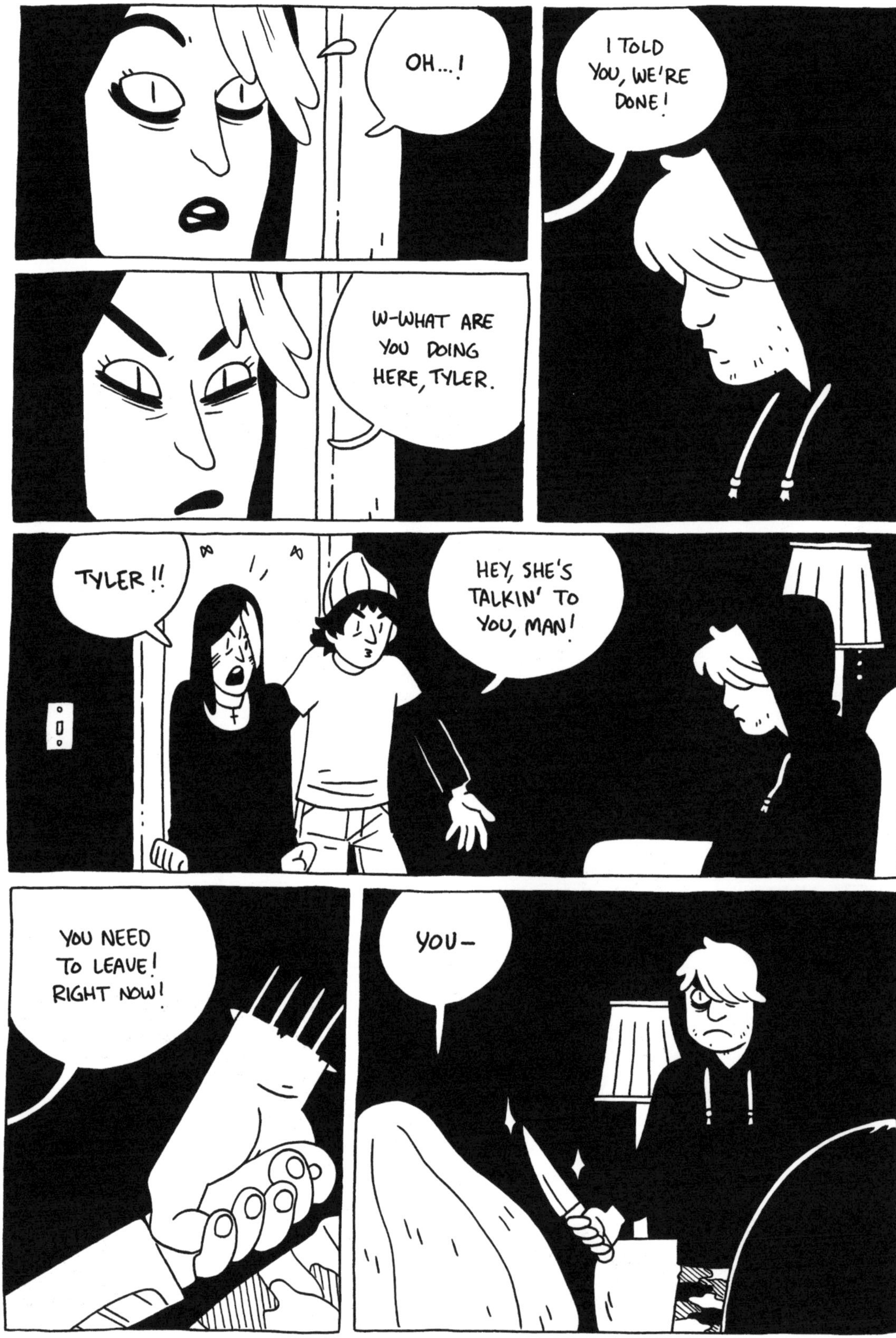
OH...!
I TOLD YOU, WE'RE DONE!
W-WHAT ARE YOU DOING HERE, TYLER.
TYLER!!
HEY, SHE'S TALKIN' TO YOU, MAN!
YOU NEED TO LEAVE! RIGHT NOW!
YOU-

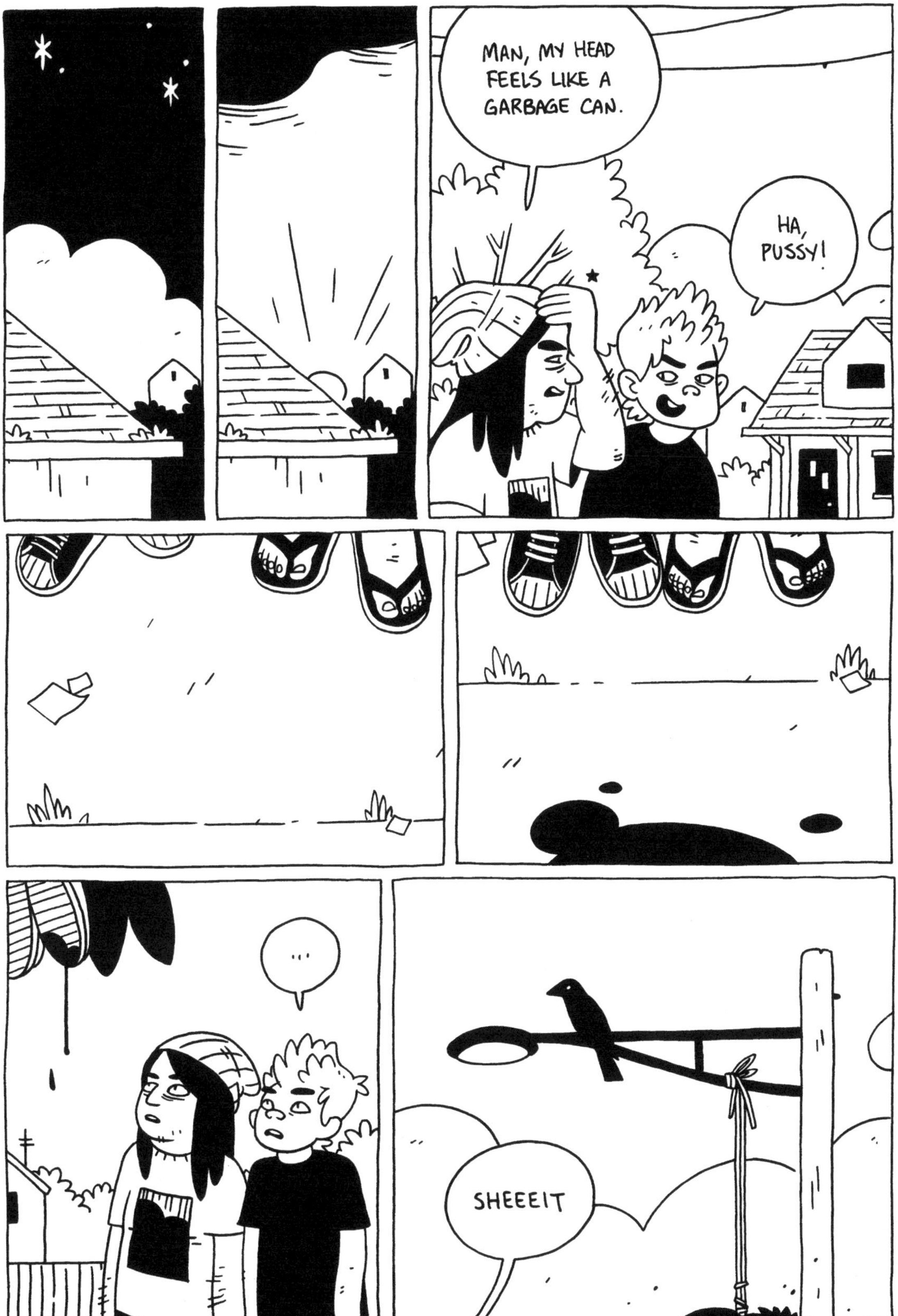
MAN, MY HEAD FEELS LIKE A GARBAGE CAN.
HA, PUSSY!
...
SHEEEIT

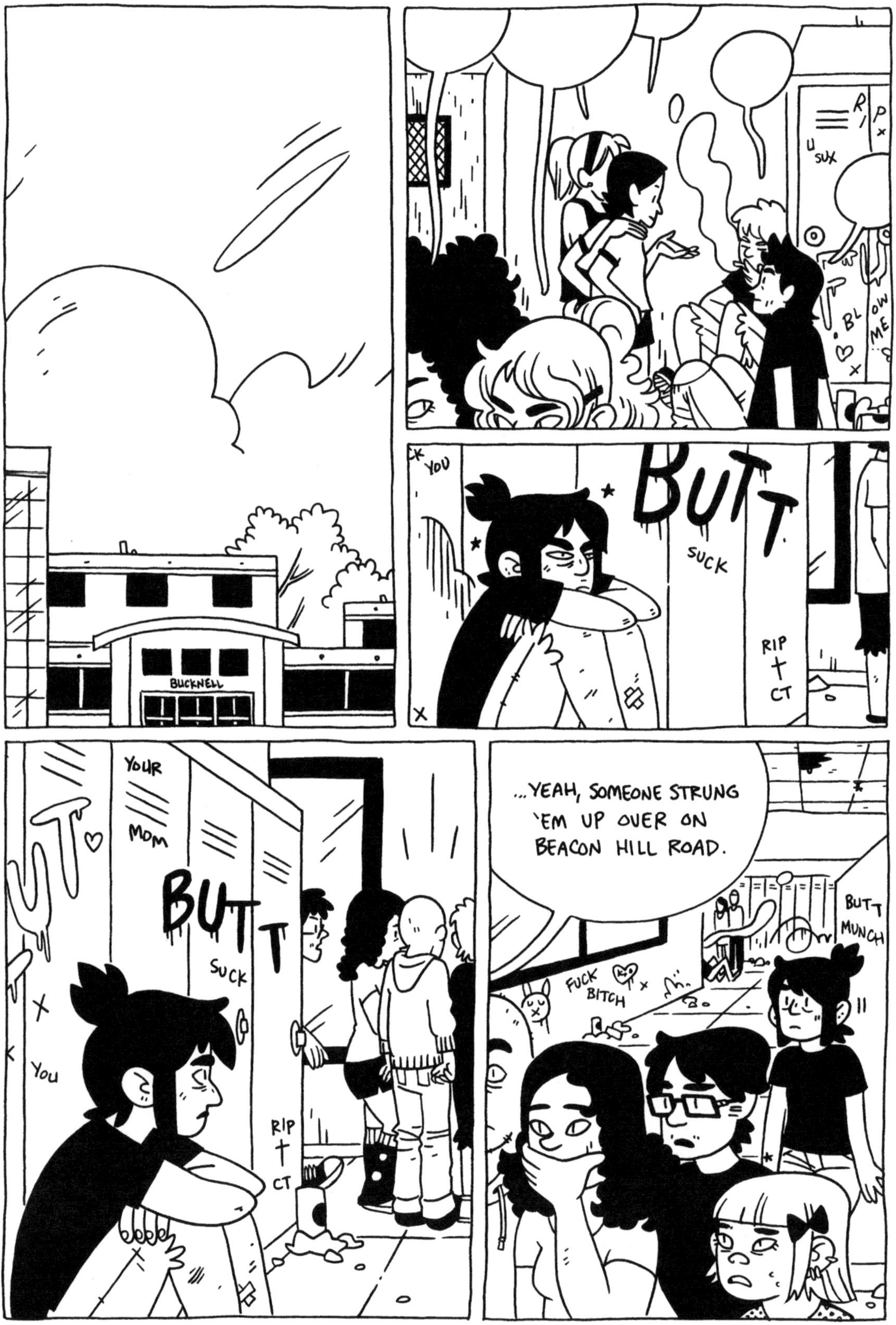
BUCKNELL
RIP
U SUX
BLOW ME
YOU
BUTT
SUCK
RIP
CT
YOUR
MOM
BUTT
SUCK
YOU
RIP
CT
...YEAH, SOMEONE STRUNG 'EM UP OVER ON BEACON HILL ROAD.
FUCK
BITCH
BUTT
MUNCH

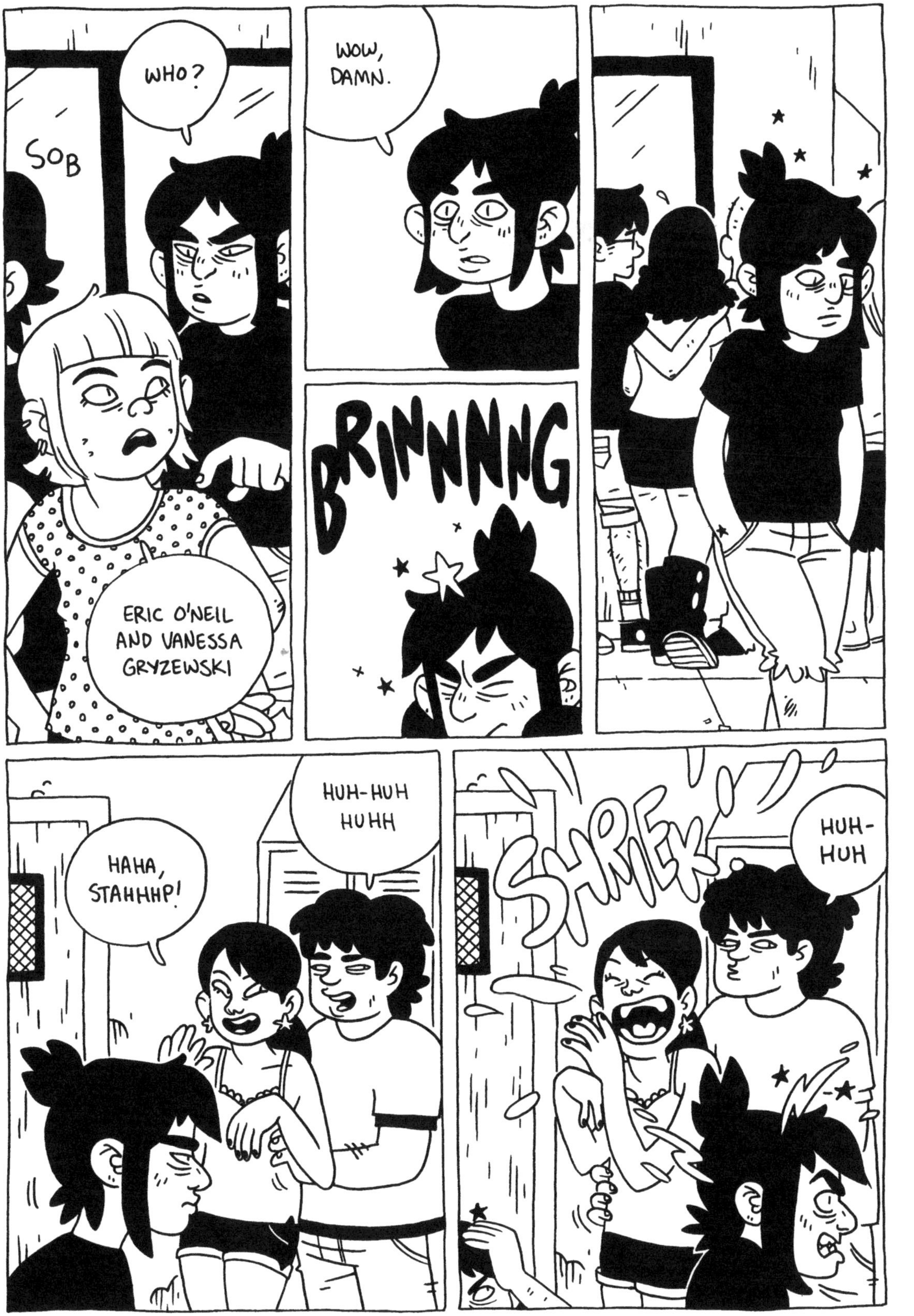
SOB
WHO?
ERIC O'NEIL AND VANESSA GRYZEWSKI
WOW, DAMN.
BRINNNNG
HAHA, STAHHHP!
HUH-HUH HUHH
SHRIEK
HUH-HUH

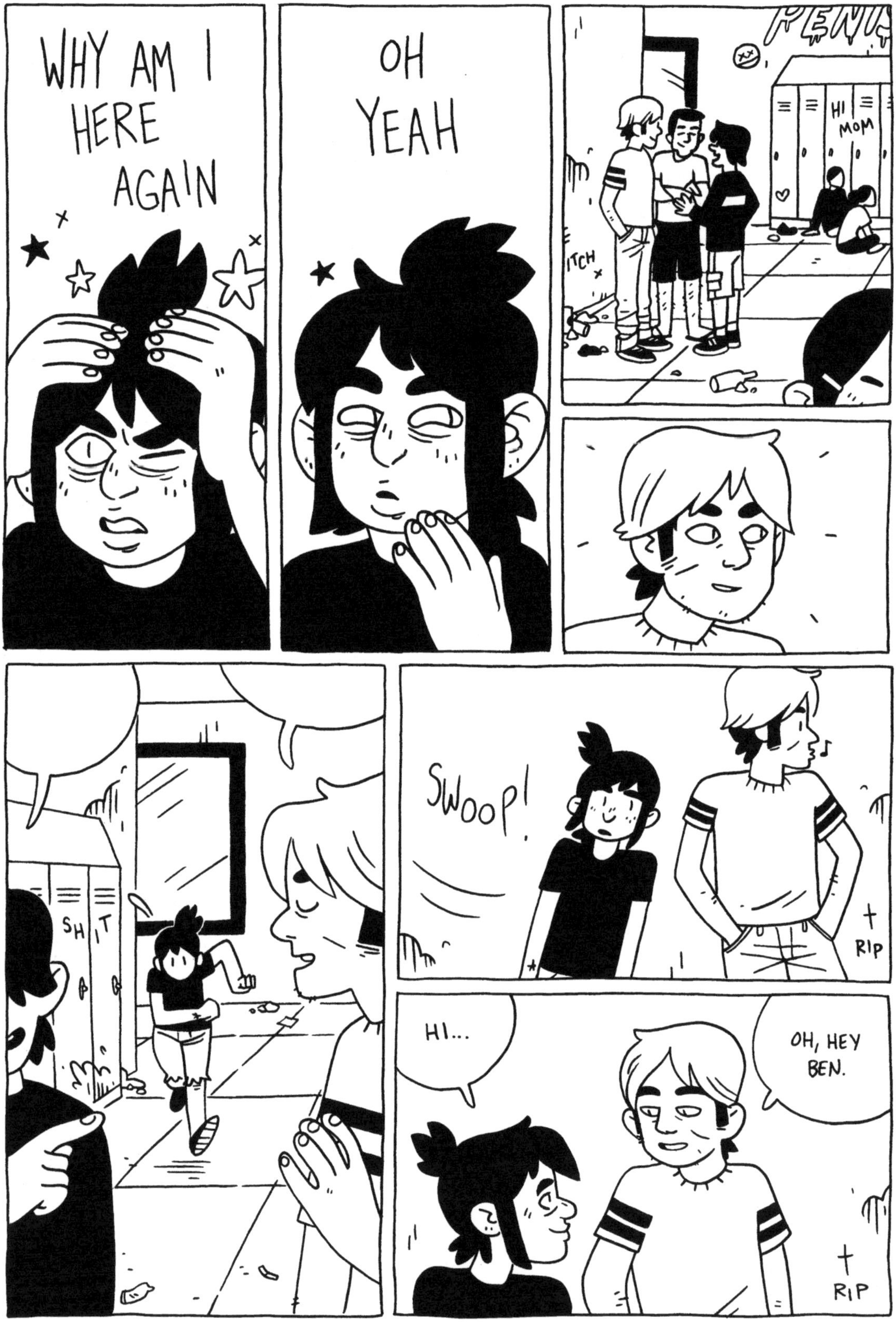
WHY AM I HERE AGAIN
OH YEAH
HI MOM
ITCH
SH IT
SWOOP!
RIP
HI...
OH, HEY BEN.
RIP

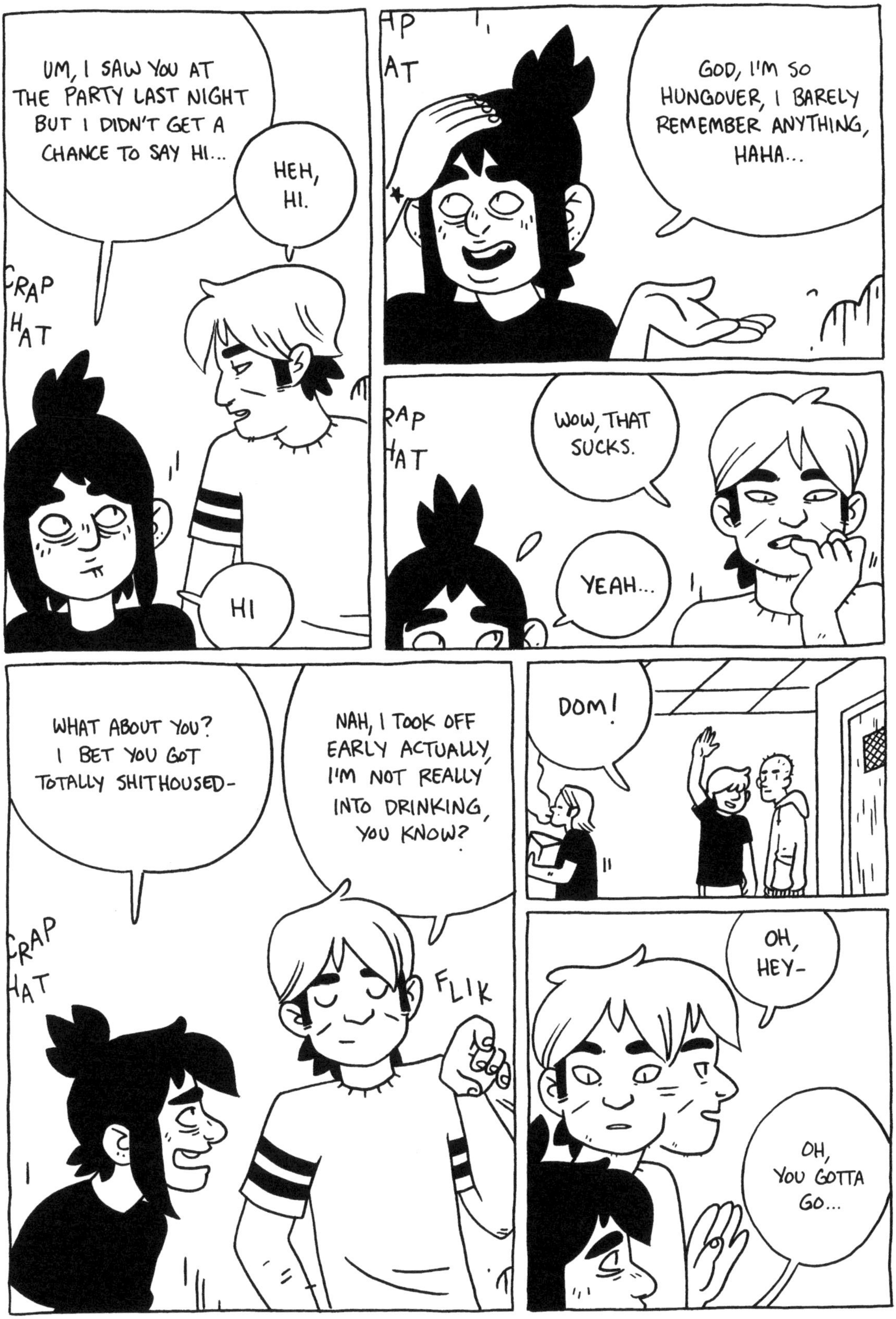
UM, I SAW YOU AT THE PARTY LAST NIGHT BUT I DIDN'T GET A CHANCE TO SAY HI...
HEH, HI.
CRAP
HAT
HI
GOD, I'M SO HUNGOVER, I BARELY REMEMBER ANYTHING, HAHA...
WOW, THAT SUCKS.
YEAH...
WHAT ABOUT YOU? I BET YOU GOT TOTALLY SHITHOUSED-
NAH, I TOOK OFF EARLY ACTUALLY, I'M NOT REALLY INTO DRINKING, YOU KNOW?
FLIK
DOM!
OH, HEY-
OH, YOU GOTTA GO...

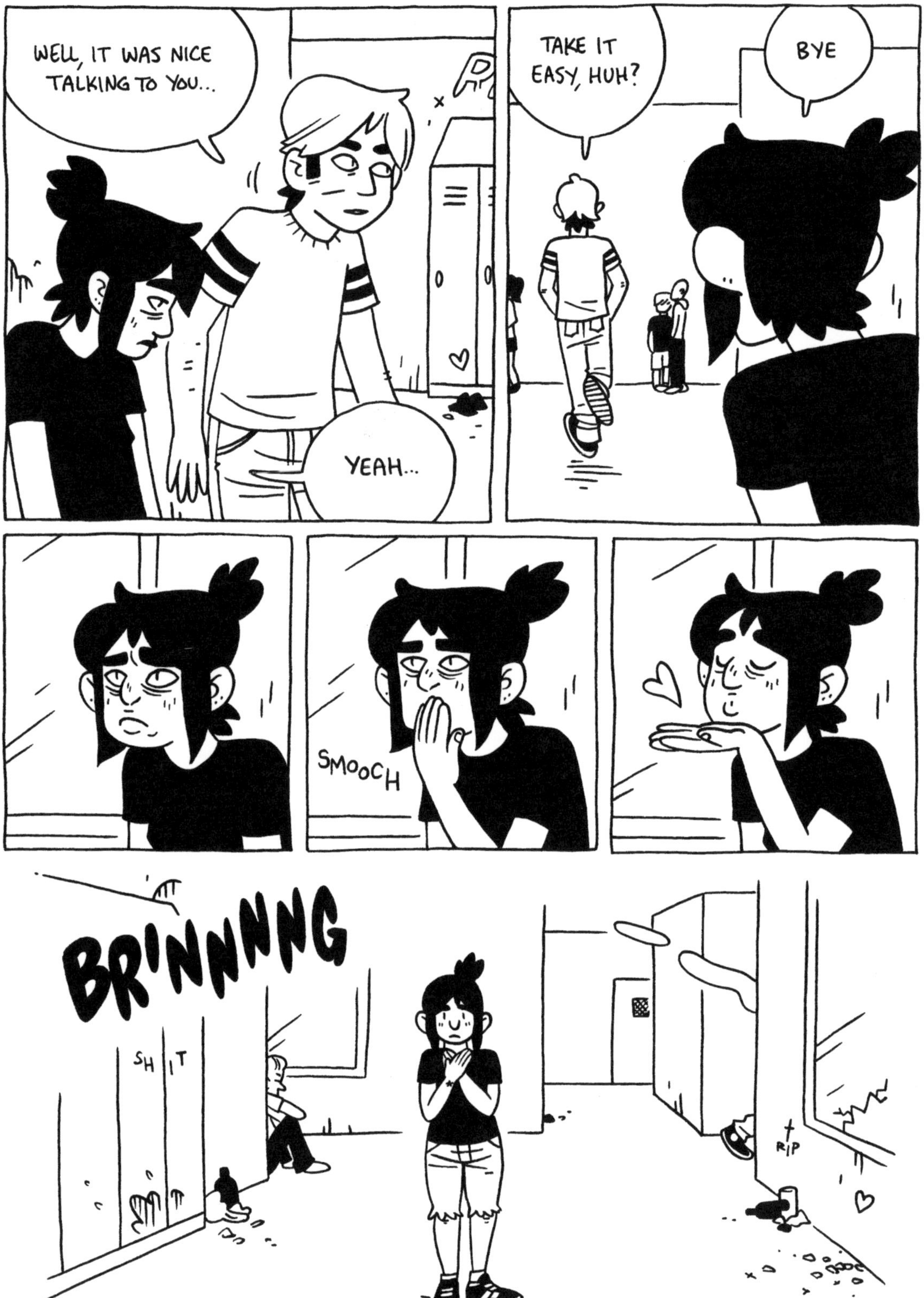
WELL, IT WAS NICE TALKING TO YOU...
YEAH...
TAKE IT EASY, HUH?
BYE
SMOOCH
BRINNNNG
SH IT
RIP

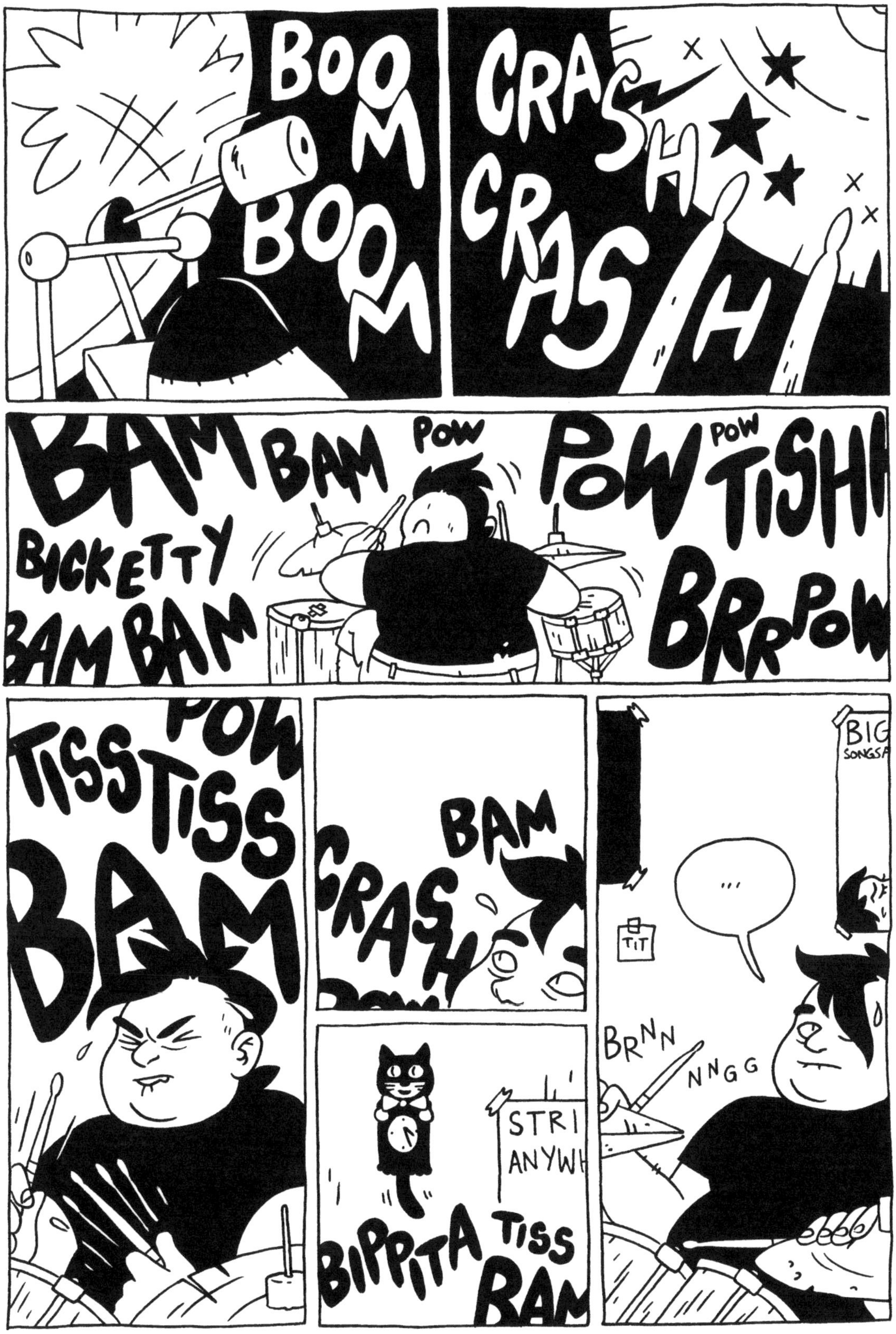
BOOM
BOOM
CRASH
CRASH
BAM BAM
POW
POW
POW
TISH
BICKETTY
BAM BAM
BRRPOW
TISS TISS
POW
BAM
BAM
CRASH
BIG
SONGS
TIT
...
BRNNNNGG
STRI
ANYWH
BIPPITA TISS
BAM

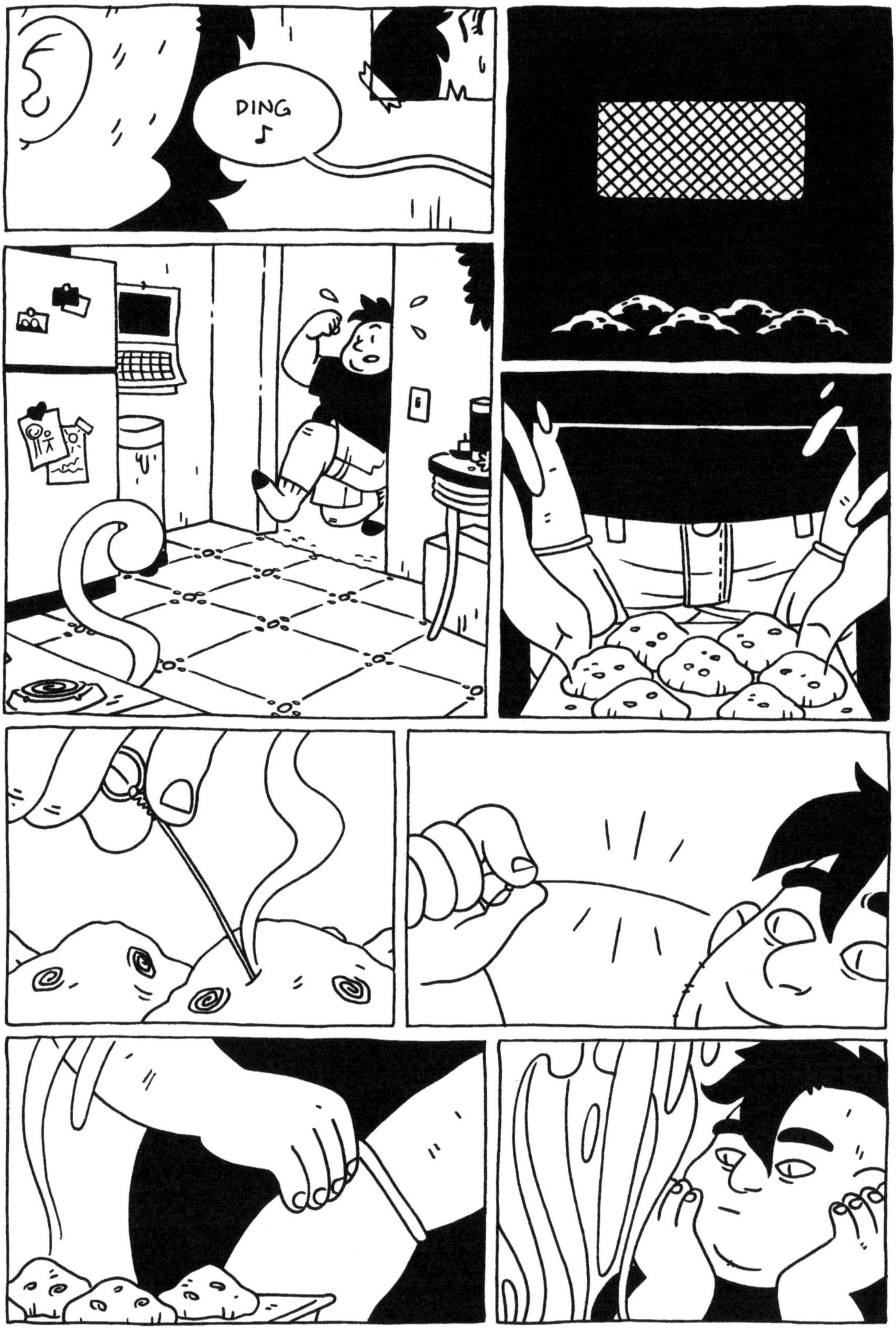
DING ♪

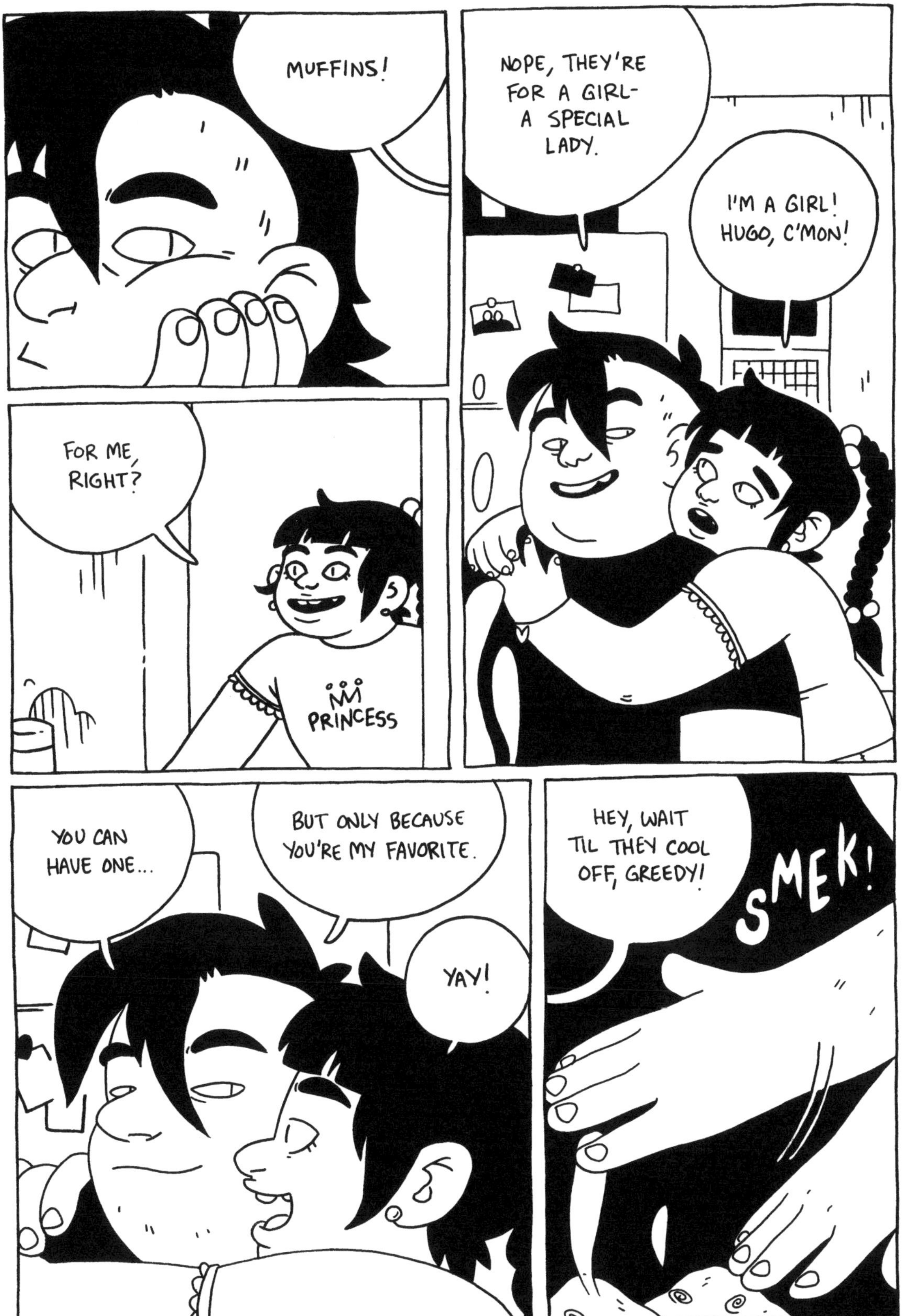
MUFFINS!
NOPE, THEY'RE FOR A GIRL- A SPECIAL LADY.
I'M A GIRL! HUGO, C'MON!
FOR ME, RIGHT?
YOU CAN HAVE ONE...
BUT ONLY BECAUSE YOU'RE MY FAVORITE.
YAY!
HEY, WAIT TIL THEY COOL OFF, GREEDY!
SMEK!
PRINCESS

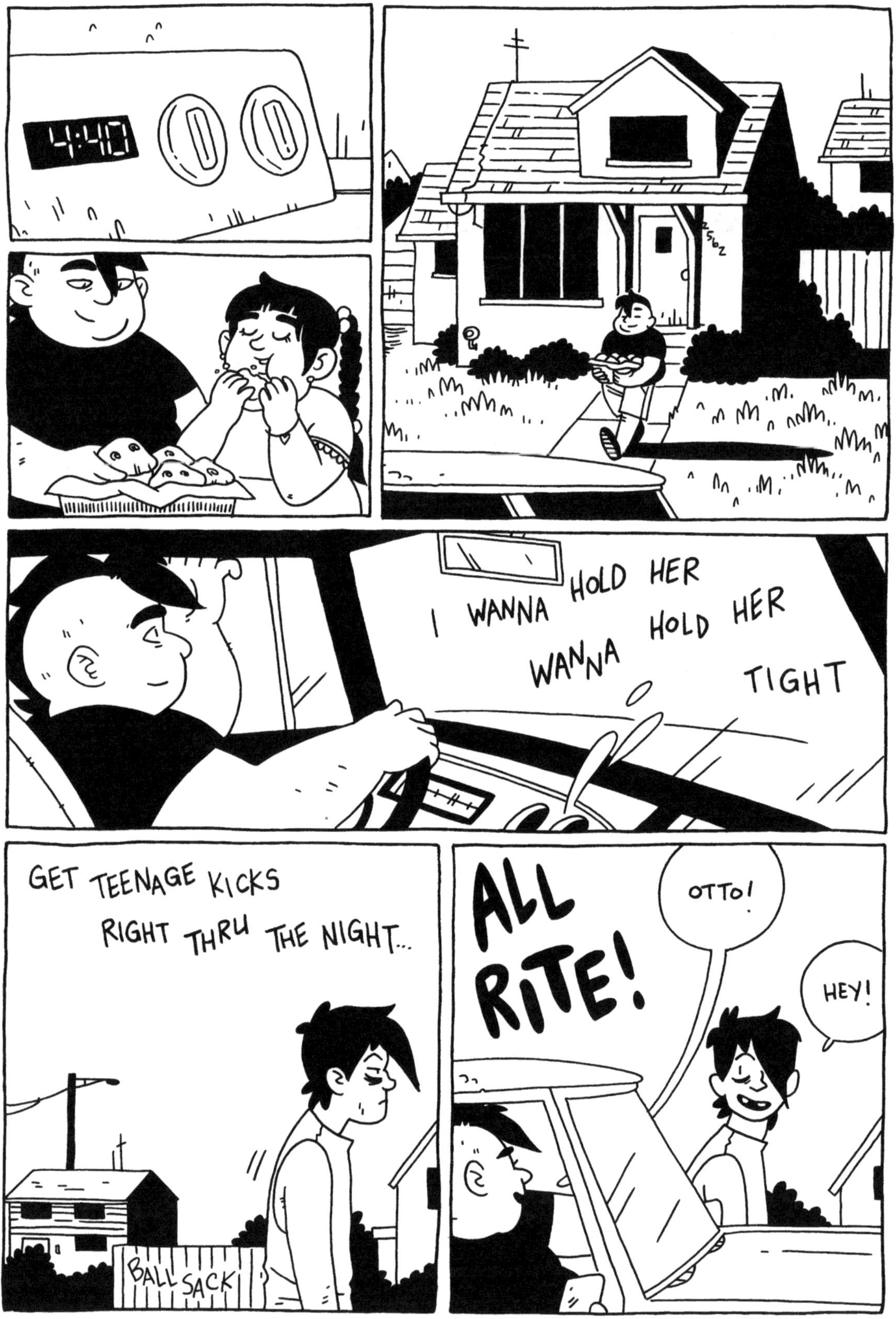
4:40
2562
I WANNA HOLD HER
WANNA HOLD HER
TIGHT
GET TEENAGE KICKS
RIGHT THRU THE NIGHT...
BALLSACK
ALL RITE!
OTTO!
HEY!

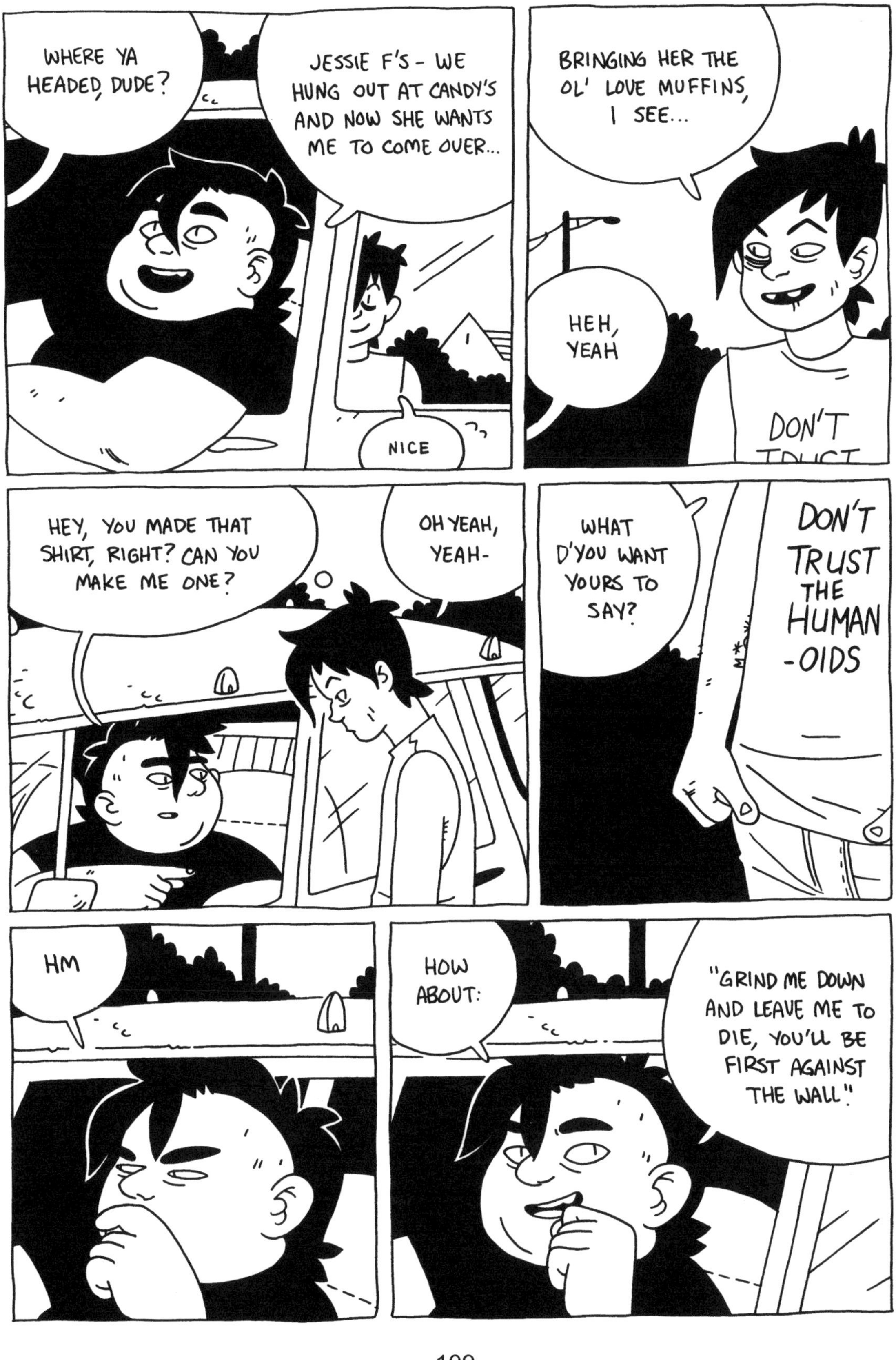
WHERE YA HEADED, DUDE?
JESSIE F'S - WE HUNG OUT AT CANDY'S AND NOW SHE WANTS ME TO COME OVER...
NICE
BRINGING HER THE OL' LOVE MUFFINS, I SEE...
HEH, YEAH
DON'T
HEY, YOU MADE THAT SHIRT, RIGHT? CAN YOU MAKE ME ONE?
OH YEAH, YEAH-
WHAT D'YOU WANT YOURS TO SAY?
DON'T TRUST THE HUMAN-OIDS
HM
HOW ABOUT:
"GRIND ME DOWN AND LEAVE ME TO DIE, YOU'LL BE FIRST AGAINST THE WALL"

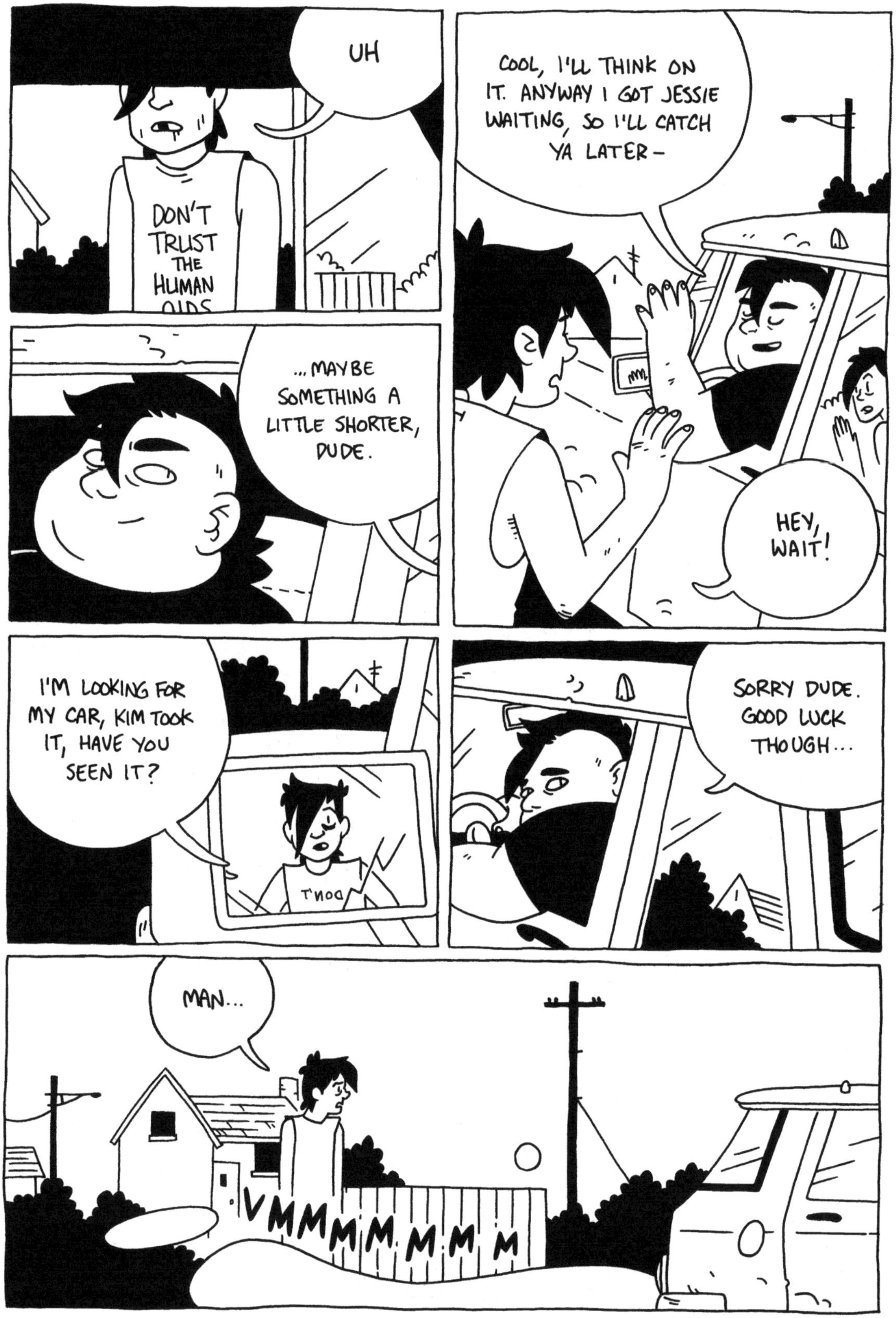
UH
DON'T TRUST THE HUMAN
COOL, I'LL THINK ON IT. ANYWAY I GOT JESSIE WAITING, SO I'LL CATCH YA LATER-
...MAYBE SOMETHING A LITTLE SHORTER, DUDE.
HEY, WAIT!
I'M LOOKING FOR MY CAR, KIM TOOK IT, HAVE YOU SEEN IT?
SORRY DUDE. GOOD LUCK THOUGH...
MAN...
VMMMMMMMM

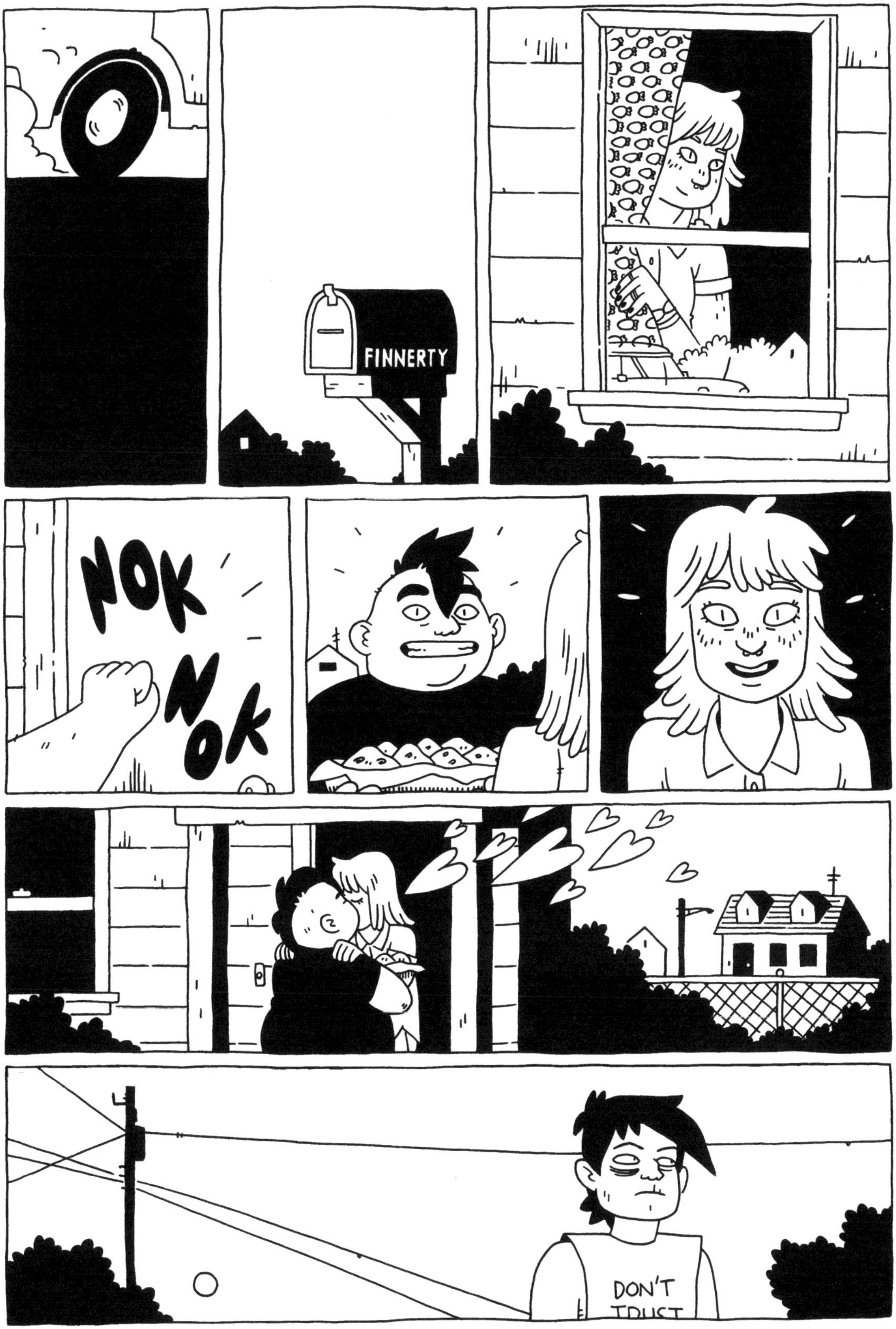
FINNERTY
NOK
NOK
NOK
DON'T

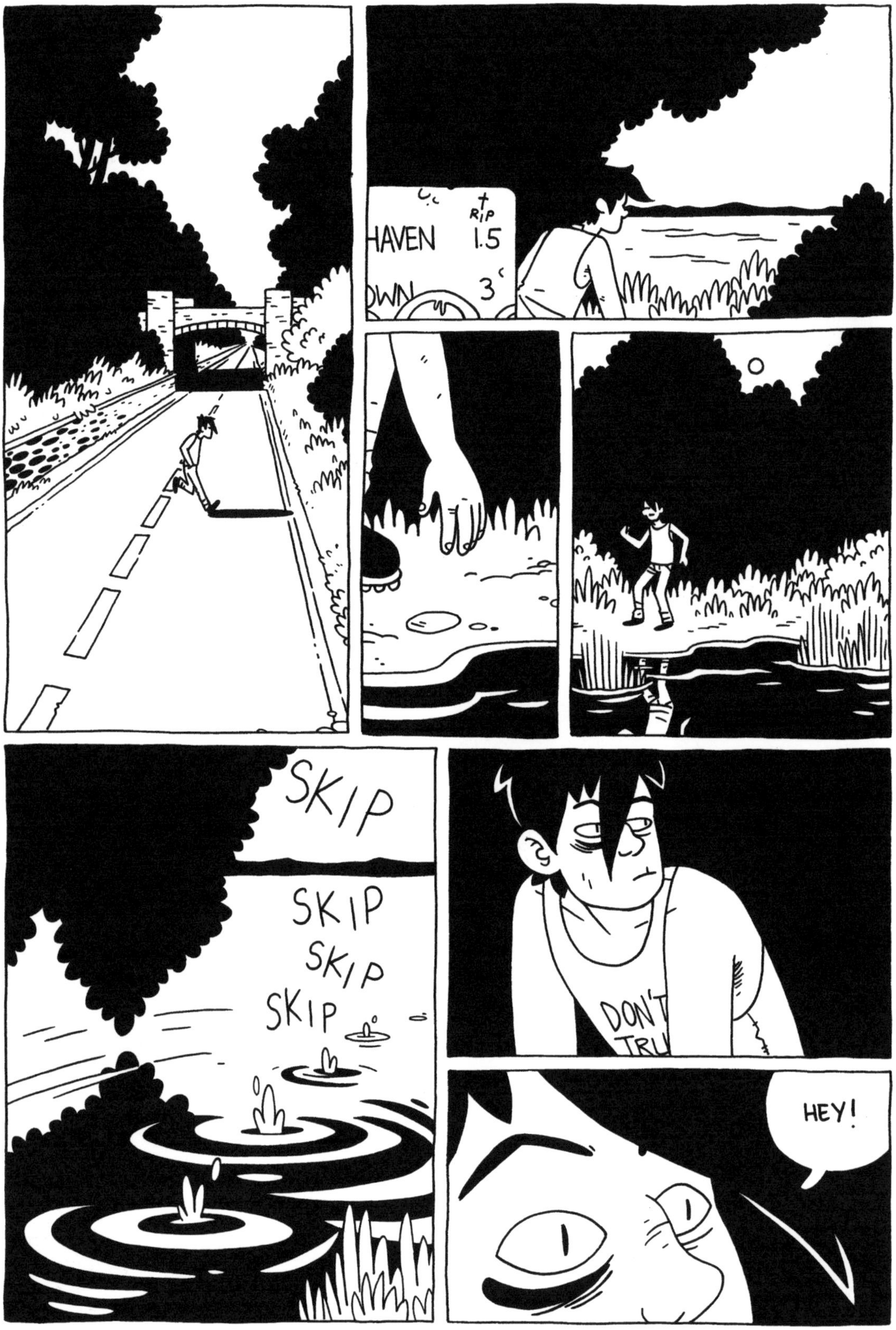
HAVEN 1.5
RIP
3
SKIP
SKIP
SKIP
SKIP
DON'T
HEY!

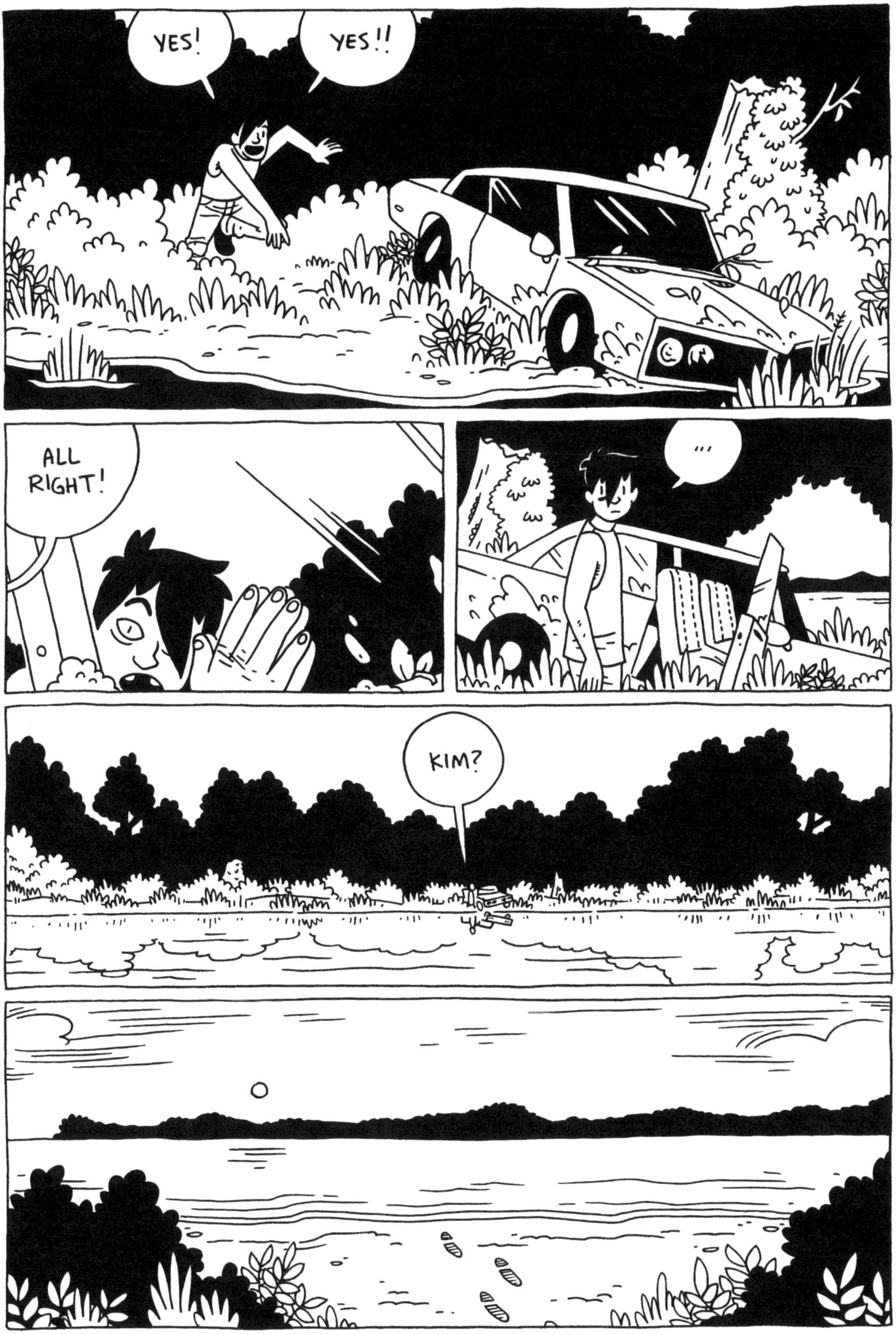
YES!
YES!!
ALL RIGHT!
...
KIM?

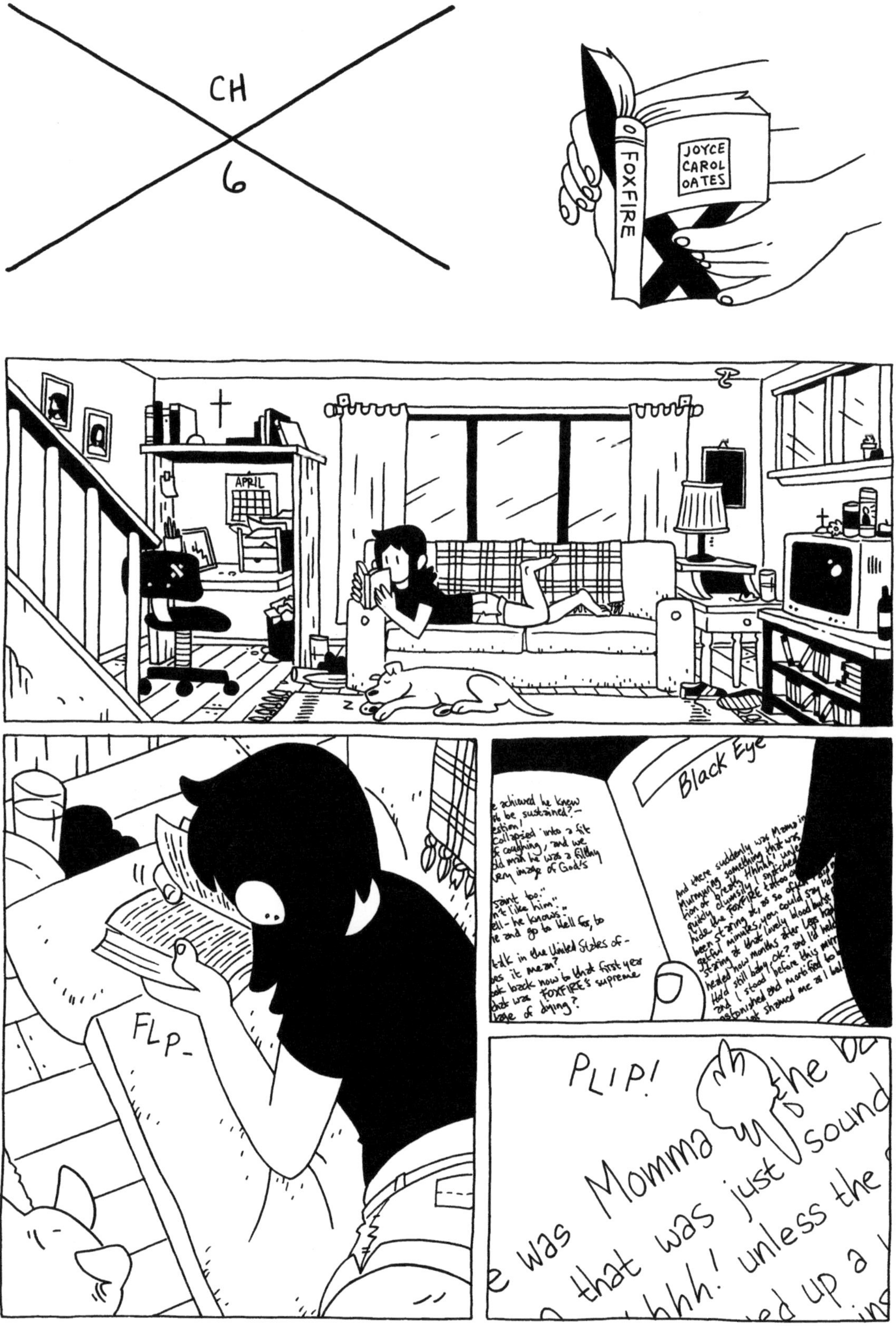
CH
6
FOXFIRE
JOYCE
CAROL
OATES
APRIL
Black Eye
FLP-
PLIP!
was Momma the
that was just sound
hhh! unless the
ed up a

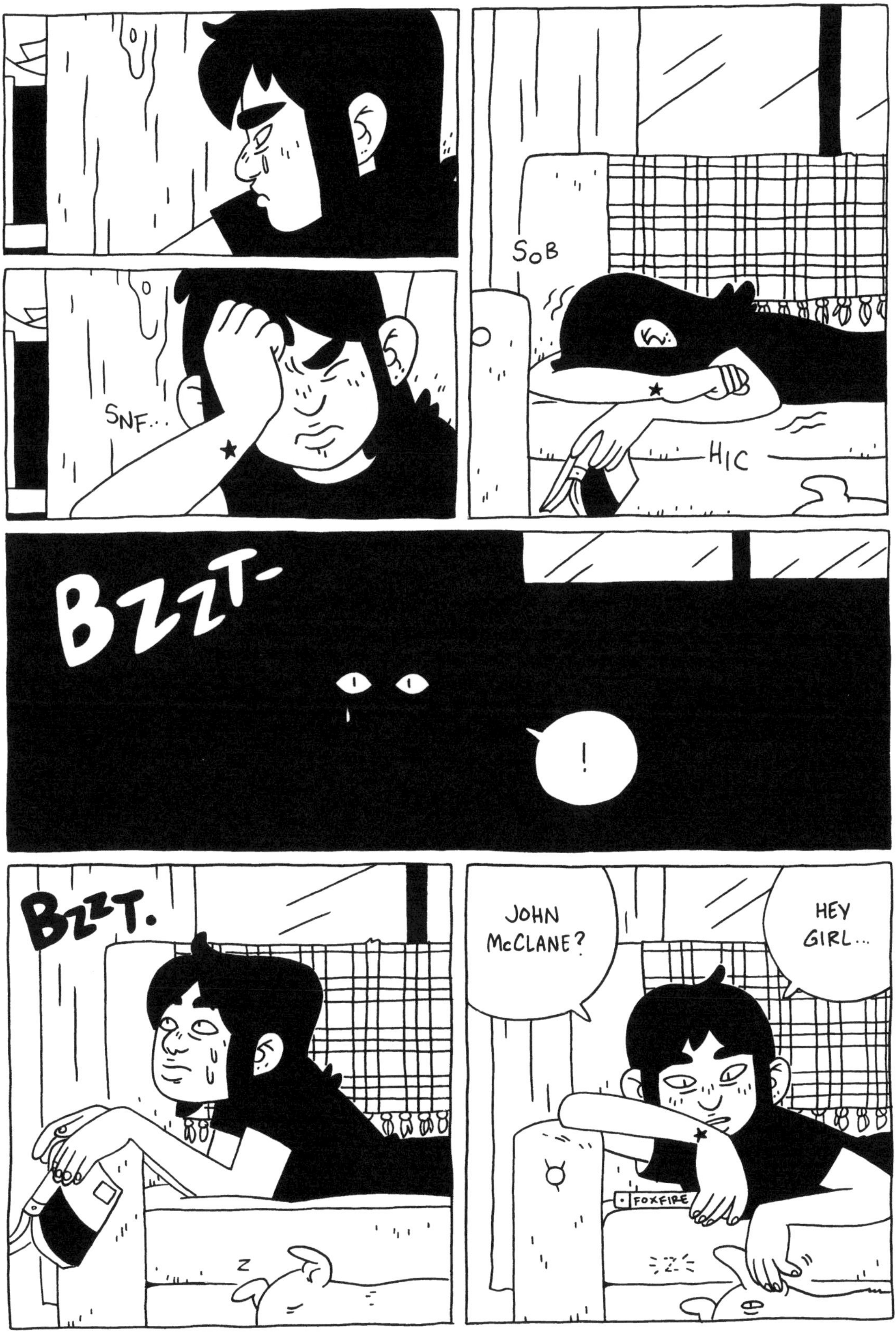
SOB
SNF...
HIC
BZZT-
!
BZZT.
JOHN McCLANE?
HEY GIRL...
Z
FOXFIRE

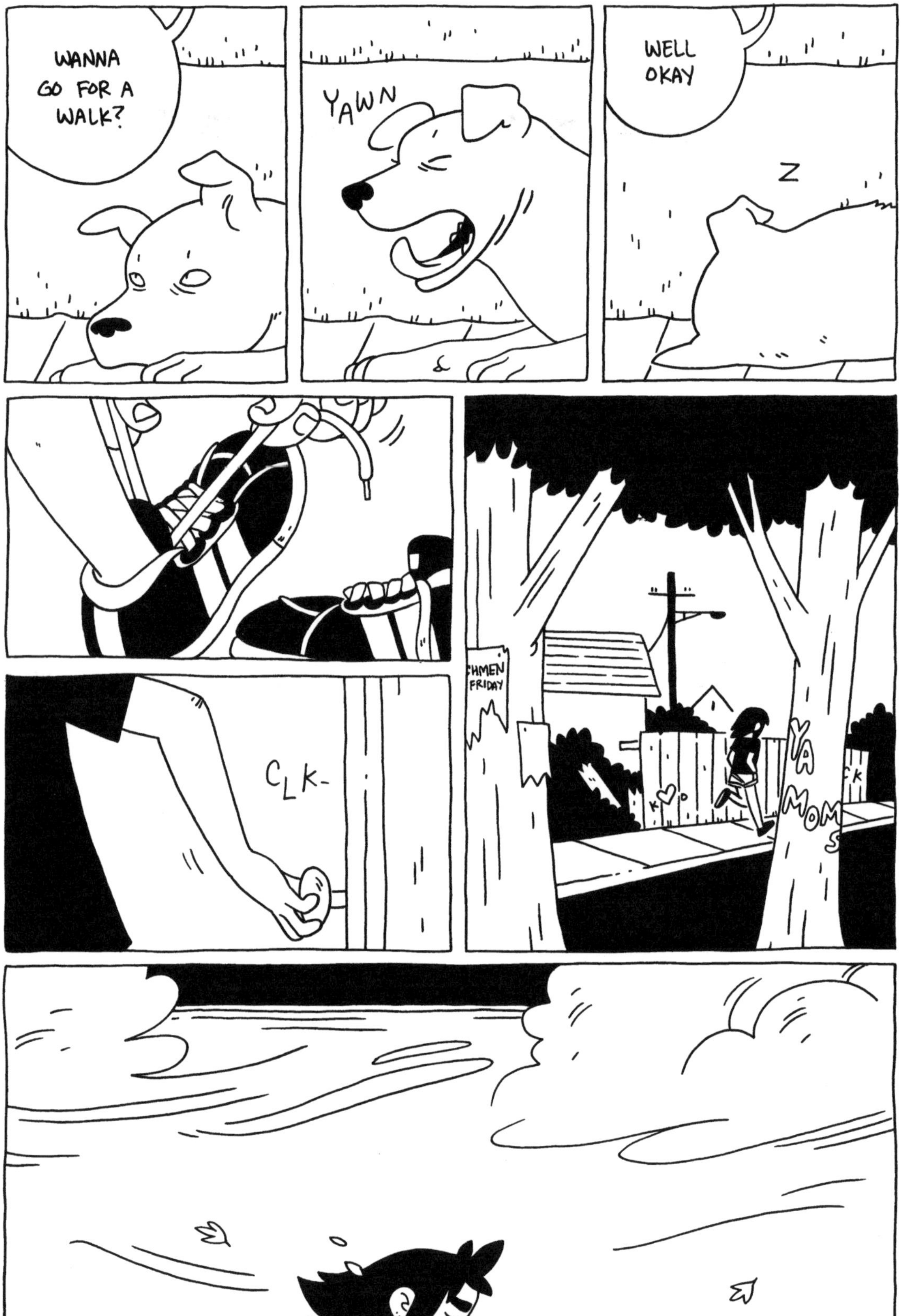
WANNA GO FOR A WALK?
YAWN
WELL OKAY
Z
CLK-
CHMEN
FRIDAY
YA MOMS

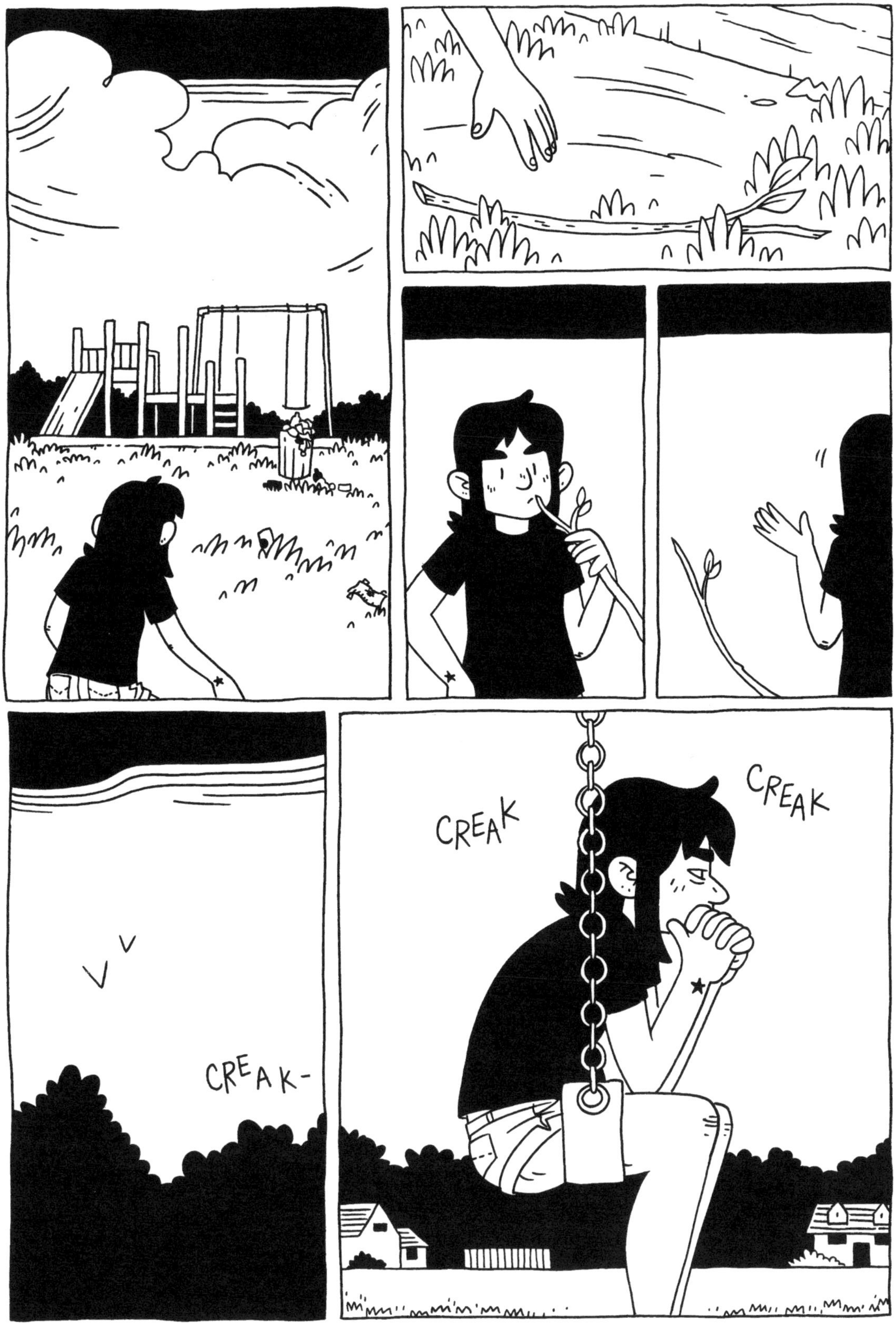
CREAK-
CREAK
CREAK

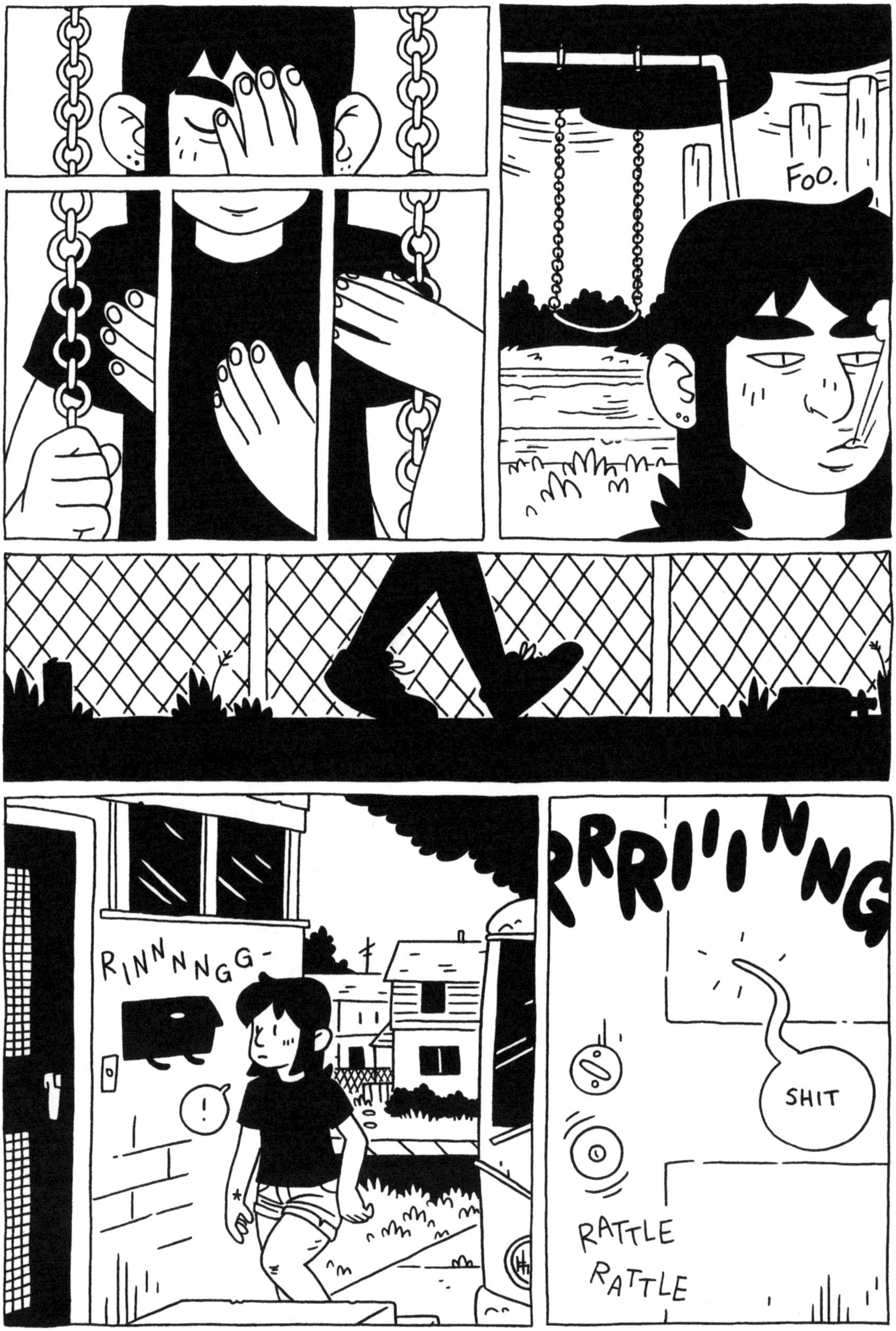
FOO.
RINNNNGG-
!
RRRI'I NNG
SHIT
RATTLE
RATTLE

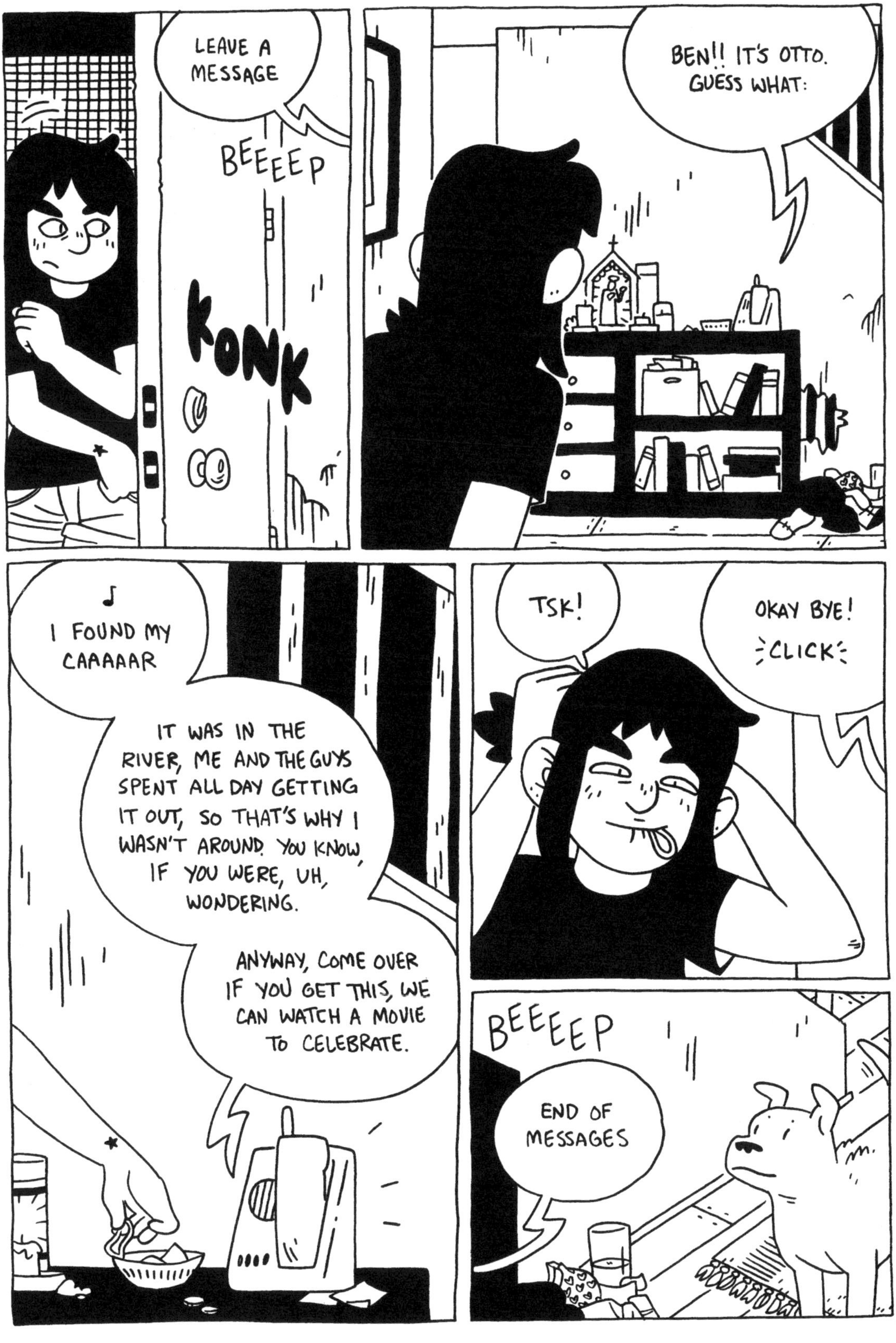
LEAVE A MESSAGE
BEEEEP
KONK
BEN!! IT'S OTTO. GUESS WHAT:
♩ I FOUND MY CAAAAAR
IT WAS IN THE RIVER, ME AND THE GUYS SPENT ALL DAY GETTING IT OUT, SO THAT'S WHY I WASN'T AROUND. YOU KNOW, IF YOU WERE, UH, WONDERING.
ANYWAY, COME OVER IF YOU GET THIS, WE CAN WATCH A MOVIE TO CELEBRATE.
TSK!
OKAY BYE!
CLICK
BEEEEP
END OF MESSAGES

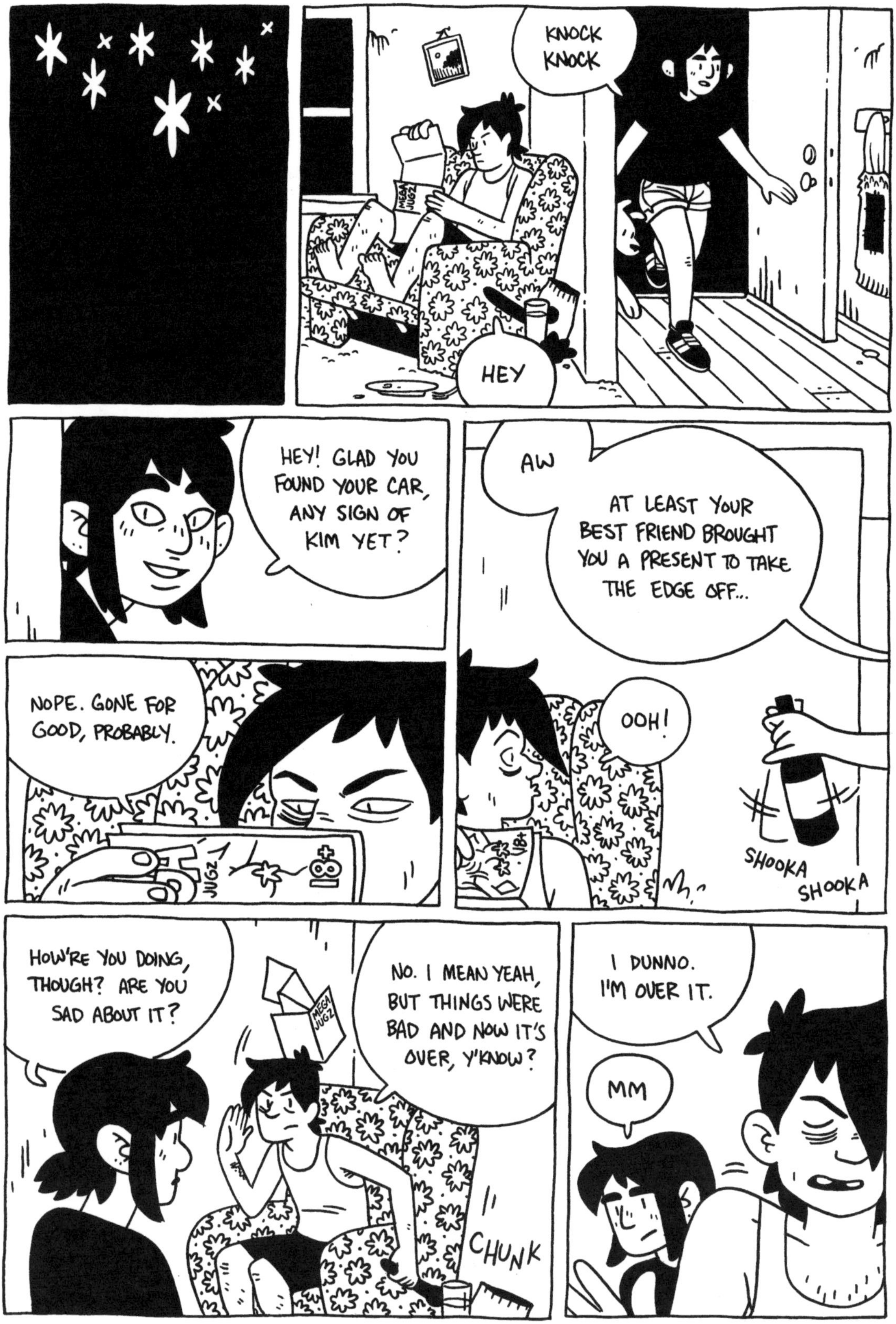
KNOCK KNOCK
MEGA JUGZ
HEY
HEY! GLAD YOU FOUND YOUR CAR, ANY SIGN OF KIM YET?
AW
AT LEAST YOUR BEST FRIEND BROUGHT YOU A PRESENT TO TAKE THE EDGE OFF...
NOPE. GONE FOR GOOD, PROBABLY.
JUGZ
OOH!
SHOOKA SHOOKA
HOW'RE YOU DOING, THOUGH? ARE YOU SAD ABOUT IT?
MEGA JUGZ
NO. I MEAN YEAH, BUT THINGS WERE BAD AND NOW IT'S OVER, Y'KNOW?
CHUNK
I DUNNO. I'M OVER IT.
MM

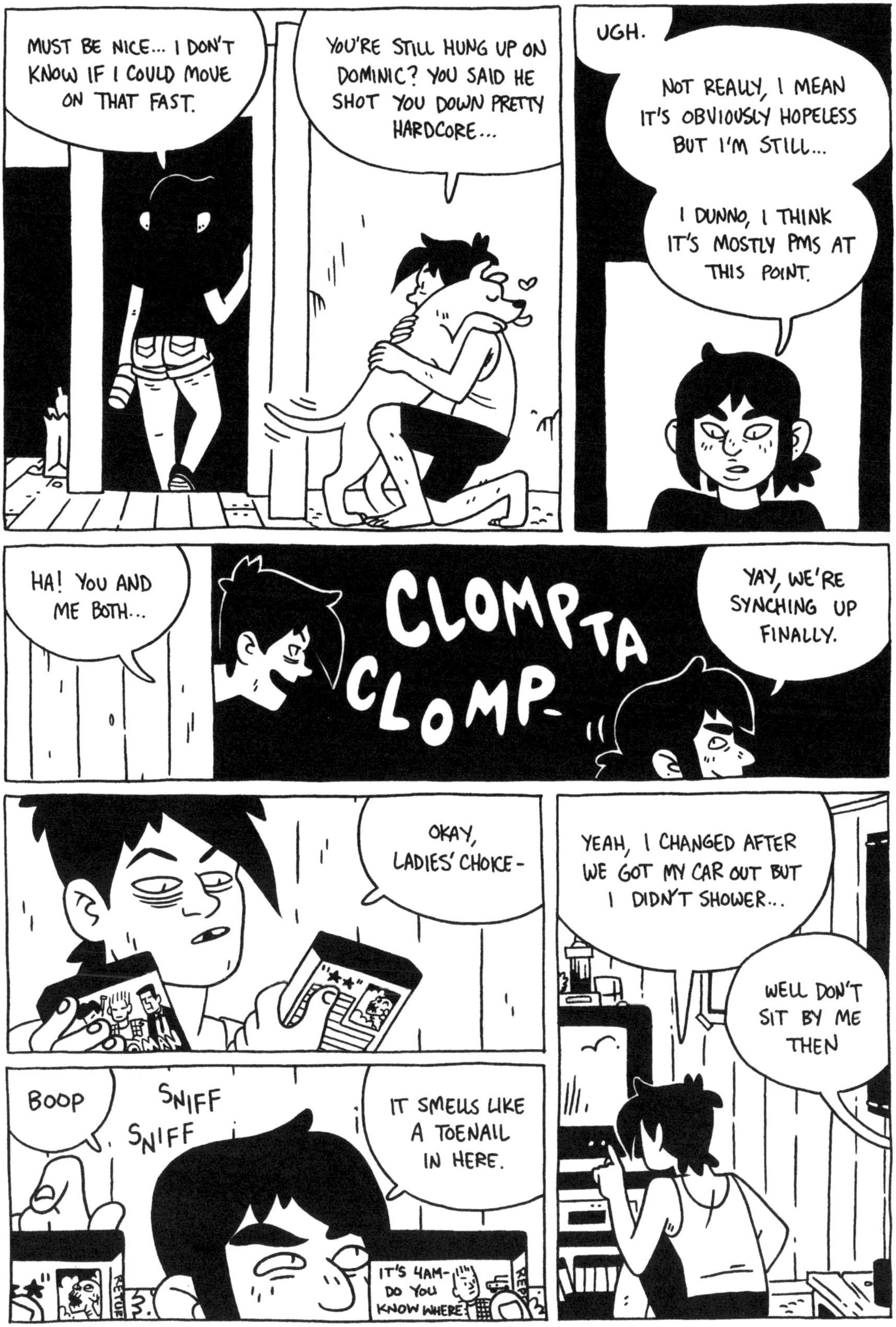
MUST BE NICE... I DON'T KNOW IF I COULD MOVE ON THAT FAST.
YOU'RE STILL HUNG UP ON DOMINIC? YOU SAID HE SHOT YOU DOWN PRETTY HARDCORE...
UGH.
NOT REALLY, I MEAN IT'S OBVIOUSLY HOPELESS BUT I'M STILL...
I DUNNO, I THINK IT'S MOSTLY PMS AT THIS POINT.
HA! YOU AND ME BOTH...
CLOMP TA CLOMP-
YAY, WE'RE SYNCHING UP FINALLY.
OKAY, LADIES' CHOICE-
BOOP
SNIFF SNIFF
IT SMELLS LIKE A TOENAIL IN HERE.
IT'S 4AM- DO YOU KNOW WHERE
YEAH, I CHANGED AFTER WE GOT MY CAR OUT BUT I DIDN'T SHOWER...
WELL DON'T SIT BY ME THEN

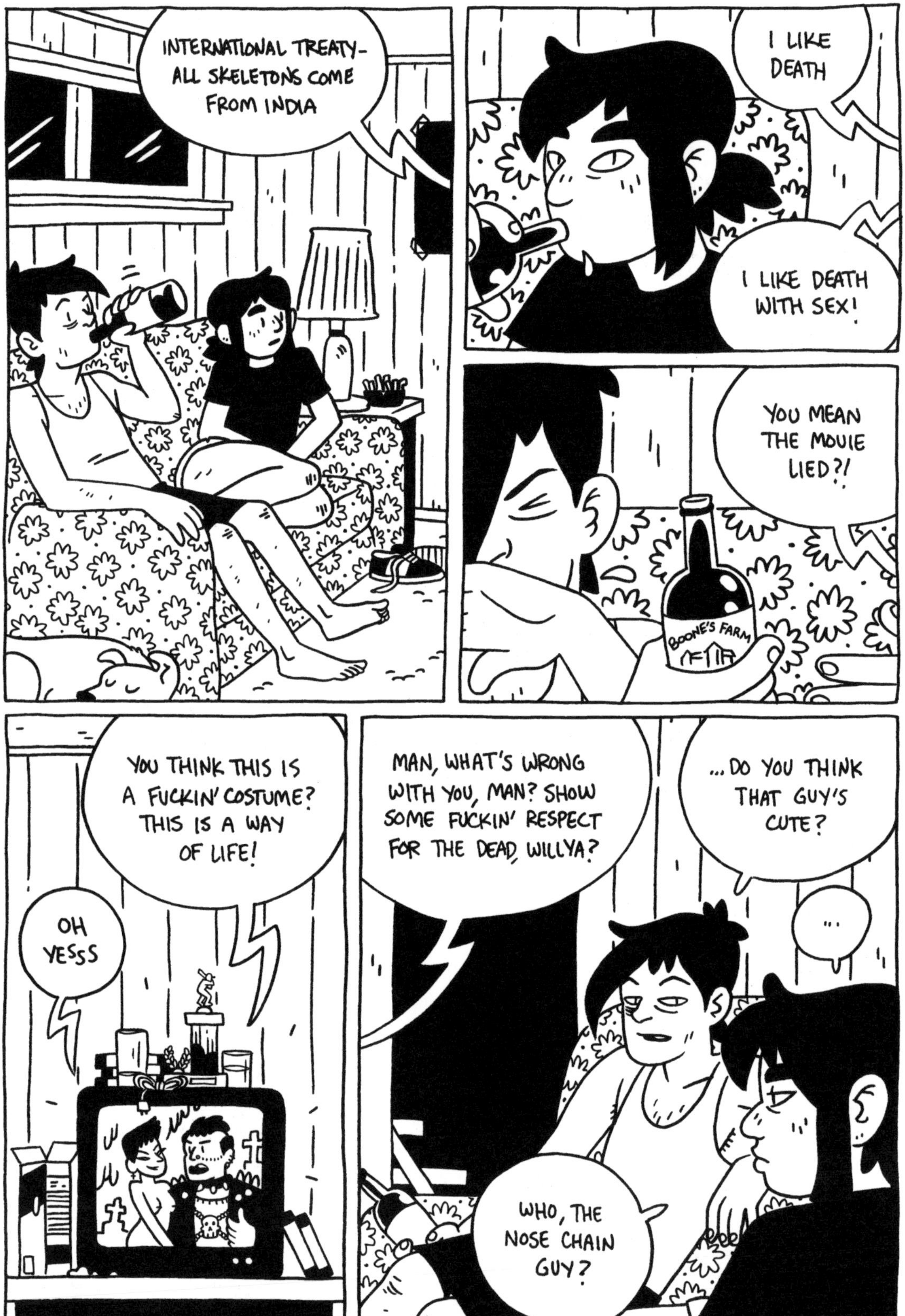
INTERNATIONAL TREATY- ALL SKELETONS COME FROM INDIA
I LIKE DEATH
I LIKE DEATH WITH SEX!
YOU MEAN THE MOVIE LIED?!
BOONE'S FARM
YOU THINK THIS IS A FUCKIN' COSTUME? THIS IS A WAY OF LIFE!
OH YESSS
MAN, WHAT'S WRONG WITH YOU, MAN? SHOW SOME FUCKIN' RESPECT FOR THE DEAD, WILLYA?
...DO YOU THINK THAT GUY'S CUTE?
...
WHO, THE NOSE CHAIN GUY?

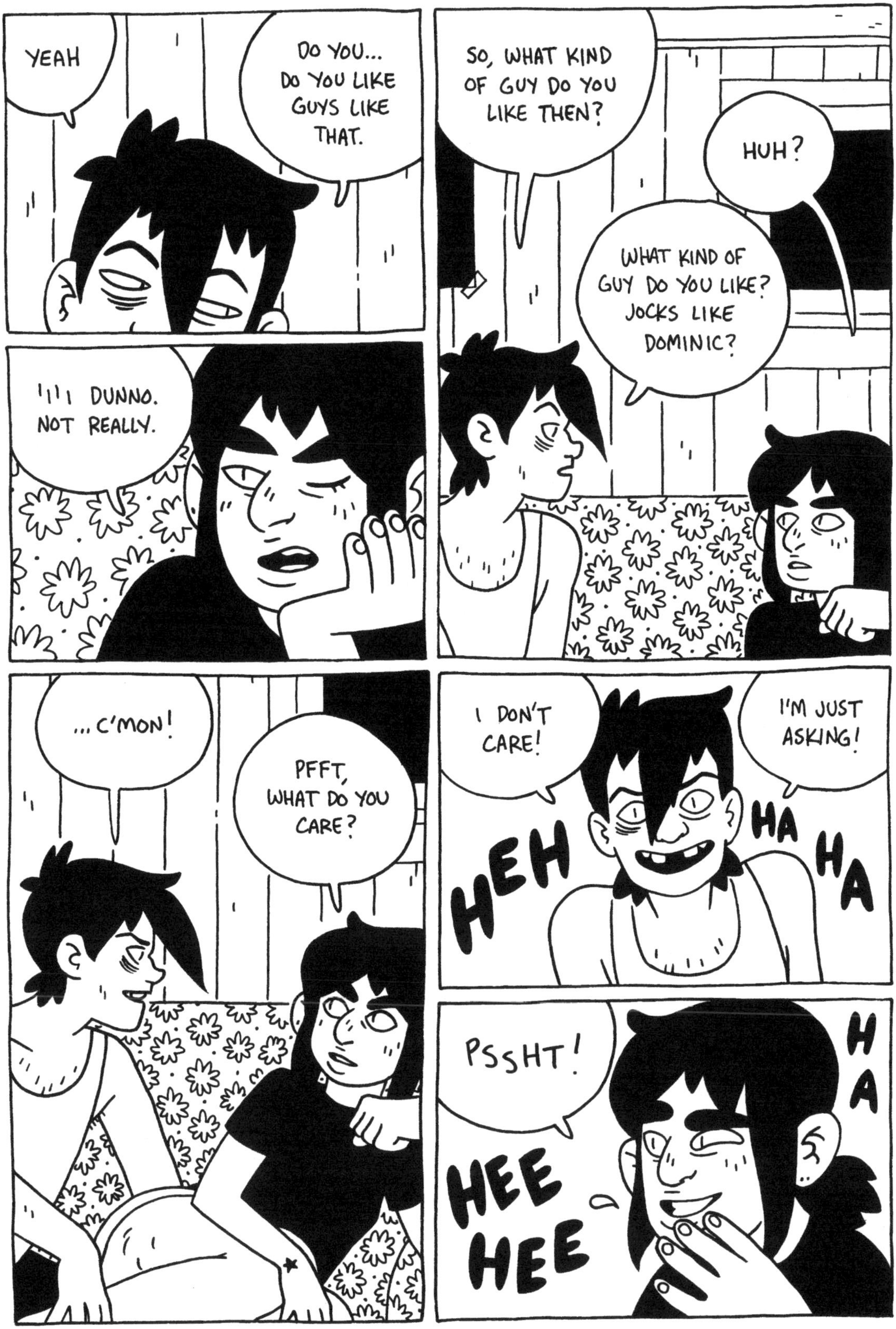
YEAH
DO YOU... DO YOU LIKE GUYS LIKE THAT.
SO, WHAT KIND OF GUY DO YOU LIKE THEN?
HUH?
WHAT KIND OF GUY DO YOU LIKE? JOCKS LIKE DOMINIC?
I DUNNO. NOT REALLY.
...C'MON!
PFFT, WHAT DO YOU CARE?
I DON'T CARE!
I'M JUST ASKING!
HEH
HA HA HA
PSSHT!
HA HA
HEE HEE

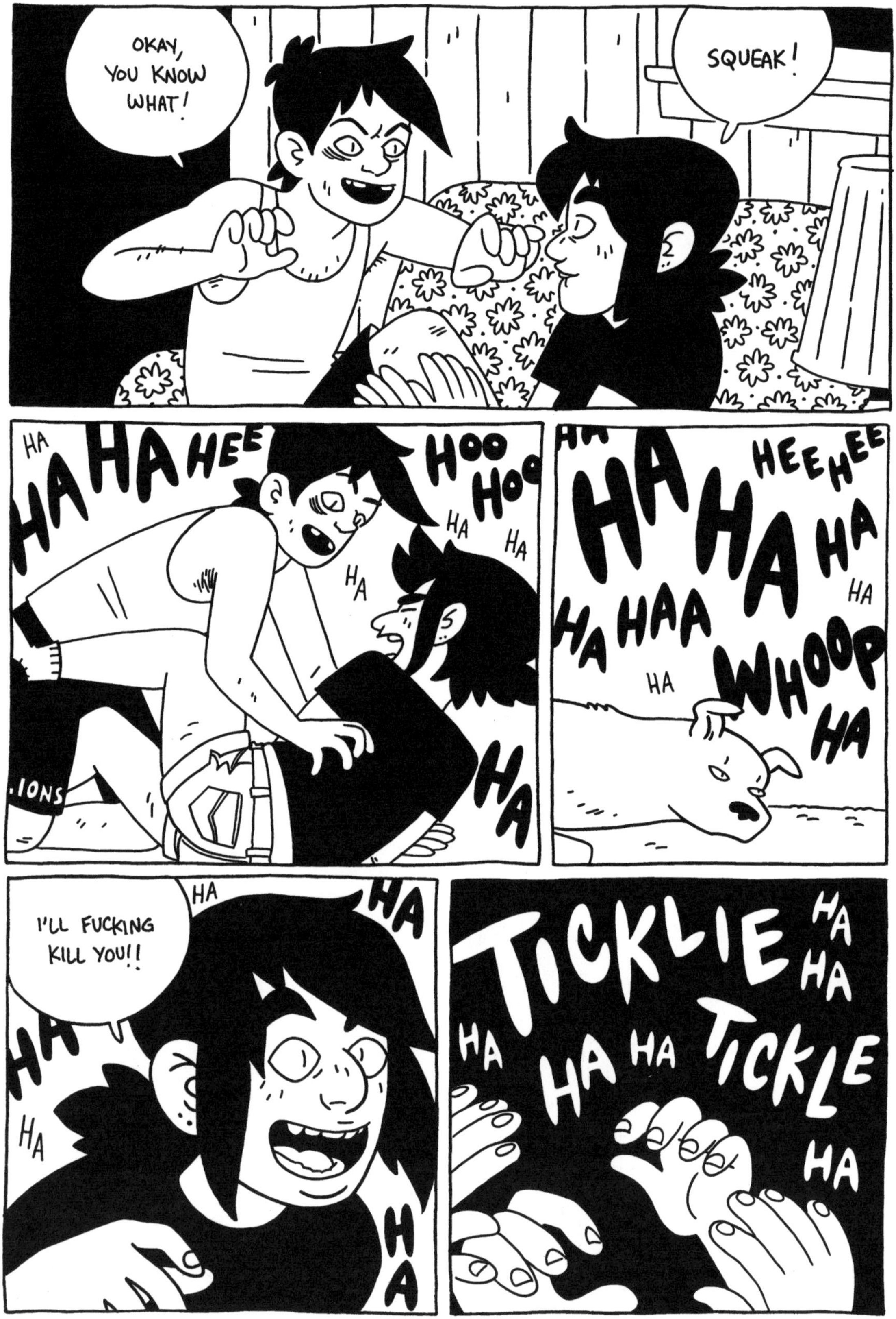

OKAY, YOU KNOW WHAT!
SQUEAK!
HA HA HA HEE
HOO HOO
HA HA
HA
HA
.IONS
HA HA HEE HEE HEE
HA HA HA
HA HA HAA
HA
WHOOP
HA
HA
I'LL FUCKING KILL YOU!!
HA
HA
HA
HA
HA
TICKLIE HA HA
HA HA HA TICKLE
HA

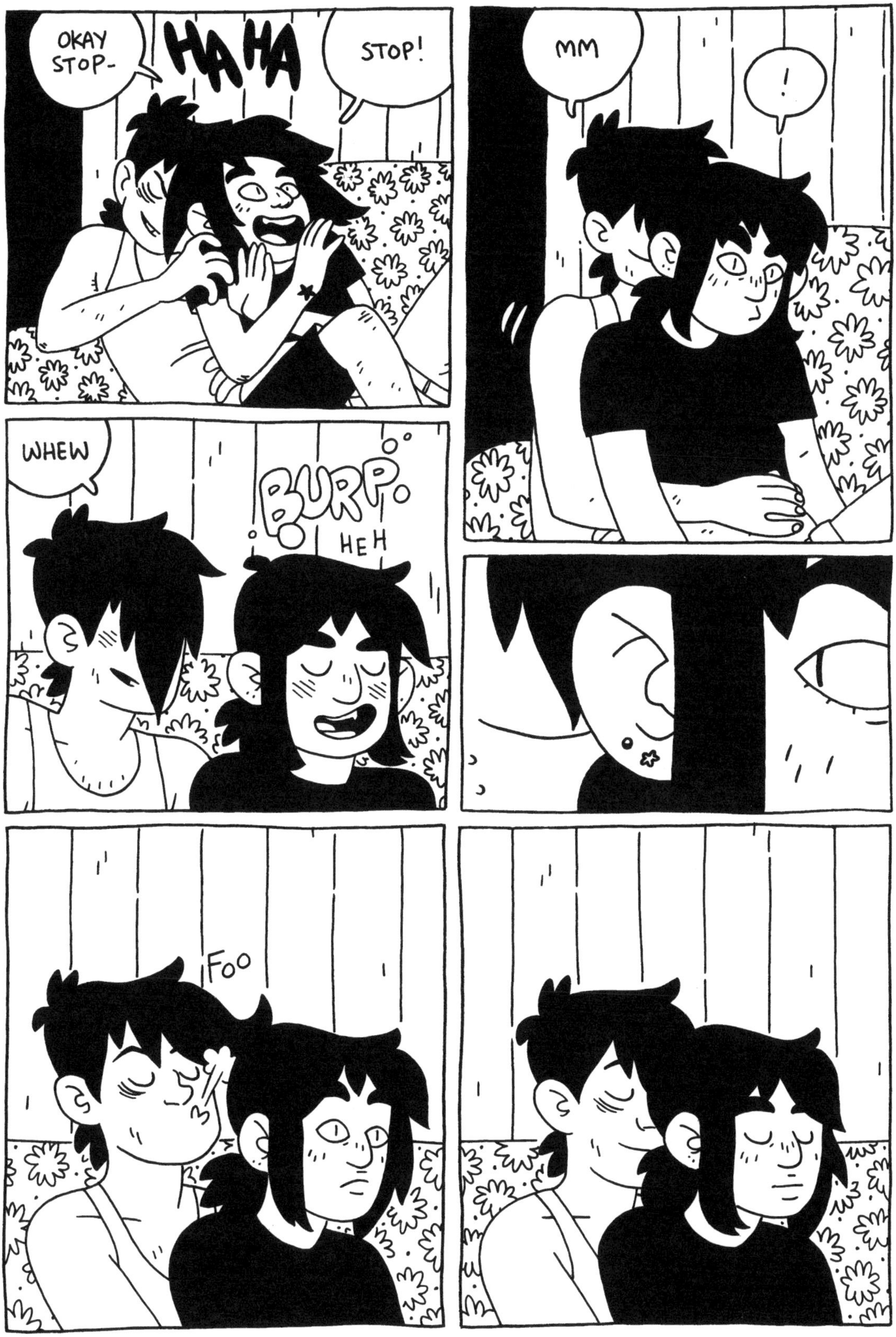
OKAY STOP-
HAHA
STOP!
MM
!
WHEW
BURP
HEH
FOO

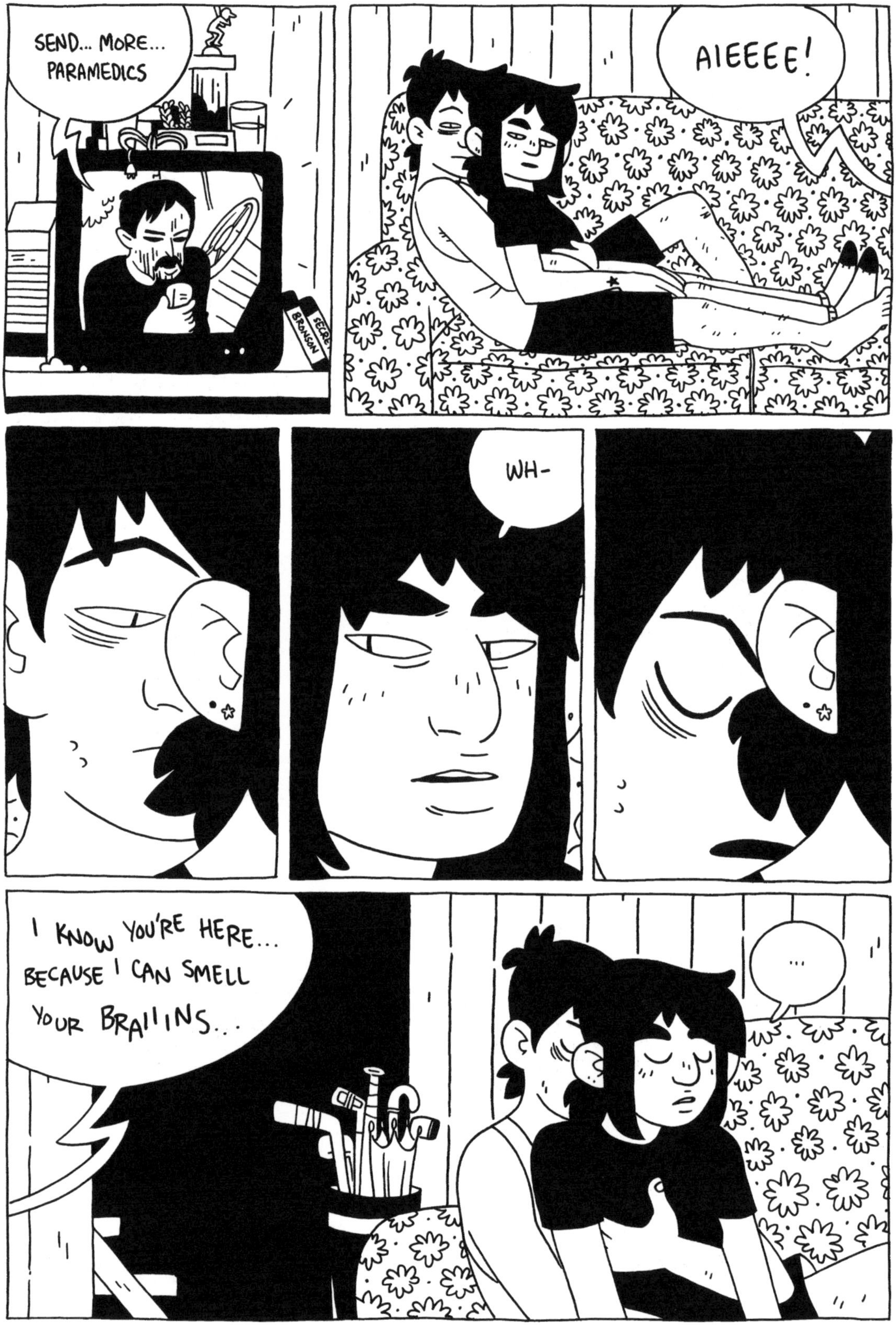
SEND... MORE... PARAMEDICS
AIEEEE!
WH-
I KNOW YOU'RE HERE... BECAUSE I CAN SMELL YOUR BRAIIINS...
...

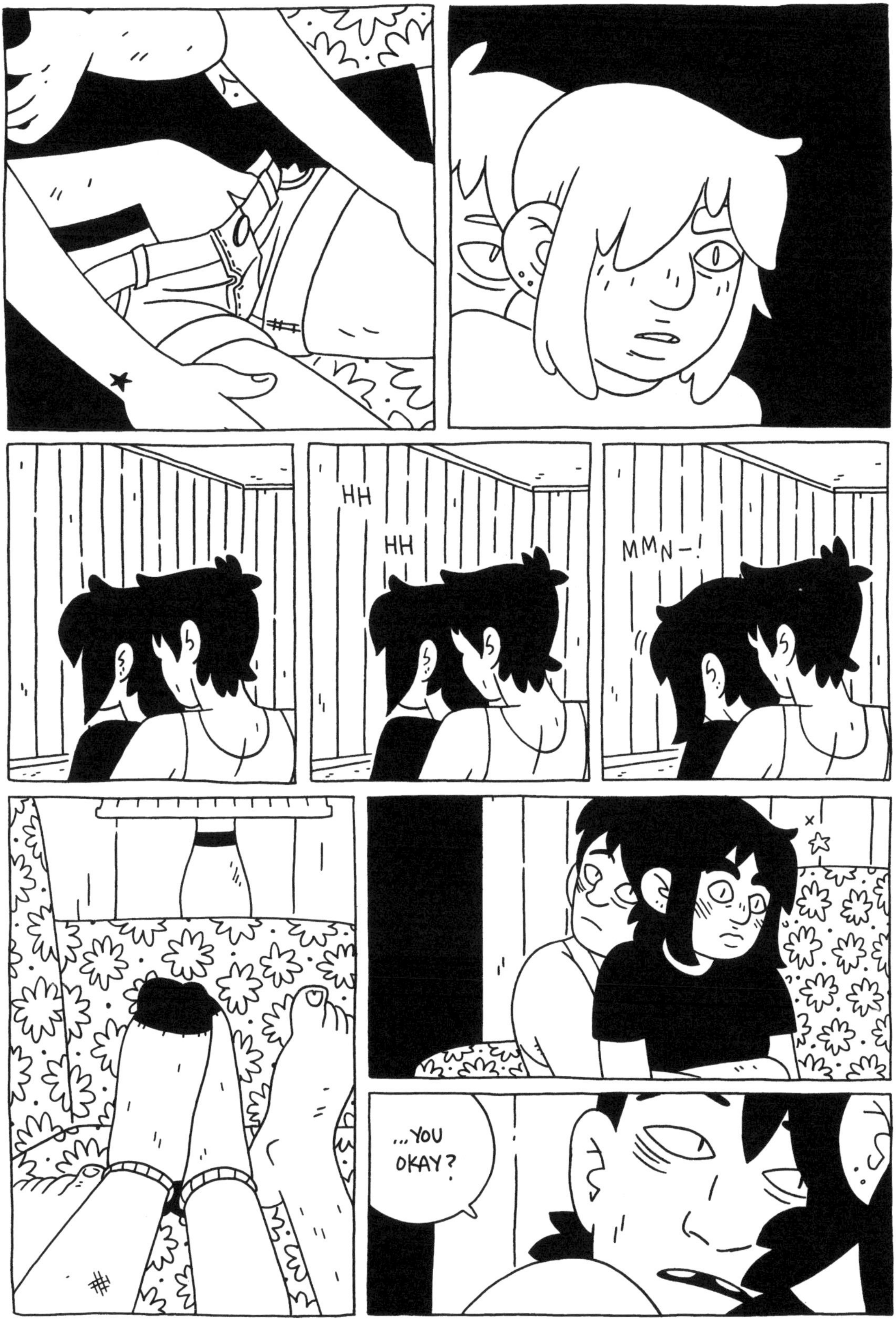
HH
HH
MMN—!
...YOU
OKAY?

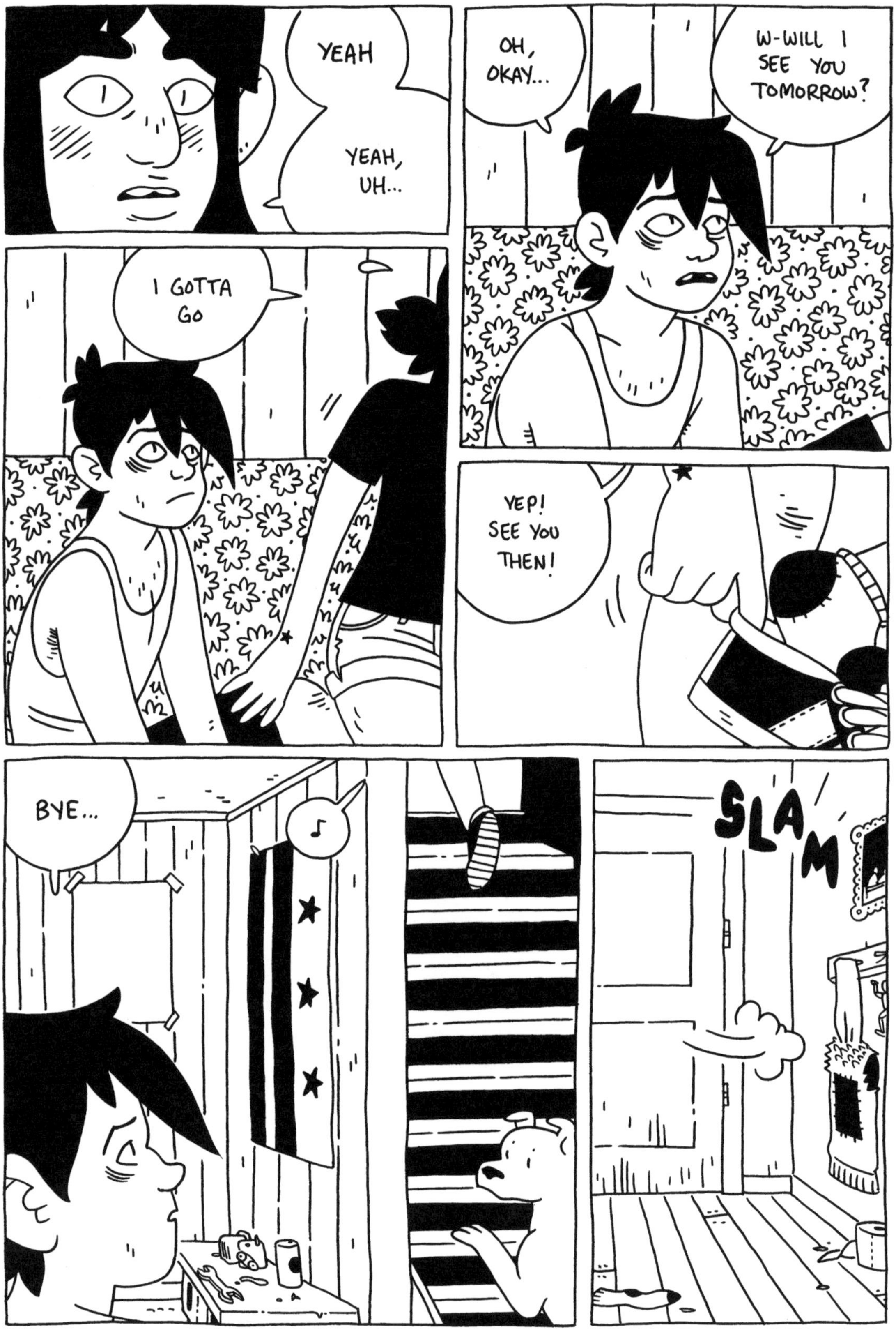
YEAH
YEAH, UH...
OH, OKAY...
W-WILL I SEE YOU TOMORROW?
I GOTTA GO
YEP! SEE YOU THEN!
BYE...
SLAM

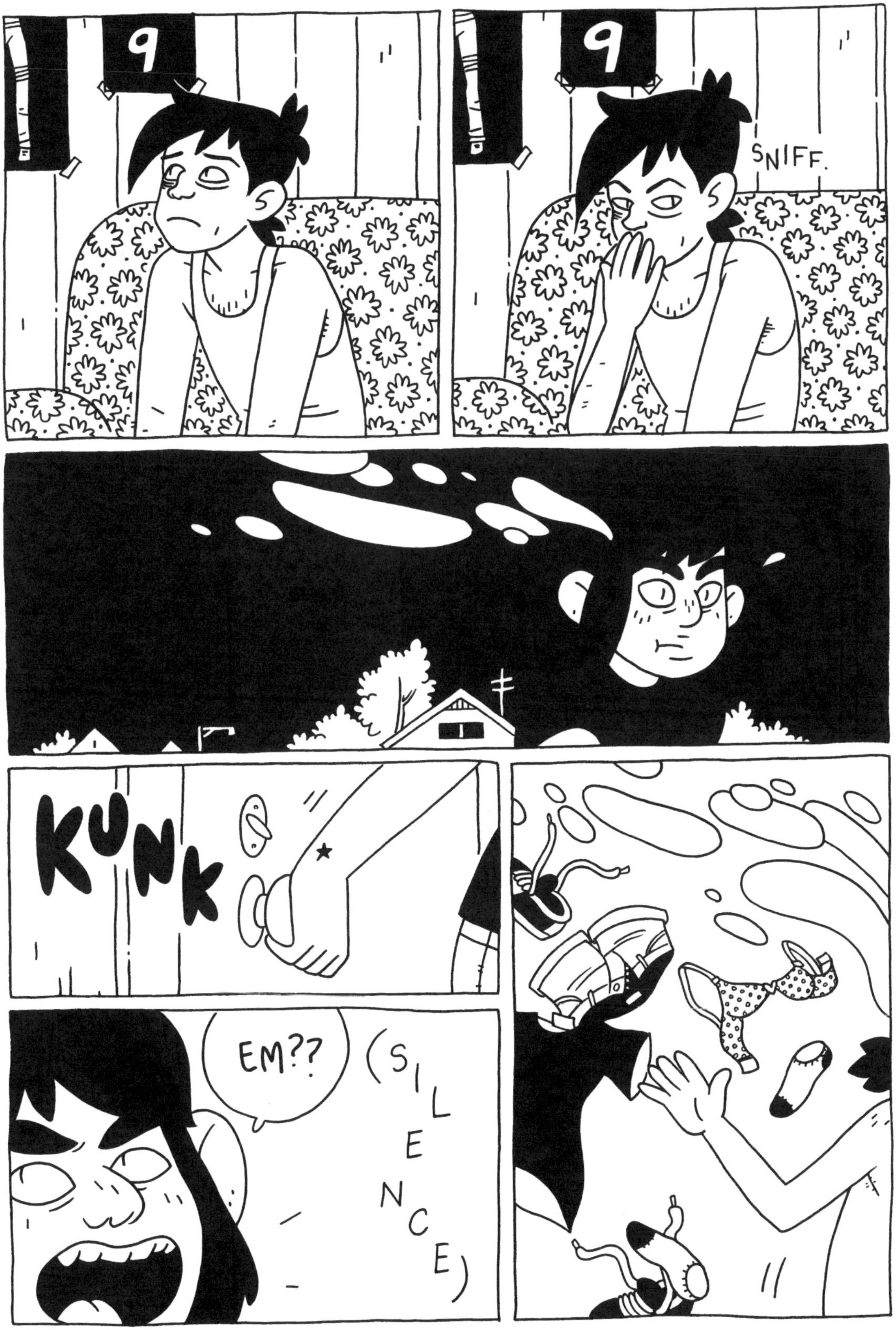
9
9
SNIFF.
KUNK
EM??
(SILENCE)

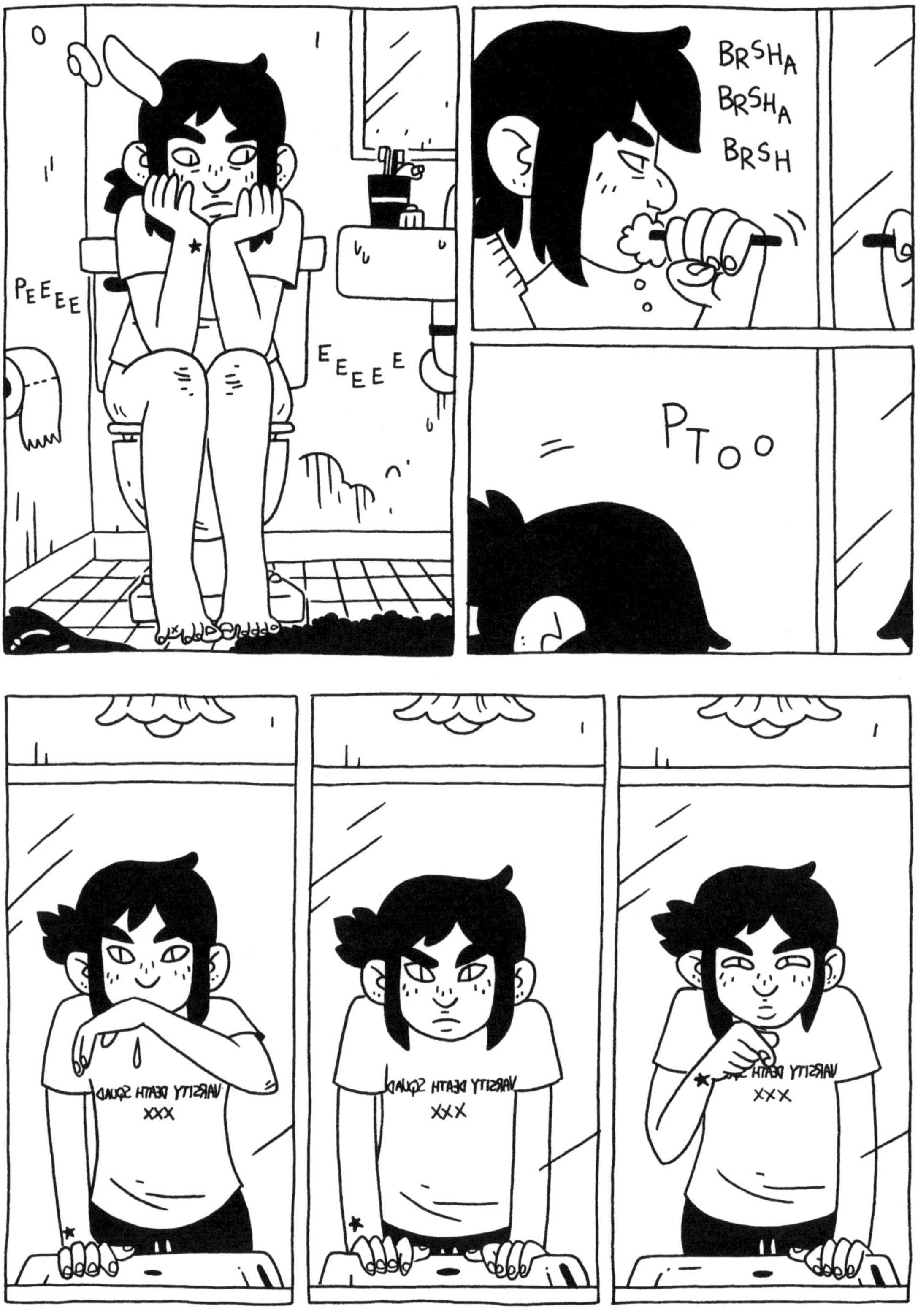
PEEEE
EEEEE
BRSHA
BRSHA
BRSH
PTOO

CH 7

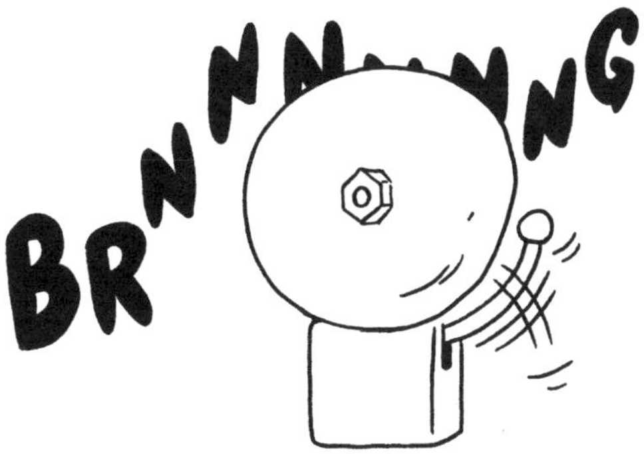
BRNNNNNNG

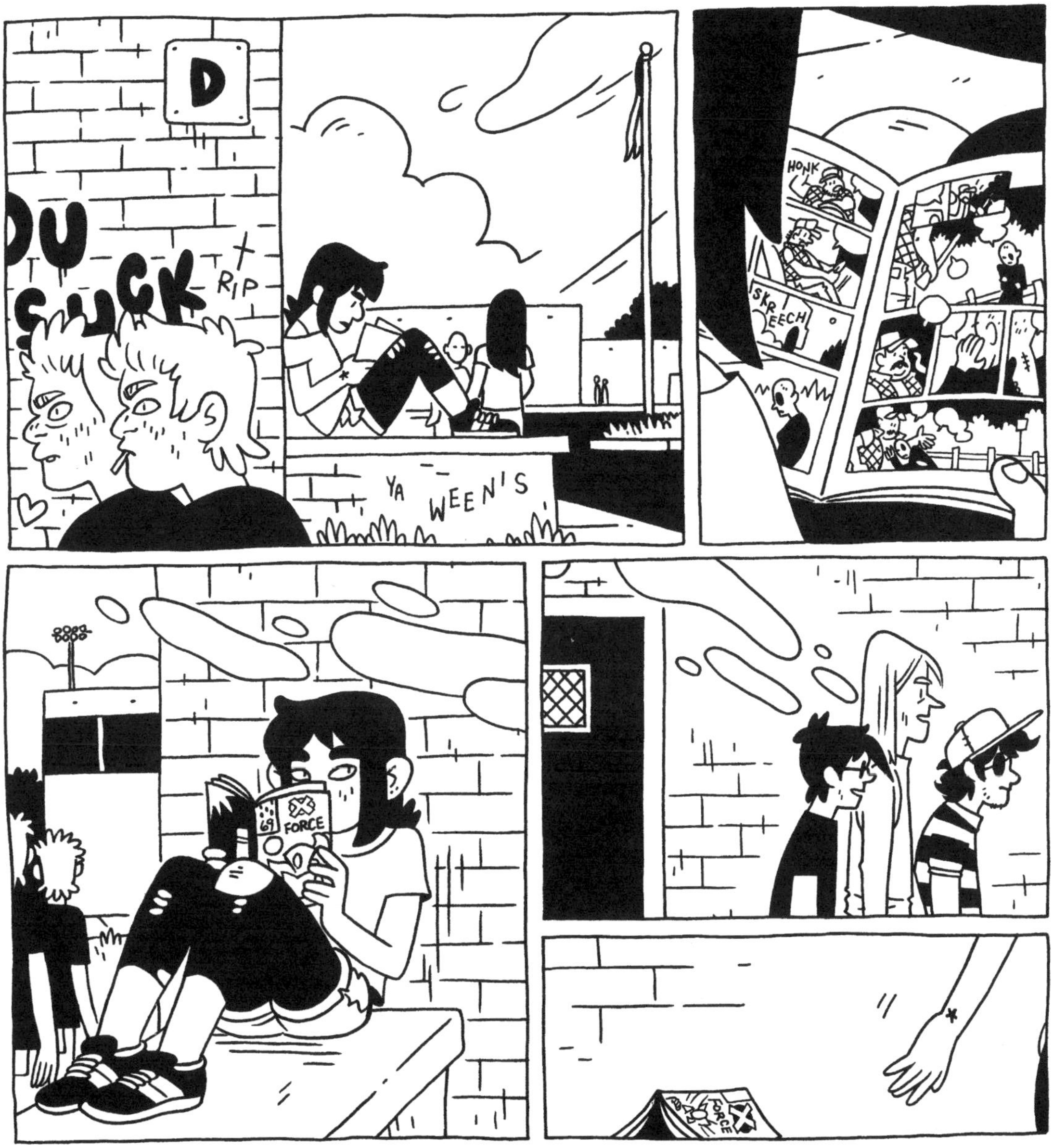
D
SUCK
RIP
YA WEEN'S
HONK
SKREECH
69
FORCE
FORCE

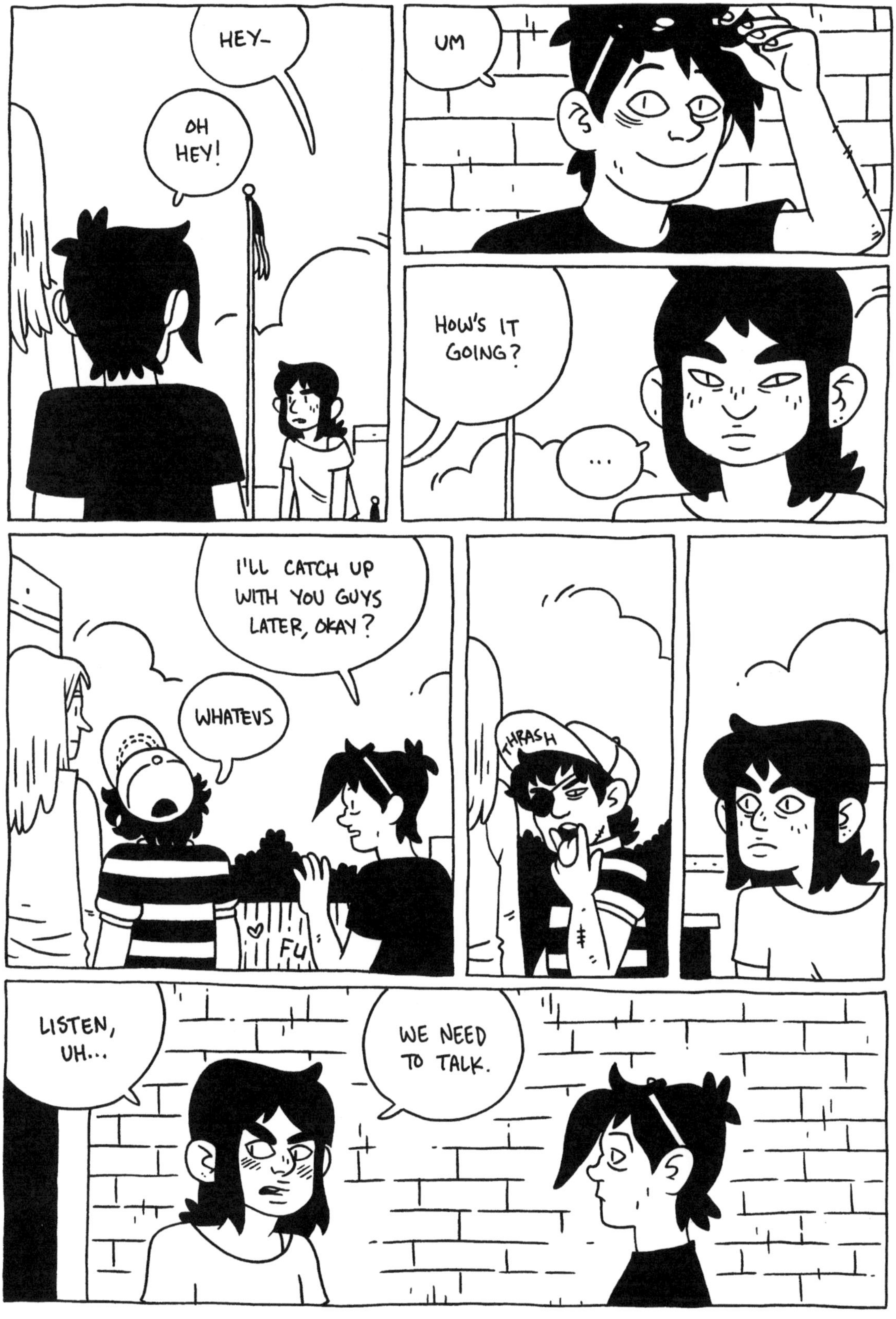
HEY-
OH HEY!
UM
HOW'S IT GOING?
...
I'LL CATCH UP WITH YOU GUYS LATER, OKAY?
WHATEVS
FU
THRASH
LISTEN, UH...
WE NEED TO TALK.

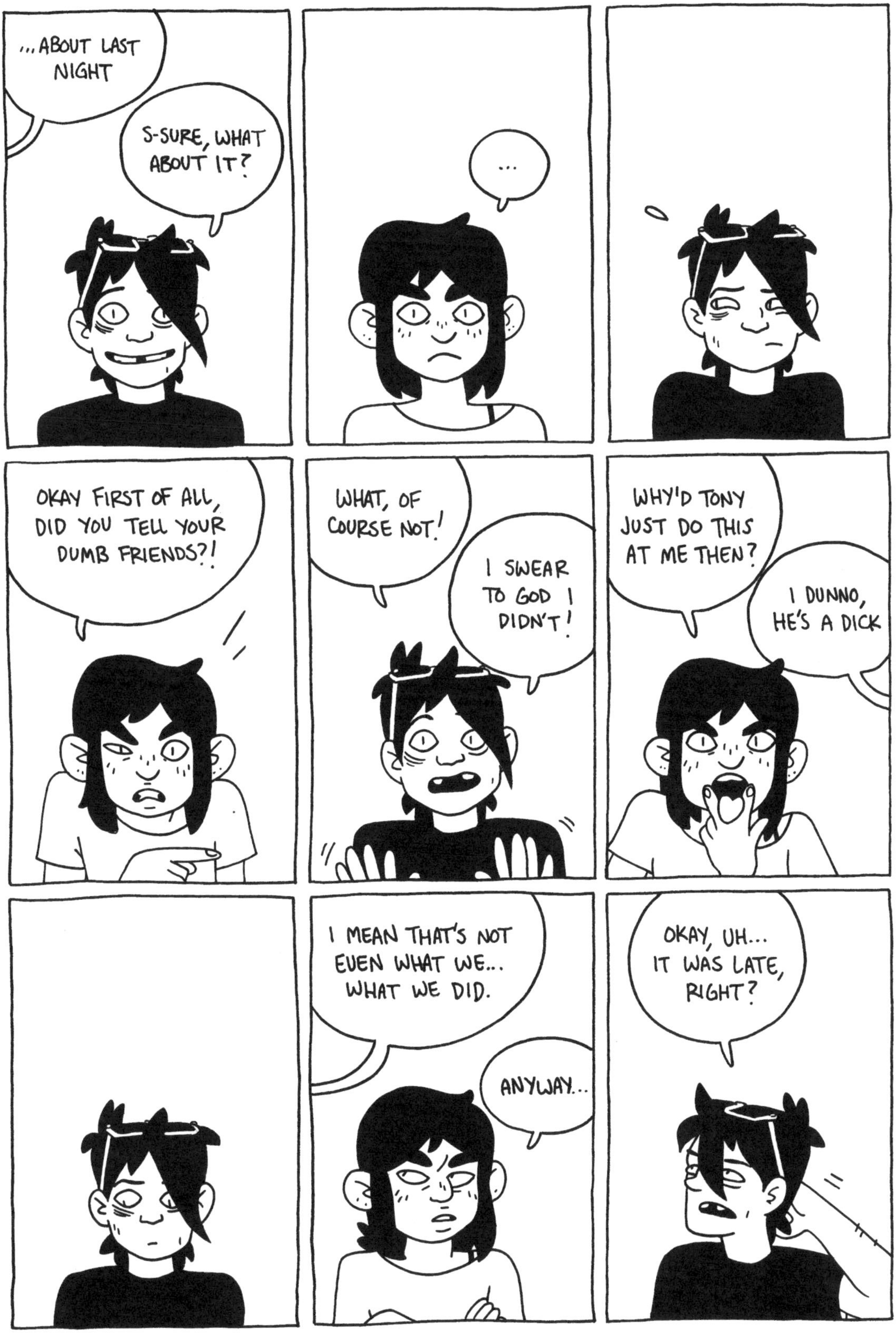

...ABOUT LAST NIGHT
S-SURE, WHAT ABOUT IT?
...
OKAY FIRST OF ALL, DID YOU TELL YOUR DUMB FRIENDS?!
WHAT, OF COURSE NOT!
I SWEAR TO GOD I DIDN'T!
WHY'D TONY JUST DO THIS AT ME THEN?
I DUNNO, HE'S A DICK
I MEAN THAT'S NOT EVEN WHAT WE... WHAT WE DID.
ANYWAY...
OKAY, UH... IT WAS LATE, RIGHT?

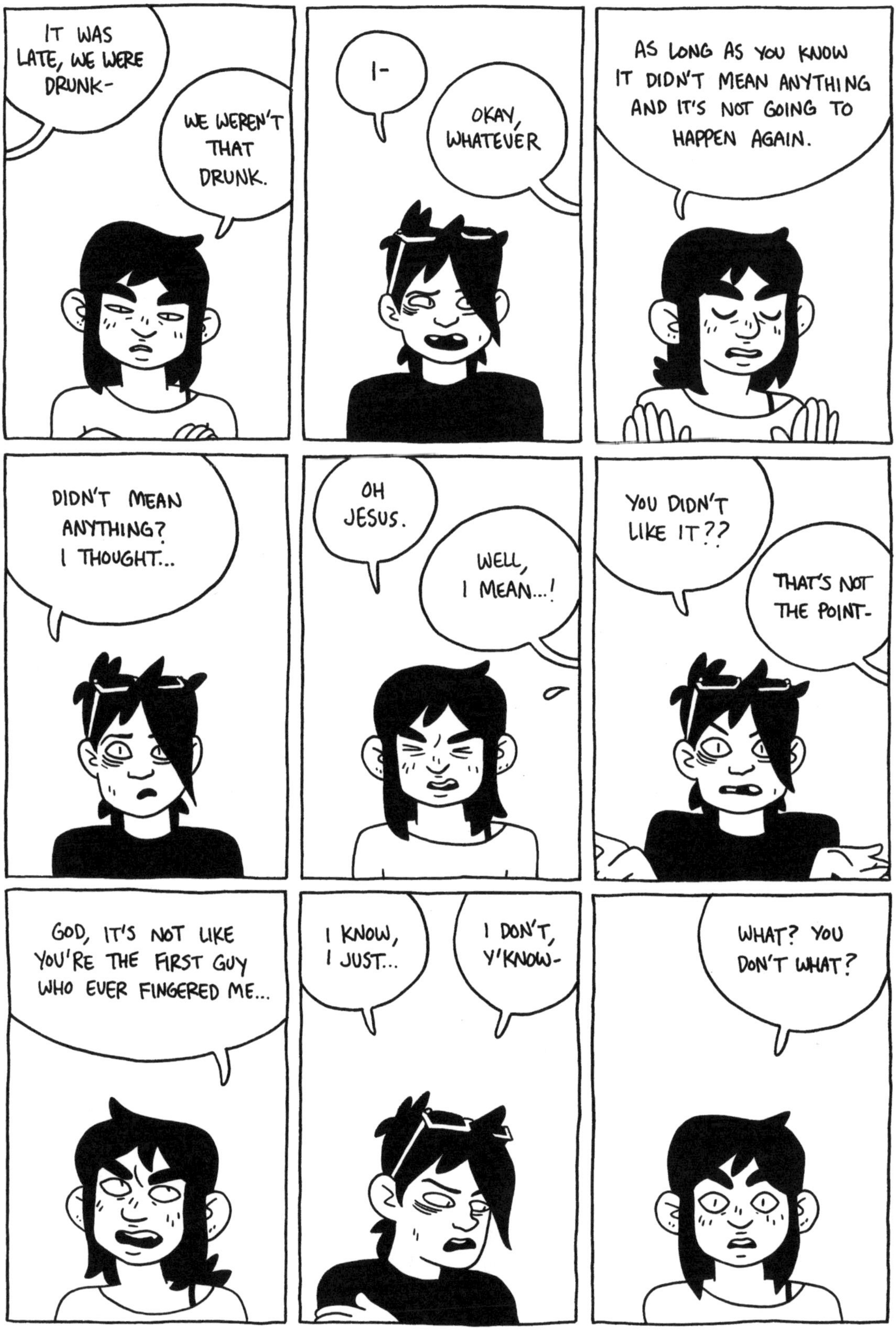
IT WAS LATE, WE WERE DRUNK-
WE WEREN'T THAT DRUNK.
I-
OKAY, WHATEVER
AS LONG AS YOU KNOW IT DIDN'T MEAN ANYTHING AND IT'S NOT GOING TO HAPPEN AGAIN.
DIDN'T MEAN ANYTHING? I THOUGHT...
OH JESUS.
WELL, I MEAN...!
YOU DIDN'T LIKE IT??
THAT'S NOT THE POINT-
GOD, IT'S NOT LIKE YOU'RE THE FIRST GUY WHO EVER FINGERED ME...
I KNOW, I JUST...
I DON'T, Y'KNOW-
WHAT? YOU DON'T WHAT?

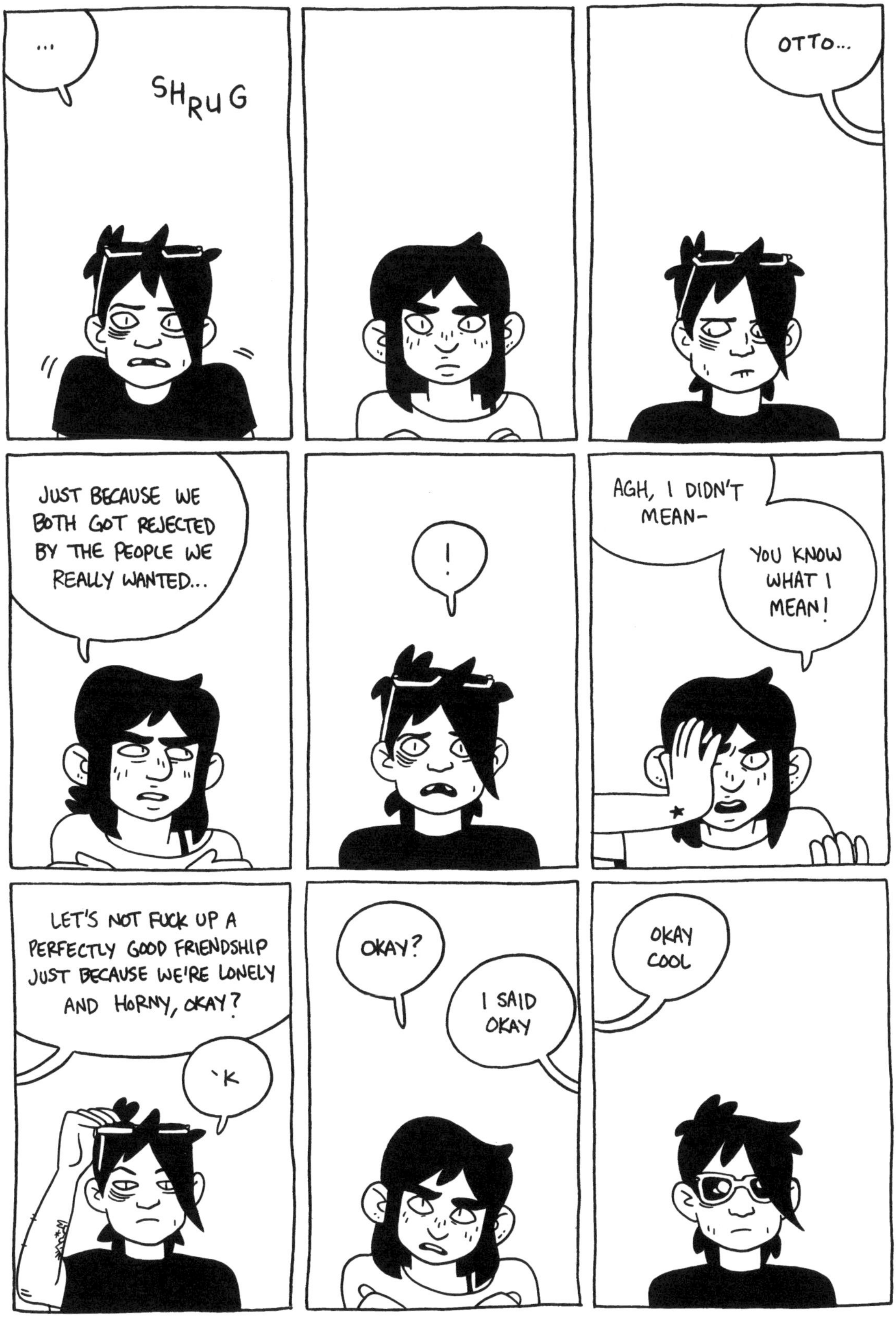
...
SHRUG
OTTO...
JUST BECAUSE WE BOTH GOT REJECTED BY THE PEOPLE WE REALLY WANTED...
!
AGH, I DIDN'T MEAN-
YOU KNOW WHAT I MEAN!
LET'S NOT FUCK UP A PERFECTLY GOOD FRIENDSHIP JUST BECAUSE WE'RE LONELY AND HORNY, OKAY?
`K
OKAY?
I SAID OKAY
OKAY COOL

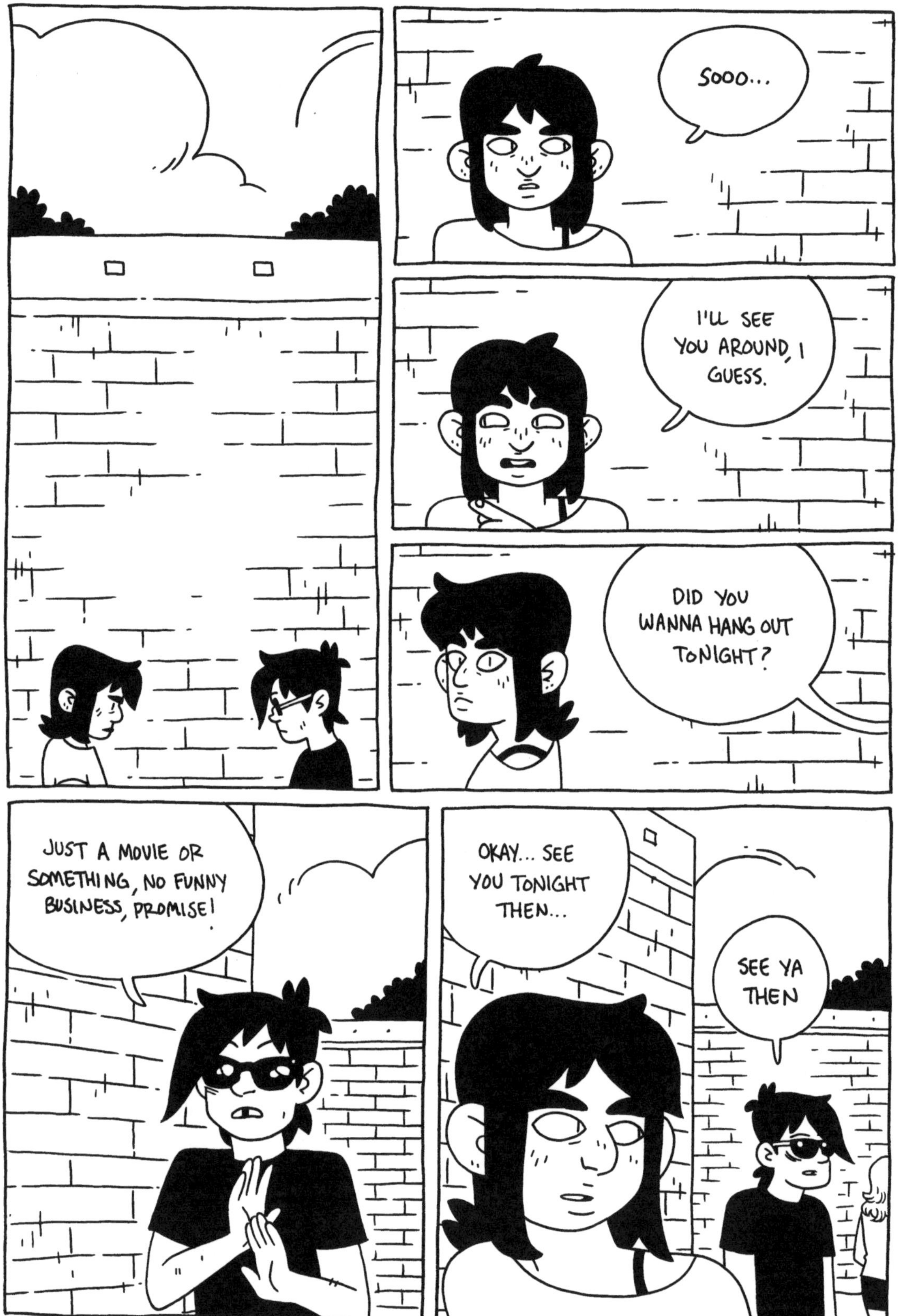
SOOO...
I'LL SEE YOU AROUND, I GUESS.
DID YOU WANNA HANG OUT TONIGHT?
JUST A MOVIE OR SOMETHING, NO FUNNY BUSINESS, PROMISE!
OKAY... SEE YOU TONIGHT THEN...
SEE YA THEN

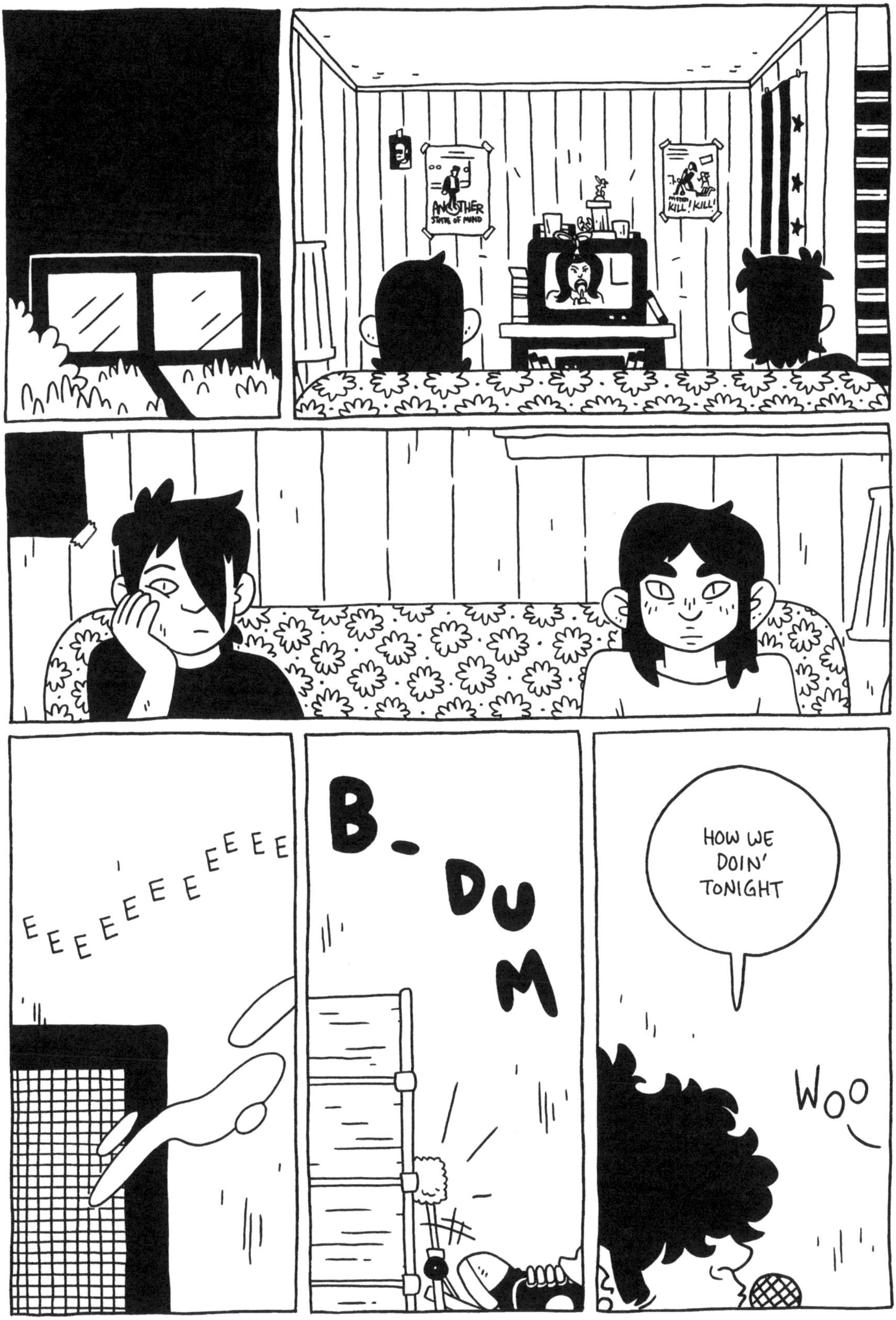
ANOTHER STATE OF MIND
KILL! KILL!
EEEEEEEEEEEEE
B-DUM
HOW WE DOIN' TONIGHT
WOO

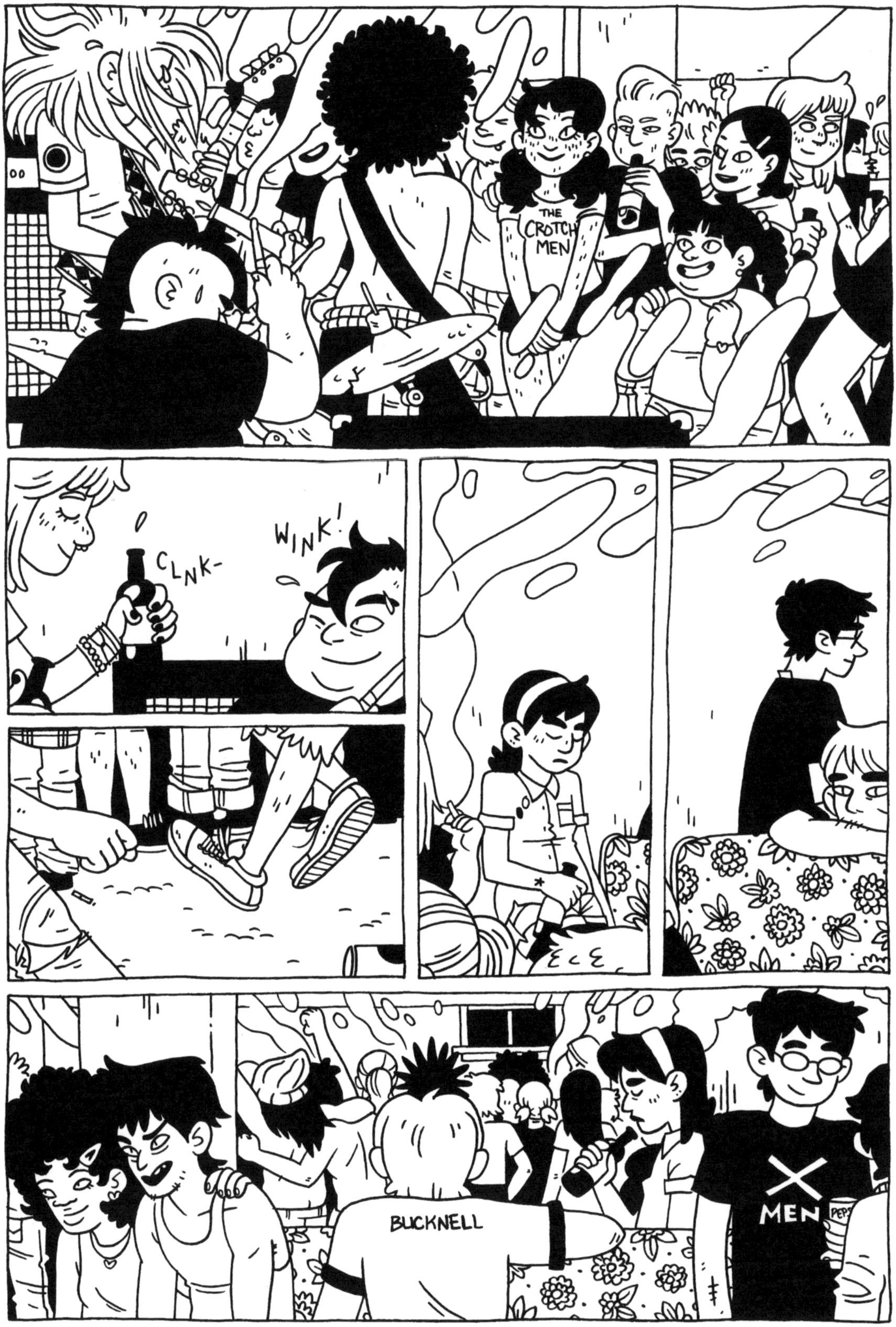
THE
CROTCH
MEN
CLNK-
WINK!
BUCKNELL
MEN

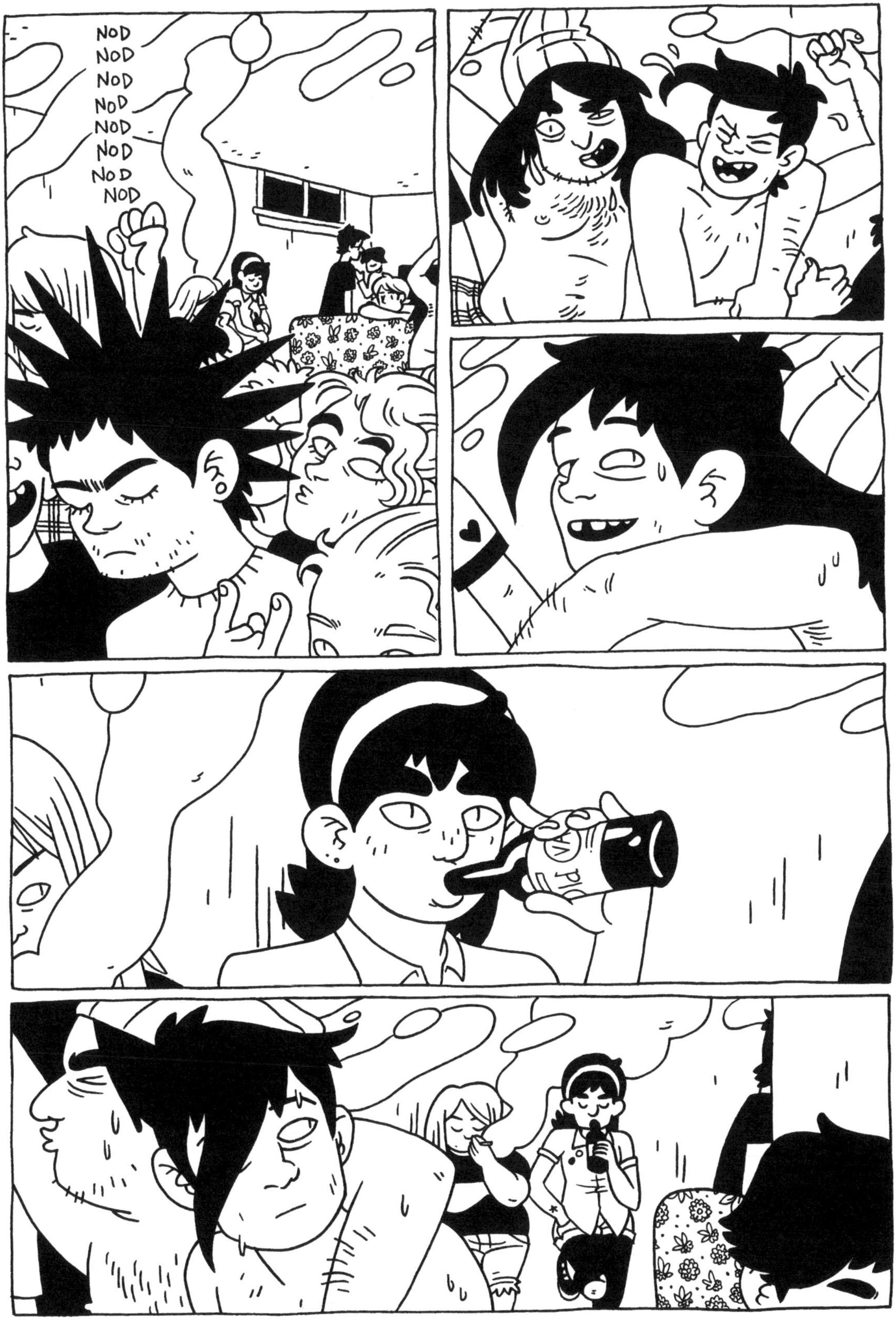
NOD
NOD
NOD
NOD
NOD
NOD
NOD
NOD

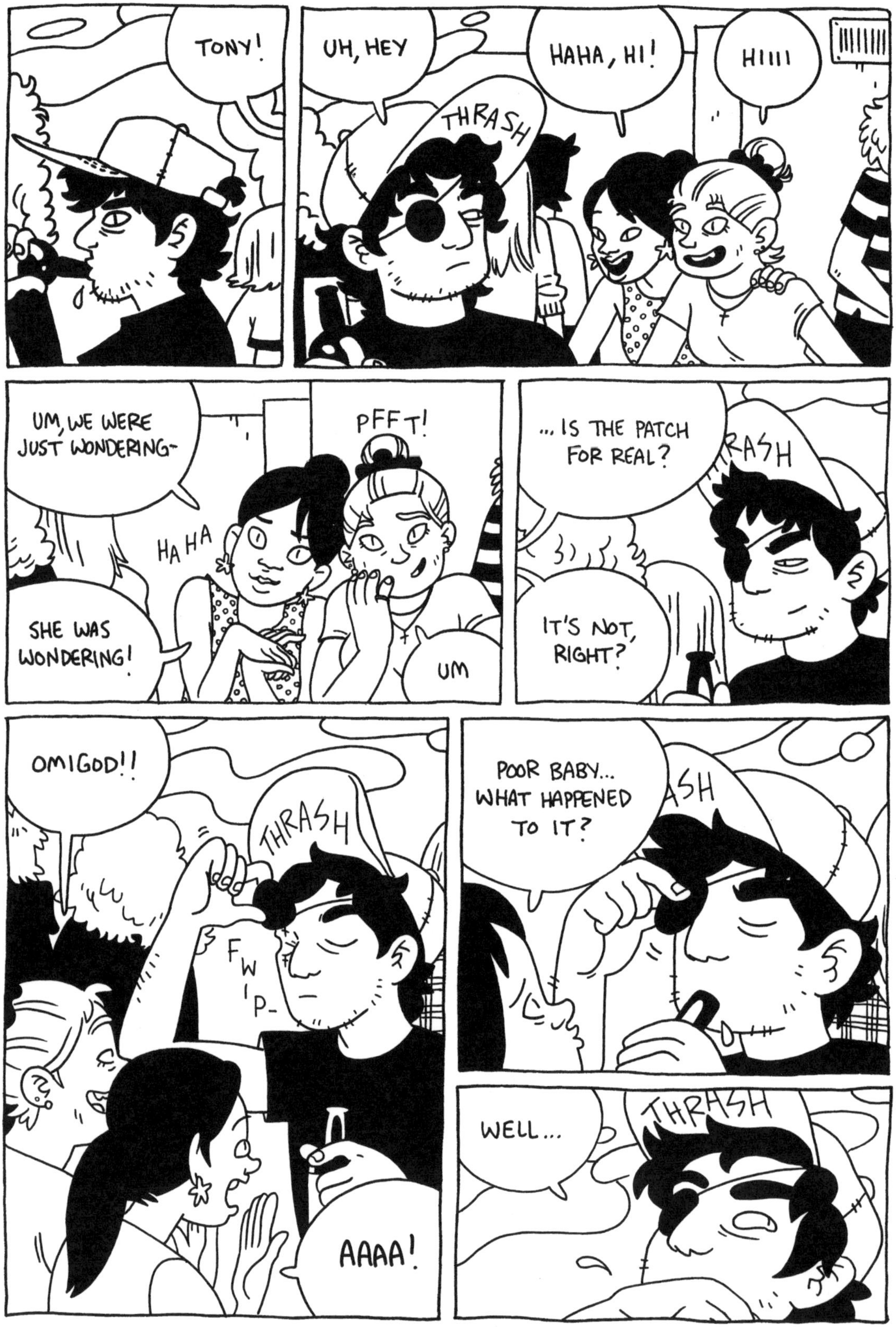
TONY!
UH, HEY
THRASH
HAHA, HI!
HIIII
UM, WE WERE JUST WONDERING-
SHE WAS WONDERING!
HAHA
PFFT!
UM
... IS THE PATCH FOR REAL?
IT'S NOT, RIGHT?
THRASH
OMIGOD!!
THRASH
FWIP-
AAAA!
POOR BABY... WHAT HAPPENED TO IT?
WELL...
THRASH

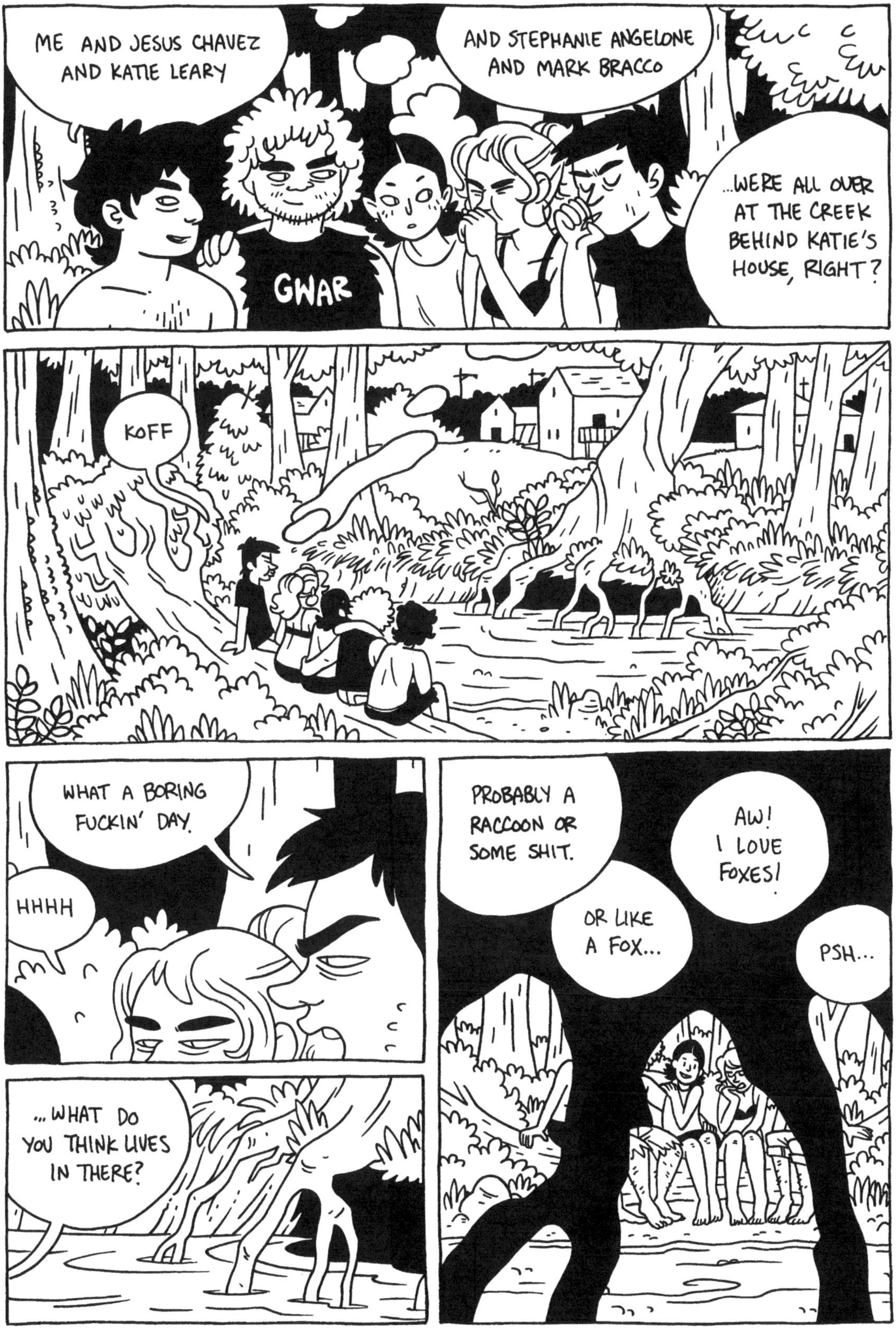
ME AND JESUS CHAVEZ AND KATIE LEARY
AND STEPHANIE ANGELONE AND MARK BRACCO
...WERE ALL OVER AT THE CREEK BEHIND KATIE'S HOUSE, RIGHT?
GWAR
KOFF
WHAT A BORING FUCKIN' DAY.
HHHH
PROBABLY A RACCOON OR SOME SHIT.
AW! I LOVE FOXES!
OR LIKE A FOX...
PSH...
...WHAT DO YOU THINK LIVES IN THERE?

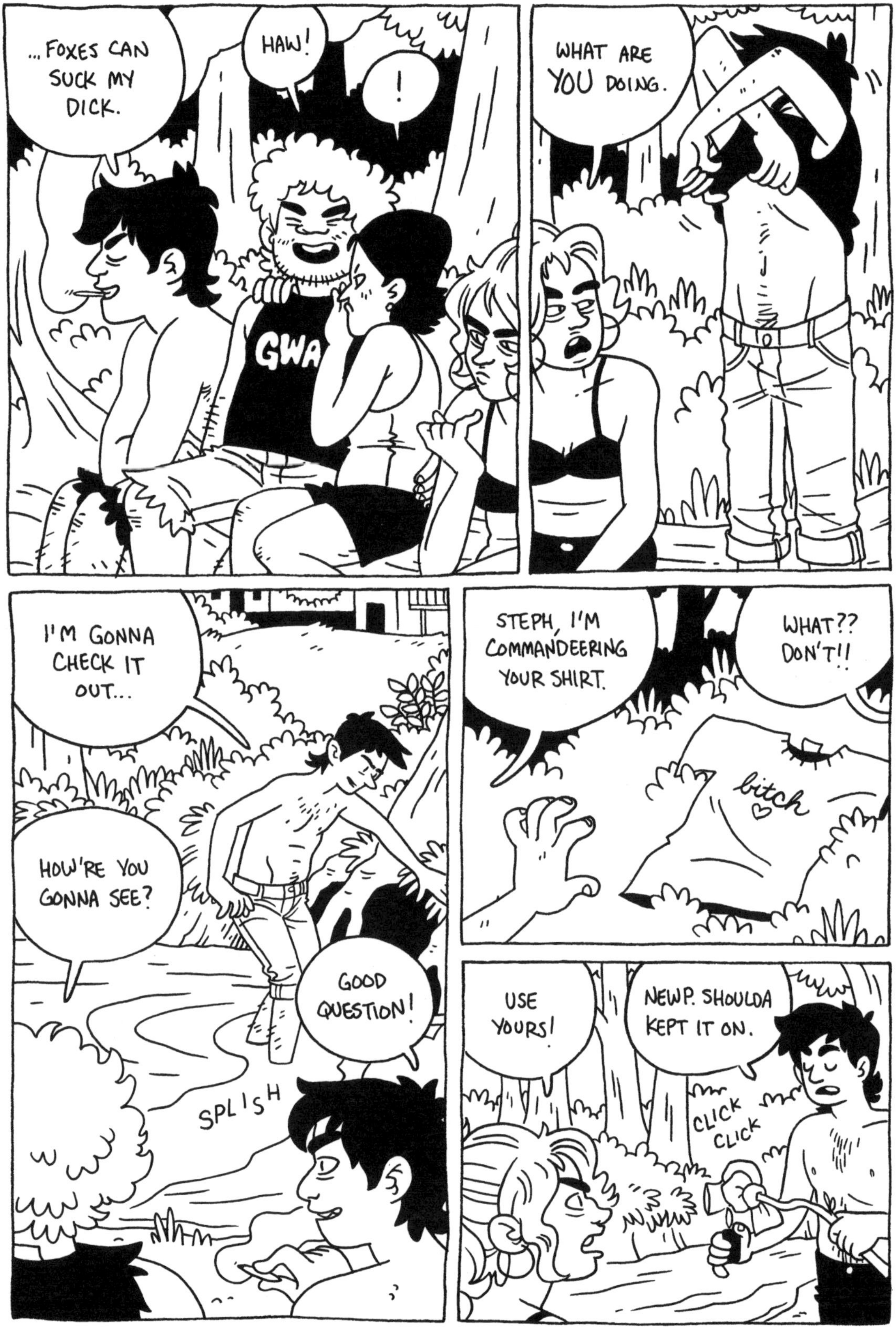
...FOXES CAN SUCK MY DICK.
HAW!
!
WHAT ARE YOU DOING.
I'M GONNA CHECK IT OUT...
HOW'RE YOU GONNA SEE?
GOOD QUESTION!
SPLISH
STEPH, I'M COMMANDEERING YOUR SHIRT.
WHAT?? DON'T!!
bitch
USE YOURS!
NEWP. SHOULDA KEPT IT ON.
CLICK CLICK

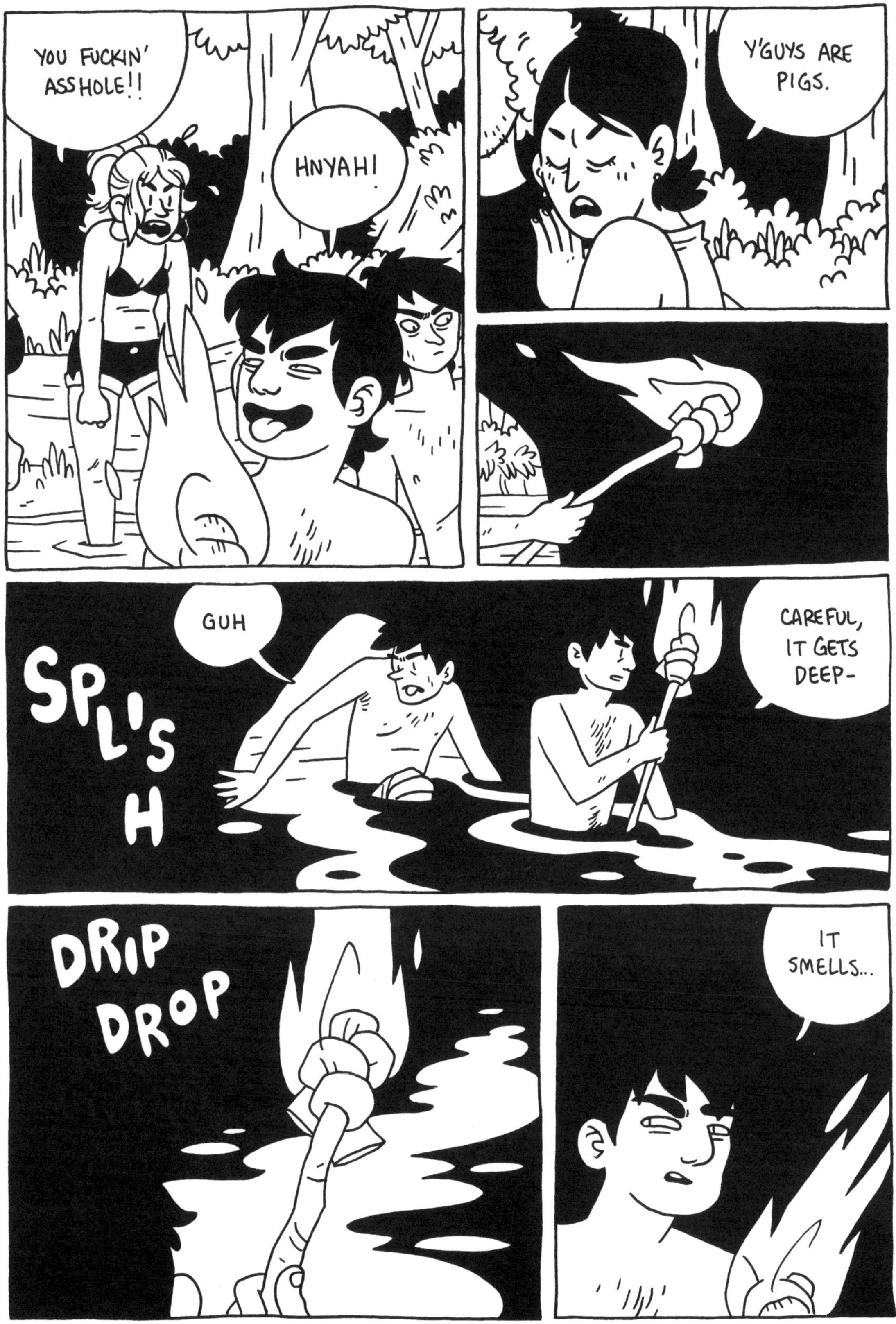
YOU FUCKIN' ASSHOLE!!
HNYAH!
Y'GUYS ARE PIGS.
SPLISH
GUH
CAREFUL, IT GETS DEEP-
DRIP DROP
IT SMELLS...

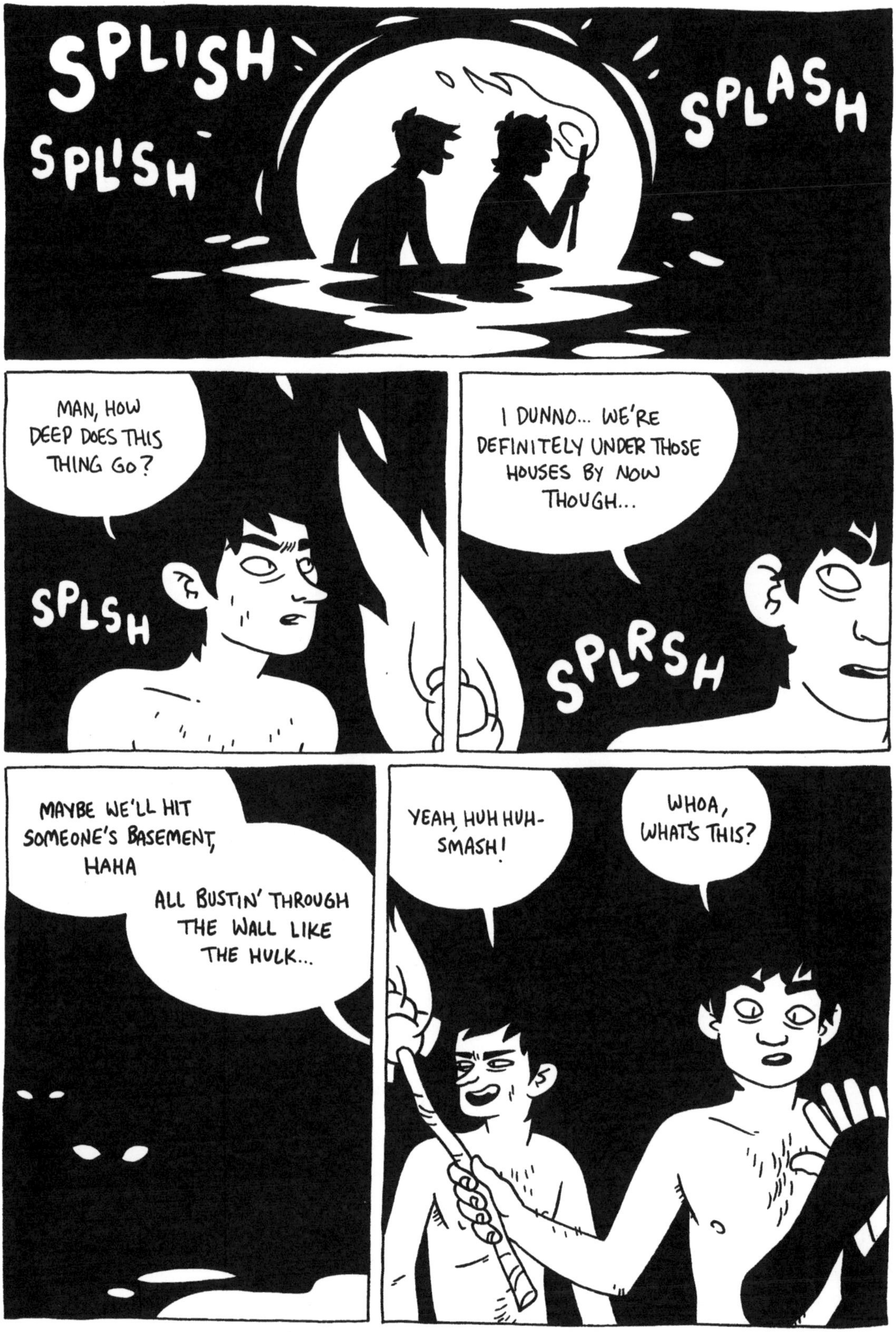
SPLISH
SPLISH
SPLASH
MAN, HOW DEEP DOES THIS THING GO?
SPLSH
I DUNNO... WE'RE DEFINITELY UNDER THOSE HOUSES BY NOW THOUGH...
SPLRSH
MAYBE WE'LL HIT SOMEONE'S BASEMENT, HAHA
ALL BUSTIN' THROUGH THE WALL LIKE THE HULK...
YEAH, HUH HUH- SMASH!
WHOA, WHAT'S THIS?

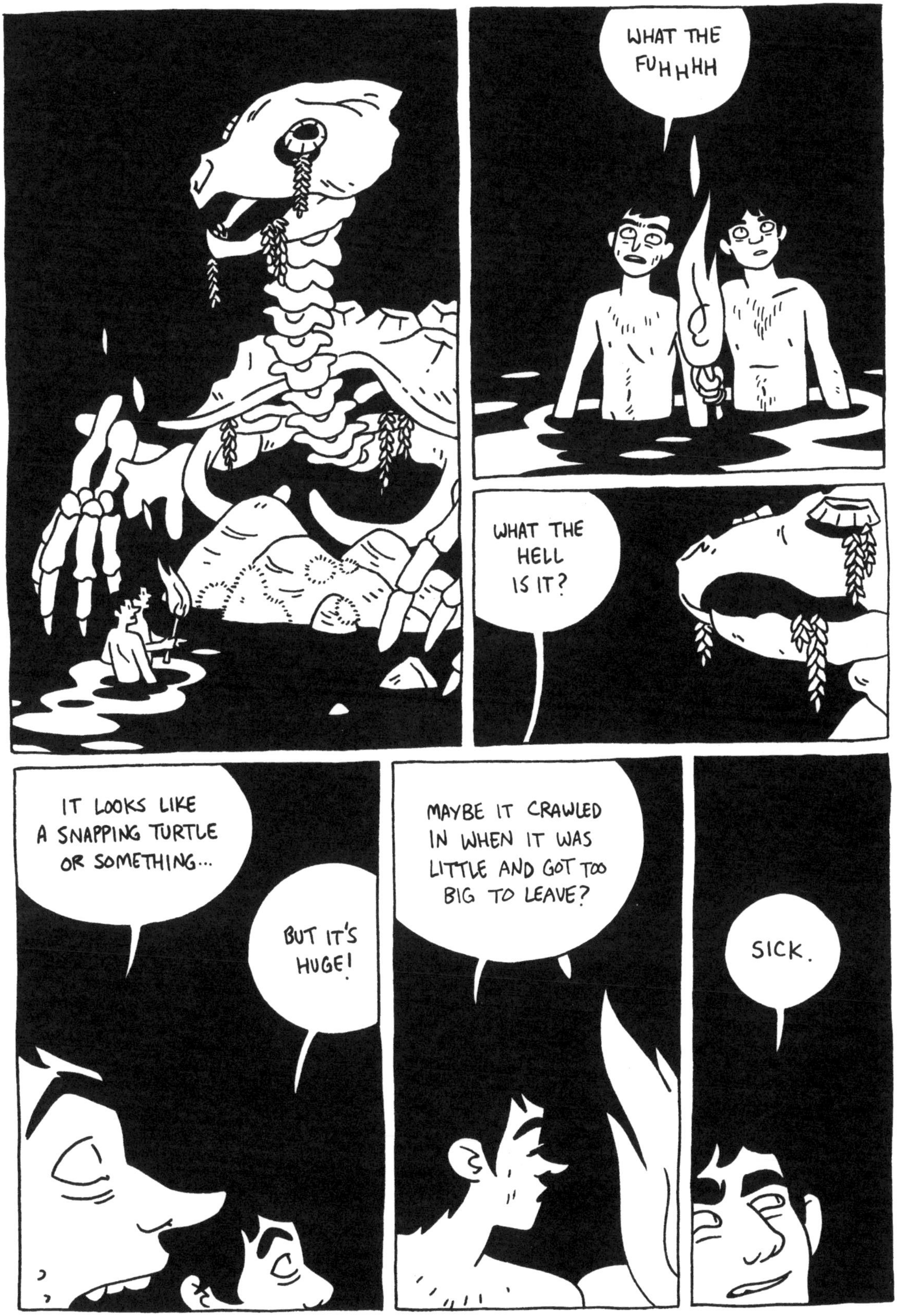

WHAT THE FUHHHH
WHAT THE HELL IS IT?
IT LOOKS LIKE A SNAPPING TURTLE OR SOMETHING...
BUT IT'S HUGE!
MAYBE IT CRAWLED IN WHEN IT WAS LITTLE AND GOT TOO BIG TO LEAVE?
SICK.

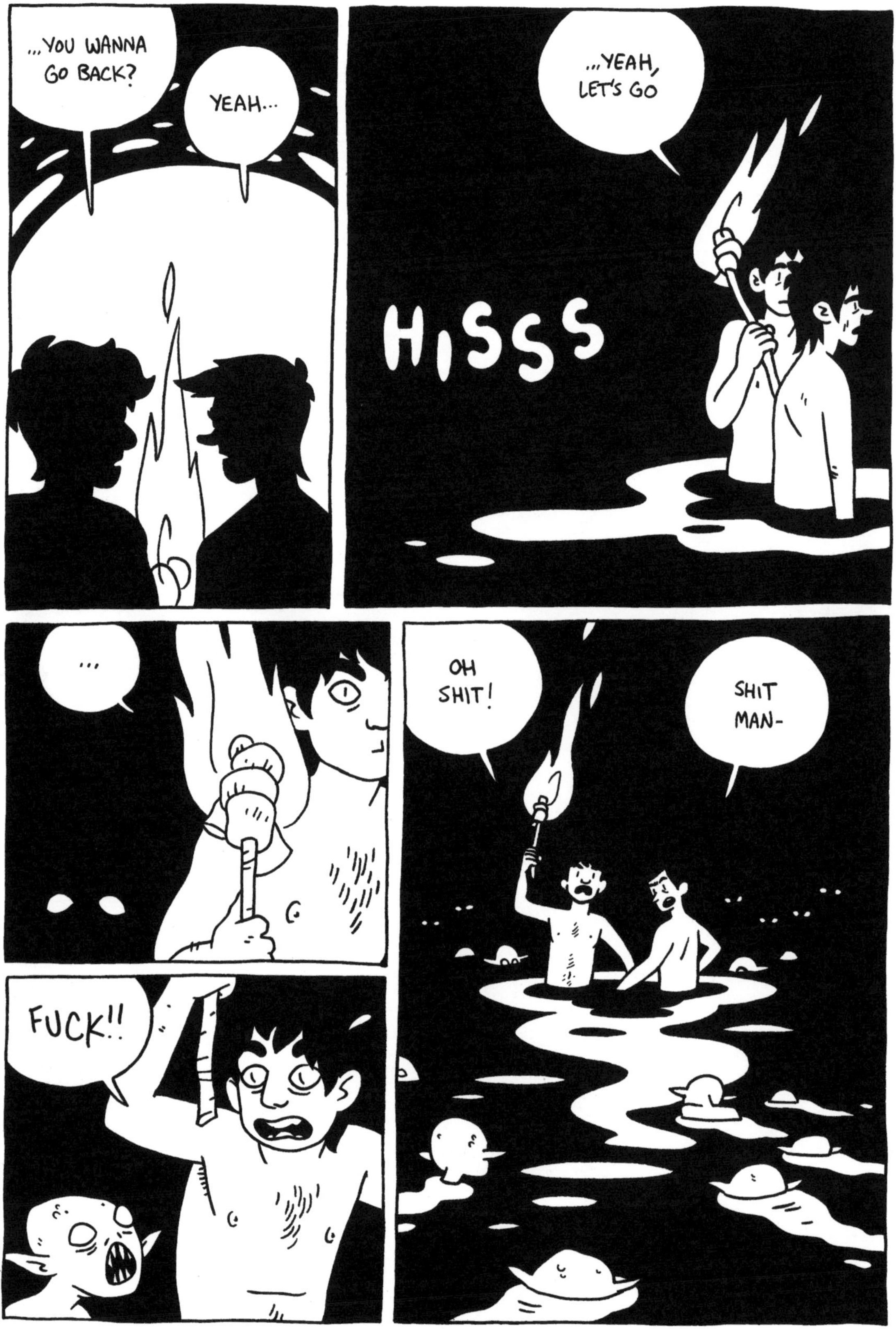
...YOU WANNA GO BACK?
YEAH...
...YEAH, LET'S GO
HISSS
...
OH SHIT!
SHIT MAN-
FUCK!!

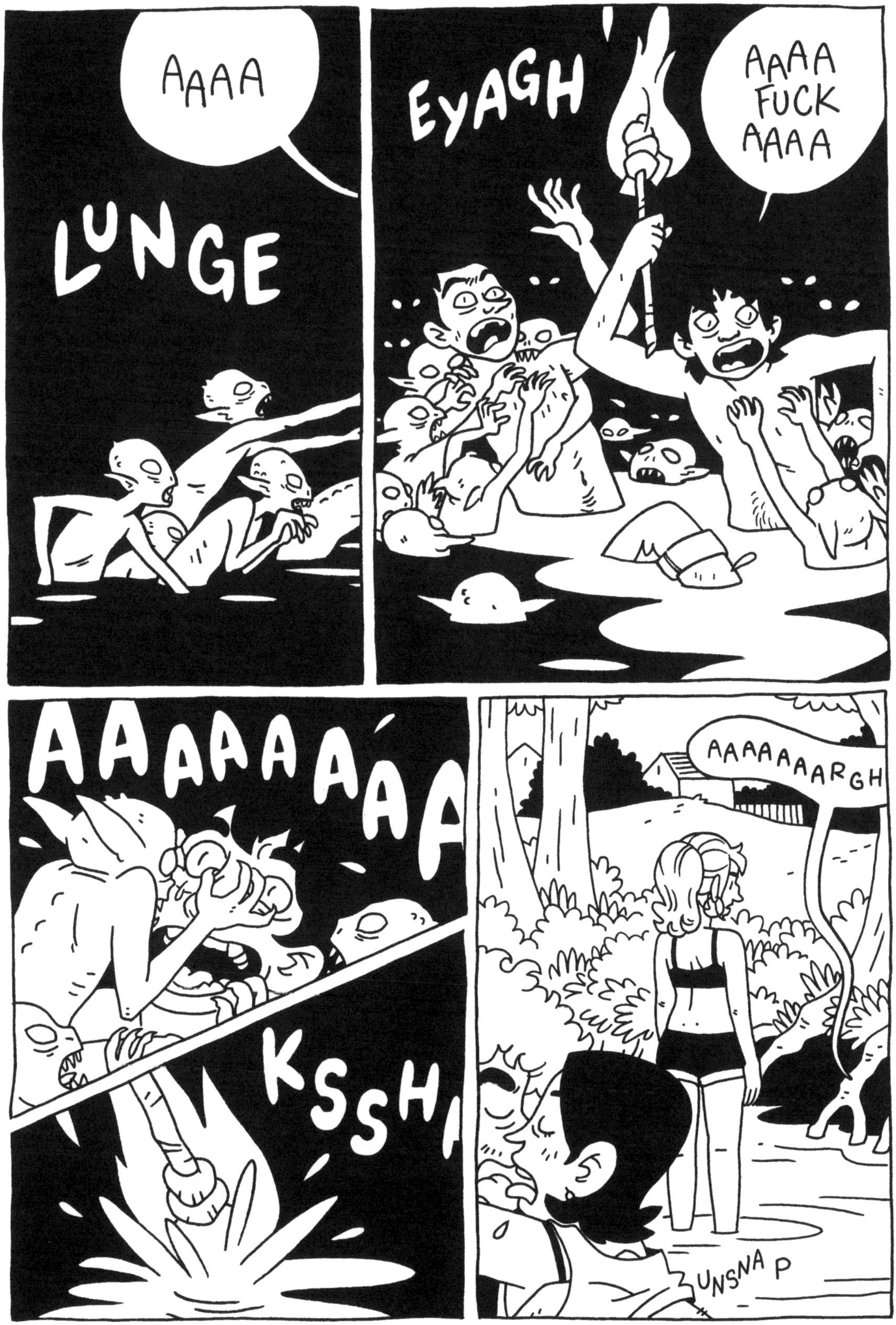
AAAA
LUNGE
EYAGH
AAAA FUCK AAAA
AAAAAAAAA
KSSH
AAAAAAARGH
UNSNAP

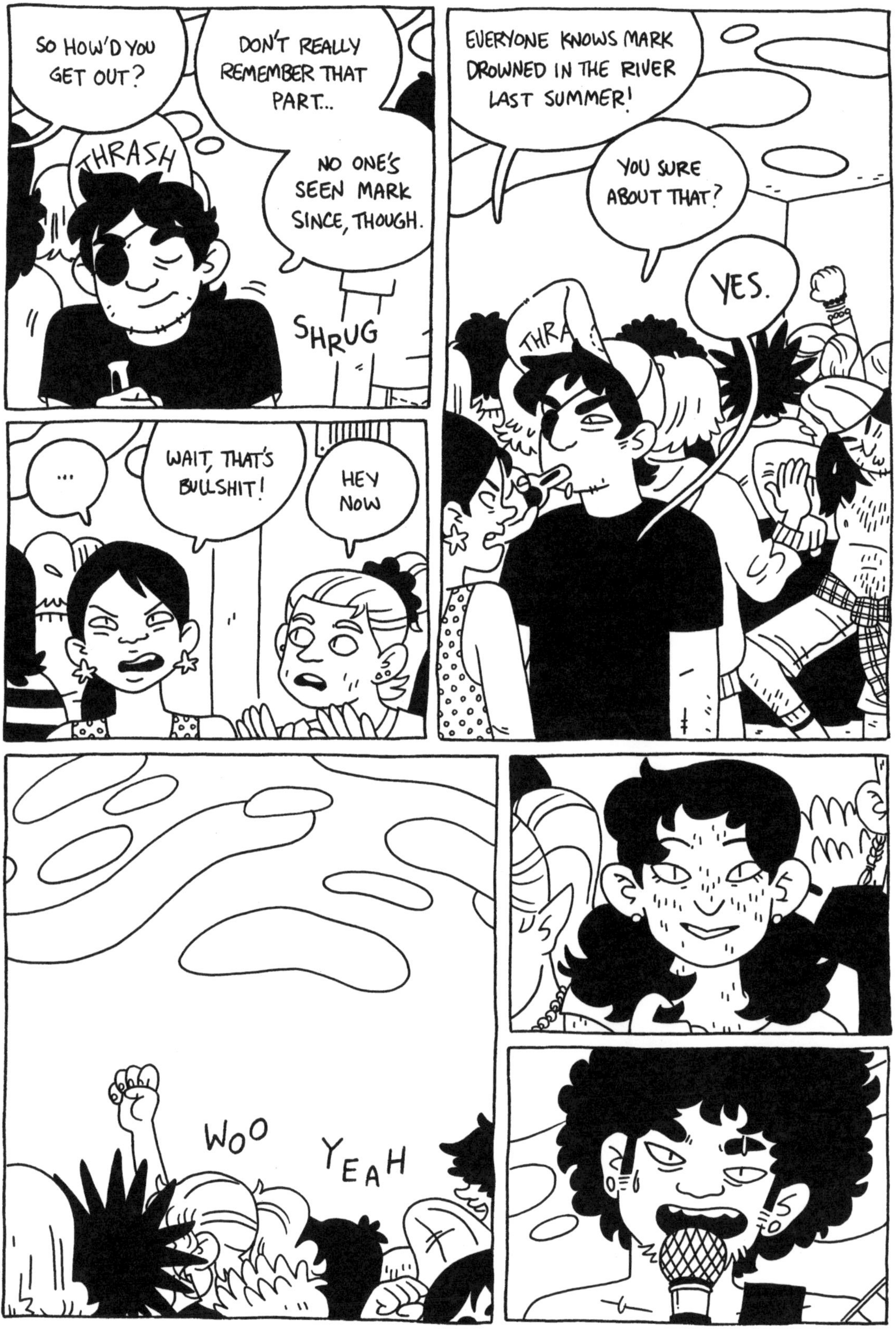
SO HOW'D YOU GET OUT?
DON'T REALLY REMEMBER THAT PART...
THRASH
NO ONE'S SEEN MARK SINCE, THOUGH.
SHRUG
EVERYONE KNOWS MARK DROWNED IN THE RIVER LAST SUMMER!
YOU SURE ABOUT THAT?
YES.
THRA
...
WAIT, THAT'S BULLSHIT!
HEY NOW
WOO
YEAH

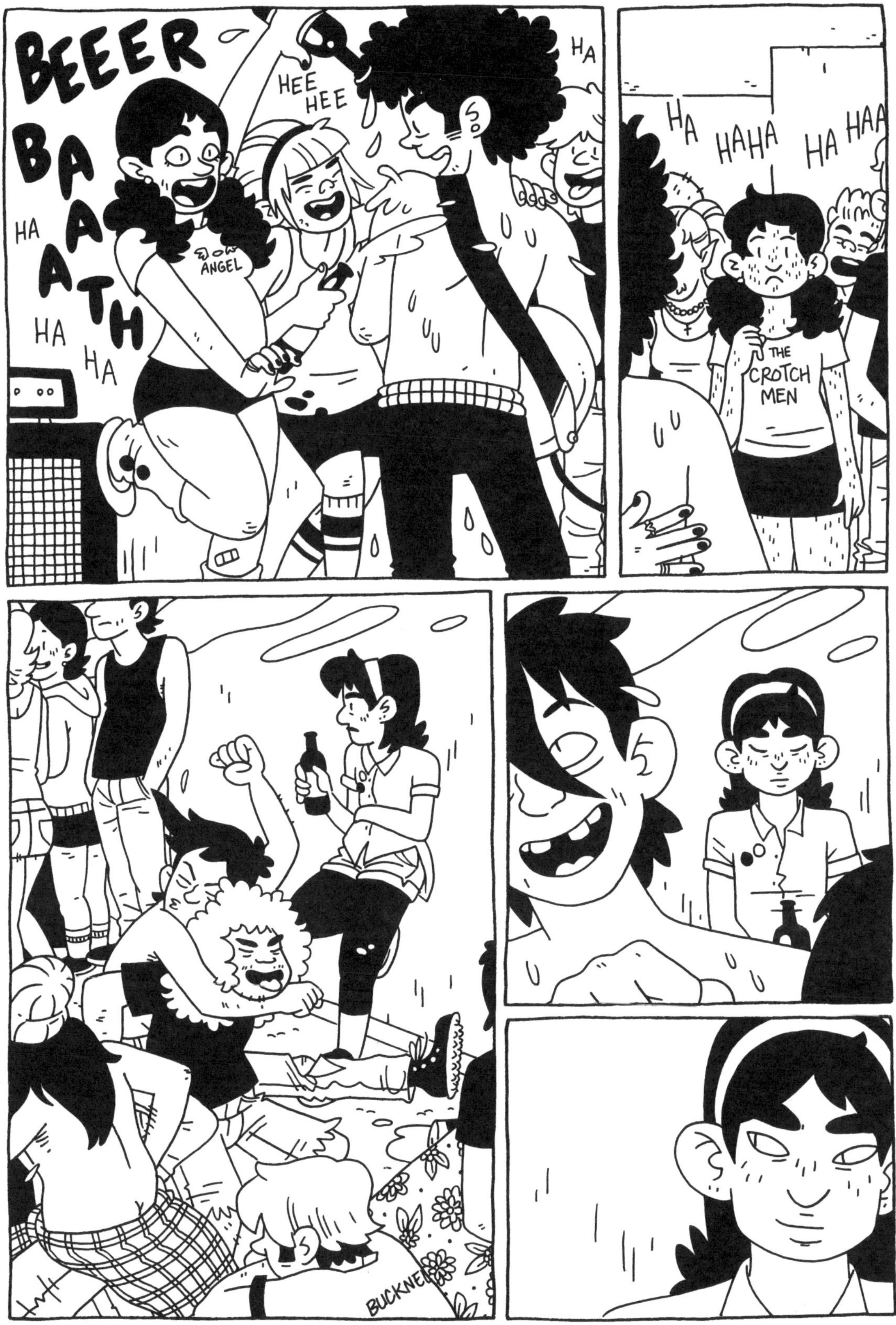
BEEER BAAATH
HEE HEE
HA
HA
HA
HA
WOW ANGEL
HA
HA HAHA HA HAA
THE CROTCH MEN
BUCKNE

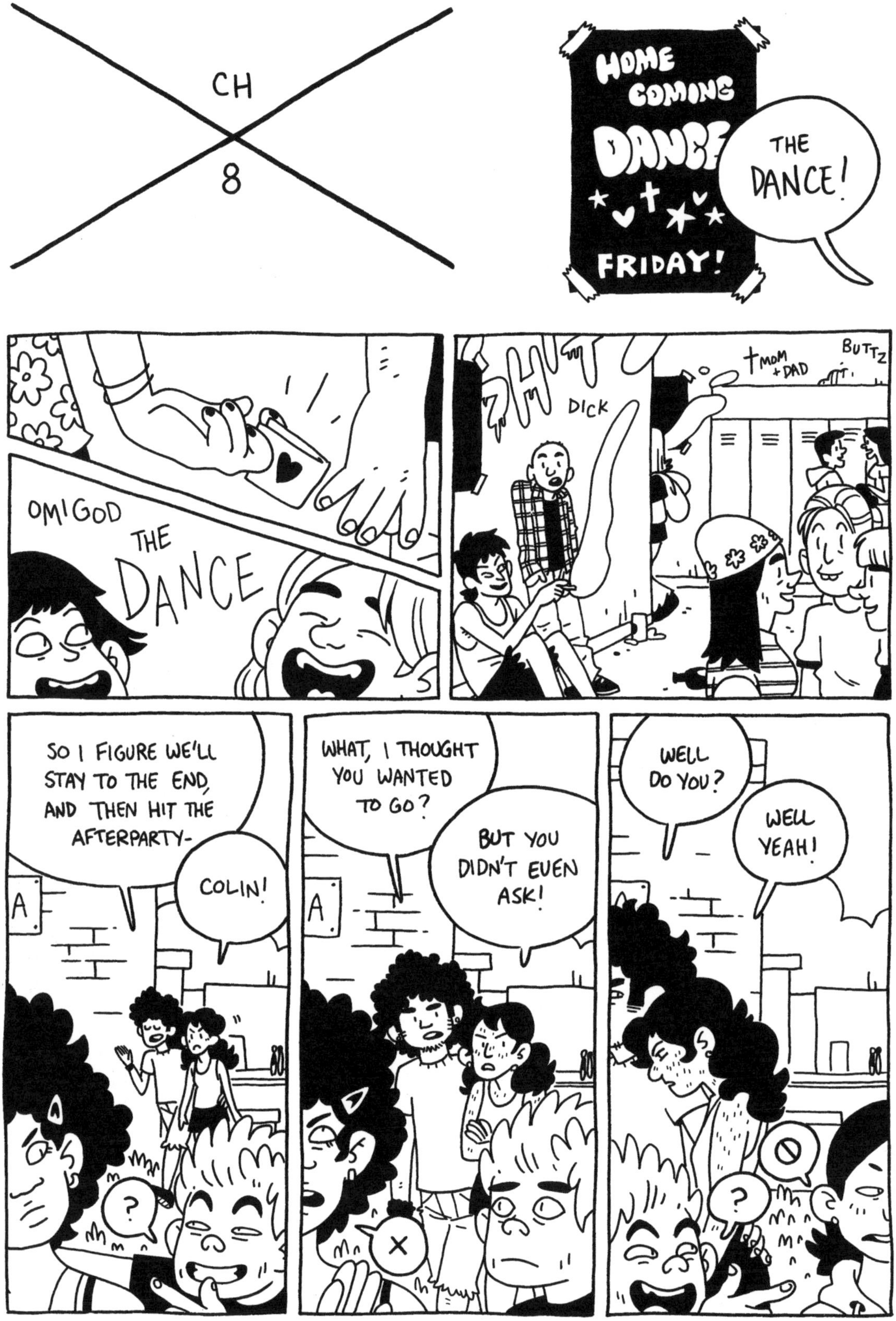
CH
8
HOME COMING
DANCE
FRIDAY!
THE DANCE!
OMIGOD
THE
DANCE
DICK
+MOM +DAD
BUTTZ
SO I FIGURE WE'LL STAY TO THE END, AND THEN HIT THE AFTERPARTY-
COLIN!
?
WHAT, I THOUGHT YOU WANTED TO GO?
BUT YOU DIDN'T EVEN ASK!
WELL DO YOU?
WELL YEAH!
?

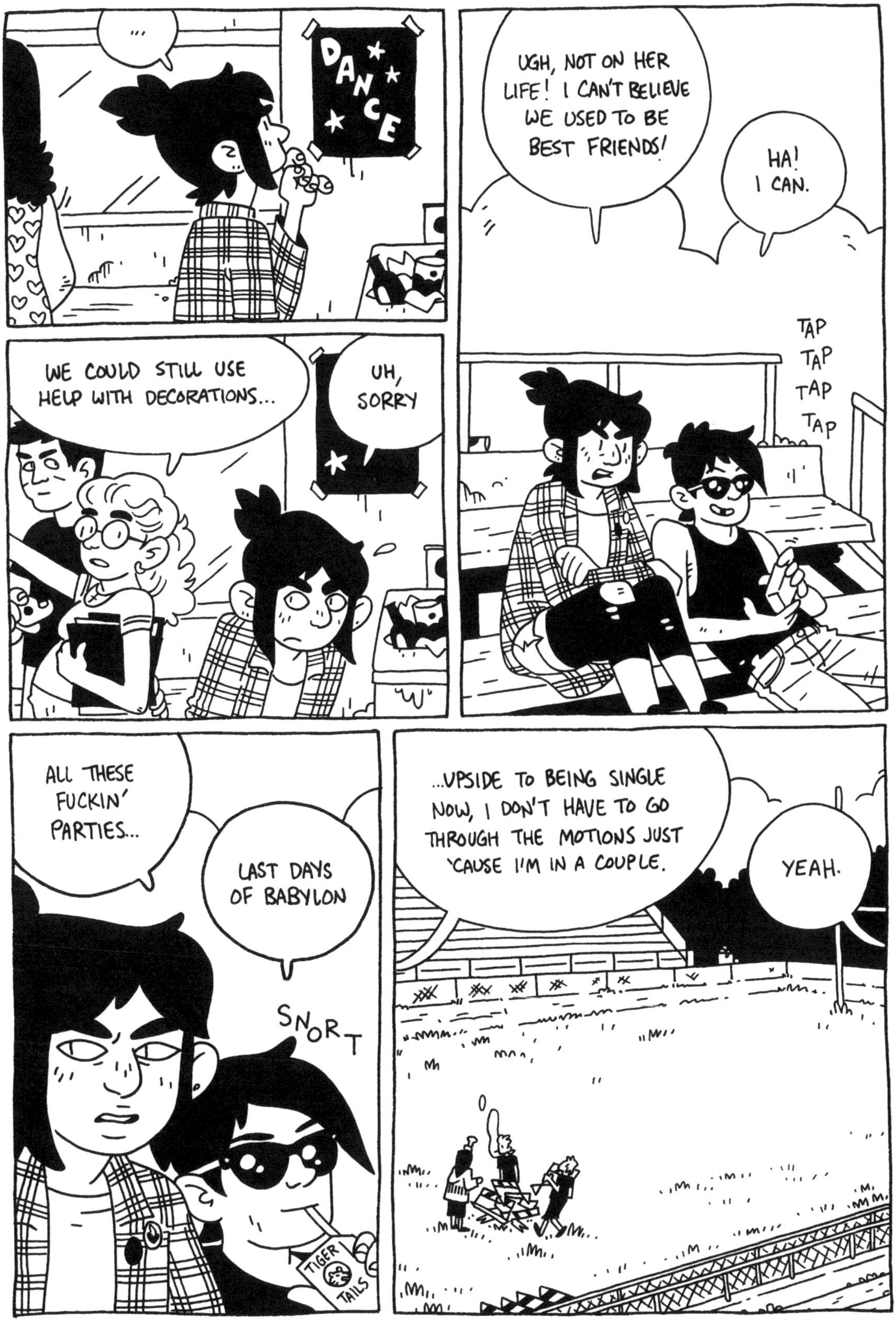
...
DANCE
UGH, NOT ON HER LIFE! I CAN'T BELIEVE WE USED TO BE BEST FRIENDS!
HA! I CAN.
WE COULD STILL USE HELP WITH DECORATIONS...
UH, SORRY
TAP TAP TAP TAP
ALL THESE FUCKIN' PARTIES...
LAST DAYS OF BABYLON
SNORT
TIGER TAILS
...UPSIDE TO BEING SINGLE NOW, I DON'T HAVE TO GO THROUGH THE MOTIONS JUST 'CAUSE I'M IN A COUPLE.
YEAH.

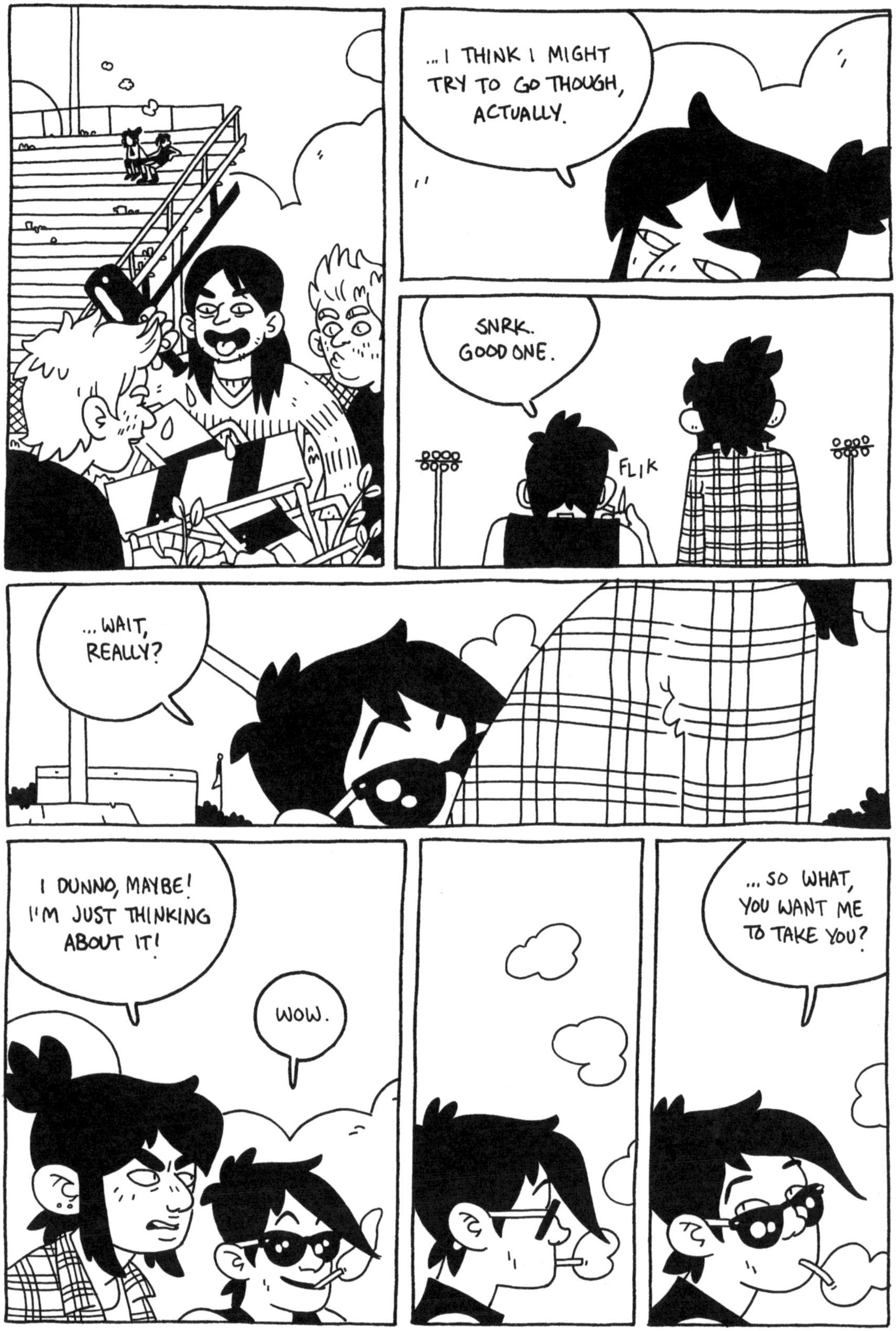
...I THINK I MIGHT TRY TO GO THOUGH, ACTUALLY.
SNRK. GOOD ONE.
FLIK
...WAIT, REALLY?
I DUNNO, MAYBE! I'M JUST THINKING ABOUT IT!
WOW.
...SO WHAT, YOU WANT ME TO TAKE YOU?

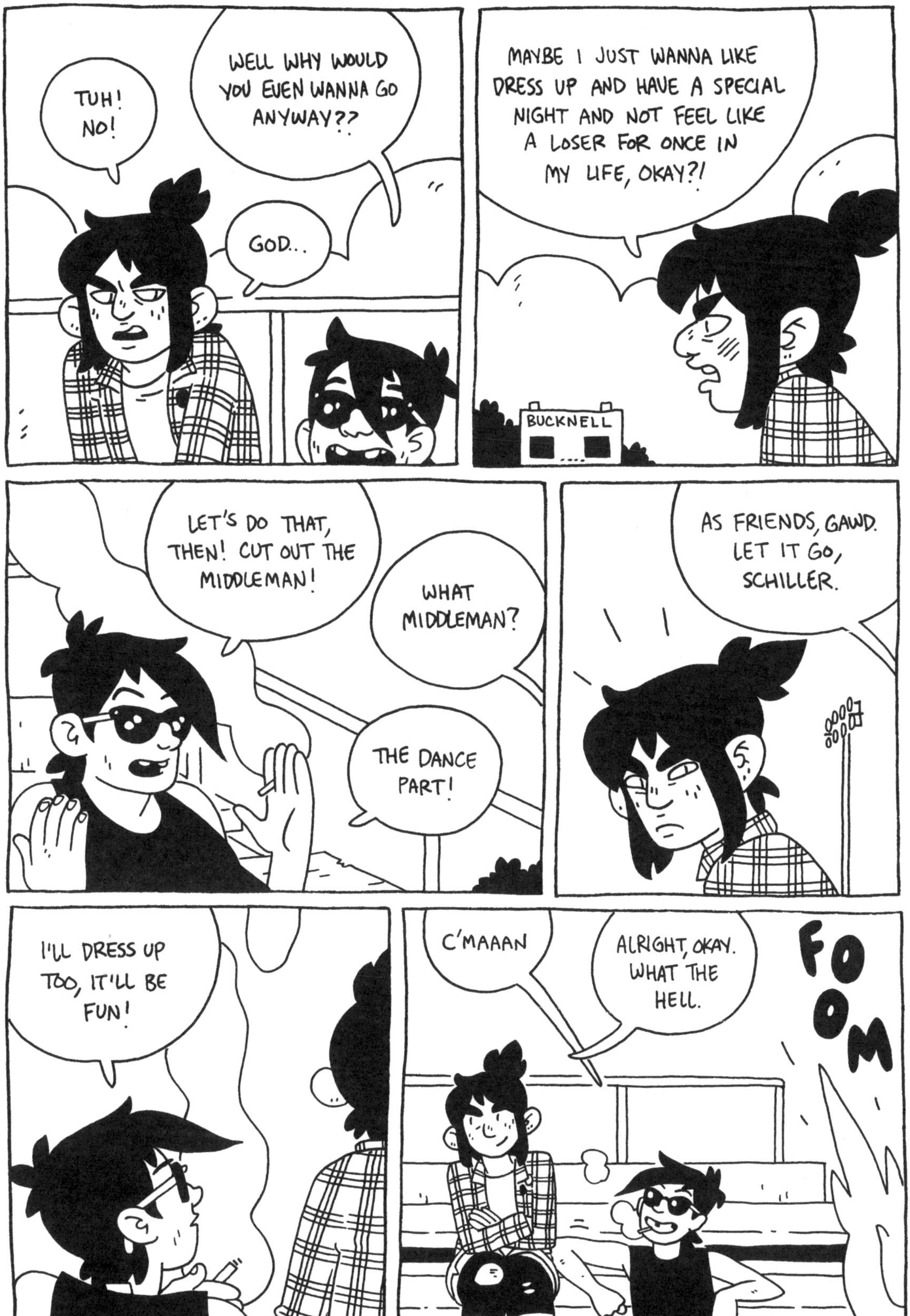
TUH! NO!
WELL WHY WOULD YOU EVEN WANNA GO ANYWAY??
GOD...
MAYBE I JUST WANNA LIKE DRESS UP AND HAVE A SPECIAL NIGHT AND NOT FEEL LIKE A LOSER FOR ONCE IN MY LIFE, OKAY?!
BUCKNELL
LET'S DO THAT, THEN! CUT OUT THE MIDDLEMAN!
WHAT MIDDLEMAN?
THE DANCE PART!
AS FRIENDS, GAWD. LET IT GO, SCHILLER.
I'LL DRESS UP TOO, IT'LL BE FUN!
C'MAAAN
ALRIGHT, OKAY. WHAT THE HELL.
FOOM

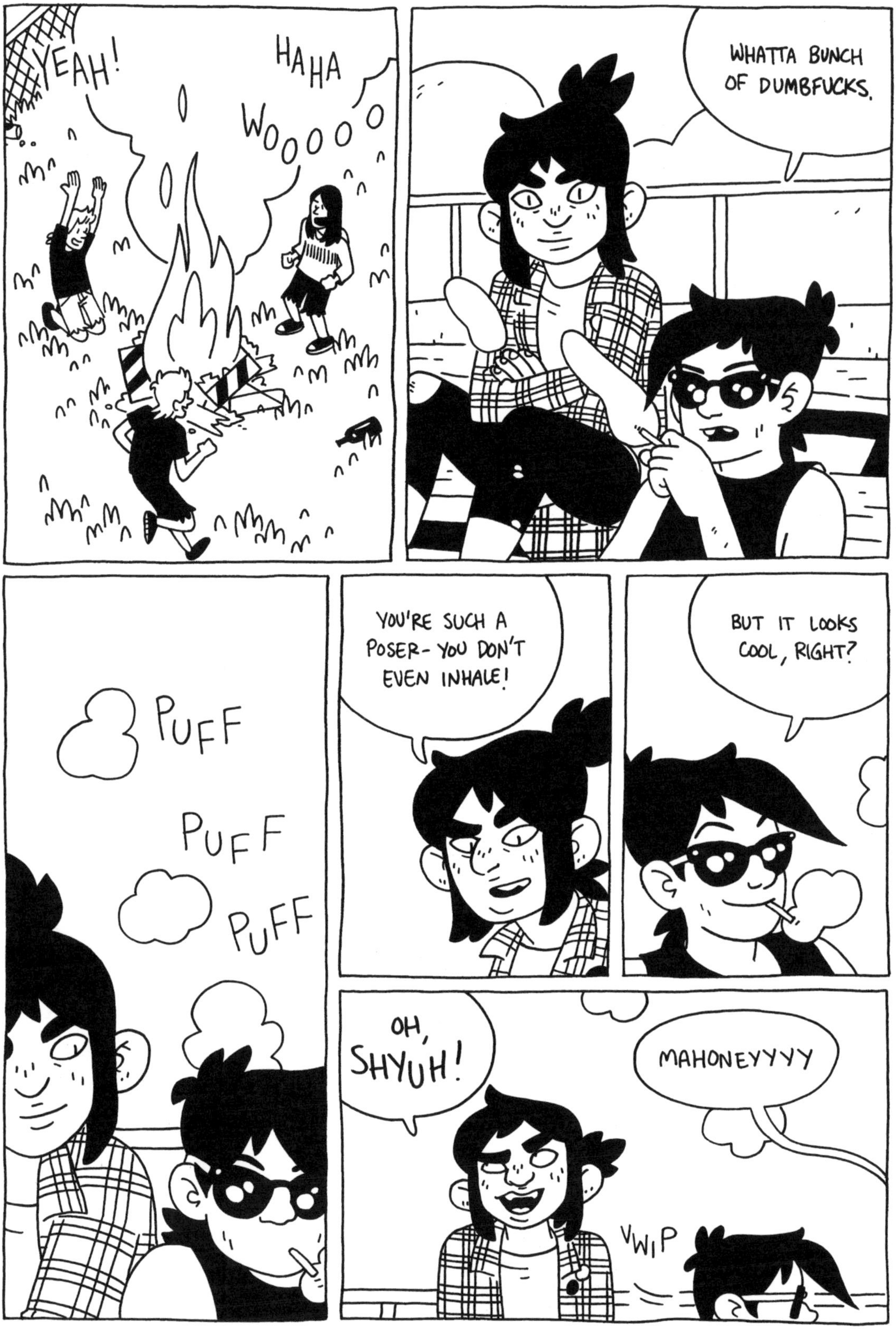
YEAH!
HAHA
WOOOOOO
WHATTA BUNCH OF DUMBFUCKS.
PUFF
PUFF
PUFF
YOU'RE SUCH A POSER- YOU DON'T EVEN INHALE!
BUT IT LOOKS COOL, RIGHT?
OH, SHYUH!
MAHONEYYYY
VWIP

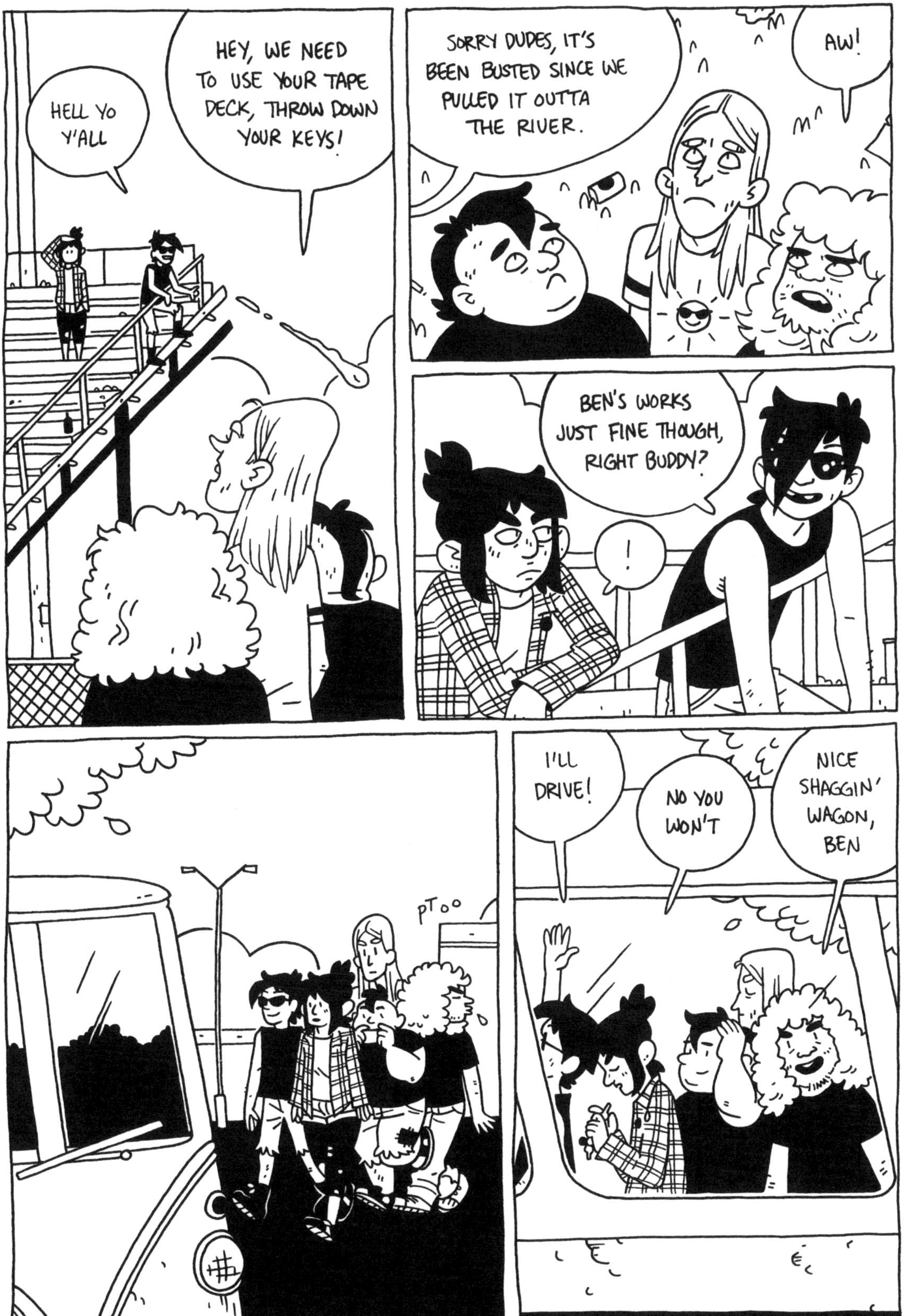
HELL YO Y'ALL
HEY, WE NEED TO USE YOUR TAPE DECK, THROW DOWN YOUR KEYS!
SORRY DUDES, IT'S BEEN BUSTED SINCE WE PULLED IT OUTTA THE RIVER.
AW!
BEN'S WORKS JUST FINE THOUGH, RIGHT BUDDY?
!
pToo
I'LL DRIVE!
NO YOU WON'T
NICE SHAGGIN' WAGON, BEN

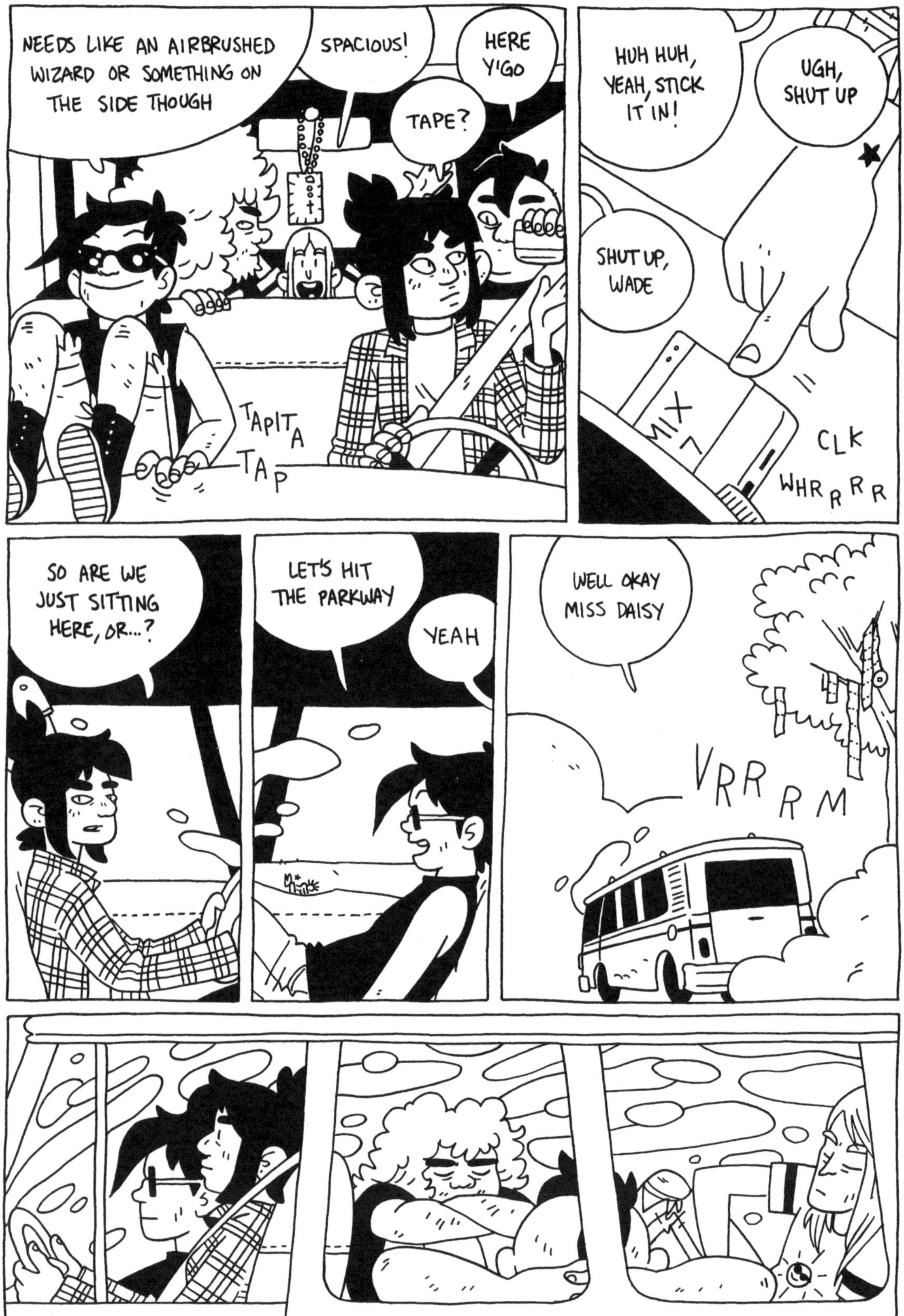
NEEDS LIKE AN AIRBRUSHED WIZARD OR SOMETHING ON THE SIDE THOUGH
SPACIOUS!
HERE Y'GO
TAPE?
TAPITA TAP
HUH HUH, YEAH, STICK IT IN!
UGH, SHUT UP
SHUT UP, WADE
MIX
CLK
WHRRRR
SO ARE WE JUST SITTING HERE, OR...?
LET'S HIT THE PARKWAY
YEAH
WELL OKAY MISS DAISY
VRRRRM

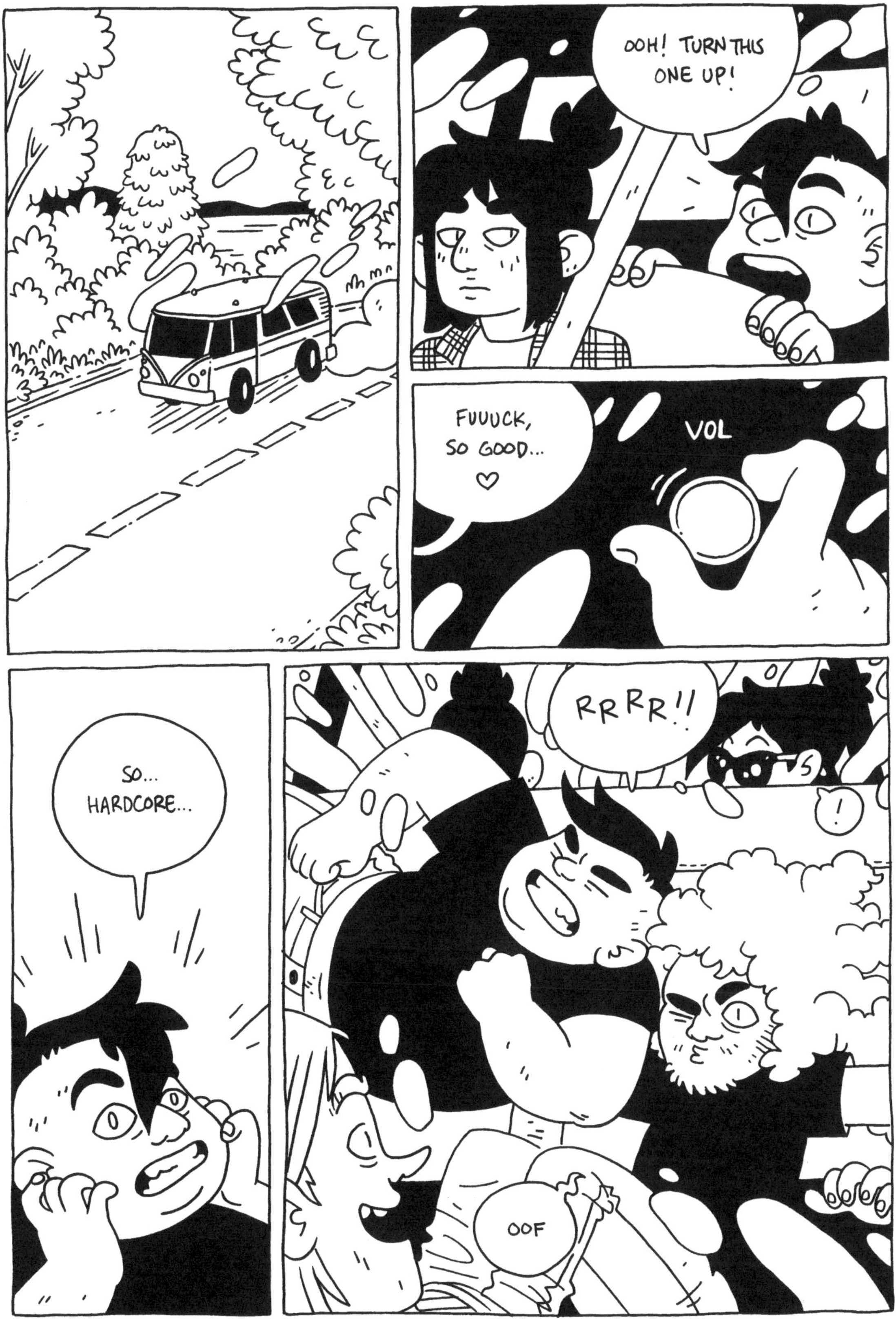
OOH! TURN THIS ONE UP!
FUUUCK, SO GOOD... ♡
VOL
SO... HARDCORE...
RRRR!!
!
OOF

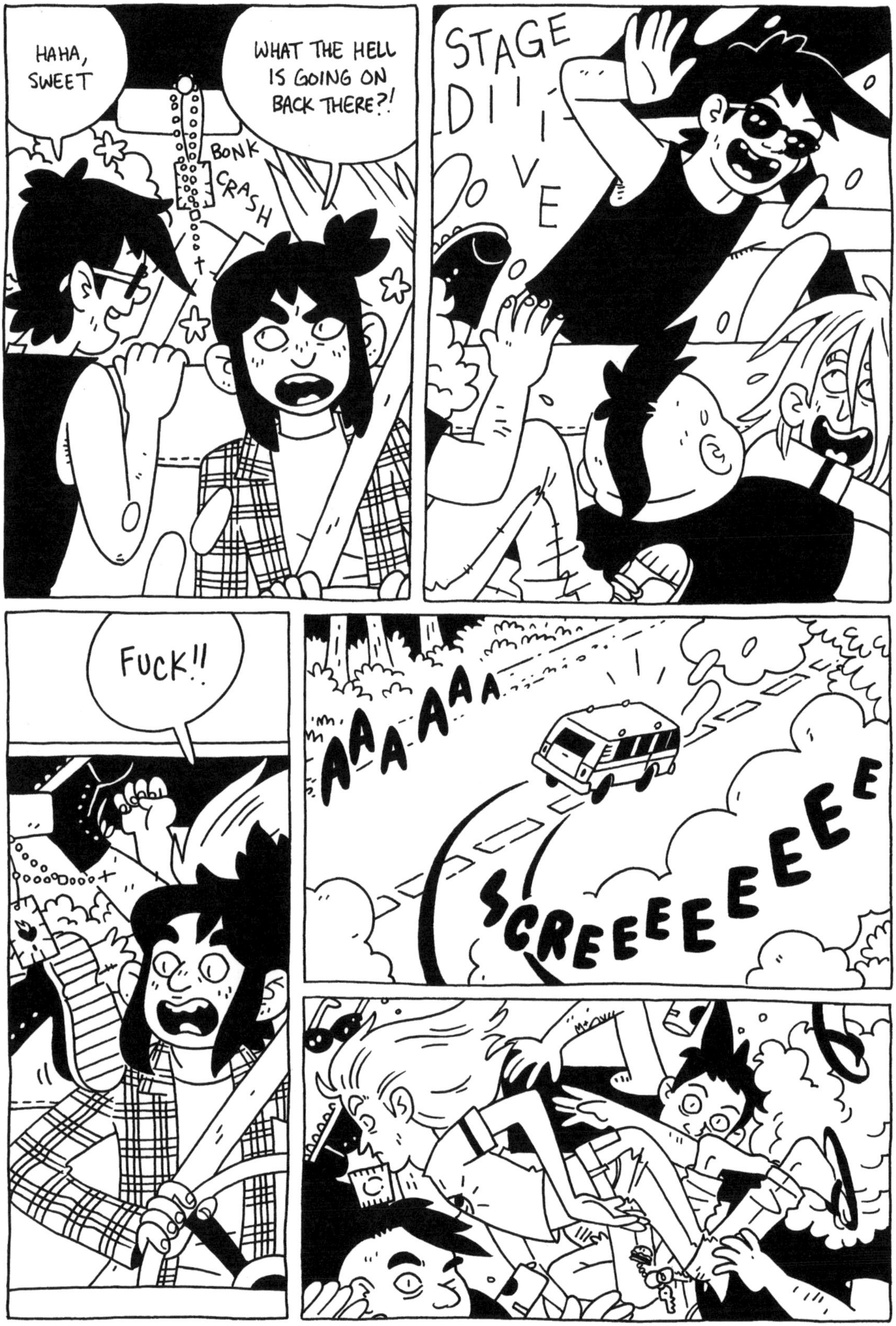
HAHA, SWEET
WHAT THE HELL IS GOING ON BACK THERE?!
BONK
CRASH
STAGE DIIIVE
FUCK!!
AAAAAAA
SCREEEEEEEEE

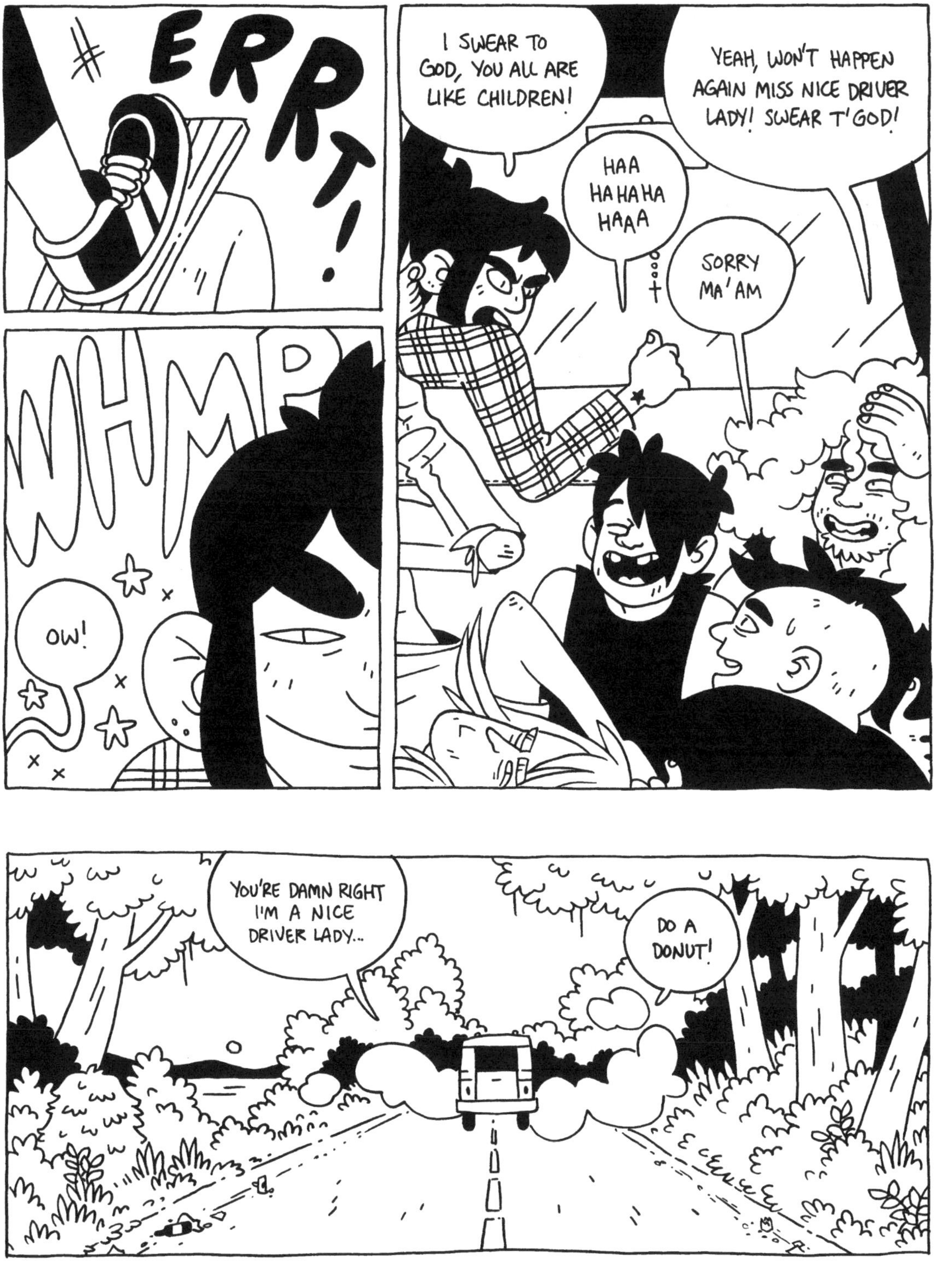
ERRT!
WHMP
OW!
I SWEAR TO GOD, YOU ALL ARE LIKE CHILDREN!
YEAH, WON'T HAPPEN AGAIN MISS NICE DRIVER LADY! SWEAR T'GOD!
HAA HAHAHA HAAA
SORRY MA'AM
YOU'RE DAMN RIGHT I'M A NICE DRIVER LADY...
DO A DONUT!

DOGGIE BREAK !

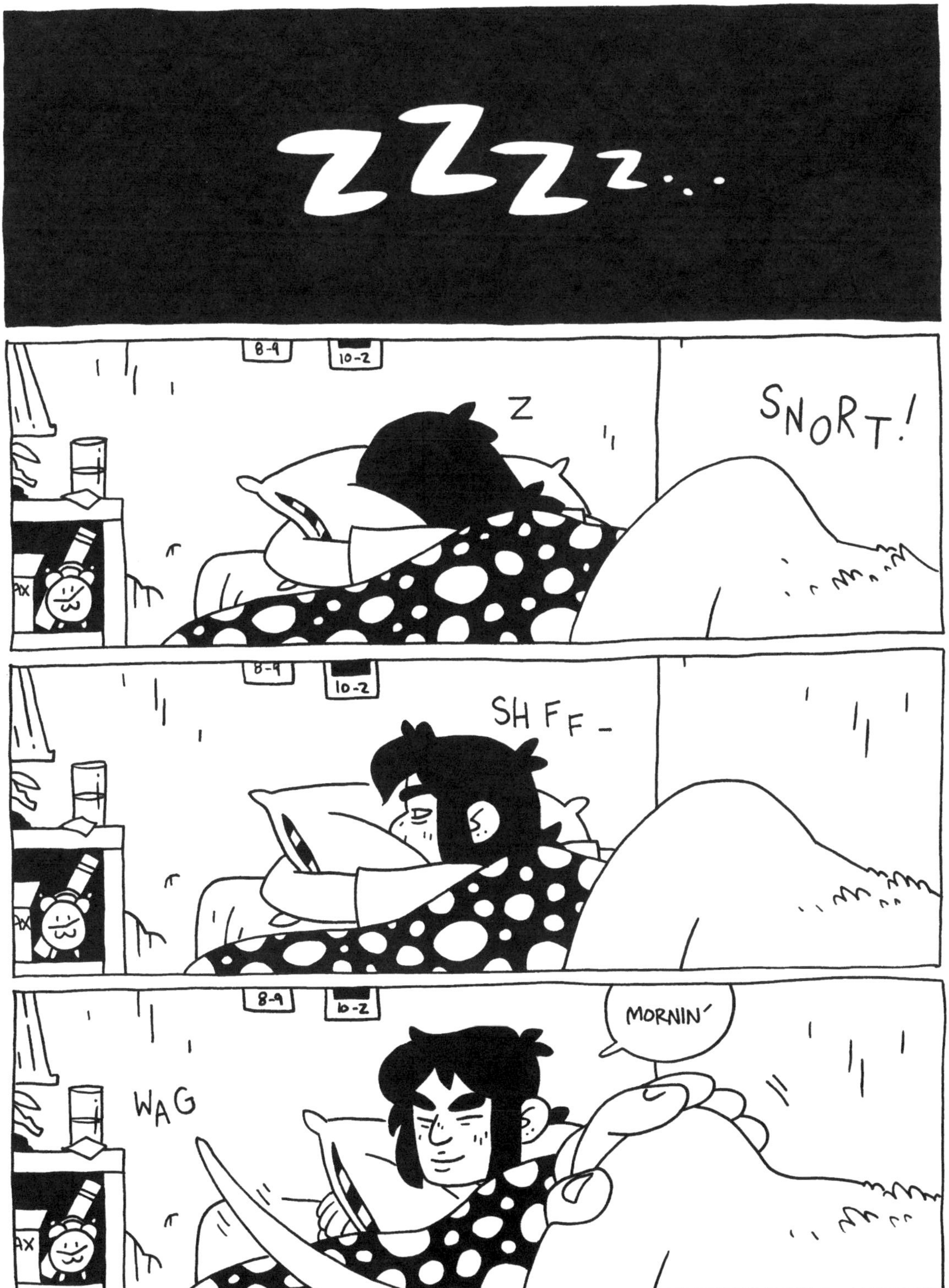
ZZZZ...
Z
SNORT!
SHFF-
WAG
MORNIN'

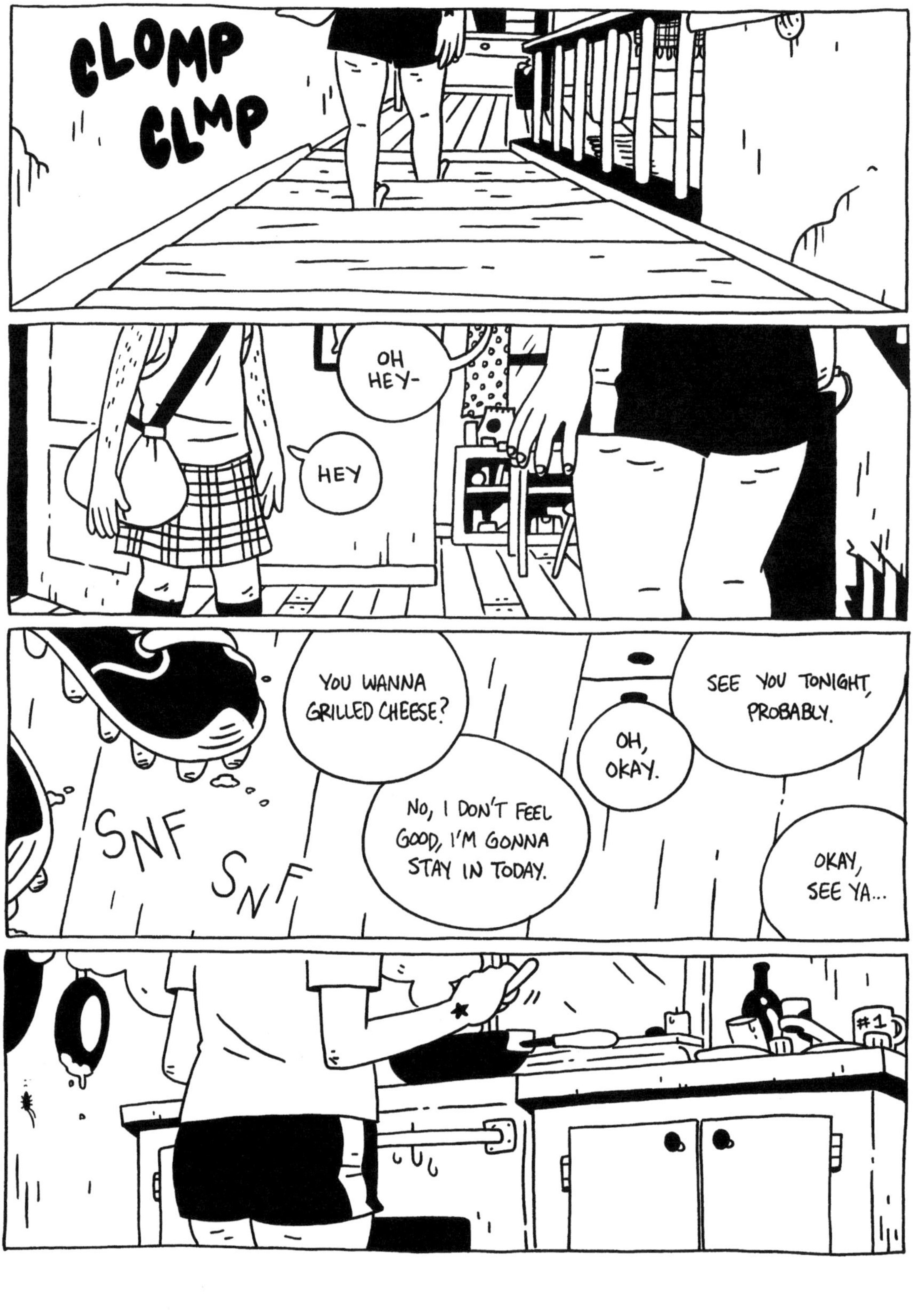
CLOMP
CLMP
OH HEY-
HEY
YOU WANNA GRILLED CHEESE?
NO, I DON'T FEEL GOOD, I'M GONNA STAY IN TODAY.
OH, OKAY.
SEE YOU TONIGHT, PROBABLY.
OKAY, SEE YA...
SNF
SNF
#1

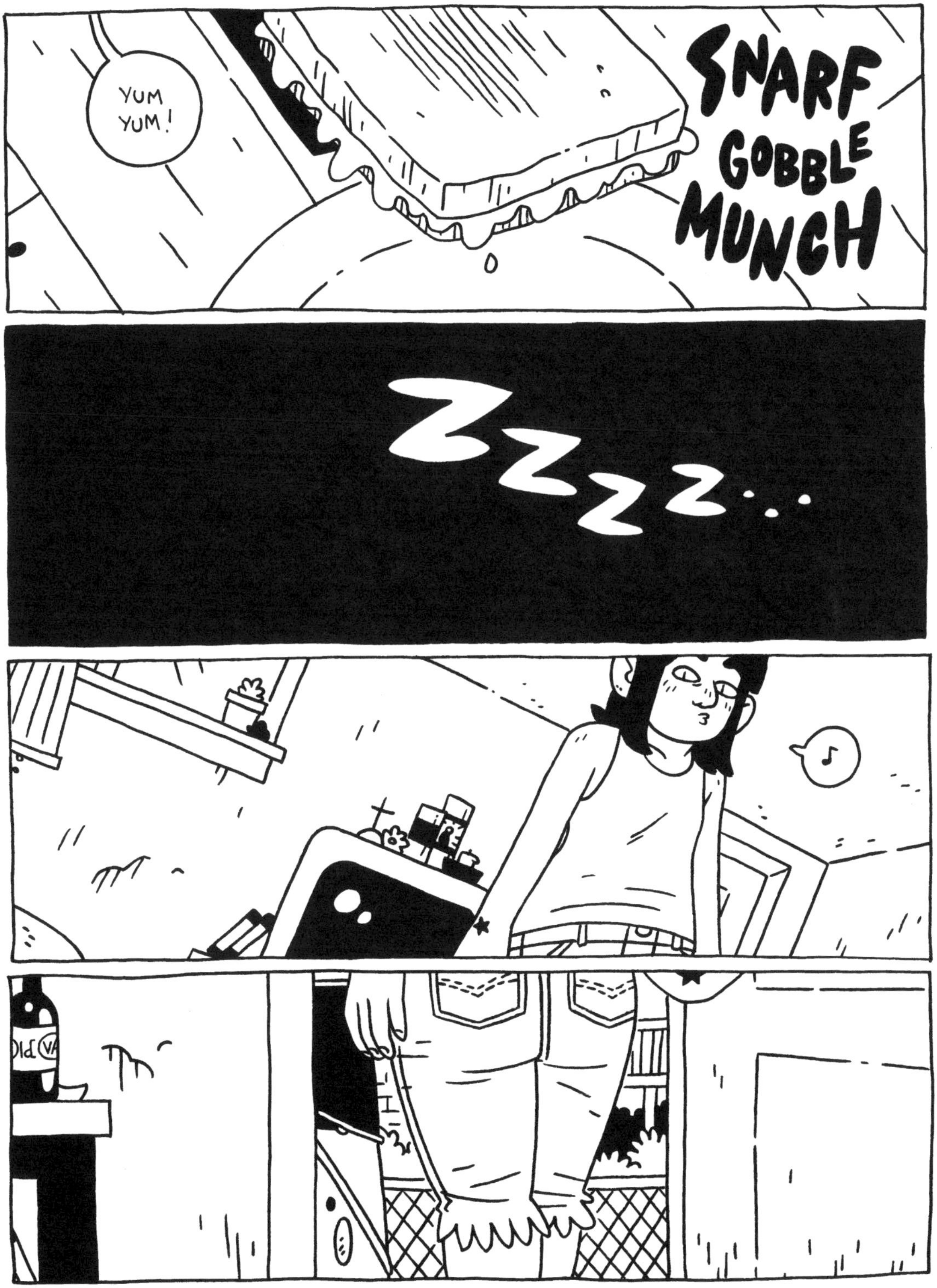
YUM YUM!
SNARF GOBBLE MUNCH
ZZZZ...

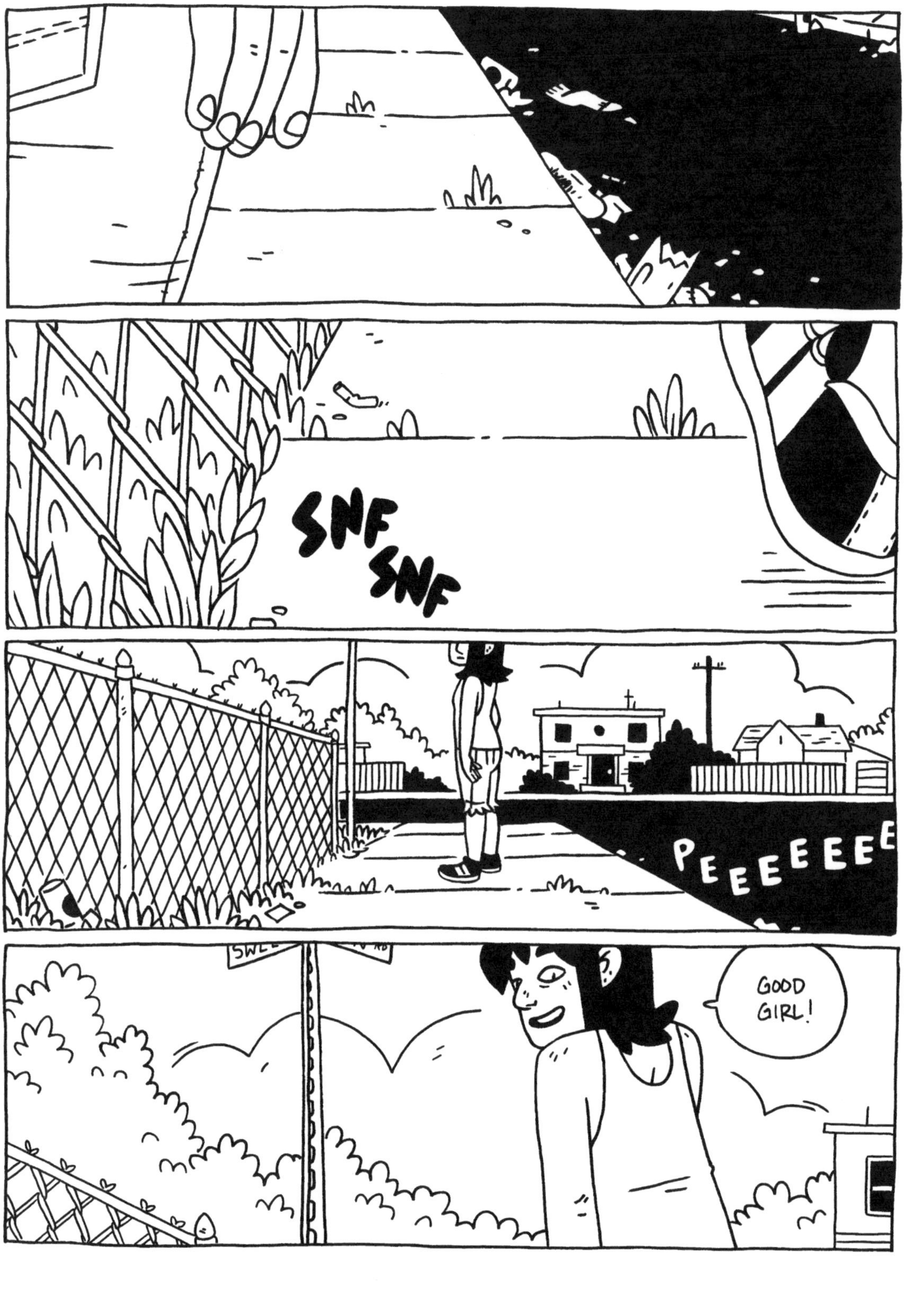
SNF SNF
PEEEEEEE
GOOD GIRL!

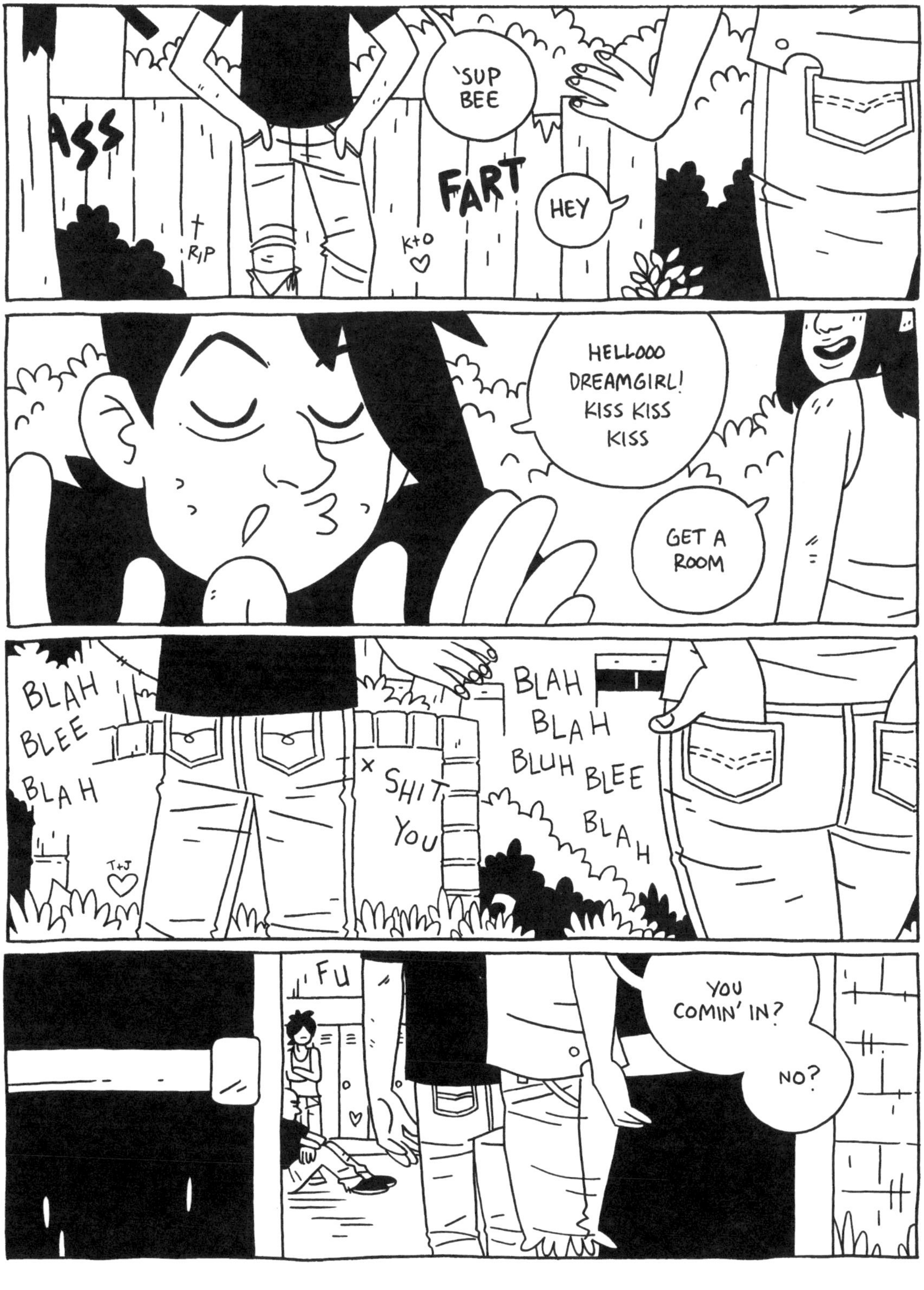
ASS
'SUP BEE
FART
RIP
K+O
HEY
HELLOOO DREAMGIRL! KISS KISS KISS
GET A ROOM
BLAH BLEE BLAH
T+J
SHIT YOU
BLAH BLAH BLUH BLEE BLAH
FU
YOU COMIN' IN?
NO?

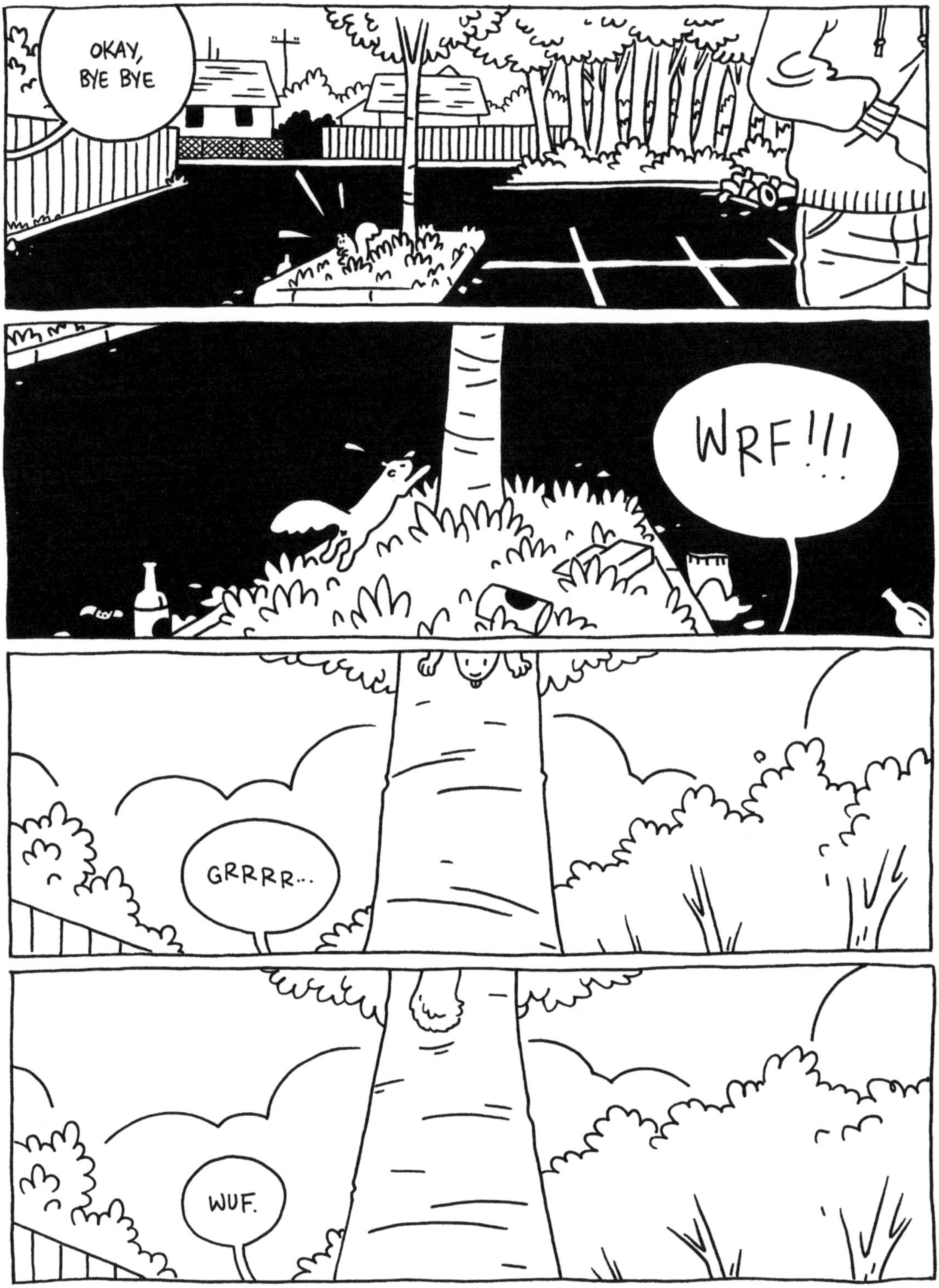
OKAY, BYE BYE
WRF!!!
GRRRR...
WUF.

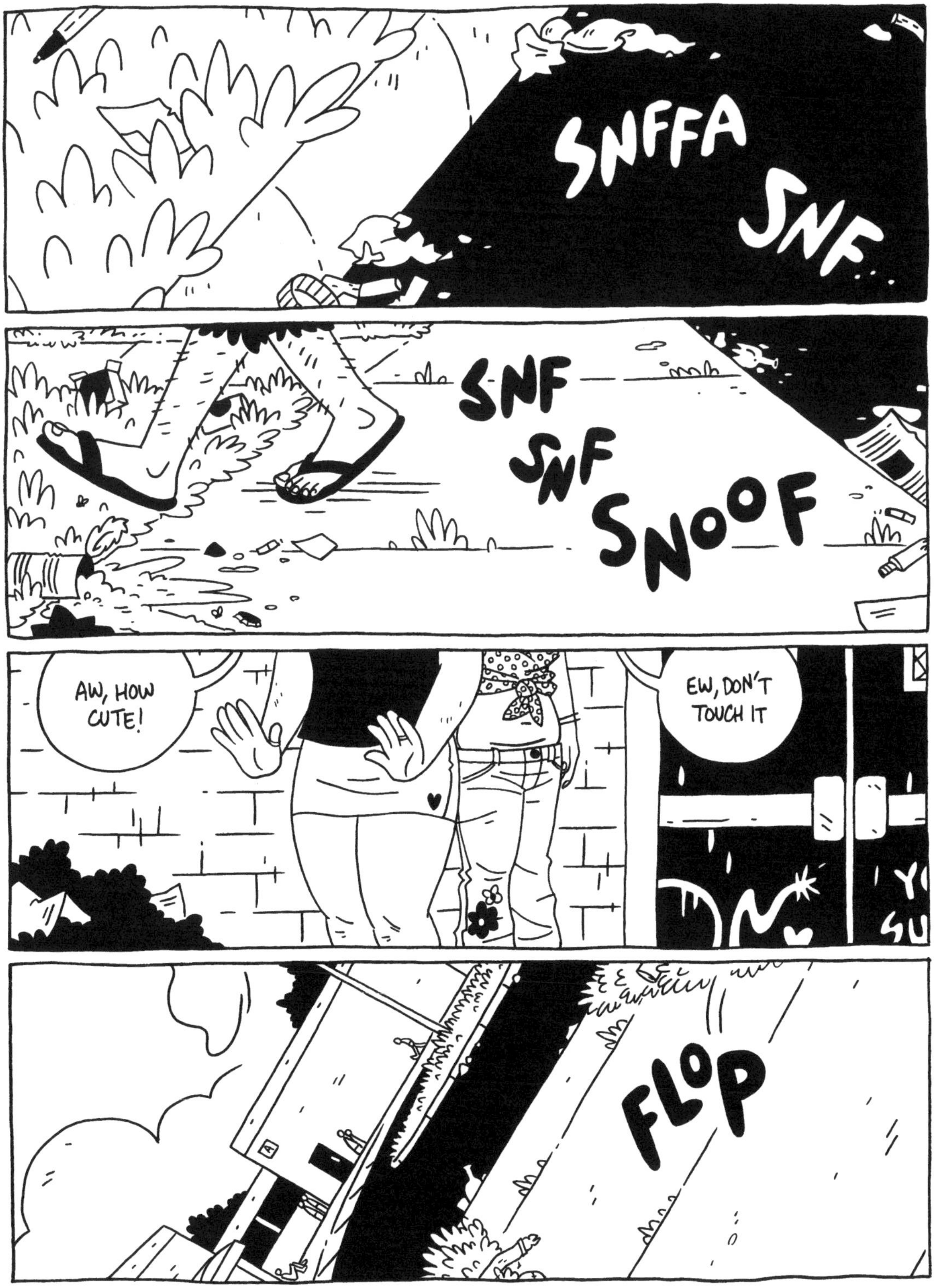
SNFFA
SNF
SNF
SNF
SNOOF
AW, HOW CUTE!
EW, DON'T TOUCH IT
FLOP

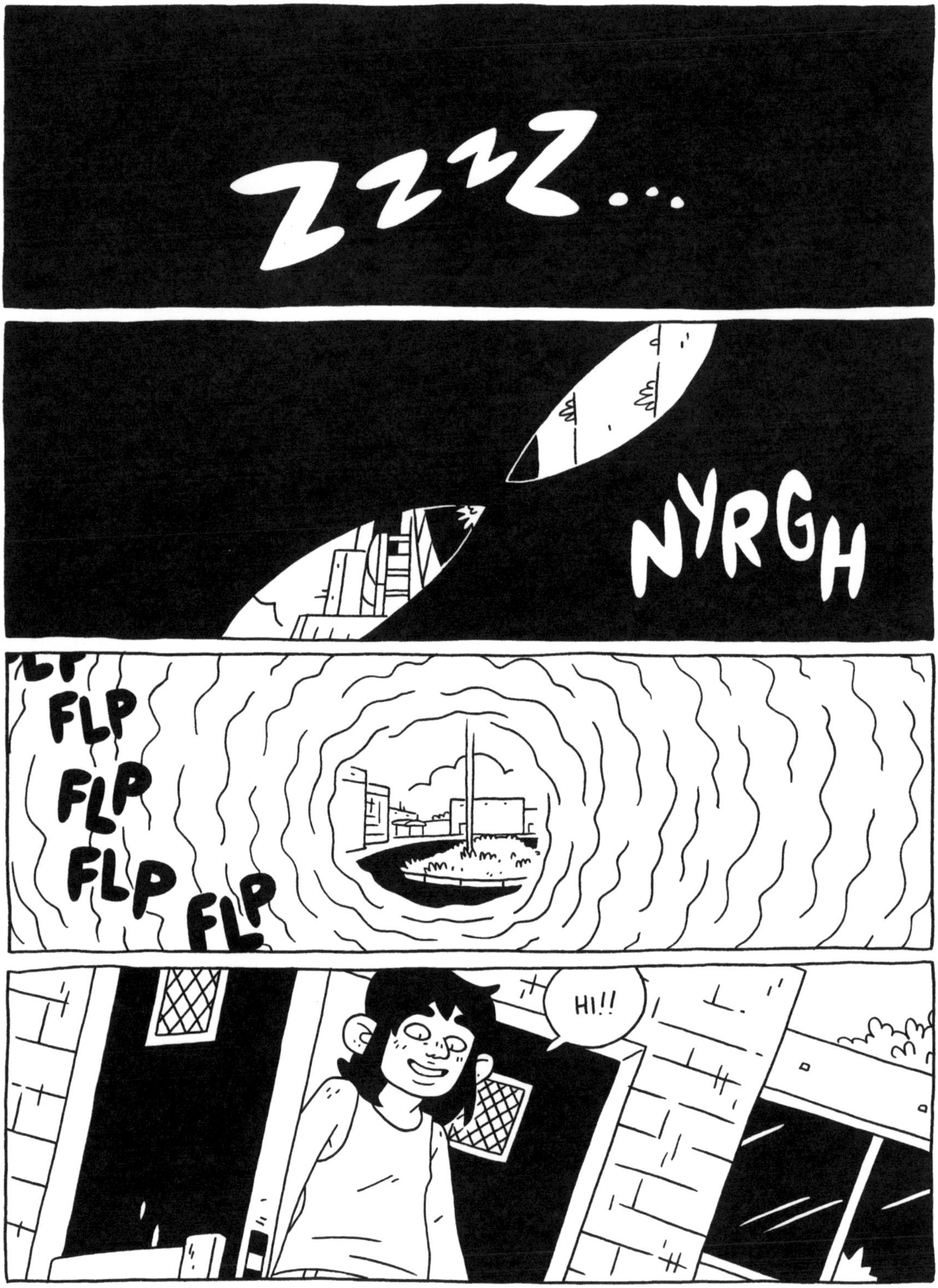
ZZZZ...
NYRGH
FLP
FLP
FLP
FLP
HI!!

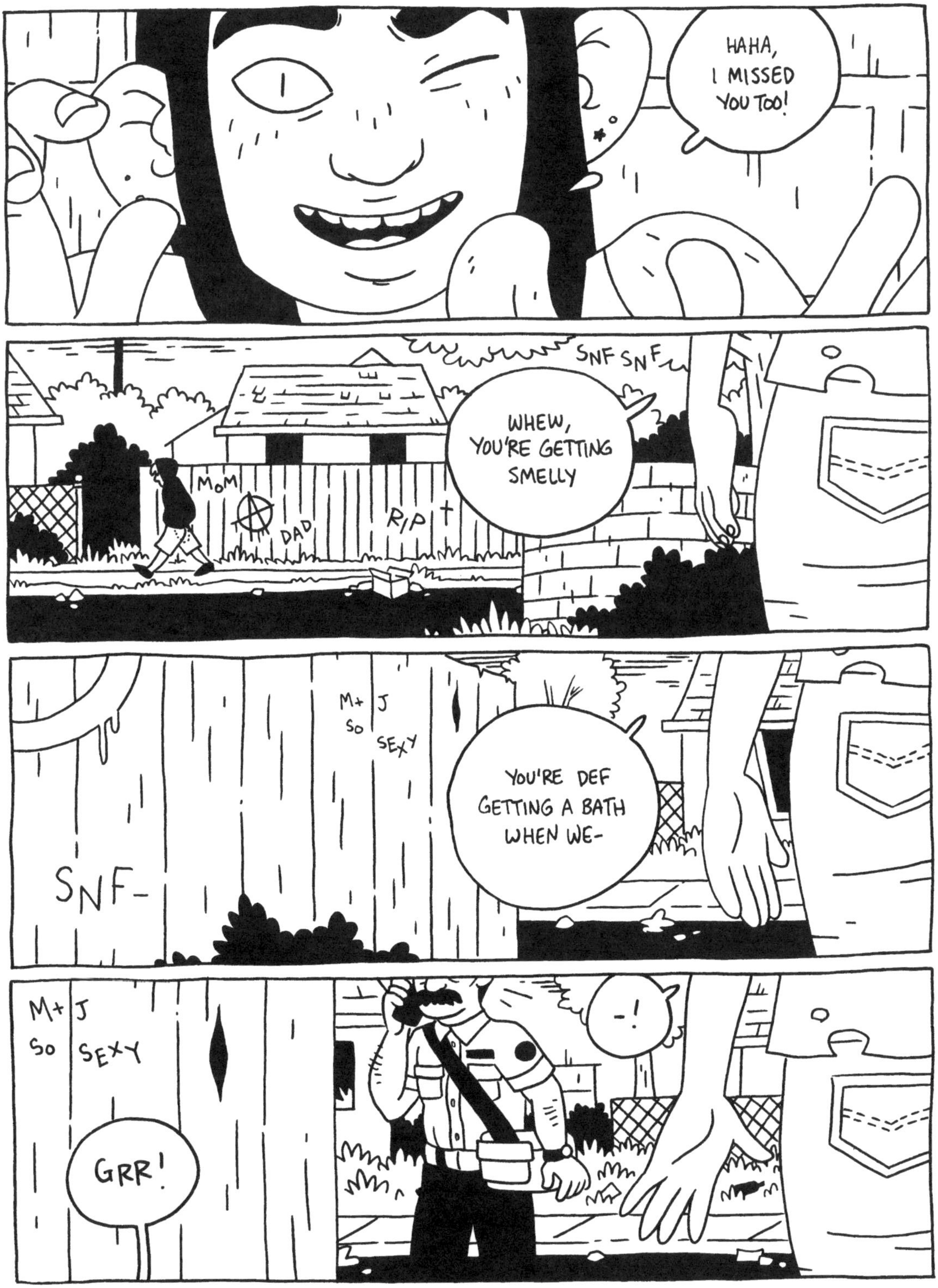
HAHA, I MISSED YOU TOO!
SNF SNF
WHEW, YOU'RE GETTING SMELLY
MOM
DAD
RIP
M+J SO SEXY
YOU'RE DEF GETTING A BATH WHEN WE-
SNF-
M+J SO SEXY
GRR!

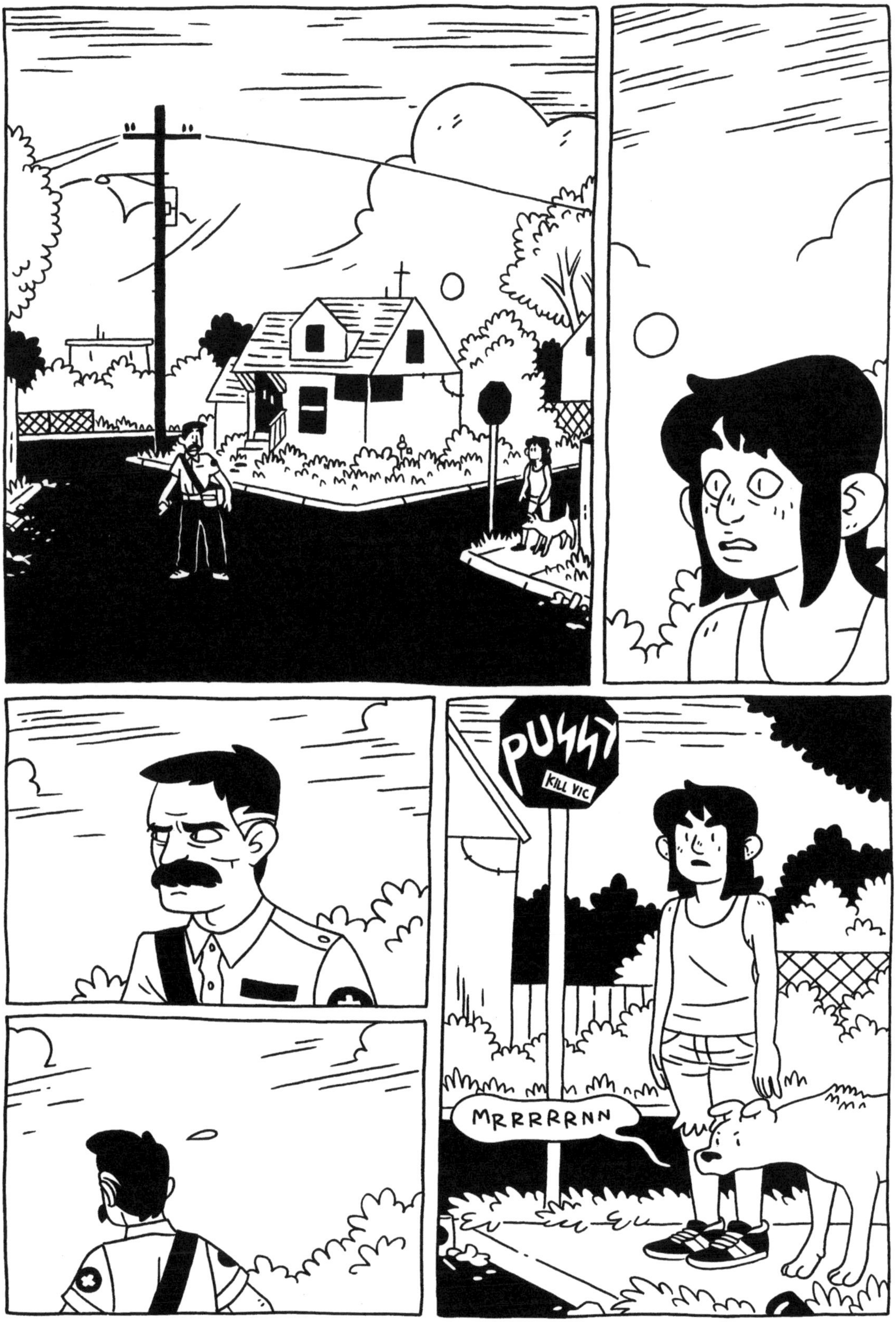
PUSSY
KILL VIC
MRRRRRNN

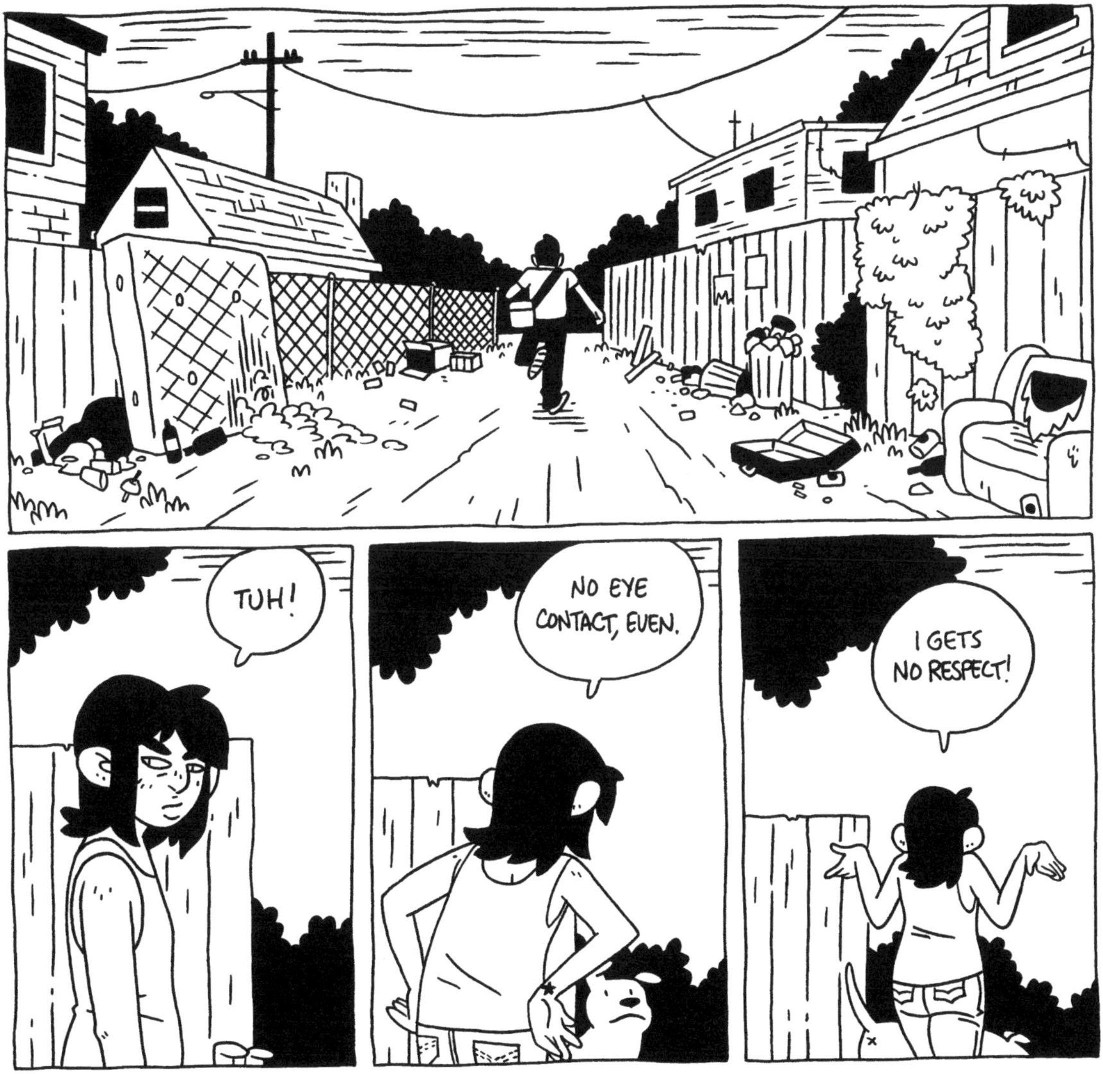
TUH!
NO EYE CONTACT, EVEN.
I GETS NO RESPECT!

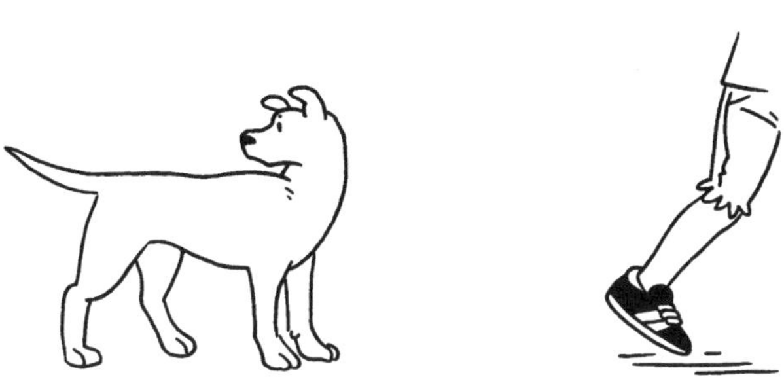

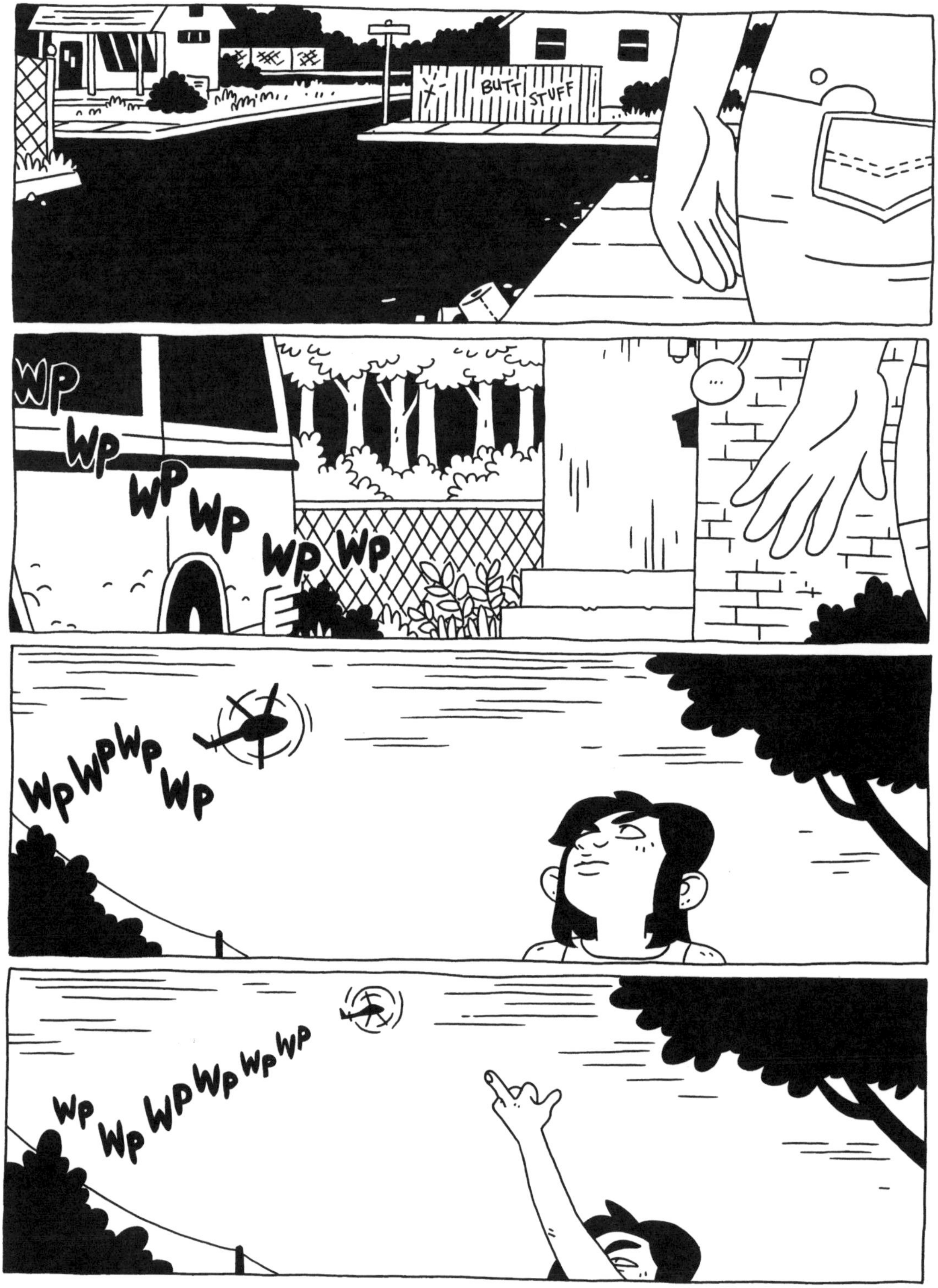

BUTT STUFF
WP WP WP WP WP WP
Wp WP Wp Wp
Wp Wp WP Wp Wp WP

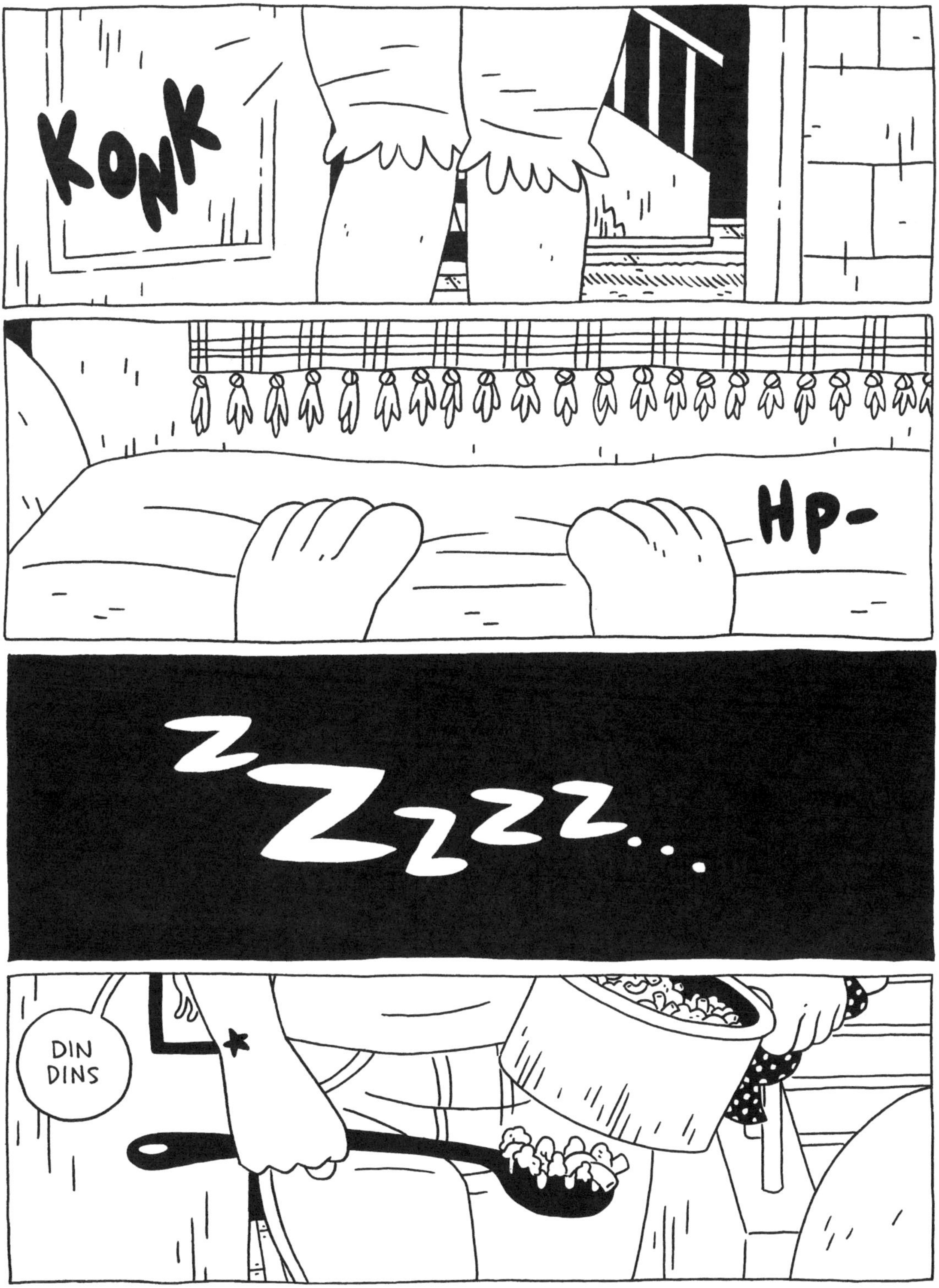
KONK
HP-
ZZZZZ...
DIN DINS

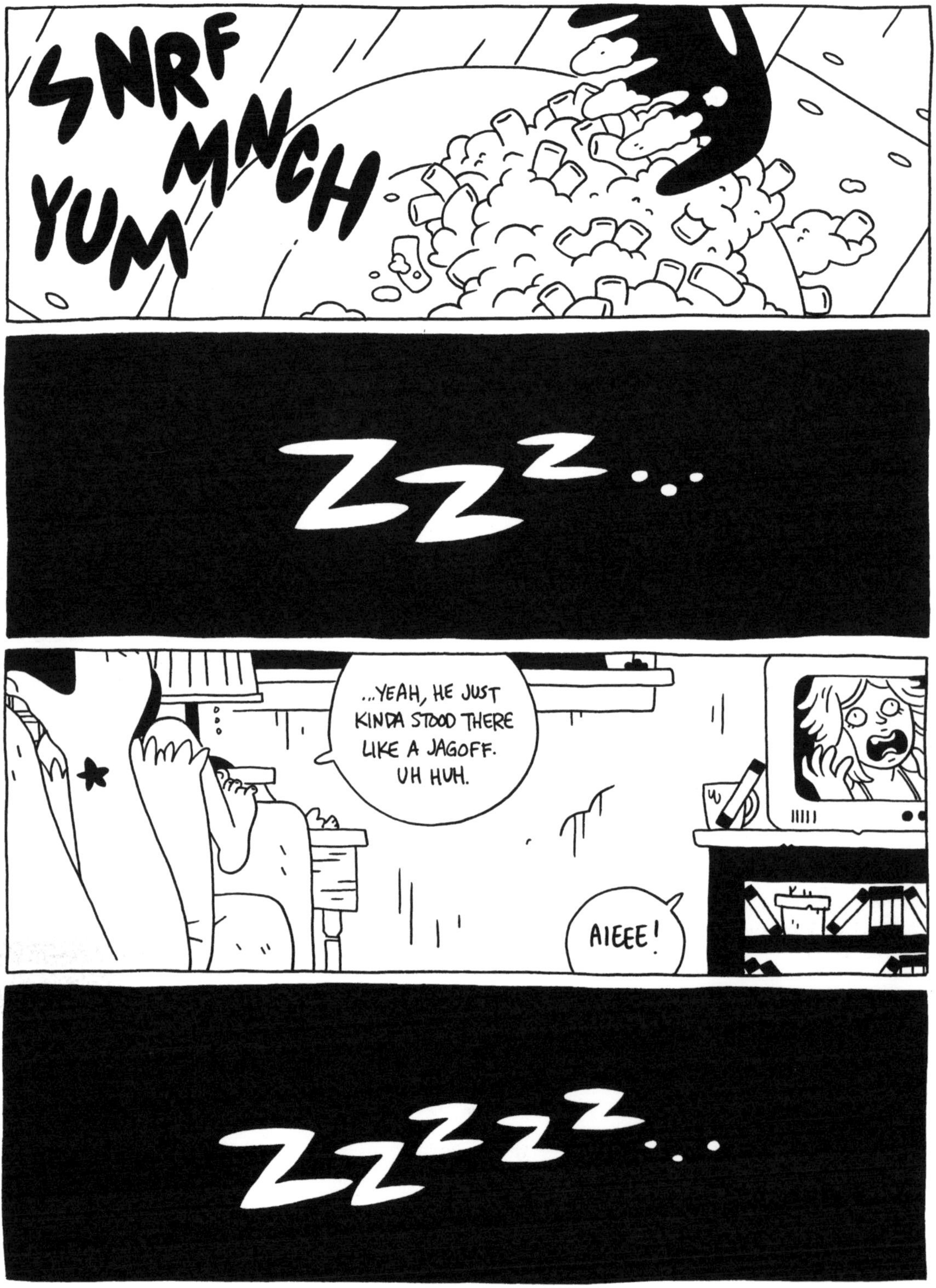
SNRF
YUM MNCH
ZZZ...
...YEAH, HE JUST KINDA STOOD THERE LIKE A JAGOFF. UH HUH.
AIEEE!
ZZZZZZ...

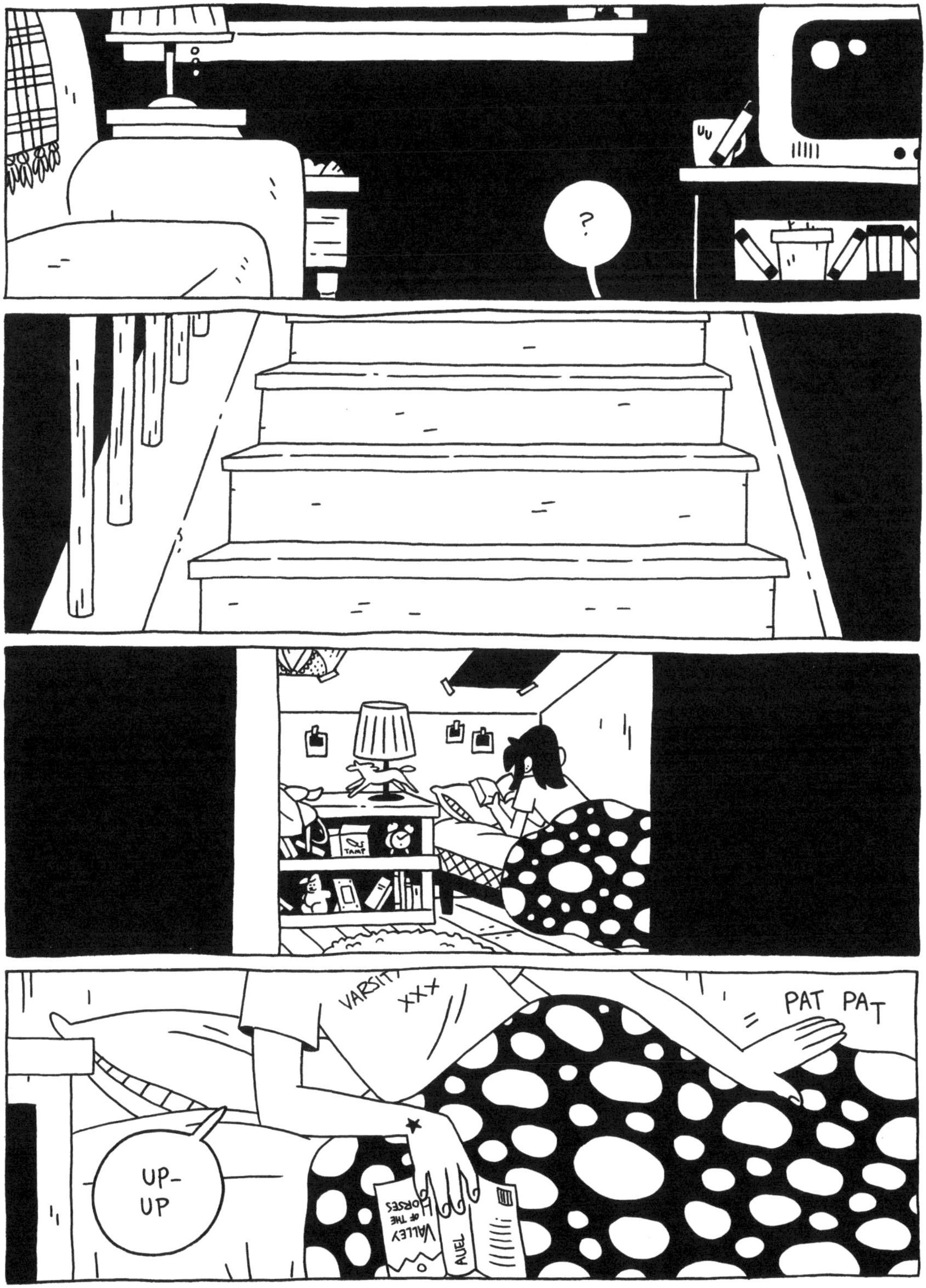
?
VARSITY
XXX
PAT PAT
UP-
UP
VALLEY OF THE HORSES
AUEL

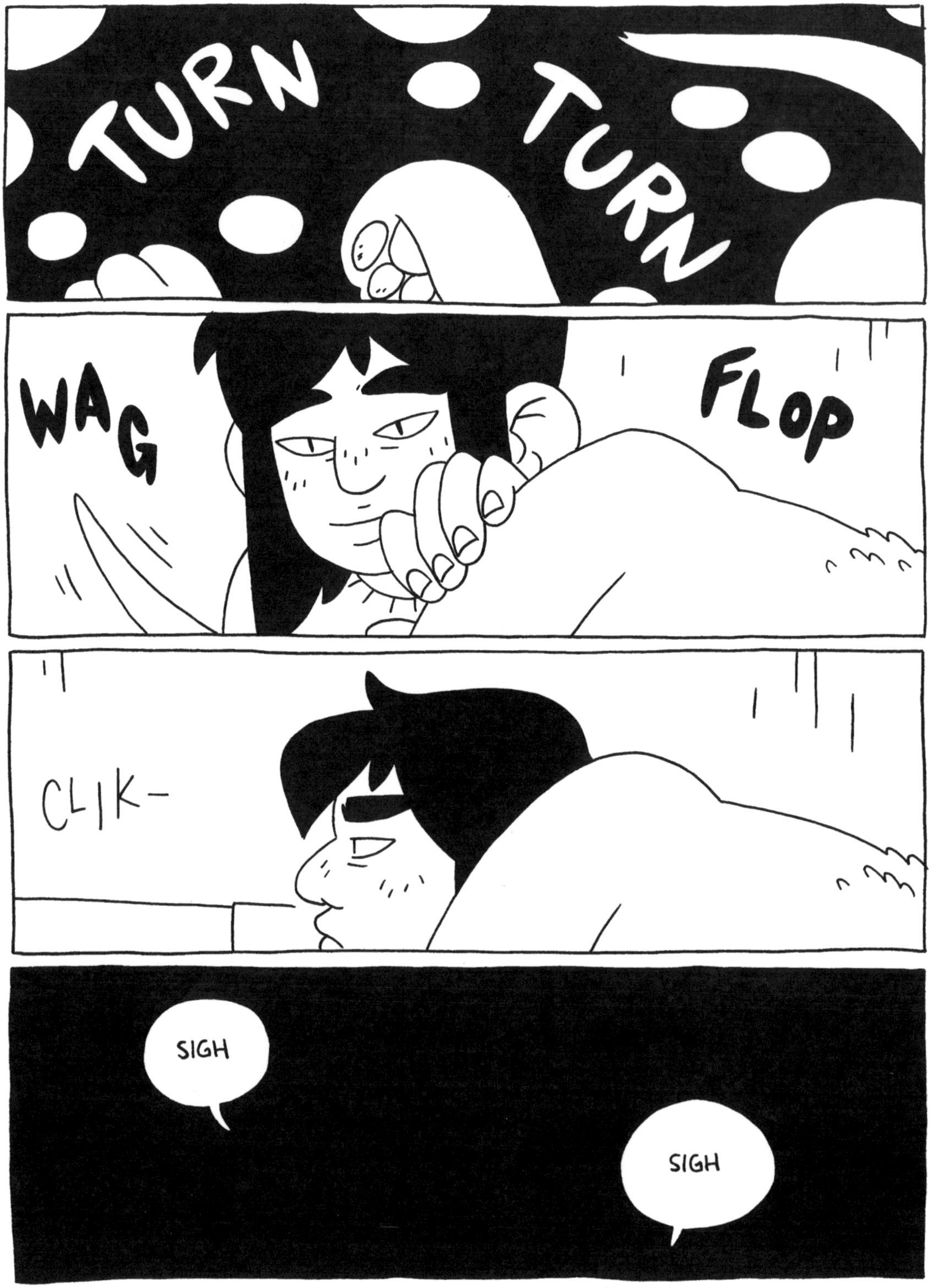
TURN
TURN
WAG
FLOP
CLIK-
SIGH
SIGH

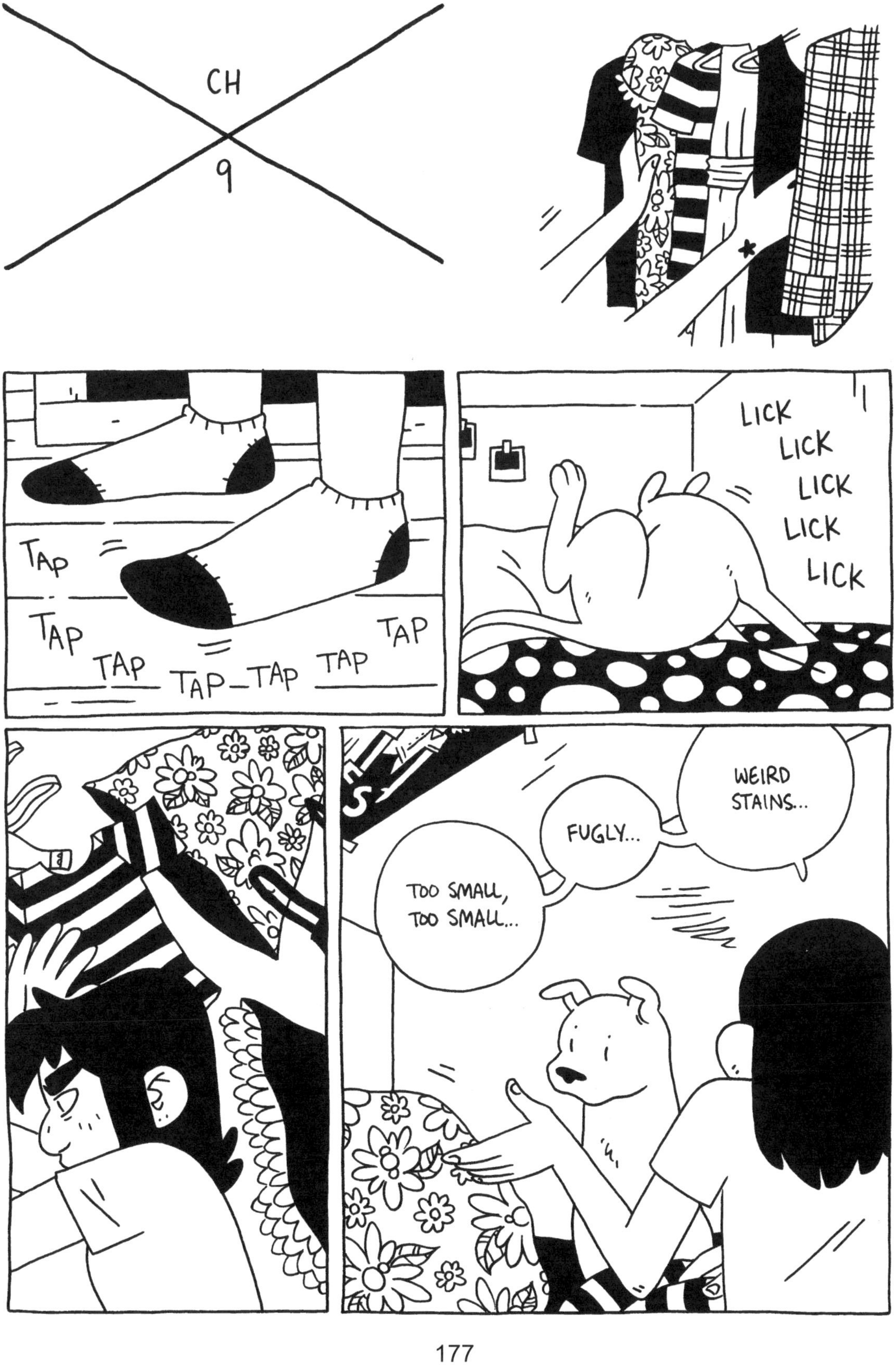
CH
9
TAP
TAP
TAP
TAP
TAP
TAP
TAP
LICK
LICK
LICK
LICK
LICK
TOO SMALL, TOO SMALL...
FUGLY...
WEIRD STAINS...

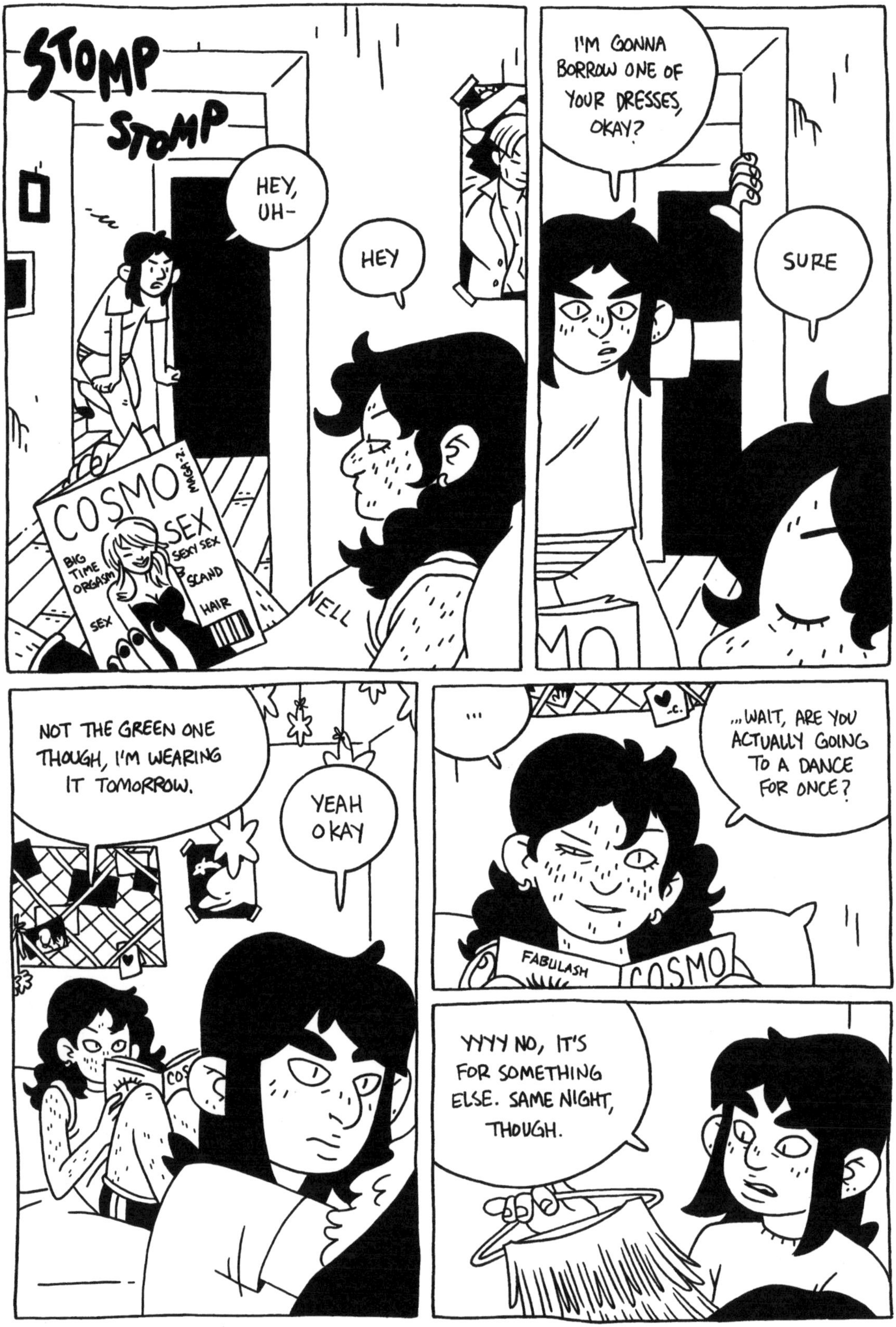
STOMP
STOMP
HEY, UH-
HEY
COSMO
MAGA-Z.
SEX
BIG TIME ORGASM
SEXY SEX
SCAND
HAIR
SEX
NELL
I'M GONNA BORROW ONE OF YOUR DRESSES, OKAY?
SURE
NOT THE GREEN ONE THOUGH, I'M WEARING IT TOMORROW.
YEAH OKAY
...
...WAIT, ARE YOU ACTUALLY GOING TO A DANCE FOR ONCE?
FABULASH
COSMO
YYYY NO, IT'S FOR SOMETHING ELSE. SAME NIGHT, THOUGH.

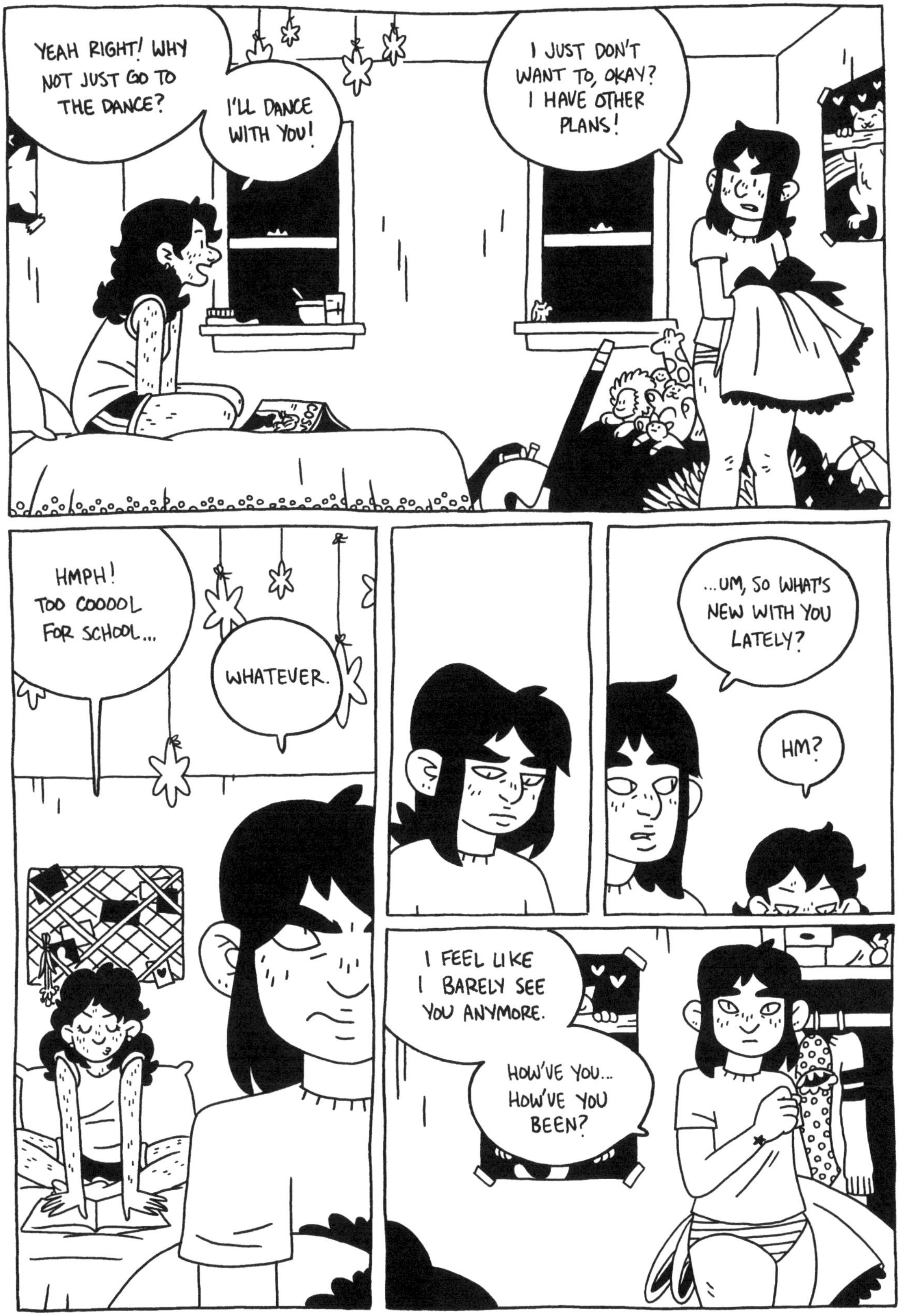
YEAH RIGHT! WHY NOT JUST GO TO THE DANCE?
I'LL DANCE WITH YOU!
I JUST DON'T WANT TO, OKAY? I HAVE OTHER PLANS!
HMPH! TOO COOOOL FOR SCHOOL...
WHATEVER.
...UM, SO WHAT'S NEW WITH YOU LATELY?
HM?
I FEEL LIKE I BARELY SEE YOU ANYMORE.
HOW'VE YOU... HOW'VE YOU BEEN?

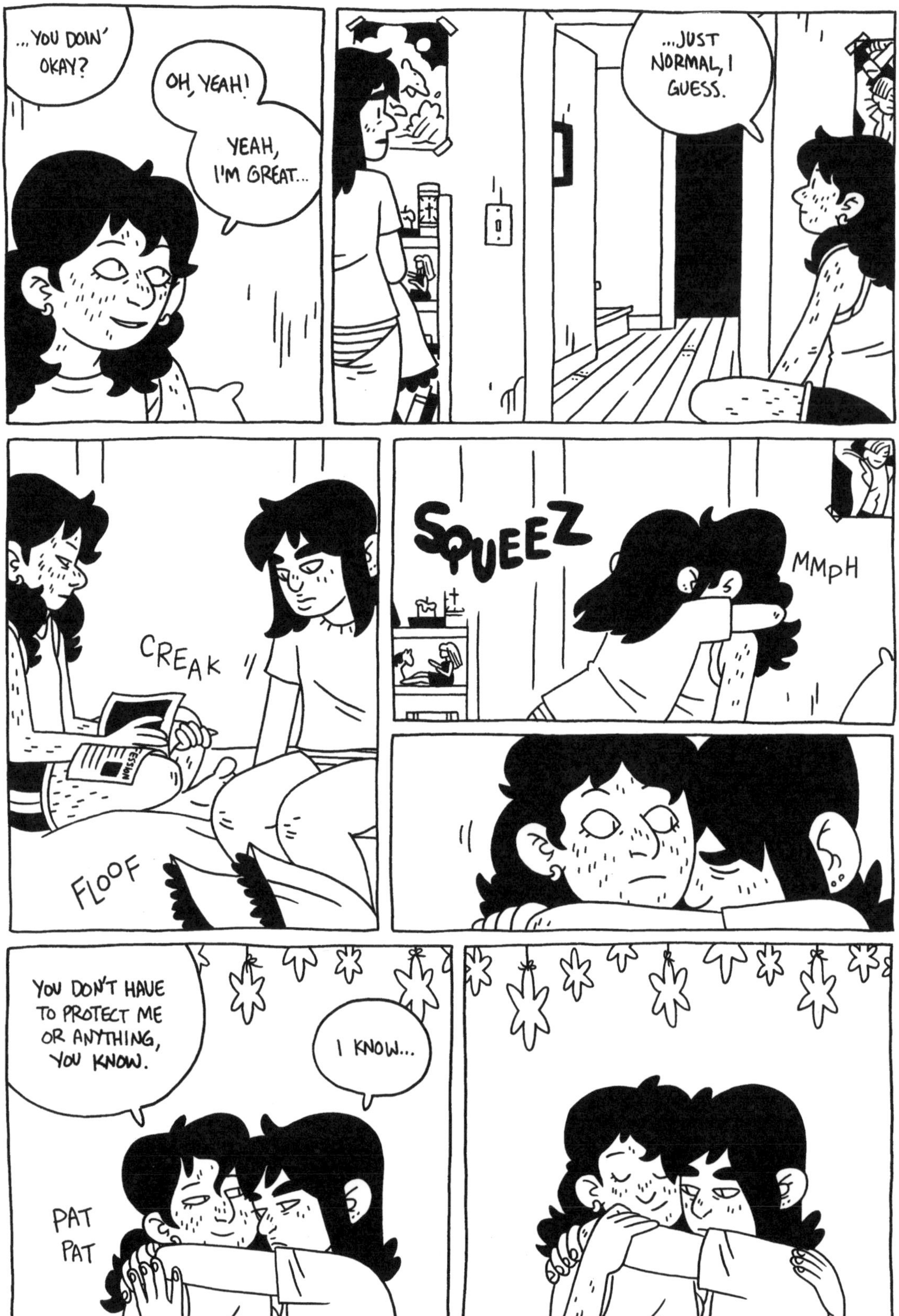
...YOU DOIN' OKAY?
OH, YEAH!
YEAH, I'M GREAT...
...JUST NORMAL, I GUESS.
CREAK
FLOOF
SQUEEZ
MMPH
YOU DON'T HAVE TO PROTECT ME OR ANYTHING, YOU KNOW.
I KNOW...
PAT PAT

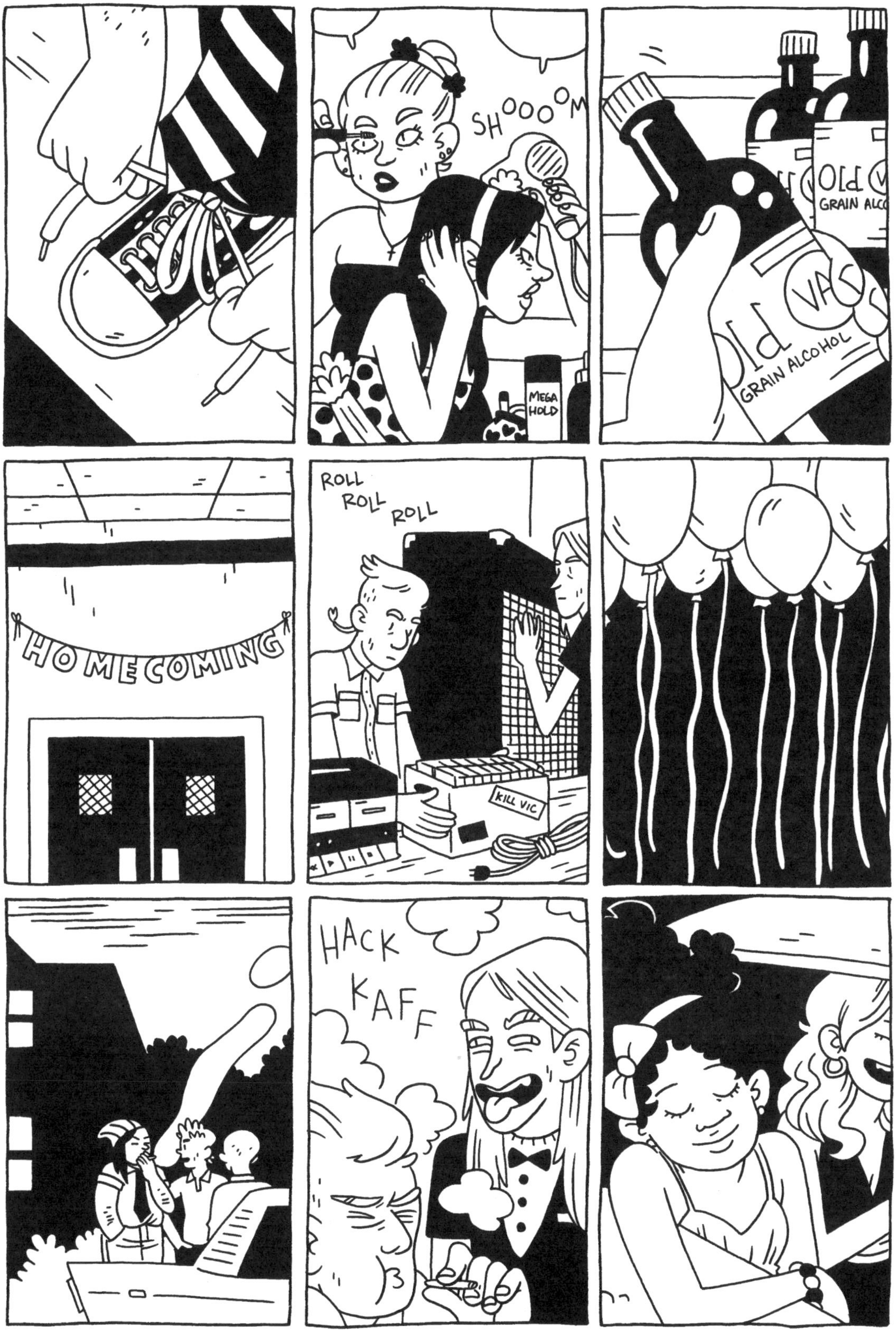
SHOOOOM
MEGA HOLD
Old VAC GRAIN ALCOHOL
HOMECOMING
ROLL ROLL ROLL
KILL VIC
HACK KAFF

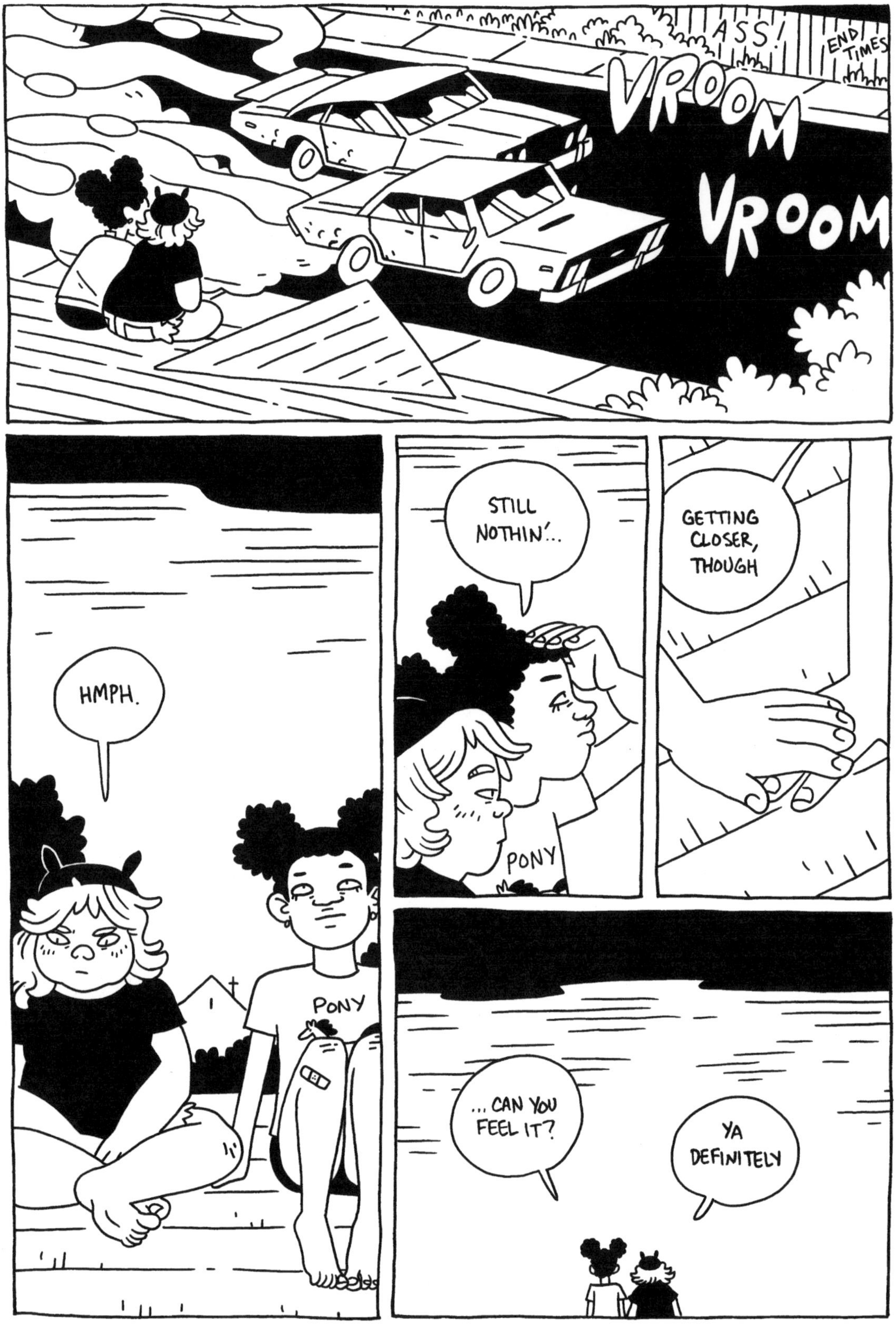
ASS!
END TIMES
VROOM
VROOM
HMPH.
STILL NOTHIN'...
PONY
GETTING CLOSER, THOUGH
PONY
... CAN YOU FEEL IT?
YA DEFINITELY

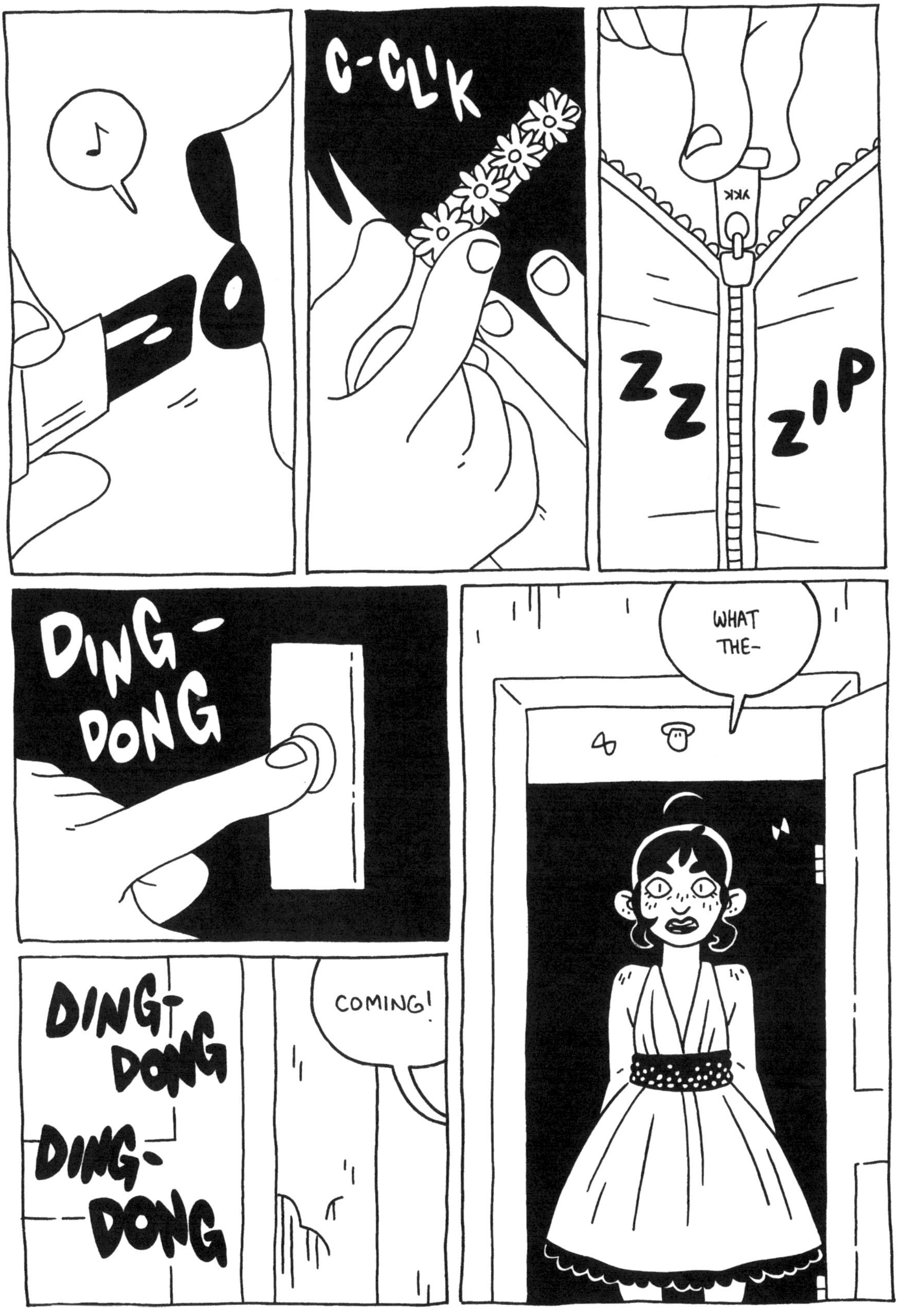
C-CLIK
ZZ ZIP
DING-DONG
DING-DONG
DING-DONG
COMING!
WHAT THE-

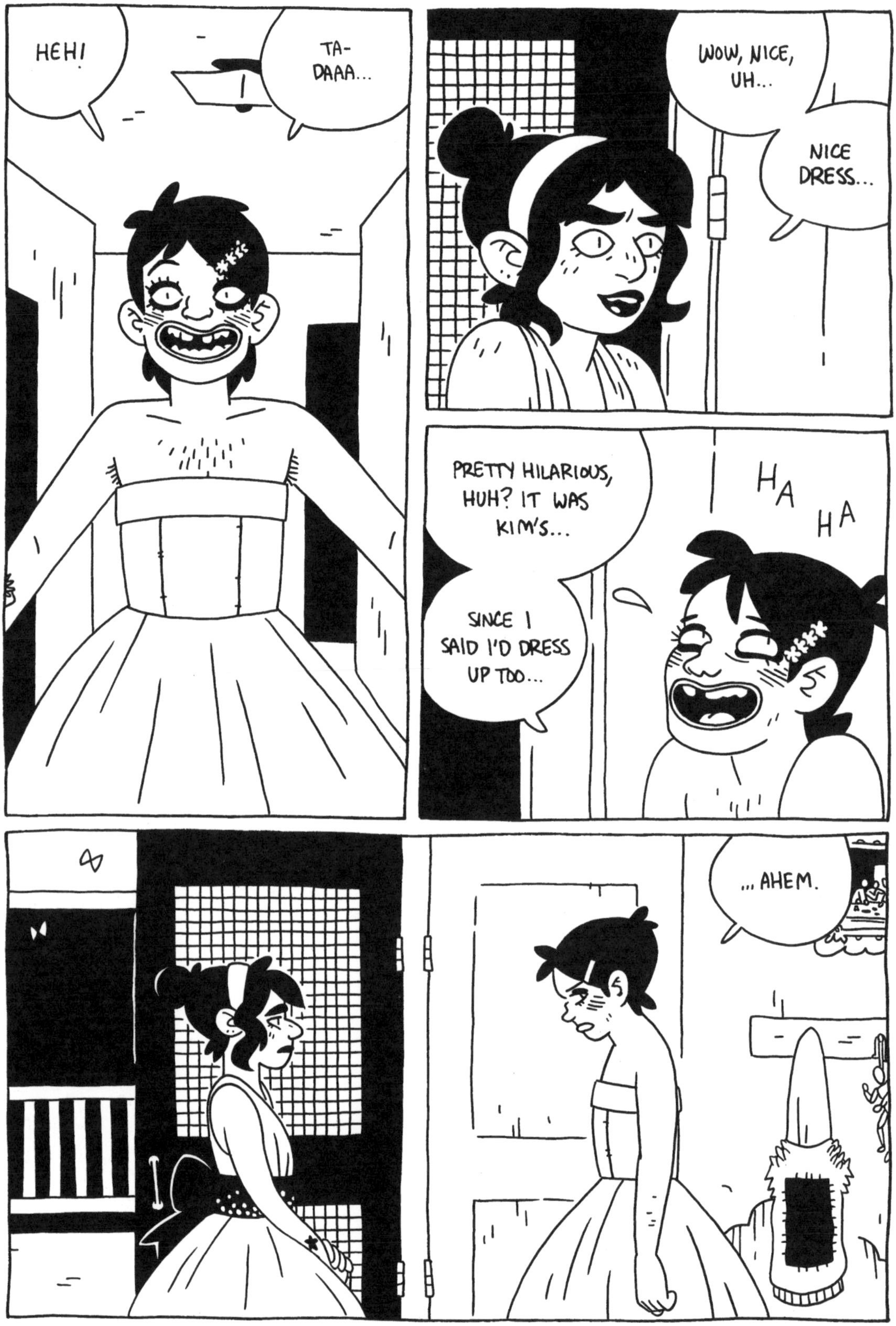
HEH!
TA-DAAA...
WOW, NICE, UH...
NICE DRESS...
PRETTY HILARIOUS, HUH? IT WAS KIM'S...
SINCE I SAID I'D DRESS UP TOO...
HA HA HA
...AHEM.

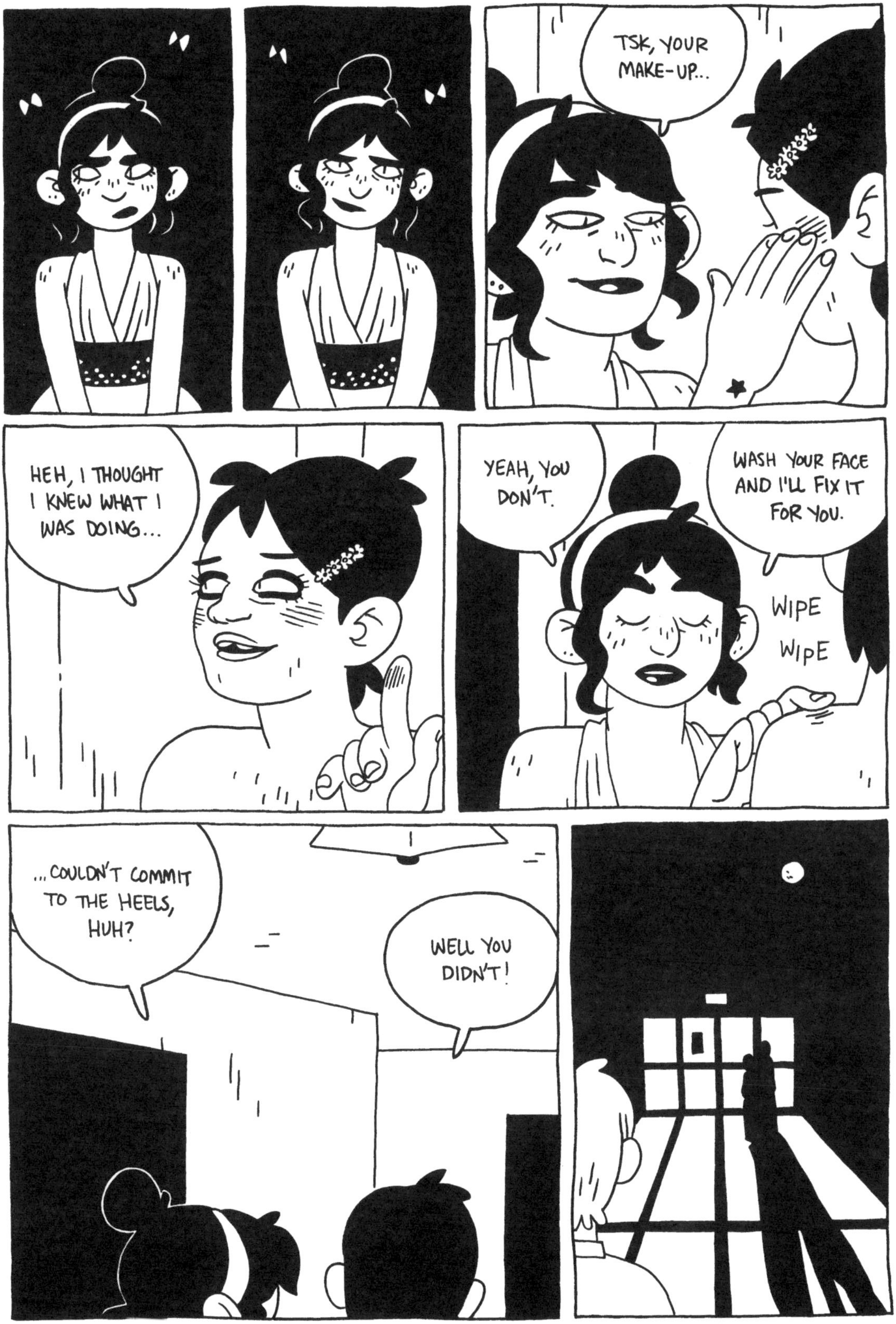
TSK, YOUR MAKE-UP...
HEH, I THOUGHT I KNEW WHAT I WAS DOING...
YEAH, YOU DON'T.
WASH YOUR FACE AND I'LL FIX IT FOR YOU.
WIPE
WIPE
...COULDN'T COMMIT TO THE HEELS, HUH?
WELL YOU DIDN'T!

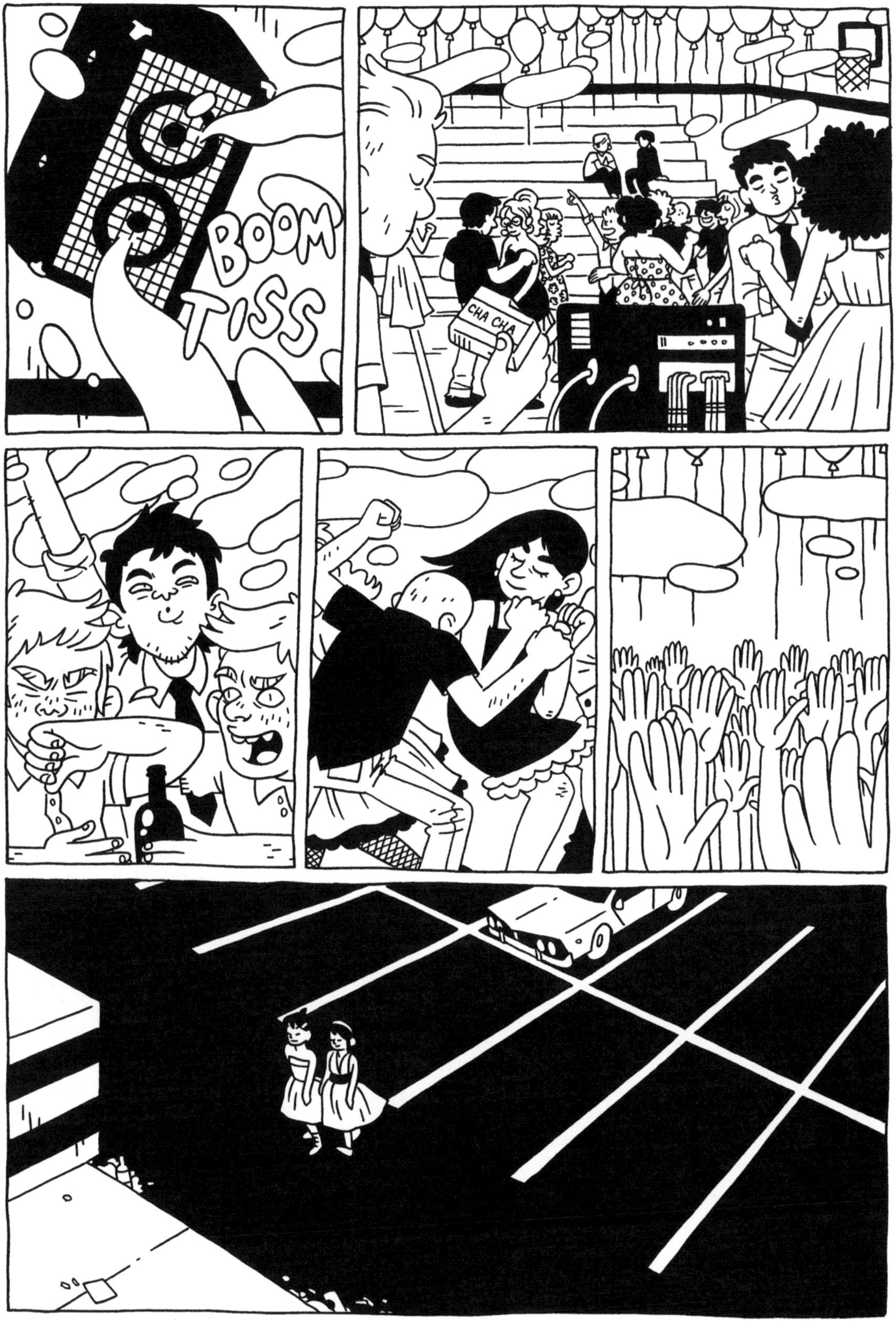
BOOM
TISS
CHA CHA

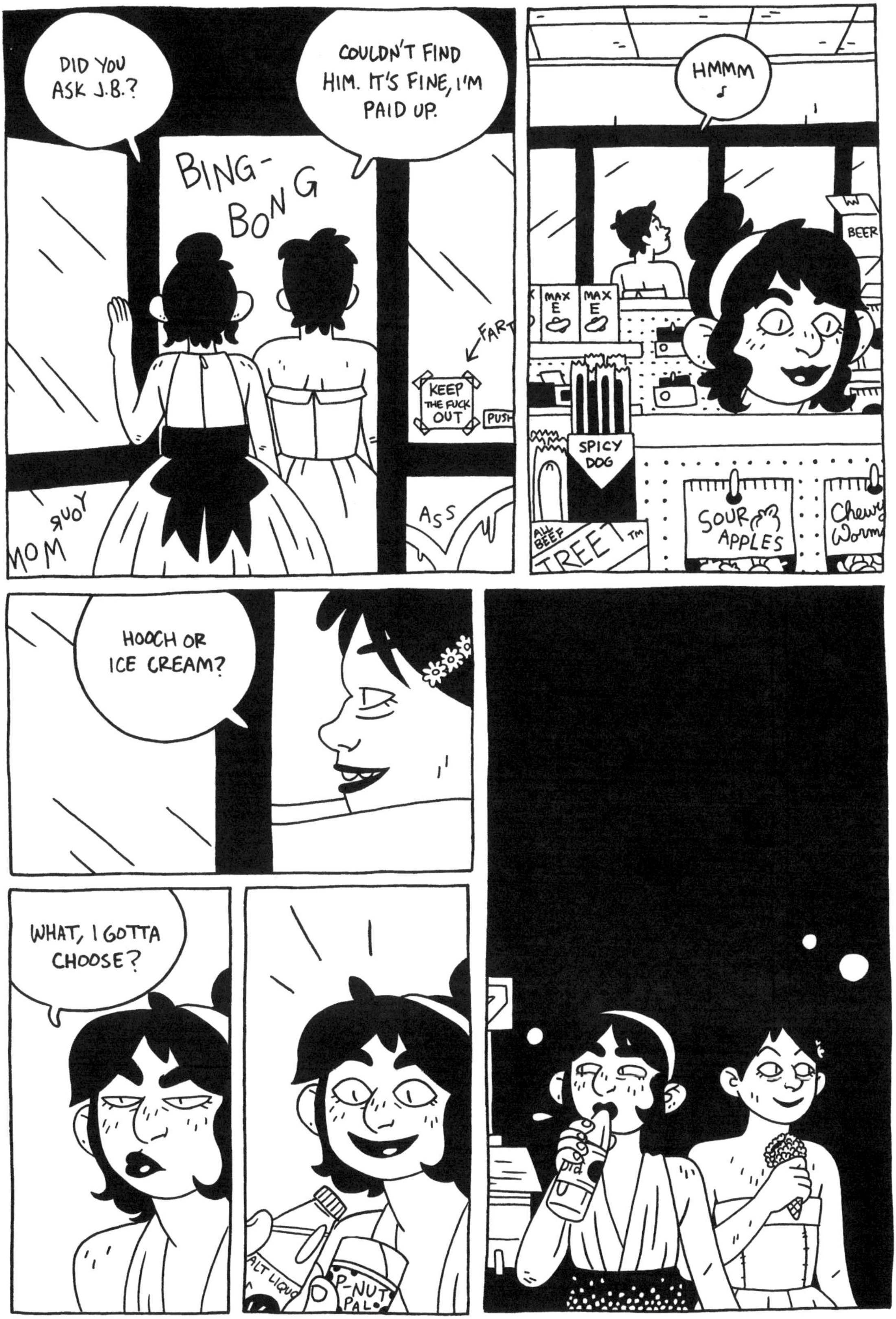
DID YOU ASK J.B.?
COULDN'T FIND HIM. IT'S FINE, I'M PAID UP.
BING-BONG
FART
KEEP THE FUCK OUT
PUSH
YOUR MOM
ASS
HMMM
MAX E
MAX E
BEER
SPICY DOG
ALL BEEF TREET TM
SOUR APPLES
Chewy Worms
HOOCH OR ICE CREAM?
WHAT, I GOTTA CHOOSE?
P-NUT PAL

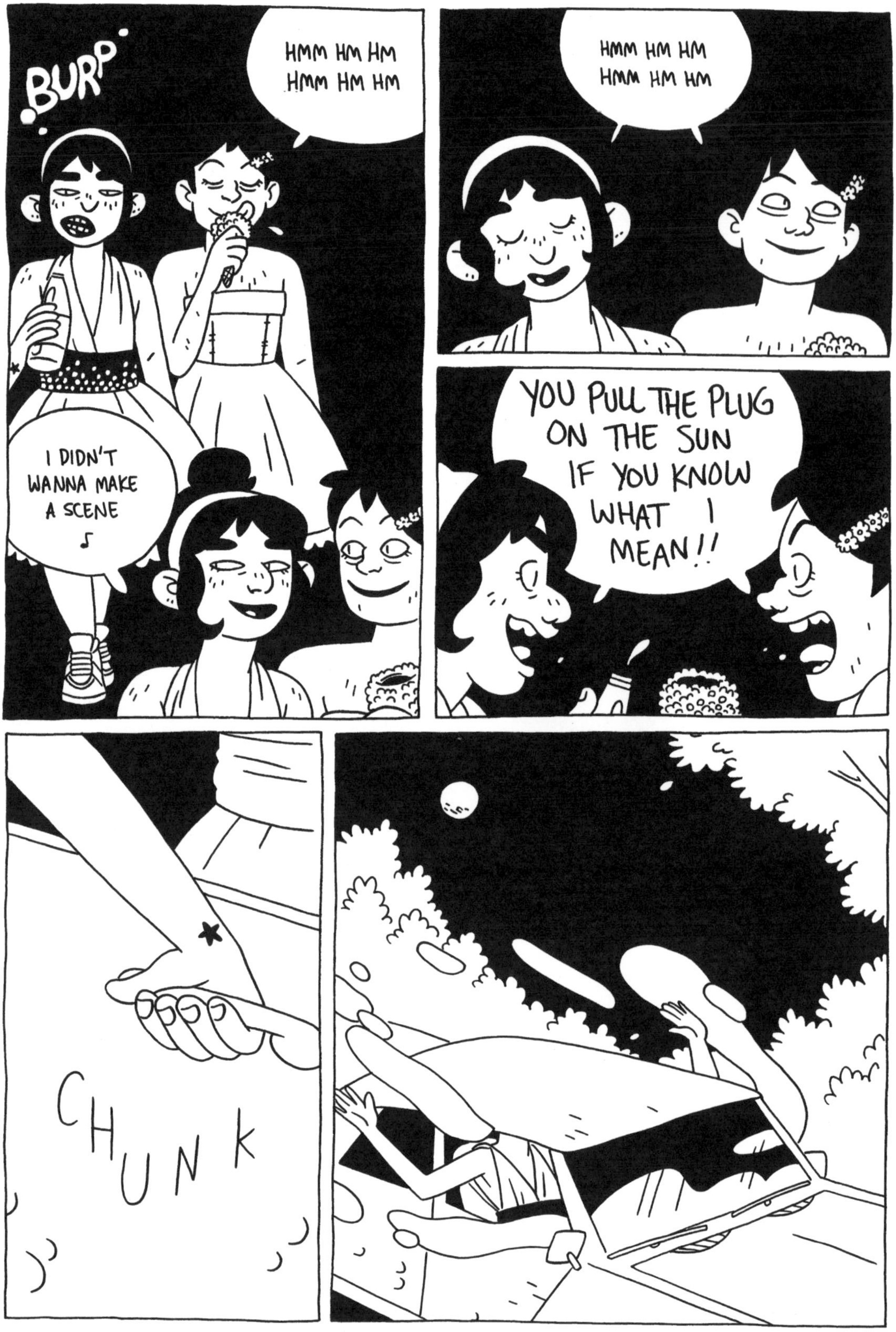
BURP
HMM HM HM HMM HM HM
I DIDN'T WANNA MAKE A SCENE ♪
HMM HM HM HMM HM HM
YOU PULL THE PLUG ON THE SUN IF YOU KNOW WHAT I MEAN!!
CHUNK

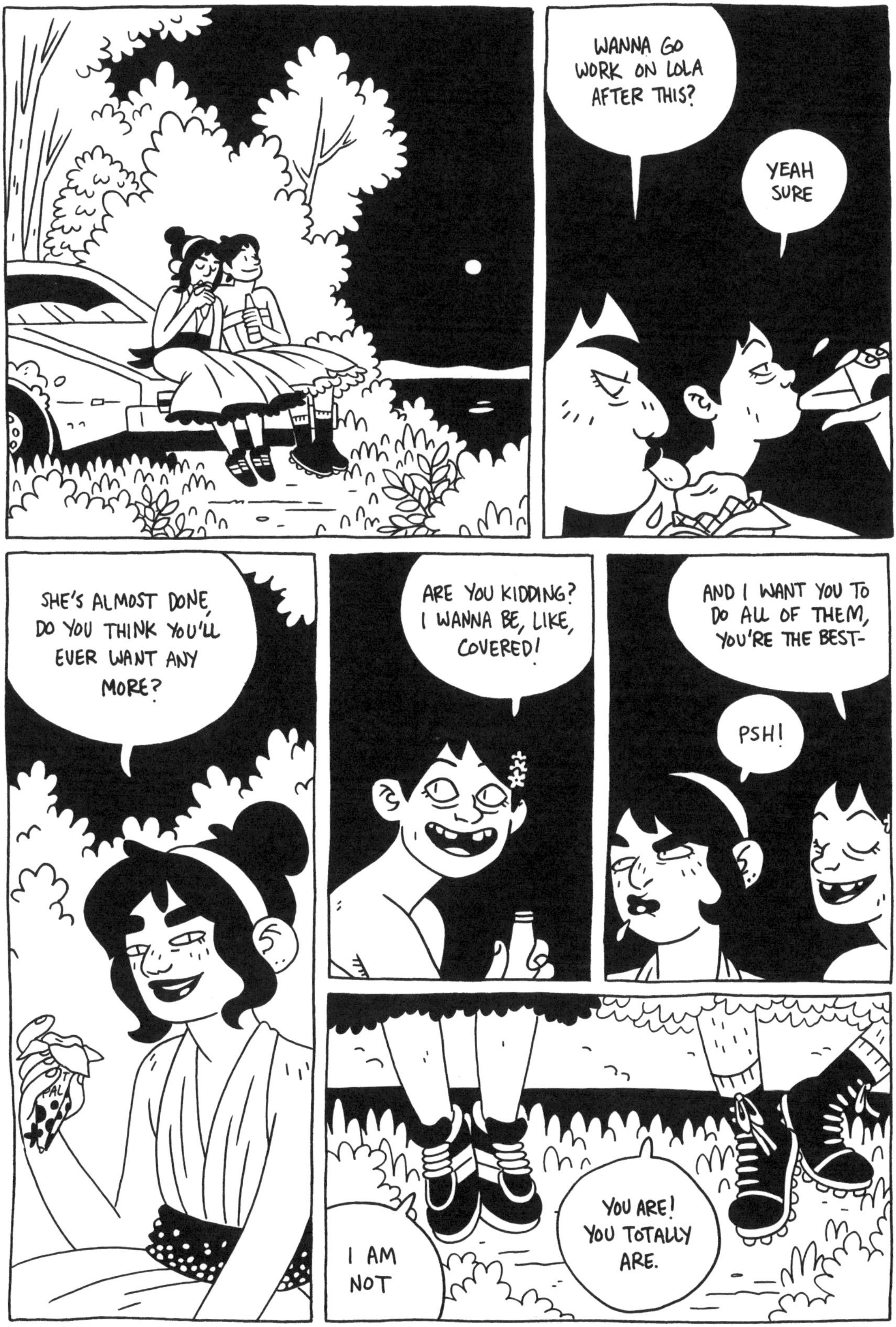
WANNA GO WORK ON LOLA AFTER THIS?
YEAH SURE
SHE'S ALMOST DONE, DO YOU THINK YOU'LL EVER WANT ANY MORE?
ARE YOU KIDDING? I WANNA BE, LIKE, COVERED!
AND I WANT YOU TO DO ALL OF THEM, YOU'RE THE BEST-
PSH!
YOU ARE! YOU TOTALLY ARE.
I AM NOT

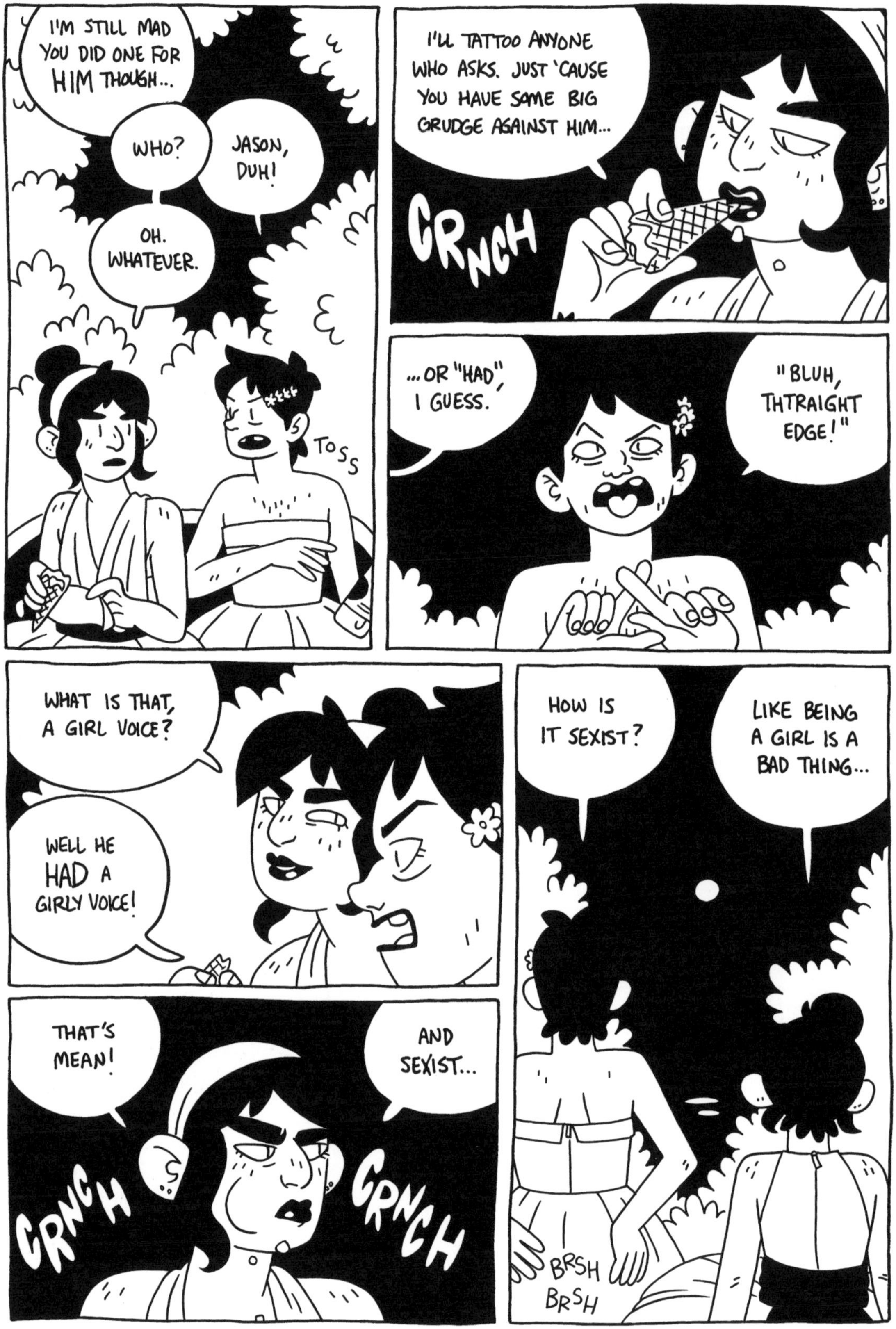
I'M STILL MAD YOU DID ONE FOR HIM THOUGH...
WHO?
JASON, DUH!
OH. WHATEVER.
TOSS
I'LL TATTOO ANYONE WHO ASKS. JUST 'CAUSE YOU HAVE SAME BIG GRUDGE AGAINST HIM...
CRNCH
...OR "HAD", I GUESS.
"BLUH, THTRAIGHT EDGE!"
WHAT IS THAT, A GIRL VOICE?
WELL HE HAD A GIRLY VOICE!
THAT'S MEAN!
AND SEXIST...
CRNCH
CRNCH
HOW IS IT SEXIST?
LIKE BEING A GIRL IS A BAD THING...
BRSH
BRSH

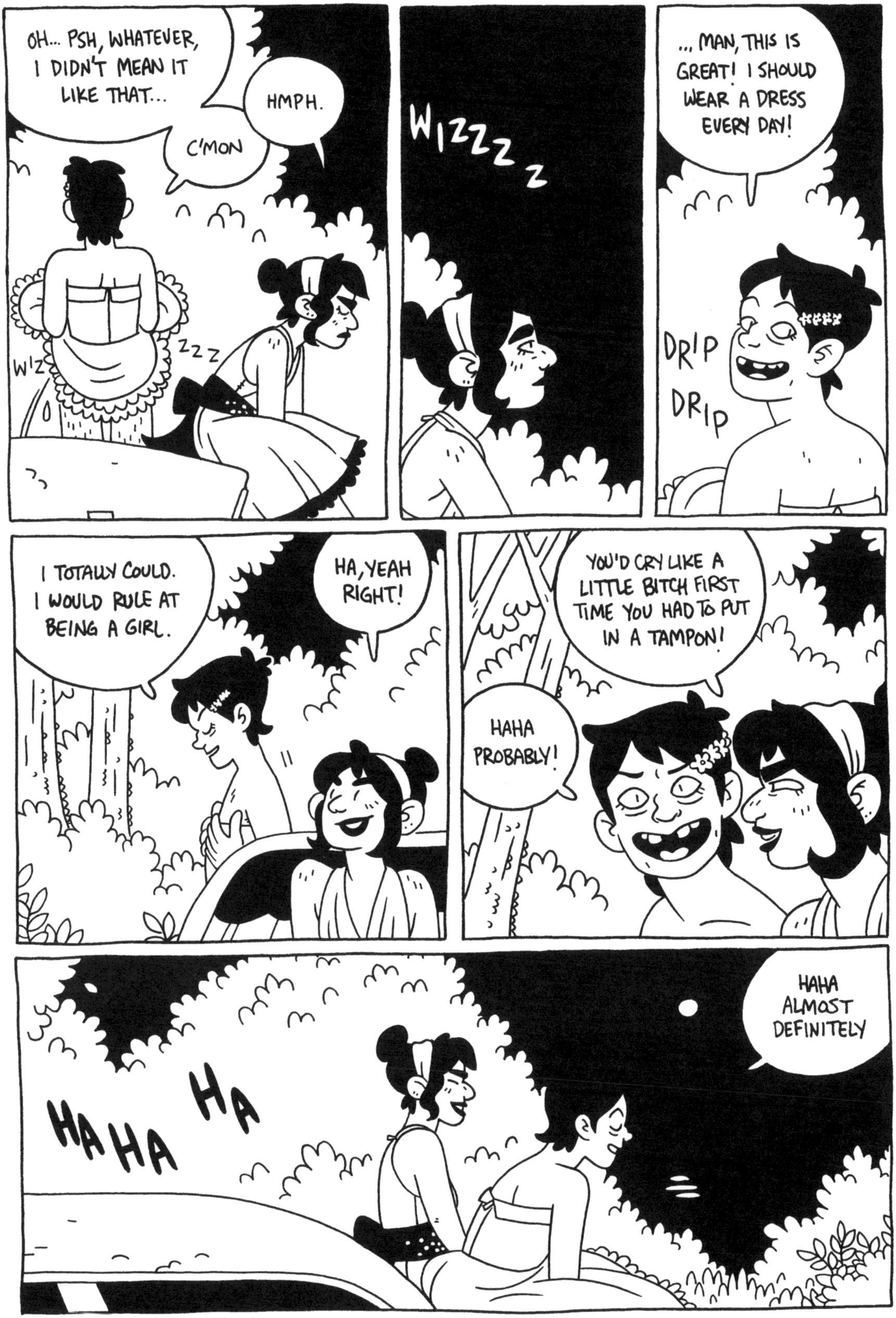
OH... PSH, WHATEVER, I DIDN'T MEAN IT LIKE THAT...
HMPH.
C'MON
W'Z
ZZZ
WIZZZZZ
..., MAN, THIS IS GREAT! I SHOULD WEAR A DRESS EVERY DAY!
DRIP
DRIP
I TOTALLY COULD. I WOULD RULE AT BEING A GIRL.
HA, YEAH RIGHT!
YOU'D CRY LIKE A LITTLE BITCH FIRST TIME YOU HAD TO PUT IN A TAMPON!
HAHA PROBABLY!
HAHA ALMOST DEFINITELY
HAHAHA
HA

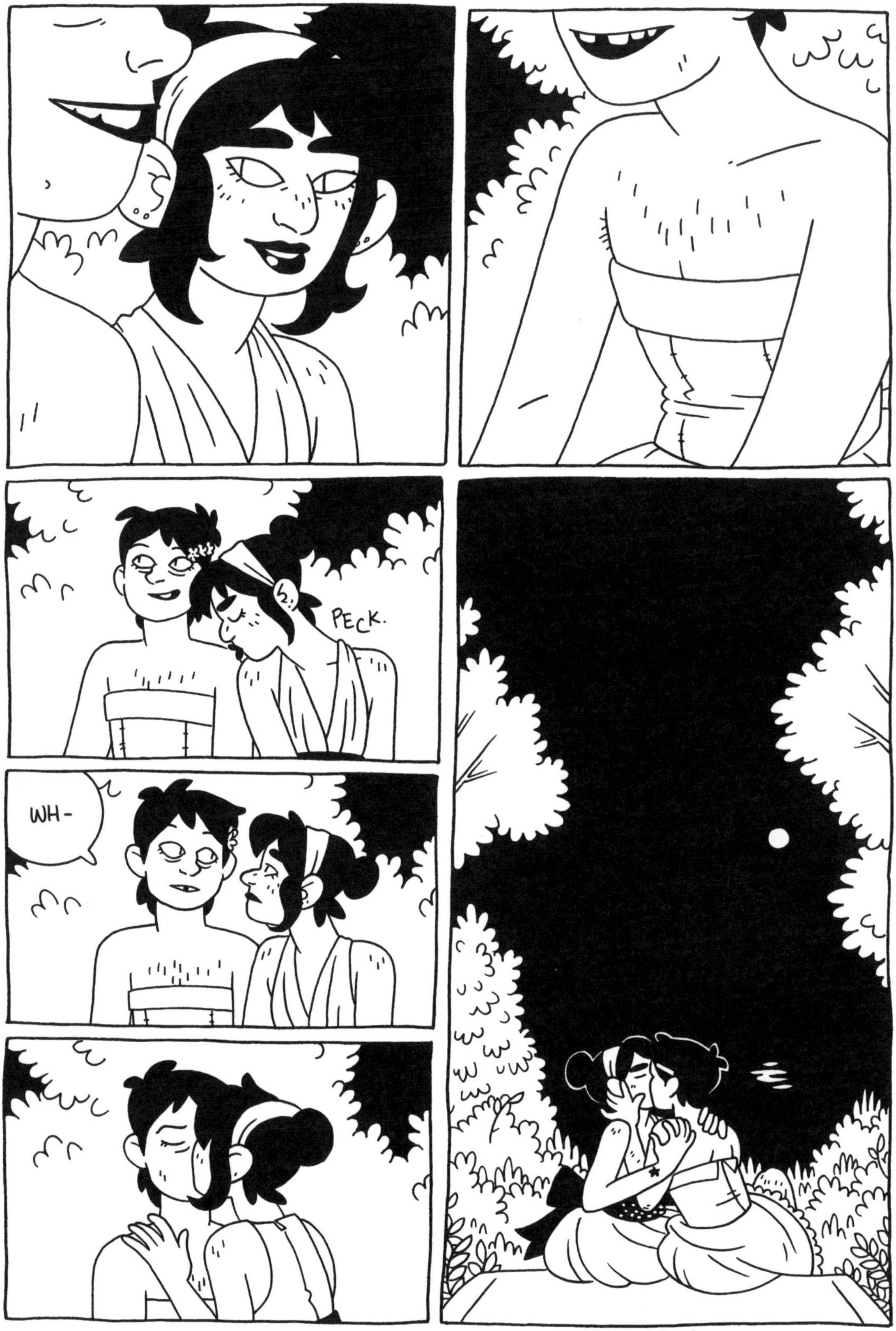
PECK.
WH-

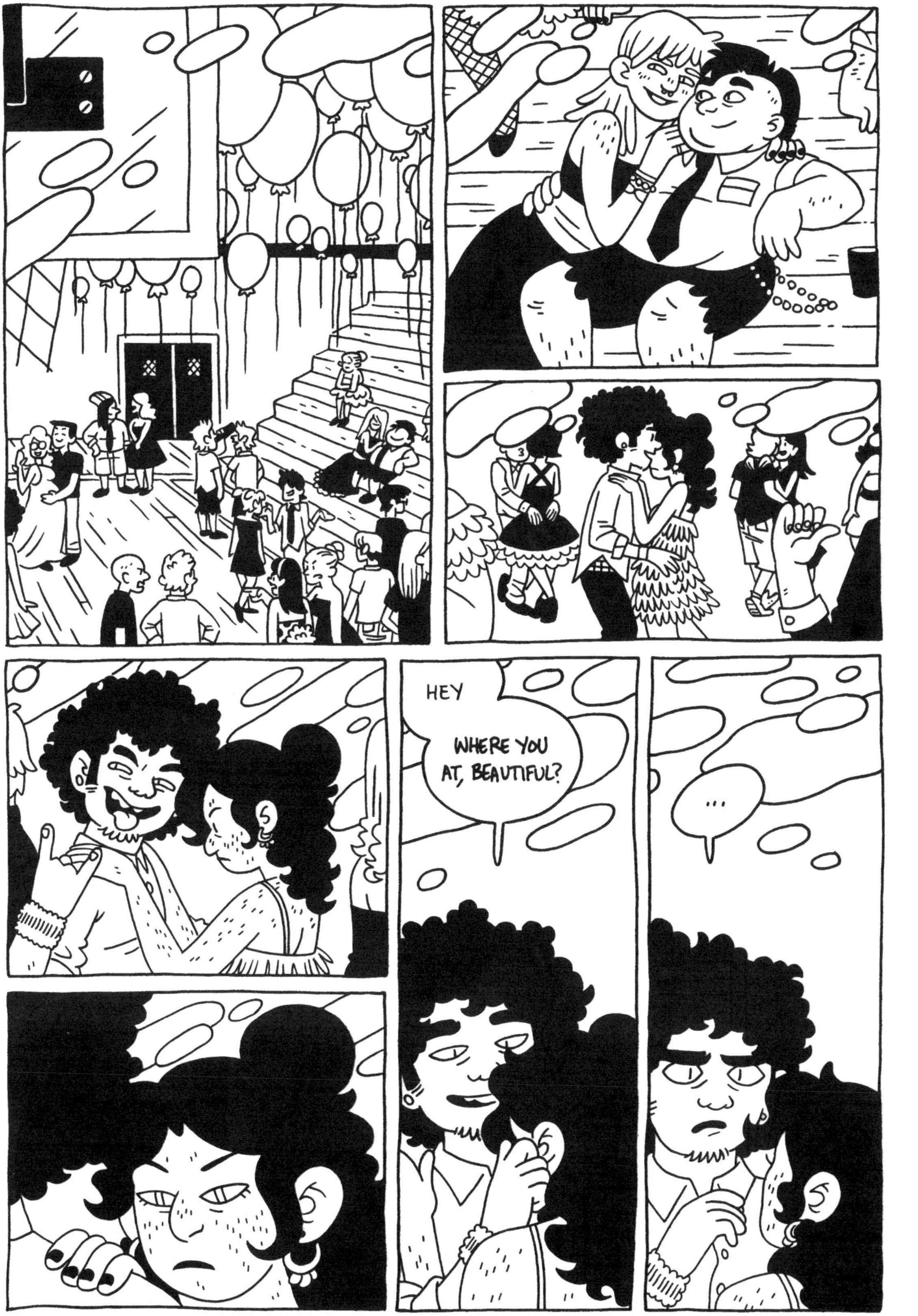
HEY
WHERE YOU AT, BEAUTIFUL?
...

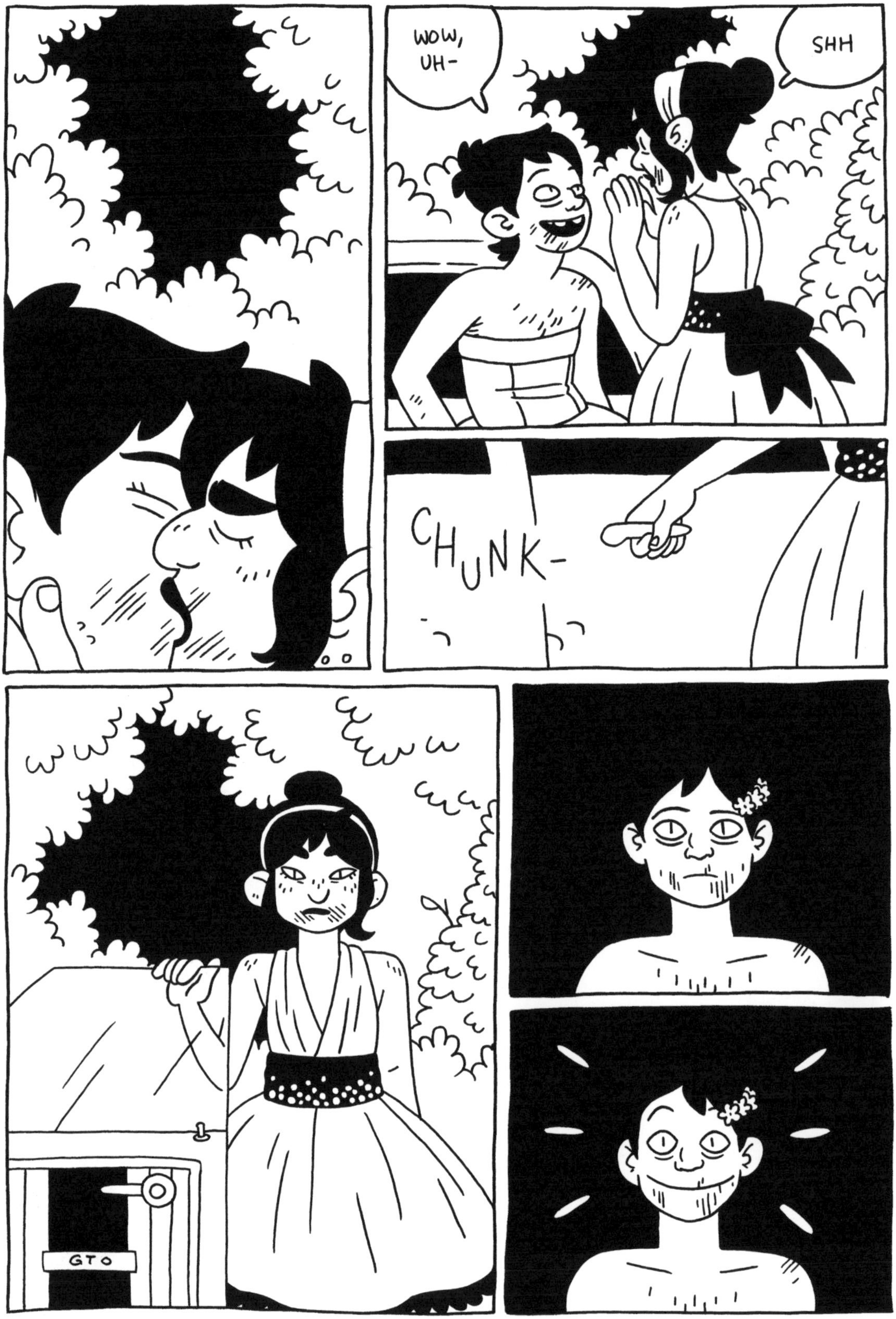
WOW,
UH-
SHH
CHUNK-
GTO

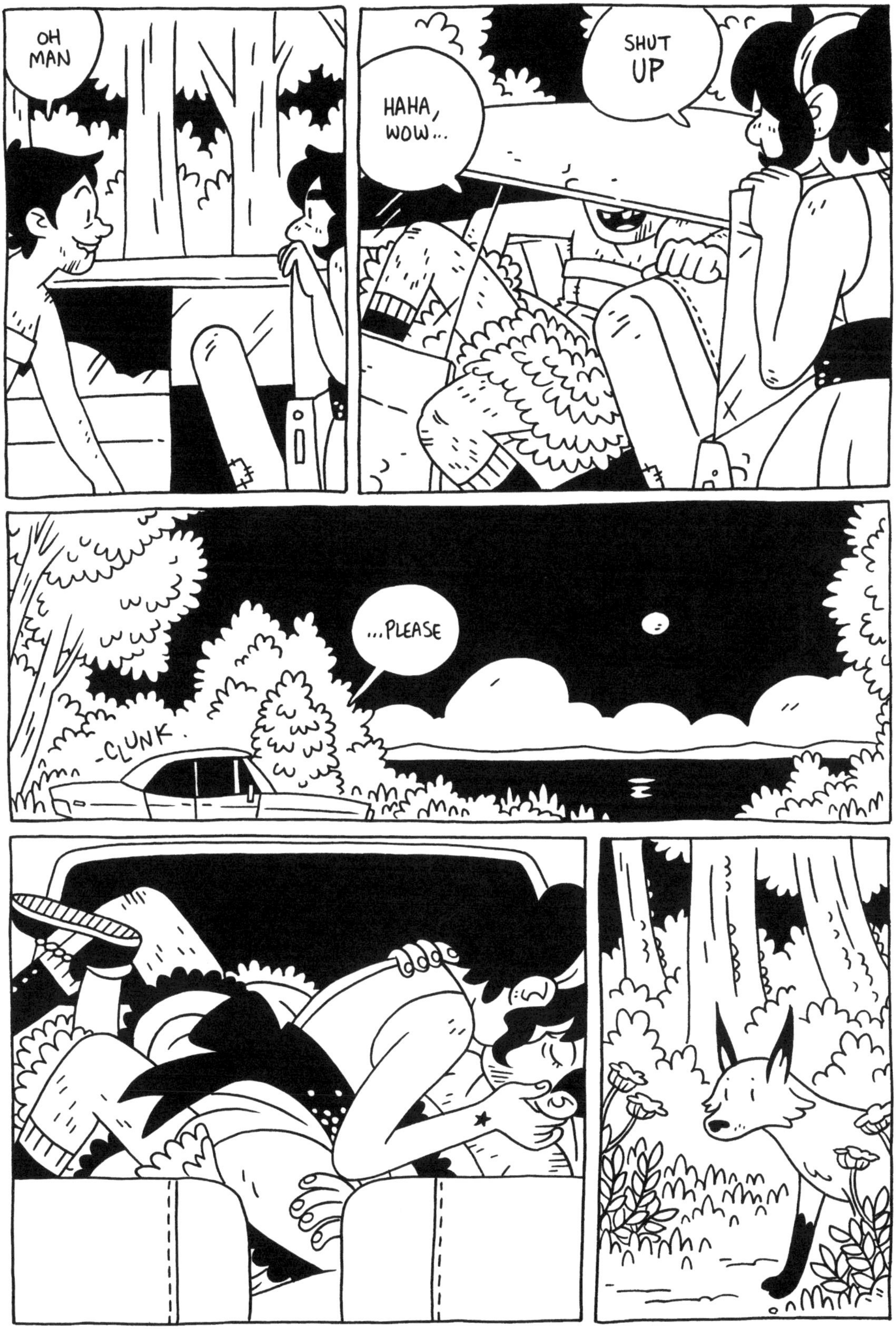
OH MAN
SHUT UP
HAHA, WOW...
...PLEASE
CLUNK

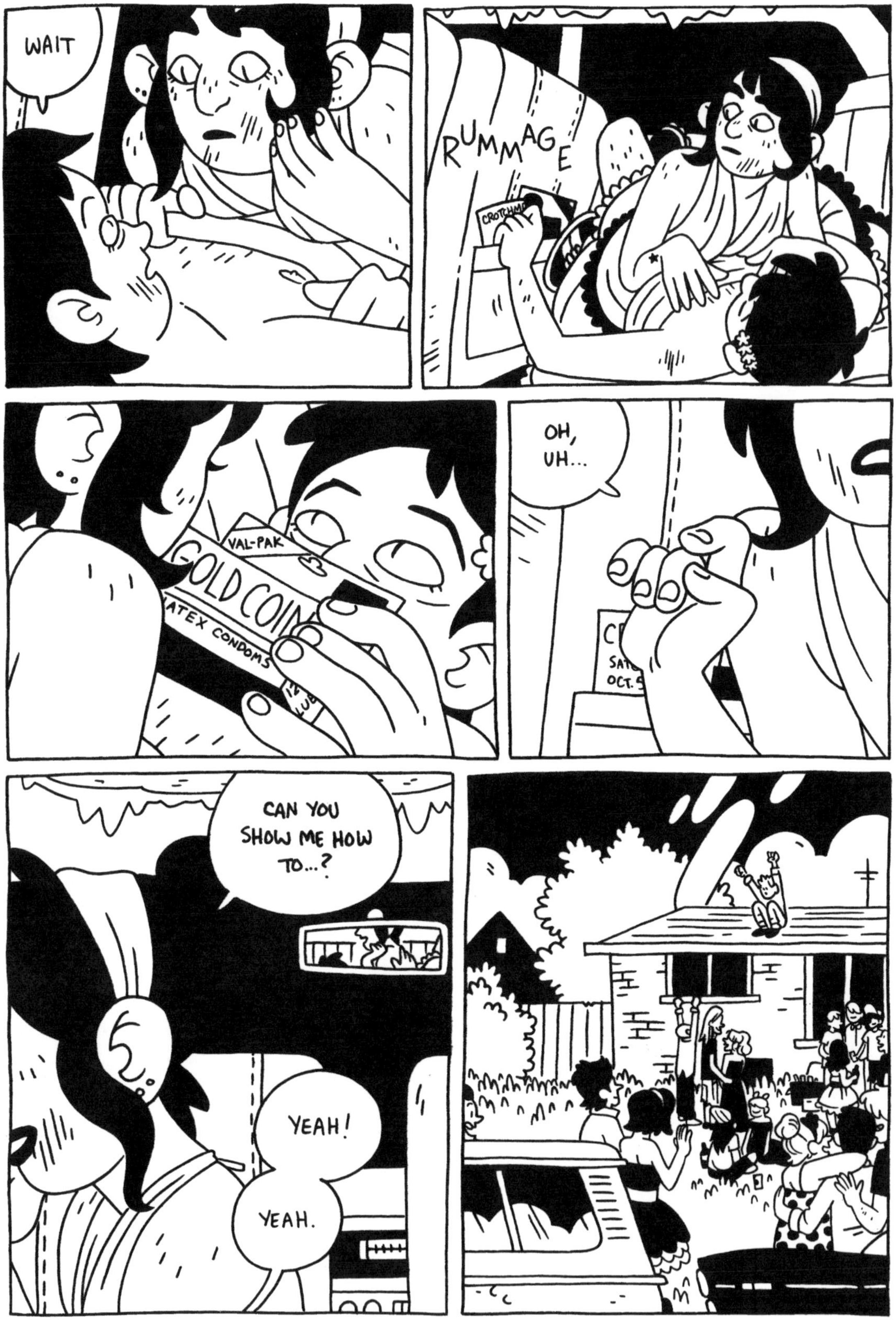
WAIT
RUMMAGE
CROTCHMA
VAL-PAK
GOLD COIN
ATEX CONDOMS
OH, UH...
SAT
OCT. 5
CAN YOU SHOW ME HOW TO...?
YEAH!
YEAH.

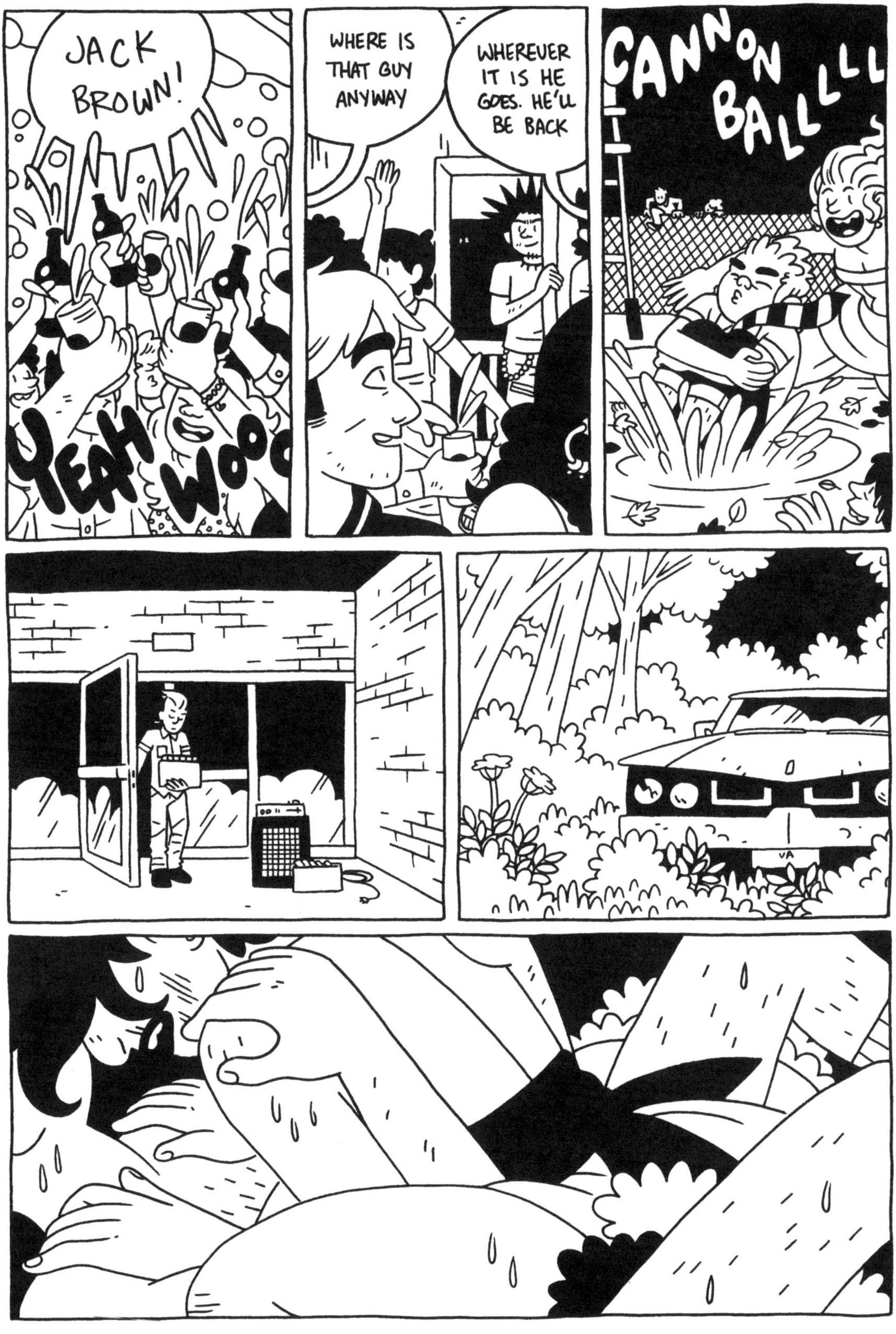
JACK BROWN!
YEAH
WOO
WHERE IS THAT GUY ANYWAY
WHEREVER IT IS HE GOES. HE'LL BE BACK
CANNONBALLLLL
VA

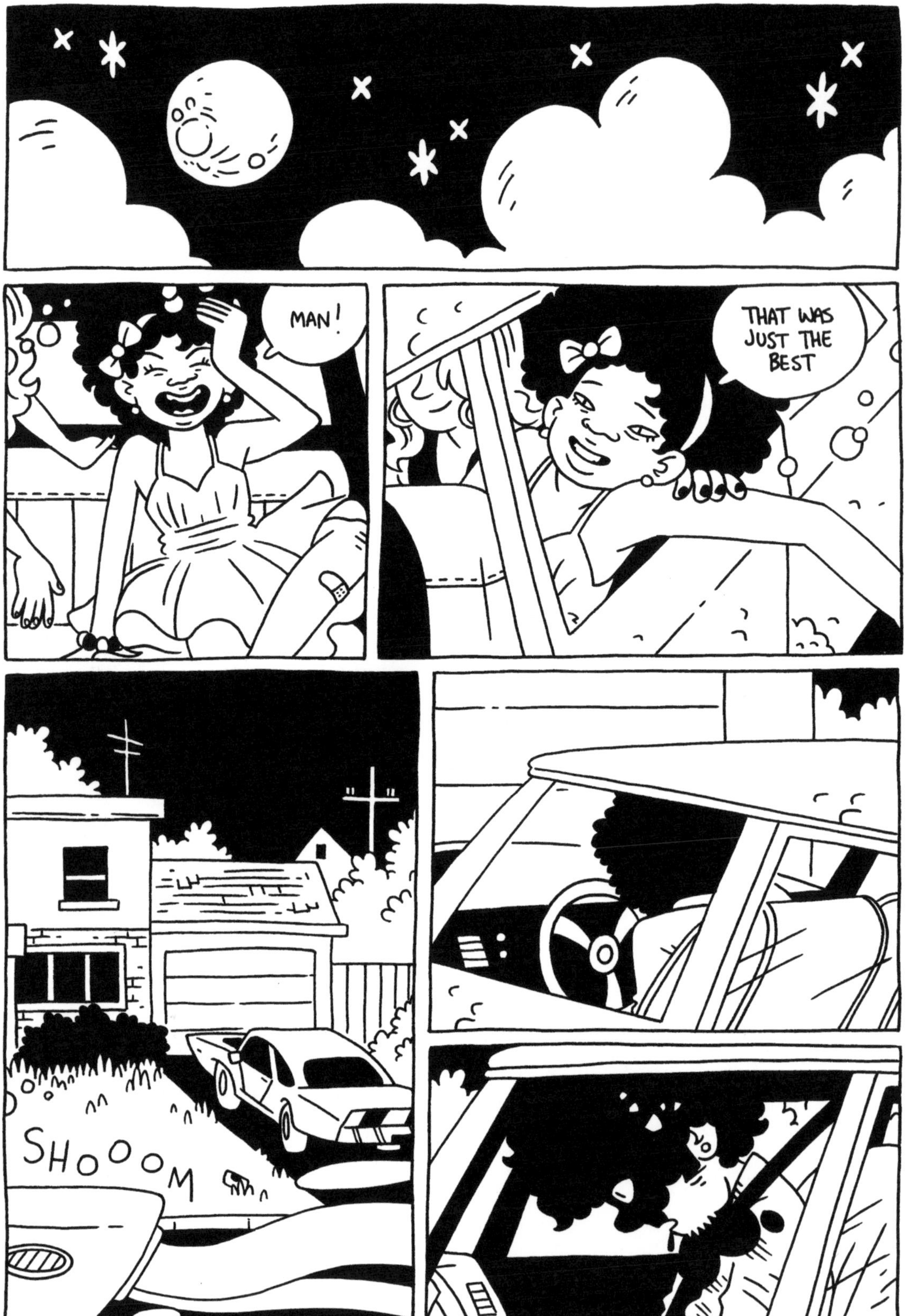
MAN!
THAT WAS JUST THE BEST
SHOOOM

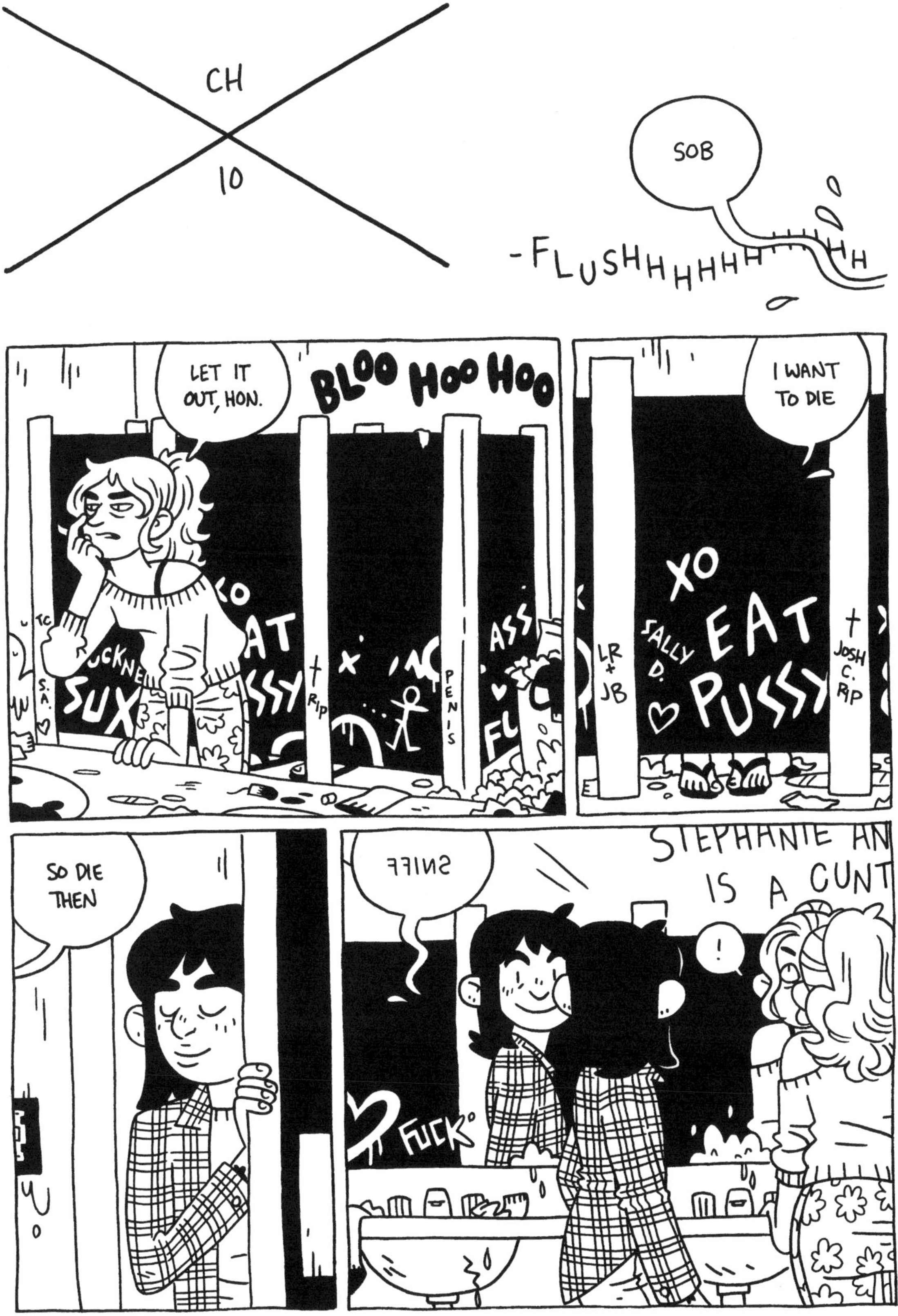
CH
10
SOB
-FLUSHHHHHHHHH
LET IT OUT, HON.
BLOO HOO HOO
SUX
EAT
RIP
PENIS
ASS
I WANT TO DIE
XO
EAT PUSSY
SALLY D.
LR + JB
JOSH C. RIP
SO DIE THEN
SNIFF
STEPHANIE AN
IS A CUNT
!
FUCK

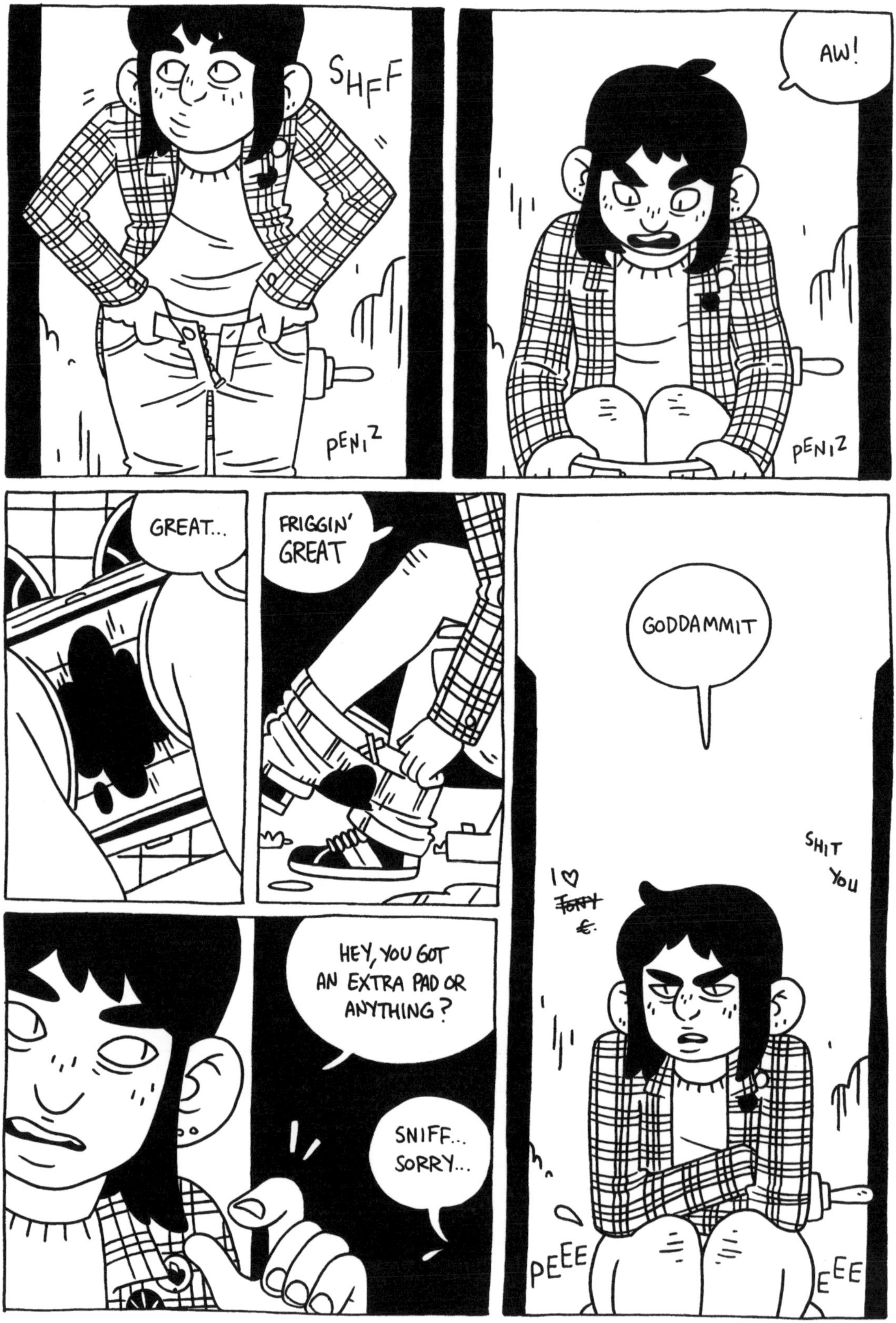
SHFF
PENIZ
AW!
PENIZ
GREAT...
FRIGGIN' GREAT
GODDAMMIT
SHIT
YOU
I ♡
PEEE
EEE
HEY, YOU GOT AN EXTRA PAD OR ANYTHING?
SNIFF... SORRY...

...?

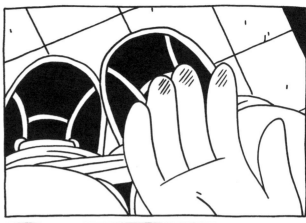

SHIT
YOU

★

PENIZ

?!

I CAN'T
BELIEVE IT!

I KNOW!

WHAT, ABOUT
COLIN BOND?

-BAM!

YA

...I CAN'T
BELIEVE HE'S
DEAD!

BAWL!!

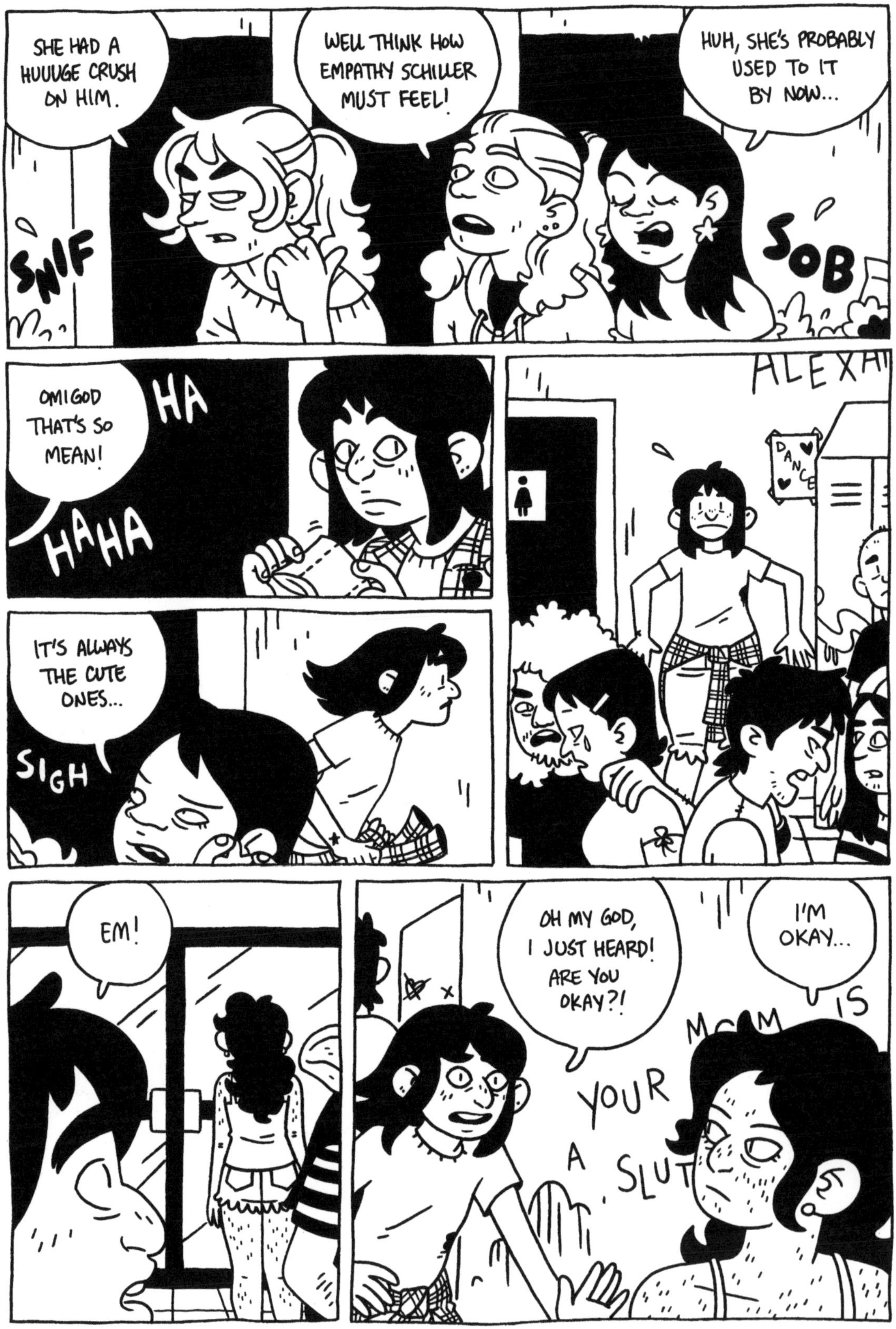
SHE HAD A HUUUGE CRUSH ON HIM.
SNIF
WELL THINK HOW EMPATHY SCHILLER MUST FEEL!
HUH, SHE'S PROBABLY USED TO IT BY NOW...
SOB
OMIGOD THAT'S SO MEAN!
HA
HAHA
ALEXA
DANCE
IT'S ALWAYS THE CUTE ONES...
SIGH
EM!
OH MY GOD, I JUST HEARD! ARE YOU OKAY?!
I'M OKAY...
YOUR MOM IS A SLUT

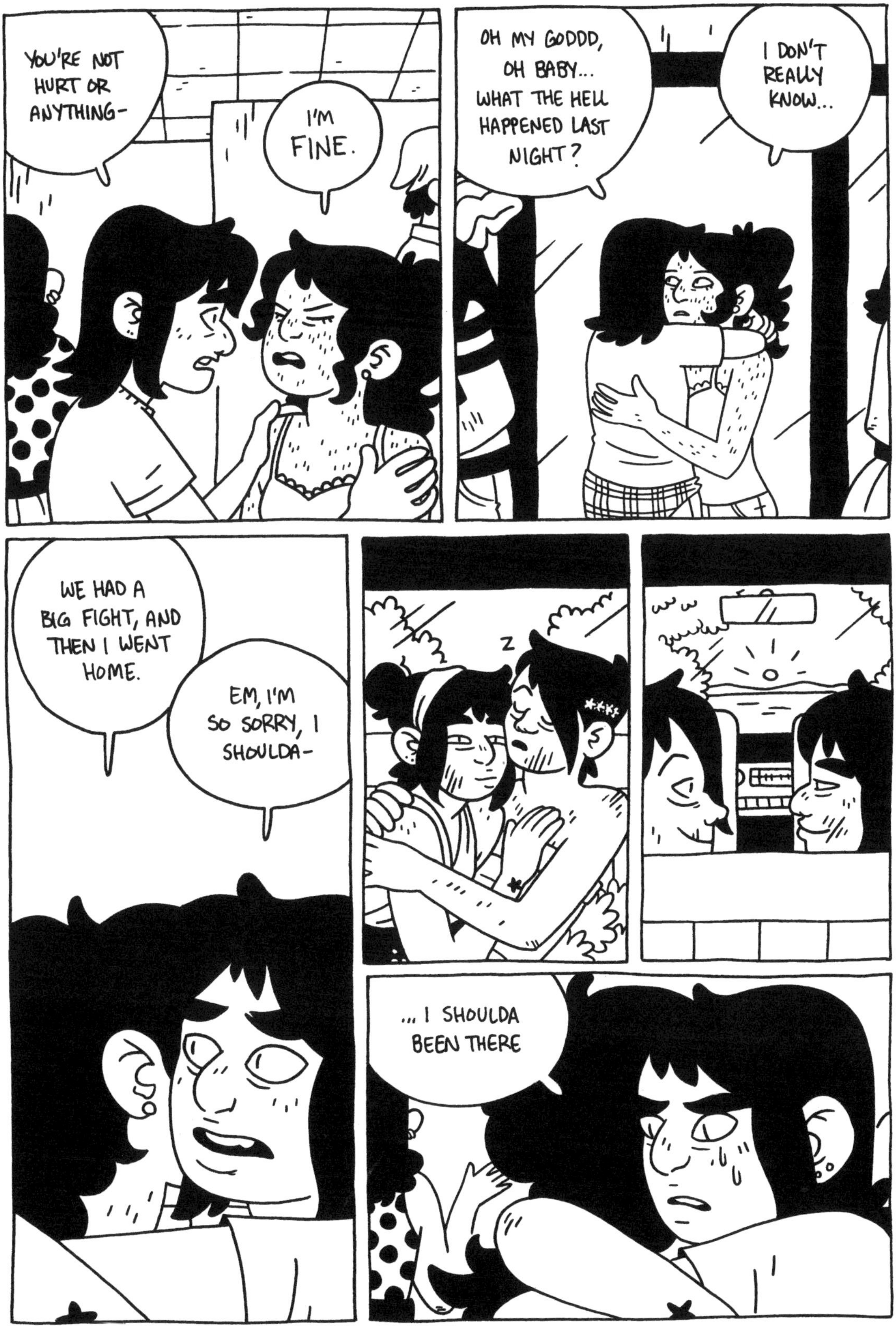
YOU'RE NOT HURT OR ANYTHING-
I'M FINE.
OH MY GODDD, OH BABY... WHAT THE HELL HAPPENED LAST NIGHT?
I DON'T REALLY KNOW...
WE HAD A BIG FIGHT, AND THEN I WENT HOME.
EM, I'M SO SORRY, I SHOULDA-
Z
...I SHOULDA BEEN THERE

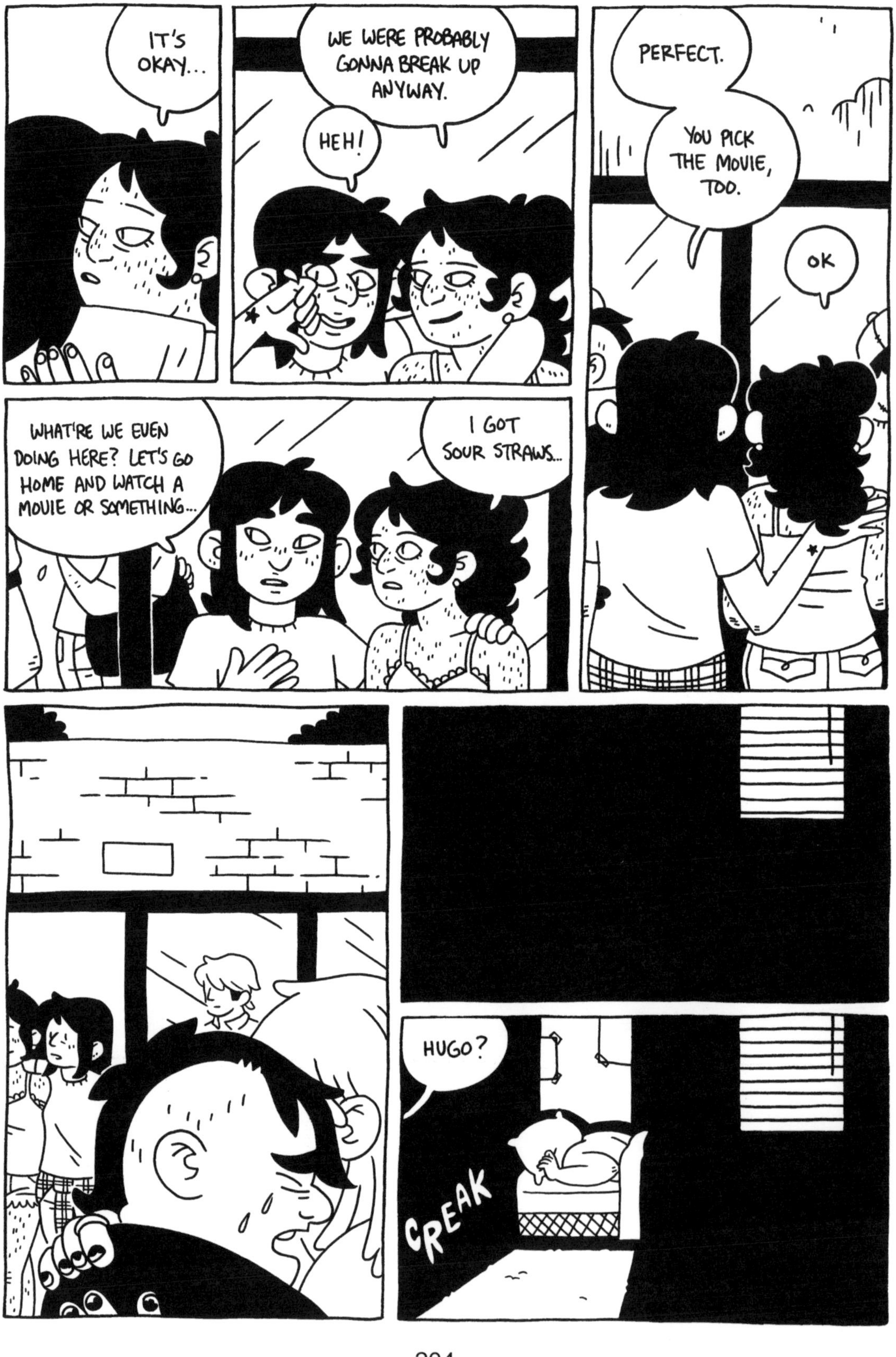
IT'S OKAY...
WE WERE PROBABLY GONNA BREAK UP ANYWAY.
HEH!
PERFECT.
YOU PICK THE MOVIE, TOO.
OK
WHAT'RE WE EVEN DOING HERE? LET'S GO HOME AND WATCH A MOVIE OR SOMETHING...
I GOT SOUR STRAWS...
HUGO?
CREAK

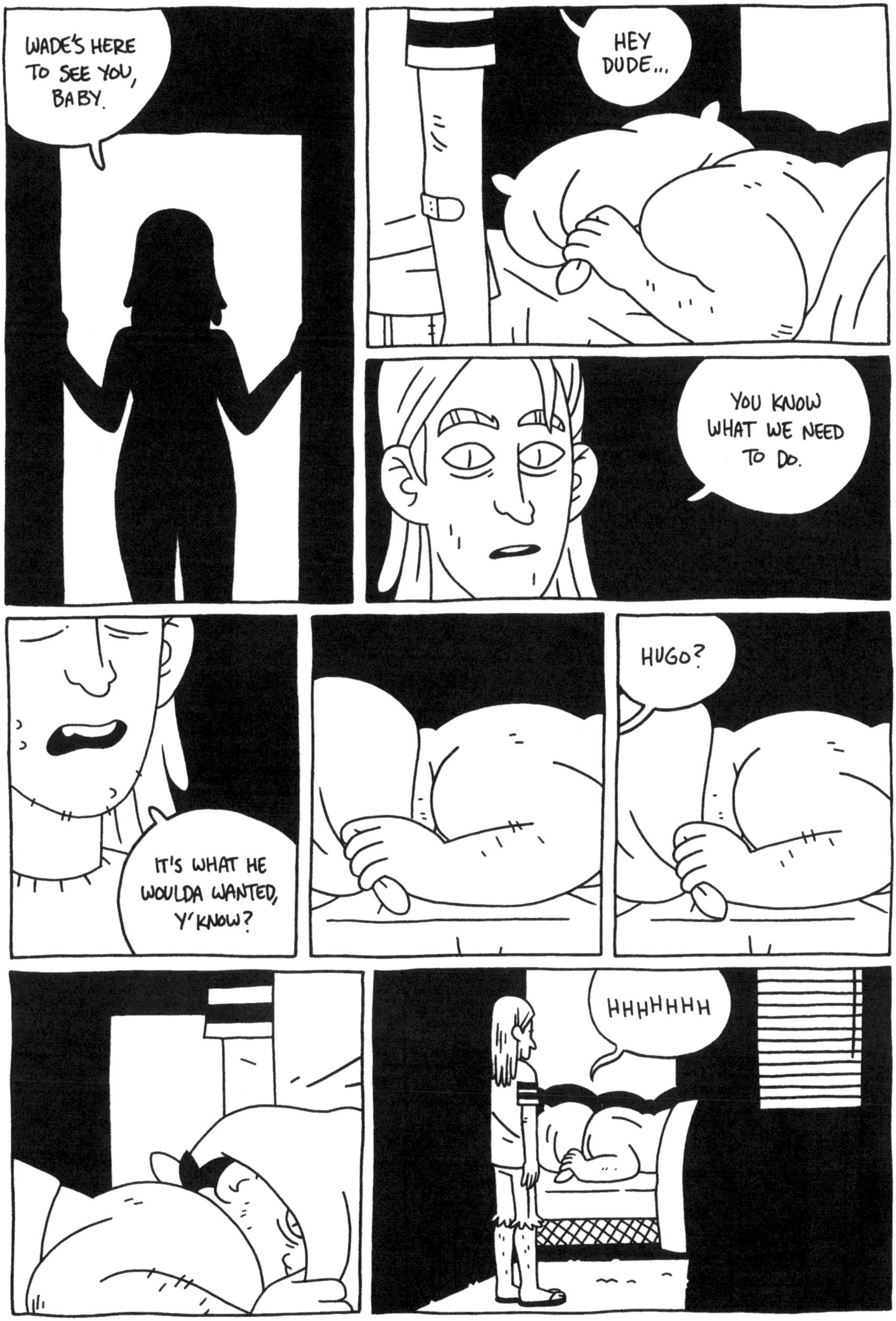
WADE'S HERE TO SEE YOU, BABY.
HEY DUDE...
YOU KNOW WHAT WE NEED TO DO.
IT'S WHAT HE WOULDA WANTED, Y'KNOW?
HUGO?
HHHHHHH

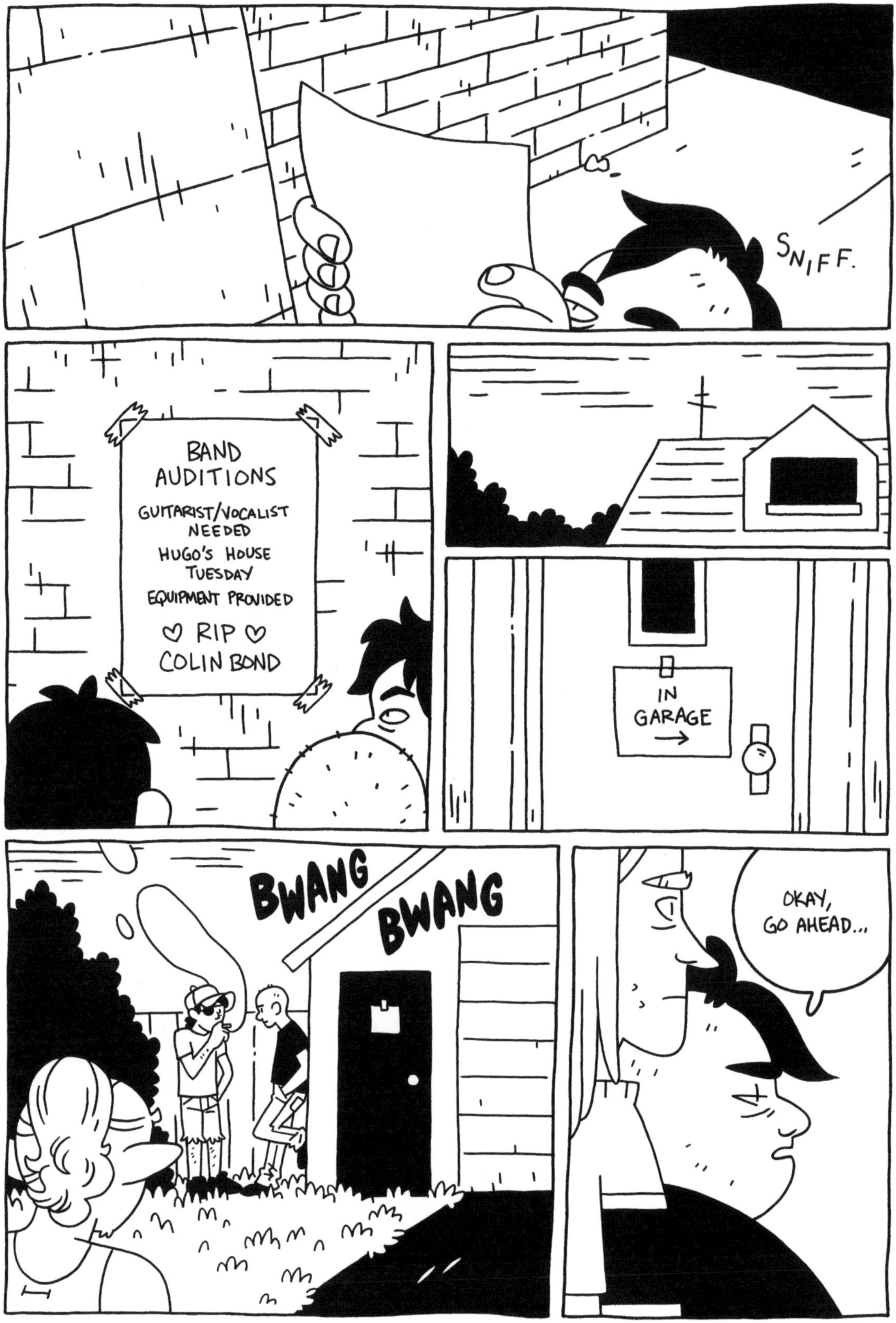
SNIFF.
BAND AUDITIONS
GUITARIST/VOCALIST NEEDED
HUGO'S HOUSE TUESDAY
EQUIPMENT PROVIDED
♡ RIP ♡
COLIN BOND
IN GARAGE →
BWANG
BWANG
OKAY, GO AHEAD...

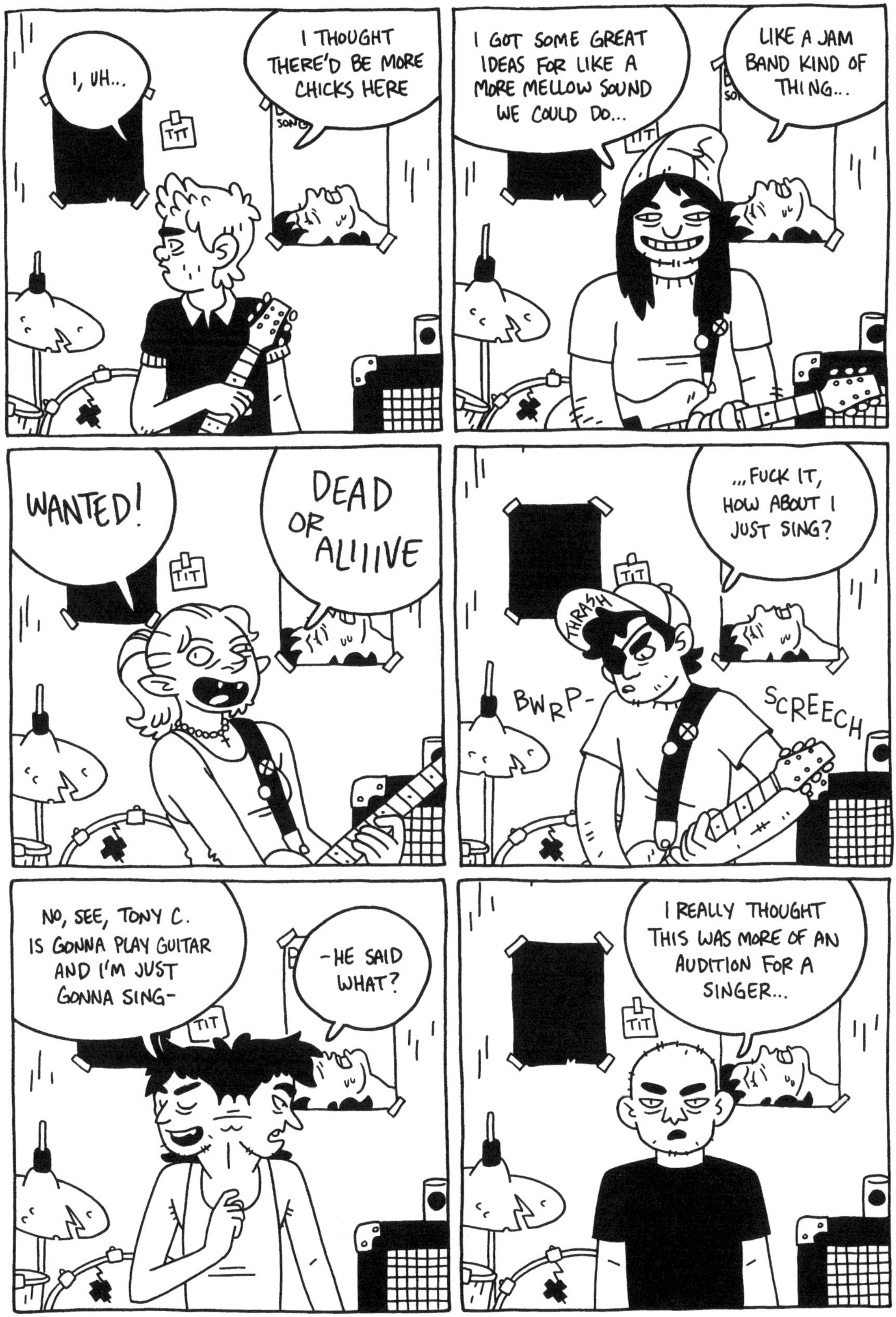
I, UH...
I THOUGHT THERE'D BE MORE CHICKS HERE
I GOT SOME GREAT IDEAS FOR LIKE A MORE MELLOW SOUND WE COULD DO...
LIKE A JAM BAND KIND OF THING...
WANTED!
DEAD OR ALIIIVE
...FUCK IT, HOW ABOUT I JUST SING?
THRASH
BWRP-
SCREECH
NO, SEE, TONY C. IS GONNA PLAY GUITAR AND I'M JUST GONNA SING-
-HE SAID WHAT?
I REALLY THOUGHT THIS WAS MORE OF AN AUDITION FOR A SINGER...

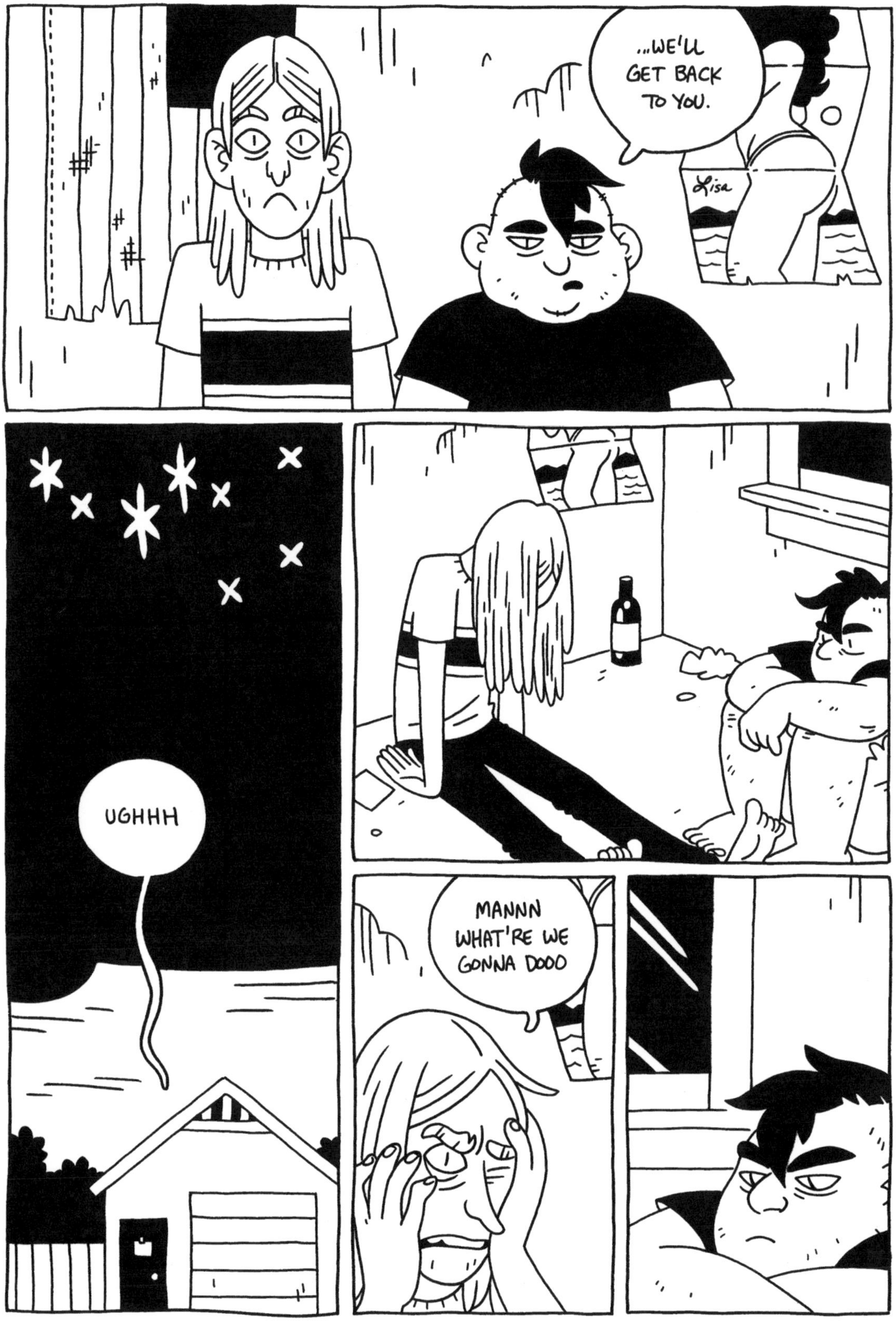
...WE'LL GET BACK TO YOU.
Lisa
UGHHH
MANNN WHAT'RE WE GONNA DOOO

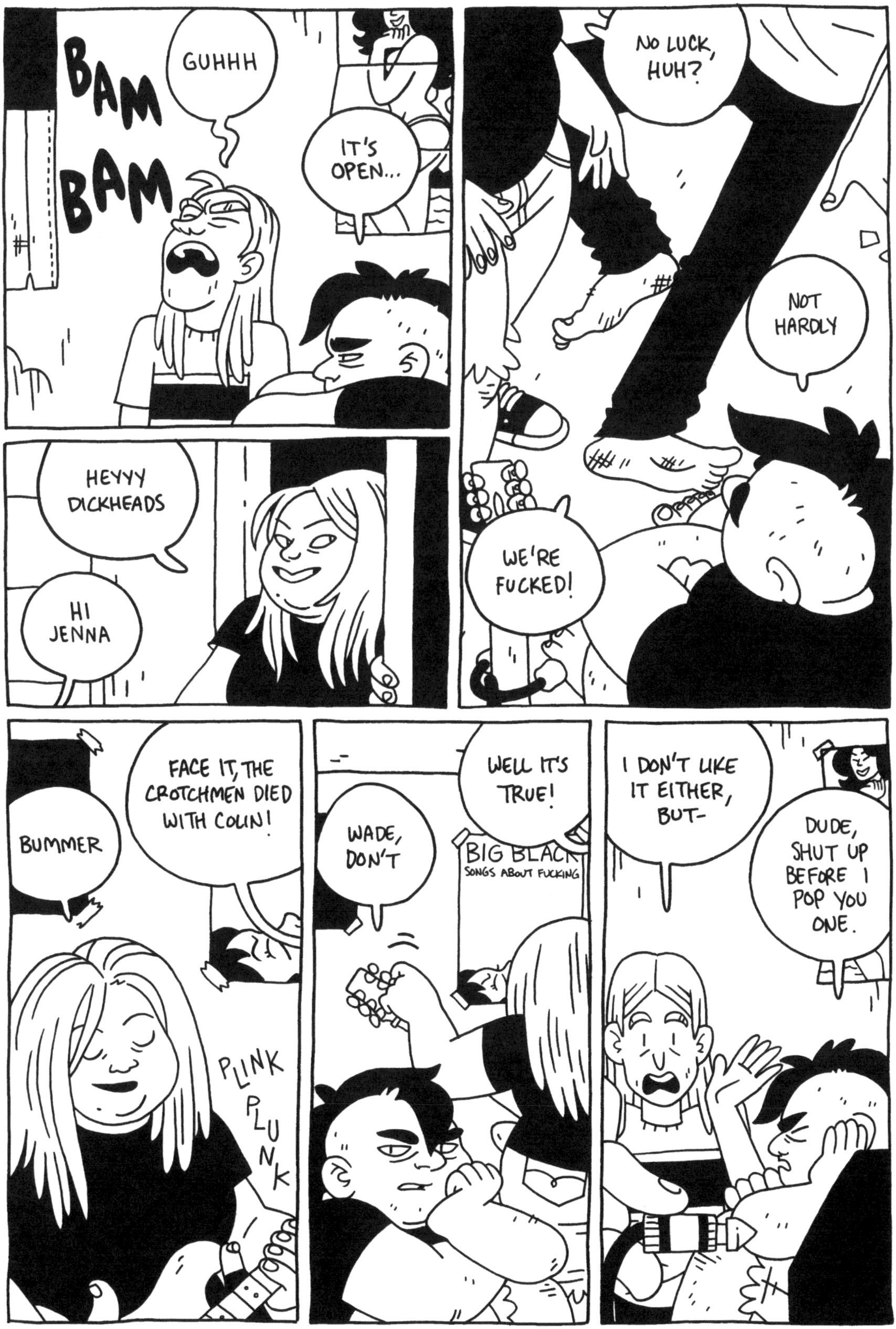
BAM BAM
GUHHH
IT'S OPEN...
NO LUCK, HUH?
NOT HARDLY
WE'RE FUCKED!
HEYYY DICKHEADS
HI JENNA
BUMMER
FACE IT, THE CROTCHMEN DIED WITH COLIN!
PLINK PLUNK
WADE, DON'T
WELL IT'S TRUE!
BIG BLACK
SONGS ABOUT FUCKING
I DON'T LIKE IT EITHER, BUT-
DUDE, SHUT UP BEFORE I POP YOU ONE.

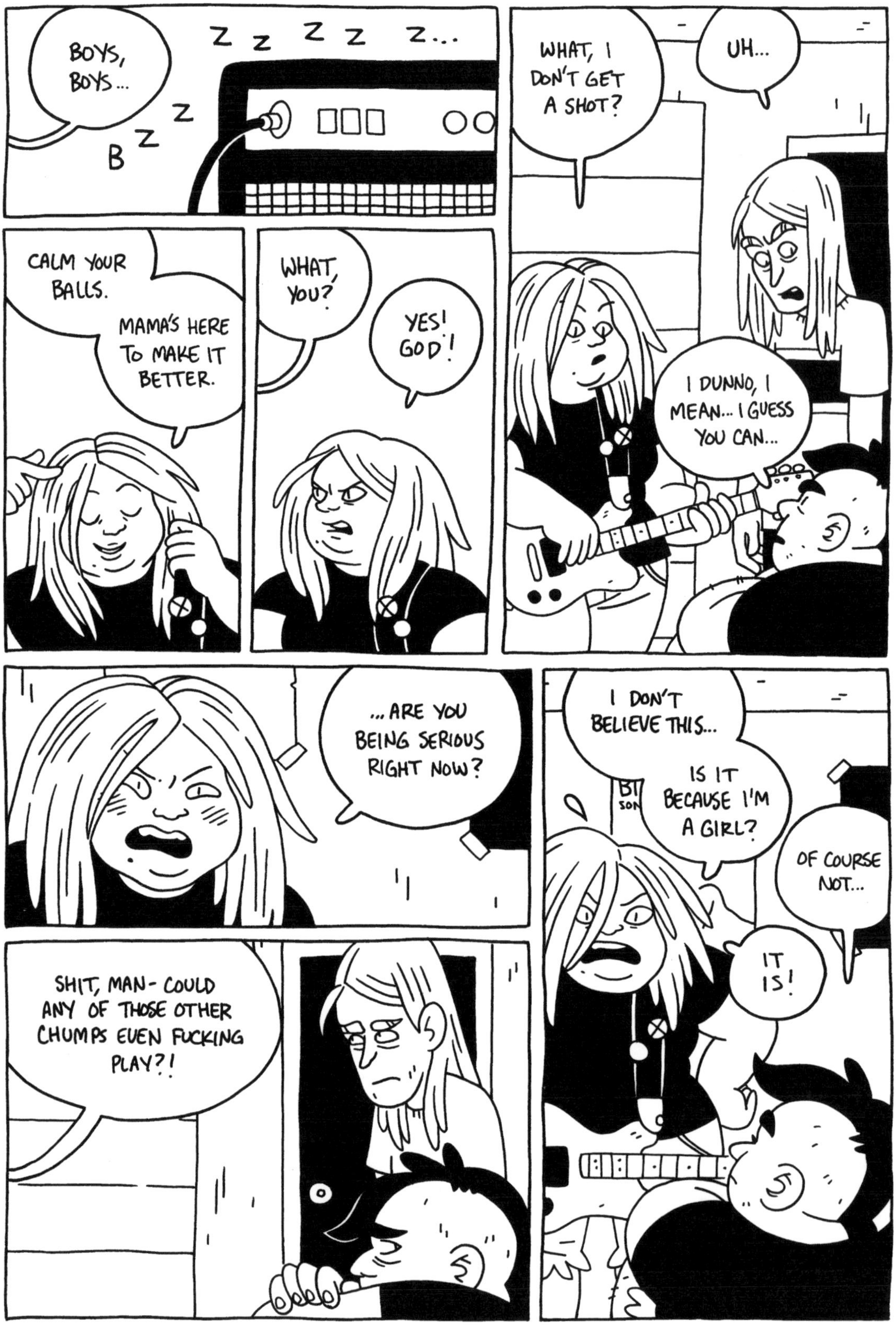
BOYS, BOYS...
Z Z Z Z Z...
B Z Z
WHAT, I DON'T GET A SHOT?
UH...
CALM YOUR BALLS.
MAMA'S HERE TO MAKE IT BETTER.
WHAT, YOU?
YES! GOD!
I DUNNO, I MEAN... I GUESS YOU CAN...
...ARE YOU BEING SERIOUS RIGHT NOW?
I DON'T BELIEVE THIS...
IS IT BECAUSE I'M A GIRL?
OF COURSE NOT...
IT IS!
SHIT, MAN- COULD ANY OF THOSE OTHER CHUMPS EVEN FUCKING PLAY?!

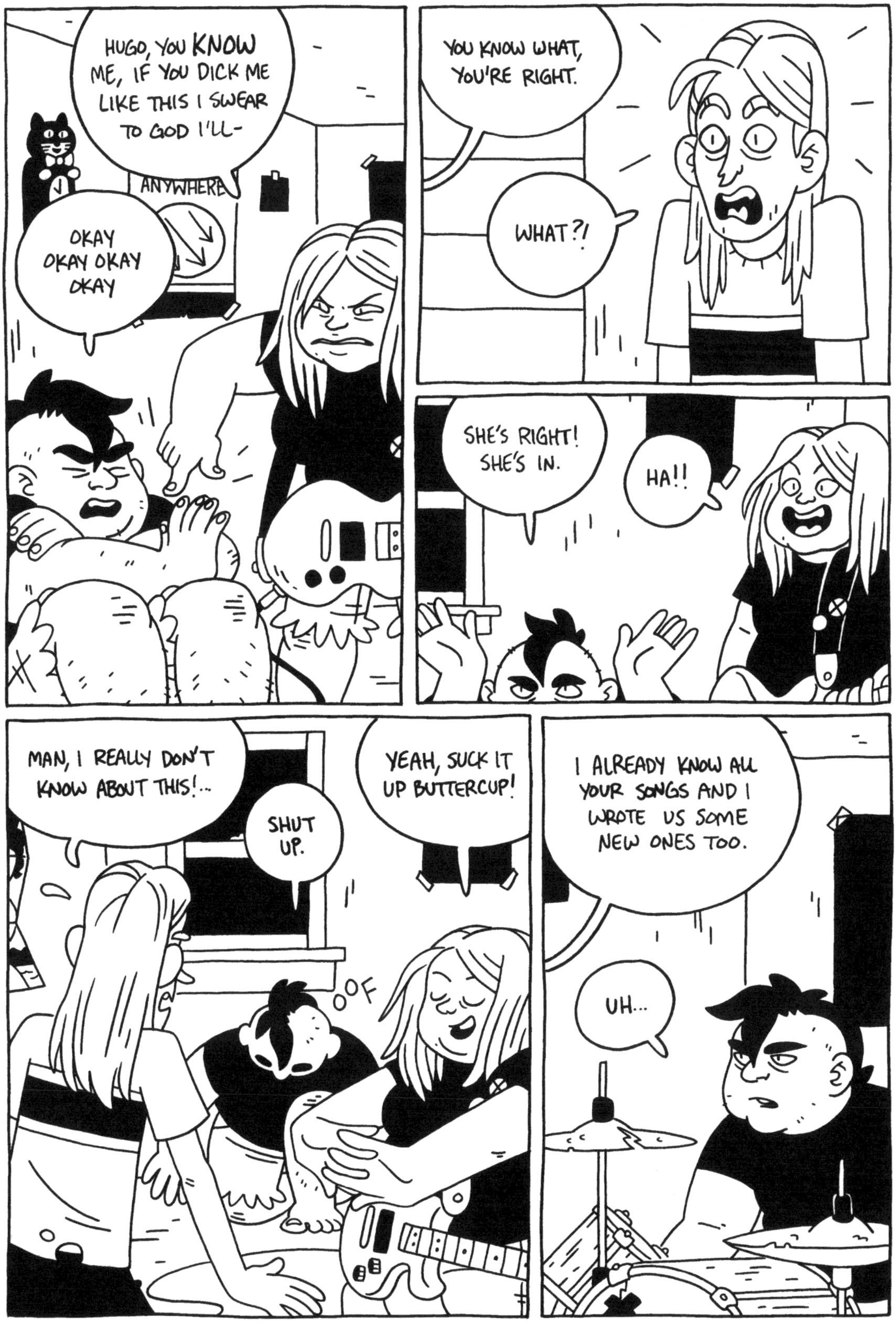
HUGO, YOU KNOW ME, IF YOU DICK ME LIKE THIS I SWEAR TO GOD I'LL-
ANYWHERE
OKAY OKAY OKAY OKAY
YOU KNOW WHAT, YOU'RE RIGHT.
WHAT?!
SHE'S RIGHT! SHE'S IN.
HA!!
MAN, I REALLY DON'T KNOW ABOUT THIS!...
SHUT UP.
YEAH, SUCK IT UP BUTTERCUP!
OOF
I ALREADY KNOW ALL YOUR SONGS AND I WROTE US SOME NEW ONES TOO.
UH...

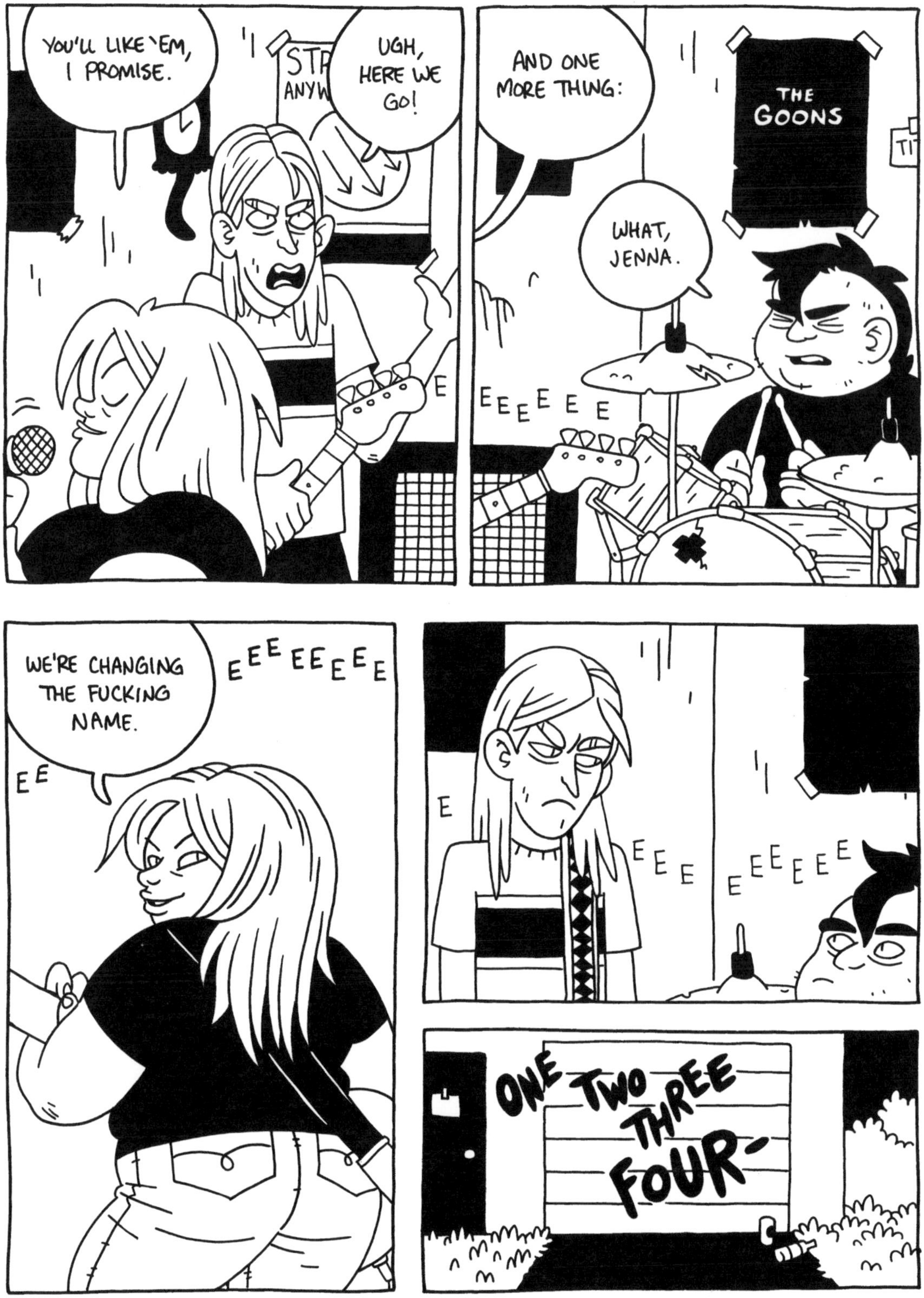
YOU'LL LIKE 'EM, I PROMISE.
UGH, HERE WE GO!
E
AND ONE MORE THING:
THE GOONS
WHAT, JENNA.
EEEEEE
WE'RE CHANGING THE FUCKING NAME.
EEEEEEEE
EE
E
EEE
EEEEEE
ONE TWO THREE FOUR-

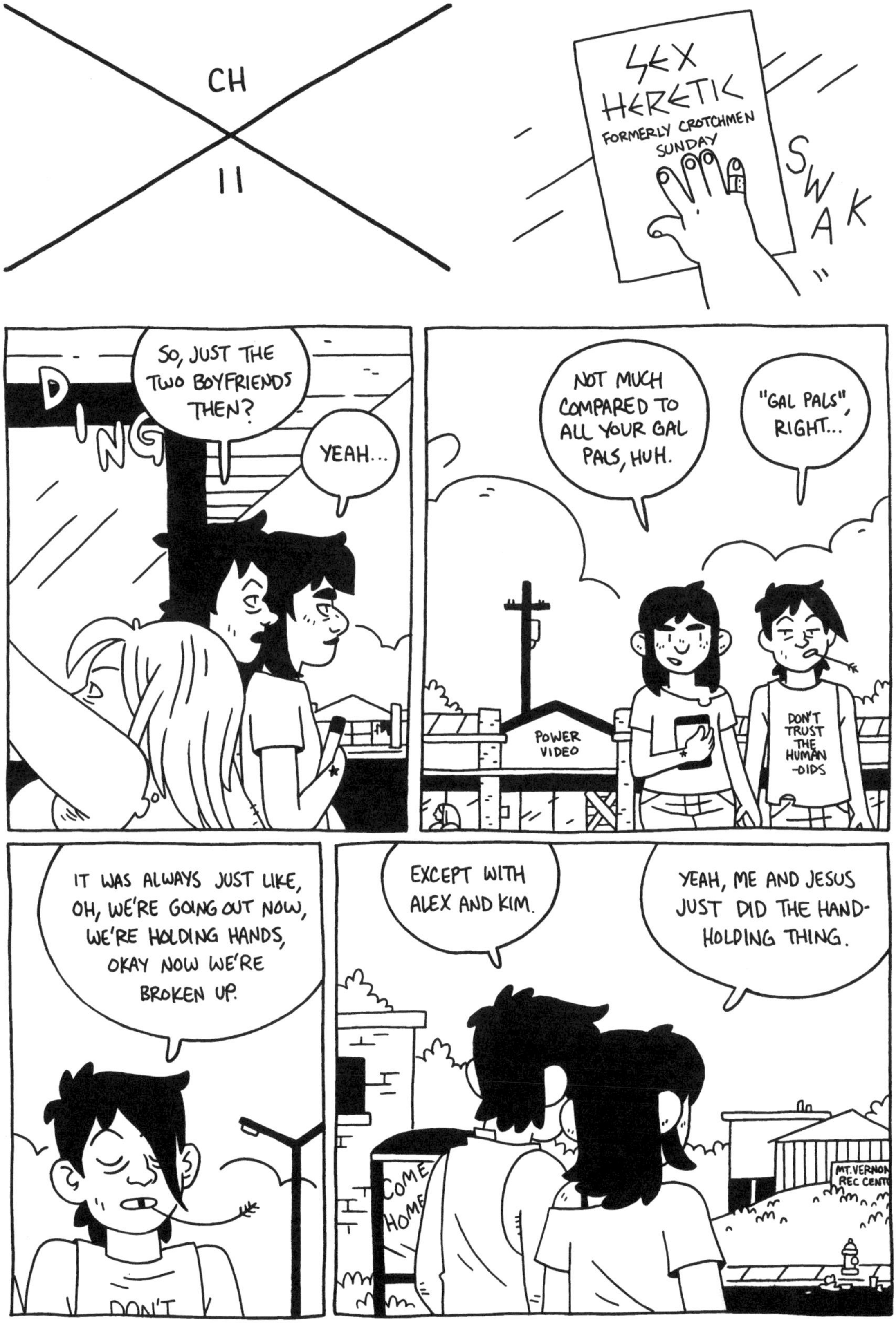
CH
11
SEX HERETIC
FORMERLY CROTCHMEN
SUNDAY
SWAK
DING
SO, JUST THE TWO BOYFRIENDS THEN?
YEAH...
NOT MUCH COMPARED TO ALL YOUR GAL PALS, HUH.
"GAL PALS", RIGHT...
POWER VIDEO
DON'T TRUST THE HUMAN-OIDS
IT WAS ALWAYS JUST LIKE, OH, WE'RE GOING OUT NOW, WE'RE HOLDING HANDS, OKAY NOW WE'RE BROKEN UP.
DON'T
EXCEPT WITH ALEX AND KIM.
YEAH, ME AND JESUS JUST DID THE HAND-HOLDING THING.
COME HOME
MT. VERNON REC CENT

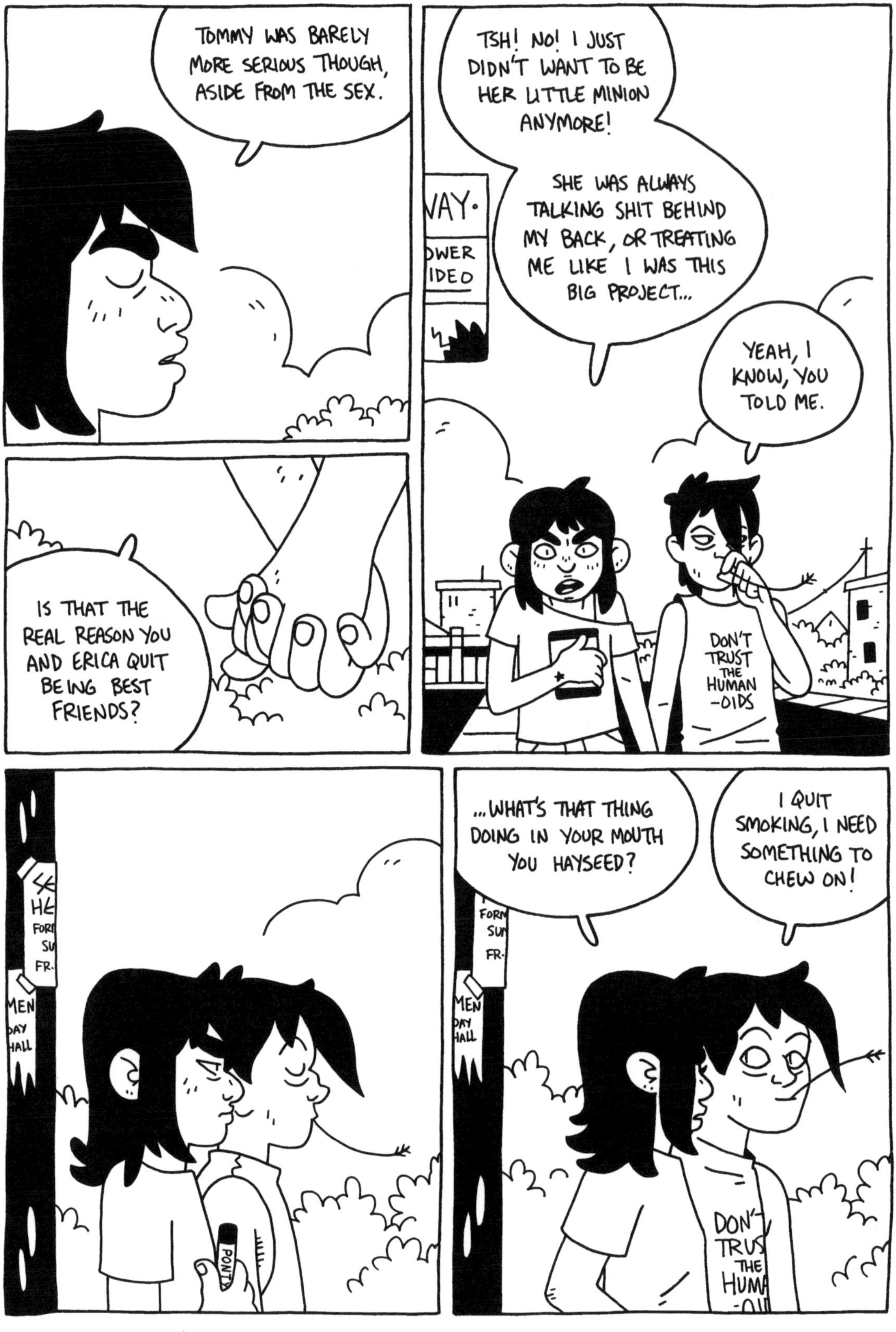
TOMMY WAS BARELY MORE SERIOUS THOUGH, ASIDE FROM THE SEX.
TSH! NO! I JUST DIDN'T WANT TO BE HER LITTLE MINION ANYMORE!
SHE WAS ALWAYS TALKING SHIT BEHIND MY BACK, OR TREATING ME LIKE I WAS THIS BIG PROJECT...
YEAH, I KNOW, YOU TOLD ME.
IS THAT THE REAL REASON YOU AND ERICA QUIT BEING BEST FRIENDS?
DON'T TRUST THE HUMAN-OIDS
...WHAT'S THAT THING DOING IN YOUR MOUTH YOU HAYSEED?
I QUIT SMOKING, I NEED SOMETHING TO CHEW ON!

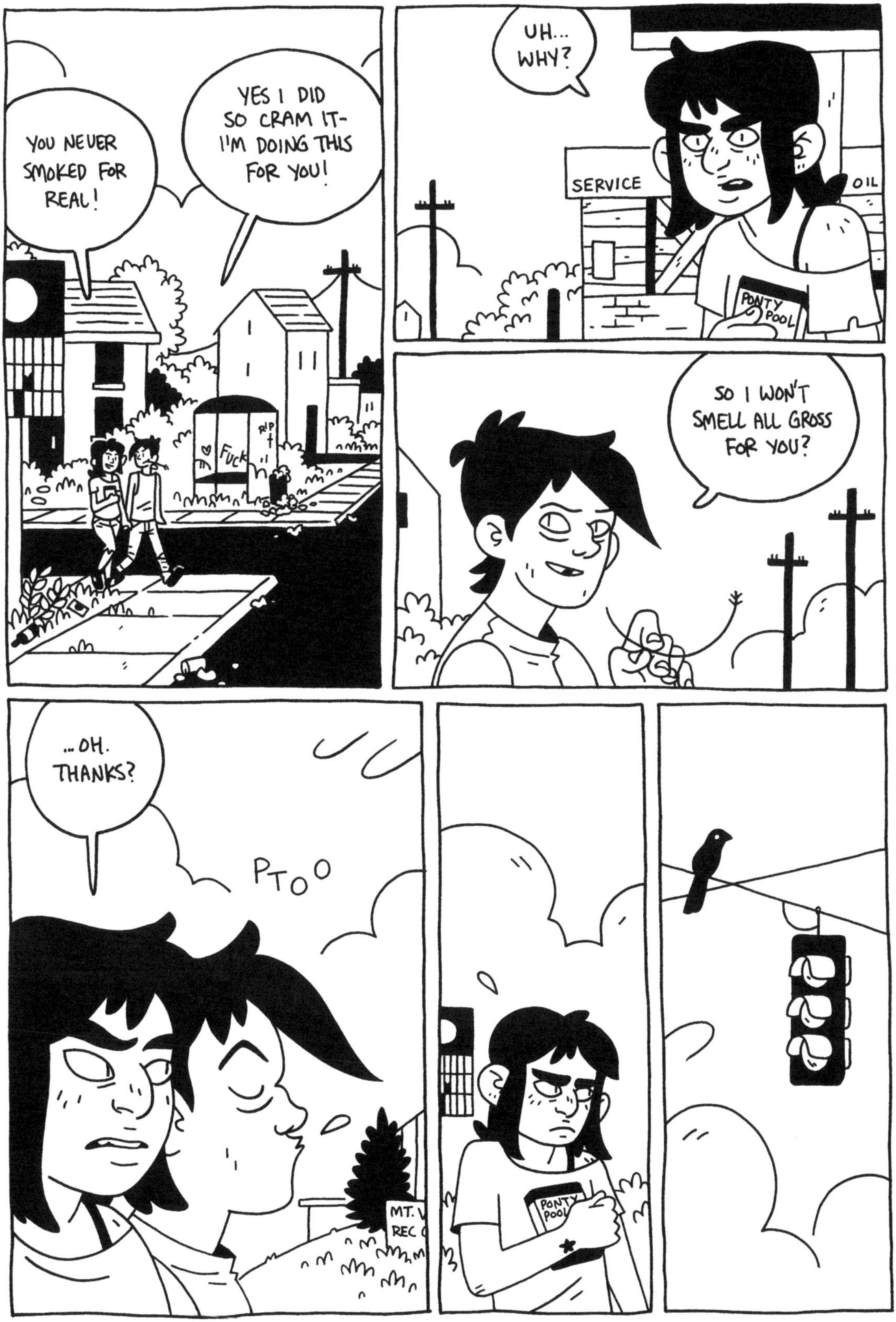
YOU NEVER SMOKED FOR REAL!
YES I DID SO CRAM IT- I'M DOING THIS FOR YOU!
RIP
FUCK
UH... WHY?
SERVICE
OIL
PONTY POOL
SO I WON'T SMELL ALL GROSS FOR YOU?
...OH. THANKS?
PTOOO
MT.
REC
PONTY POOL

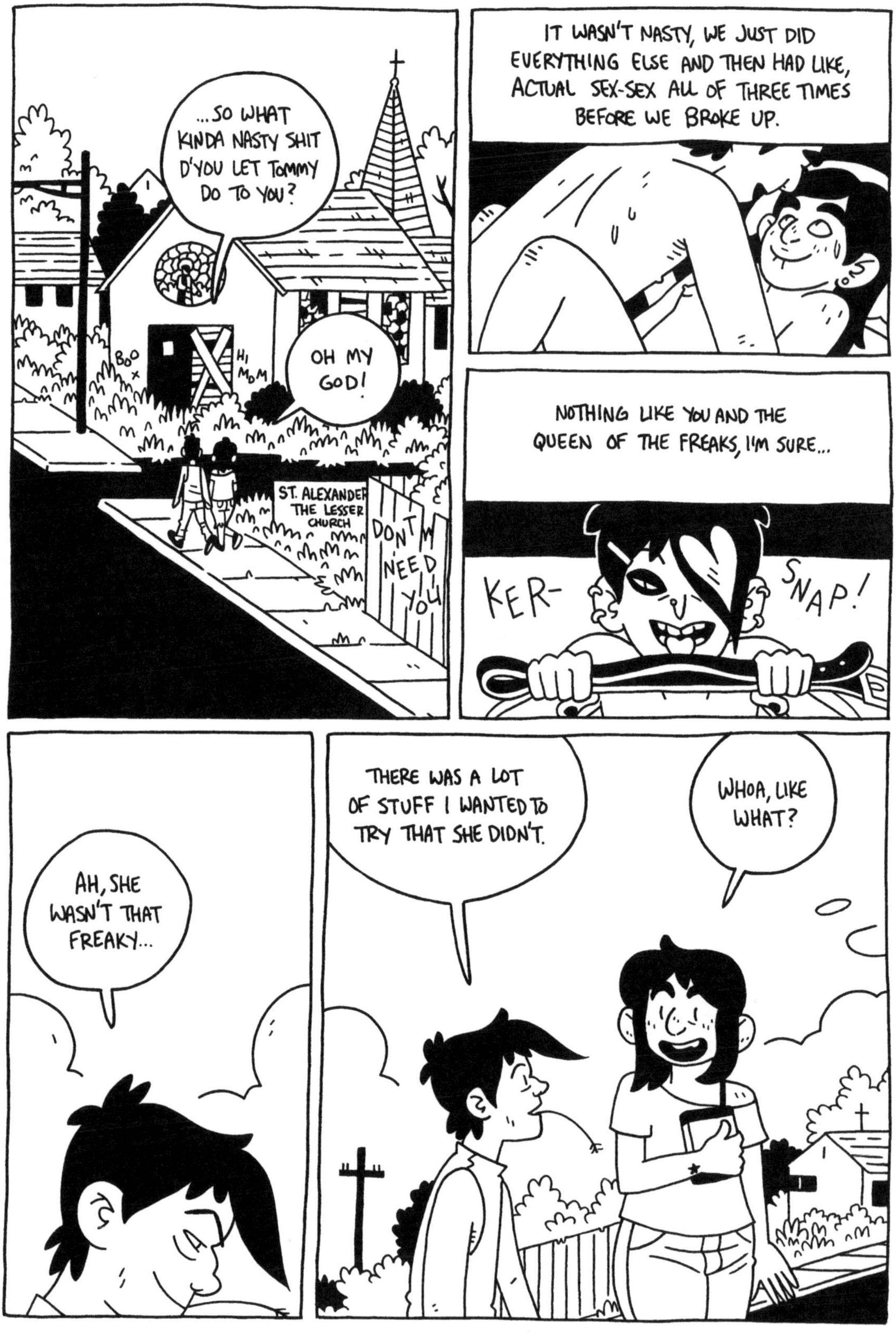
...SO WHAT KINDA NASTY SHIT D'YOU LET TOMMY DO TO YOU?
BOO x
HI MOM
OH MY GOD!
ST. ALEXANDER THE LESSER CHURCH
DON'T NEED YOU
IT WASN'T NASTY, WE JUST DID EVERYTHING ELSE AND THEN HAD LIKE, ACTUAL SEX-SEX ALL OF THREE TIMES BEFORE WE BROKE UP.
NOTHING LIKE YOU AND THE QUEEN OF THE FREAKS, I'M SURE...
KER-
SNAP!
AH, SHE WASN'T THAT FREAKY...
THERE WAS A LOT OF STUFF I WANTED TO TRY THAT SHE DIDN'T.
WHOA, LIKE WHAT?

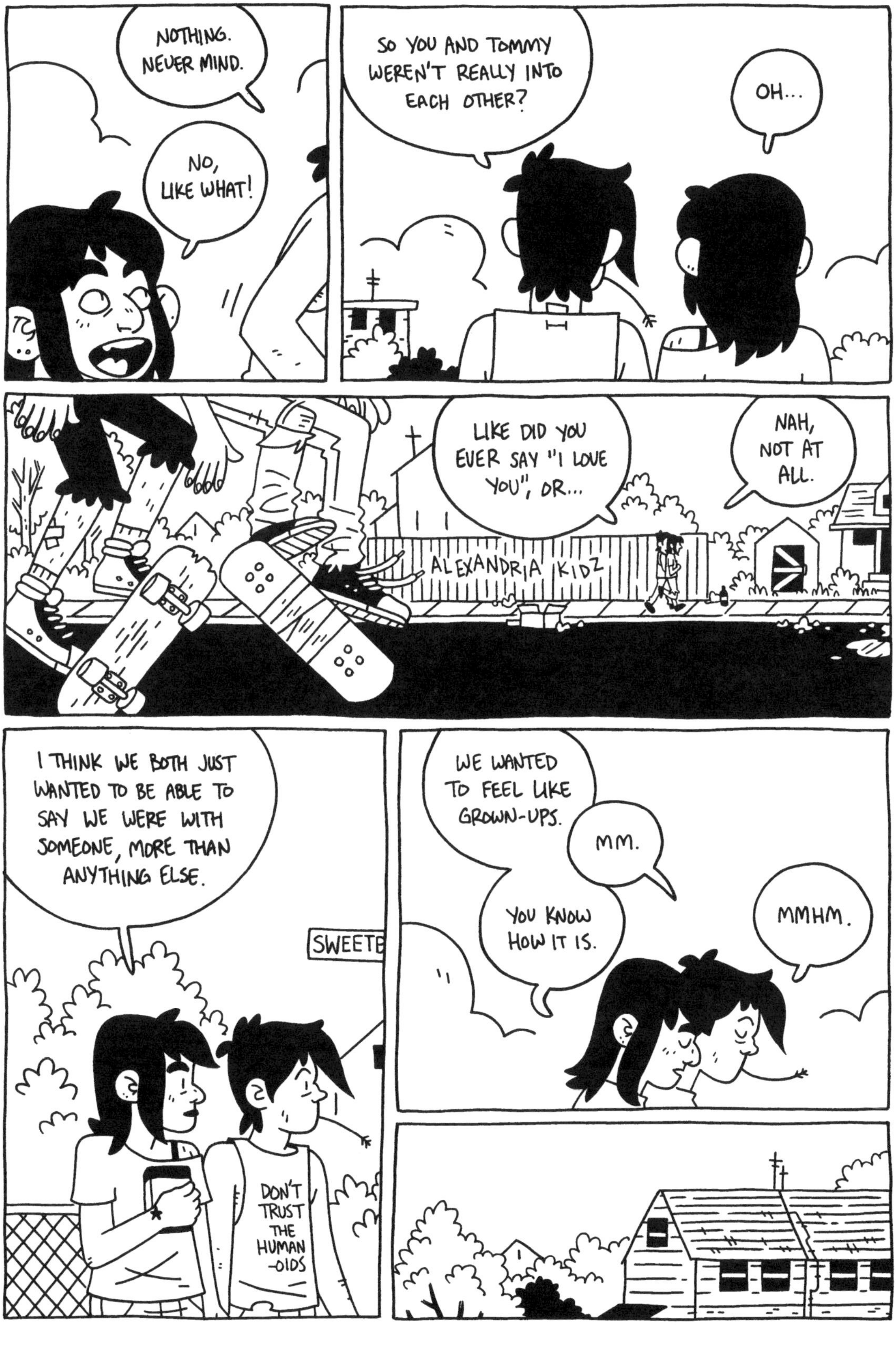

NOTHING. NEVER MIND.
NO, LIKE WHAT!
SO YOU AND TOMMY WEREN'T REALLY INTO EACH OTHER?
OH...
LIKE DID YOU EVER SAY "I LOVE YOU", OR...
NAH, NOT AT ALL.
ALEXANDRIA KIDZ
I THINK WE BOTH JUST WANTED TO BE ABLE TO SAY WE WERE WITH SOMEONE, MORE THAN ANYTHING ELSE.
SWEETE
DON'T TRUST THE HUMAN-OIDS
WE WANTED TO FEEL LIKE GROWN-UPS.
MM.
YOU KNOW HOW IT IS.
MMHM.

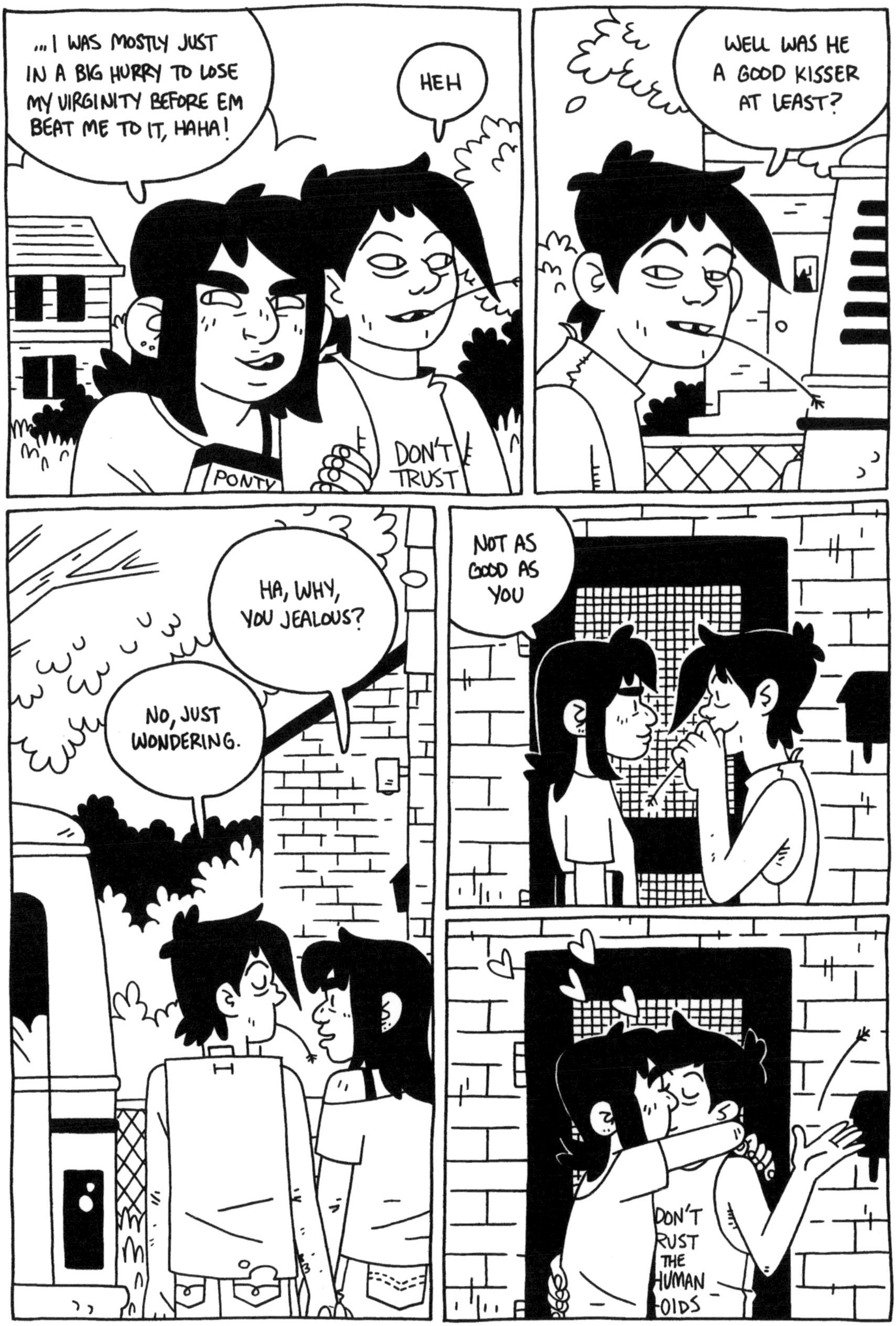
...I WAS MOSTLY JUST IN A BIG HURRY TO LOSE MY VIRGINITY BEFORE EM BEAT ME TO IT, HAHA!
HEH
PONTY
DON'T TRUST
WELL WAS HE A GOOD KISSER AT LEAST?
HA, WHY, YOU JEALOUS?
NO, JUST WONDERING.
NOT AS GOOD AS YOU
DON'T RUST THE HUMAN OIDS

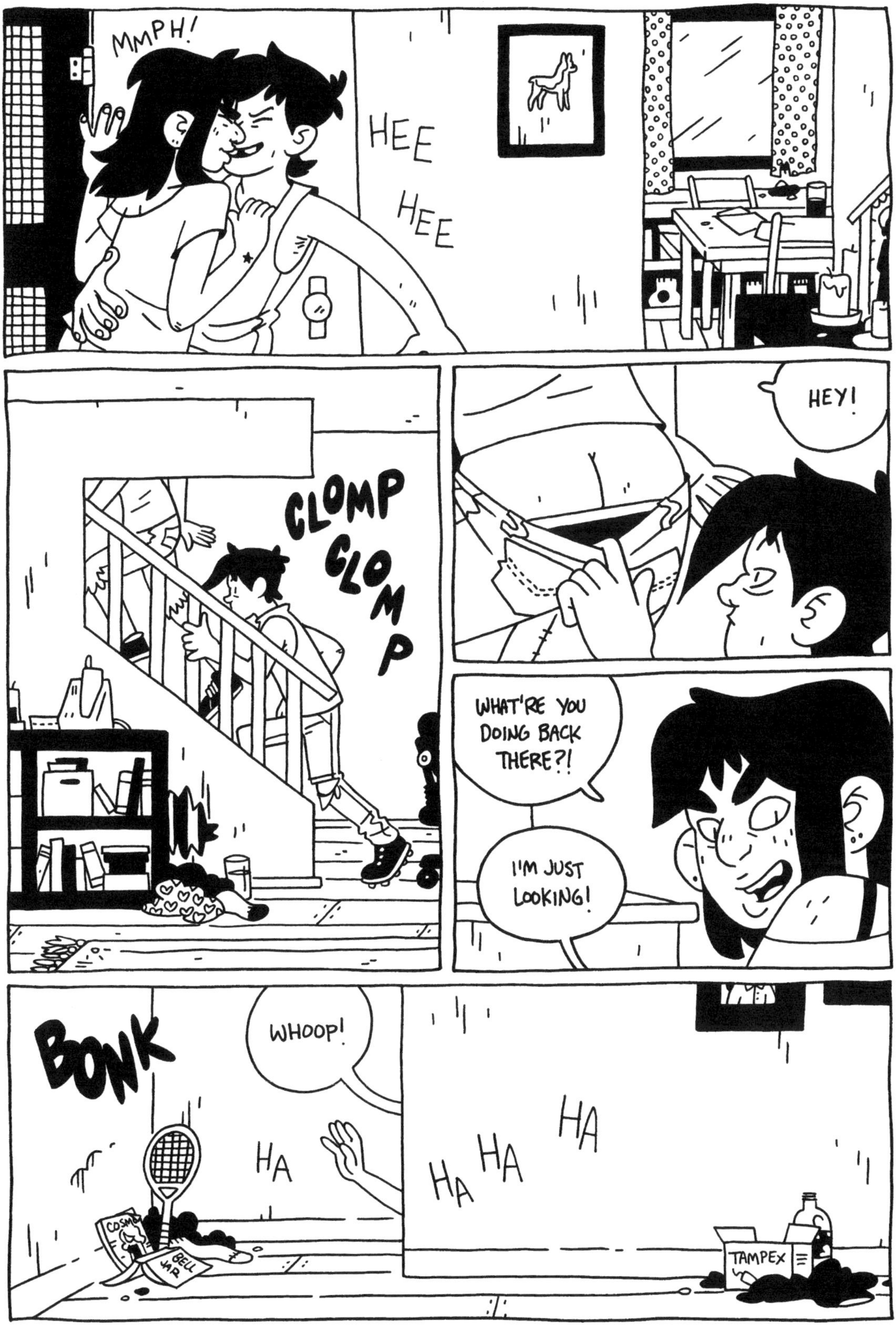
MMPH!
HEE
HEE
CLOMP
CLOMP
HEY!
WHAT'RE YOU DOING BACK THERE?!
I'M JUST LOOKING!
BONK
WHOOP!
HA
COSMO
BELL JAR
HA
HA
HA
TAMPEX

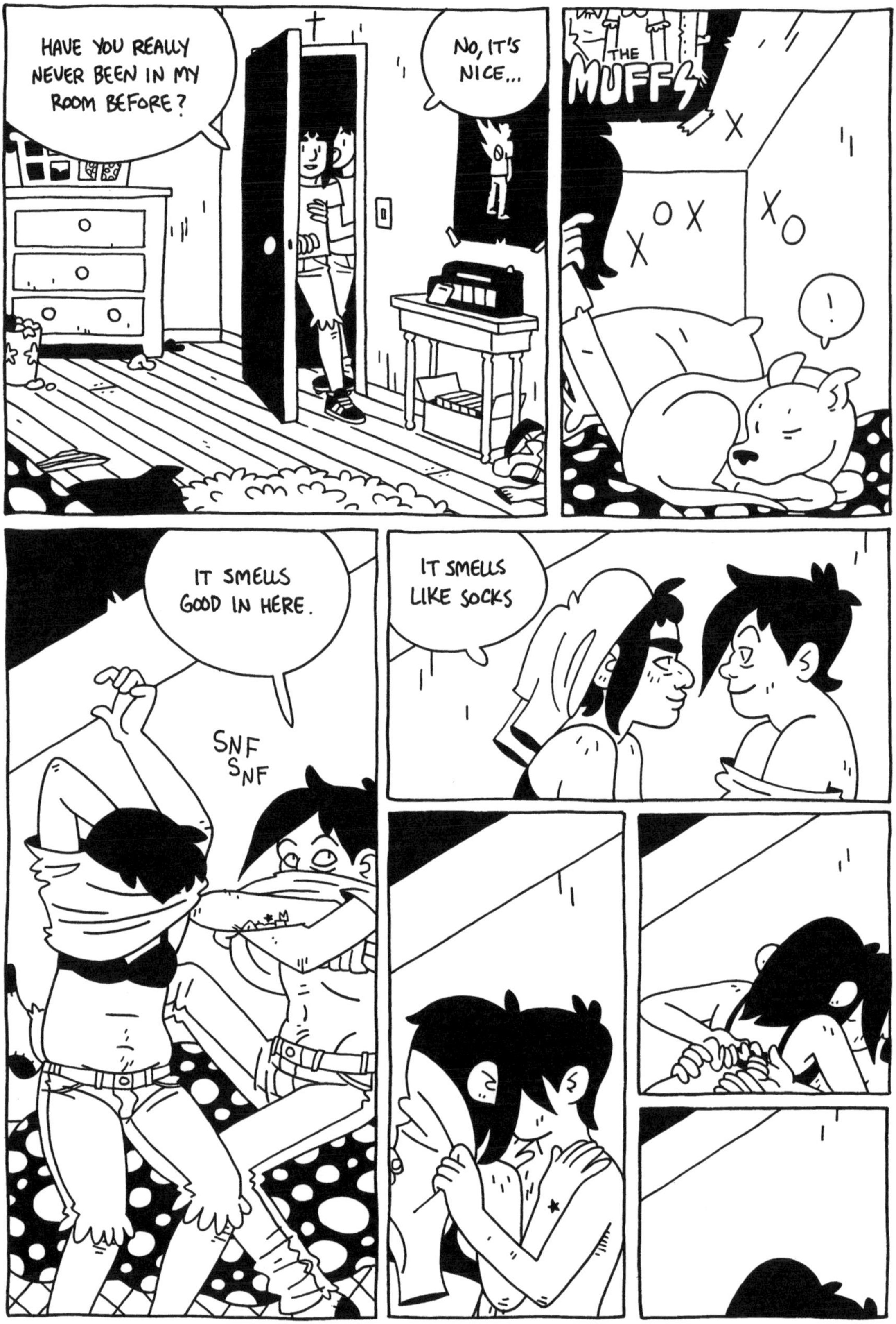
HAVE YOU REALLY NEVER BEEN IN MY ROOM BEFORE?
NO, IT'S NICE...
THE MUFFS
X O X
X O
!
IT SMELLS GOOD IN HERE.
SNF SNF
IT SMELLS LIKE SOCKS

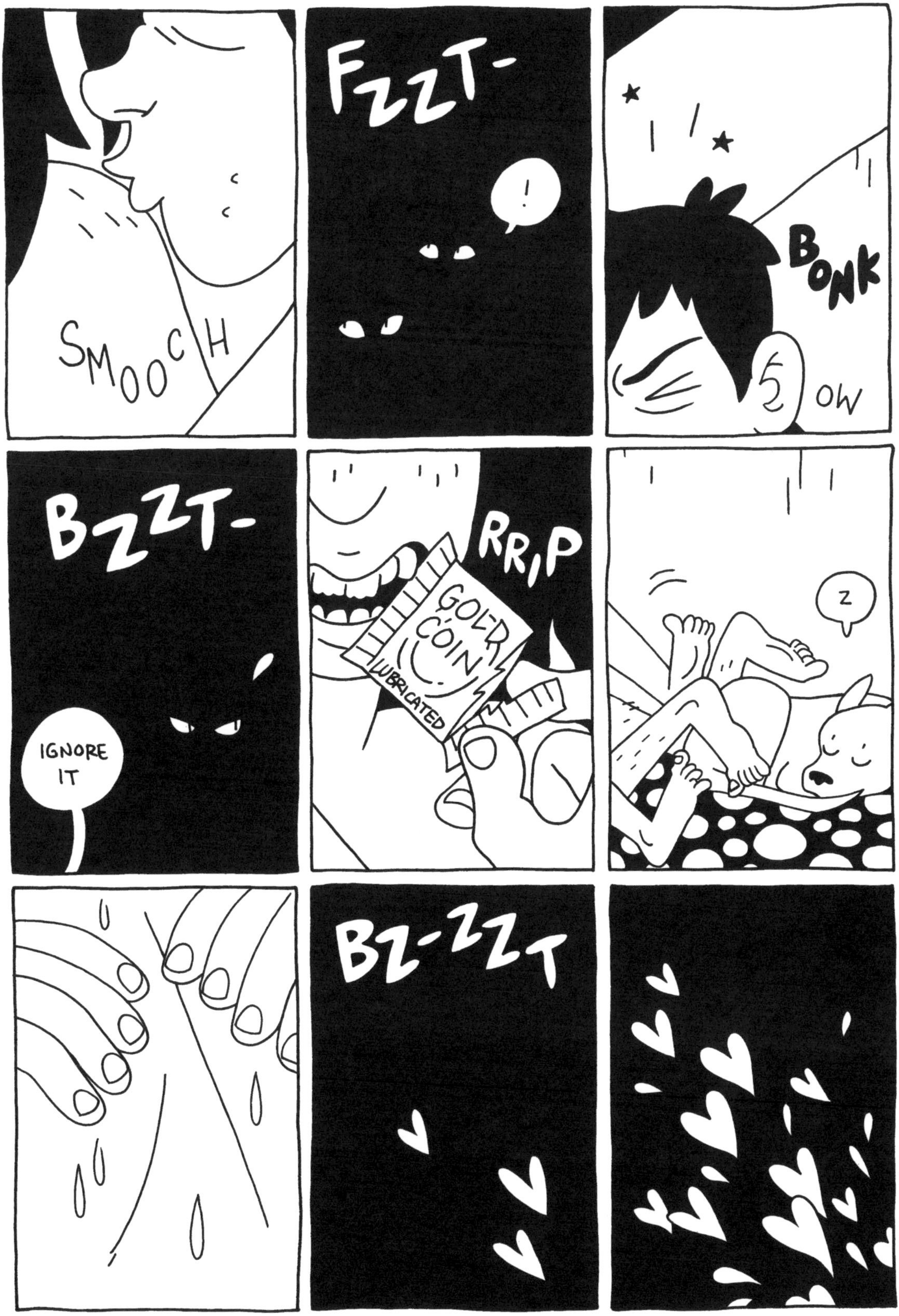
SMOOCH
FZZT-
!
BONK
OW
BZZT-
IGNORE IT
RRIP
GOL'D COIN
LUBRICATED
Z
BZ-ZZT

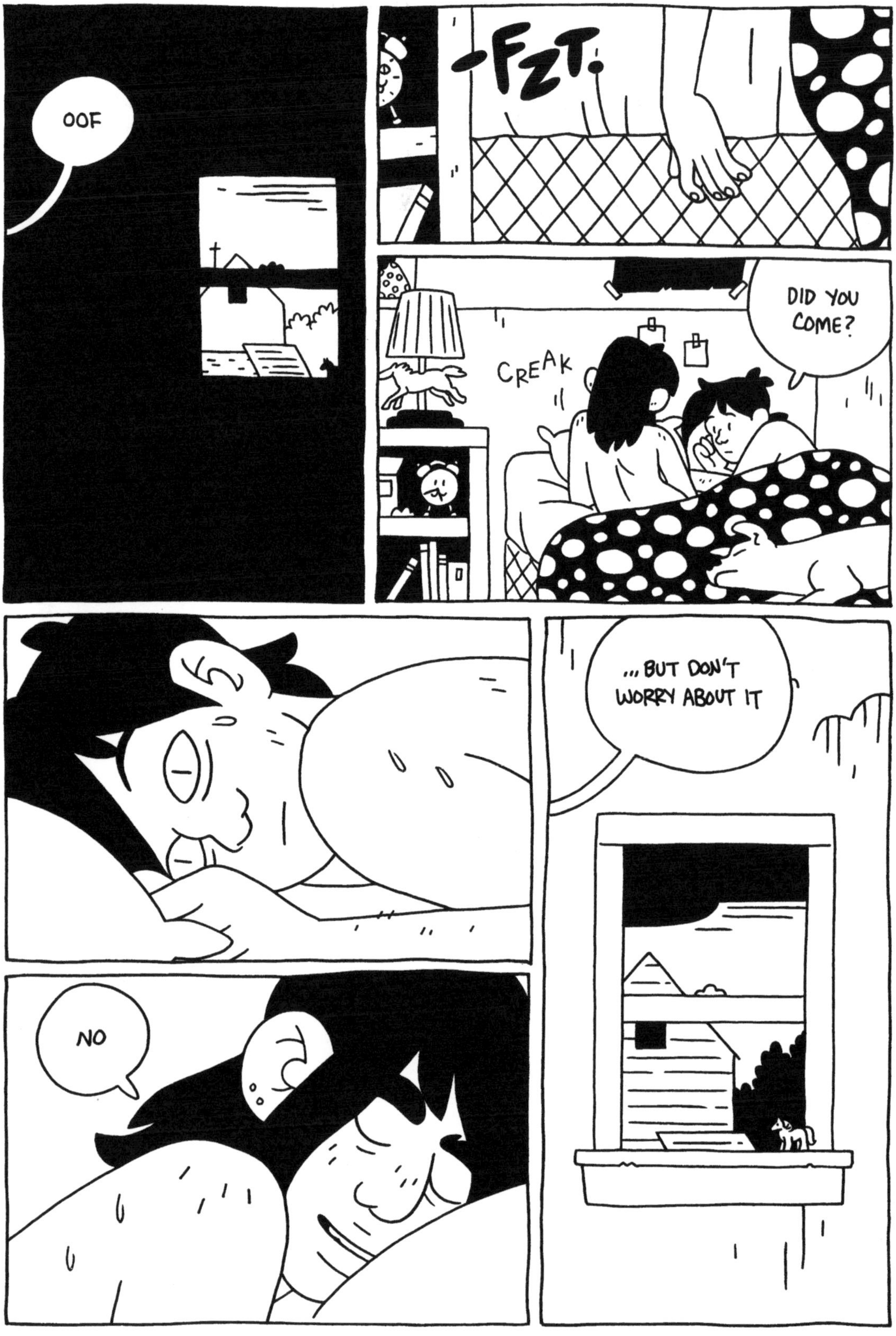
OOF
-FZT-
CREAK
DID YOU COME?
...BUT DON'T WORRY ABOUT IT
NO

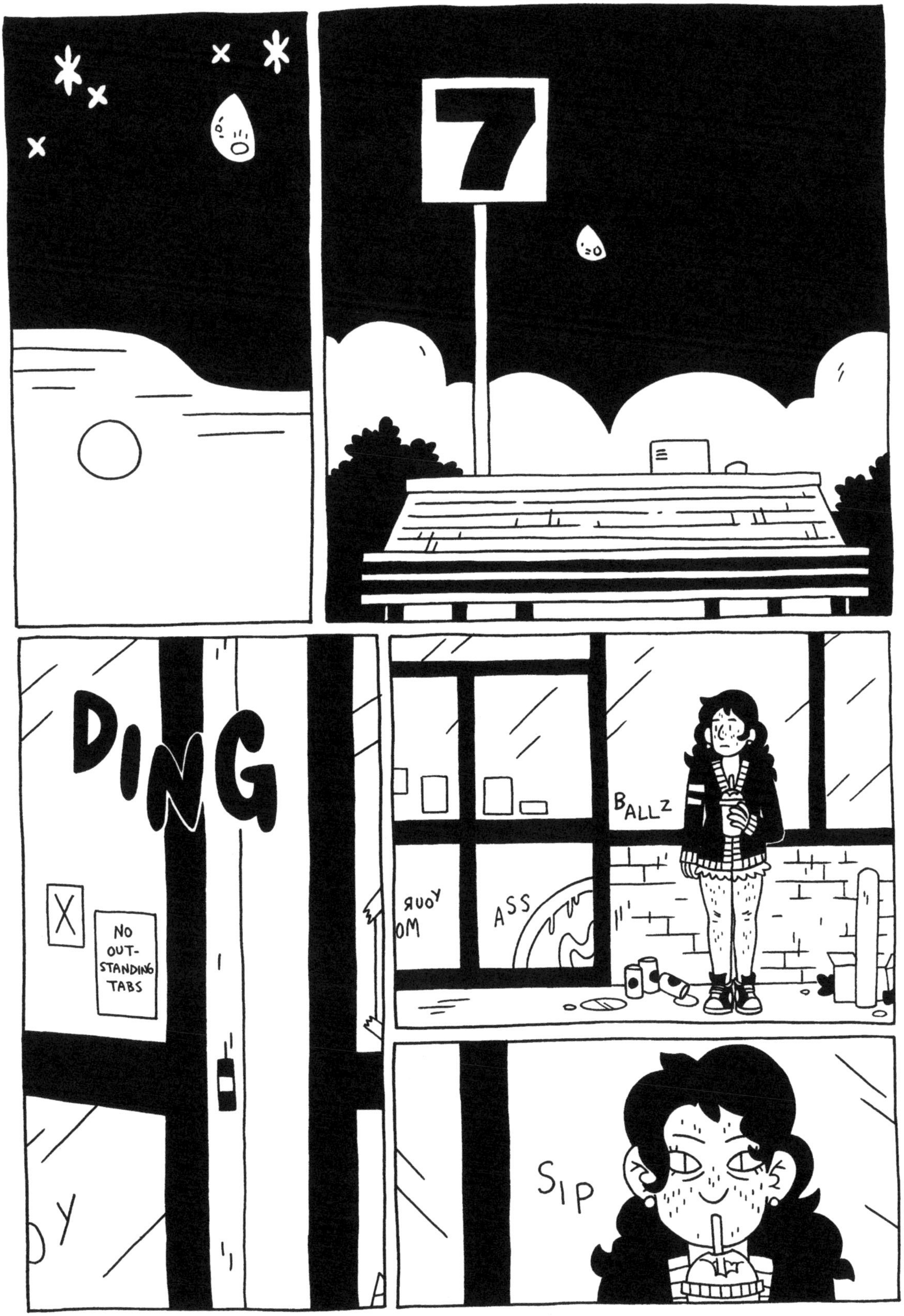
DING
NO OUT-STANDING TABS
BALLZ
YOUR MO
ASS
SIP

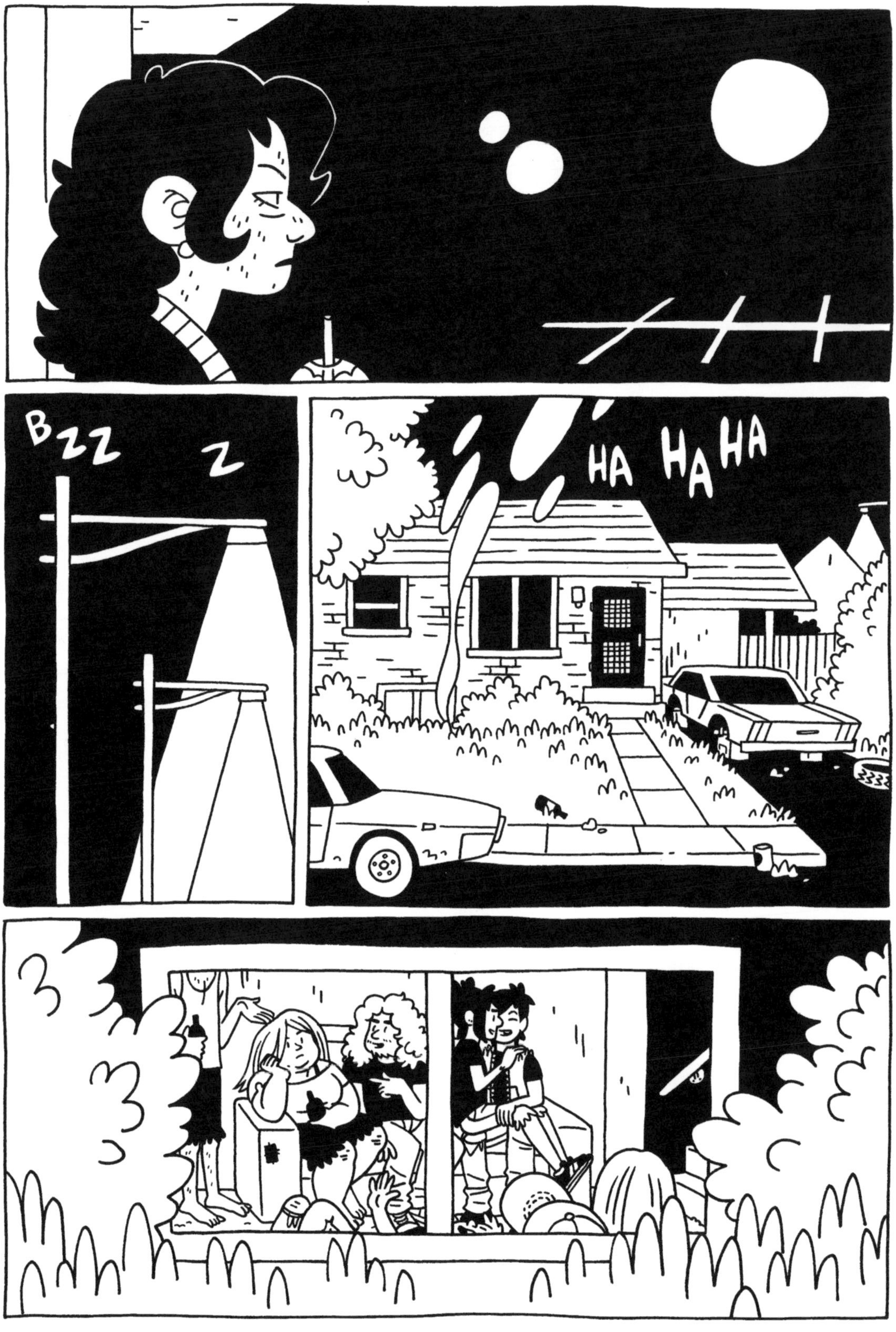
BZZZ
Z
HA HA HA HA

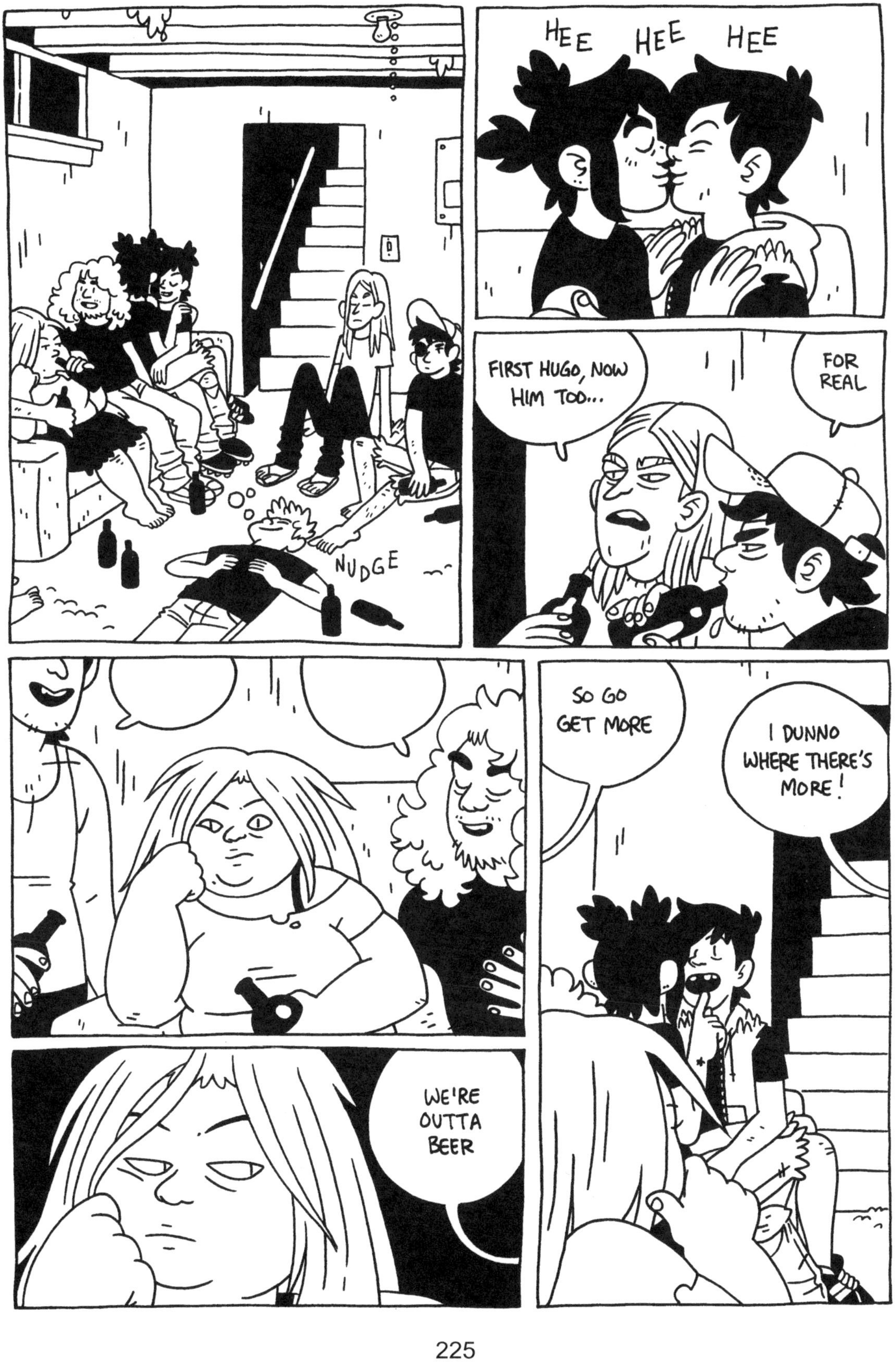
NUDGE
HEE HEE HEE
FIRST HUGO, NOW HIM TOO...
FOR REAL
WE'RE OUTTA BEER
SO GO GET MORE
I DUNNO WHERE THERE'S MORE!

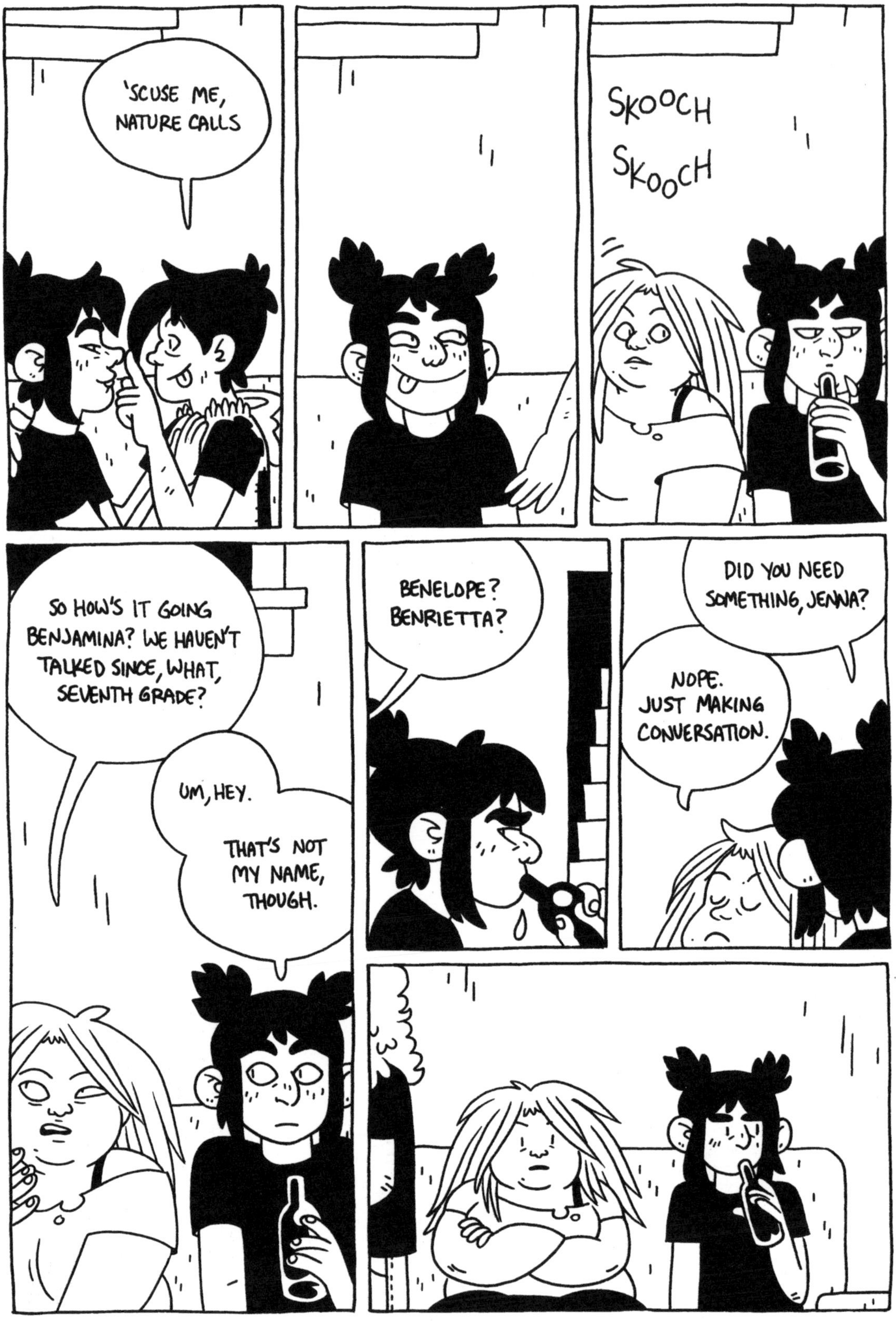
'SCUSE ME, NATURE CALLS
SKOOCH
SKOOCH
SO HOW'S IT GOING BENJAMINA? WE HAVEN'T TALKED SINCE, WHAT, SEVENTH GRADE?
UM, HEY.
THAT'S NOT MY NAME, THOUGH.
BENELOPE? BENRIETTA?
DID YOU NEED SOMETHING, JENNA?
NOPE. JUST MAKING CONVERSATION.

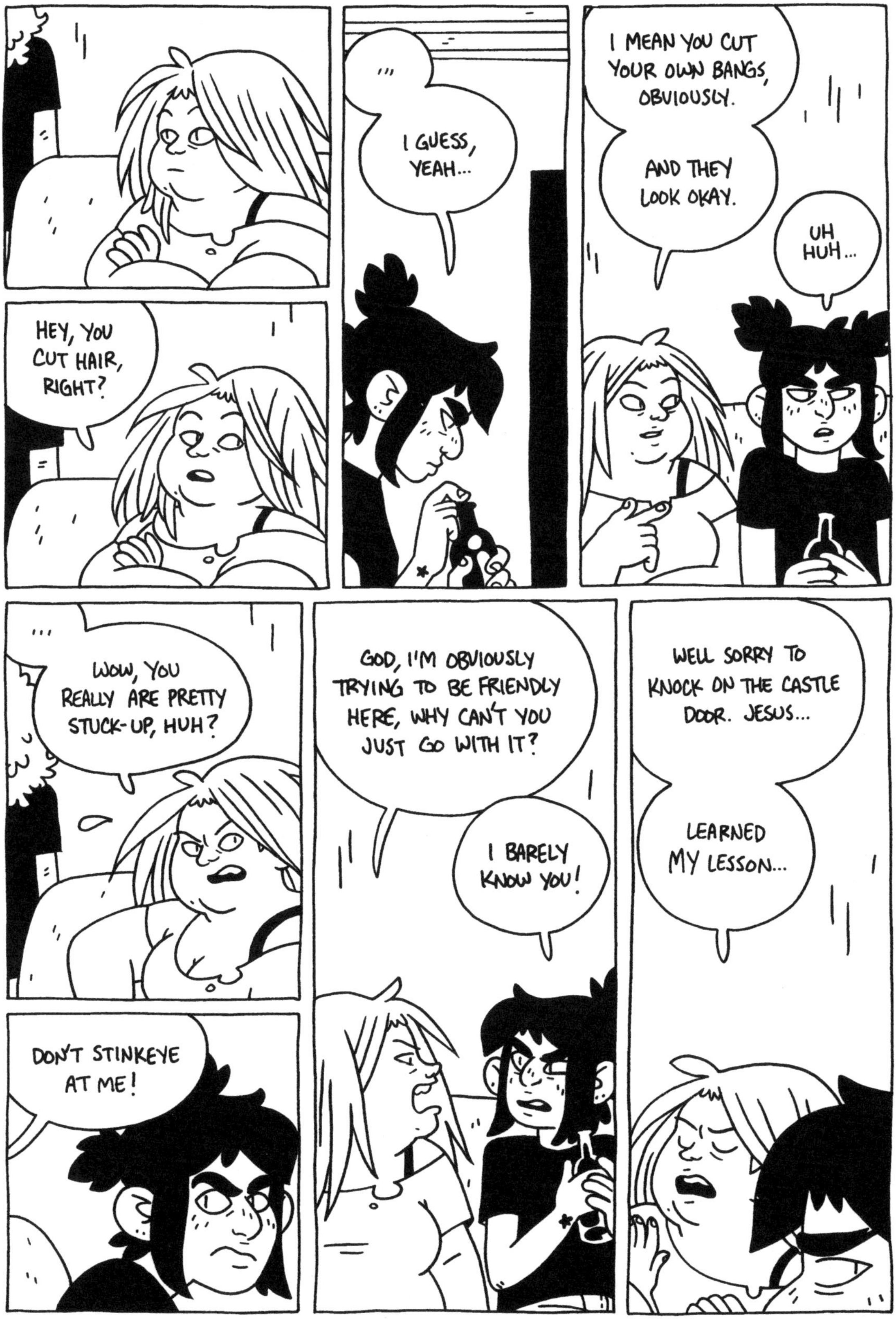
HEY, YOU CUT HAIR, RIGHT?
...
I GUESS, YEAH...
I MEAN YOU CUT YOUR OWN BANGS, OBVIOUSLY.
AND THEY LOOK OKAY.
UH HUH...
...
WOW, YOU REALLY ARE PRETTY STUCK-UP, HUH?
DON'T STINKEYE AT ME!
GOD, I'M OBVIOUSLY TRYING TO BE FRIENDLY HERE, WHY CAN'T YOU JUST GO WITH IT?
I BARELY KNOW YOU!
WELL SORRY TO KNOCK ON THE CASTLE DOOR. JESUS...
LEARNED MY LESSON...

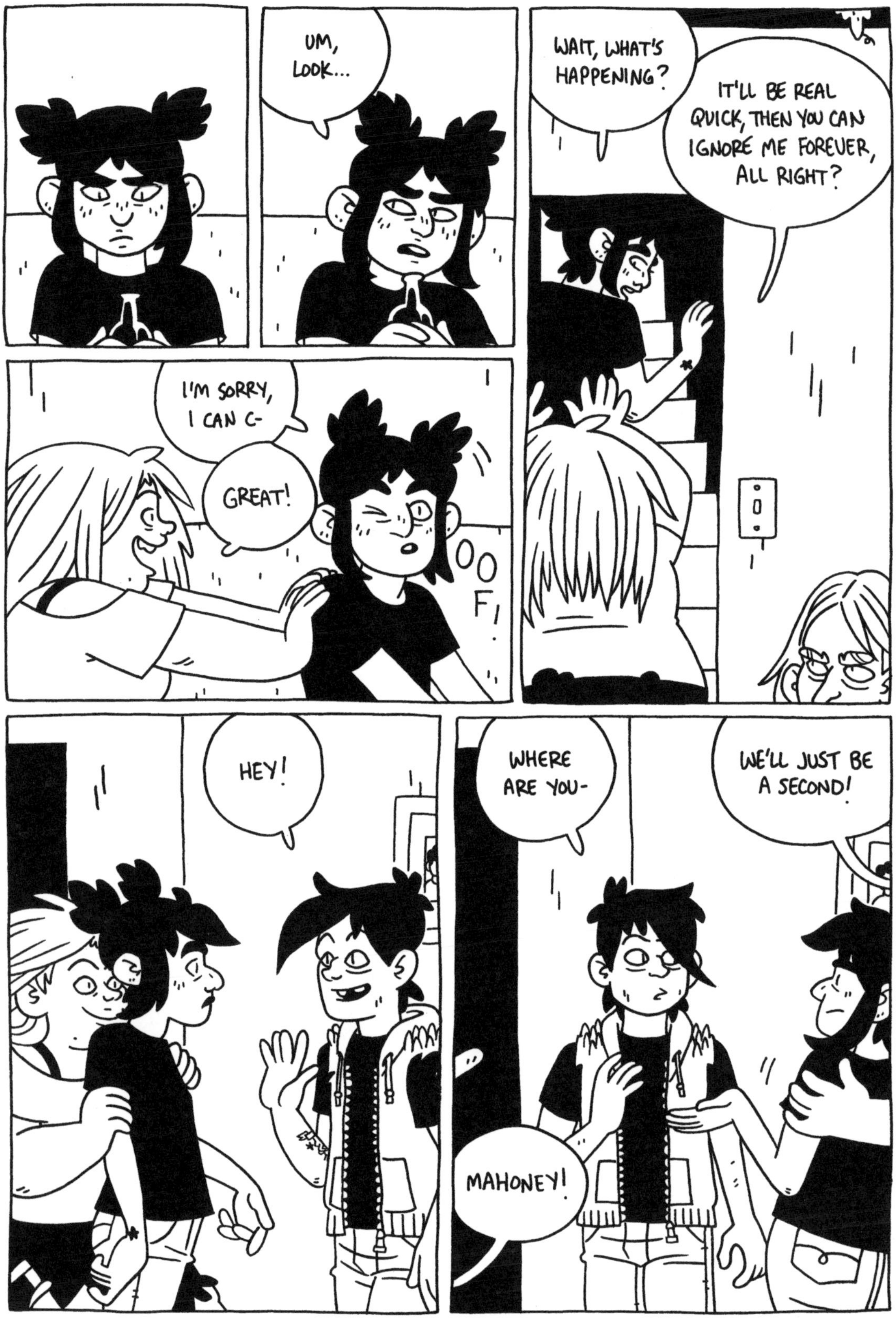
UM, LOOK...
WAIT, WHAT'S HAPPENING?
IT'LL BE REAL QUICK, THEN YOU CAN IGNORE ME FOREVER, ALL RIGHT?
I'M SORRY, I CAN C-
GREAT!
OOF!
HEY!
WHERE ARE YOU-
WE'LL JUST BE A SECOND!
MAHONEY!

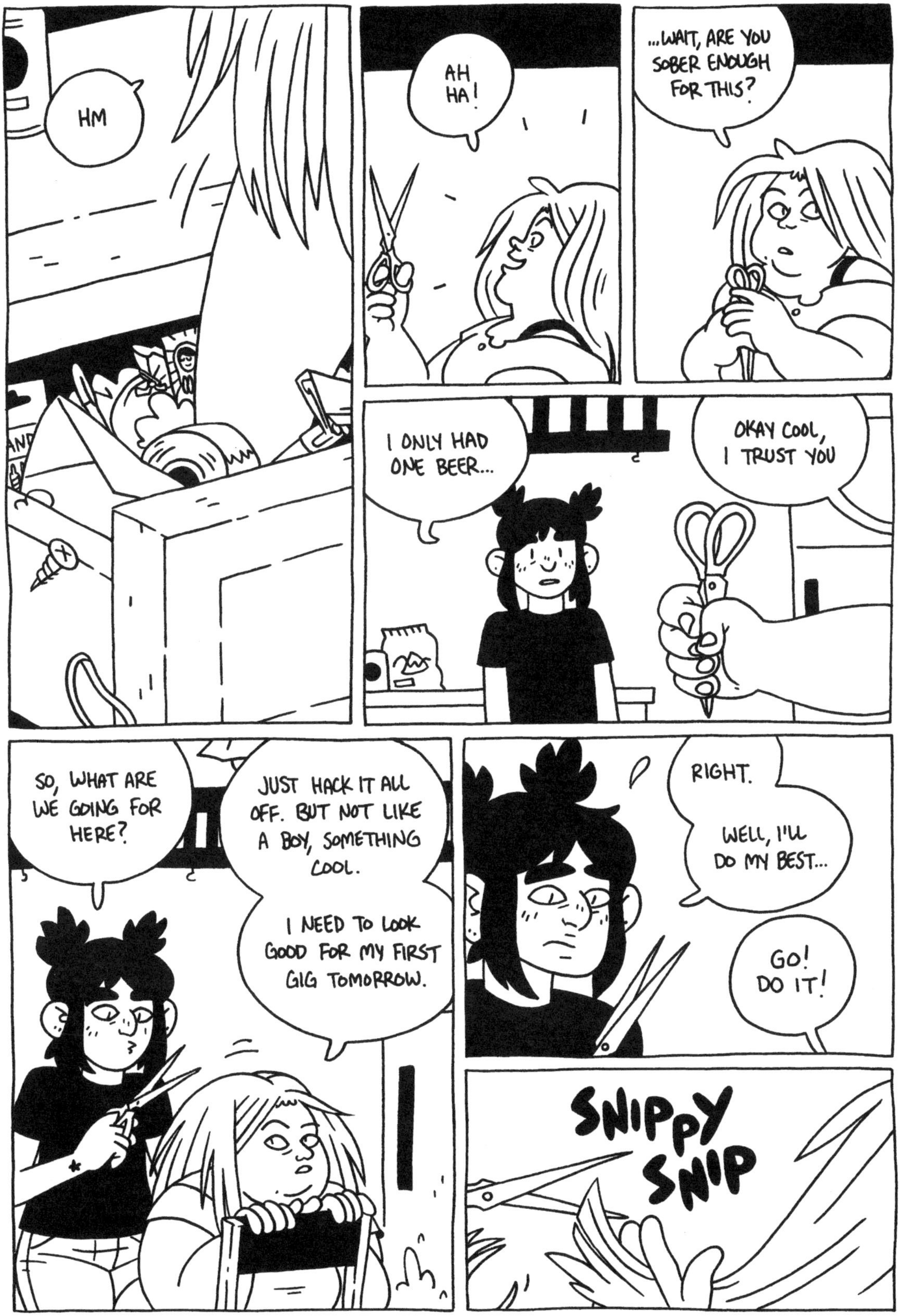
HM
AH HA!
...WAIT, ARE YOU SOBER ENOUGH FOR THIS?
I ONLY HAD ONE BEER...
OKAY COOL, I TRUST YOU
SO, WHAT ARE WE GOING FOR HERE?
JUST HACK IT ALL OFF. BUT NOT LIKE A BOY, SOMETHING COOL.
I NEED TO LOOK GOOD FOR MY FIRST GIG TOMORROW.
RIGHT.
WELL, I'LL DO MY BEST...
GO! DO IT!
SNIPPY SNIP

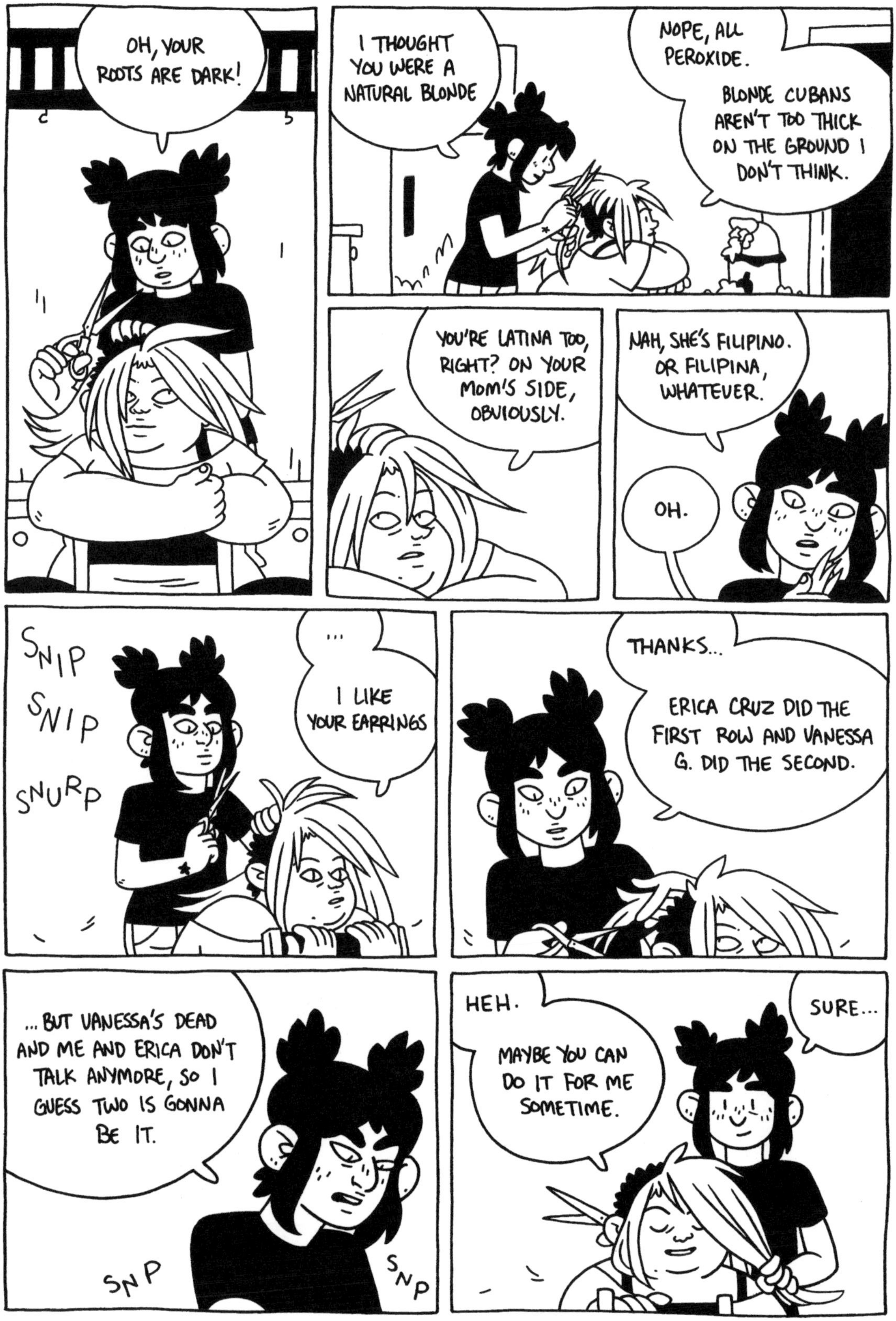

OH, YOUR ROOTS ARE DARK!
I THOUGHT YOU WERE A NATURAL BLONDE
NOPE, ALL PEROXIDE.
BLONDE CUBANS AREN'T TOO THICK ON THE GROUND I DON'T THINK.
YOU'RE LATINA TOO, RIGHT? ON YOUR MOM'S SIDE, OBVIOUSLY.
NAH, SHE'S FILIPINO. OR FILIPINA, WHATEVER.
OH.
SNIP
SNIP
SNURP
...
I LIKE YOUR EARRINGS
THANKS...
ERICA CRUZ DID THE FIRST ROW AND VANESSA G. DID THE SECOND.
...BUT VANESSA'S DEAD AND ME AND ERICA DON'T TALK ANYMORE, SO I GUESS TWO IS GONNA BE IT.
SNP
SNP
HEH.
MAYBE YOU CAN DO IT FOR ME SOMETIME.
SURE...

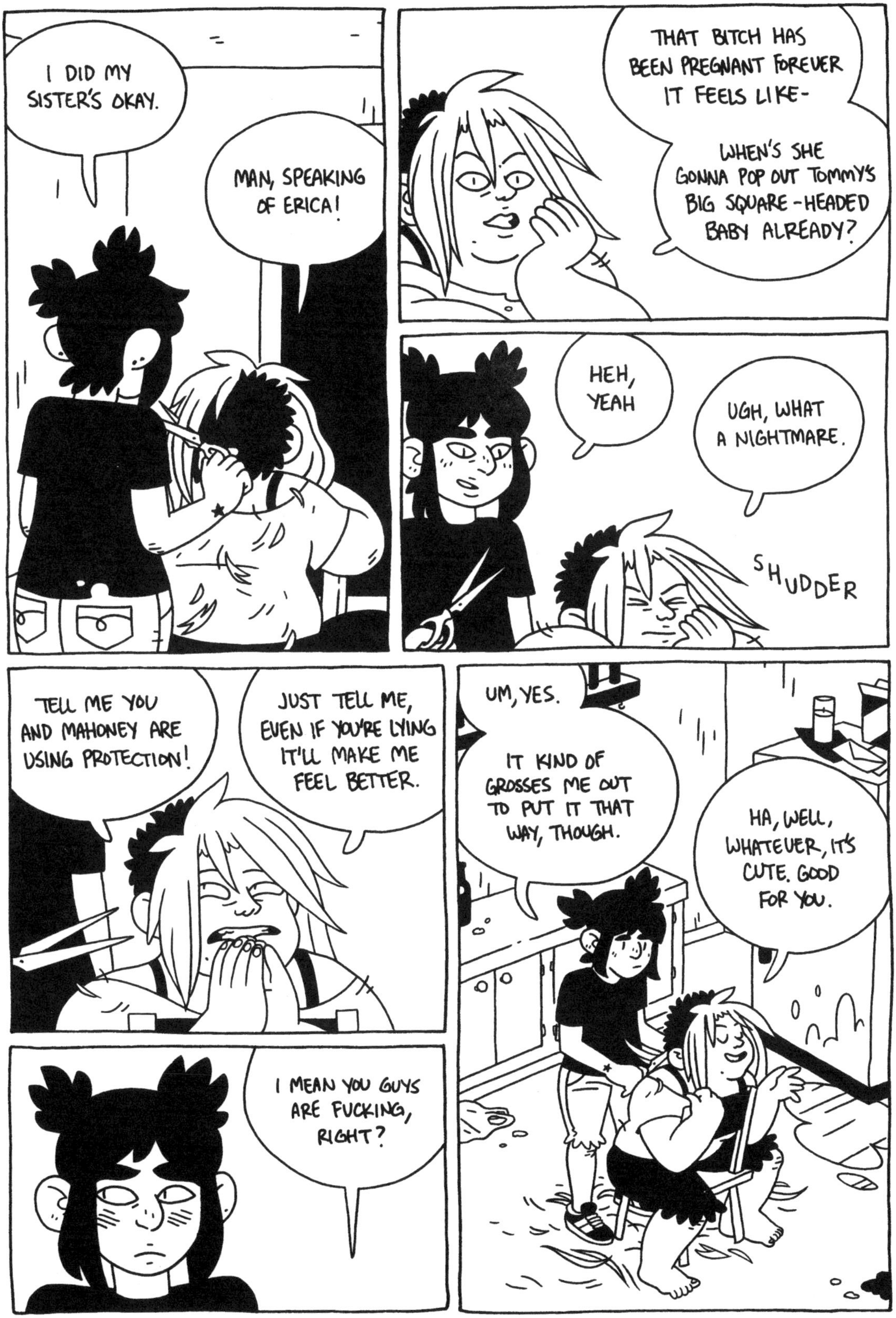
I DID MY SISTER'S OKAY.
MAN, SPEAKING OF ERICA!
THAT BITCH HAS BEEN PREGNANT FOREVER IT FEELS LIKE-
WHEN'S SHE GONNA POP OUT TOMMY'S BIG SQUARE-HEADED BABY ALREADY?
HEH, YEAH
UGH, WHAT A NIGHTMARE.
SHUDDER
TELL ME YOU AND MAHONEY ARE USING PROTECTION!
JUST TELL ME, EVEN IF YOU'RE LYING IT'LL MAKE ME FEEL BETTER.
I MEAN YOU GUYS ARE FUCKING, RIGHT?
UM, YES.
IT KIND OF GROSSES ME OUT TO PUT IT THAT WAY, THOUGH.
HA, WELL, WHATEVER, IT'S CUTE. GOOD FOR YOU.

WHAT ABOUT YOU, ARE YOU SEEING ANYONE?

THBBT

NAH.

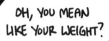

OH, YOU MEAN LIKE YOUR WEIGHT?

I DON'T THINK THAT'D BE A PROBLEM, I MEAN LOOK AT HUGO AND JESSIE...

THERE'S, UH, NOT REALLY ANYBODY MY TYPE AROUND HERE, YOU KNOW?

NOT THAT WOULD GO FOR A GIRL LIKE ME, ANYWAY.

I DIDN'T MEAN MY WEIGHT.

OH, UH...

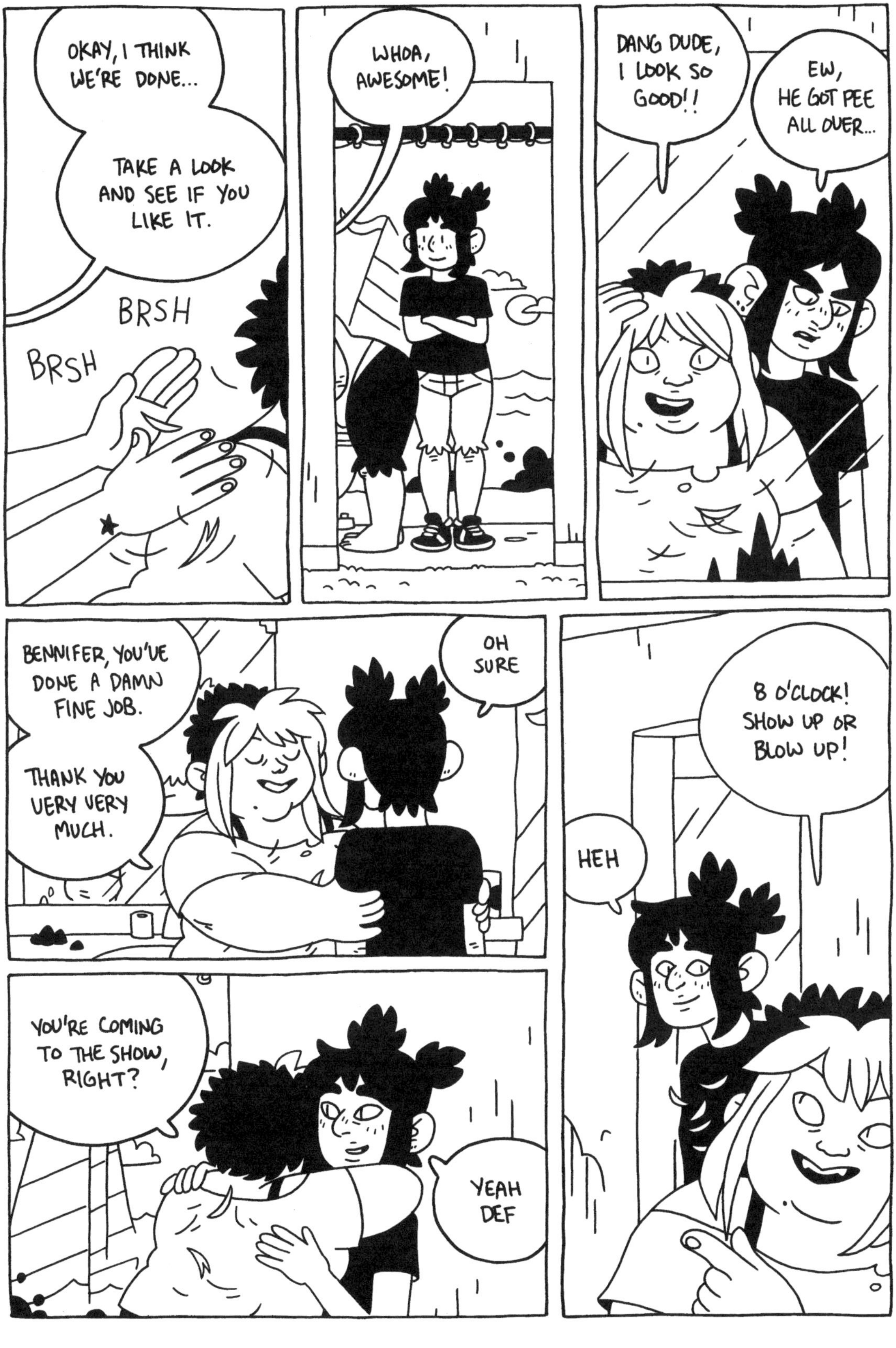
OKAY, I THINK WE'RE DONE...
TAKE A LOOK AND SEE IF YOU LIKE IT.
BRSH
BRSH
WHOA, AWESOME!
DANG DUDE, I LOOK SO GOOD!!
EW, HE GOT PEE ALL OVER...
BENNIFER, YOU'VE DONE A DAMN FINE JOB.
THANK YOU VERY VERY MUCH.
OH SURE
YOU'RE COMING TO THE SHOW, RIGHT?
YEAH DEF
8 O'CLOCK! SHOW UP OR BLOW UP!
HEH

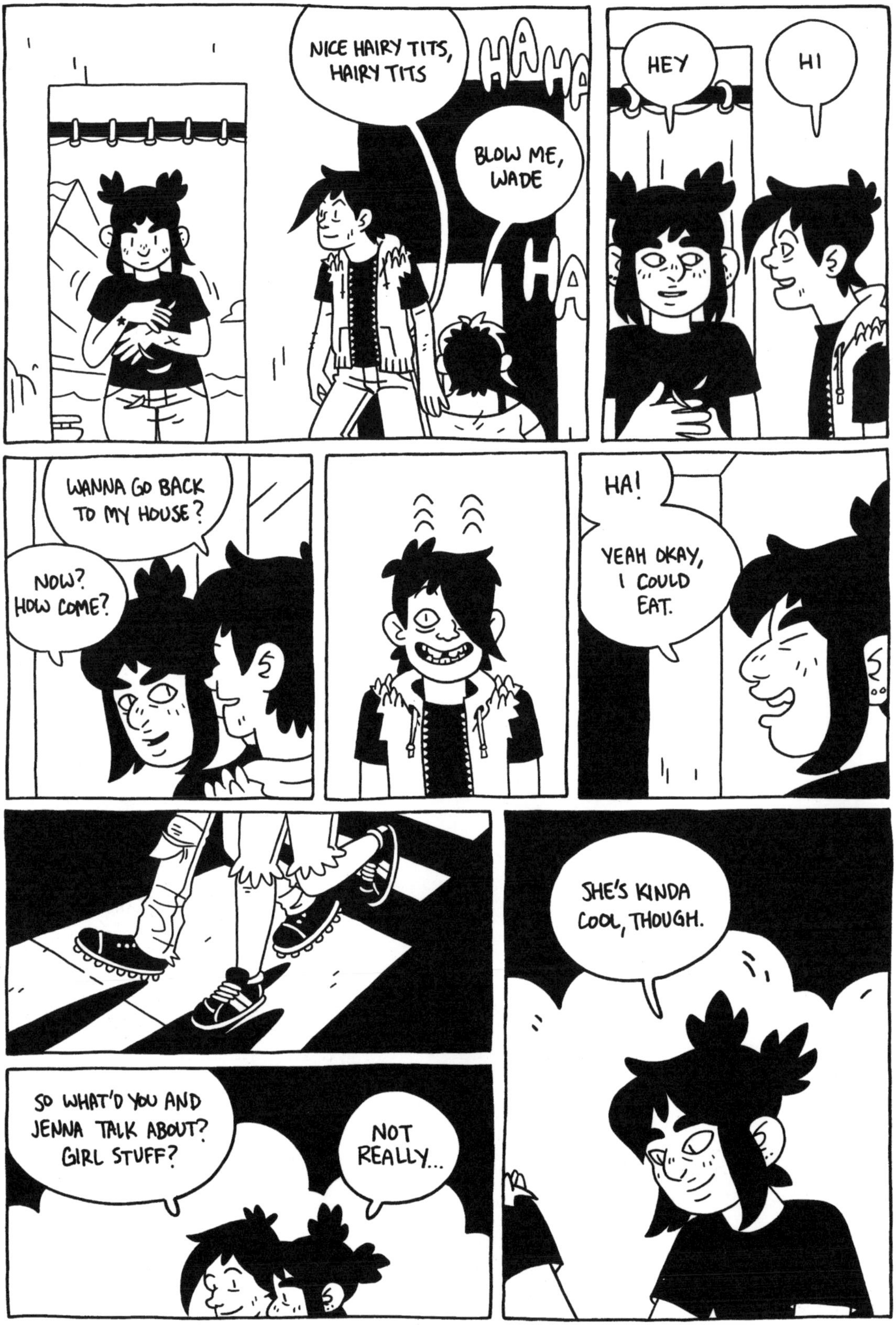
NICE HAIRY TITS, HAIRY TITS
HA HA HA
BLOW ME, WADE
HA
HEY
HI
WANNA GO BACK TO MY HOUSE?
NOW? HOW COME?
HA!
YEAH OKAY, I COULD EAT.
SHE'S KINDA COOL, THOUGH.
SO WHAT'D YOU AND JENNA TALK ABOUT? GIRL STUFF?
NOT REALLY...

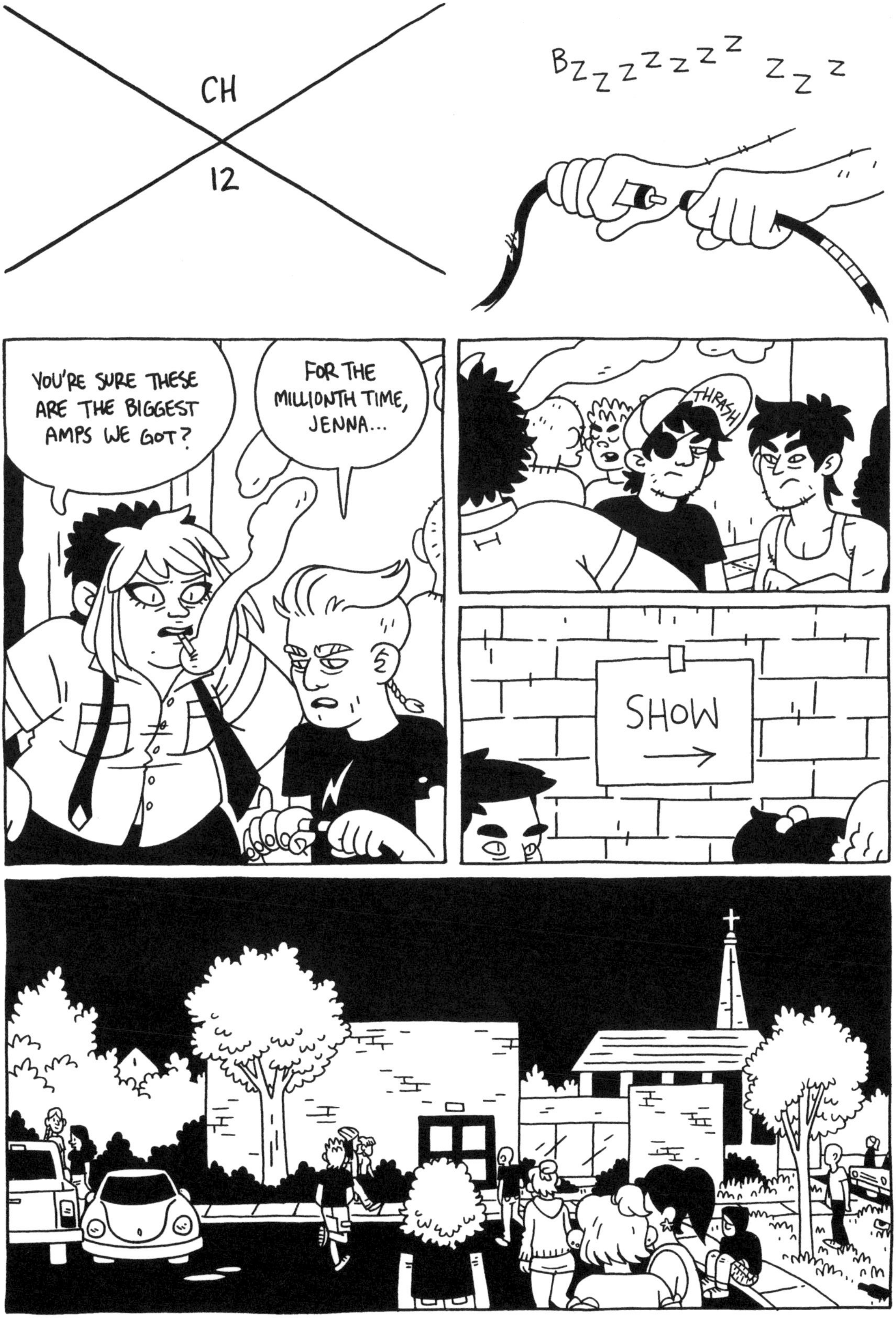
CH
12
BZZZZZZZZ ZZZ
YOU'RE SURE THESE ARE THE BIGGEST AMPS WE GOT?
FOR THE MILLIONTH TIME, JENNA...
THRASH
SHOW

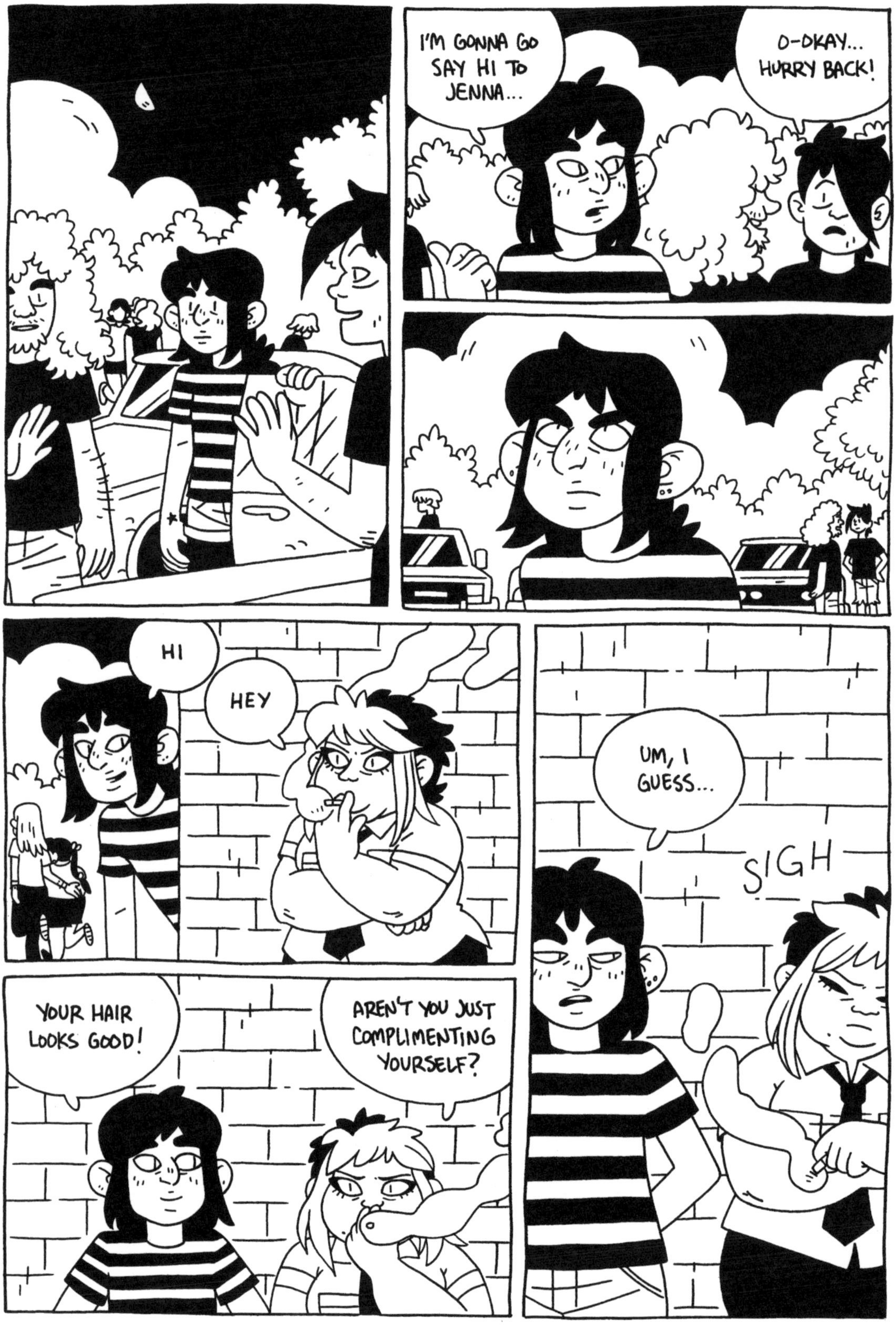
I'M GONNA GO SAY HI TO JENNA...
O-OKAY... HURRY BACK!
HI
HEY
YOUR HAIR LOOKS GOOD!
AREN'T YOU JUST COMPLIMENTING YOURSELF?
UM, I GUESS...
SIGH

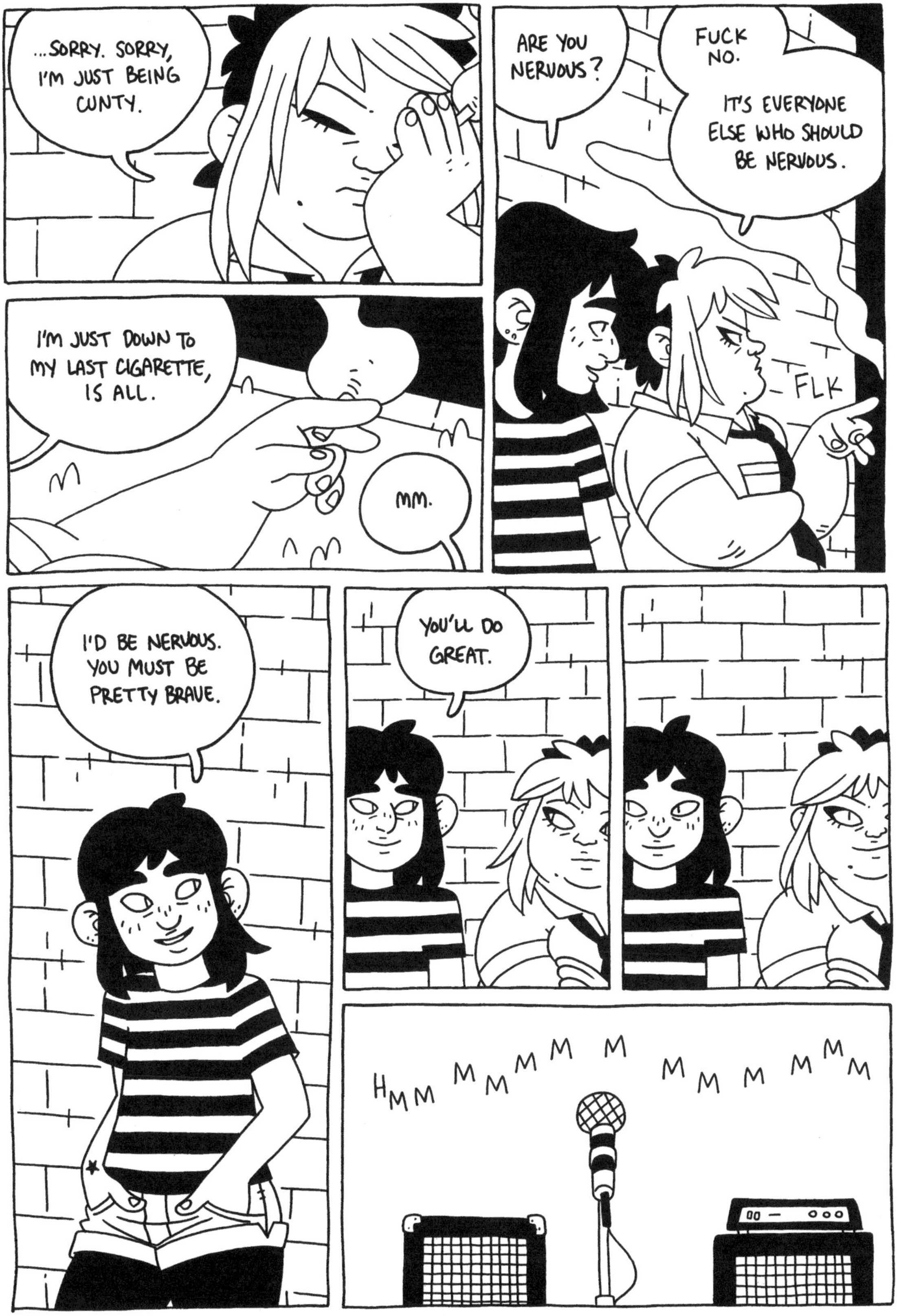
...SORRY. SORRY, I'M JUST BEING CUNTY.
ARE YOU NERVOUS?
FUCK NO.
IT'S EVERYONE ELSE WHO SHOULD BE NERVOUS.
I'M JUST DOWN TO MY LAST CIGARETTE, IS ALL.
MM.
FLK
I'D BE NERVOUS. YOU MUST BE PRETTY BRAVE.
YOU'LL DO GREAT.
HMM MMMMM M MMMMMM

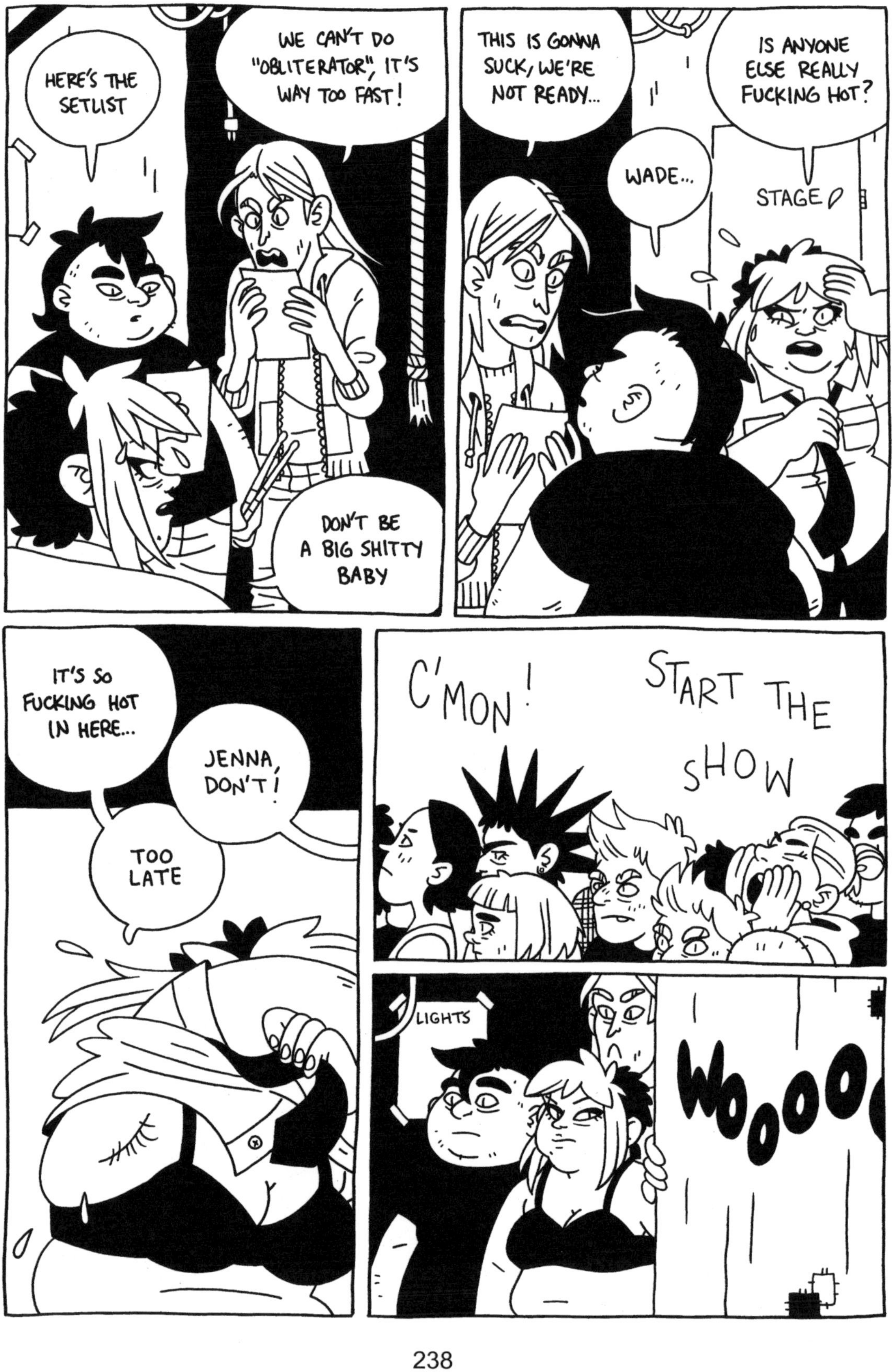
HERE'S THE SETLIST
WE CAN'T DO "OBLITERATOR", IT'S WAY TOO FAST!
DON'T BE A BIG SHITTY BABY
THIS IS GONNA SUCK, WE'RE NOT READY...
WADE...
IS ANYONE ELSE REALLY FUCKING HOT?
STAGE
IT'S SO FUCKING HOT IN HERE...
JENNA, DON'T!
TOO LATE
C'MON!
START THE SHOW
LIGHTS
WOOOO

OW OW A WHIIITE WHALE
THRASH
420
MOOOOOOO
PUT IT ON!
HA HA HA
BZZZ-EEEEEEEE

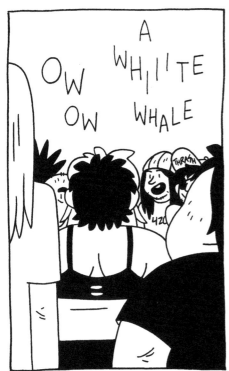

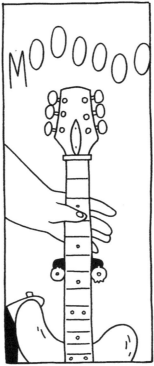

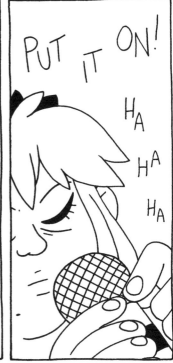

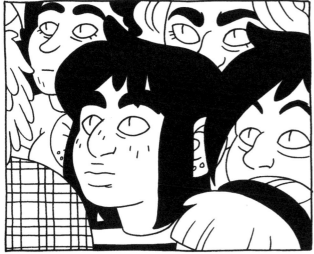

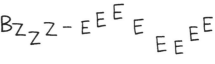

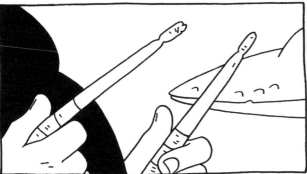

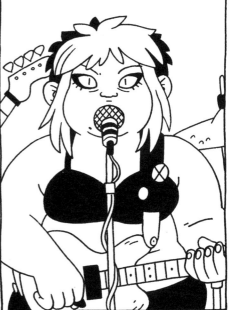

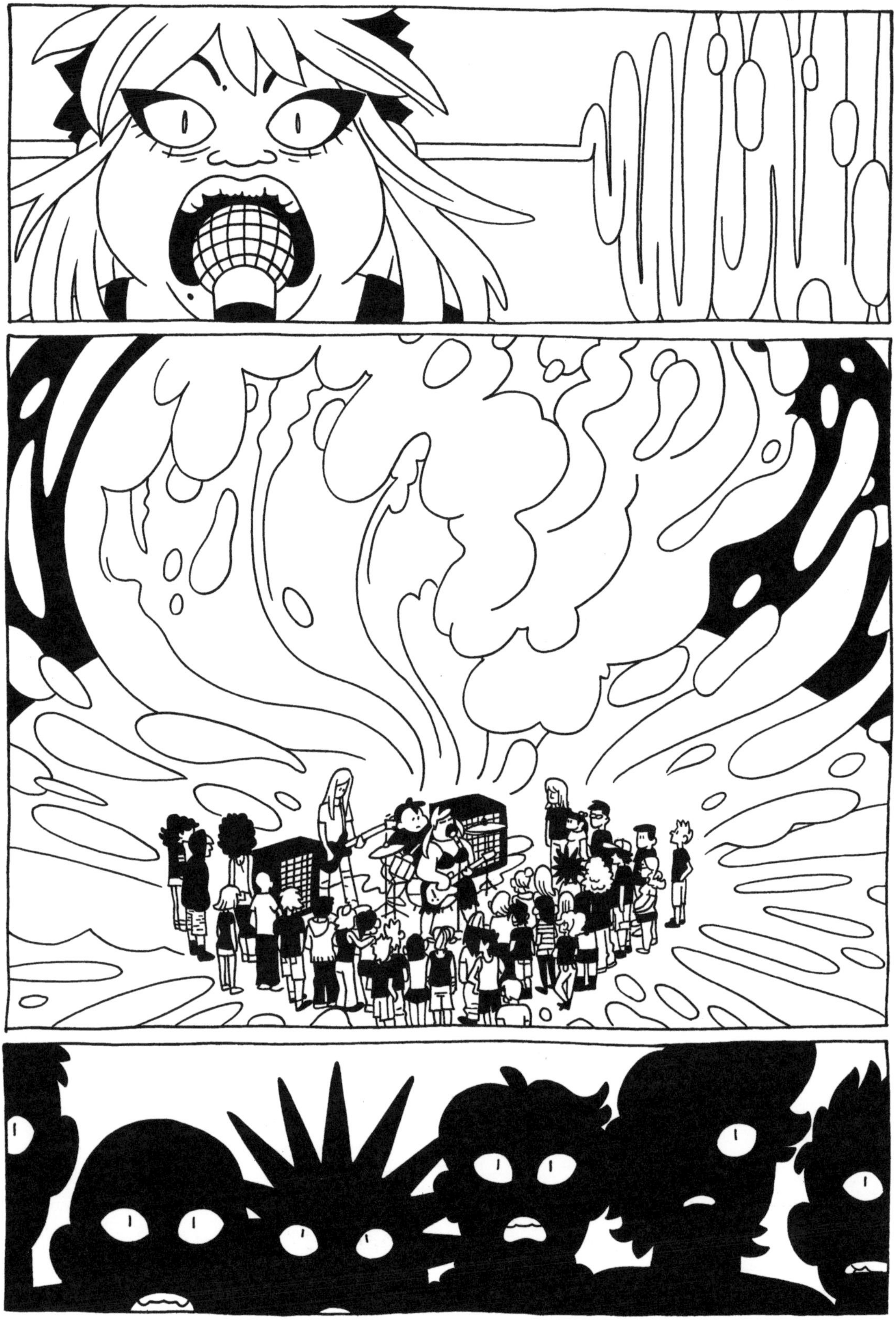

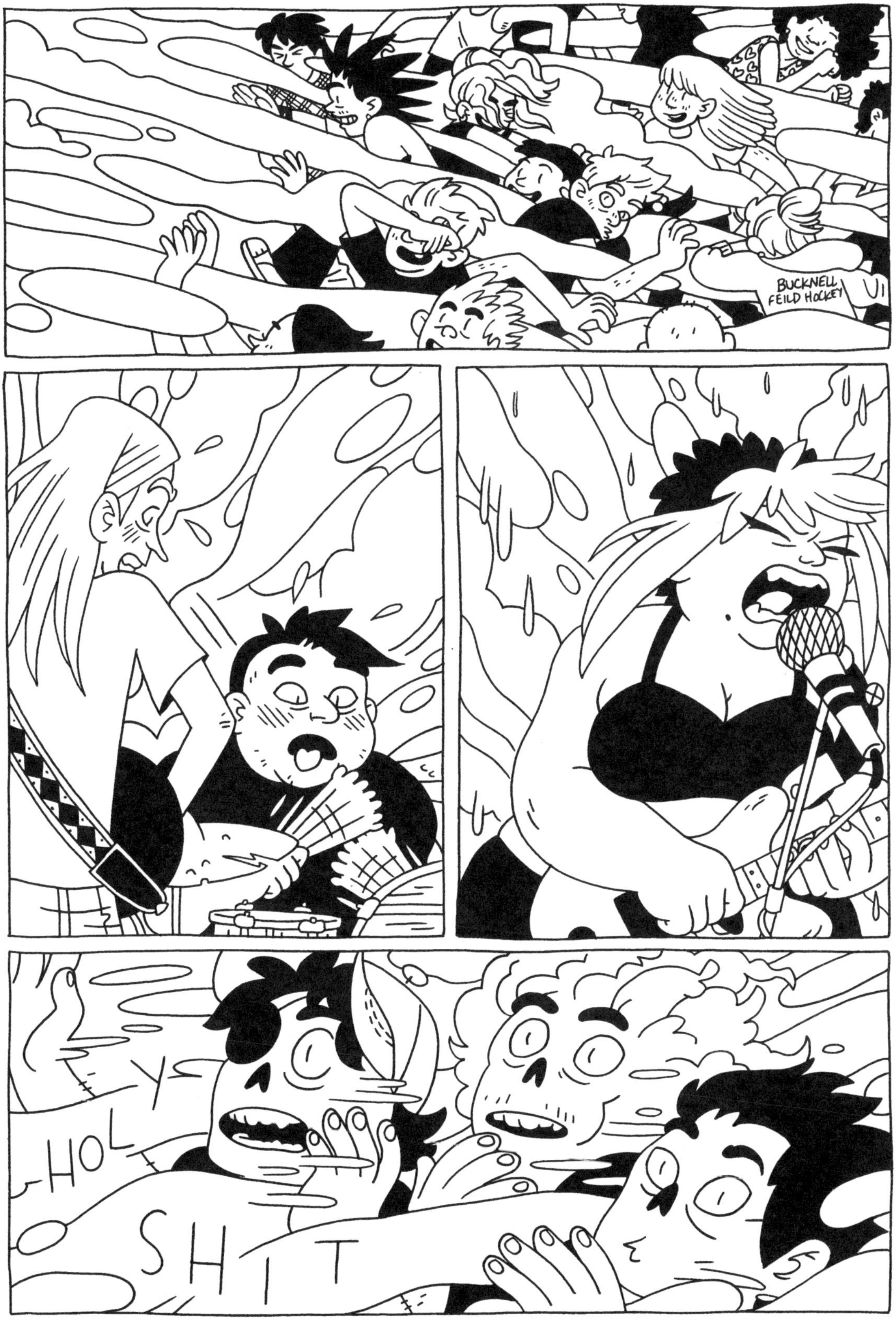
BUCKNELL
FEILD HOCKEY
HOLY
SHIT

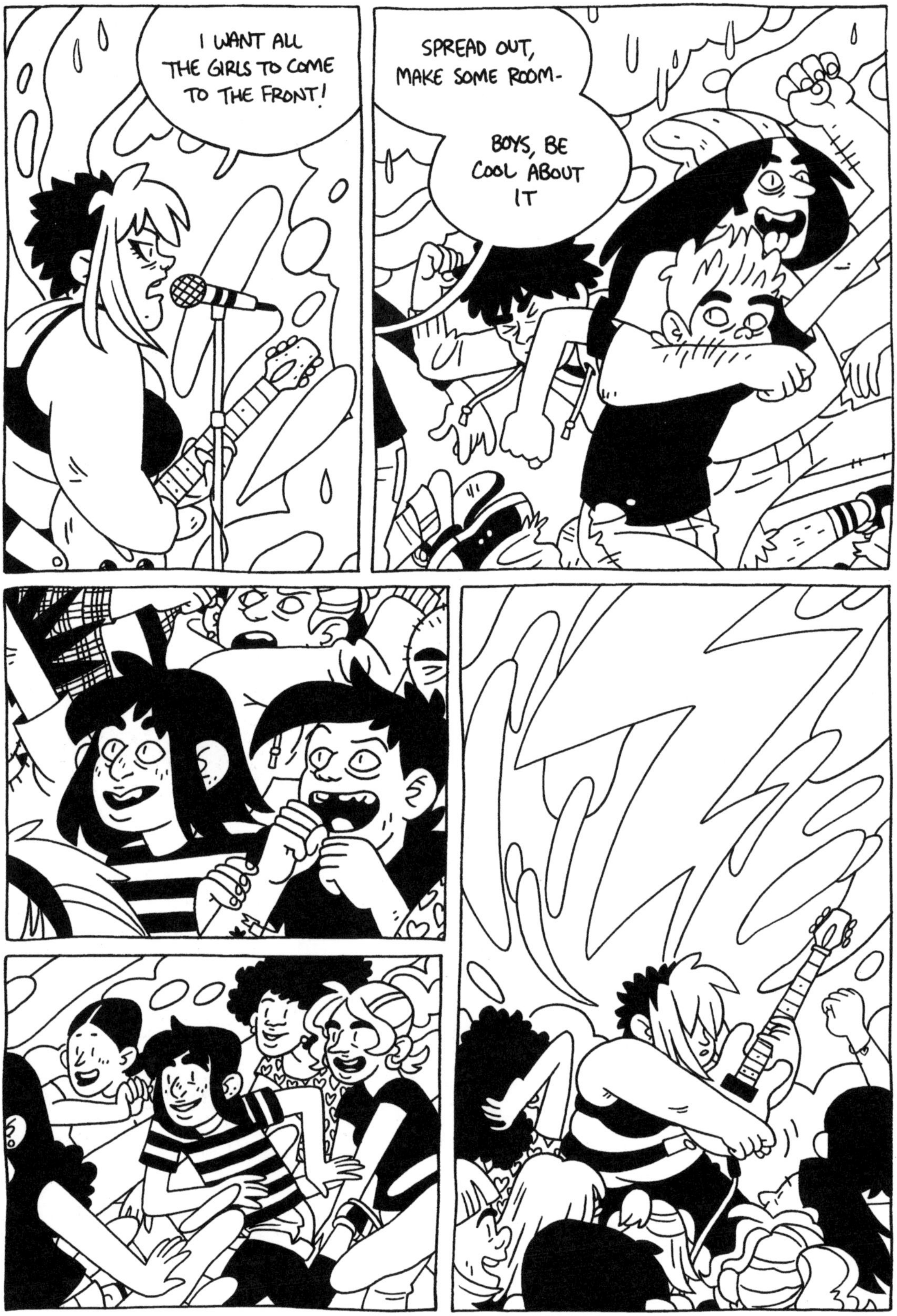
I WANT ALL THE GIRLS TO COME TO THE FRONT!
SPREAD OUT, MAKE SOME ROOM-
BOYS, BE COOL ABOUT IT

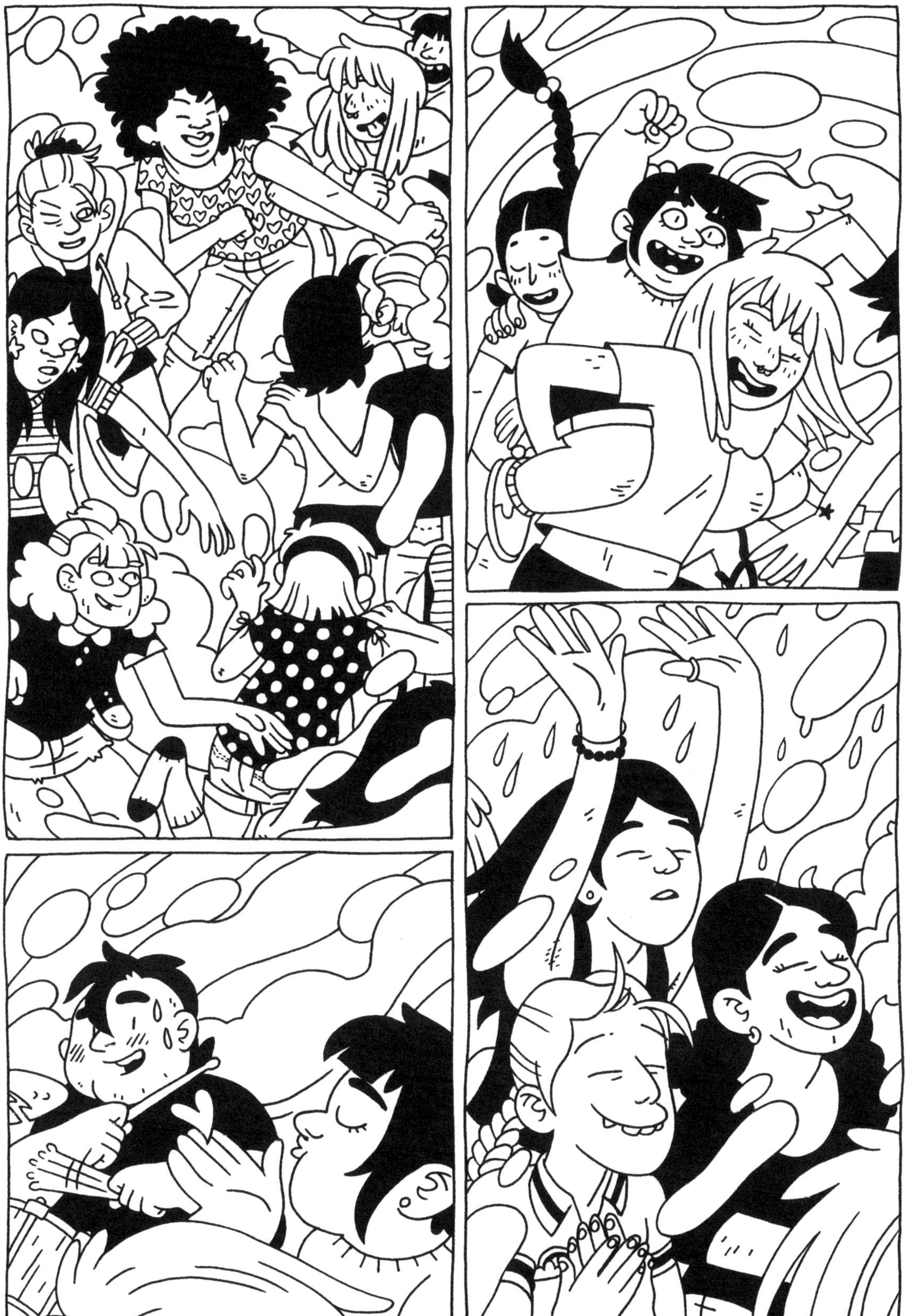

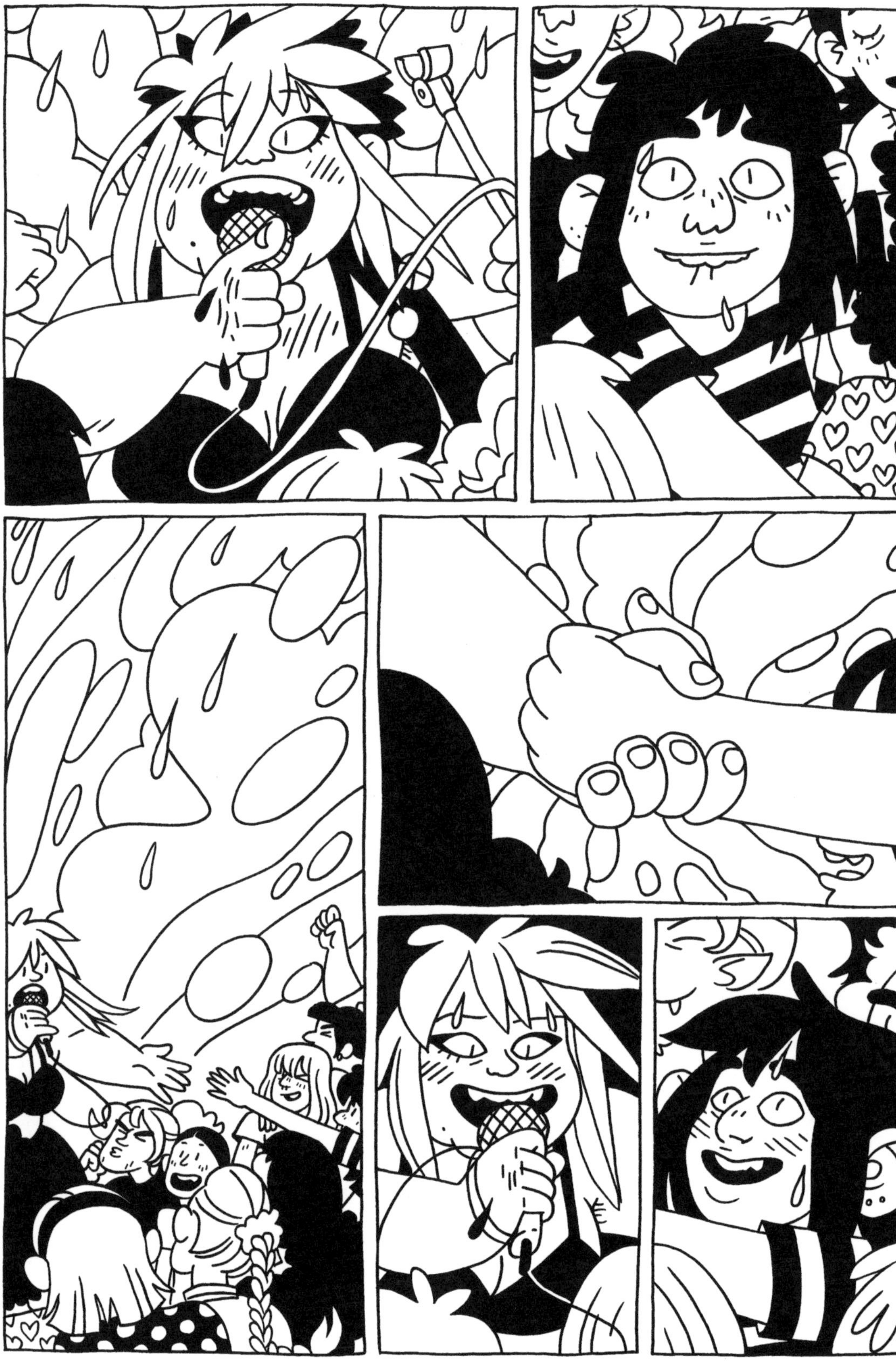

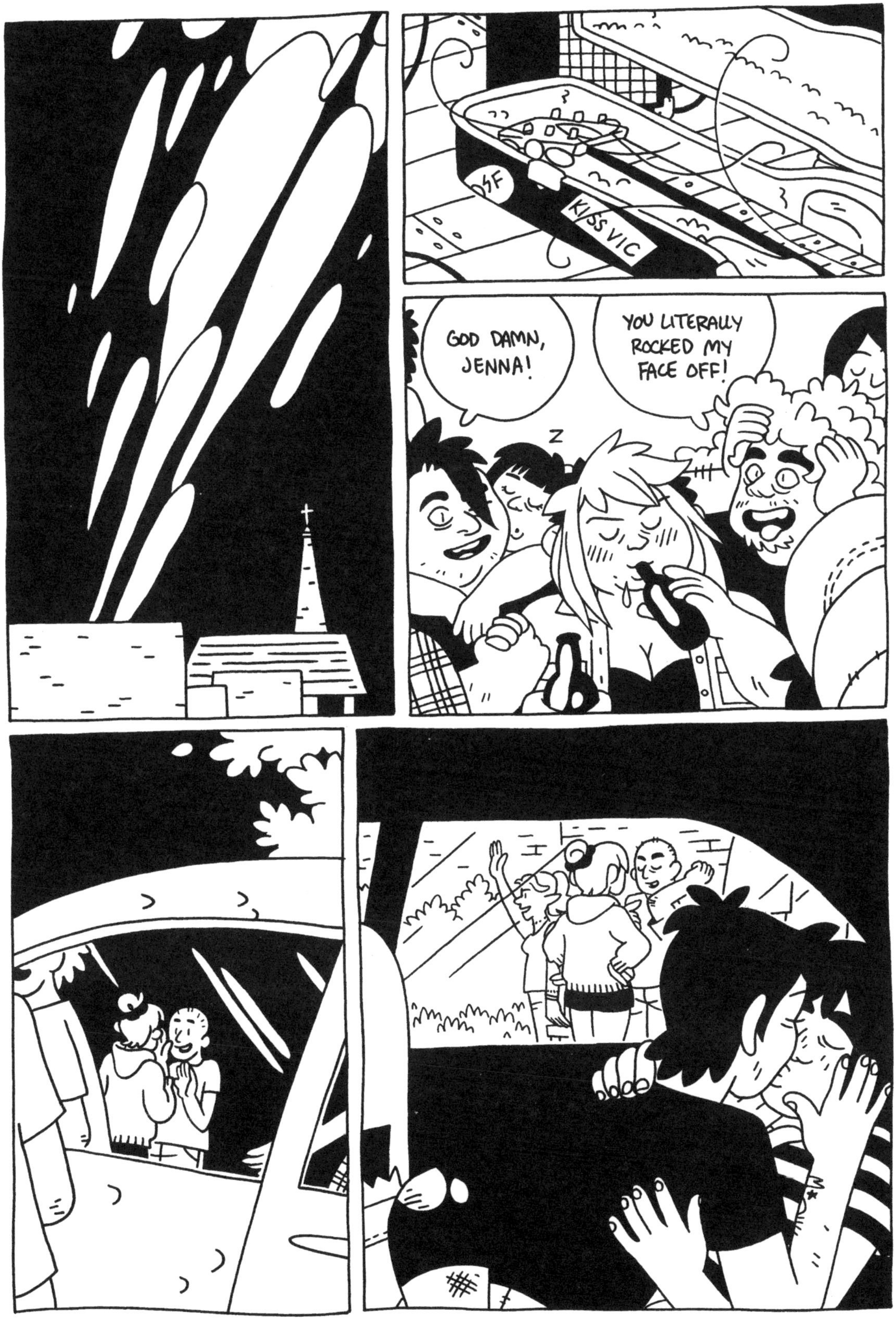
SF
KISS VIC
GOD DAMN, JENNA!
YOU LITERALLY ROCKED MY FACE OFF!
Z

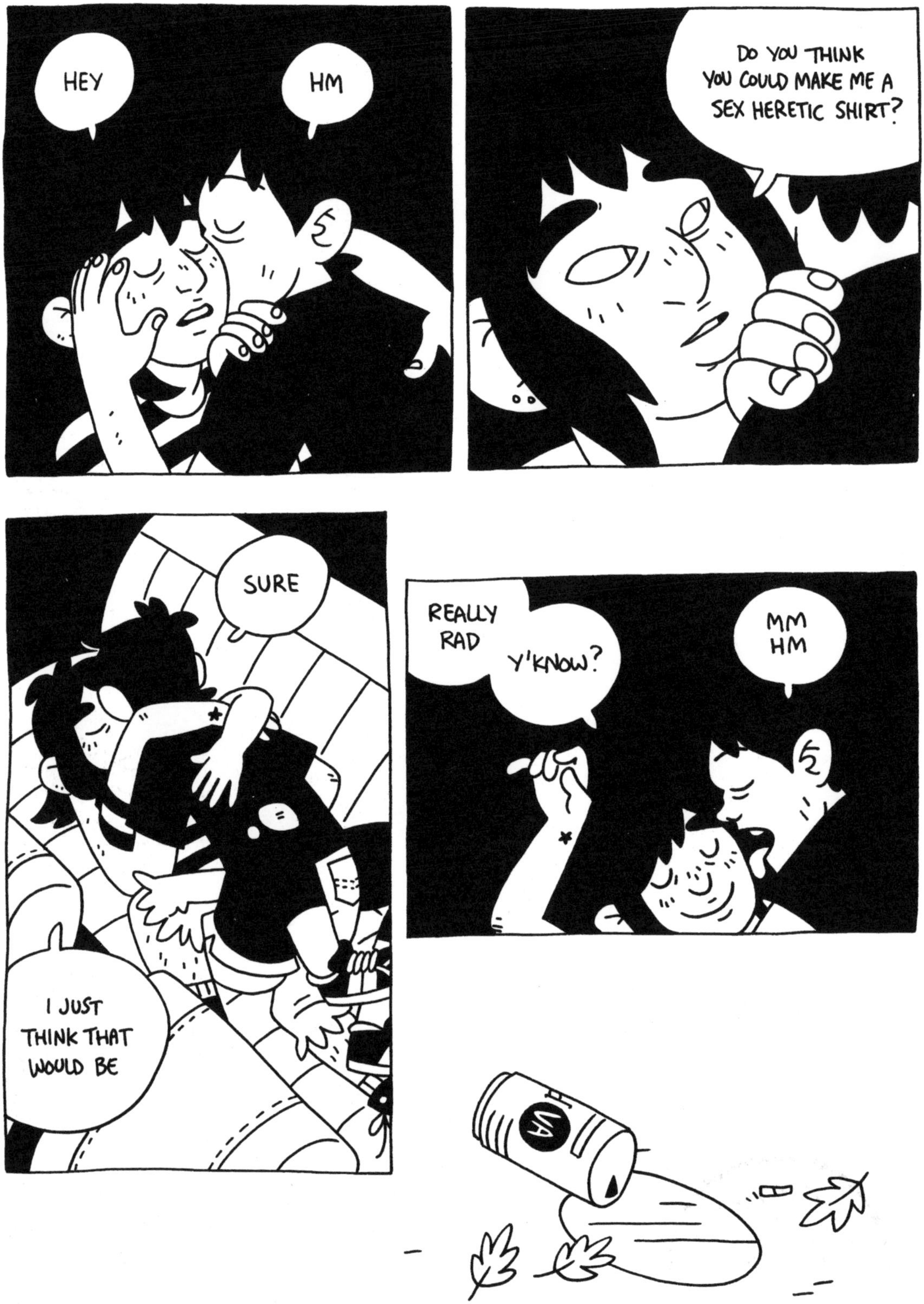
HEY
HM
DO YOU THINK YOU COULD MAKE ME A SEX HERETIC SHIRT?
SURE
I JUST THINK THAT WOULD BE
REALLY RAD
Y'KNOW?
MM HM

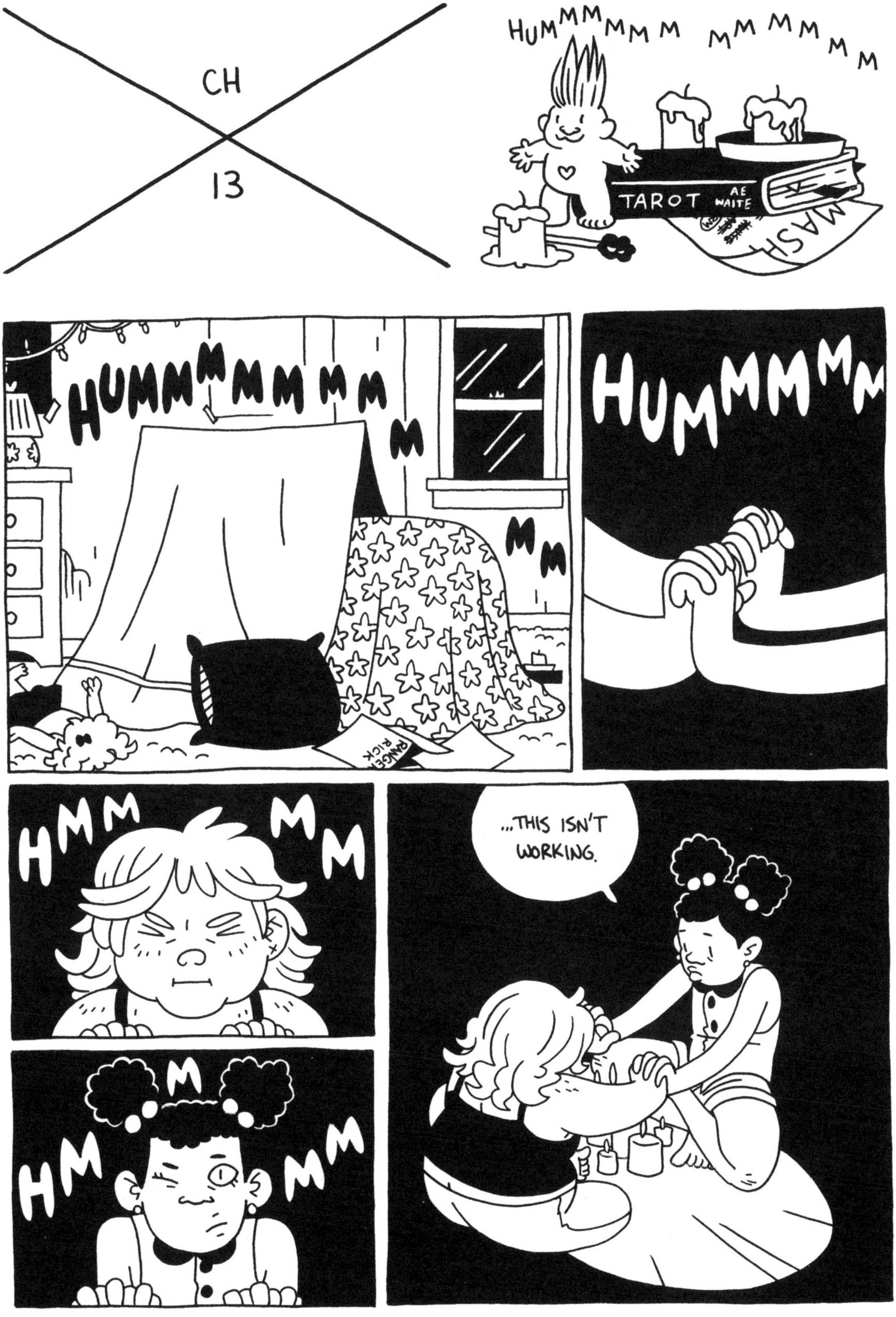
CH
13
HUMMMMMMM MMMMMMM
TAROT
AE WAITE
MASH
HUMMMMMMMMM
MM
RANGER RICK
HUMMMMMM
HMM MM
...THIS ISN'T WORKING.
HM M MM

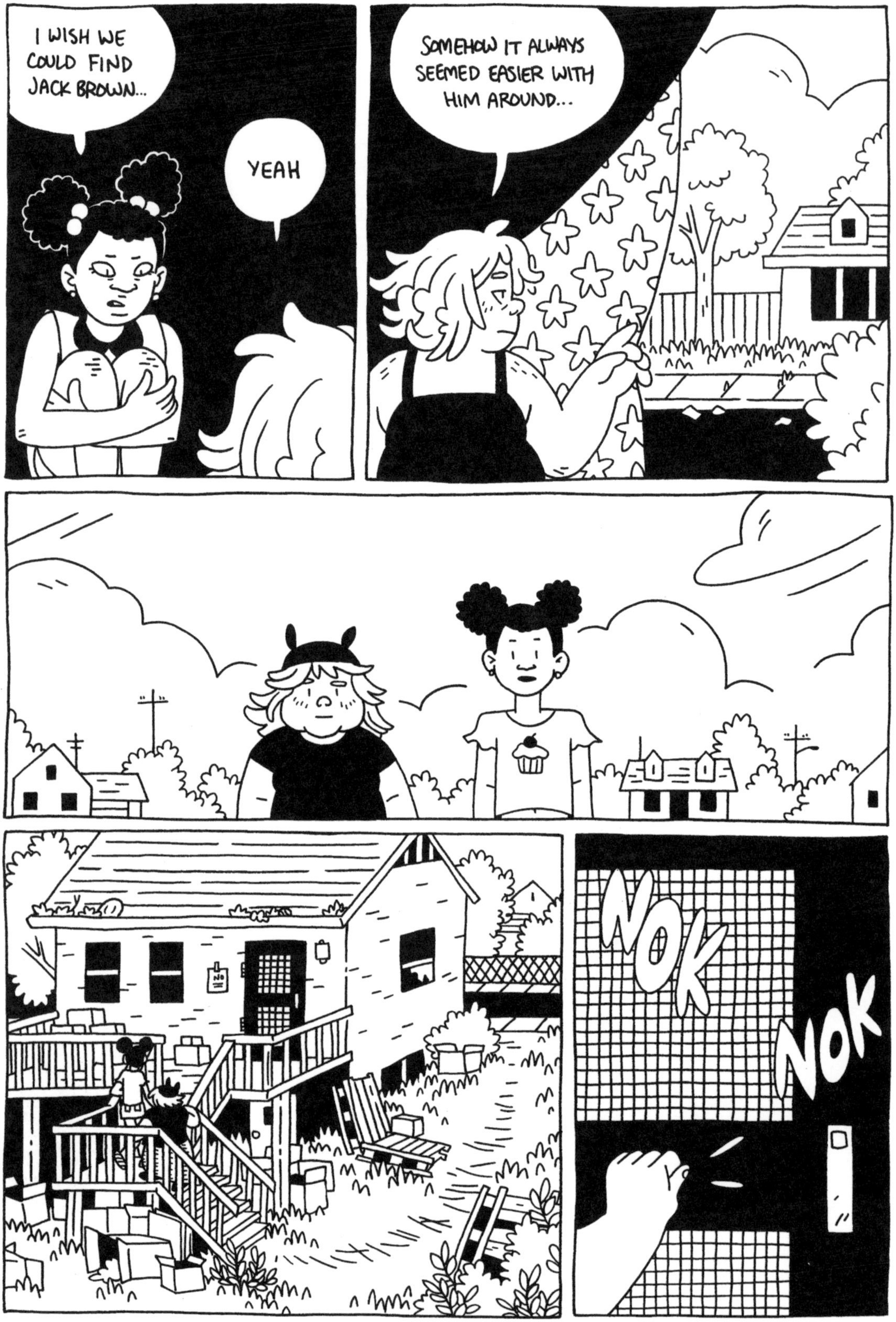
I WISH WE COULD FIND JACK BROWN...
YEAH
SOMEHOW IT ALWAYS SEEMED EASIER WITH HIM AROUND...
NO
NOK
NOK

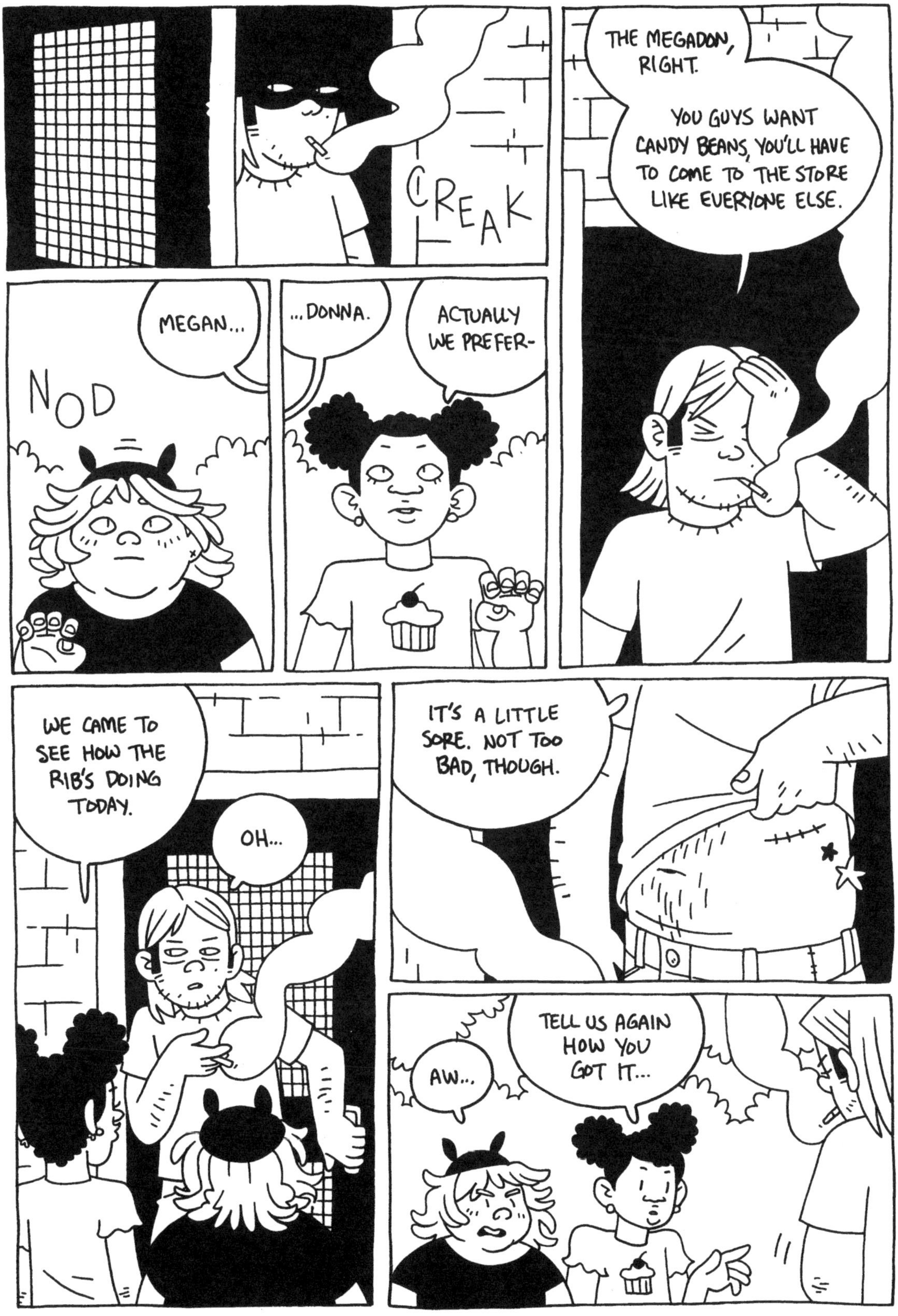
CREAK
THE MEGADON, RIGHT.
YOU GUYS WANT CANDY BEANS, YOU'LL HAVE TO COME TO THE STORE LIKE EVERYONE ELSE.
NOD
MEGAN...
...DONNA.
ACTUALLY WE PREFER-
WE CAME TO SEE HOW THE RIB'S DOING TODAY.
OH...
IT'S A LITTLE SORE. NOT TOO BAD, THOUGH.
AW...
TELL US AGAIN HOW YOU GOT IT...

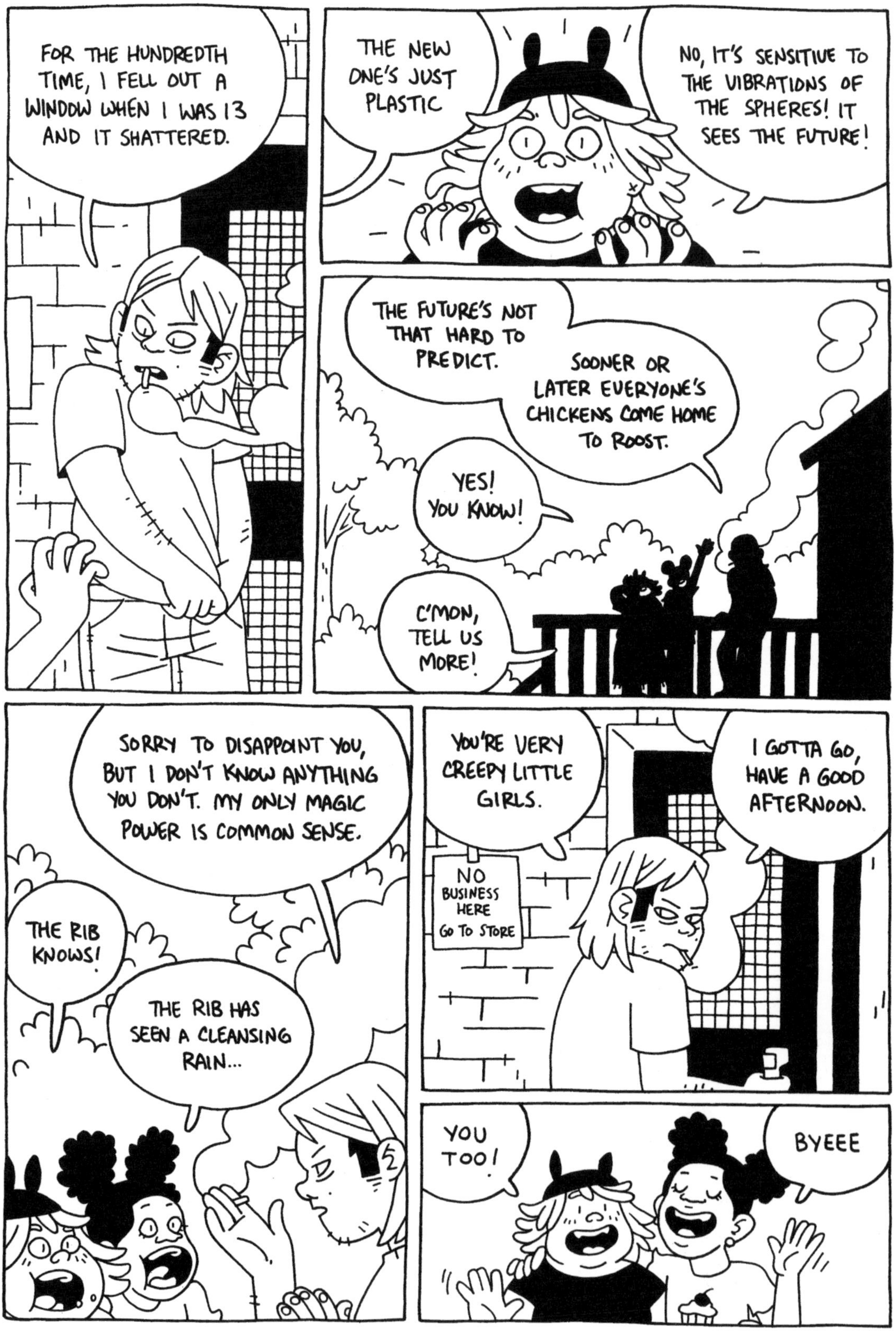
FOR THE HUNDREDTH TIME, I FELL OUT A WINDOW WHEN I WAS 13 AND IT SHATTERED.
THE NEW ONE'S JUST PLASTIC
NO, IT'S SENSITIVE TO THE VIBRATIONS OF THE SPHERES! IT SEES THE FUTURE!
THE FUTURE'S NOT THAT HARD TO PREDICT.
SOONER OR LATER EVERYONE'S CHICKENS COME HOME TO ROOST.
YES! YOU KNOW!
C'MON, TELL US MORE!
SORRY TO DISAPPOINT YOU, BUT I DON'T KNOW ANYTHING YOU DON'T. MY ONLY MAGIC POWER IS COMMON SENSE.
THE RIB KNOWS!
THE RIB HAS SEEN A CLEANSING RAIN...
YOU'RE VERY CREEPY LITTLE GIRLS.
NO BUSINESS HERE GO TO STORE
I GOTTA GO, HAVE A GOOD AFTERNOON.
YOU TOO!
BYEEE

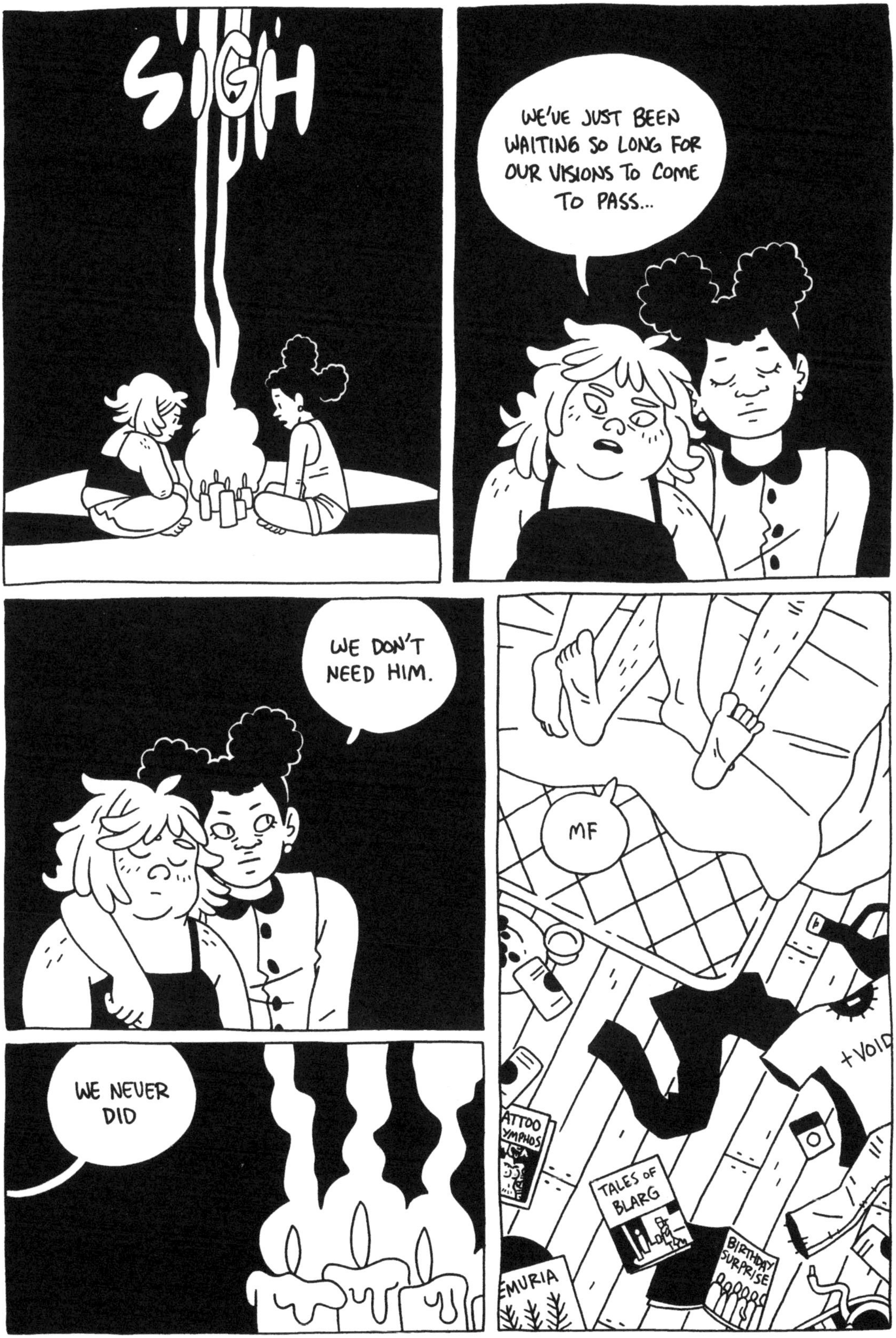
SIGH
WE'VE JUST BEEN WAITING SO LONG FOR OUR VISIONS TO COME TO PASS...
WE DON'T NEED HIM.
WE NEVER DID
MF
+VOID
TATTOO SYMPHOS
TALES OF BLARG
BIRTHDAY SURPRISE
EMURIA

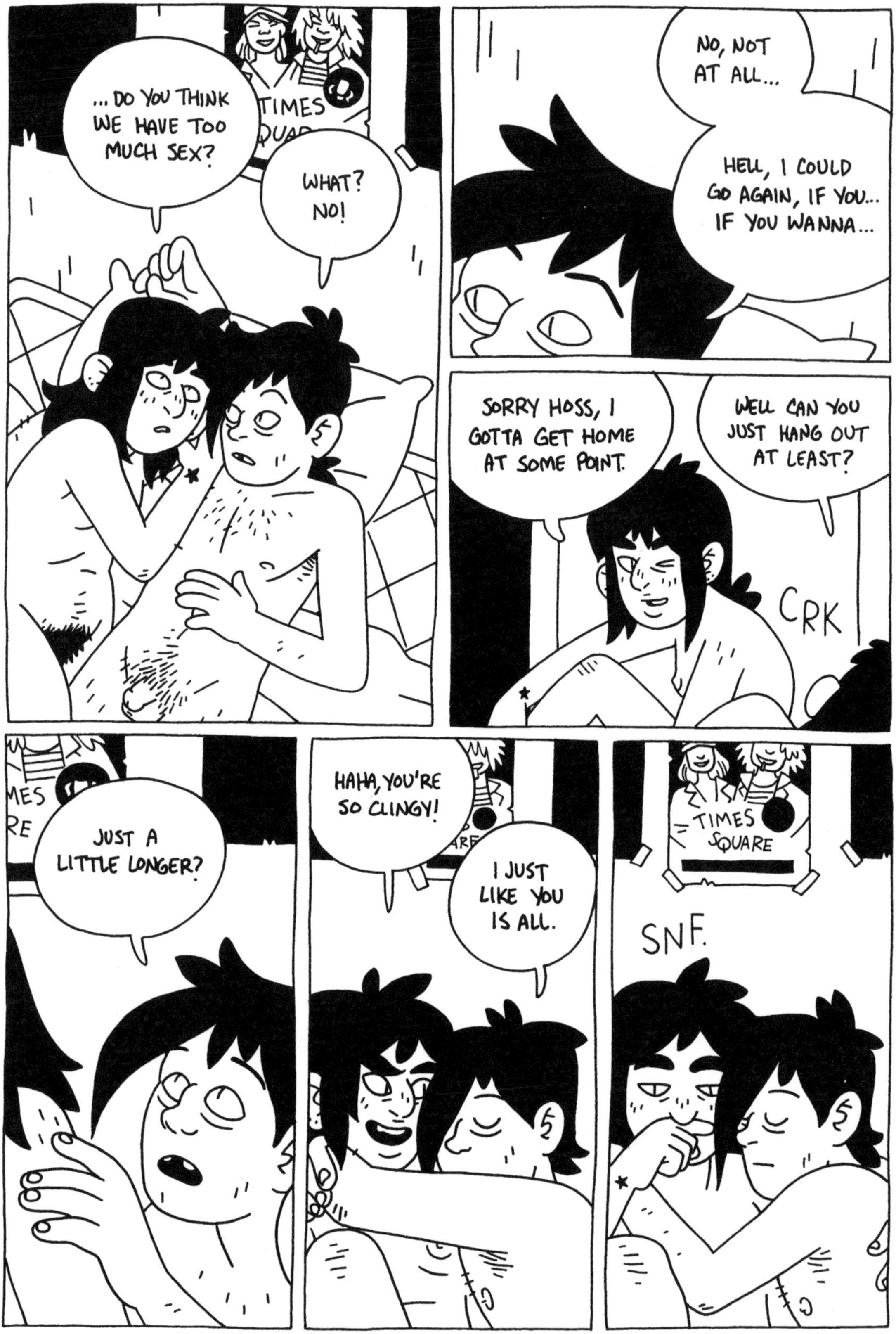
TIMES SQUARE
...DO YOU THINK WE HAVE TOO MUCH SEX?
WHAT? NO!
NO, NOT AT ALL...
HELL, I COULD GO AGAIN, IF YOU... IF YOU WANNA...
SORRY HOSS, I GOTTA GET HOME AT SOME POINT.
WELL CAN YOU JUST HANG OUT AT LEAST?
CRK
JUST A LITTLE LONGER?
HAHA, YOU'RE SO CLINGY!
I JUST LIKE YOU IS ALL.
TIMES SQUARE
SNF.

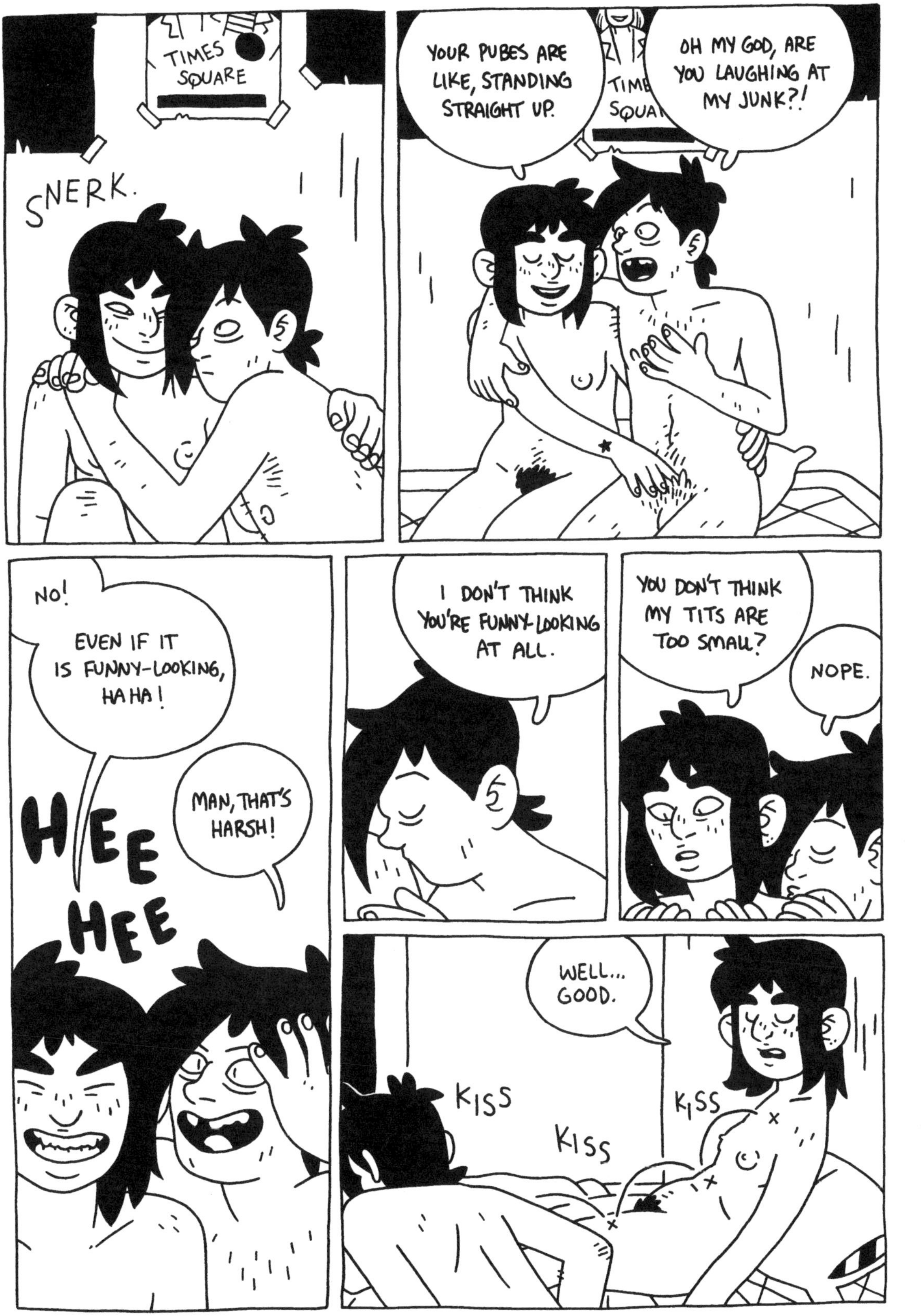

TIMES SQUARE
SNERK.
YOUR PUBES ARE LIKE, STANDING STRAIGHT UP.
OH MY GOD, ARE YOU LAUGHING AT MY JUNK?!
NO!
EVEN IF IT IS FUNNY-LOOKING, HA HA!
HEE HEE
MAN, THAT'S HARSH!
I DON'T THINK YOU'RE FUNNY-LOOKING AT ALL.
YOU DON'T THINK MY TITS ARE TOO SMALL?
NOPE.
WELL... GOOD.
KISS
KISS
KISS

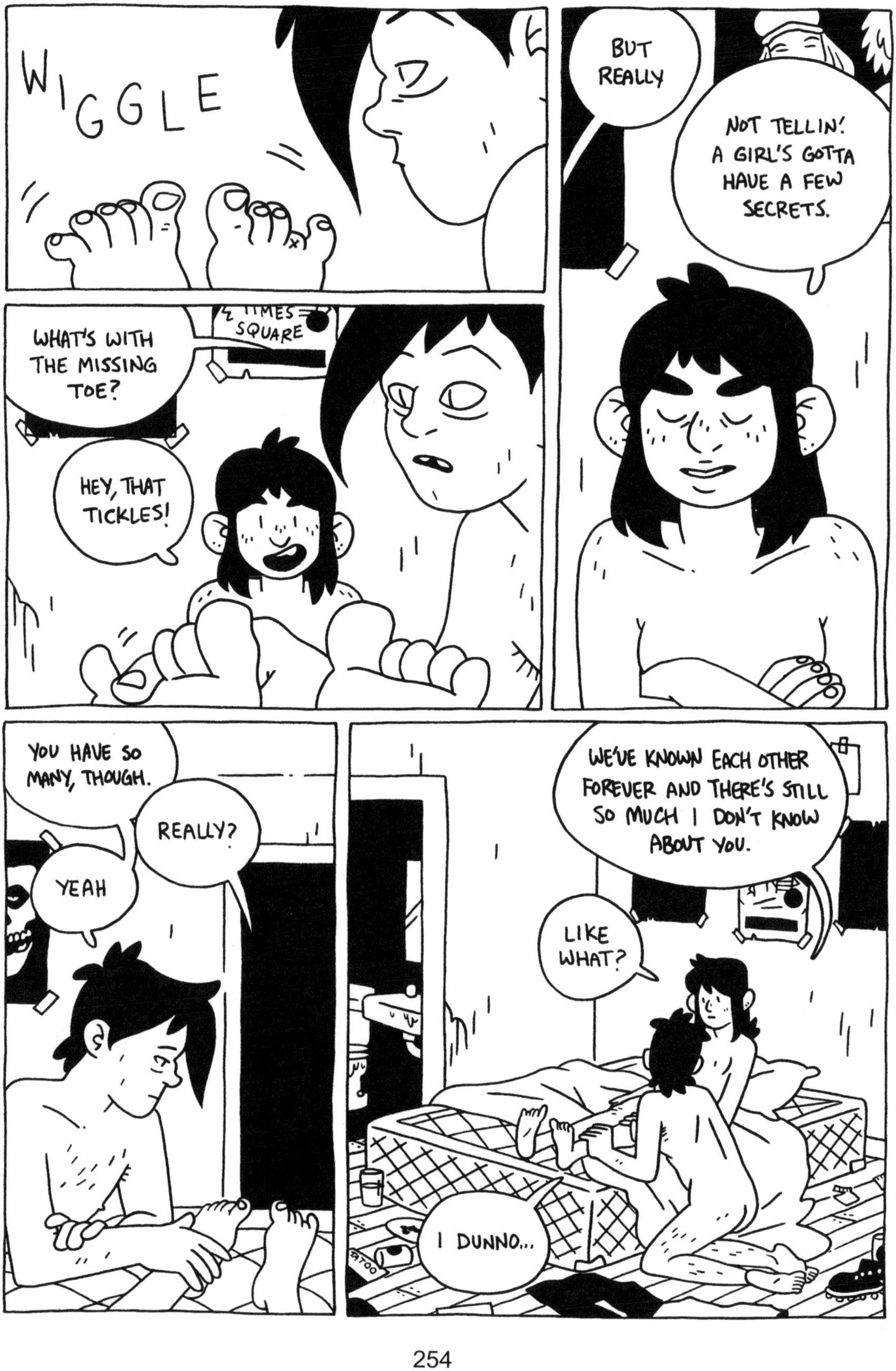
WIGGLE
BUT REALLY
NOT TELLIN'! A GIRL'S GOTTA HAVE A FEW SECRETS.
TIMES SQUARE
WHAT'S WITH THE MISSING TOE?
HEY, THAT TICKLES!
YOU HAVE SO MANY, THOUGH.
REALLY?
YEAH
WE'VE KNOWN EACH OTHER FOREVER AND THERE'S STILL SO MUCH I DON'T KNOW ABOUT YOU.
LIKE WHAT?
I DUNNO...
TATOO

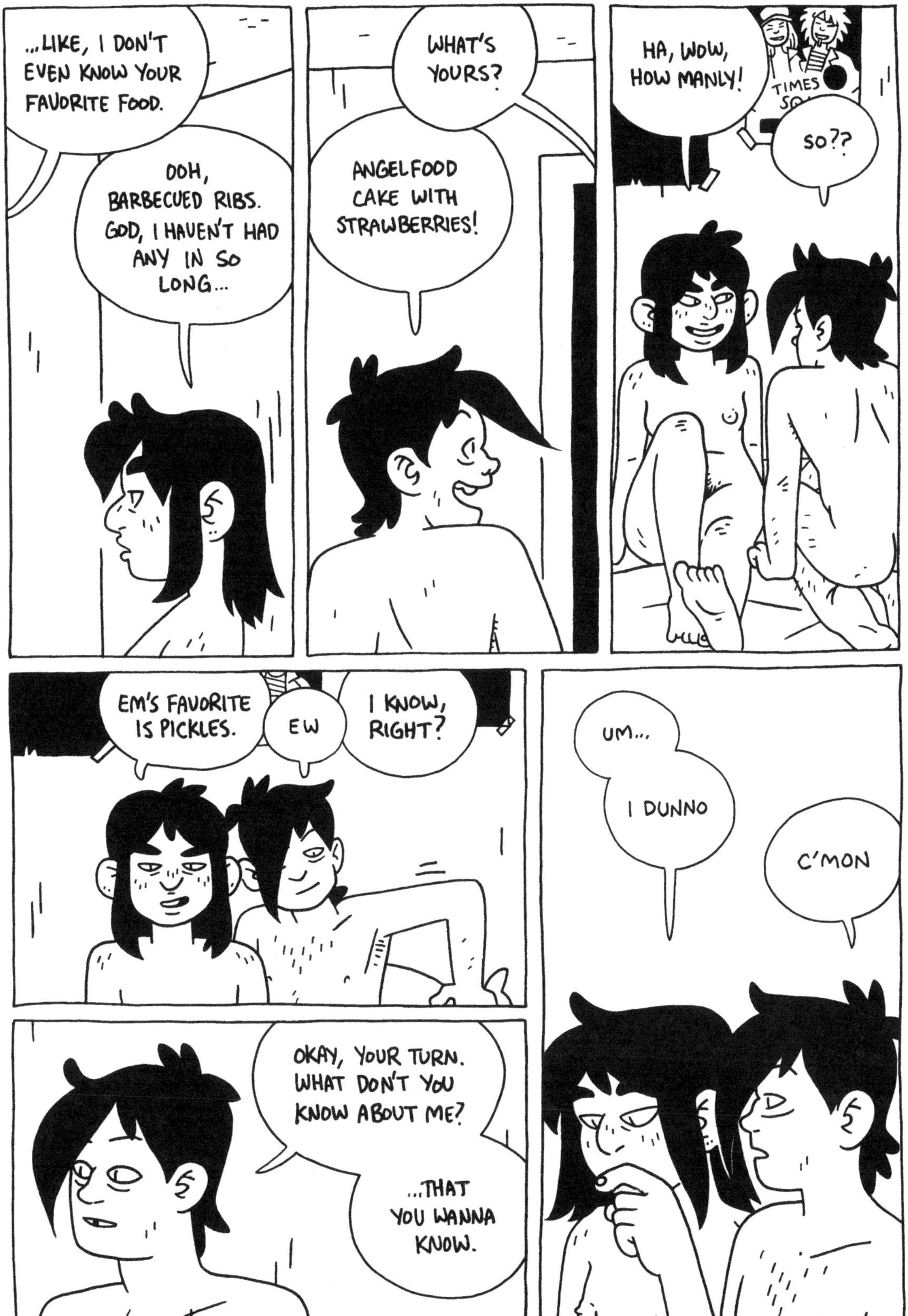
...LIKE, I DON'T EVEN KNOW YOUR FAVORITE FOOD.
OOH, BARBECUED RIBS. GOD, I HAVEN'T HAD ANY IN SO LONG...
WHAT'S YOURS?
ANGELFOOD CAKE WITH STRAWBERRIES!
HA, WOW, HOW MANLY!
TIMES
SO??
EM'S FAVORITE IS PICKLES.
EW
I KNOW, RIGHT?
OKAY, YOUR TURN. WHAT DON'T YOU KNOW ABOUT ME?
...THAT YOU WANNA KNOW.
UM...
I DUNNO
C'MON

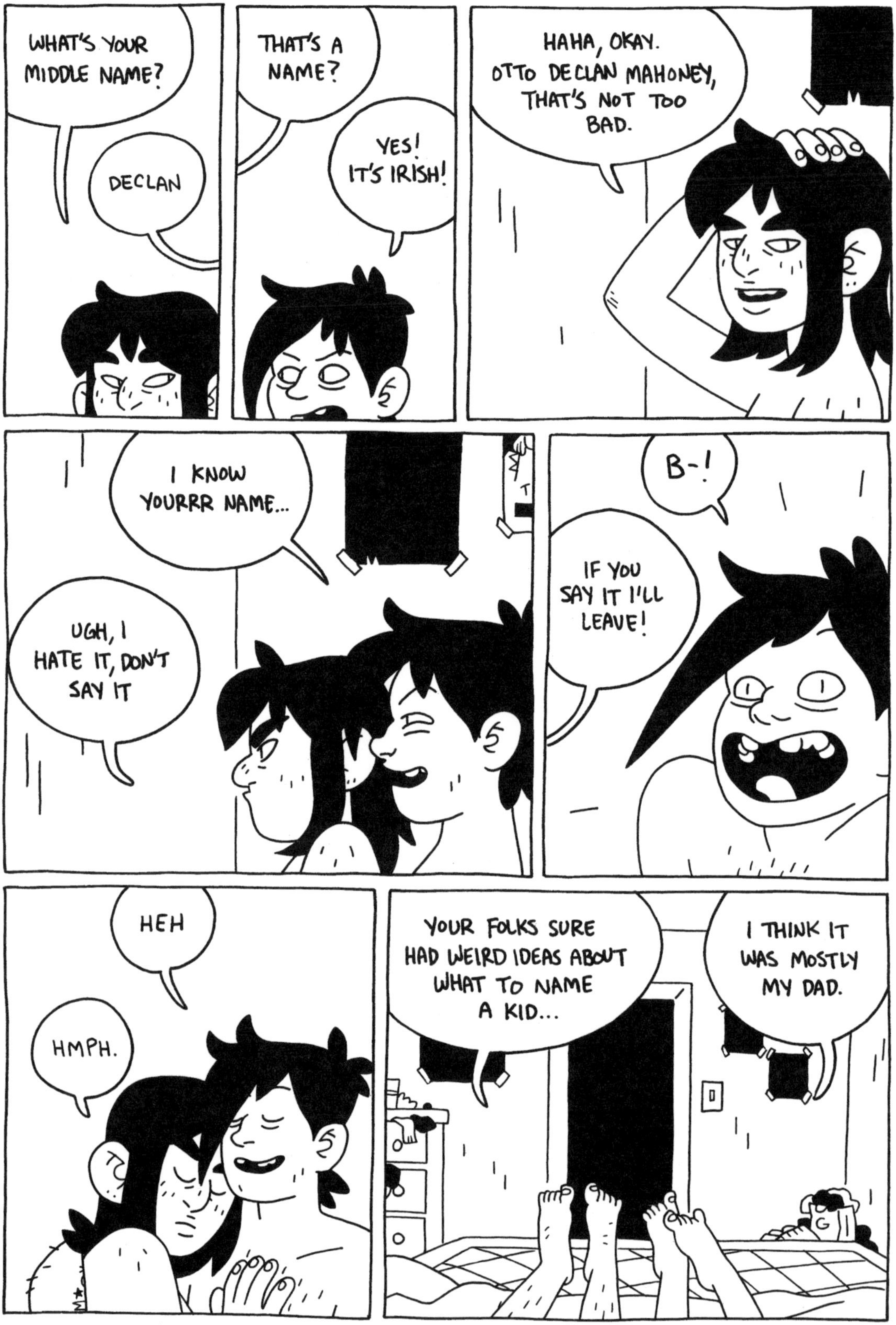
WHAT'S YOUR MIDDLE NAME?
DECLAN
THAT'S A NAME?
YES! IT'S IRISH!
HAHA, OKAY. OTTO DECLAN MAHONEY, THAT'S NOT TOO BAD.
I KNOW YOURRR NAME...
UGH, I HATE IT, DON'T SAY IT
B-!
IF YOU SAY IT I'LL LEAVE!
HEH
HMPH.
YOUR FOLKS SURE HAD WEIRD IDEAS ABOUT WHAT TO NAME A KID...
I THINK IT WAS MOSTLY MY DAD.

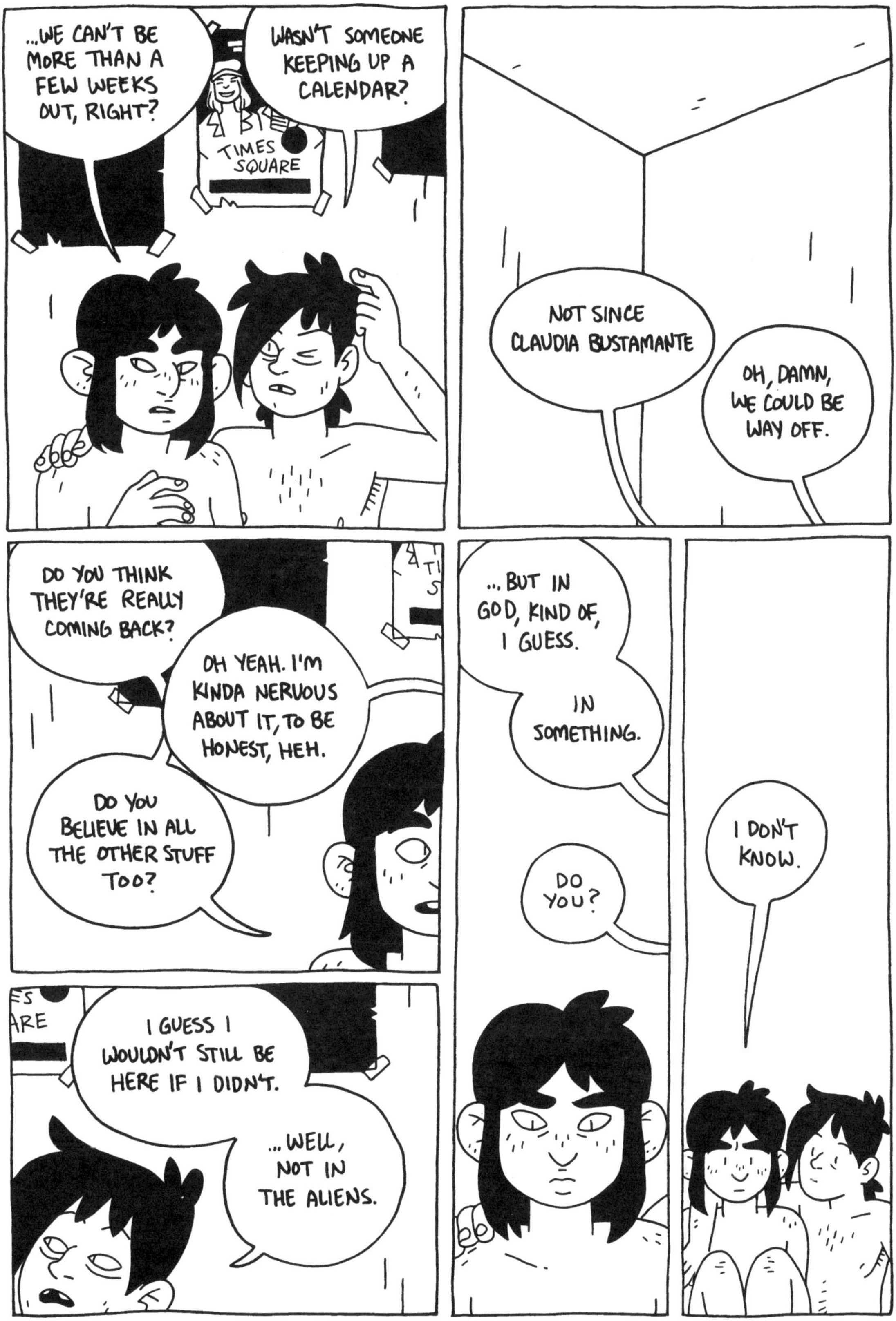
...WE CAN'T BE MORE THAN A FEW WEEKS OUT, RIGHT?
WASN'T SOMEONE KEEPING UP A CALENDAR?
TIMES SQUARE
NOT SINCE CLAUDIA BUSTAMANTE
OH, DAMN, WE COULD BE WAY OFF.
DO YOU THINK THEY'RE REALLY COMING BACK?
OH YEAH. I'M KINDA NERVOUS ABOUT IT, TO BE HONEST, HEH.
DO YOU BELIEVE IN ALL THE OTHER STUFF TOO?
I GUESS I WOULDN'T STILL BE HERE IF I DIDN'T.
...WELL, NOT IN THE ALIENS.
...BUT IN GOD, KIND OF, I GUESS.
IN SOMETHING.
DO YOU?
I DON'T KNOW.

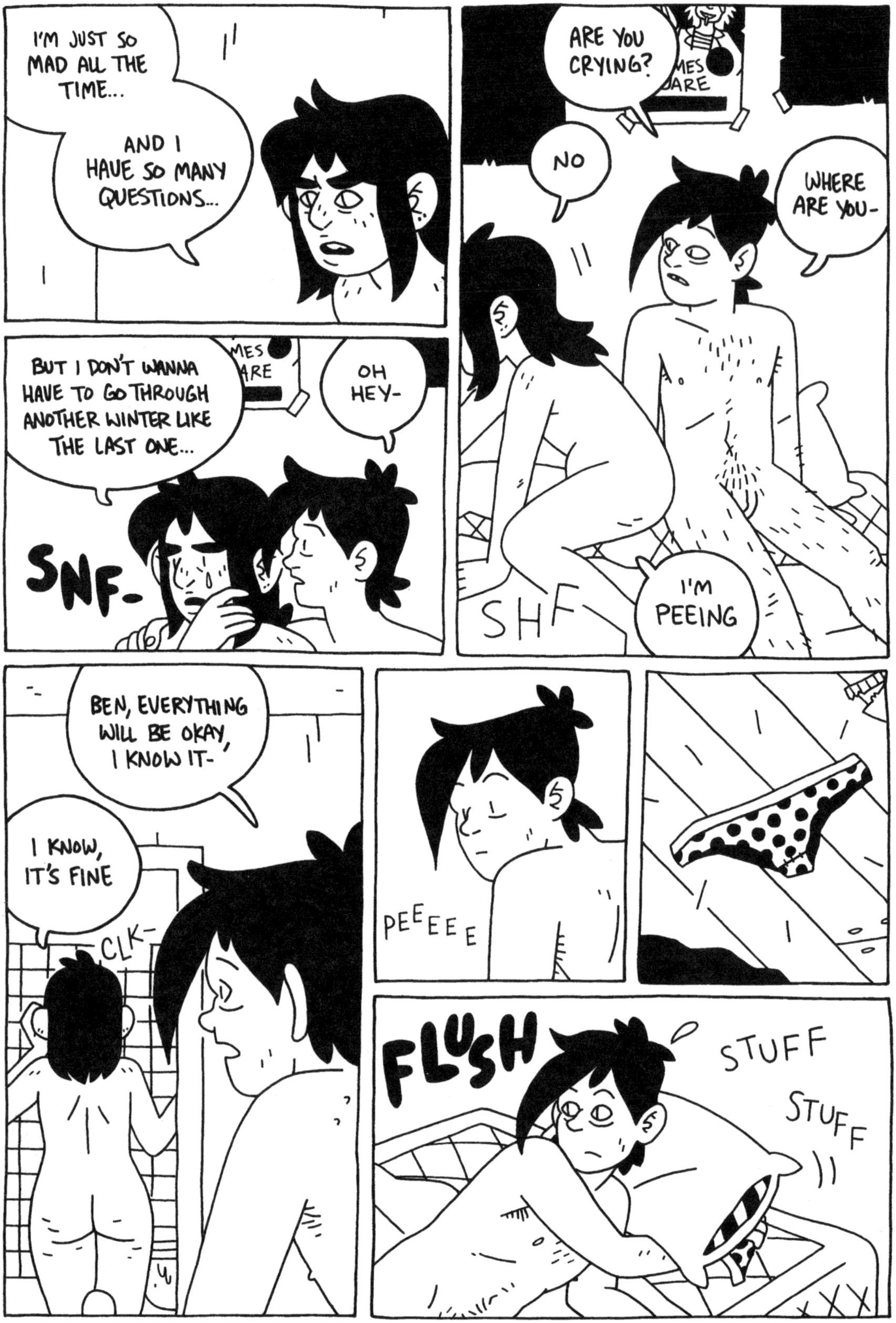
I'M JUST SO MAD ALL THE TIME...
AND I HAVE SO MANY QUESTIONS...
ARE YOU CRYING?
NO
WHERE ARE YOU-
SHF
I'M PEEING
BUT I DON'T WANNA HAVE TO GO THROUGH ANOTHER WINTER LIKE THE LAST ONE...
OH HEY-
SNF-
BEN, EVERYTHING WILL BE OKAY, I KNOW IT-
I KNOW, IT'S FINE
CLK-
PEEEEEE
FLUSH
STUFF
STUFF

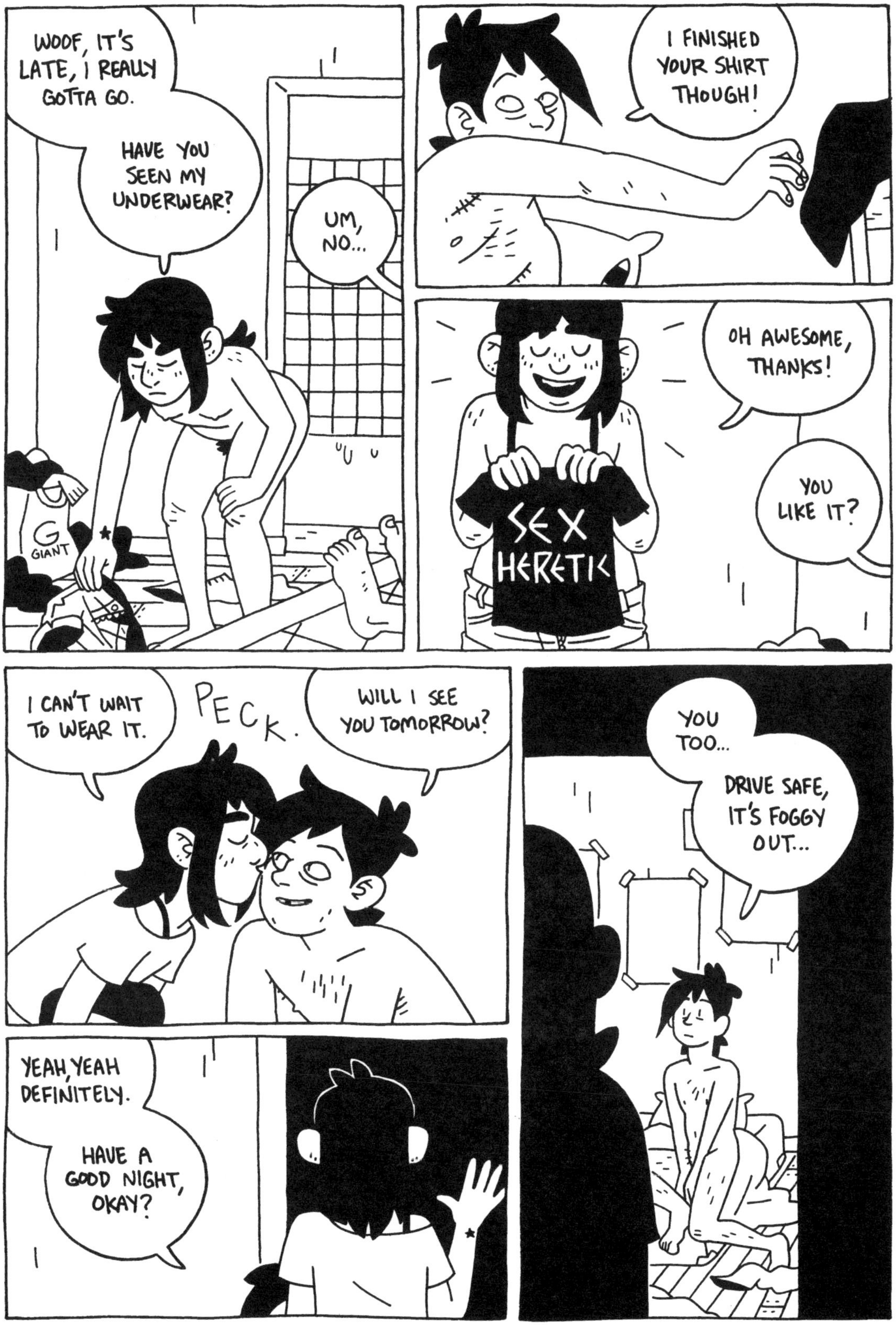
WOOF, IT'S LATE, I REALLY GOTTA GO.
HAVE YOU SEEN MY UNDERWEAR?
UM, NO...
I FINISHED YOUR SHIRT THOUGH!
OH AWESOME, THANKS!
YOU LIKE IT?
SEX HERETIC
I CAN'T WAIT TO WEAR IT.
PECK.
WILL I SEE YOU TOMORROW?
YEAH, YEAH DEFINITELY.
HAVE A GOOD NIGHT, OKAY?
YOU TOO...
DRIVE SAFE, IT'S FOGGY OUT...
GIANT

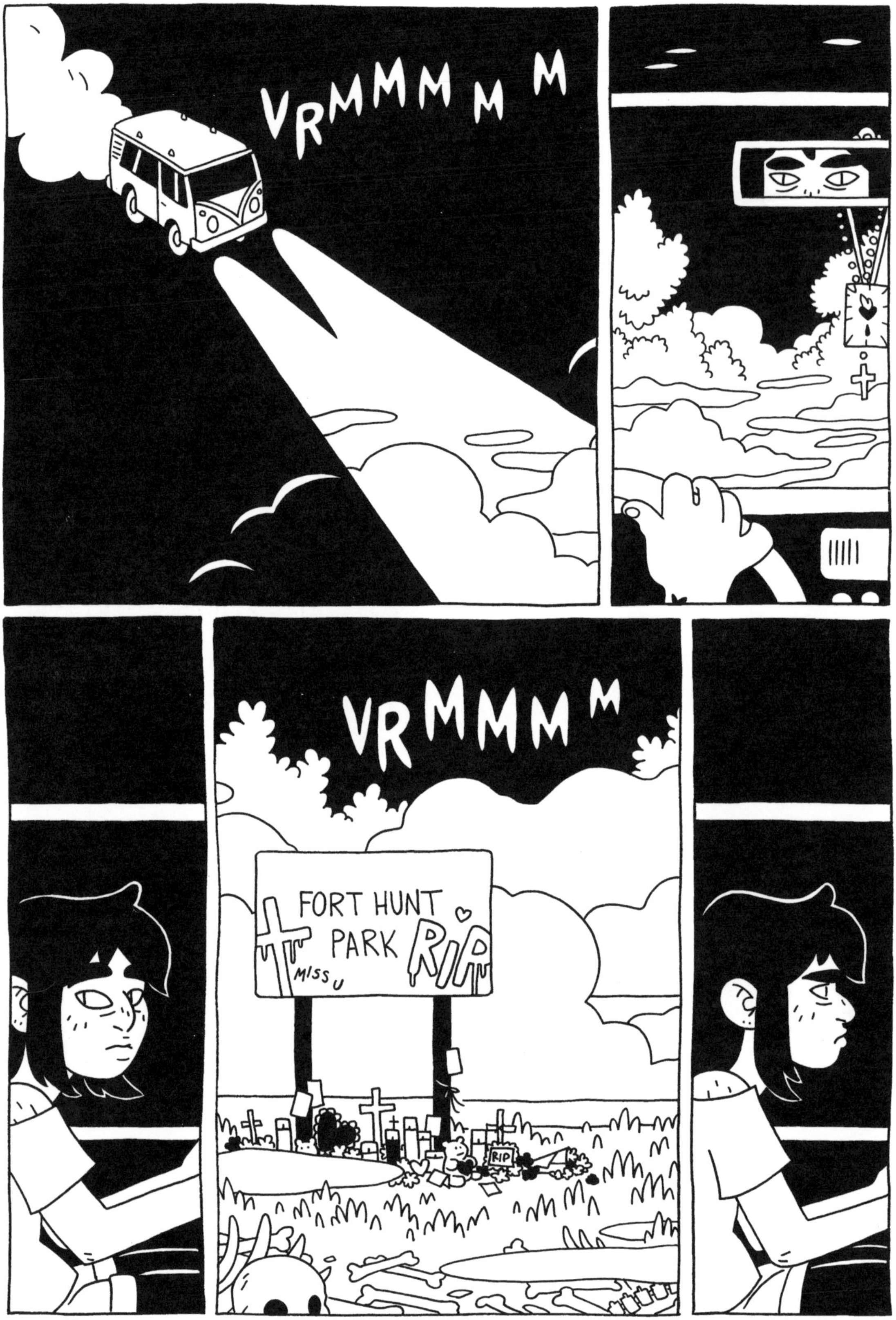
VRMMMM M M
VRMMMM
FORT HUNT PARK
RIP
MISS U
RIP

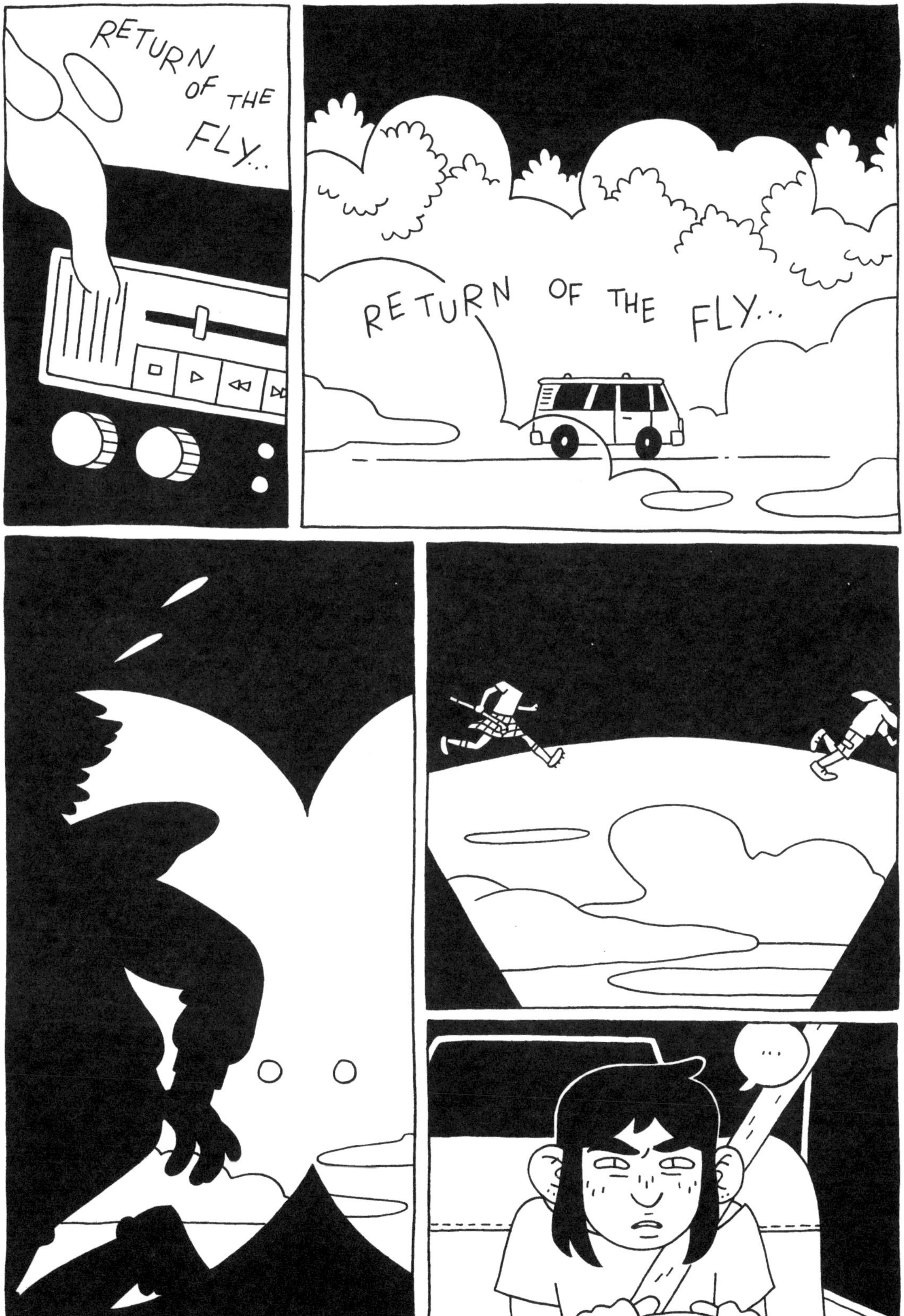
RETURN OF THE FLY...
RETURN OF THE FLY...
...

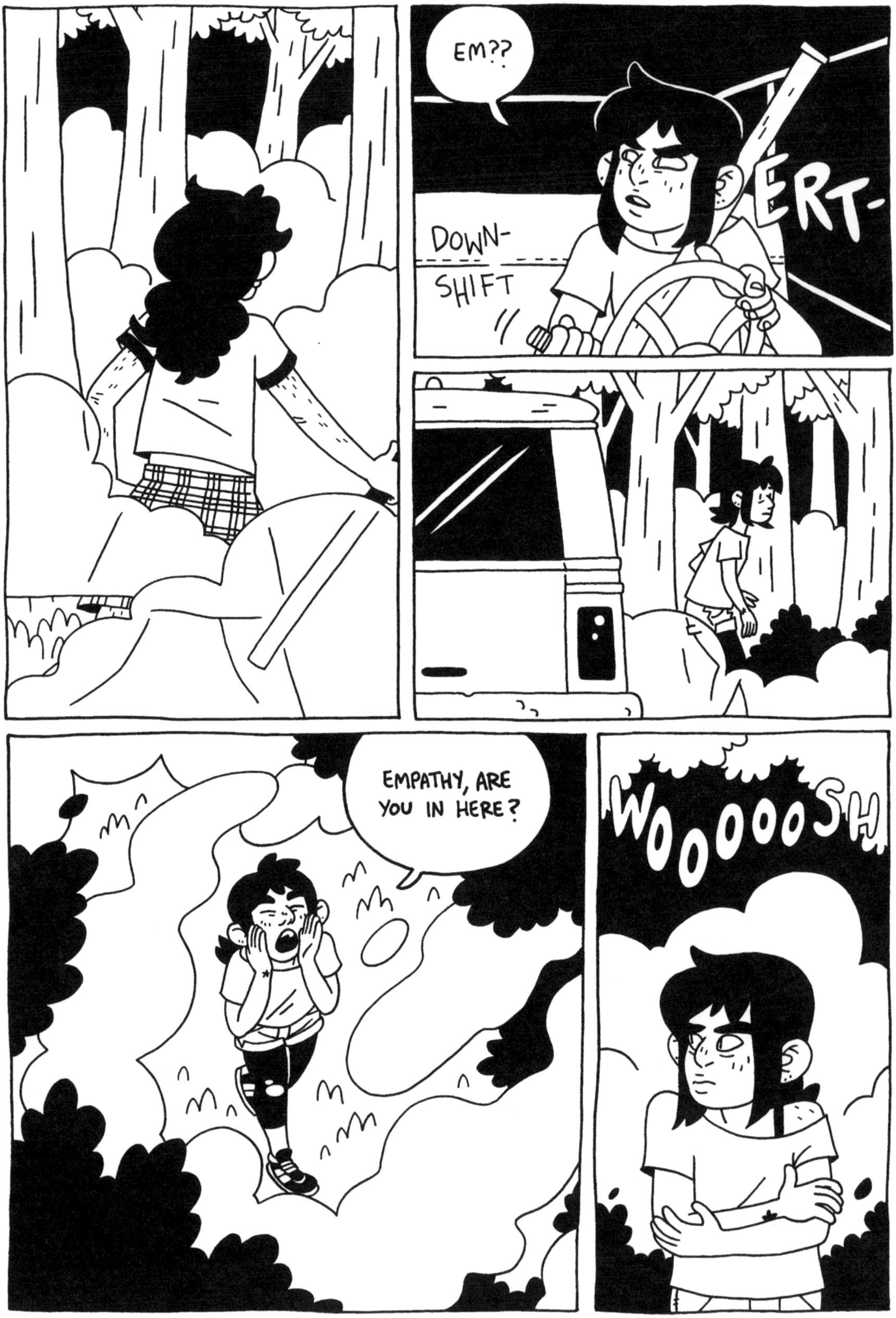
EM??
DOWN-
SHIFT
ERT-
EMPATHY, ARE YOU IN HERE?
WOOOOOOSH

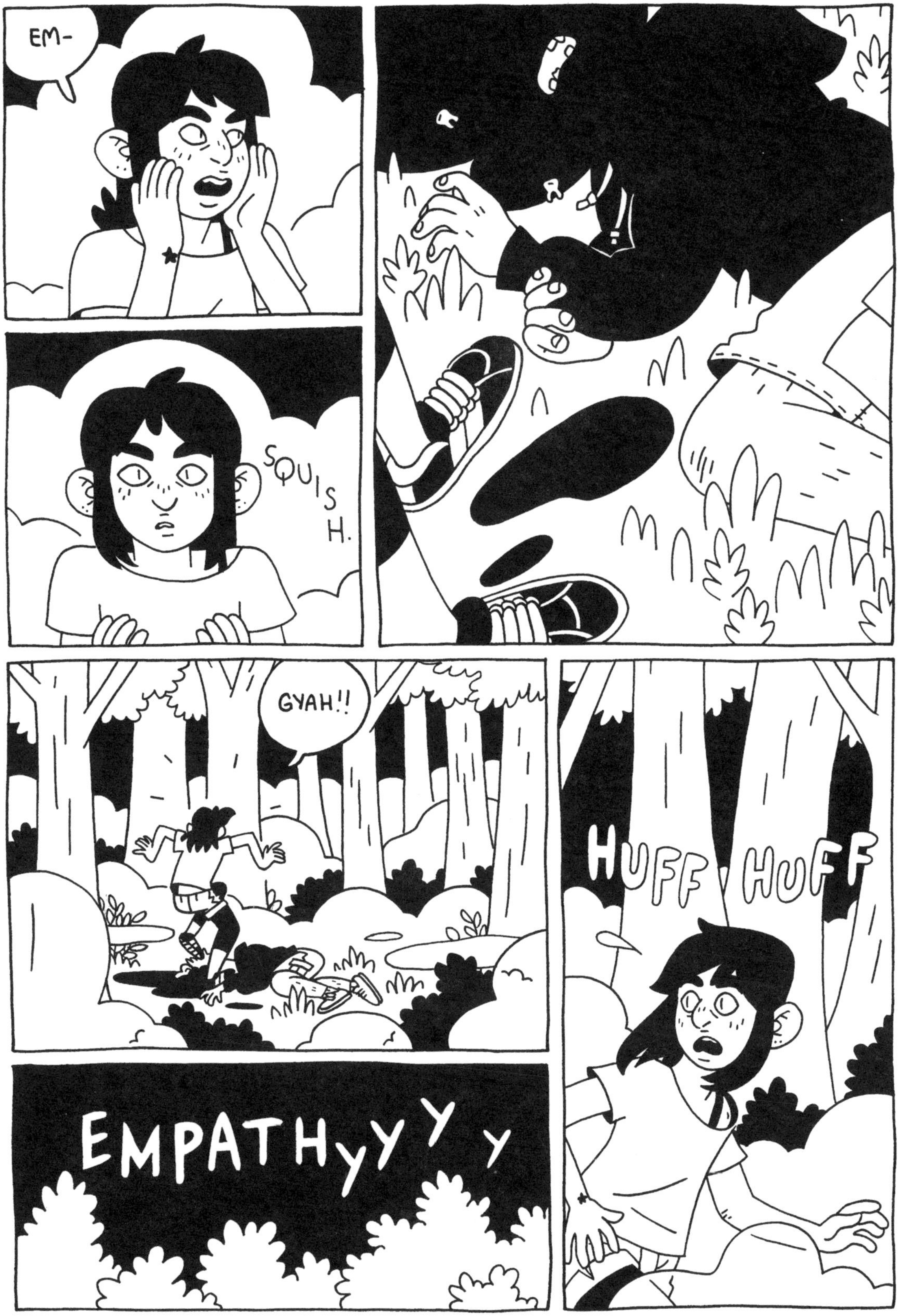
EM-
SQUISH.
GYAH!!
HUFF HUFF
EMPATHyyYYy

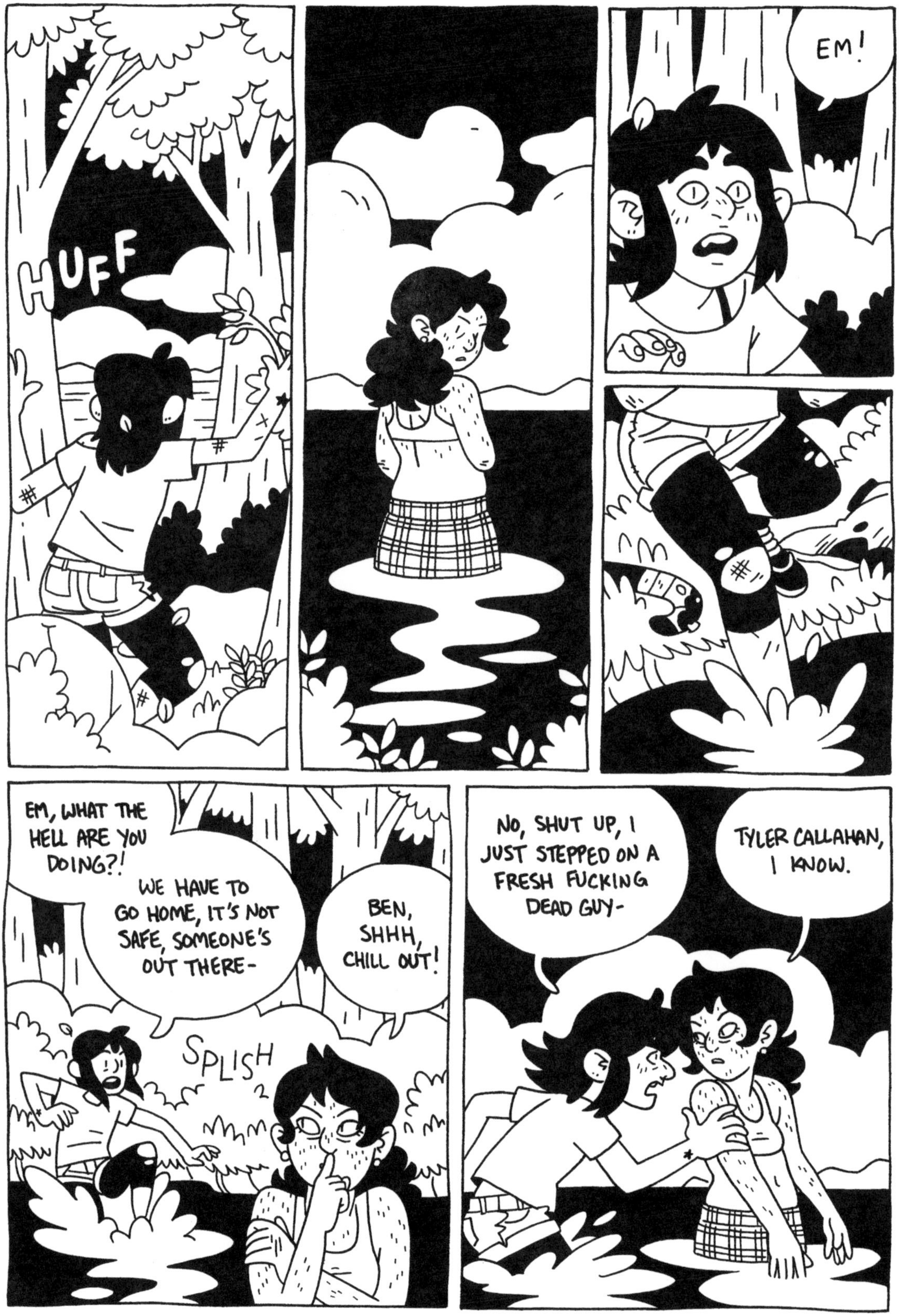
HUFF
EM!
EM, WHAT THE HELL ARE YOU DOING?!
WE HAVE TO GO HOME, IT'S NOT SAFE, SOMEONE'S OUT THERE-
BEN, SHHH, CHILL OUT!
SPLISH
NO, SHUT UP, I JUST STEPPED ON A FRESH FUCKING DEAD GUY-
TYLER CALLAHAN, I KNOW.

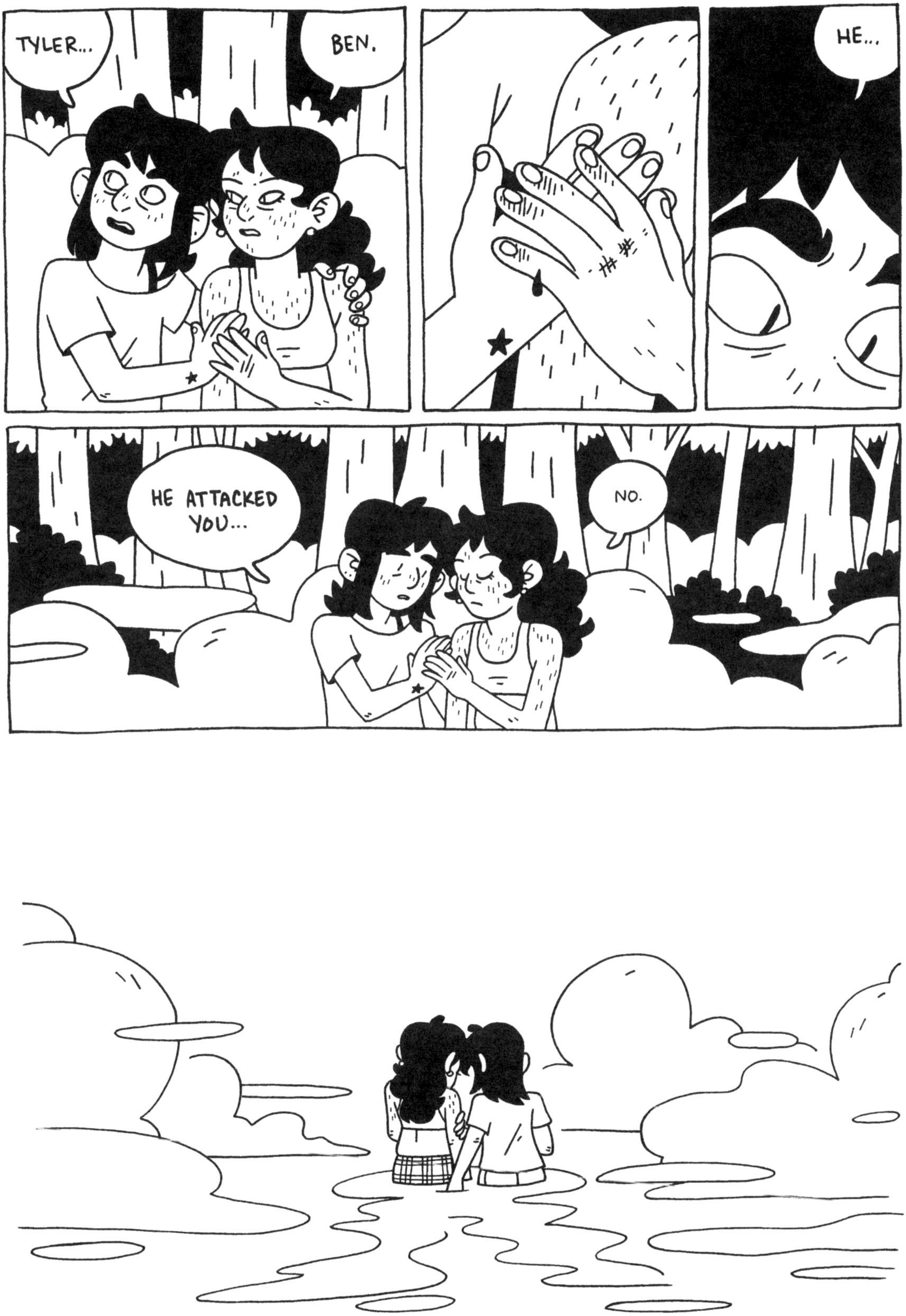
TYLER...
BEN.
HE...
HE ATTACKED YOU...
NO.

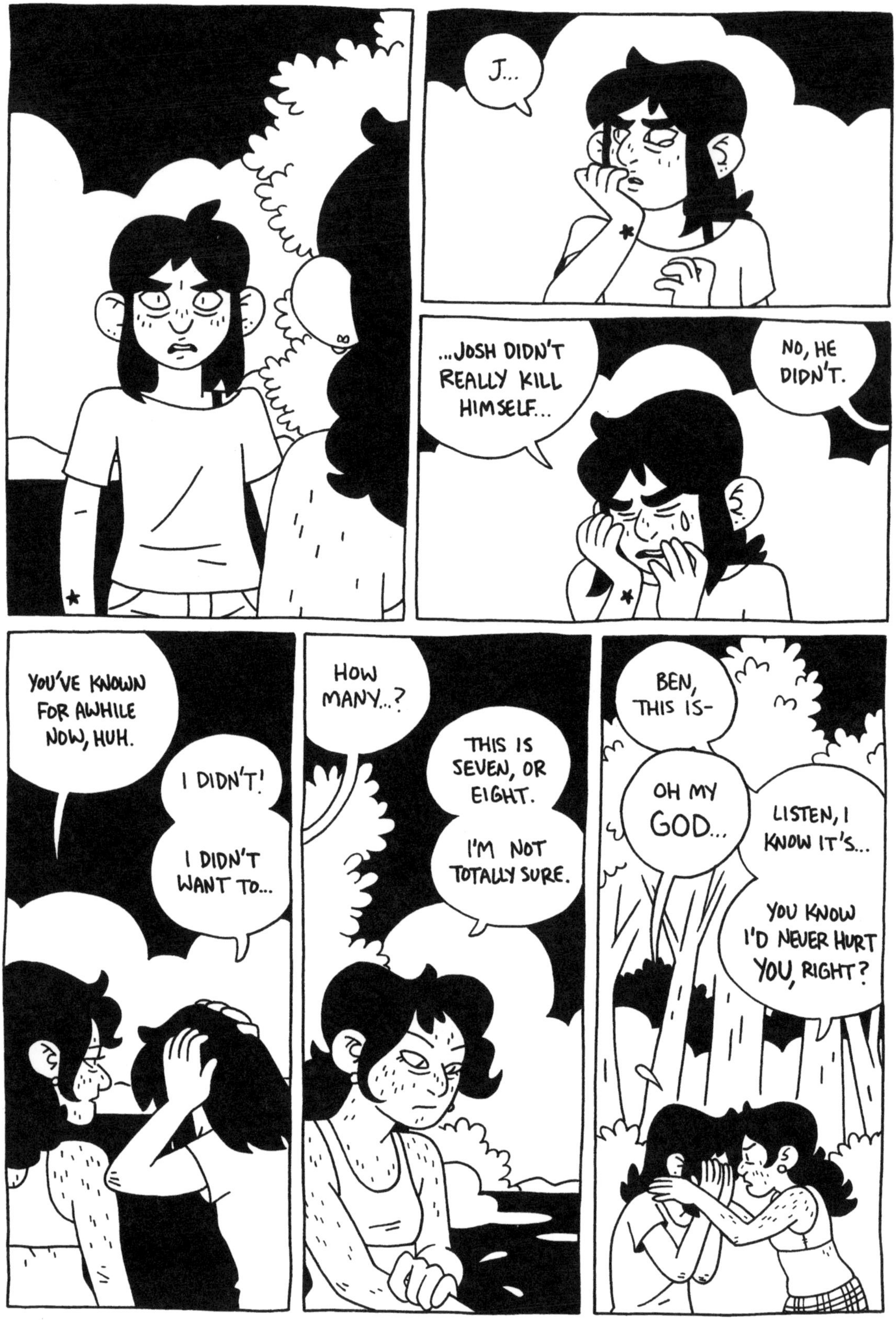
J...
...JOSH DIDN'T REALLY KILL HIMSELF...
NO, HE DIDN'T.
YOU'VE KNOWN FOR AWHILE NOW, HUH.
I DIDN'T!
I DIDN'T WANT TO...
HOW MANY...?
THIS IS SEVEN, OR EIGHT.
I'M NOT TOTALLY SURE.
BEN, THIS IS-
OH MY GOD...
LISTEN, I KNOW IT'S...
YOU KNOW I'D NEVER HURT YOU, RIGHT?

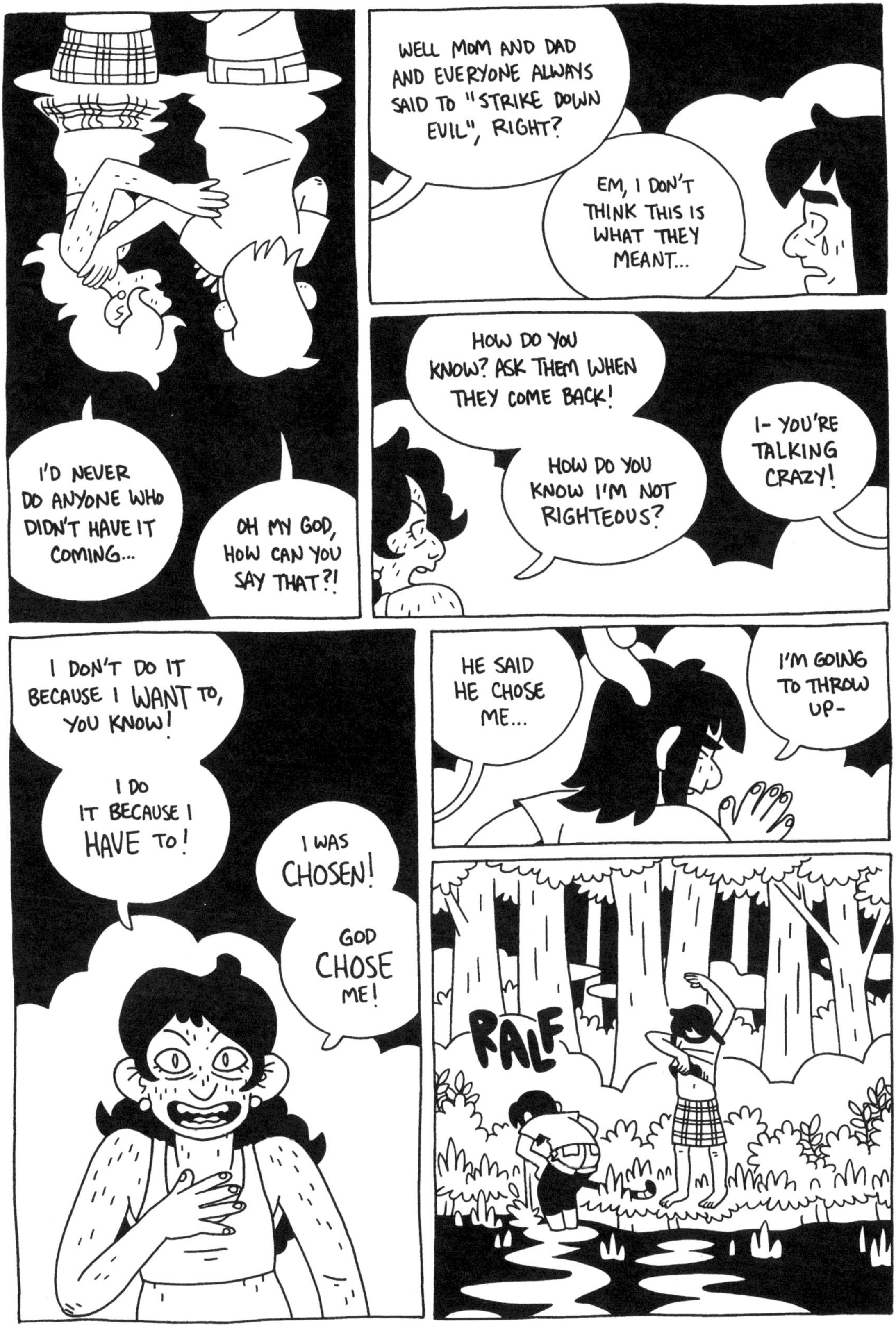
WELL MOM AND DAD AND EVERYONE ALWAYS SAID TO "STRIKE DOWN EVIL", RIGHT?
EM, I DON'T THINK THIS IS WHAT THEY MEANT...
I'D NEVER DO ANYONE WHO DIDN'T HAVE IT COMING...
OH MY GOD, HOW CAN YOU SAY THAT?!
HOW DO YOU KNOW? ASK THEM WHEN THEY COME BACK!
HOW DO YOU KNOW I'M NOT RIGHTEOUS?
I- YOU'RE TALKING CRAZY!
I DON'T DO IT BECAUSE I WANT TO, YOU KNOW!
I DO IT BECAUSE I HAVE TO!
I WAS CHOSEN!
GOD CHOSE ME!
HE SAID HE CHOSE ME...
I'M GOING TO THROW UP-
RALF

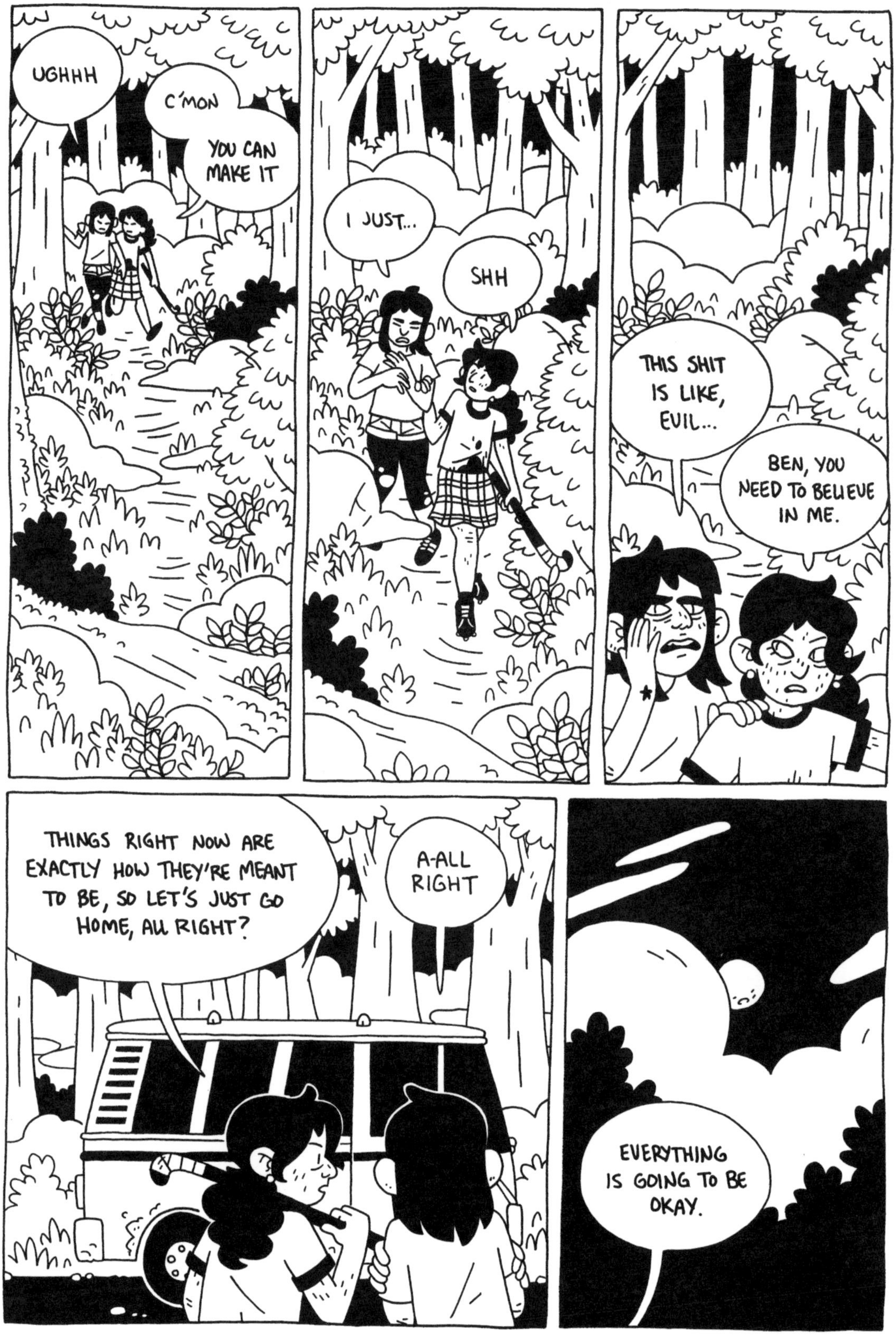
UGHHH
C'MON
YOU CAN MAKE IT
I JUST...
SHH
THIS SHIT IS LIKE, EVIL...
BEN, YOU NEED TO BELIEVE IN ME.
THINGS RIGHT NOW ARE EXACTLY HOW THEY'RE MEANT TO BE, SO LET'S JUST GO HOME, ALL RIGHT?
A-ALL RIGHT
EVERYTHING IS GOING TO BE OKAY.

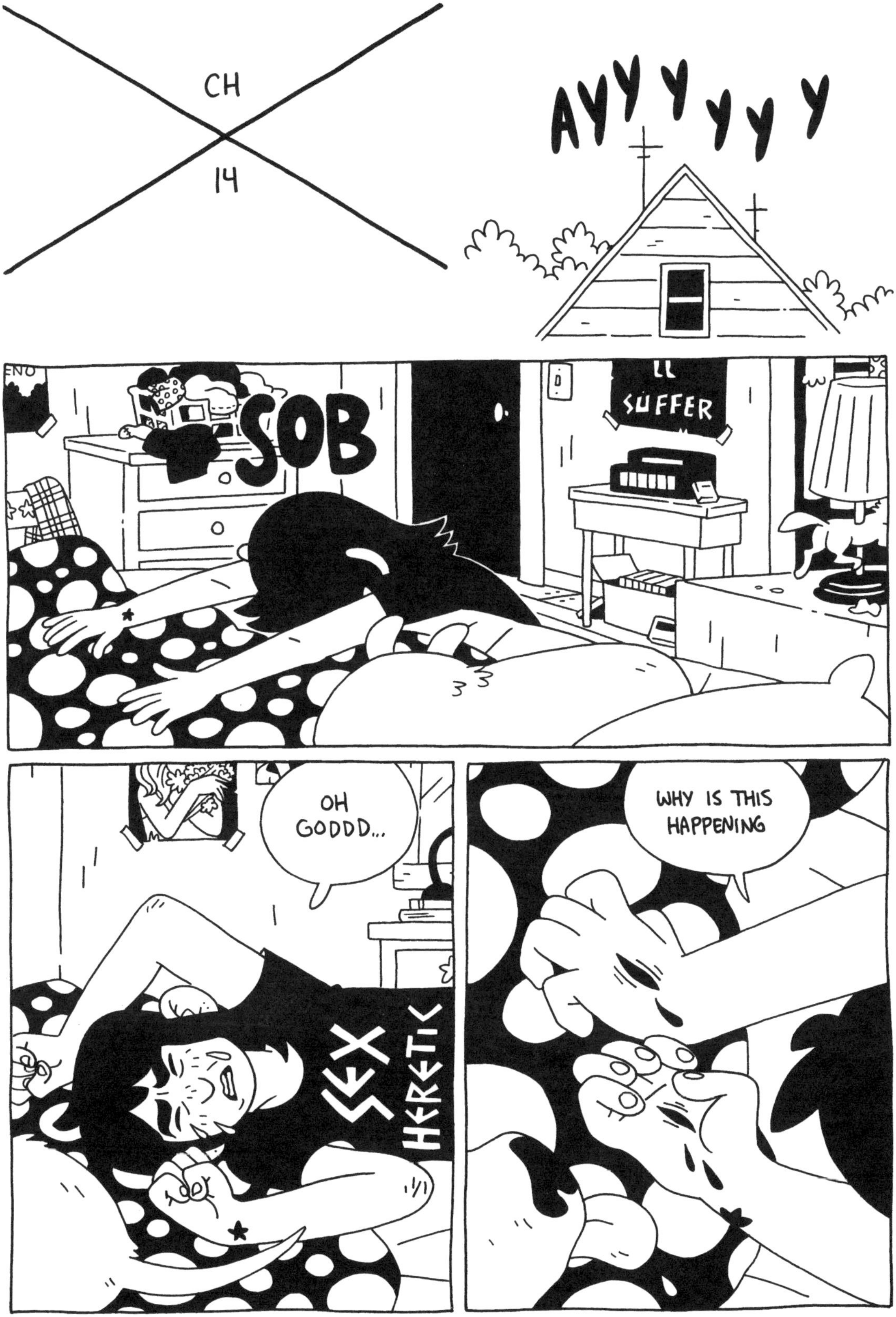
CH 14
AYYYYYY
SOB
LL SUFFER
OH GODDD...
SEX HERETIC
WHY IS THIS HAPPENING

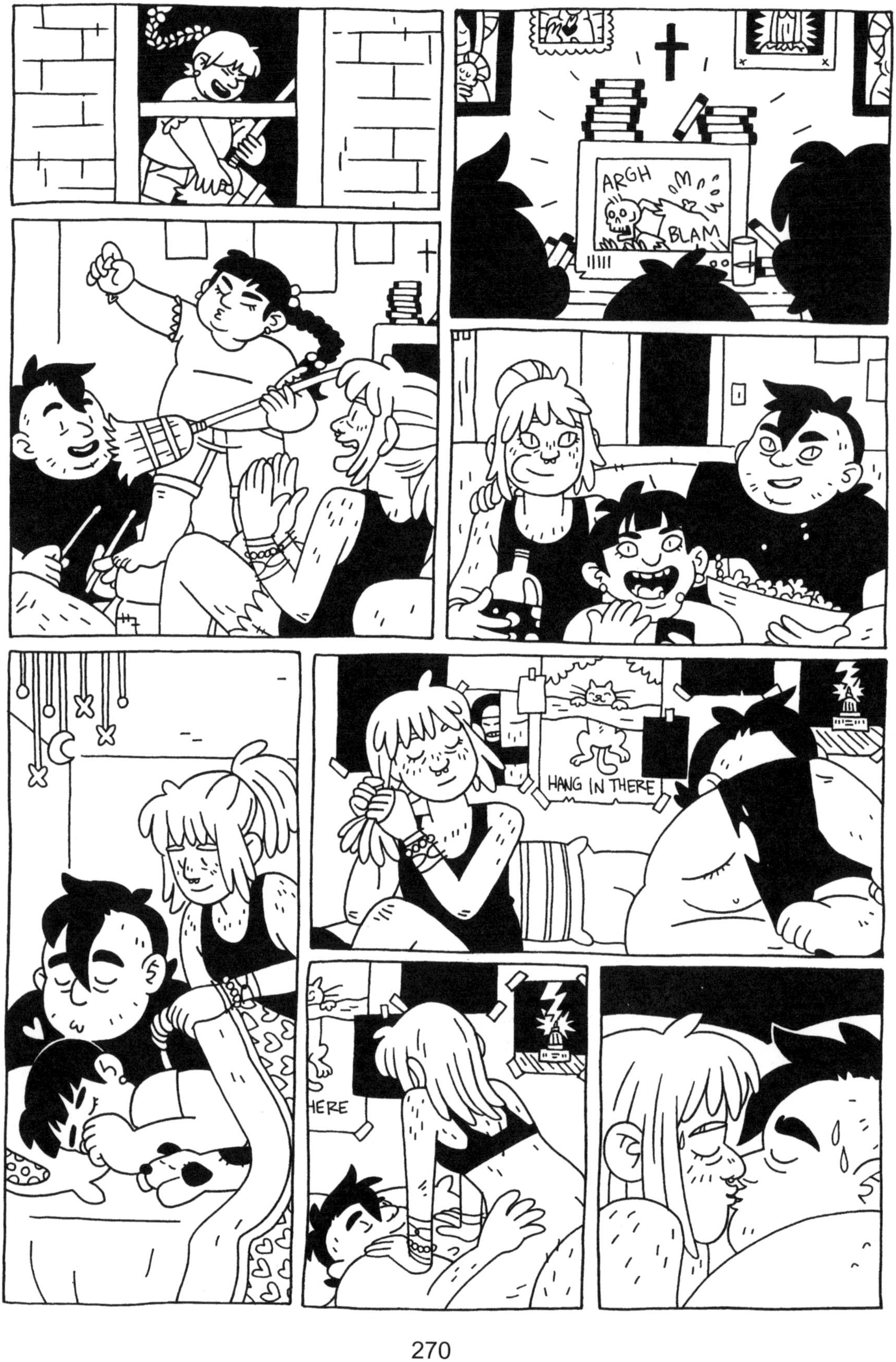
ARGH
BLAM
HANG IN THERE
HERE

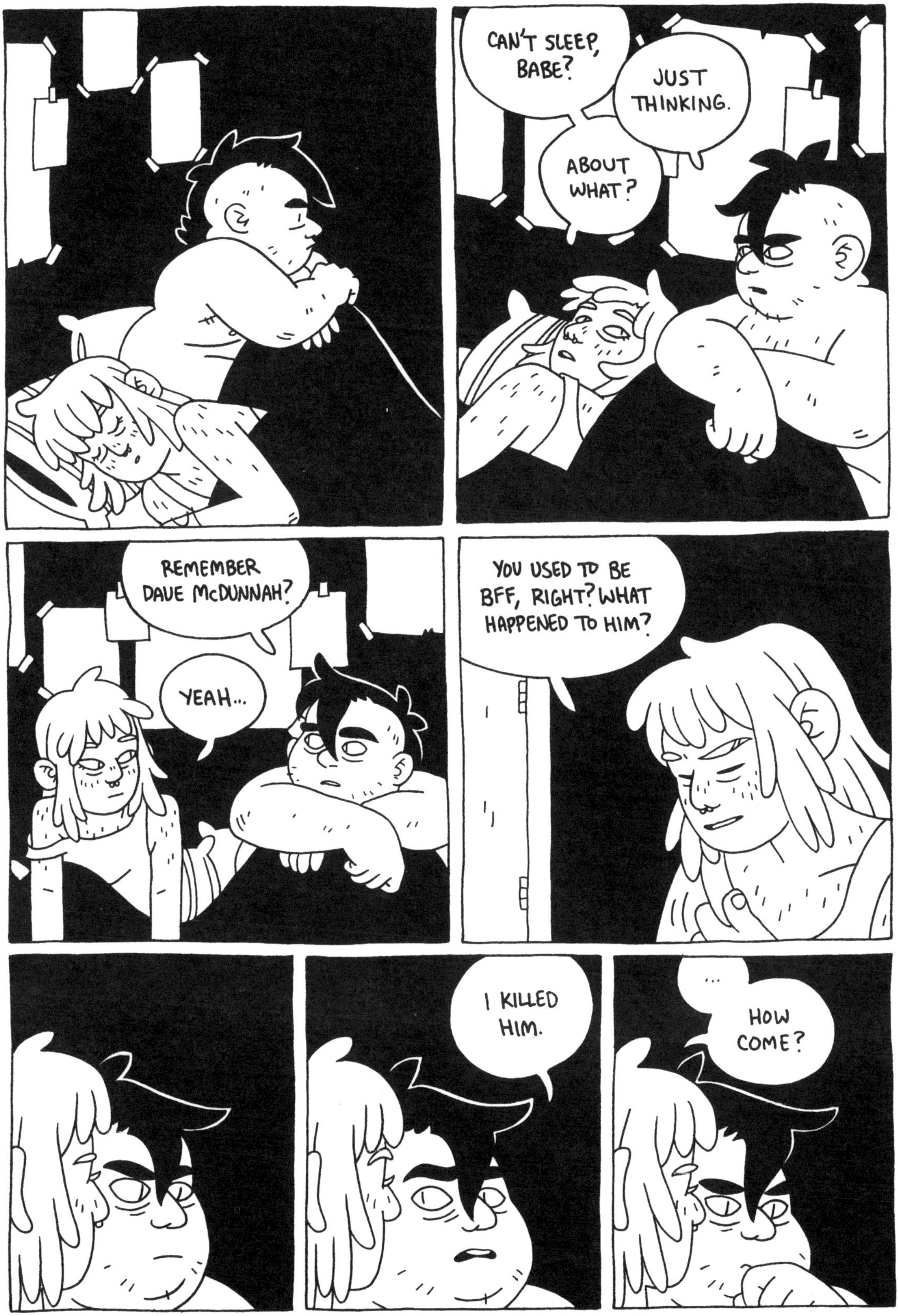
CAN'T SLEEP, BABE?
JUST THINKING.
ABOUT WHAT?
REMEMBER DAVE McDUNNAH?
YEAH...
YOU USED TO BE BFF, RIGHT? WHAT HAPPENED TO HIM?
I KILLED HIM.
...
HOW COME?

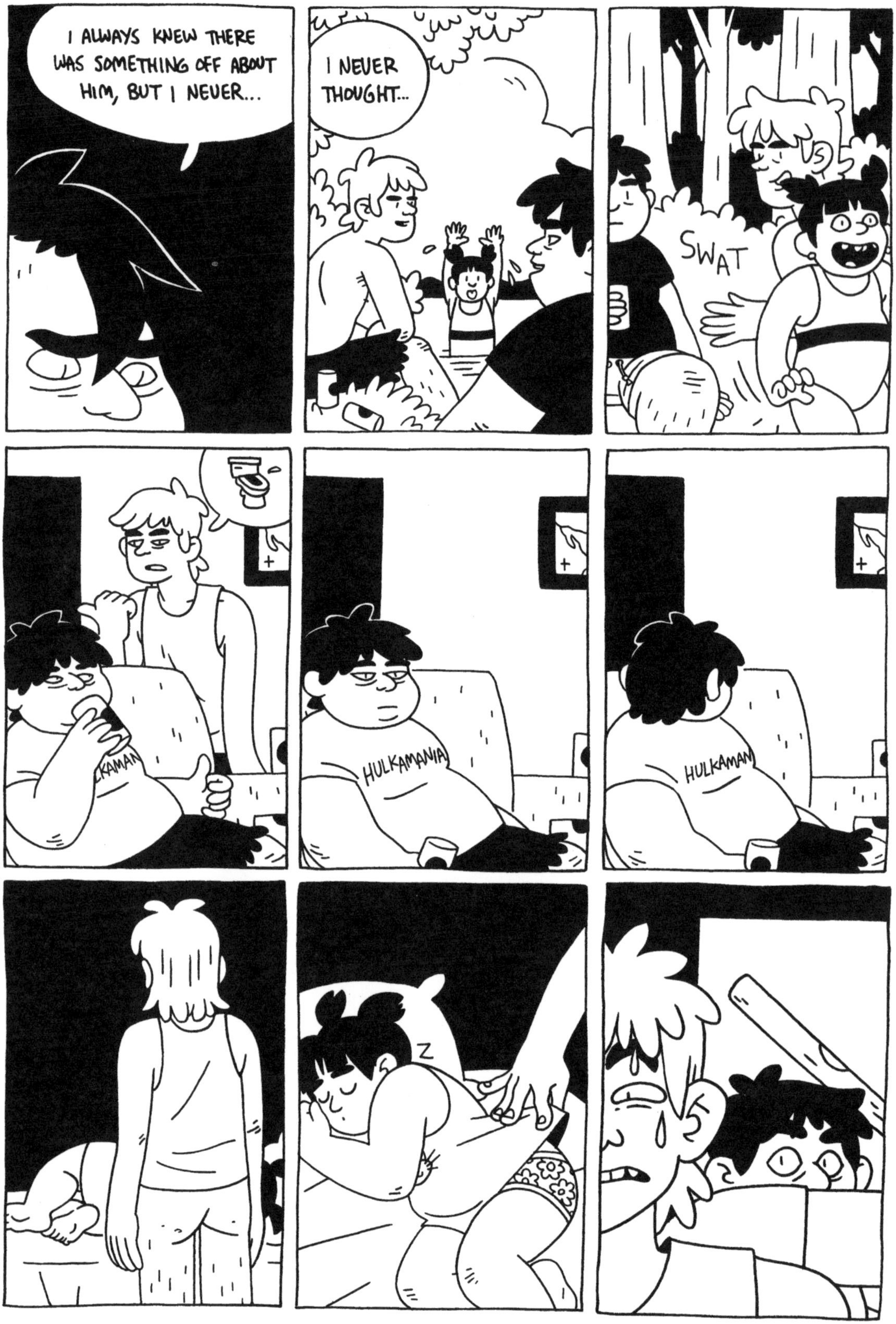
I ALWAYS KNEW THERE WAS SOMETHING OFF ABOUT HIM, BUT I NEVER...
I NEVER THOUGHT...
SWAT
HULKAMANIA
HULKAMANIA
HULKAMAN
Z

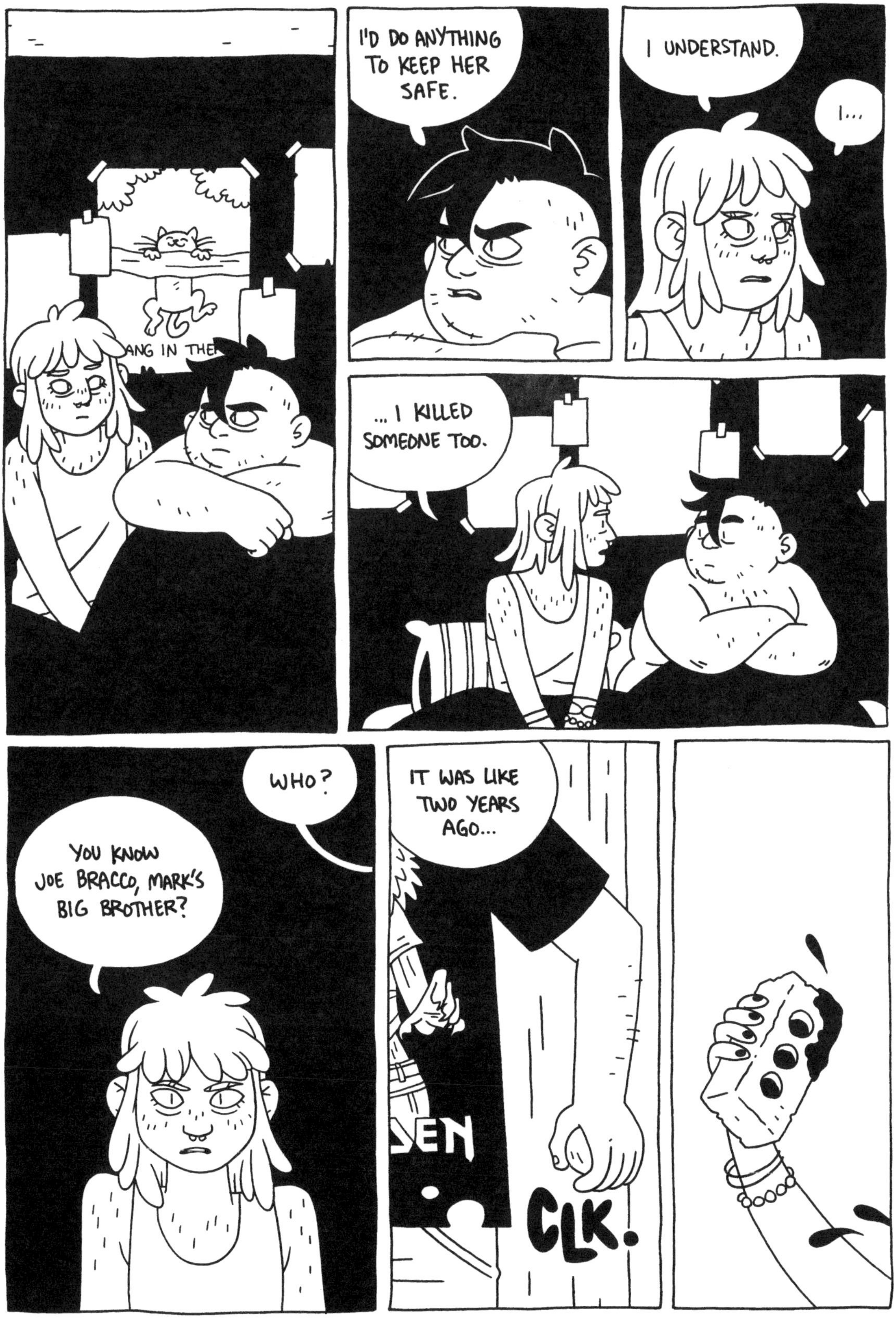
ANG IN THE
I'D DO ANYTHING TO KEEP HER SAFE.
I UNDERSTAND.
I...
...I KILLED SOMEONE TOO.
WHO?
YOU KNOW JOE BRACCO, MARK'S BIG BROTHER?
IT WAS LIKE TWO YEARS AGO...
SEN
CLK.

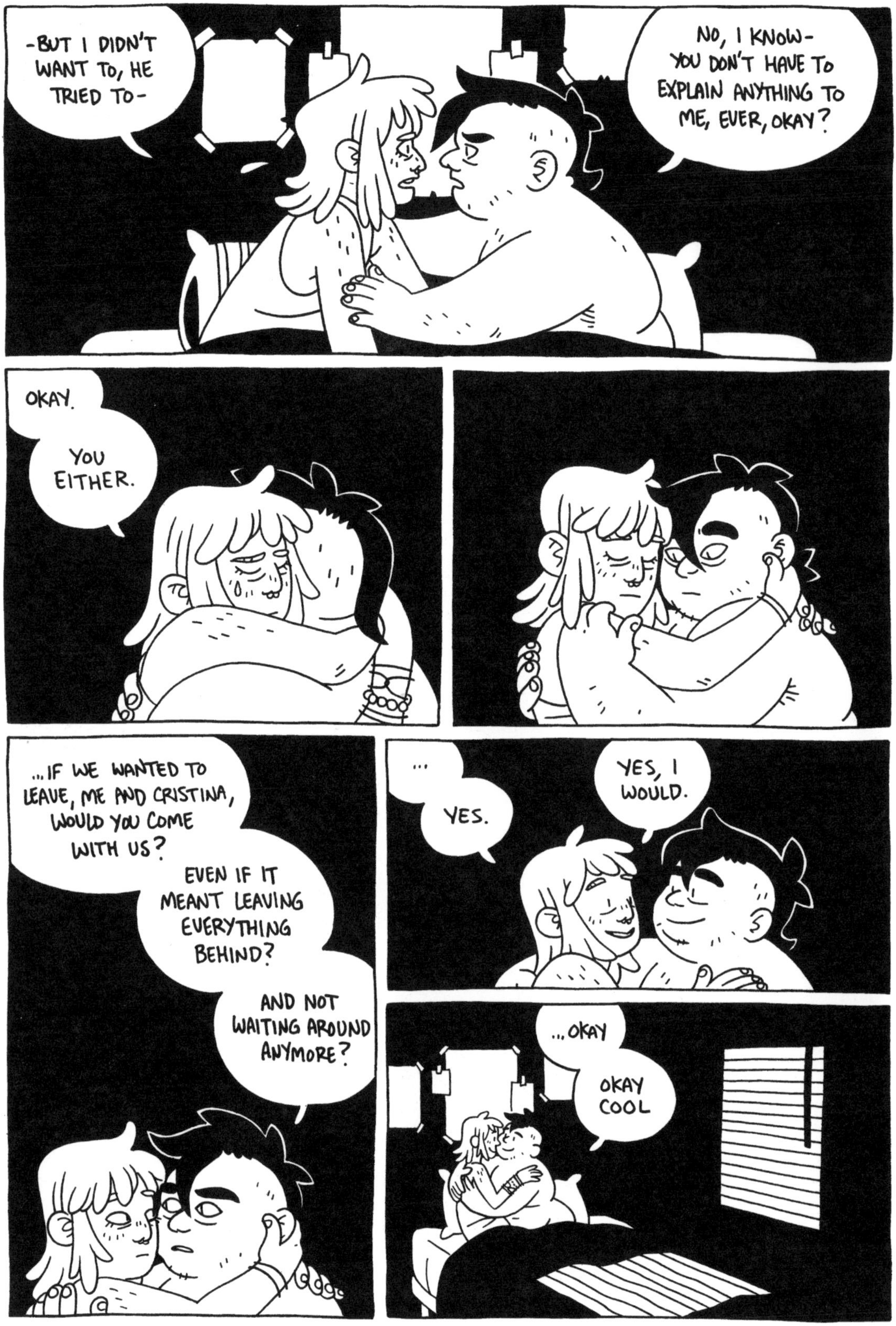
-BUT I DIDN'T WANT TO, HE TRIED TO-
NO, I KNOW- YOU DON'T HAVE TO EXPLAIN ANYTHING TO ME, EVER, OKAY?
OKAY.
YOU EITHER.
...IF WE WANTED TO LEAVE, ME AND CRISTINA, WOULD YOU COME WITH US?
EVEN IF IT MEANT LEAVING EVERYTHING BEHIND?
AND NOT WAITING AROUND ANYMORE?
...
YES.
YES, I WOULD.
...OKAY
OKAY COOL

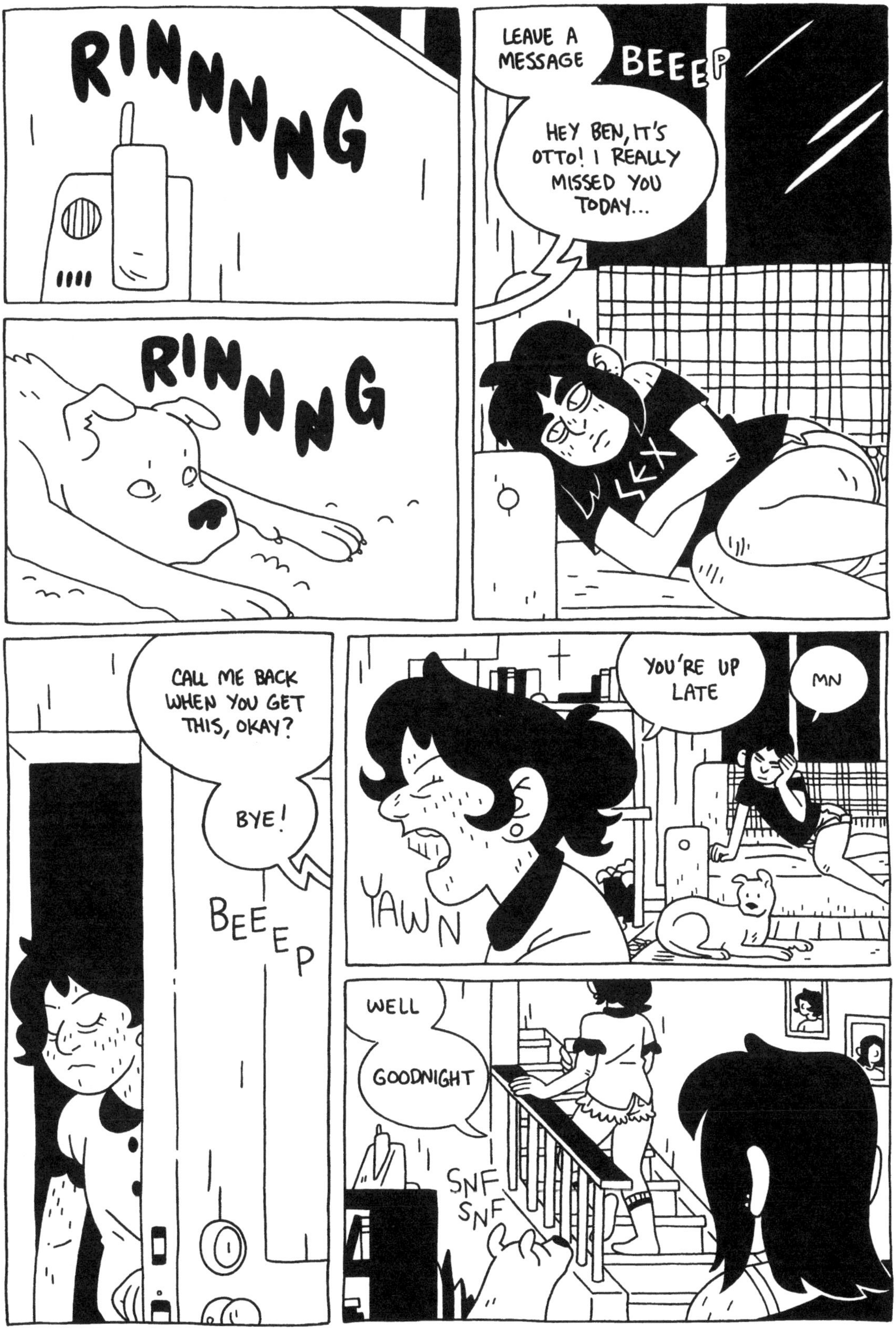
RINNNNG
LEAVE A MESSAGE
BEEEP
HEY BEN, IT'S OTTO! I REALLY MISSED YOU TODAY...
RINNNG
CALL ME BACK WHEN YOU GET THIS, OKAY?
BYE!
BEEEP
YAWN
YOU'RE UP LATE
MN
WELL
GOODNIGHT
SNF SNF

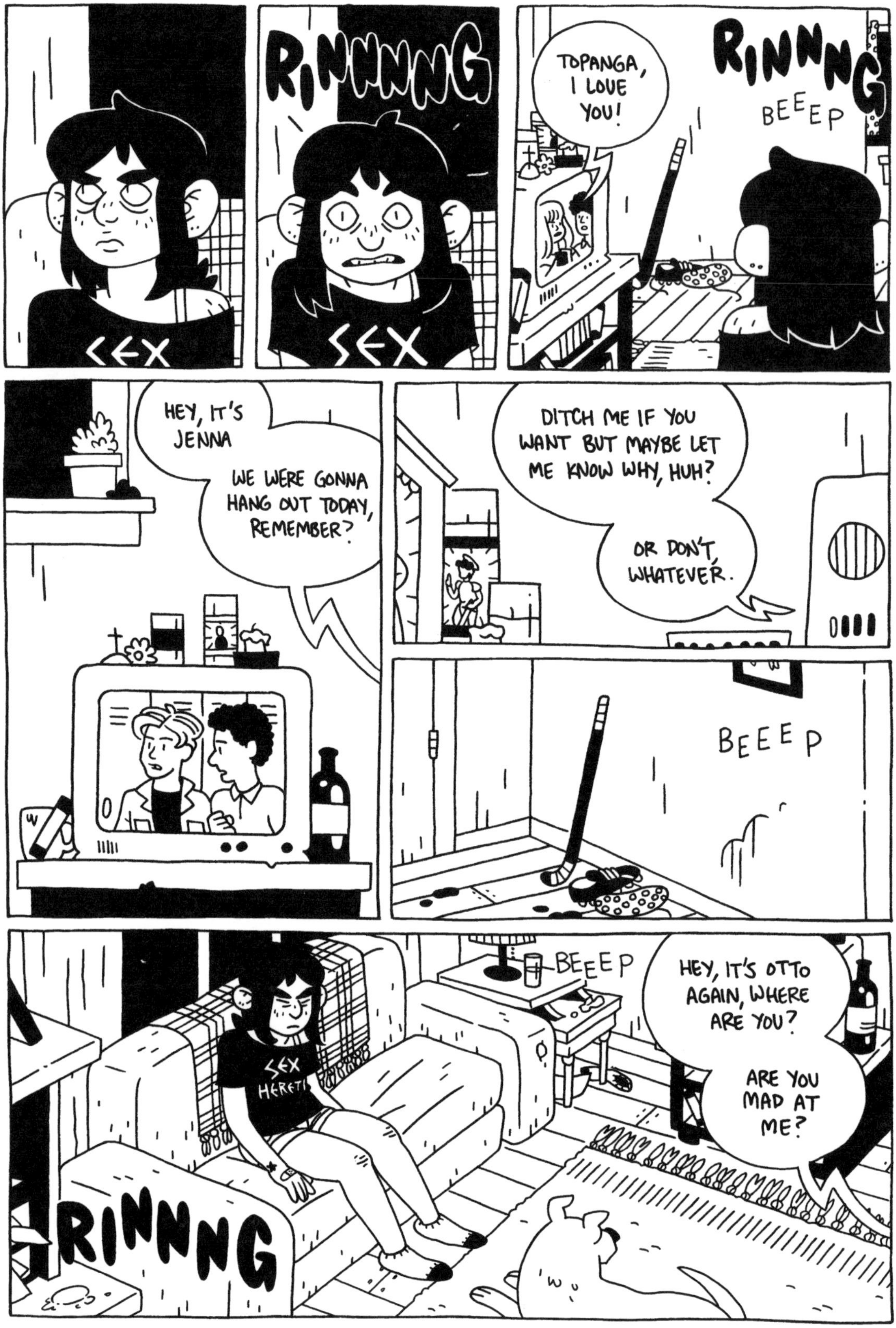
SEX
RINNNNG
SEX
TOPANGA, I LOVE YOU!
RINNNG
BEEEP
HEY, IT'S JENNA
WE WERE GONNA HANG OUT TODAY, REMEMBER?
DITCH ME IF YOU WANT BUT MAYBE LET ME KNOW WHY, HUH?
OR DON'T, WHATEVER.
BEEEP
BEEEP
HEY, IT'S OTTO AGAIN, WHERE ARE YOU?
ARE YOU MAD AT ME?
SEX HERETI
RINNNG

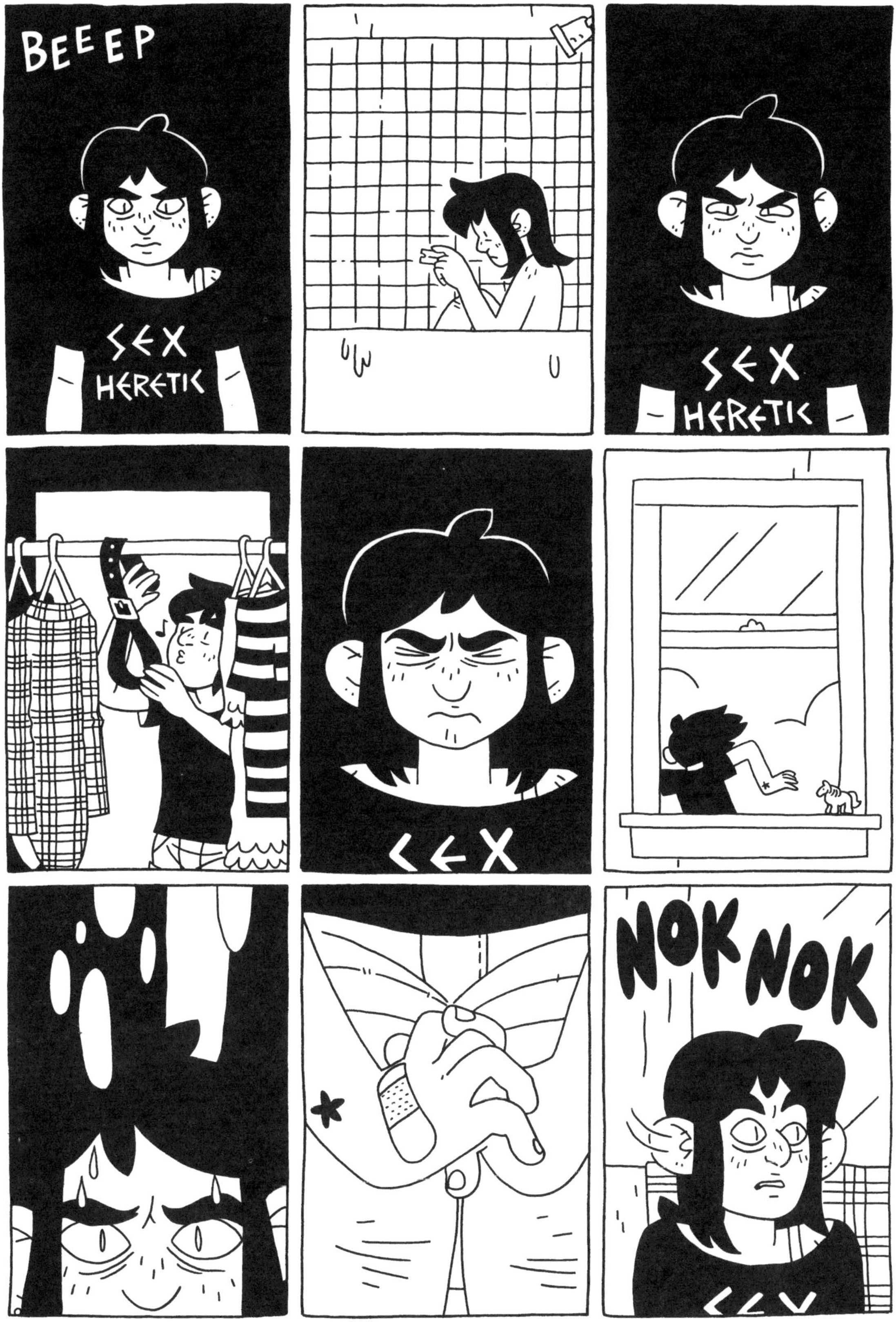
BEEEP
SEX HERETIC
SEX HERETIC
SEX
NOK NOK

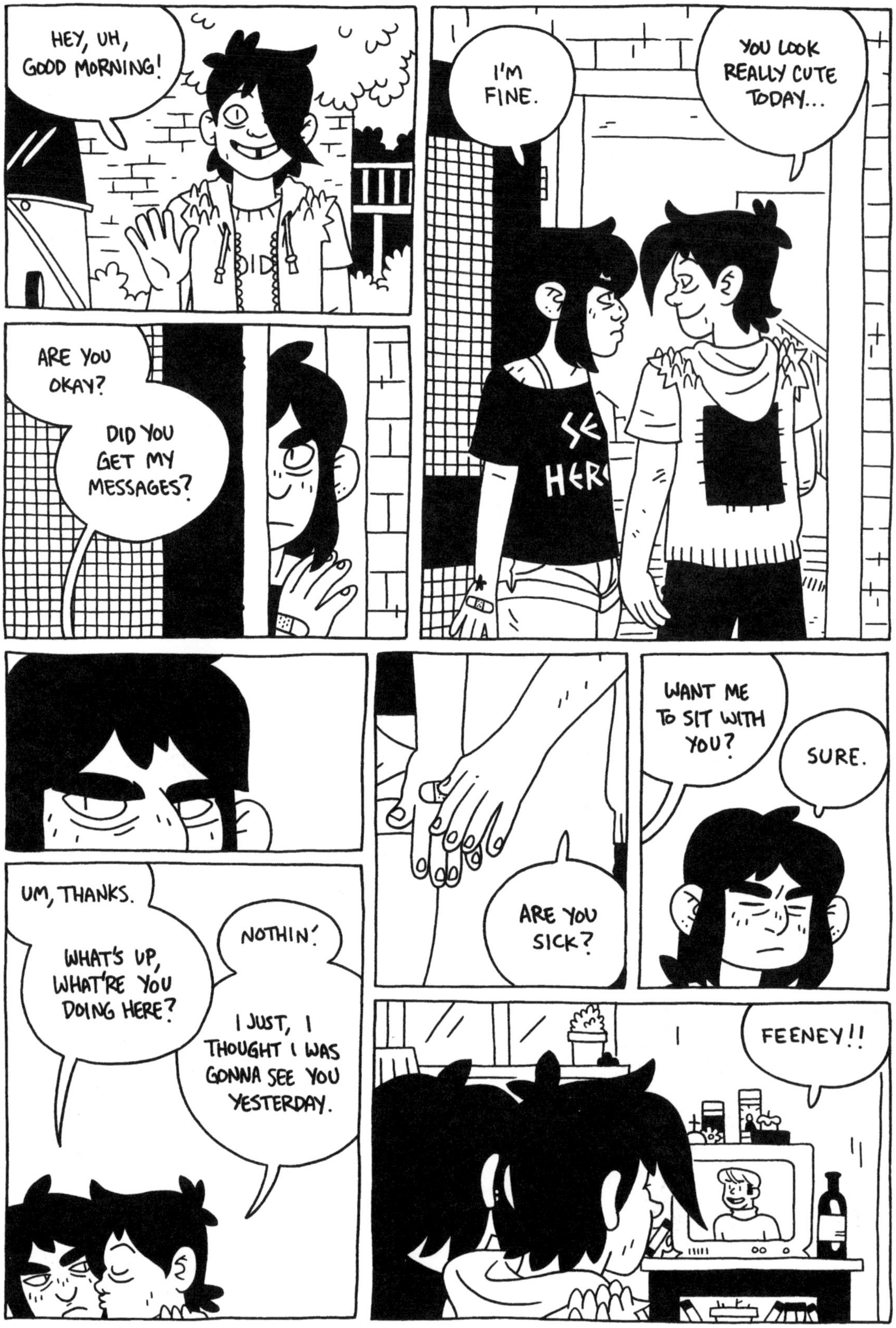
HEY, UH, GOOD MORNING!
I'M FINE.
YOU LOOK REALLY CUTE TODAY...
ARE YOU OKAY?
DID YOU GET MY MESSAGES?
ARE YOU SICK?
WANT ME TO SIT WITH YOU?
SURE.
UM, THANKS.
WHAT'S UP, WHAT'RE YOU DOING HERE?
NOTHIN'.
I JUST, I THOUGHT I WAS GONNA SEE YOU YESTERDAY.
FEENEY!!

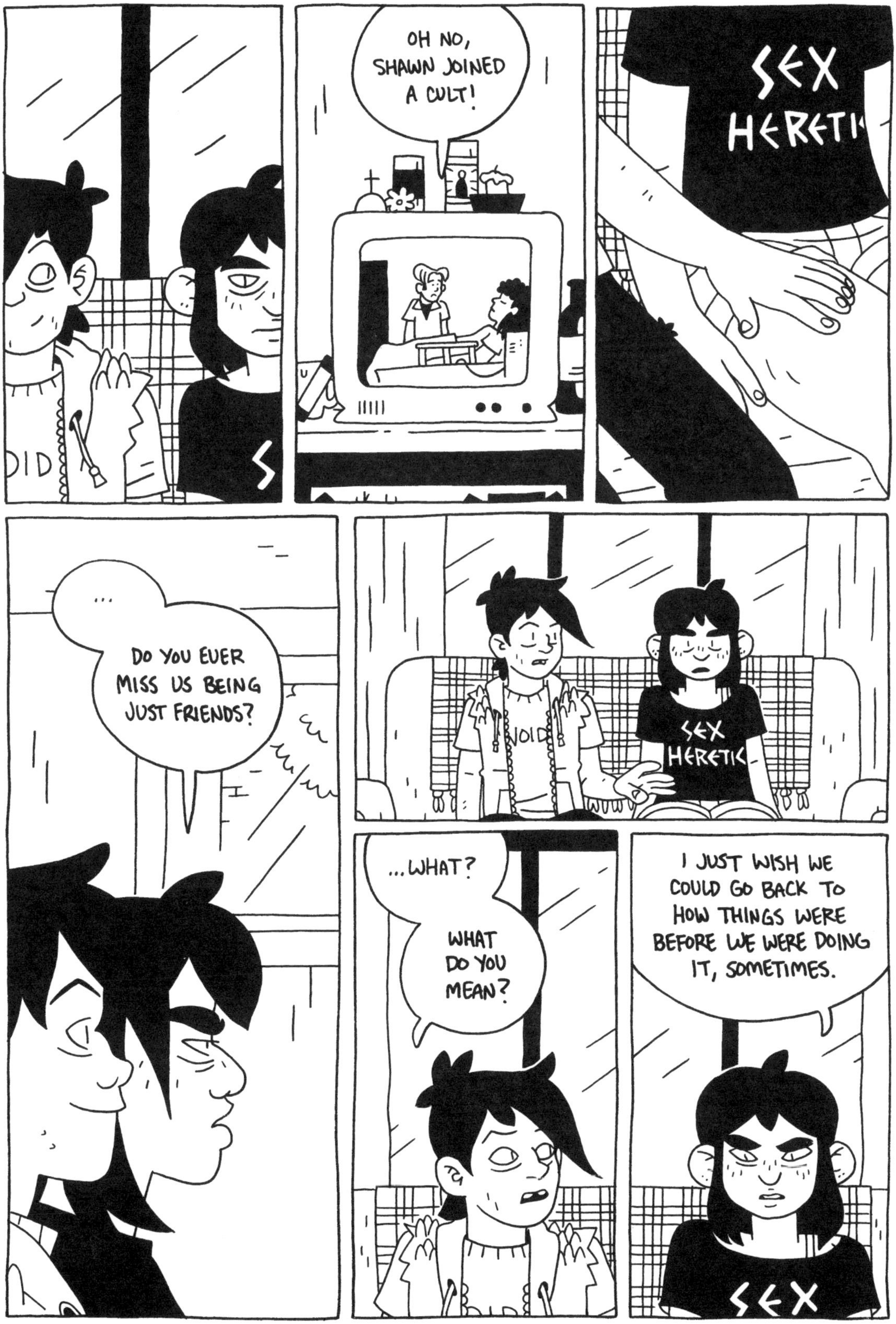
VOID
S
OH NO, SHAWN JOINED A CULT!
SEX HERETIC
...
DO YOU EVER MISS US BEING JUST FRIENDS?
VOID
SEX HERETIC
...WHAT?
WHAT DO YOU MEAN?
I JUST WISH WE COULD GO BACK TO HOW THINGS WERE BEFORE WE WERE DOING IT, SOMETIMES.
SEX

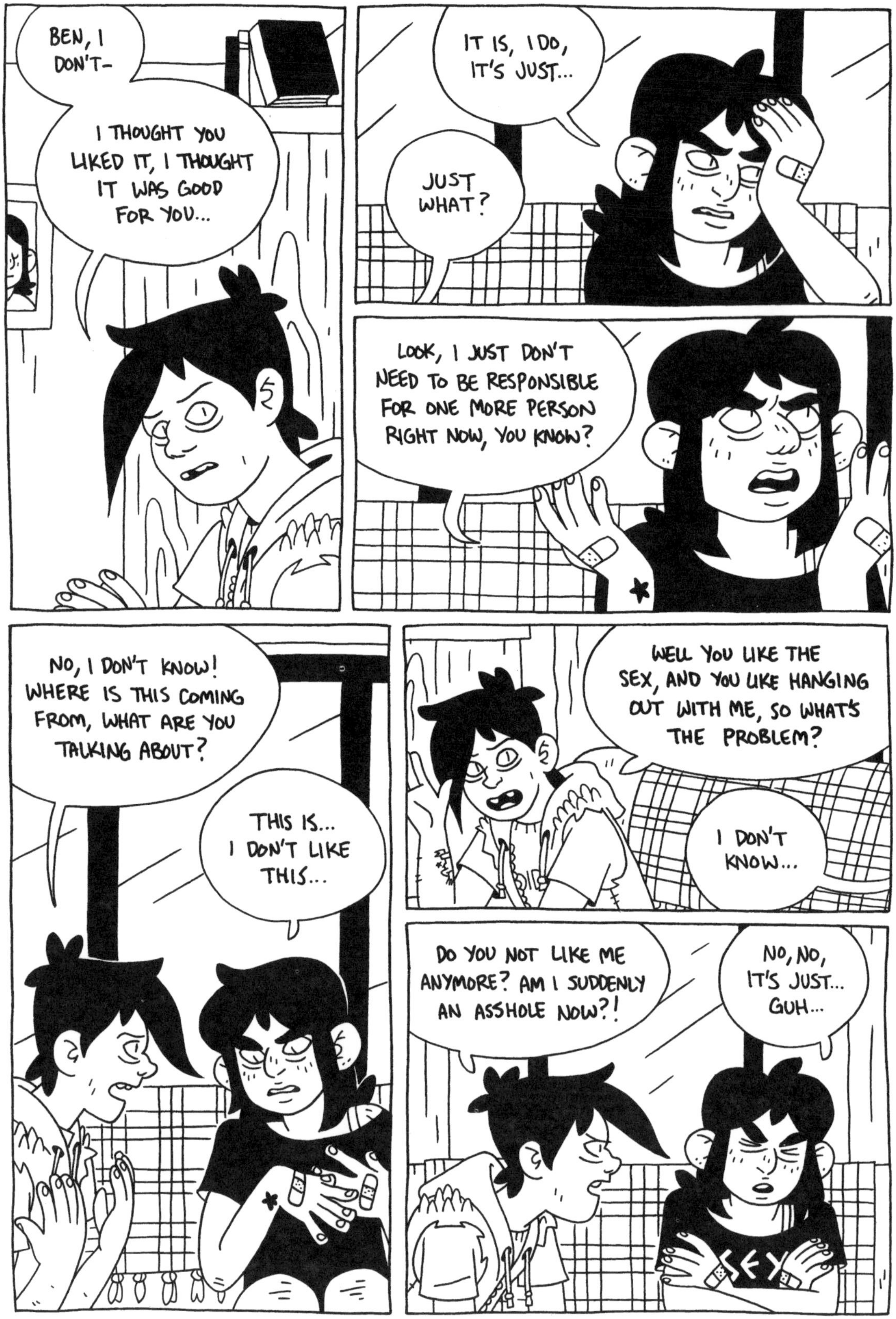
BEN, I DON'T-
I THOUGHT YOU LIKED IT, I THOUGHT IT WAS GOOD FOR YOU...
IT IS, I DO, IT'S JUST...
JUST WHAT?
LOOK, I JUST DON'T NEED TO BE RESPONSIBLE FOR ONE MORE PERSON RIGHT NOW, YOU KNOW?
NO, I DON'T KNOW! WHERE IS THIS COMING FROM, WHAT ARE YOU TALKING ABOUT?
THIS IS... I DON'T LIKE THIS...
WELL YOU LIKE THE SEX, AND YOU LIKE HANGING OUT WITH ME, SO WHAT'S THE PROBLEM?
I DON'T KNOW...
DO YOU NOT LIKE ME ANYMORE? AM I SUDDENLY AN ASSHOLE NOW?!
NO, NO, IT'S JUST... GUH...
SEX

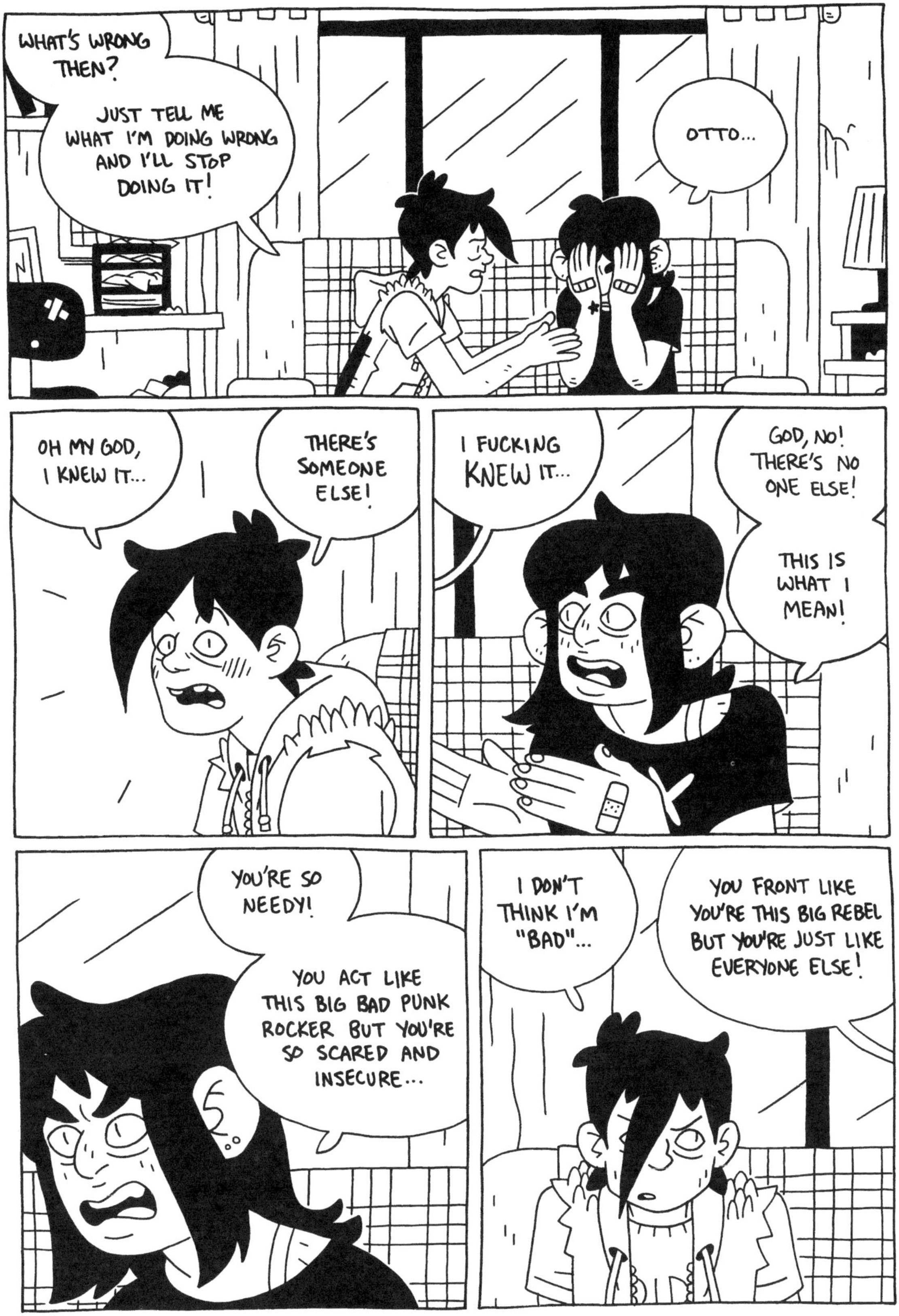
WHAT'S WRONG THEN?
JUST TELL ME WHAT I'M DOING WRONG AND I'LL STOP DOING IT!
OTTO...
OH MY GOD, I KNEW IT...
THERE'S SOMEONE ELSE!
I FUCKING KNEW IT...
GOD, NO! THERE'S NO ONE ELSE!
THIS IS WHAT I MEAN!
YOU'RE SO NEEDY!
YOU ACT LIKE THIS BIG BAD PUNK ROCKER BUT YOU'RE SO SCARED AND INSECURE...
I DON'T THINK I'M "BAD"...
YOU FRONT LIKE YOU'RE THIS BIG REBEL BUT YOU'RE JUST LIKE EVERYONE ELSE!

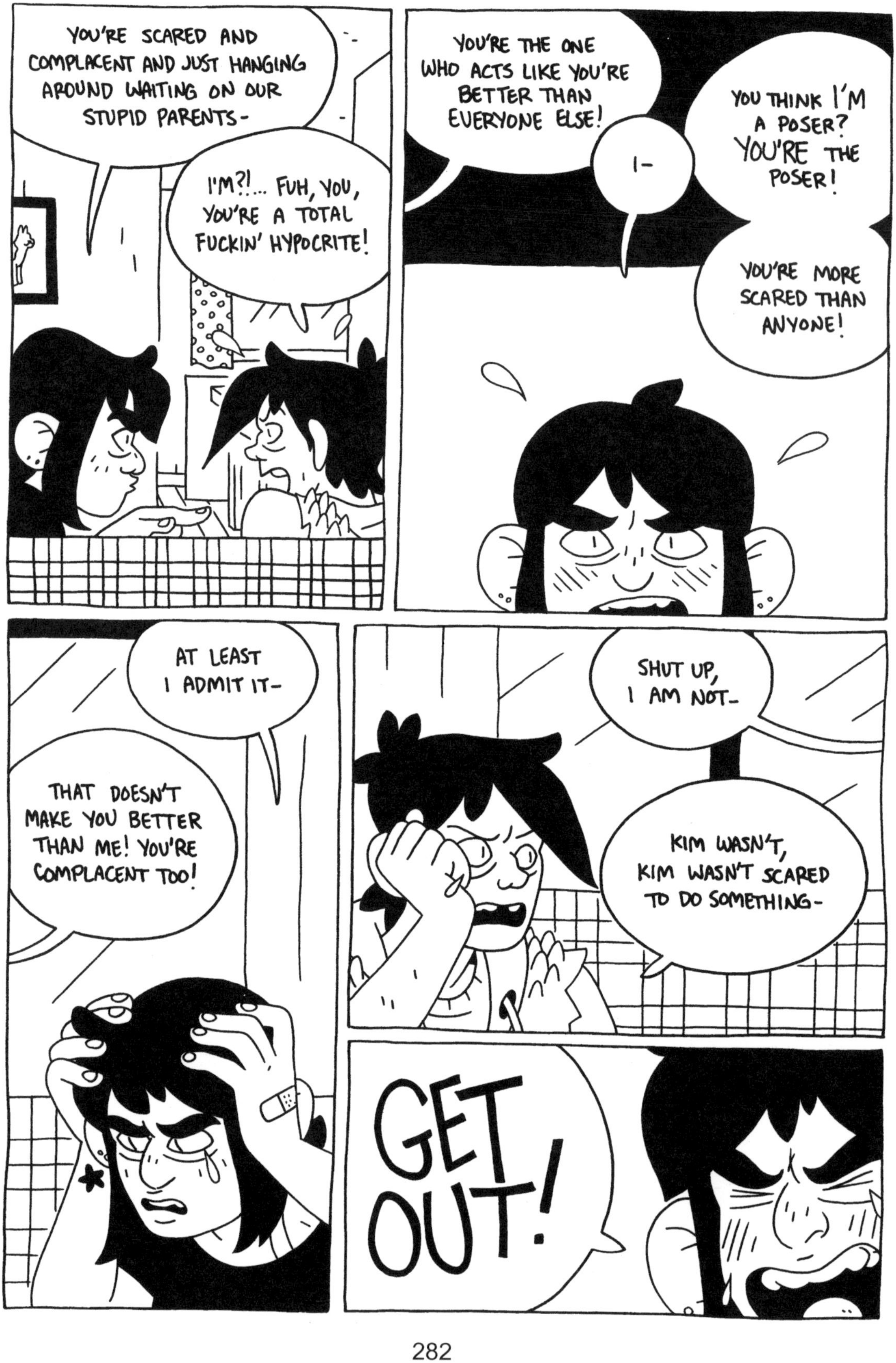
YOU'RE SCARED AND COMPLACENT AND JUST HANGING AROUND WAITING ON OUR STUPID PARENTS-
I'M?!.... FUH, YOU, YOU'RE A TOTAL FUCKIN' HYPOCRITE!
YOU'RE THE ONE WHO ACTS LIKE YOU'RE BETTER THAN EVERYONE ELSE!
I-
YOU THINK I'M A POSER? YOU'RE THE POSER!
YOU'RE MORE SCARED THAN ANYONE!
AT LEAST I ADMIT IT-
THAT DOESN'T MAKE YOU BETTER THAN ME! YOU'RE COMPLACENT TOO!
SHUT UP, I AM NOT-
KIM WASN'T, KIM WASN'T SCARED TO DO SOMETHING-
GET OUT!

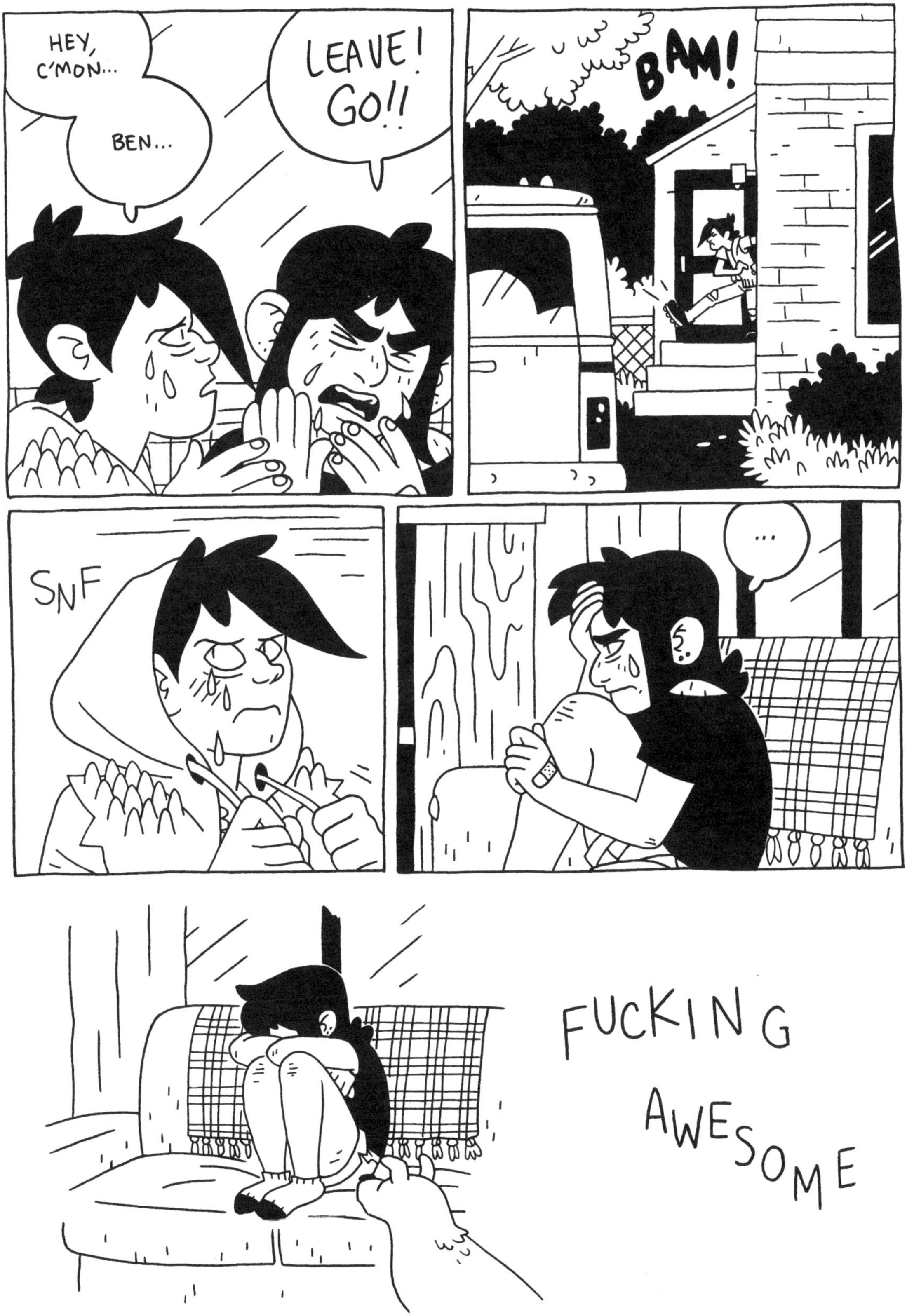
HEY, C'MON...
BEN...
LEAVE! GO!!
BAM!
SNF
...
FUCKING AWESOME

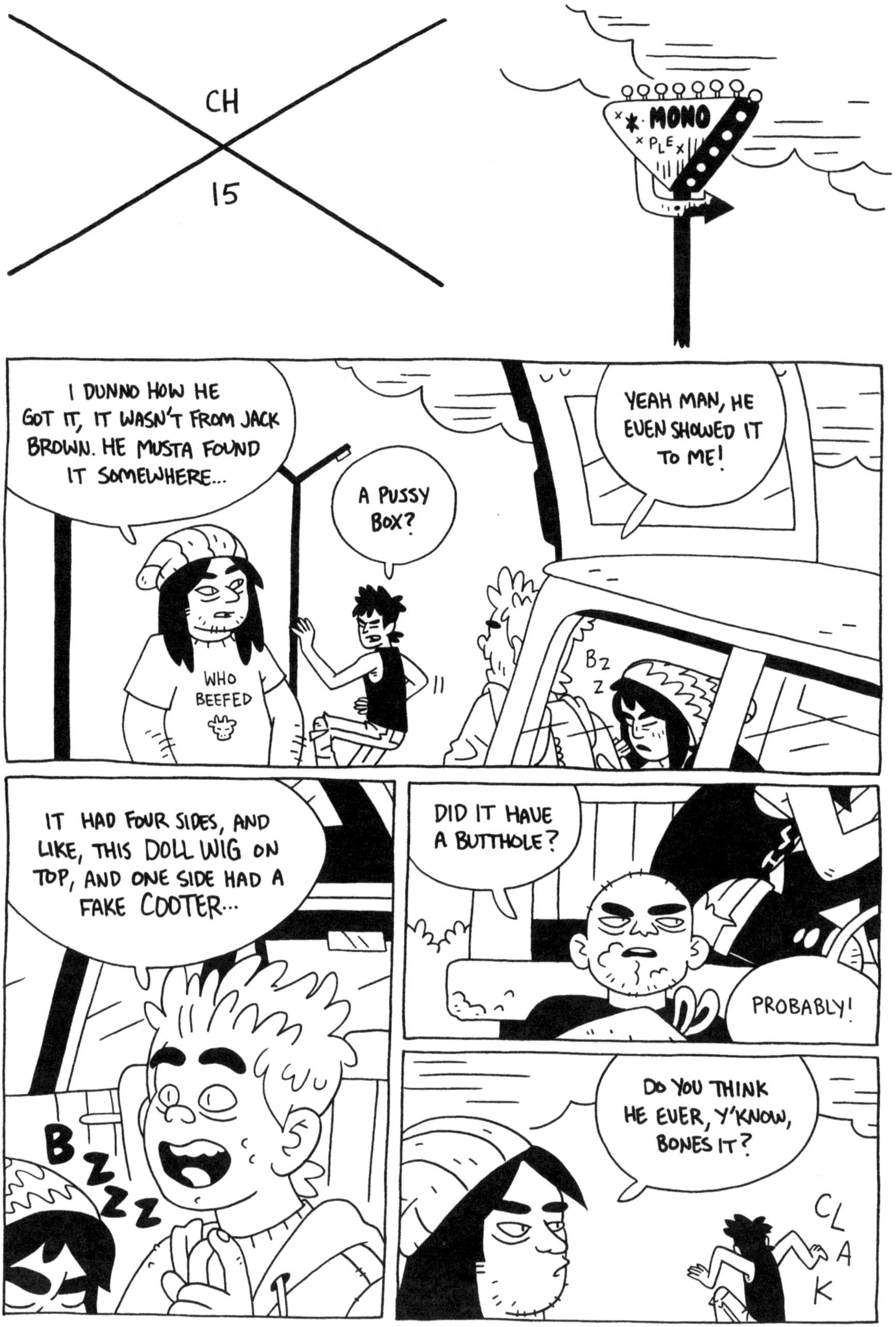
CH 15
MONO PLEX
I DUNNO HOW HE GOT IT, IT WASN'T FROM JACK BROWN. HE MUSTA FOUND IT SOMEWHERE...
A PUSSY BOX?
YEAH MAN, HE EVEN SHOWED IT TO ME!
WHO BEEFED
BZZ
IT HAD FOUR SIDES, AND LIKE, THIS DOLL WIG ON TOP, AND ONE SIDE HAD A FAKE COOTER...
BZZZ
DID IT HAVE A BUTTHOLE?
PROBABLY!
DO YOU THINK HE EVER, Y'KNOW, BONES IT?
CLAK

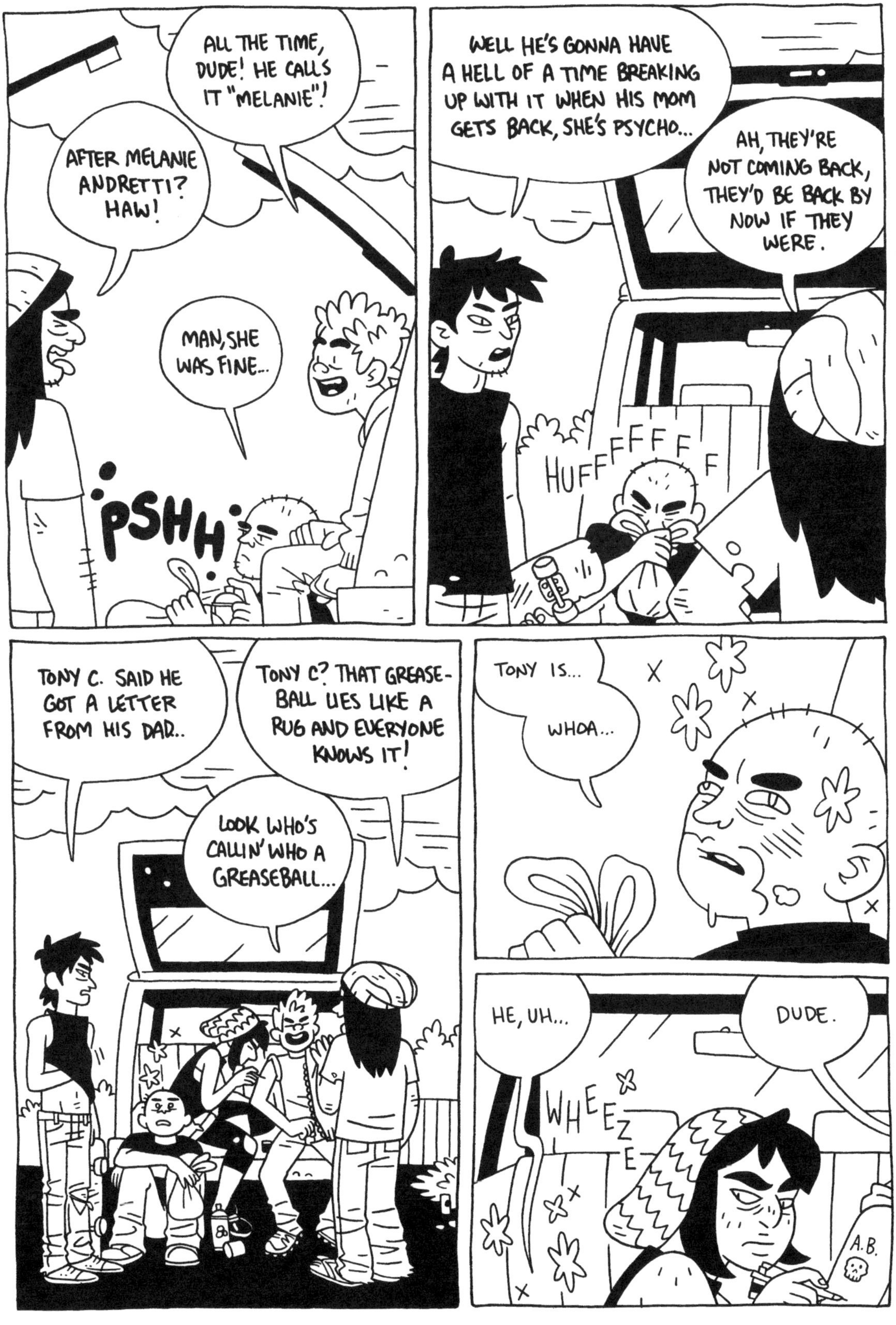
ALL THE TIME, DUDE! HE CALLS IT "MELANIE"!
AFTER MELANIE ANDRETTI? HAW!
MAN, SHE WAS FINE...
PSHH
WELL HE'S GONNA HAVE A HELL OF A TIME BREAKING UP WITH IT WHEN HIS MOM GETS BACK, SHE'S PSYCHO...
AH, THEY'RE NOT COMING BACK, THEY'D BE BACK BY NOW IF THEY WERE.
HUFFFFFFF
TONY C. SAID HE GOT A LETTER FROM HIS DAD..
TONY C? THAT GREASE-BALL LIES LIKE A RUG AND EVERYONE KNOWS IT!
LOOK WHO'S CALLIN' WHO A GREASEBALL...
TONY IS...
WHOA...
HE, UH...
DUDE.
WHEEZE
A.B.

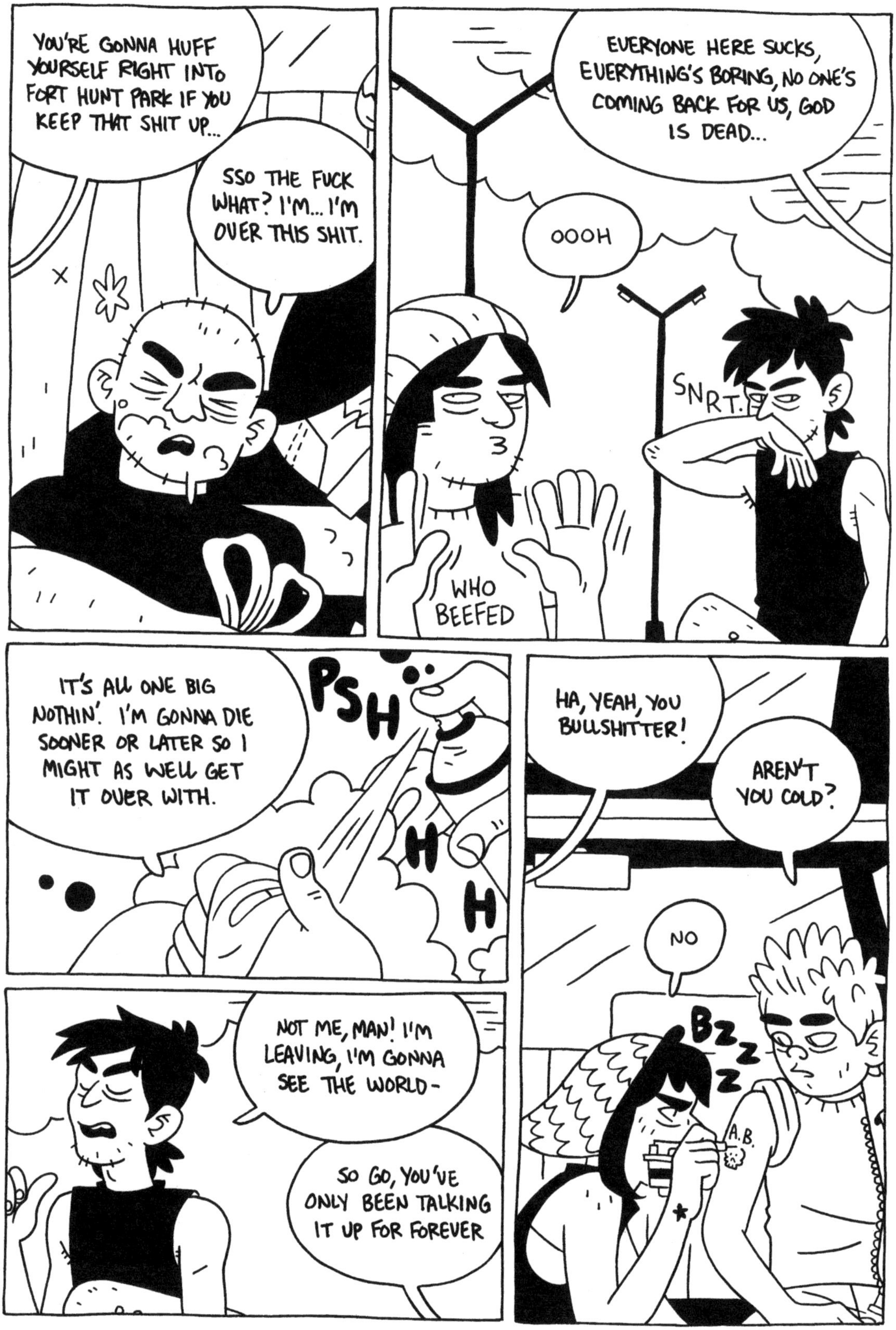
YOU'RE GONNA HUFF YOURSELF RIGHT INTO FORT HUNT PARK IF YOU KEEP THAT SHIT UP...
SSO THE FUCK WHAT? I'M... I'M OVER THIS SHIT.
EVERYONE HERE SUCKS, EVERYTHING'S BORING, NO ONE'S COMING BACK FOR US, GOD IS DEAD...
OOOH
SNRT.
WHO BEEFED
IT'S ALL ONE BIG NOTHIN'. I'M GONNA DIE SOONER OR LATER SO I MIGHT AS WELL GET IT OVER WITH.
PSH
H
H
HA, YEAH, YOU BULLSHITTER!
AREN'T YOU COLD?
NO
BZZZ
A.B.
NOT ME, MAN! I'M LEAVING, I'M GONNA SEE THE WORLD-
SO GO, YOU'VE ONLY BEEN TALKING IT UP FOR FOREVER

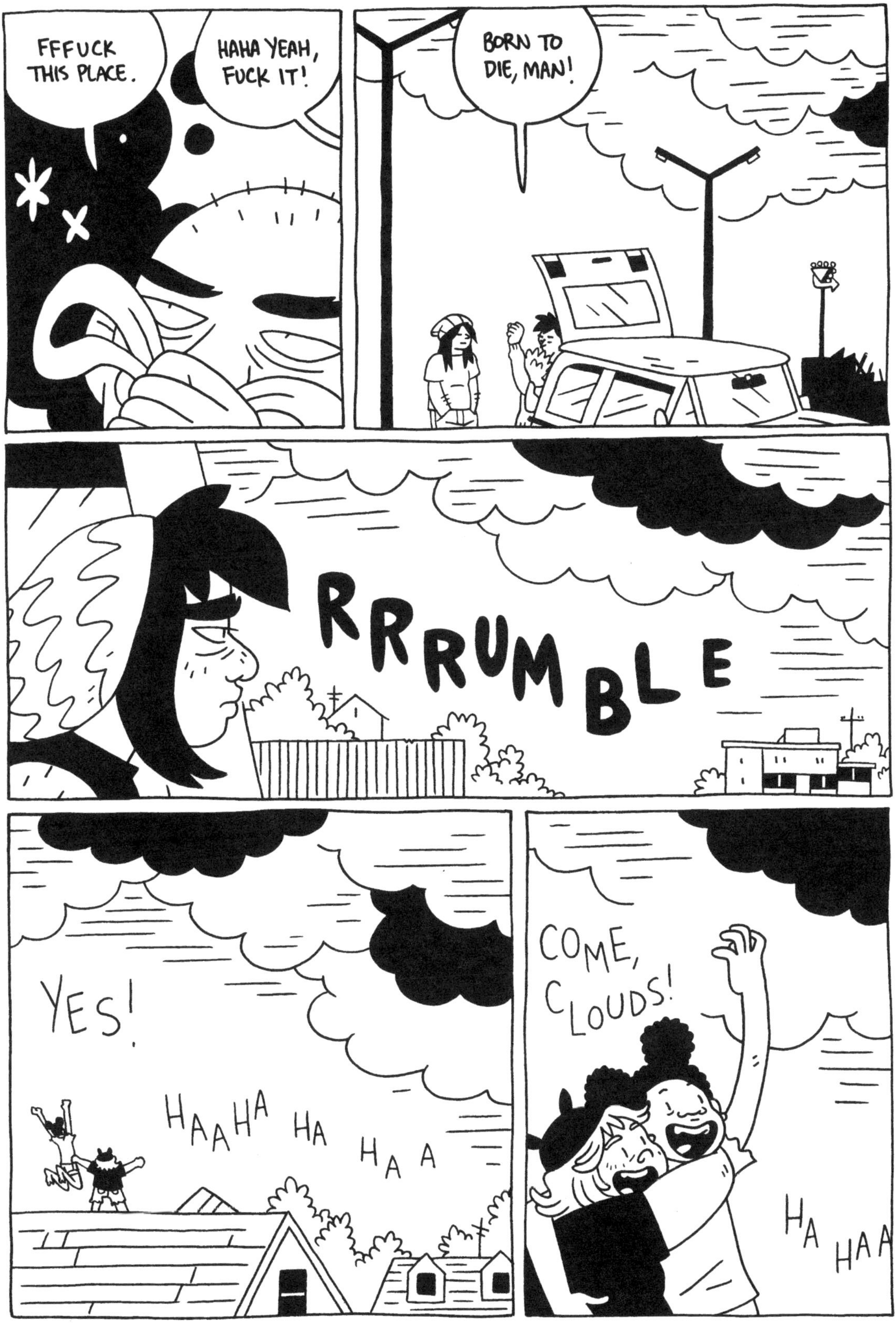
FFFUCK THIS PLACE.
HAHA YEAH, FUCK IT!
BORN TO DIE, MAN!
RRRUMBLE
YES!
HAAHA HA HA A
COME, CLOUDS!
HA HAA

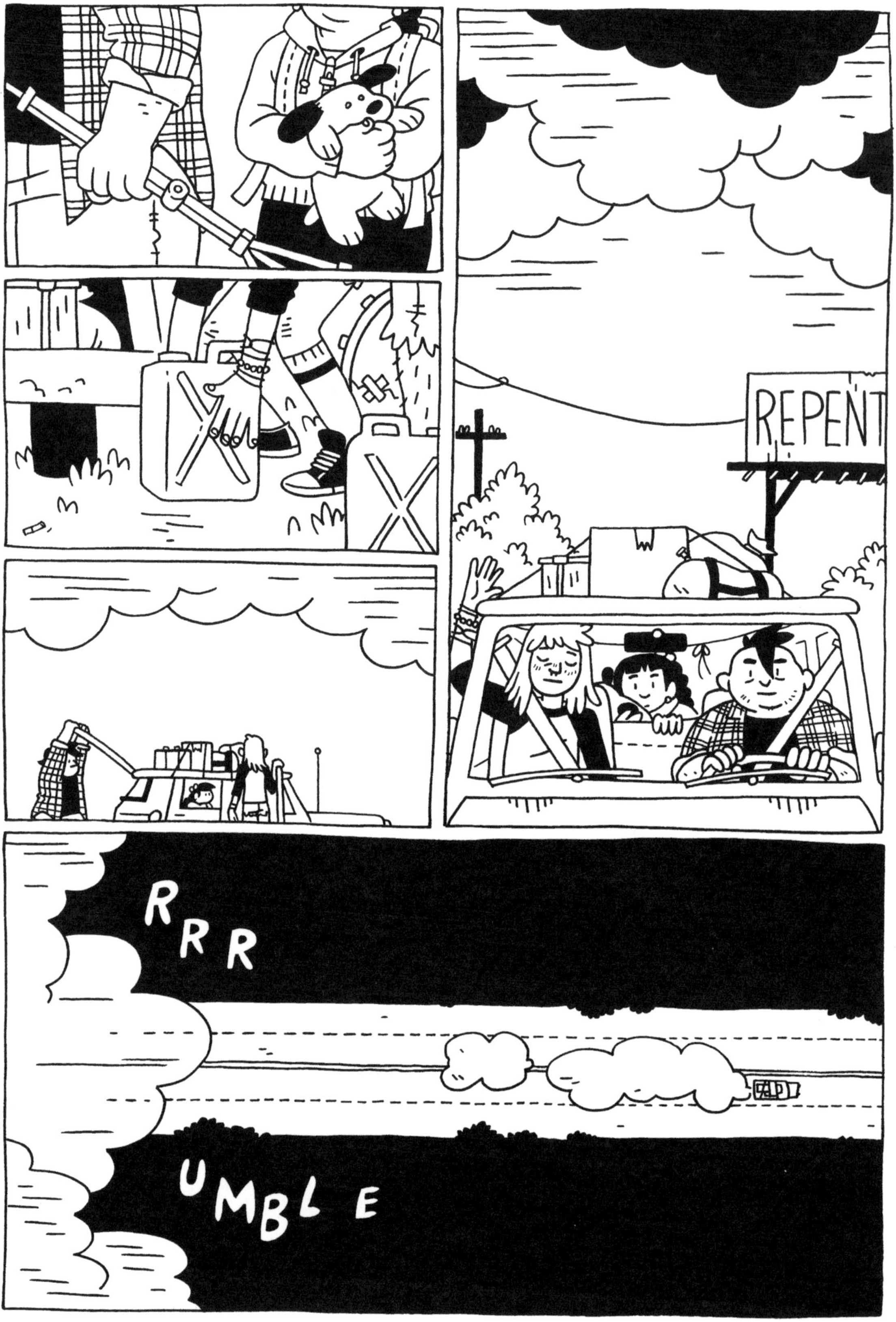
REPENT
RRR
UMBLE

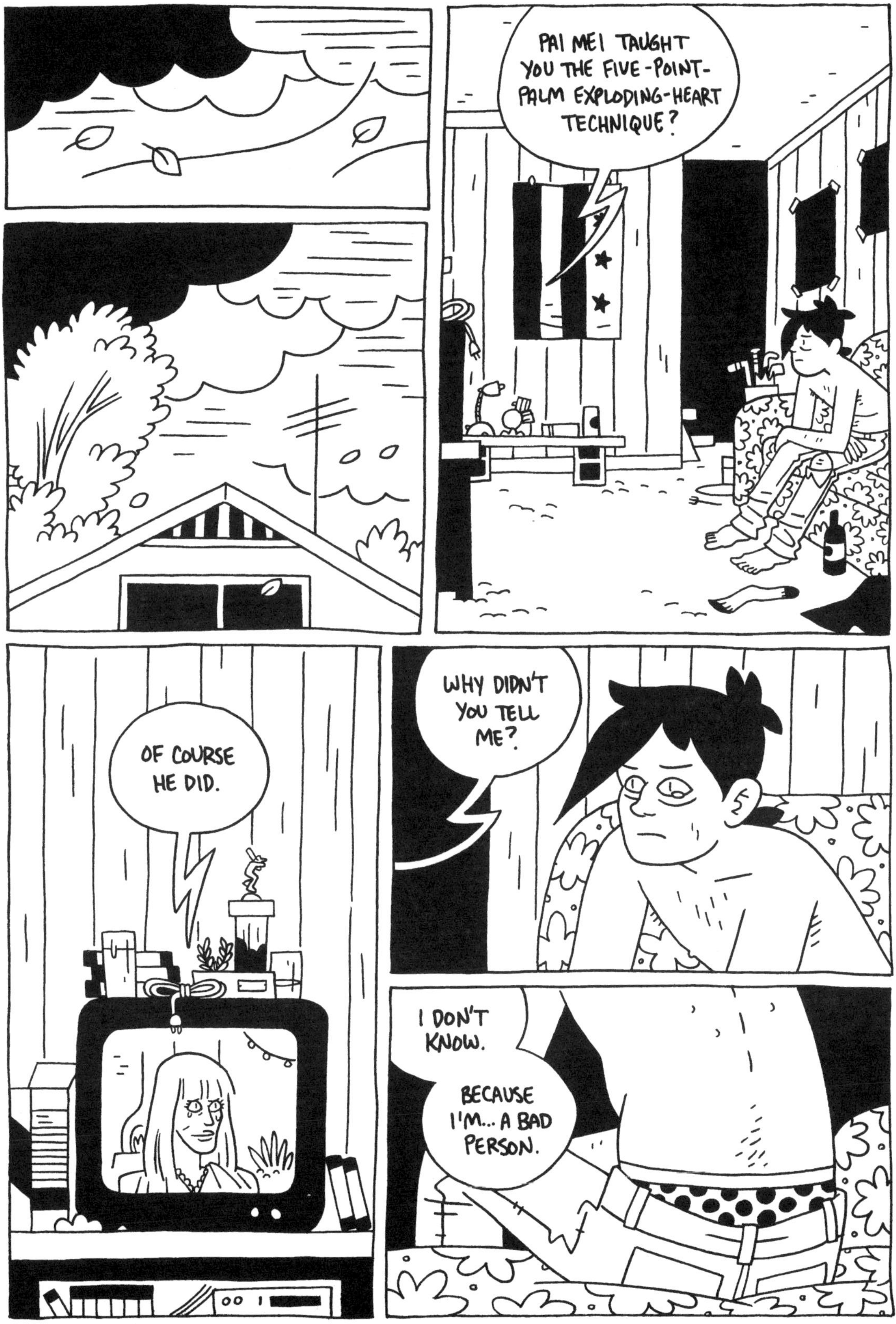
PAI MEI TAUGHT YOU THE FIVE-POINT-PALM EXPLODING-HEART TECHNIQUE?
OF COURSE HE DID.
WHY DIDN'T YOU TELL ME?
I DON'T KNOW.
BECAUSE I'M... A BAD PERSON.

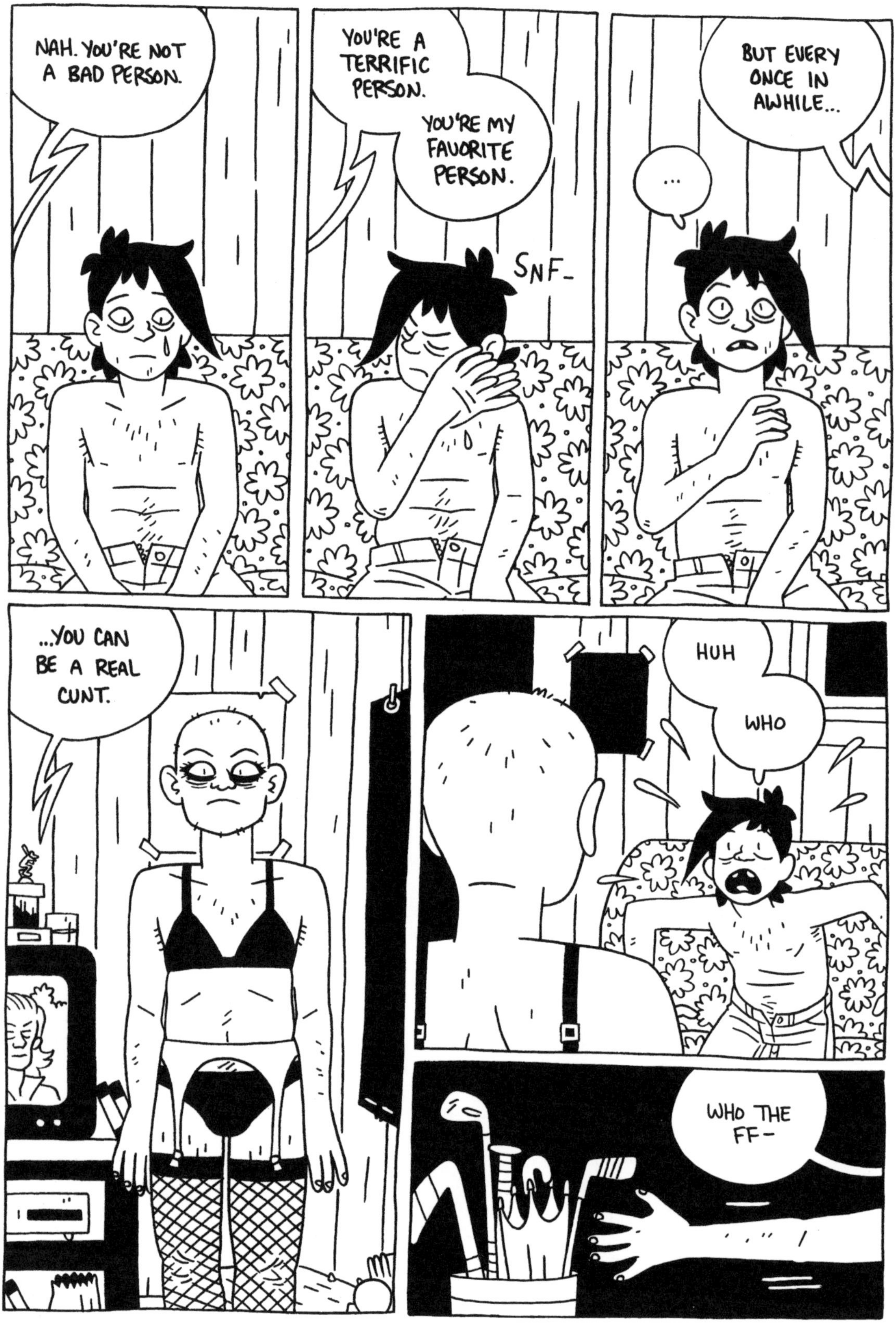
NAH. YOU'RE NOT A BAD PERSON.
YOU'RE A TERRIFIC PERSON.
YOU'RE MY FAVORITE PERSON.
SNF-
BUT EVERY ONCE IN AWHILE...
...
...YOU CAN BE A REAL CUNT.
HUH
WHO
WHO THE FF-

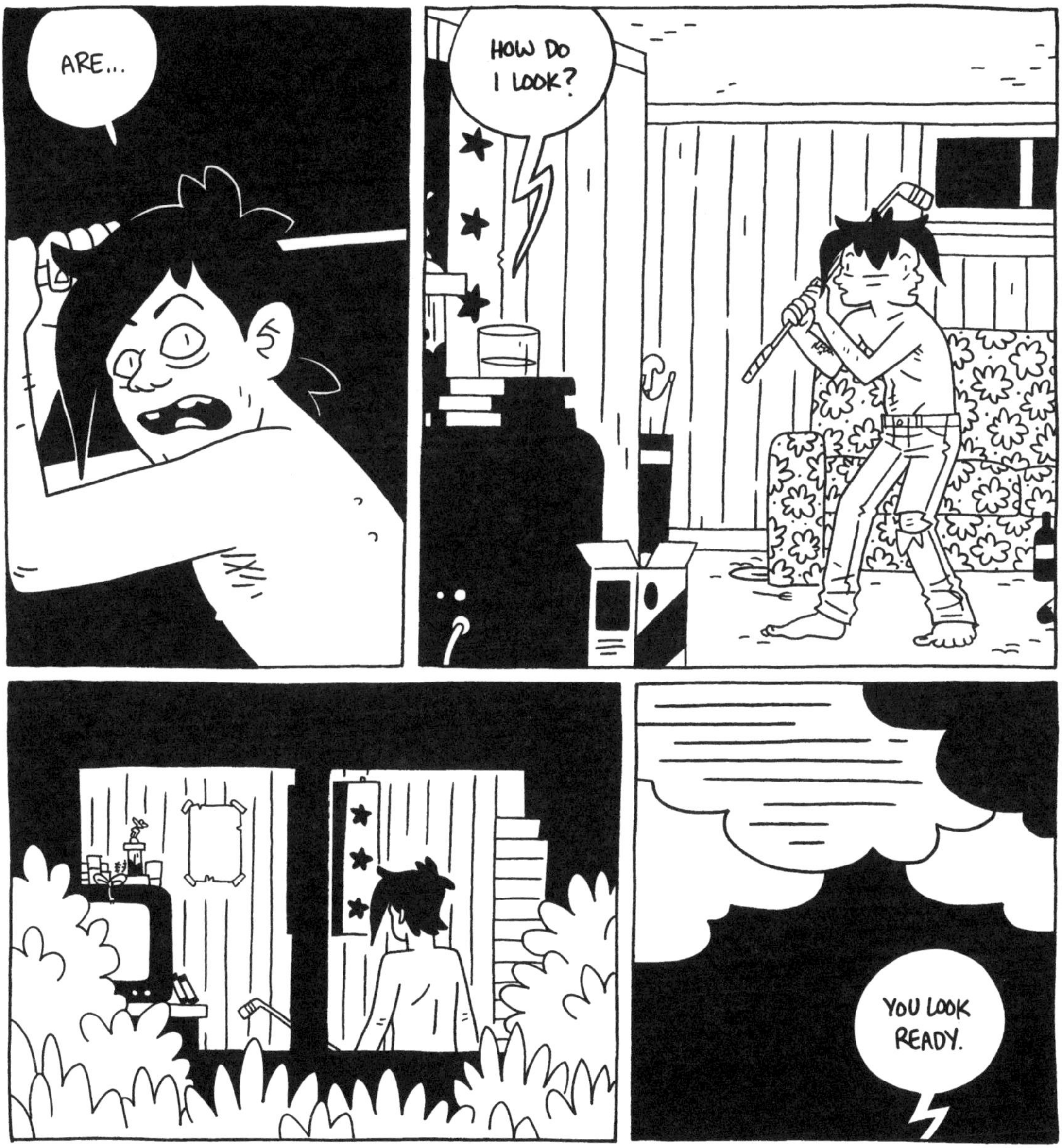
ARE...
HOW DO I LOOK?
YOU LOOK READY.

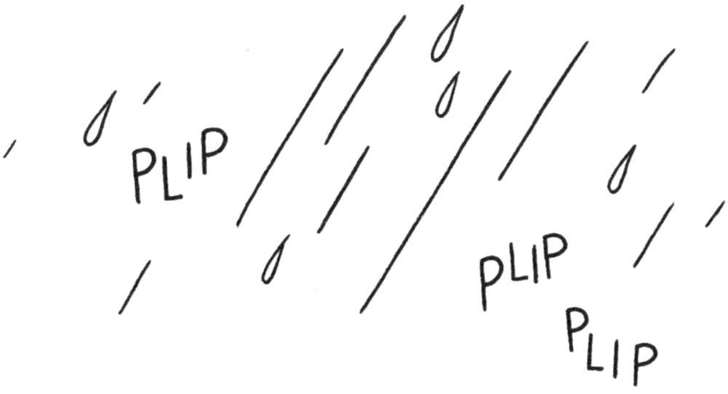
PLIP
PLIP
PLIP

CH 16

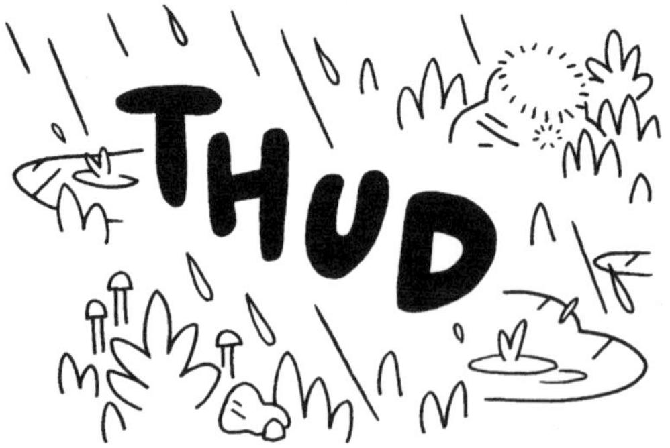
THUD

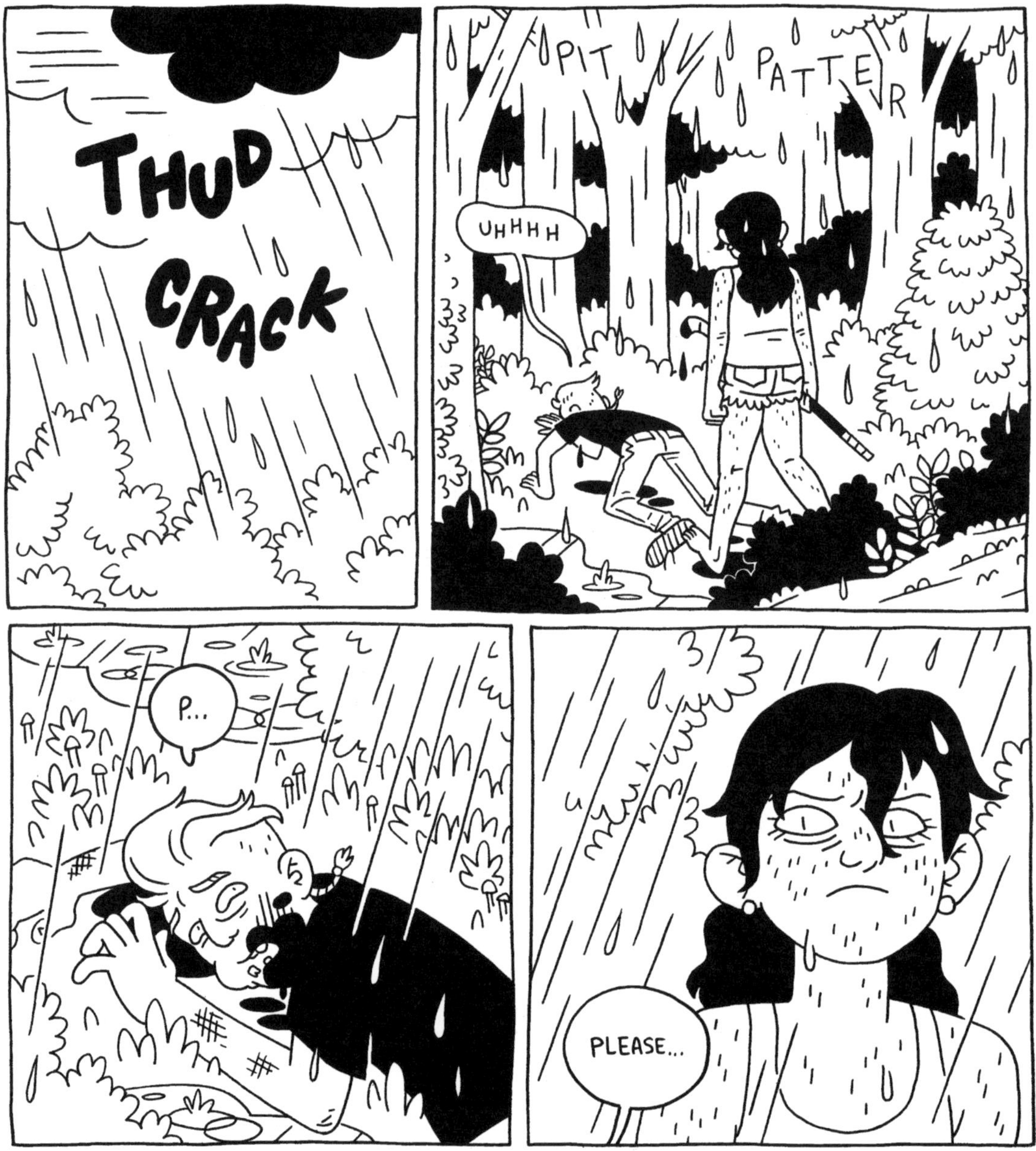
THUD
CRACK
PIT
PATTER
UHHHH
P...
PLEASE...

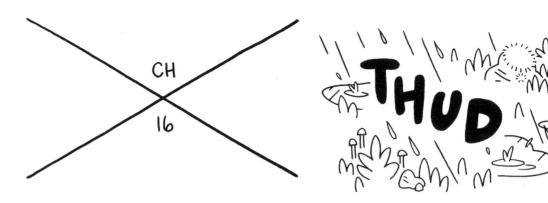

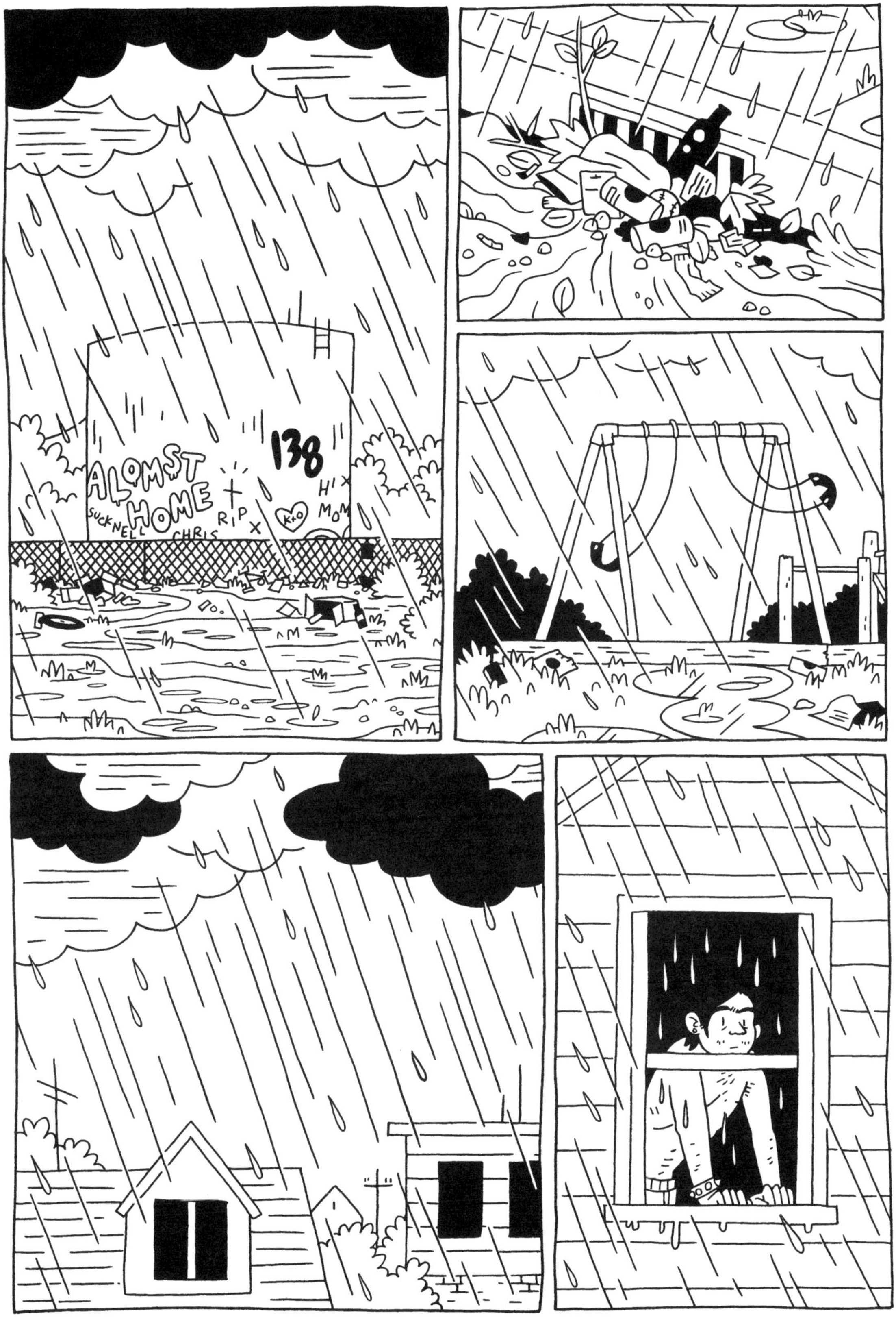
ALOMST HOME
138
SUCKNELL
CHRIS
RIP

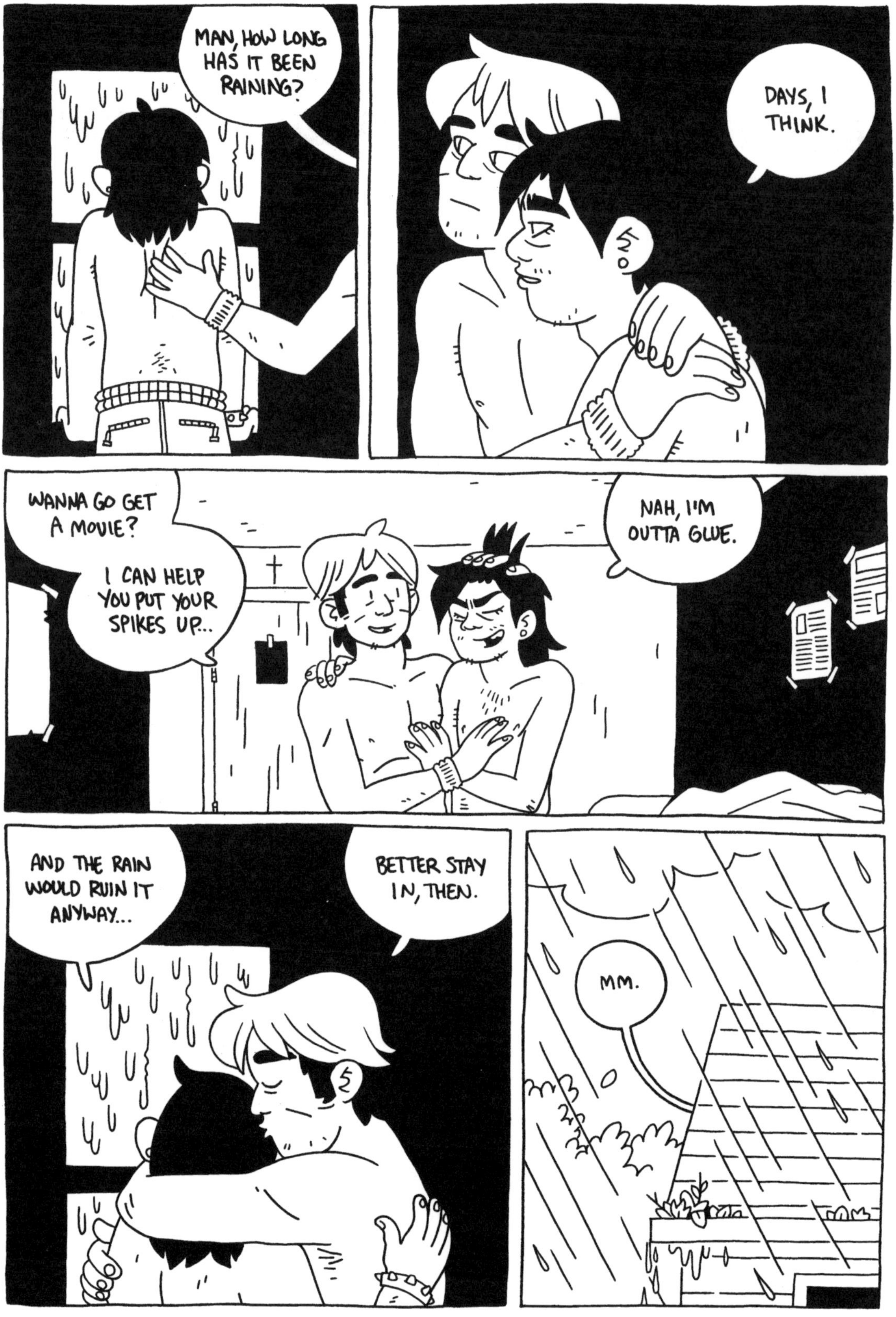

MAN, HOW LONG HAS IT BEEN RAINING?
DAYS, I THINK.
WANNA GO GET A MOVIE?
I CAN HELP YOU PUT YOUR SPIKES UP...
NAH, I'M OUTTA GLUE.
AND THE RAIN WOULD RUIN IT ANYWAY...
BETTER STAY IN, THEN.
MM.

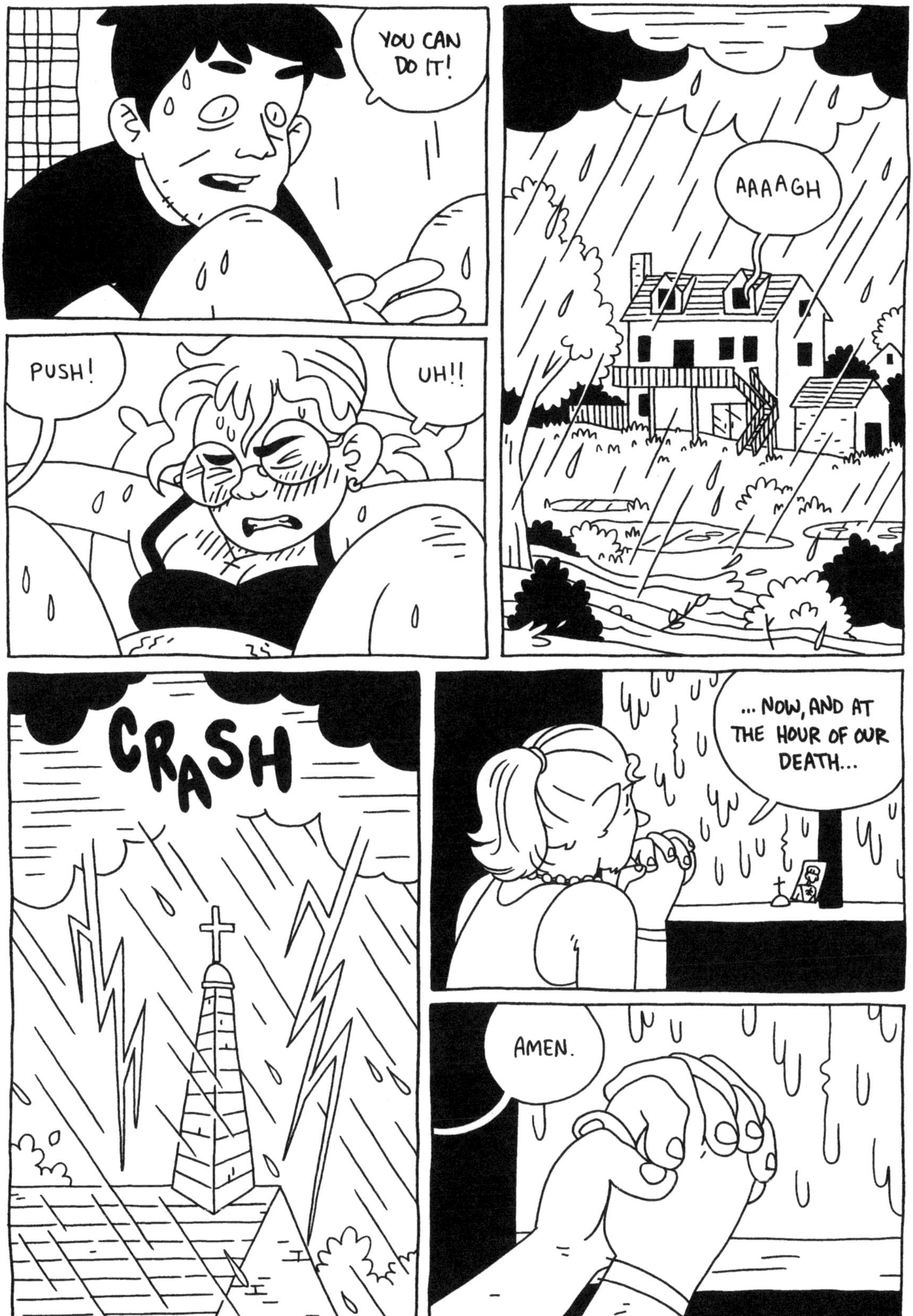
YOU CAN DO IT!
AAAAGH
PUSH!
UH!!
CRASH
... NOW, AND AT THE HOUR OF OUR DEATH...
AMEN.

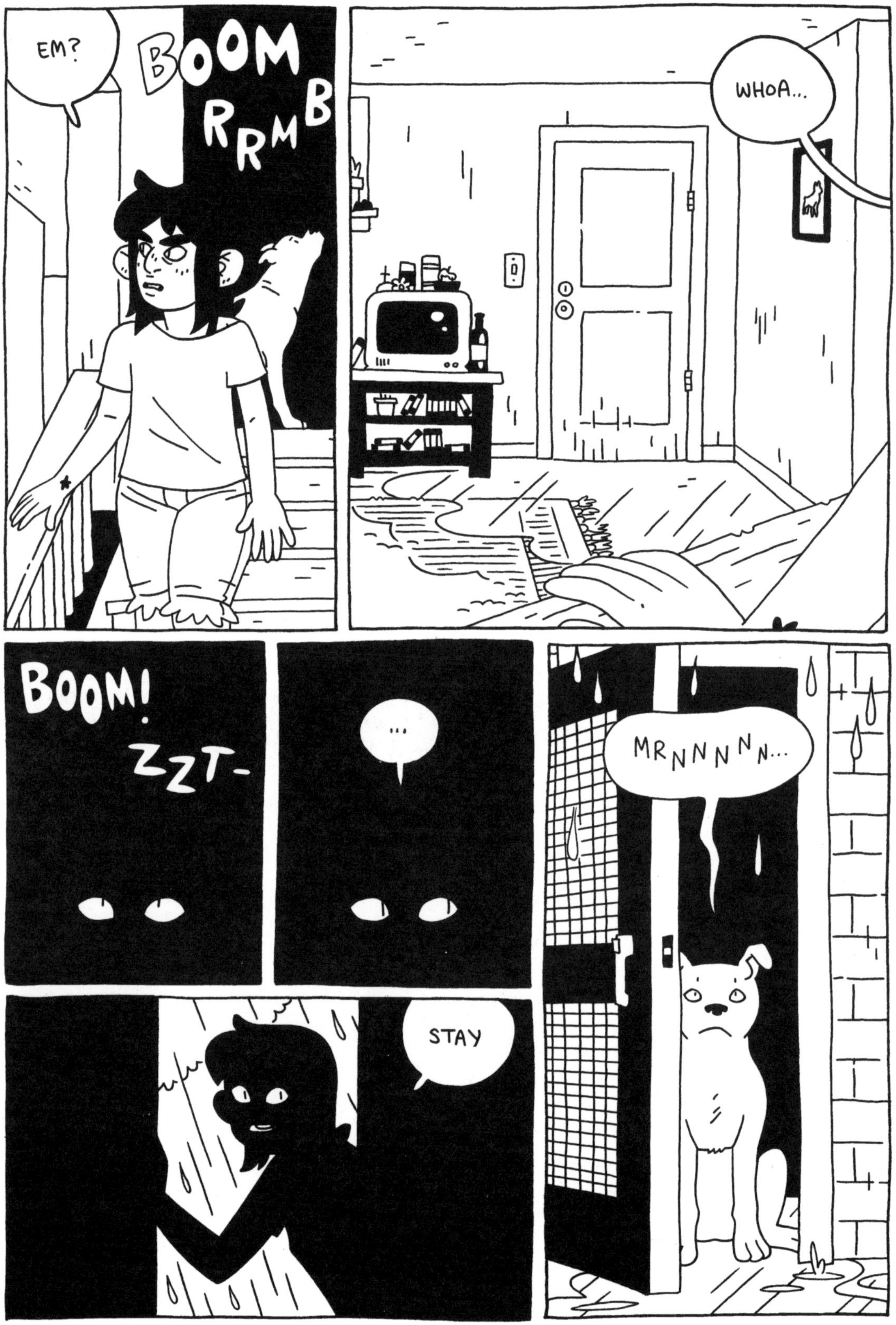
EM?
BOOM
RRMB
WHOA...
BOOM!
ZZT-
...
MRNNNNN...
STAY

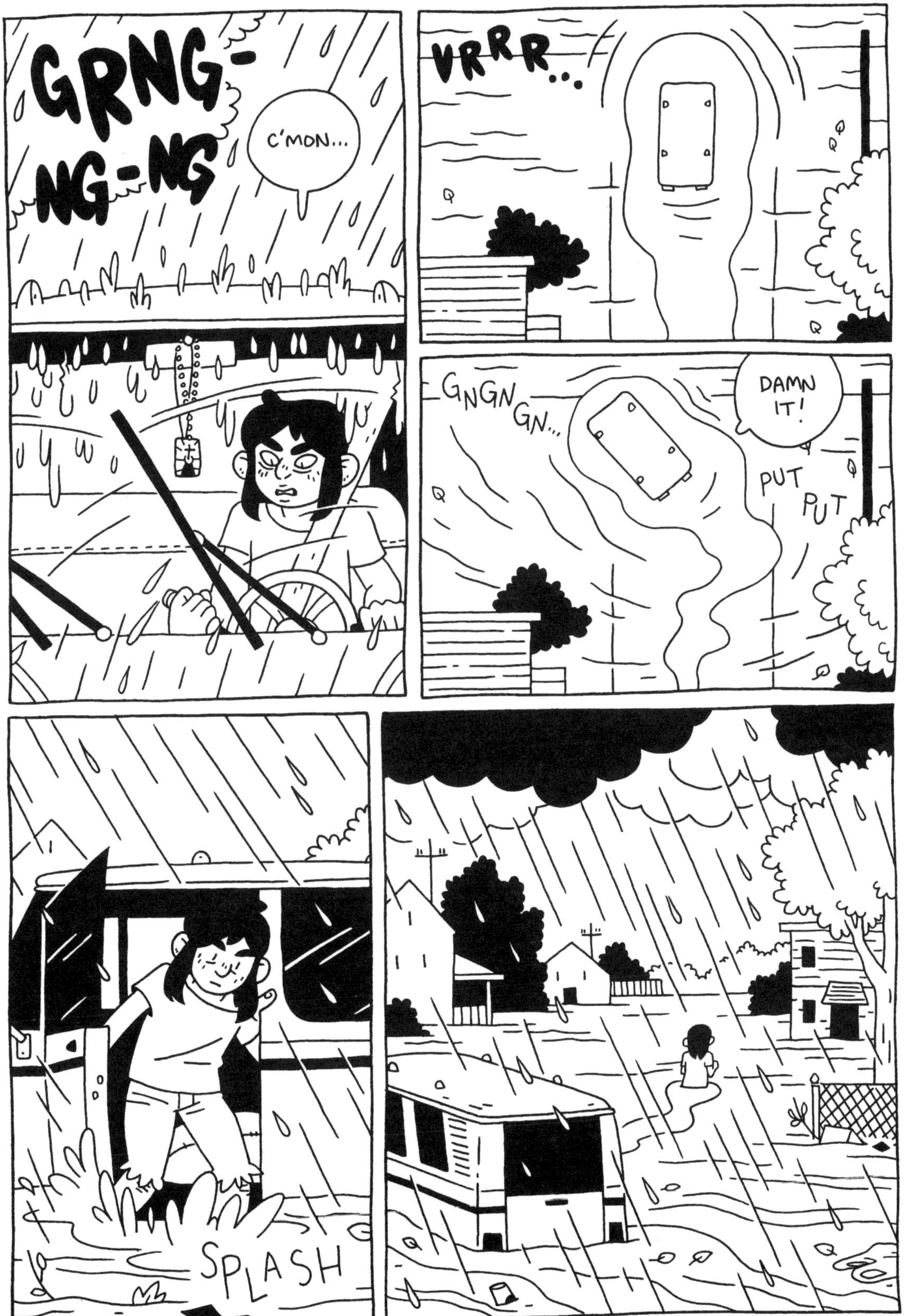
GRNG-NG-NG
C'MON...
VRRR...
GNGNGN...
DAMN IT!
PUT PUT
SPLASH

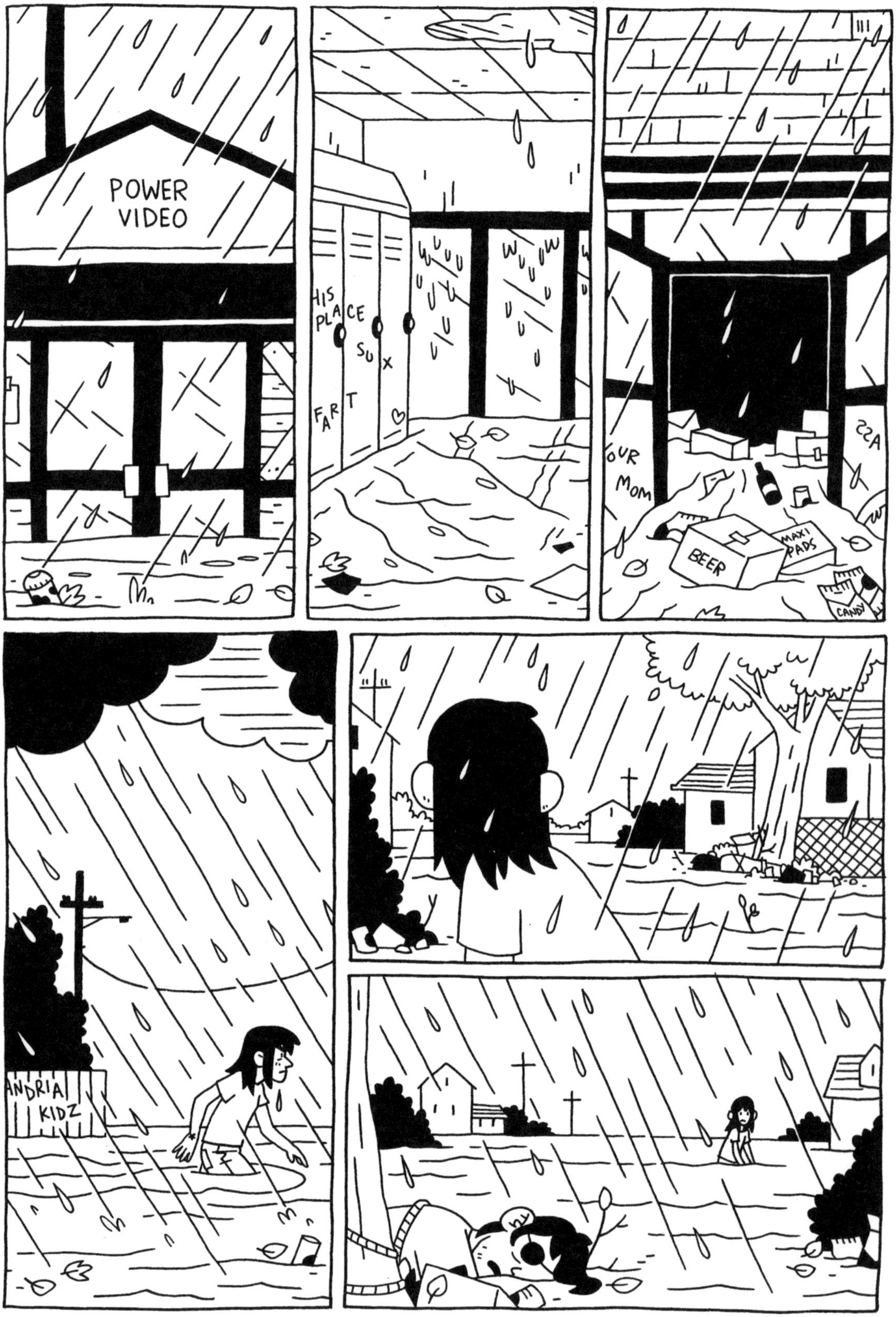
POWER
VIDEO
HIS PLACE SUX
FART
OUR MOM
BEER
MAXI PADS
CANDY
ANDRIA KIDZ

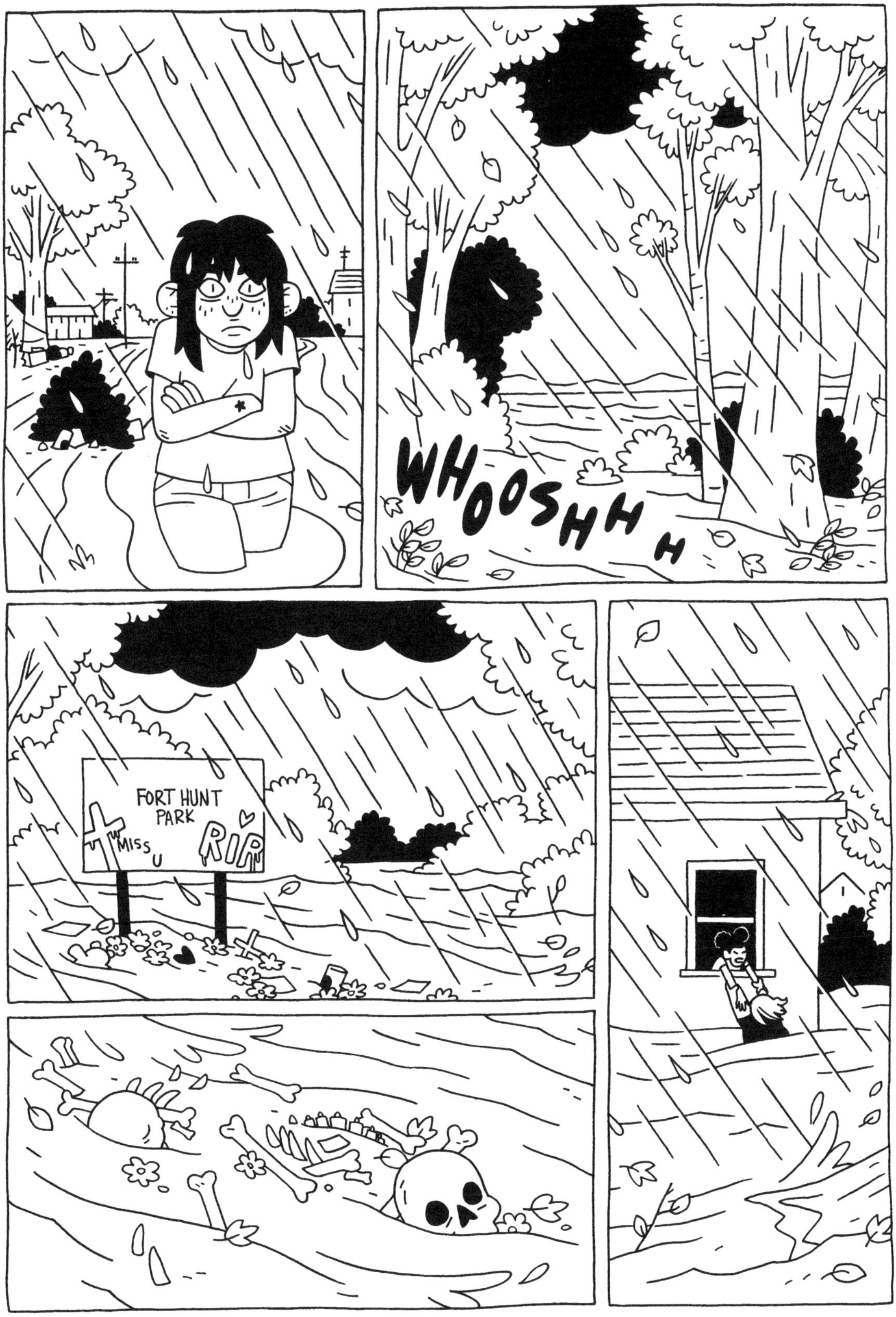
WHOOSHHH
FORT HUNT PARK
MISS U
RIP

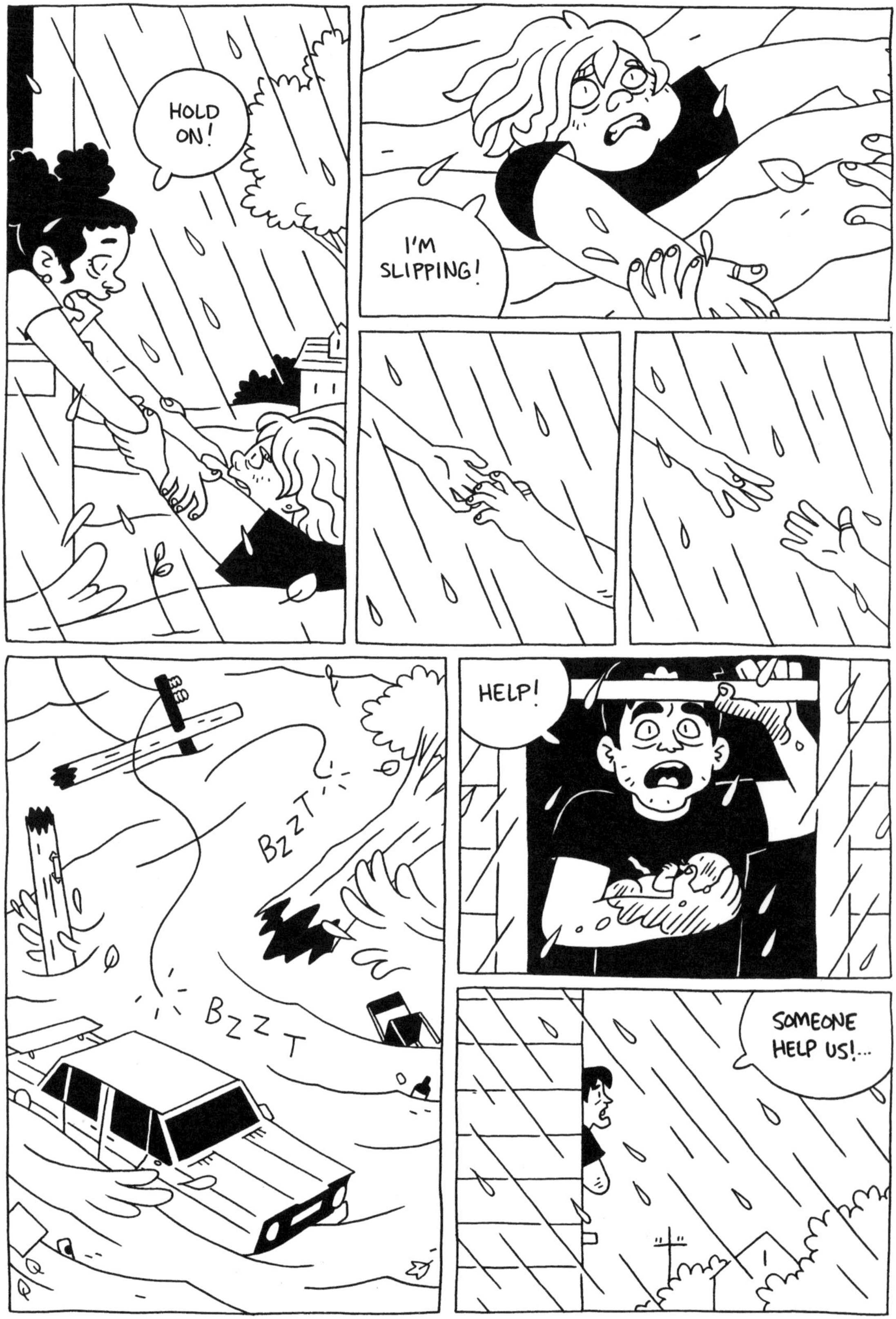
HOLD ON!
I'M SLIPPING!
BZZT
BZZT
HELP!
SOMEONE HELP US!...

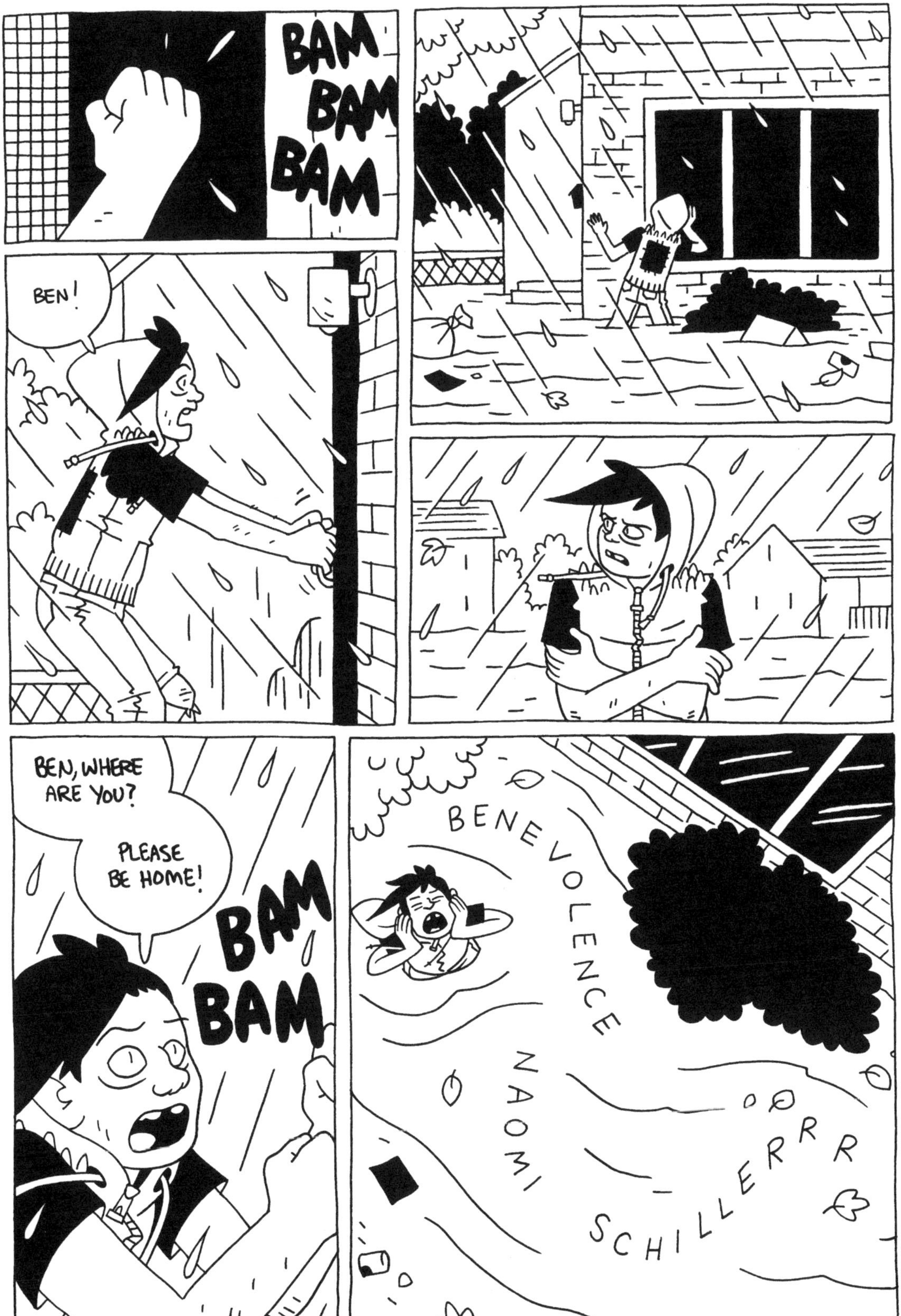
BAM
BAM
BAM
BEN!
BEN, WHERE ARE YOU?
PLEASE BE HOME!
BAM
BAM
BENEVOLENCE
NAOMI
SCHILLERRRR

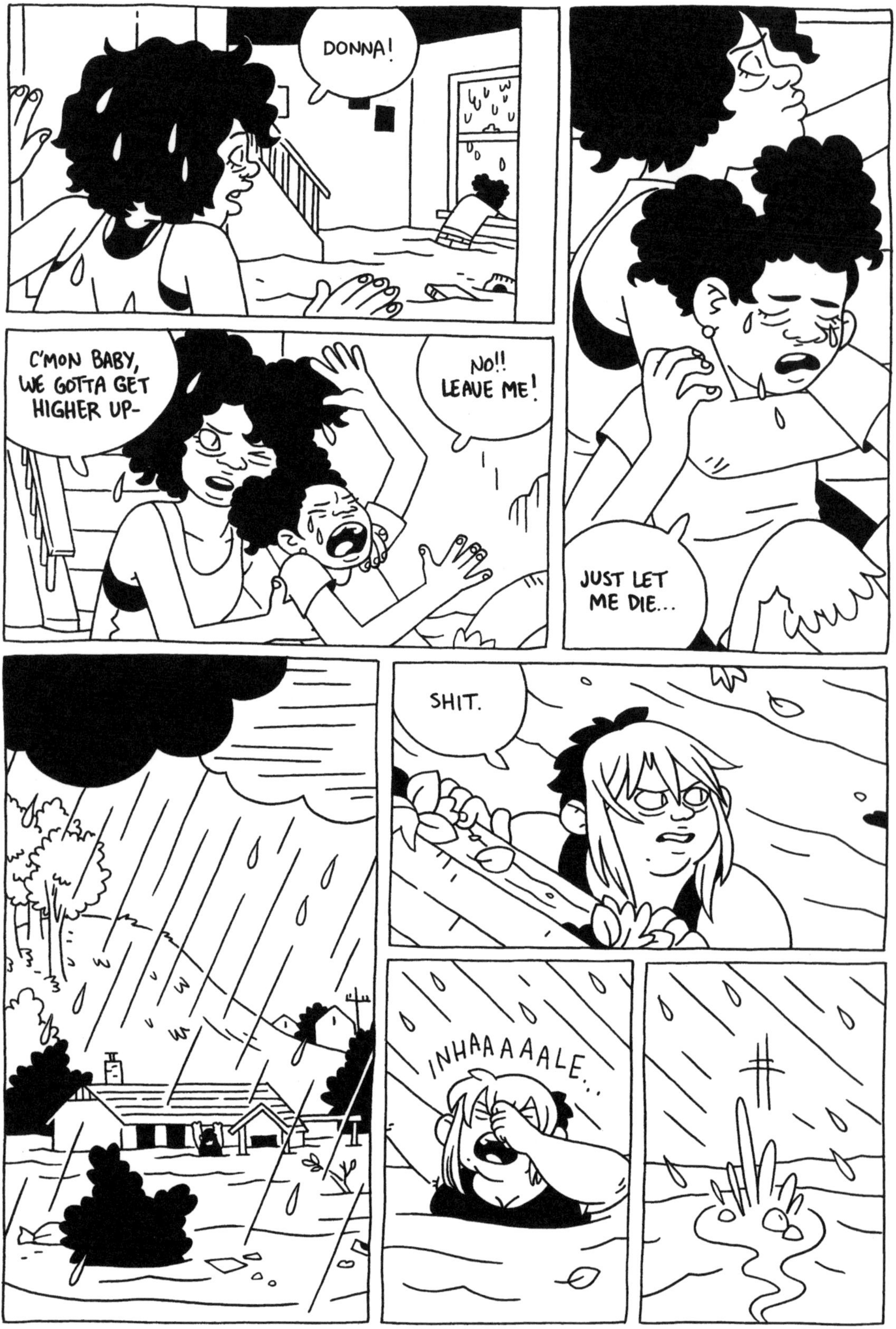
DONNA!
C'MON BABY, WE GOTTA GET HIGHER UP-
NO!! LEAVE ME!
JUST LET ME DIE...
SHIT.
INHAAAAALE...

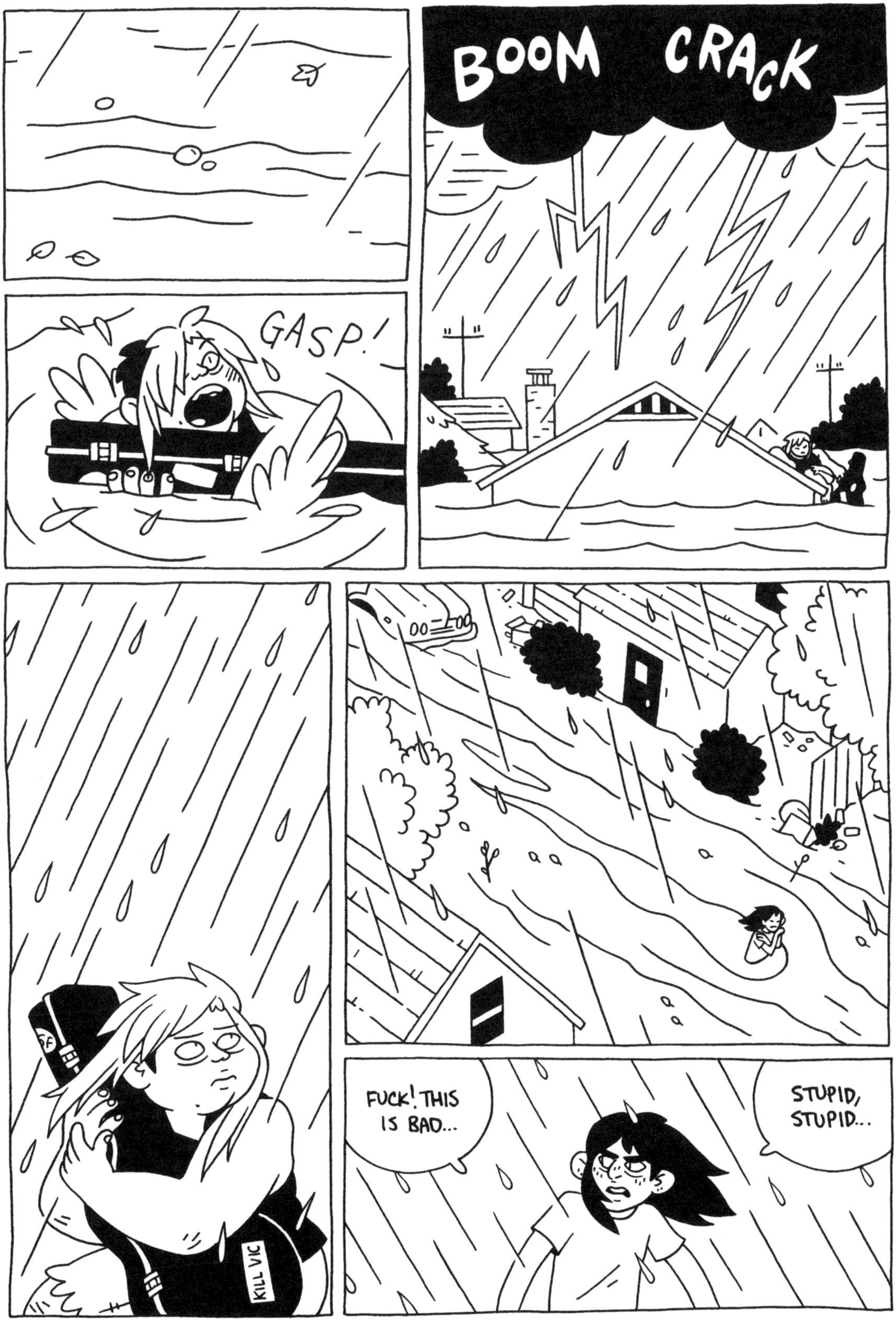
BOOM CRACK
GASP!
KILL VIC
FUCK! THIS IS BAD...
STUPID, STUPID...

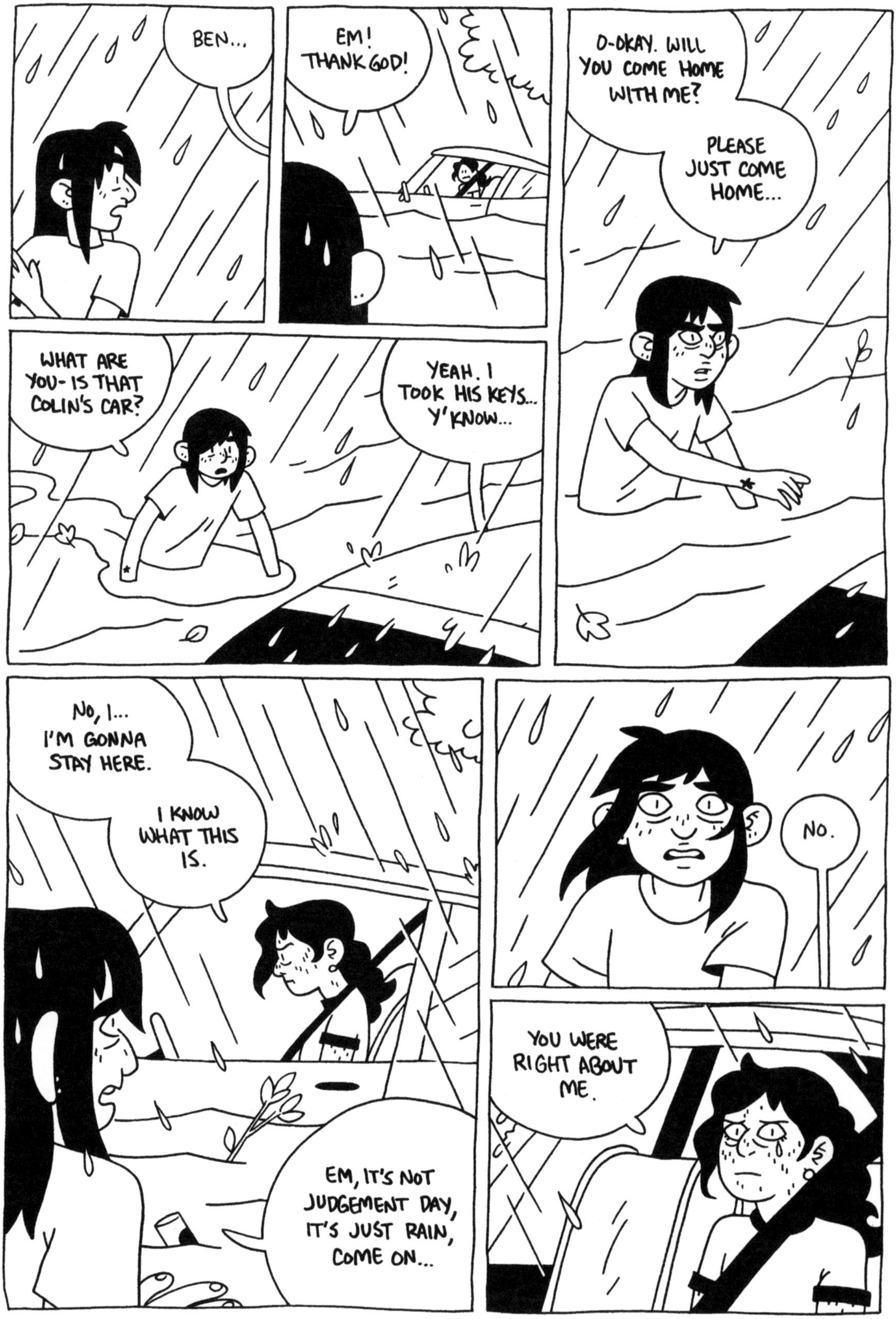
BEN...
EM! THANK GOD!
O-OKAY. WILL YOU COME HOME WITH ME?
PLEASE JUST COME HOME...
WHAT ARE YOU- IS THAT COLIN'S CAR?
YEAH. I TOOK HIS KEYS... Y'KNOW...
NO, I... I'M GONNA STAY HERE.
I KNOW WHAT THIS IS.
EM, IT'S NOT JUDGEMENT DAY, IT'S JUST RAIN, COME ON...
NO.
YOU WERE RIGHT ABOUT ME.

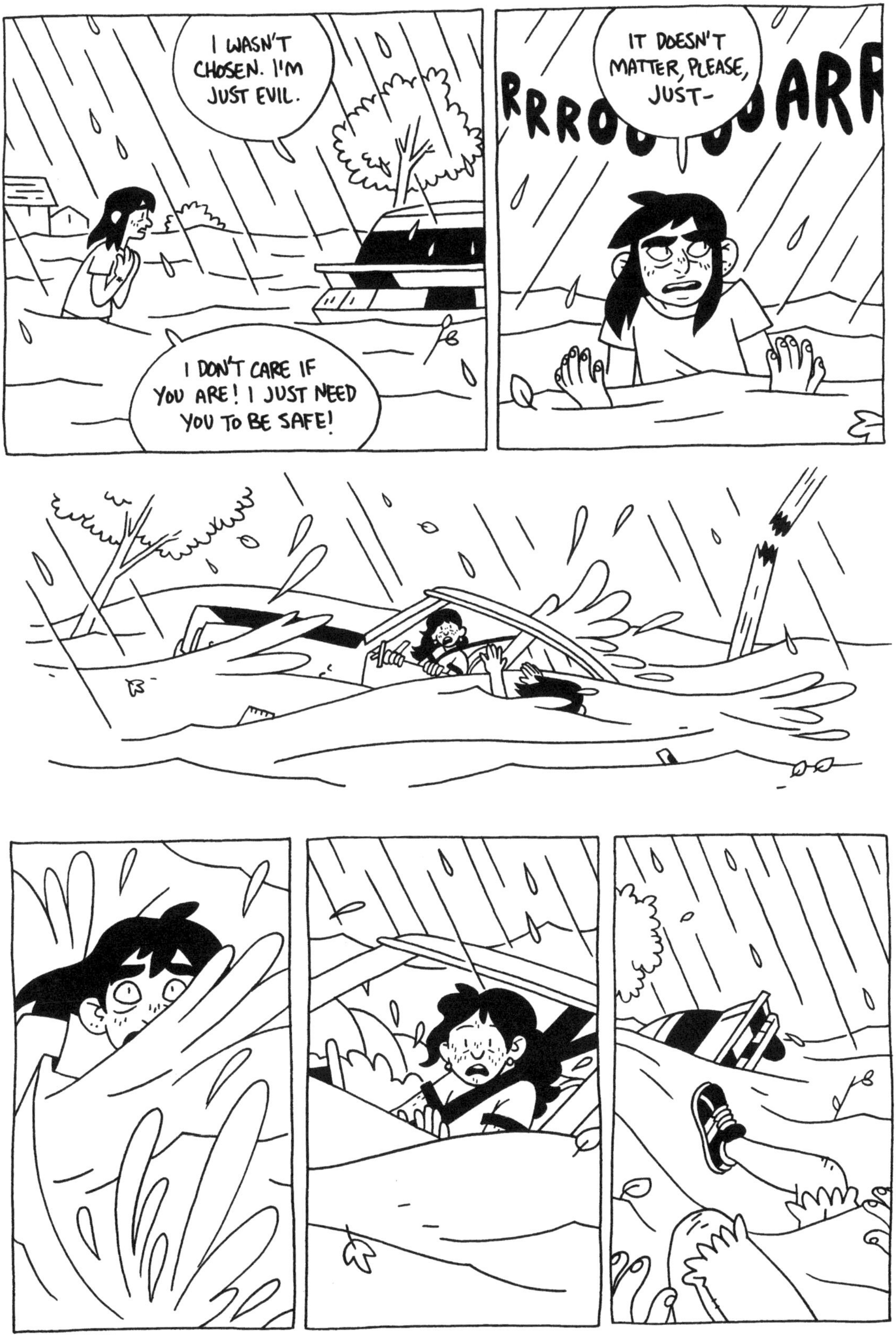
I WASN'T CHOSEN. I'M JUST EVIL.
I DON'T CARE IF YOU ARE! I JUST NEED YOU TO BE SAFE!
IT DOESN'T MATTER, PLEASE, JUST-
RRROOOOOARR

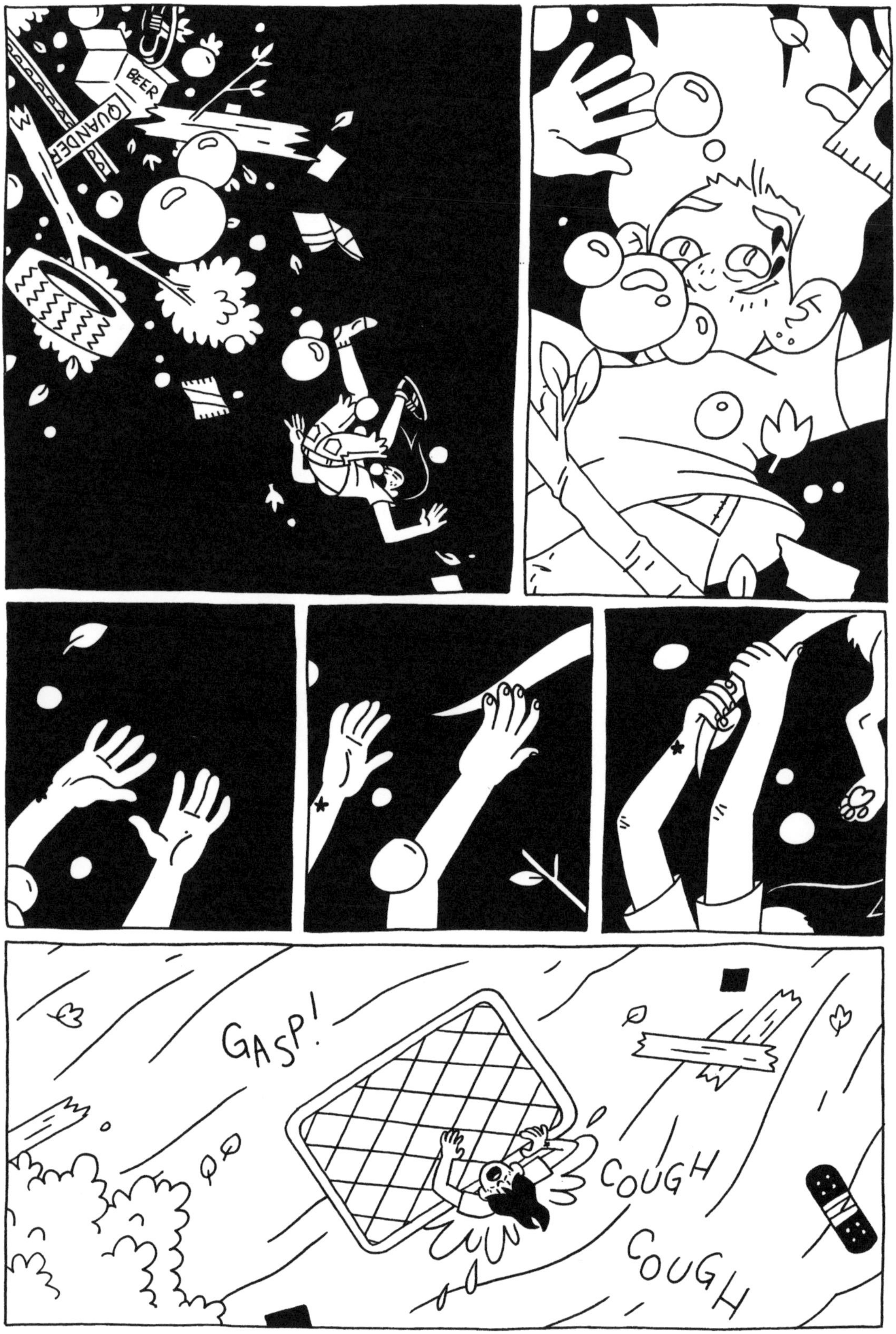
BEER
QUANDER
GASP!
COUGH
COUGH

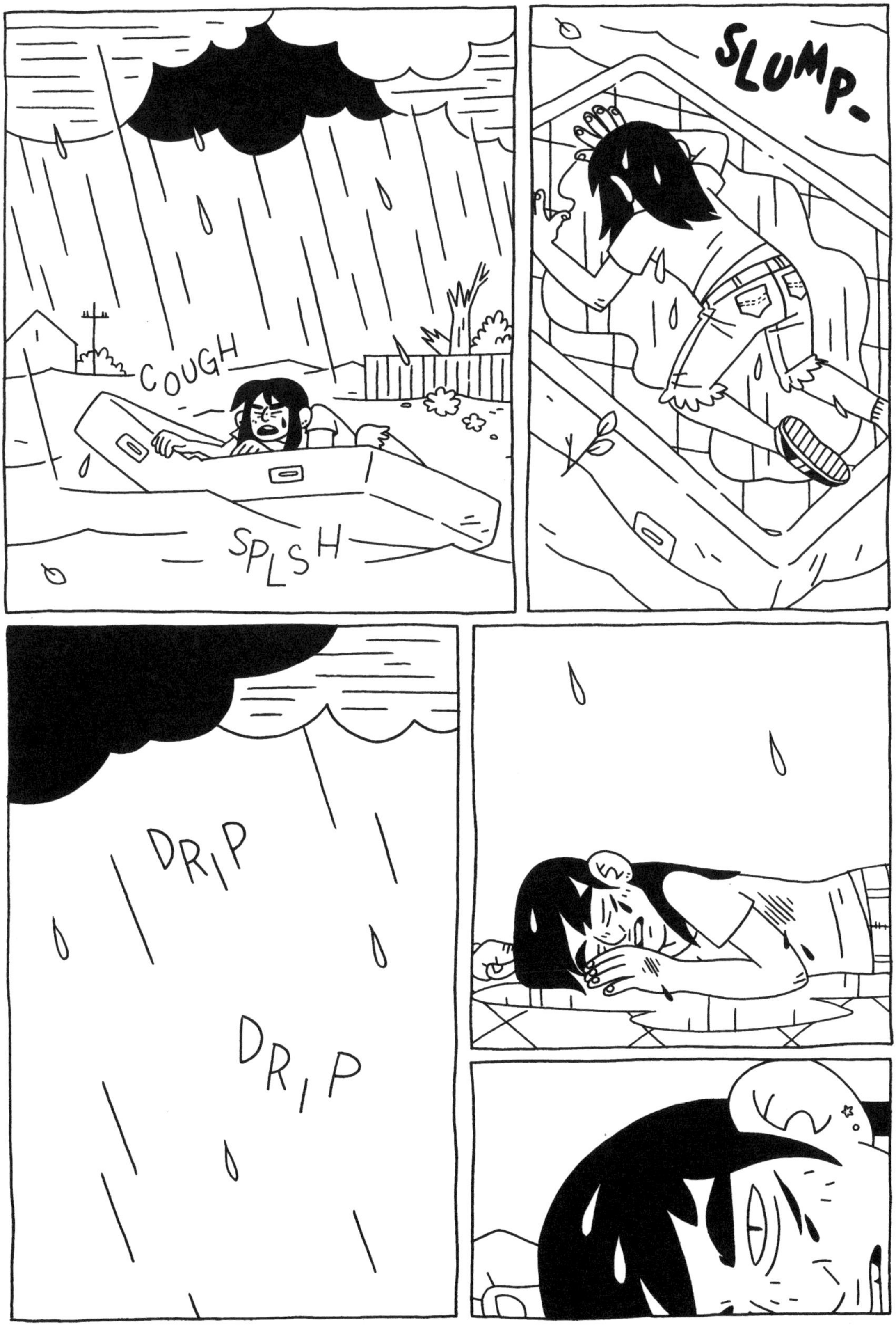
COUGH
SPLSH
SLUMP-
DRIP
DRIP

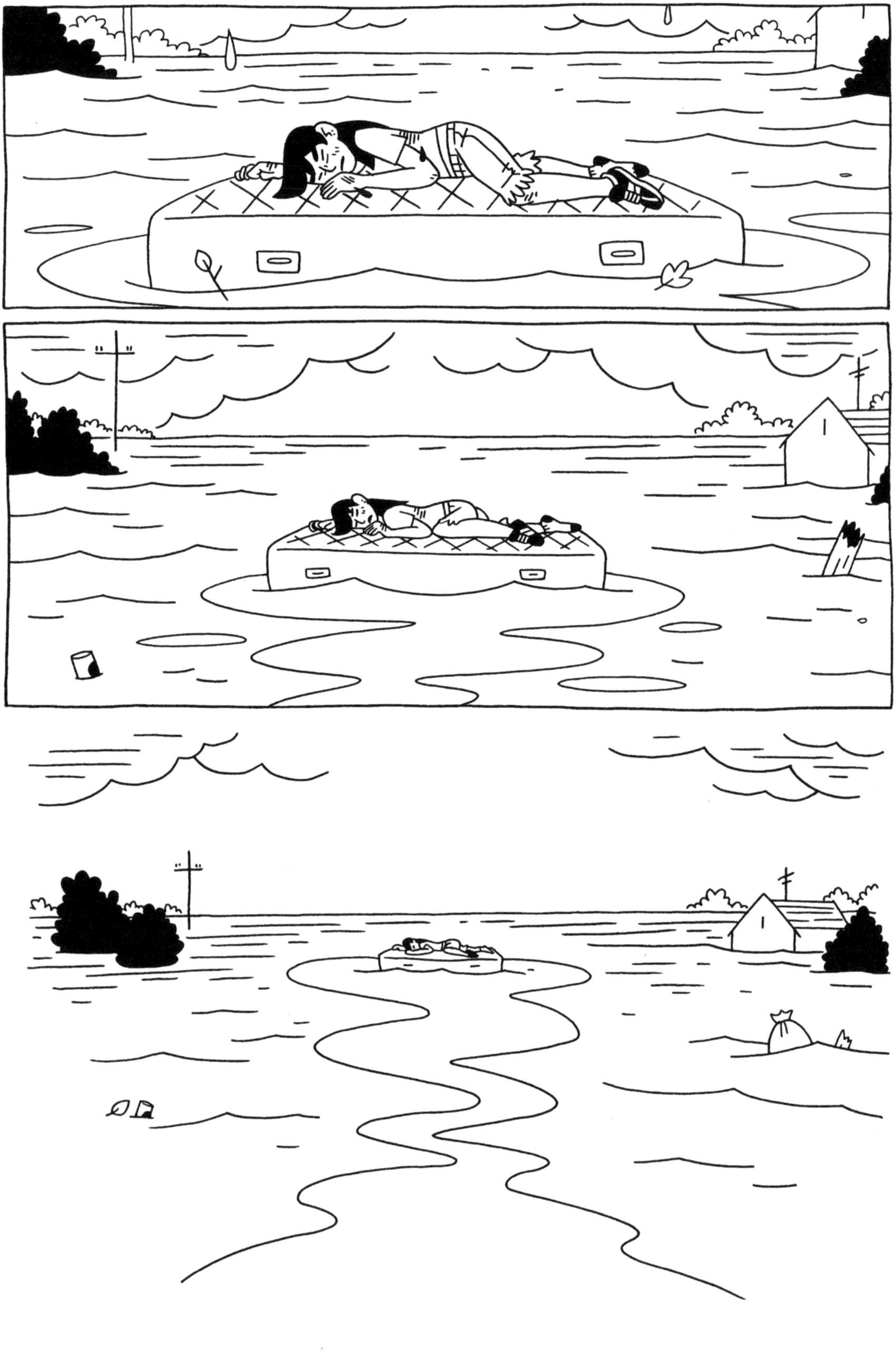

THE POST
CULT COMPOUND OBLITERATED
BY STORM OF THE CENTURY

T B C

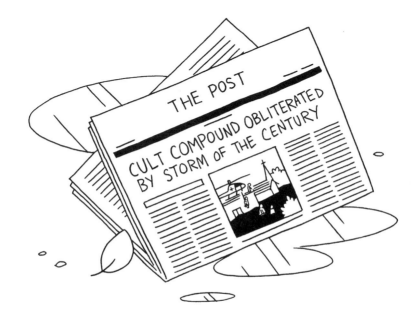

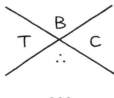

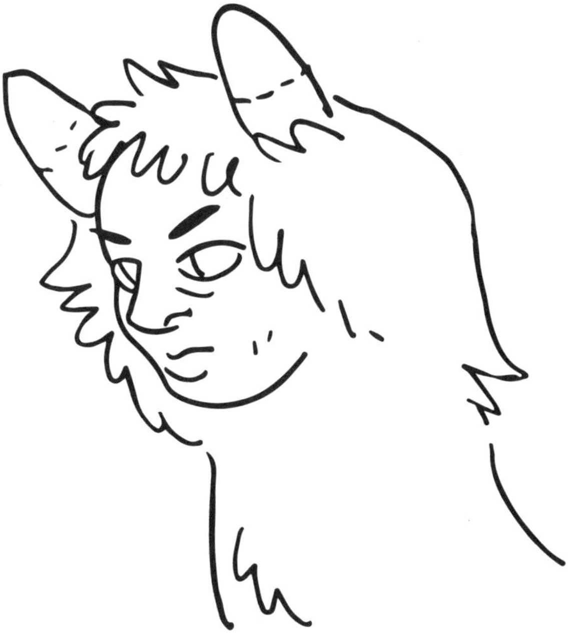

Liz Suburbia currently lives in Nevada.
This is her first book.

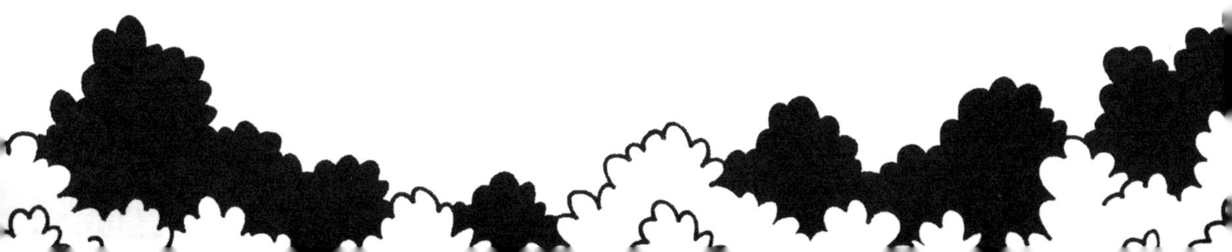

FANTAGRAPHICS BOOKS INC.

7563 Lake City Way NE

Seattle, Washington, 98115

Editor and associate publisher: Eric Reynolds

Book Design: Liz Suburbia with Michael Heck

Production: Paul Baresh

Publisher: Gary Groth

ISBN 978-1-60699-841-0

Library of Congress Control Number: 2015942121

First printing: September 2015

Printed in Singapore